An
ITALIAN
LOVE STORY

SURPRISE AND JOY ON THE
~AMALFI COAST~

CAMPAGNA BOOKS by JAMES ERNEST SHAW

AN ITALIAN JOURNEY
A Harvest of Revelations in the Olive Groves of Tuscany

AN AMERICAN JOURNEY
Travels with Friday in Search of America and Americans

AN ITALIAN JOURNEY
Celebrating the Sweet Life of Tuscany
(*An Italian Journey* with more than 40 color photos added)

An ITALIAN LOVE STORY

SURPRISE AND JOY ON THE AMALFI COAST

JAMES ERNEST SHAW

CAMPAGNA

First Edition

ISBN 978-0-9846585-4-1 (paperback, b/w photos, pen-and-ink drawings)
ISBN 978-0-9846585-5-8 (paperback, color photos, pen-and-ink drawings)
ISBN 978-0-9846585-6-5 (hardcover, dust jacket, b/w photos, pen-and-ink drawings)
ISBN 978-0-9846585-7-2 (hardcover, dust jacket, color photos, pen-and-ink drawings)
ISBN 978-0-9846585-9-6 (hardcover, case laminate, b/w photos, pen-and-ink drawings)

The text in this book is composed in Minion Pro.

Cover design by George Foster
Interior design and typesetting by Sue Knopf
Illustrations by Jonathan Edward Shaw
Photographs by James Ernest Shaw

Publisher's Cataloging-in-Publication Data
Shaw, James Ernest, 1946.
An Italian Love Story: Surprise and Joy on the Amalfi Coast / James Ernest Shaw.
1. Amalfi Coast (Italy). 2. Basilicata (Italy). 3. Campania (Italy – Description and travel).
4. Italy – Traditions, social life, and customs. 5. Farming – Italy. 6. Local food – Italy.
7. Family and relationships – Marriage and long-term relationships.
8. Christianity – Roman Catholicism.

Campagna Books, Wisconsin
http://www.facebook.com/Campagna

Printed in the United States of America

10 9 8 7 6 5 4 3 2 1

Contents

An ITALIAN LOVE STORY

SURPRISE AND JOY ON THE
AMALFI COAST

Illustrations by
JONATHAN EDWARD SHAW

We Didn't Go on a Honeymoon

You may have the universe if I may have Italy.
GIUSEPPE VERDI

■

The world is a book, and those who do not travel read only one page.
SAINT AUGUSTINE

$\mathcal{D}$o any of us really know the beginning of the stories we tell? This Italian love story might have begun with the hundred or so books I read every year as a child, or one of the movies I saw each Saturday night with my friends, or maybe the Italian girl I had a crush on when I was barely old enough to have crushes, but the best place and time, it seems to me, to begin this story is forty-some years ago in the courthouse of my small southwestern Nebraska hometown when the beautiful young girl I was marrying had to sit down at the judge's desk to type up our marriage license. I think it may have been the first time that Judge Bodeman had been called upon to perform a marriage ceremony and he was a bit overwhelmed. He was more farmer than judge— too nervous, too flustered to operate a typewriter. He also had typical farmer hands—fingers too big to hit just one key at a time.

We didn't have time for a church wedding, nor did we have the money. We weren't eloping but it was about as close to a secret wedding as you can get. That morning we had told my parents we were getting married, but they were a bit shy and opted not to come. Mardi's mom, a widow, also knew we were getting married, but she lived three hundred miles away. None of our friends were there—no best man, no maid of honor—and no pastor to convey blessings on our union. Our wedding cake was a pumpkin pie with a dollop of heart-shaped whipped cream on top. Despite the humble beginnings, our marriage has survived almost half a century.

We didn't go on a honeymoon. Nothing about our wedding was traditional. The whole thing was tailor made to match our budget. We were barely able to afford a night in a motel room halfway across the state, as we made our way to Omaha where two days later I was scheduled to swear allegiance to the Constitution of the United States and be inducted into the U.S. Army.

Ours had been a whirlwind romance—love at first sight when we met a few months earlier—and we had been together ever since. We didn't feel we needed a honeymoon to get to know each other and even if we had felt we needed it, or could have afforded it, we wouldn't have had time. The induction notice stated that my presence on May 7th was not optional. We told ourselves that we would eventually find time and money for a honeymoon—or if push came to shove, to use a favorite saying of my mom—we would just wait until I got out of the army.

But life got in the way of those plans. First it was making a living, then starting a business, and after that it was raising children, and then it was a horrendous almost life-ending automobile crash, which prompted our decision to have more children, and then it was hard times, and college educations, followed by the marriages of our five children, and then the births of grandchildren and now almost fifty years later we are ready turn our attention back to the honeymoon we never got to take. In turning our attention back to that honeymoon, we also turned our attention back to each other and the attraction that overwhelmed us across a crowded room so many years ago.

Mardi and I have been on a *Two for the Road* marriage adventure that has seen its share of good times and bad times, but we are now ready to celebrate our forty-six years of marriage—ready to rekindle the passionate love we once had for each other. Our choice of where to go was easy. The good life we are now living is the result of a solo trip I took to Italy. Seven years ago I volunteered to pick olives for Tuscan farmers with the hope of finding the answer to a question that had long perplexed me—why are Italians and Italy so beloved? Working alongside these passionate people I discovered what I believe is the answer to my question and I wrote of my conviction in the bestselling book *An Italian Journey: A Harvest of Revelations in the Olive Groves of Tuscany.*

What I learned greatly impacted my life—in ways that influence me more with every passing year.

I know I am not alone in my love and admiration of Italy and Italians. Thousands of followers turn each day to *An Italian Journey's* Facebook page and hundreds of people take the time to leave comments about their passion for Italy or their desire to travel to that ancient, storied land—many even go so far as to share their dream of someday living in Italy. Having discovered what I feel is the reason Italy and Italians are so beloved, it now seems right to turn my attention to an exploration of the impact that this appreciation for the Italian way of life has had on how I live my life.

As Saint Augustine noted we are greatly influenced by travel. *An Italian Love Story: Surprise and Joy on the Amalfi Coast* is the story of the Italy, and the Italians, we've gotten to know—and how we, as well as our marriage, have been changed by *il Bel Paese, The Beautiful Country,* as Dante called it. You will also find woven into this tale the story of that honeymoon we waited almost fifty years to take.

Wedding Day ~ May 5, 1970.

CHAPTER ONE

Wisconsin ~ Winter

Eating Our Way to Italy at Twenty Miles an Hour

You don't have to be rich to travel well.
EUGENE FODOR

■

A great marriage is not
when the 'perfect couple' comes together.
It is when an imperfect couple
learns to enjoy their differences.
DAVE MEURER

*W*hy did I live so much of my life not knowing what a glorious time awaited me if only I would cross an ocean by boat? I've always been adventurous. What prevented me from realizing that I should do whatever necessary to experience the delight of being humbled each daybreak as the sky changes from the deep black of a lightless night through all the colors of the spectrum as the sun appears to slowly rise out of the expanse of the ocean? Surely in my almost seven decades on this earth I should have read a book or crossed the path of someone who might have stressed how perfectly civilized it is, and how much it would do for my marriage, to relax for two weeks at sea, eat divine food all day, dance the night away, make love with playful abandon, then sleep as long as I want, and arrive in Europe refreshed and ready for the wonders of Italy?

I have known from a very young age the glories of traveling slowly on land. I've written books that tout the benefits of wandering about America and

Italy by bicycle, of the advantages that accrue to the person who throws off the isolating armor of an automobile's steel and glass to open himself to the lives of the people encountered each day. But somehow it had never occurred to me that in this era of relatively inexpensive airline travel, people are still crossing the ocean at the speed of a bicycle, loving it, and doing it at what seems to me a reasonable cost.

Before this journey I knew so little about big ships that I didn't even realize they move at about the same speed I pedal my bicycle on my daily rides. Twenty miles an hour doesn't get you very far when compared to the seventy miles an hour of a car or the four hundred miles an hour of a jetliner, but at some point in our lives, if we live long enough, we come to realize that speed isn't everything, just as we eventually learn that money is not the final arbiter of all things. Bicycle speed multiplied by twenty-four hours can carry you quite a distance; multiply that by seven, and you discover that it is possible to get from America to Europe in just a little over a week.

The choice of transportation for our journey of a lifetime followed the course of a pinball bouncing through an arcade game rather than the flight of an arrow whistling toward a target. Italy was our destination, of that we were sure. On my first journey to Italy, I picked olives for seven weeks on farms scattered throughout Tuscany. I heard the stories of farmers and got to know them and their families. This proved to be one of the most rewarding adventures I have ever come up with. Thinking outside the box has always come naturally to me, and I found myself wondering if my wife and I could find jobs on a working ship traveling from America to Italy—with the opportunity to sit down to meals with the crew and hear their stories as we sailed.

I didn't find any opportunities to work or even volunteer, but I did discover that it is possible to book berths on the cargo ships of the world. Most container ships have room for up to a dozen paying customers. The accommodations are austere, entertainment is limited, and you must have a bit of patience as the longshoremen load and unload cargo in the various ports along the way—but on most ships you do eat with the crew.

As I continued my search, looking for a ship that matched our schedule and would get us to Italy in a reasonable amount of time, I discovered deep discounts on what the travel industry calls *repositioning cruises*. I was shocked to learn that the cost is even cheaper than freighter excursions, and the schedules lined up better with our desire to arrive in Italy before Mardi's birthday. I had mistakenly thought that only the super rich could afford to travel by cruise ship, but when I did the math I discovered that it is possible to travel to Italy in luxury at a cost in line with the daily tab for a modest motel and inexpensive meals.

Despite finding the cost reasonable, we were still not convinced that our journey should be by boat. We noted that on the initial leg—from Ft. Lauderdale to Portugal—we would be at sea for eight days, a long time to be seasick. Both of us have sailed enough to know that the only sure cure, once motion sickness has set in, is to get to land. Twenty years ago I was seasick for eight hours on a sailboat cruising from Massachusetts to Maine. I still shudder at the memory of those wretched hours. I cannot imagine such misery dragging on for eight days.

But that wasn't the only factor keeping us from booking the incredibly cheap cruise to Civitavecchia, Italy. Roger, a good friend, was battling prostate cancer. Burning in my memory was a phone conversation with Craig, a cousin my age who had called to tell me he was in a hospital being treated for cancer, that he was certain he was going to recover, and that he would, within a few months, be beating me on the tennis courts again. I made plans to fly to the East Coast to be with him early the following week. But before the week was over his sister called to tell me that he was very frail and the whole family was flying out immediately to see him. He was able to hold onto life only long enough to say goodbye to them.

Roger's optimism and that of his wife, Bev, as well as their encouragement for us to do what they no longer could, lessened our fears, but we never lost sight of the fact that at any moment we might have to interrupt our journey and return to America to be with our friends. We knew we were increasing the risk by traveling by boat, but we wanted to slow our clocks down—to get on *Italian time*, both literally and figuratively, before we got to Italy. Almost every year of my life I have bicycled between five and ten thousand miles. Many of those years I have put more miles on the bikes I ride than on the cars I drive. Weather, road surfaces, even wind direction can cause me to alter my route when I journey by bike, and I apply that mentality to travel in general. I call it *pinball traveling*—allowing myself to be affected by the opportunities as well as the roadblocks that come my way.

You don't demand to exert your will—you let the game come to you, to use a sports metaphor, traveling according to your passions and desires as well as those of the people you meet on your journey. If you see something you like, you have the freedom to explore it. If someone extends a hand of friendship along the way, you have the opportunity to accept it. It helps me approach travel with a mindset that allows me to absorb the *daily-ness* of life.

For many, an open calendar is frightening—a schedule with only the word *Italy* penciled in every day for a month is a bit too serendipitous. Our calendar for the two weeks preceding our arrival in Italy was only slightly less redundant—at sea for thirteen days with three port calls, one in Portugal and two in Spain before arriving in Civitavecchia, on the third of April, three days before Mardi's birthday.

I wanted Mardi to experience Italy intimately, just as I had on my first journey, but since no Italian farmers had accepted our offer to help, I switched gears and began concentrating on making this journey as much like a honeymoon as is possible for old folks. As I researched the possibilities for a romantic celebration I became convinced that Portofino in Cinque Terre or Positano on the Amalfi Coast should be at the top of our list. Andrea Bocelli chose Portofino as the site of what I feel is his most romantic concert—a concert I have watched at least a half dozen times on DVD, and every time I am swept away by the beauty of that idyllic seacoast village. This side of heaven, I didn't know a town could look so perfect.

But Positano won out for a very pragmatic reason. I wanted to introduce Mardi to the people of Italy and everyone I talked to said that if warm and friendly people are for you the main attraction of Italy, the warmest and friendliest will be found in the South. I should also mention that Mardi is of German heritage—penny-pinching and practical. She would not find any hotel romantic, or the town in which it was located idyllic, if it cost more than the motels we find on our road trips to Wyoming to visit our ranching son Christopher and his family.

With all this in mind I visited *Hotels.com* and began my search for a romantic hotel in Positano that also happened to be cheap. I soon found what looked like an offer I couldn't pass up—a bed and breakfast with a beautiful view from a gorgeous terrace for a price similar to a Motel 6 in the States, with free cancellation until a week before our intended stay. This *pensione* boasted of a breakfast that numerous guests had raved about. The reviews also mentioned lots of stairs and that the place was a bit hard to find, but I rationalized that for a great breakfast and incredible views, Mardi would be willing to climb a few steps and talk to the locals if we couldn't find the place. But mostly I was relying on the free cancellation policy—if I found something that suited us better, we could cancel and book another hotel.

Once we had made the no-turning-back decision of paying for the cruise, we had exactly two months to get ready. The phrase *missing the boat* took on an ominous significance as we contemplated what would happen if a spring snowstorm delayed or canceled an early morning flight to Fort Lauderdale the day of our departure. Whether we were on that boat or not, we were going to pay for the journey, so we decided to arrive a day early. Staying at a hotel in Florida for a night would cost much less than trip insurance.

We were also more than a little concerned about gaining weight. Our research confirmed that ocean cruises feature great cooking. I mentioned that Mardi is a penny-pincher, but I should admit that I too am a bit cheap. However, our frugality was not going to keep us from overindulging on this journey—meals were included in the fare. Our only hope was that with no other responsibilities on board we would find plenty of time to exercise. We penciled in on our calendar the goal of gaining no more than four or five pounds eating our way to Italy.

The weeks of winter rolled by. I began biking outdoors again, enjoying long uninterrupted sessions on the backroads of Wisconsin making decisions as I pedaled—choosing which books to take, which clothes not to take, how many bags we wanted to deal with getting in and out of hotels, buses, and trains. Our goal—maybe I should say *my* goal—was to take one large suitcase and two carry-ons, plus one backpack. This led to our first disagreement about the trip. Mardi wanted to also pack a rolling duffel bag—one that I used on my first journey to Italy. But I had discovered that it didn't track well if the weight wasn't distributed perfectly.

If we were going to take an extra bag, I wanted a new suitcase—one with four wheels that would be easy to move through airport lines—like the rest of our luggage. We agreed to a trial run. Mardi let me buy a new medium-sized suitcase, knowing she could take it back if we found we didn't need it. We thought we were being ruthless in our packing choices, but we found we needed the extra suitcase—both for space and for the ease of moving our suitcases about. Ten or twenty years ago we might have had a fight over such a difference of opinion, but it seems that somewhere along the line we may have learned a thing or two about getting along.

In preparation for our journey we checked out dozens of books and DVDs from the library—travel guides and photo books—as well as films and movies that had anything to do with Italy. *An Affair to Remember,* a Cary Grant/Deborah Kerr film from the 1950s about a shipboard romance, captured our attention. I felt I had seen it before, possibly when I was a kid. It may have shaped my thoughts about adventure, and even about marriage. The opening song contains the lyrics, *Our love affair, may it always be a flame to burn through eternity, that we may share a love affair to remember.* Even though the word *affair* is in the title song as well as the film's title, the movie is really about the sacredness of marriage. Watching Cary Grant and Deborah Kerr fall in love helped us lose our fear of getting seasick. We were also beginning to feel that two weeks aboard a ship might be the perfect way to a launch a honeymoon.

We were calling this our *journey of a lifetime*. We had no doubts about putting this adventure at the top of our list even though we have been blessed over the years with some special trips. We sailed among the Ionian Islands of Greece in our thirties. A few years later we moved our whole family to New Zealand for three months where I commuted by ferry from the coastal town of Devonport to downtown Auckland to work on a series of adventure films. Our kids attended public school and we all walked together to the neighborhood markets to shop for meals. But we hoped this journey would be in a class by itself. It would be our first trip abroad during which all other concerns had been set aside, either by choice or by life's circumstances. The previous fall, our only unmarried child had vowed to God and to his girlfriend of two years to love, honor, and cherish her for the rest of his life. Even though we knew that our jobs of parenting weren't over (we had the example of four other adult children to convince us of that), we felt that we had reached a stage in our lives when, for the first time, our presence wasn't needed—by either a child or a parent—and it was liberating.

The question of how long to stay in Italy also led to some conflict, which we never did fully resolve. Mardi didn't think we could afford to stay in Italy as long as I wanted. I also wondered if she was truly convinced that our kids could survive without us. I decided to not press the point. She might be right—maybe it *would* cost more than I had set aside. If we found no opportunities to trade our labor for room and board, we would be spending a lot more than I had budgeted. My romantic vision pictured that our sojourn in Italy would last from my wife's sixty-ninth birthday on April 6 to our forty-sixth wedding anniversary on May 5, but we began our journey with no firm concept of when it would end.

For most of the days getting ready I was confident and excited, but that didn't prevent me from occasionally fearing that it might not turn out to be the journey I was dreaming it would be. This trip was going to be just for ourselves. The New Zealand adventure was for a film project. The same was true for our idyllic days sailing around the Ionian Islands. We were beginning to feel guilty about spending so much on ourselves. Even the amount I was spending on books about Italy was beginning to add up. I bought the Touring Club Italiano's highly detailed road map—a three-and-a-half-pound monstrosity that delineates nearly every path and certainly shows every road. For my first trip to Italy I had carried a large folding map that had the same exacting detail and found it invaluable as I sought interesting routes through the villages of

Tuscany. But this time we had no idea where we might end up, so I bought one large, expensive bound book detailing the backroads of every village in the whole country.

Night after night I pored over the maps, noting distances between towns whose streets I wanted to walk and whose people I wanted to get to know. If this was going to be our journey of a lifetime, I wanted to be both prepared and knowledgeable—besides, I found the research extremely enjoyable. I was still relying on our pinball travel approach, but I was developing ideas about where I hoped the bouncing ball would lead us.

I planned to do all I could to encourage our pinball to get flung up to the little town of Aliano in the mountains of Basilicata, but getting there was going to be difficult. The town was too remote to have train service, and bus service even looked problematic. If you've heard of Aliano, you most likely either have a relative from that part of Italy or you've read Carlo Levi's masterpiece *Christ Stopped at Eboli*. I was delighted to discover that Eboli was only a hundred kilometers from Positano, and that the people Levi had fallen in love with lived only another one hundred fifty kilometers down the road. We of course wanted to see the beauty of Italy, but we had learned in our previous travels that the true beauty of a country resides in its people. That's where we hoped the pinball effect would carry us—to the people of Italy.

By the time the day of our departure rolled around we had developed a thorough checklist, and we adhered to it religiously. The flight to Florida was uneventful. The only thing out of the ordinary was that I made the rookie mistake of not having the phone number of our hotel saved on my phone. We encountered the unique situation that the hotel we booked had changed ownership and hotel chain affiliation, as well as name, since I'd made the reservation—not something you normally have to worry about—but then when you're traveling, anything you can do to make sure the unexpected doesn't cause needless frustration is usually worth doing.

When at last we found the right shuttle bus, we discovered only one other traveler waiting to have his luggage loaded. He was totally relaxed—nonchalant even. It was obvious that the driver knew him by the body language both exhibited. Once we were under way he eagerly volunteered his story. He was a happy traveler. He had lost count of the cruises he had enjoyed over the years and was flabbergasted that we were taking our first. He could not imagine that at our age we had not once been on a cruise ship. What he said about cruises reminded me of the passion people hold for Italy: *at least once in your life you owe yourself a trip to Italy.*

The next day we discovered another rookie mistake—one that had the potential to be disastrous. Seated near us in the breakfast room of the hotel was a man about our age who seemed distracted. When I offered him the sports section of the newspaper, he immediately opened up to us, revealing that he was from Ohio and a Buckeye fan. He also shared the reason for his subdued demeanor. He and his wife had departed on a cruise the week before—their twentieth. But this time the unthinkable happened. His wife suffered a heart attack. The medical staff on board was able to stabilize her, but they felt she needed the attention that only a major hospital could provide. She had to be evacuated by helicopter to the nearest airfield and from there flown by jet back to Fort Lauderdale. He told us the bill for the evacuation and the medical treatment was over seventy-five thousand dollars—twenty-five thousand for just one item—the medevac flight by jet from Colombia to the Broward County Hospital.

The reason he was telling us all this was, of course, to share his burden, but it was also to encourage us to do what he had done—purchase travel insurance. After praying with him I went to our room and called his insurance company. The agent interviewed me for a half hour, asking question after question. The last question she asked should have been the first—*When are you leaving on this cruise?*

"In about six hours," I answered.

"Before midnight?"

"We're set to sail at five," I said.

"Sorry, we can't cover you. You have to purchase this insurance the day before you leave."

End of discussion. If either of us experienced a major medical emergency in the next thirteen days, we'd have to pay for it ourselves.

Despite the time spent on the phone with the insurance agent, our morning was relaxed. The window for getting on the boat was large—about seven hours. We chose a time slot in the middle—just after lunch. On the shuttle bus ride from the hotel to the boat, only one other person was aboard—the same man we had ridden with from the airport to the hotel. We introduced ourselves. Andy was not as upbeat this time, even though his clothes were festive, almost island-like. But his smile and enthusiasm were missing.

He once again opened up to us. In a severe twist of fortune, he explained, the young woman he had planned to marry was bringing assault charges against him. The story didn't make sense, but we were certain there were more chapters and that we would hear them once we were aboard the *Oosterdam*.

The ship was the size of a small village, and I figured it wouldn't be unusual to cross paths frequently with people you had come to know.

The process of boarding a vessel capable of carrying two thousand souls went more quickly than we imagined. The friendly crew took photos and issued identification cards, and we were soon walking the gangplank. The excitement of being aboard was palpable. Adventure was calling. We felt at home right away. As a former military man, I liked the order and the cleanliness of the ship, seeing the crew in uniform, being aware of the chain of command. We were struck by the attention to detail of our cabin, how compact and shipshape everything was. Our doubts about paying extra for a balcony quickly vanished. We felt like kids on Christmas morning as we read through the information packets and discovered just how much first class entertainment would be available to us for the next two weeks. But before we could set sail everyone had to attend a safety drill. I liked the feeling of standing in line near our assigned lifeboat for roll call. It conveyed the sense that while this was a pleasure cruise, we were under the direction of the captain, and our lives might depend on following his instructions.

As our huge vessel maneuvered through the crowded harbor, I felt a surge of adrenalin. We climbed to the observation deck and watched the hotels along the shore become shorter and shorter until at last they sank into the sea. The silvery patterns created by the bow slicing through the crests of the waves captivated us. A line from *An Affair to Remember* came to mind as we stood together at the railing watching Florida disappear. Deborah Kerr's character, Terry, whispered to Nicky (Cary Grant), "Why can't we do this forever?"

"I'll talk to the captain," Nicky quipped. We suddenly understood the feeling.

Life aboard the ship felt more civilized than traveling by air. Our whims were catered to in every way. Meals were delightful—they were also very international. At our first dinner we were joined by a couple from Illinois, but we were also sitting next to a couple from Canada and a couple from England. We quickly discovered that we were the oddities at the table—first-timers. They all wanted to know how we had the courage to choose a trans-Atlantic crossing for our first cruising experience.

That question drove home the point that not only were we newbies, but our reason for being aboard was unique as well. We weren't going on a cruise—we wanted to get from America to Italy and we wanted to do it slowly. That we would also be wined, dined, and entertained every mile of the way did not fully enter our consciousness until we began to realize how quickly time was passing.

We had thought we'd get bored. We brought books to pass the time, but we never opened them. I brought cycling jerseys, shorts, and shoes, but not once did I put them on. We were informed on the first day that the ship charged ten dollars an hour to ride the stationary bikes to offset the cost of injuries passengers might suffer while riding them. That kept me—and apparently everyone else aboard—from riding; not once in our two weeks at sea did we see even one of the dozen bikes in use. But I think that was our only complaint, unless you would consider it a complaint that we didn't feel we were adequately warned about the necessity of boarding the ship with a huge measure of self-restraint.

We had been warned that the food on cruise ships was good, but we didn't comprehend how good and how available it would be. Breakfast was served beginning at six and overlapped lunch, which was overlapped by the hamburger and Mexican food bar, which overlapped the choice of four dining rooms for dinner. Following dinner a slight gap was encountered. The late night dining room didn't start serving until 11:30. You had to pace yourself to span that two-hour gap when no fresh food was coming out of the kitchen. However, if you found yourself desperate during those hours, most of the ship's bars had light snacks for sale.

On our third day at sea I ordered early morning room service. Mardi thought that was overly indulgent—and a lot of work for our stewards. But what a luxury it was to eat breakfast in bed and then slip into our bathrobes and head out to our private balcony to enjoy our tea and croissants as the ocean slid silently by below us.

But we didn't make a habit of that luxury. We enjoyed the freedom of letting each day develop its own leisurely rhythm—ordering breakfast in bed required forethought—we had to choose the night before what time we wanted to be awakened by a knock on our door. We found we preferred letting our bodies and minds tell us when to get up each day—or even whether to get up. We had plenty of fruit and nuts and yogurt and the fixings for tea in our cabin whenever we felt the need. Some mornings we headed to the Hudson Room at eight for devotions, other mornings we got up before the sun to walk a few miles on the decks and watch the sun emerge from the ocean, and on some mornings the sun was high in the sky before we opened our eyes.

Life aboard the ship truly was like living in the heart of a small, very interesting, very entertaining town with lots to do just down the street. We could stop by the bar to listen to big band music, work out, meet people from all over the world, soak in a hot tub, marvel at the sleight of hand of a magician, learn to play poker or dance, watch a first-run movie, take a class on the use of digital cameras, and see people who were in love walking arm in arm to dinner. Those people especially caught our eye.

We found our favorite places to eat, our preferred tables, and the dining room staff we enjoyed sharing our mornings with. They quickly learned our habits and greeted us enthusiastically each morning. Each day we learned a little more about their lives—some would be away for as many as nine months, but they were making money they could send back home.

We also found that we had our favorite places to hang out during the day, even which table we preferred in the library, or our favorite nook in the piano bar, and of course our favorite patio chairs on the back deck, where we could catch the warming rays of the sun as we slipped steadily eastward toward Europe.

One sunny but rather chilly day we were relaxing on the back deck drinking hot tea. A man with a huge paunch caught my eye as he ambled into the smoking area on the other side of the ship wearing a tent for a shirt. Despite his girth he moved with ease as he settled into a chaise lounge. The waiter, a man half his size, appeared immediately and took his card. No words were exchanged. He apparently knew the man's drink. The man pulled out a delicately carved red pipe. Even though he was on the other side of the ship, and a swimming pool separated us, the fragrance of his pipe smoke filled my senses. The sensation was not at all unpleasant. I loved the memories it evoked of my childhood. My father, for a brief time, smoked a pipe after his doctors convinced him that cigarettes were going to kill him.

Dad gained a few extra years giving up cigarettes, but not enough. He died very young. He was only seventy-two. I am sixty-nine and don't feel anywhere near close to death. My father at sixty-nine had no such confidence. He could go nowhere without his portable oxygen tank. It had been that way since my sophomore year in high school—the year Dad turned fifty-nine.

My father struggled mightily to breathe the last twenty years of his life. I accepted his condition as the price of growing old. I no longer feel that way. My father's death at a young age may have been at least partially responsible for me remaining very serious about trying to maintain the fitness of an athlete all my life. Riding my bike thousands of miles a year takes a bit of time, but to my mind it is a good investment. I saw how many days and years of Dad's life were spent in doctors' offices and hospitals, not to mention the many hours he lost to coughing.

"Do you mind if I join you?" I heard a man ask. I looked up, surprised to see Andy standing beside our table.

"Please do," I answered. Few days had gone by in which we did not talk to Andy or at least wave to him. Many days we ate breakfast or another meal together, and we heard about his difficulties. The assault charges had been dropped by his fiancée, who we discovered was not a passenger, but was from Indonesia and worked aboard the ship. I suppose he sought us out because he wanted what we have—he had already been in two marriages and had given up on both. He was intrigued when we told him that our marriage and our relationship had not always been as he was observing it to be—that may have encouraged him to open up to us—to ask so many questions about our relationship.

His curiosity may have led me to notice *Acedia & Me,* a book in the ship's library about marriage. It was written by Kathleen Norris, an author whose work I had read before. I looked up the meaning of *acedia* and found that it means sloth, or laziness or indifference in religious matters, but Norris described it as *soul weariness.* I was hooked when I realized she was writing about the transformation of her marriage—the very subject that was on my mind, on our minds, as Mardi and I returned, often at the promptings of Andy, to discussions of the journey she and I had been on since the summer of 1969.

And what of the dead times in a marriage, when the romance has faded, and happily ever after seems a cruel sham? Norris was putting words to the feelings Mardi and I had experienced not so long ago. I felt I could trust the author not only because I had read and appreciated her work before but also because she was from the kind of people I was from. She was raised on the plains of South Dakota and had even returned to the stark beauty of those vast oceans of grass to pursue her craft. The book grabbed me also because Norris, like me, wanted to better understand the writings of that great Italian author, Dante Alighieri. When I read a line well into her book, *Love is the whole purpose of Dante's journey, and also its goal,* I knew we were kindred spirits.

Watching the deep blue waters of the ocean slide by day after day filled us with anticipation for the adventures awaiting us. Listening to English spoken in accents from all over the world added to the feeling of mystery and intrigue. A German woman explaining to an Englishman the intricacies of reading books on a Kindle put me in touch with my childhood dreams that travel would open to me the possibility of getting to know people who lived lives much different than mine.

A young Japanese woman, walking beside a European man I was certain she had just met, clenched her fists tightly on the first two circuits of the promenade deck. But each time she walked by the snippets of conversation became more and more relaxed until on the third circuit her fists opened, her arms moved freely, and her fingers were wide and extended. She at last looked as if she was truly enjoying the man's company. No longer were they interviewing each other—they were sharing common interests in free-flowing conversation.

Mardi and I were convinced that many of the lovers we were noticing were married folks like us, devoting time to their spouses that they had not felt they could afford earlier in their lives. We did a little inquiring and discovered we were correct—three honeymooners were aboard, an equal number of couples renewing their marriage vows, and thirty-seven couples celebrating wedding anniversaries, and who knows how many couples like us who were discovering the luxury of having nothing on your agenda but enjoying yourself and your spouse.

Traveling at the speed of a bicycle does wondrous things for the mind and body. Watching the motion of the waves bouncing off the side of the ship has a definite calming effect—I never did tire of stepping onto the verandah and feeling the immensity of the ocean and the power of the wind and the waves. No matter how large the swells, our ship cut through the water with very little wake. We had learned in a captain's meeting that the big, bulbous bow was responsible. It seemed counterintuitive that something big and round on the front of a ship would not only cut down on the size of our wake but increase fuel efficiency as well.

Such tidbits of information kept us coming back day after day to the captain's meeting. I was fascinated by all facets of the ship and navigation. I enjoyed studying our movement through the water, and guessing our speed, which I could verify by looking at the twenty-four/seven coverage of the ship's progress on our television monitor. Not only could we see where in the world we were, 1469 nautical miles to Funchal, Portugal and 1834 nm from FLL, but we could also see the course we were following, our exact speed, the apparent wind speed on deck, and the local time, as well as sunset at our present position.

We knew Italy awaited us at the end of our ocean journey, but we loved the luxury and adventure of being on the high seas—too much, it seemed. We had planned to study Italian each day, but we found far too much to do—or maybe we were just enjoying the time away from time so much that we were not eager for this portion of our journey to end. I don't quite know how else to put it, nor could I really make sense of it. I am a production-oriented person. I want to get things done. Yet what was I getting done each day? On the surface of it, not much.

However I was sensing a transformation—a subtle shift—that we may not have noticed had we not been able to look at ourselves through Andy's eyes. He helped us see that we were becoming gentler with each other—more focused on each other's needs and less concerned about motives. In short we were wooing each other—no longer taking each other for granted. We were approaching our relationship in the same way that travel is approached, where the everyday things are appreciated, even scrutinized.

Time—lots of it—was transforming us. I hoped that we could carry this feeling of oneness, and completeness in time, with us to Italy. When I was in Italy the first time, working as a laborer on farms, I came to realize that Italians view time differently. I was eager to find out if what I was feeling on the ship was what Italians feel every day. I sensed that it was.

CHAPTER TWO

MS Oosterdam ~ Tuesday March 29 ~ 62 & Partly Cloudy

Taking a Fresh Look

To travel is to take a journey into yourself.
DANNY KAYE

■

The highest happiness on earth is marriage.
WILLIAM LYON PHELPS

𝓐 week and a day into our journey I woke up to an unusual sight—lights on land. I slipped into my robe and stepped onto our verandah to watch the lights draw nearer. We were over thirty-two hundred miles from Fort Lauderdale and less than ten from Funchal. I slowly became aware that one light had begun moving. Quite a few minutes passed before I figured out that it was the light of a small fishing boat heading our way. Soon after, I saw two more small boats motoring into the early morning fog to begin a day of fishing even before the sun had made its appearance. Behind them I could barely make out mountains reaching into low-hanging clouds. As we worked our way closer and closer to the shore I saw houses stair-stepping up the hills. It was a strange sensation after so many days of seeing just water.

Mardi joined me on the verandah, pressed herself against my back, and asked me what I would give up to make it possible to cruise the oceans of the world at least once a year for the rest of our lives. I swear she and I have angels surrounding us that prompt our thoughts—it's bizarre how often what she is thinking is what I am thinking. When I was a kid I learned that this was called ESP—extrasensory perception—a scientific sounding name for *we don't know what the heck it is.* There are an awful lot of things in life that we really don't have an explanation for. The mysterious relationship between husband and wife is one of those phenomena. *And the two shall become one* is the best explanation I know.

Mardi's question made my day. We didn't have to come up with an answer. Just knowing she was loving this life as much as I was meant that we would work together to make it happen. We had already discovered we enjoyed living with our youngest son, Jimi, and his wife, Kristin—and that was saving us a bunch of money. At first it would have been more accurate to say that they were living with us, but with the birth of our granddaughter Chloe last year, it seemed that we were now living with them. The knowledge that our house is not empty when we live in Italy, or Colorado, or Nebraska, or Wyoming for varying lengths of time is very liberating.

I thought I'd be in a rush to get off the ship to tour Funchal, but I felt no such compunction. We joined Edward and Mary, the English couple we had dined with our first night aboard, for a leisurely breakfast. They told us they planned to tour the island of Madeira by private taxi and mentioned a couple of compatriots with a strong connection to Funchal—George Bernard Shaw had taken dance lessons at Reid's Palace and Sir Winston Churchill had a favorite room at the world famous hotel. Edward and Mary had toured Funchal on a previous cruise and described an exhilarating ride down its steep streets in a basket. I think they were a little surprised that we weren't more interested in seeing the sights.

We told them we were going to allow our curiosity to guide us to the old part of town where we hoped to find a coffee shop where locals hang out. It turned out to be on a busy street filled with people, not cars. The clientele was young professionals—a sure sign of a fast Internet connection. We claimed a couple of stools separated by a small table that had a perfect view of the street. Our waiter knew no English. We knew no Portuguese. We thought we had ordered coffee with a touch of milk in it. What we got was black coffee and a large pot of warm milk.

While we were worked our way through the hundreds of emails that had built up during the week, we discovered that language barriers are real. Even though we were in the midst of Portuguese society, our contact with Portuguese people was limited. We had not felt isolated when we sat in the coffee shops and restaurants of Rome or Bolzano the previous fall when Mardi gave volunteering as a farm laborer a try. We were definitely not fluent in Italian, but the time we had spent learning the language allowed us to comprehend enough of what was being said around us that we didn't feel cut off.

Some of the isolation we felt in Funchal may have been because we were in a city deluged with tourists getting off ships. We would be there a very short time. We felt like tourists and we were treated like tourists—not necessarily poorly, but we weren't investing a lot in the locals and they had no reason to invest a lot in us. We were here today, gone tomorrow as far as they were concerned. However, we were there long enough, thanks to a huge storm that dropped torrents of rain on the city, to use that whole pot of milk to flavor our coffees and then our teas.

The sun drew us out after lunch and we walked through the city's glistening gardens marveling at the intricate mosaics of its sidewalks, and watched the lineup of taxis being pushed forward by hand in the queue across from the Ritz. The drivers inched their cars forward, being careful to not crash into each other. Accompanying this amusing display of saving fuel was an Elvis Presley wannabe serenading the taxi drivers with his rendition of "It's Now or Never." The song reminded me of the captain's warning that had been playing like a stuck record in my mind all day—*The ship will set sail without you if you are not on board at five thirty*. I felt a great sense of relief as we walked up the gangplank at 1701 and were informed that two hundred twenty-five people were not yet on board. We went to the observation deck to watch the last of our fellow passengers scurrying down the quay. All day I had been imagining that *we'd* be the ones running toward the ship, the horn blaring. I'm sure the captain had some leeway built into his admonition, but no one tested his resolve, and we were soon maneuvering out of the harbor.

Mardi and I settled back into our routines. Even though we had walked over six miles on the charming streets of Funchal, we made our way down to the promenade deck to walk and watch the sun sink into the ocean. Of all the things we loved to do aboard, that was the one thing we made sure we did every day—that and eating of course—and sleeping, which we did quite well that night.

We had planned to get up early the next morning to walk, but with no sun to lure us to the promenade deck we stayed in bed and exercised, then fell back to sleep. Nine o'clock rolled around and we were still moving at the pace of the ocean slipping by—a pace that was slower than usual—the captain informed us that since we were ahead of schedule, he had slowed the ship's speed from eighteen to seventeen knots.

With one port down and only two to go, the feeling aboard changed. The end was in sight. It was time to consider some commemorative purchases. Mardi bought a Holland America windbreaker for me and I bought an iPhone holder/wallet for her.

During the final few days of the cruise Andy dined with us often. We found out he was a successful businessman from suburban Chicago with three children—daughters aged twenty-five and thirty-one, and a son, twenty-eight—and that he sometimes took his grandkids cruising with him. He also shared that his fiancée was half his age, had a three-year-old daughter, and took care of her mother, who was in poor health.

As he discussed his situation he began to understand how different his expectations were from those of his fiancée. He was comparing his life to ours, and our relationship to the one he feared he would have with a woman whose values and culture were so different. When he heard himself say that she didn't actually know how to love, realization flashed in his eyes. He began wondering how he had gotten himself into a situation where he was spending tens of thousands of dollars cruising the world to be near a woman he barely knew. By his own admission *he was a man in his sixties acting as if he was in his twenties wooing a woman in her thirties.* Watching Andy take a fresh look at his life, I was reminded of Thomas Merton's aphorism *It takes real courage to recognize that we ourselves are the cause of our own unhappiness.*

As we were nearing our second landfall I heard a three-generation family loudly discussing their vacation. They talked at length of where they were going and where they had been. The grandfather began telling a story about a vineyard he had particularly enjoyed. His son asked him what country it was in. The old man said that he had no idea. I couldn't relate to his story at the time, but that was before I visited two ports in two days, both in Spain.

We were delivered to Malaga and Cartagena with little effort on our part— we hadn't spent months planning and dreaming about these ports of call. We saw a military parade in Cartagena—or was that Malaga, Picasso's birthplace? There was a Ferris wheel in Malaga and a merry-go-round in Cartagena, right? And where did we see that man transporting a mattress balanced on a bicycle? Andy joined us for dinner and showed us a video of him giving his fiancée flowers and taking her for a carriage ride. Was that after Malaga or Cartagena? I do recall it was the night he said he was still thinking of marrying her.

On the penultimate day of the cruise Andy joined us for lunch. He began mid-thought, not realizing that the fears that were keeping him from sleeping had not yet been shared with us. He backed up and confided that he had been told that his fiancée may be seeing other men. As if to emphasize the indiscretions, or maybe his indecision, he held his mouth open and cocked to the side after he finished talking. I couldn't tell whether he believed what he had heard, but I did note that he used the phrase *disastrous relationship* when he asked what we thought he should do. We attempted to help him by asking questions—hoping the answers would help him see his situation more clearly. He teared up as he told us he had been following her around the world for two years, and was hoping that marrying her would give them a different life.

Even though we were eating one of his favorite lunches—a spicy shredded beef sandwich topped off with a piece of pecan pie—Andy was too worked up to eat. It was one of my favorite meals too, but the meal was more noteworthy for feelings of loneliness. Seated nearby, and situated so that she was looking right at us, was a lone woman. I had no idea what her story was—only that her face looked sad. Her countenance reminded me of difficult days in our own marriage—of times when we were like Andy, facing decisions that should, in retrospect, have been easy for us but somehow weren't.

Our discussions with Andy were making me deeply aware that no matter what our situation, we are all on journeys—sometimes difficult, sometimes joyous. I hoped that we had helped him. The decision he was about to make was going impact him greatly—and his kids and grandkids as well. He was obviously open to advice—in fact crying out for it. I remember those times in our marriage, and in my career, when we were asking for help in our decisions. Those seasons of life when you fear your prayers aren't being answered can feel like dark days indeed.

Our last night aboard was bittersweet. We were happy knowing that when we woke up the next morning we'd be in Italian waters, but we had come to love the rhythms of the sea and life aboard the ship. Standing on our verandah and watching the ocean slide by was a sensation I never tired of—a private space to experience the immensity of this earth drew me outside every time we set foot in our cabin. I wondered if standing on that balcony gave me a sense of how little I control and of how much my happiness depends upon accepting that fact. I was not in charge of where the ship was headed, nor how fast it was going, nor anything about the voyage. My only contribution was to pay for a portion of it, and in exchange I was given a space in which to enjoy the movement of the ship, the sea, the sky, and this earth. That is one of the reasons I was so enamored with monitoring our progress around the globe—seeing where it was day and where it was night—where storms were rocking the earth and where it was calm and beautiful. On this trip calm and beautiful seemed to be wherever our ship was.

The same seems true of our relationship. We have been through the storms of not getting along, not trusting each other, not affirming each other. Now we are enjoying the smooth sailing of the lessons we've learned on our journey. We've learned of the benefits of a slight change in attitude. We've also learned the benefits of being totally attentive to each other's needs. I'm not sure this cruise taught us that, but it certainly gave us a great opportunity to practice it.

The next day, as we were preparing to get off the ship, Andy came rushing up to tell us that he viewed meeting us as God's plan for his life. It made me feel good to hear him say that. Every time we spoke with Andy, Mardi and I spent a good portion of the next day wondering whether what we had shared with him about marriage had been helpful. As Andy talked about the failures of his previous marriages, I was reminded of the mistakes I had made and the mistakes I almost made—especially those related to the amount of time I dedicated to running my business. How easy it would have been for me be in Andy's shoes, without a companion in my senior years to share my life. The essence of Andy's story was that he was lonely. He shared with us that he saw something in the relationship that Mardi and I have that he wanted. I regret now that I didn't get his email address. I would love to know the rest of his story.

While thinking about Andy—wondering what he had decided to do, an epiphany about the word *rest* struck me. It has two entirely different meanings, both pertaining to Andy. He is looking for rest—in the Biblical sense of the word—*Come to me, all you who are weary and burdened, and I will give you rest.* And then there's that other very different meaning, the completion, what comes next. Are we all looking for the rest of our journey—that part of our story where we finally give up doing it our way and rest.

As I pondered these thoughts it hit me that this might be the secret of Italian time.

CHAPTER THREE

Civitavecchia ~ Sunday April 3 ~ 69 & Sunny

A Two for the Road Beginning

Certainly, travel is more than the seeing of sights;
it is a change that goes on, deep and permanent,
in the ideas of living.
MARY RITTER BEARD

■

To get the full value of joy
you must have someone to divide it with.
MARK TWAIN

Our first day in Italy began in stateroom 5158 of the *Oosterdam*. As I was leaving the nirvana of my dreams and returning to the heaven on earth of our last thirteen days, I opened my eyes and saw glistening lights lining the harbor of one of Italy's oldest cities. The lights weren't getting larger or smaller, just hanging there. As I slowly became aware of the implications of those stationary lights, my pulse quickened. The ship's travel experts had given us a glimpse of the day that lay ahead of us; they assured me that we could travel from Civitavecchia to the Amalfi Coast in one day using buses and trains, but in no way did their seasoned advice prepare me for the adventure that awaited us.

Even our last breakfast aboard didn't go as I thought it would. I wanted to eat in the Vista Dining Room on deck two—down near water level—for a more regal sendoff. Mardi, however, convinced me that we should eat where we always ate—in the Lido Café up on level nine where we had managed to secure a window seat every morning. While Mardi brewed our early morning Earl Grey tea, I went in search of a table with a view. We loved starting each day watching the mesmerizing rhythm of the waves as they rolled by into the vast expanse beyond. It was humbling and energizing at the same time. For my last meal aboard I chose what had become my favorite breakfast—the *Oosterdam's* delicious French toast, but on this morning I couldn't eat all of it. I was too excited—too nervous about the day ahead.

Seated at a nearby table was a woman who would soon play a large and recurring role in the story of our day. I hadn't noticed her earlier in the voyage, but her smile as we walked out of the restaurant made the day feel right—a fellow passenger acknowledging that one very good portion of our adventure was ending and another beginning once we stepped away from the familiar routines of the ship.

We returned to our stateroom, put our toiletries in our suitcases, and wheeled them to the midships lobby. That in itself was memorable—it would be our first elevator ride aboard the *Oosterdam*. On our first day we encountered a long line of people waiting for the elevator. We opted to carry our bags up three flights of stairs. That gave us the idea of making stair-climbing part of our exercise program for the next two weeks. On some days we climbed over one hundred flights as we made our way from meal to meal, event to event, and deck to deck, our iPhones faithfully recording it all. Often we climbed as many as eight flights two or three times a day to get from the promenade deck on the second floor to the tenth deck, where the library and the observation platform were located.

Now that we were in Italy, we were in a hurry to get off the boat and through customs—and we didn't want to be slowed waiting for the stewards to deliver our bags to us onshore. But all of our bags were more than we could handle in the crowded stairways, so we punched the elevator's down button and waited and waited. Finally the door opened, however the elevator looked full. We told the folks we would catch the next one, but a woman in the back said, "Hop on, we can make room." We started to protest but she insisted: "You'll regret it if you don't take this one." Reluctantly the people in front gave up some personal space and we squeezed in. As I turned to thank her for her thoughtfulness, I recognized her. She was the woman who had smiled at us as we were leaving the restaurant. Whether you attribute it to Providence or good luck, it seemed like our journey was getting off to a good start—or it might have been naive optimism coloring my judgment.

The elevator stopped at every floor. Each time the door opened we saw at least a dozen people waiting. In the crush of people getting off the elevator Mardi and I got separated. She followed a group that missed a turn. I thought she was following me, and so did she. When I discovered she wasn't, I took a calculated risk and left my suitcases to go find her. After a few minutes of nervous searching I found her. We hurried back to our suitcases, which, I was thankful to discover, were right where I had left them. One crisis averted. We queued up.

I expected a formal clearing of customs, but this line was for the sole purpose of scanning our stateroom keys to insure that we were off the ship. We shuffled like lemmings down the gangplank and into the terminal, moving with the flow of people. We walked past numerous officials in uniforms. At any moment I expected one of them to ask for my *passaporto*. We kept inching forward until at last we found ourselves outside the terminal, no longer surrounded by uniformed officials, standing near a line of motor coaches.

I took a deep breath of the chilly morning air and immediately felt at one with Italy—we were hearing the Italian language—delivered at full volume and with a passionate cadence. As we made our way past the buses in the direction I had been told we would find the train station, it suddenly hit me that once again we were in Italy with no official proof of our entry. This time Italian officials had not even glanced at our passports.

The last time, they had at least looked at them. Mardi and I had taken a bus from Bolzano in northern Italy to Munich, to catch a nonstop Lufthansa flight to Chicago. The German customs agent asked me, with what sounded like bewilderment, how we had been able to drive to Germany. I didn't understand why he couldn't figure out from my passport that I had flown from the USA to Rome, spent a few weeks in Italy, and had arrived in Munich by bus. When I mentioned *Italy*, he said, "Ah, now I understand. You've come from Italy and not America. The Italians are not so diligent about stamping passports..." and then his thought trailed off and with a wave of his hand he signified that we should proceed and that the Italians should be forgiven for their lack of attention to details—for their *laissez-faire* attitude to use a French term—which I have defined since my days of high school French as an attitude of letting things take their own course without interfering. We didn't yet know, as we tucked our passports safely into our bags, that we would soon be treated to yet another exchange that was Italian to the core.

We continued walking toward what we presumed was the train station, visible about a mile or so away. Several of our fellow *Oosterdam* passengers, who had disembarked at Civitavecchia on previous journeys, had told us that it was possible to walk from the ship to the train station. We had our eyes focused on a building that had what looked like Trenitalia's logo on it. But just to be sure I asked a policeman if we were indeed heading in the right direction. He assured us that we were, but he said it was three kilometers and we should take the free shuttle.

"*Ci piace camminare,*" I said.

"*Ma è a tre chilometri,*" he said again, to make sure we had understood.

"*Questo non è molto lontano,*" I said trying to emphasize with hand gestures that we didn't think that was such a long way to walk.

He did the same to me, using not only his hands but his whole body. He ended the performance with that beautiful Italian shrug that includes a jutting forward of the chin while lifting his eyebrows that says *As you wish. If you like to walk I won't try to talk you out of it.*

We soon discovered that the policeman had failed to mention what seemed to be a very important fact to us. The smooth sidewalk that had delivered us to the policeman suddenly ended after the last bus. I should have remembered what I had learned on my previous visits to Italy—Italians are somewhat reluctant to offer a counter-argument when confronted with resolve. It hadn't fazed us when the policeman repeated the warning about the three-kilometer walk. Had he mentioned that we'd have to walk on the side of a highway to get to the train station—that would have fazed us.

We stopped to take our first picture in Italy. Mardi posed with our suitcases—two carry-ons plus one full-sized and one medium-sized bag—all of them on casters. Mardi looked decidedly festive in a bright pink jacket. She was also sporting a huge smile. Before I put my phone away, I glanced at the image to make sure we had a good photograph to remember this auspicious juncture—the moment we set off on the Italian portion of our journey of a lifetime.

As we made our way along the road we debated our decision to walk. Rather than turn back, we relied on the fact that others had done it. We were certain we were fit enough to handle the walk, and surely we would get to a sidewalk again. About a hundred yards ahead we could see that the road turned right. We expected to find a sidewalk after the turn. We didn't. We found instead a rough road with potholes, but we were too far into the game to turn back. Our eyes were on the Trenitalia logo on the building ahead of us. We were certain it would be our deliverance. To our dismay, as we got closer, we discovered that Trenitalia and the Port of Civitavecchia have similar logos—the building we thought was the train station was not. Beyond it, a couple of more football-field-lengths, we saw another building that looked like it could be the train station—so we began wheeling our suitcases toward it. It turned out to be another terminal for cruise ships. It was beginning to dawn on me that there were a lot of places for the big ships to dock at Civitavecchia, and some of them were a lot closer than ours to the main part of town. Our advice-givers must have walked to the train station from one of those docks.

When at last we got to that third terminal we saw no people, but we did find large buses. We were relieved to find a driver inside the first one. He opened his door as we approached. I explained our situation. With a flourish of hospitality he invited us aboard, telling us that he could get us within a ten-minute walk of the station. I was surprised. I was sure it wasn't his job to shuttle passengers from a different terminal to town. As he drove us to the drop-off point I watched the route. I could not imagine how we would have gotten across the motorway on foot. The only possible route seemed to be the exact one we were following—a busy roadway.

I turned around to take a picture of Mardi to contrast with our first photo in Italy. She was still wearing a huge smile—the seats of the big, beautifully decked out bus stretched out behind her—all of them empty. From the comfort of the bus I thought back to our grand entrance into Italy—shuffling along a road dragging our suitcases, hoping that a taxi would come along or a generous motorist would offer us a ride. It brought to mind a similar scene from one of my favorite movies, *Two for the Road,* which I first saw when I was in college. Audrey Hepburn and Albert Finney play Joanna and Mark, two college students traveling around Europe. Mark is alone and Joanna is with a group of friends. Their paths cross. Unlike Mardi and me, they didn't like each other at first. But an outbreak of chickenpox among Joanna's traveling companions forced the two of them to team up to travel around France.

Jump to the end of the movie. Joanna and Mark are once again traveling around Europe. This time, however, they are driving an expensive Mercedes convertible. They are married. She is sophisticated and beautiful. He is a successful architect. They are at a border crossing, passing from France into Italy. In addition to gorgeous, Joanna is also cool-headed and organized. In a scene reminiscent of numerous other moments in their marriage, Mark is in full panic mode searching through his bags, thinking he has lost his passport. Joanna opens the glove box, pulls out his passport, and calmly hands it to him. He calls her a *b-word.* She calls him a *b-word* as well. But this time the words are said softly, with respect—a twinkle in their eyes. To my eye it was obvious that they had come not only to appreciate each other but also to love each other. That movie has always held a special place in my heart because it showed that a good marriage is not one that never has conflict but one that has *survived* conflict and has gone on to flourish and prosper.

As Mardi and I dragged our suitcases down that rough, narrow road skirting potholes, we questioned our decision, but neither of us turned on the other. That cannot be said of our whole marriage, however. At various points in our forty-six years together, one or both of us might have said something snarky. But on this morning we laughed at ourselves—feeling that walking thirty minutes was better than waiting in a bus. We felt even better about our decision when we looked back and saw that none of the buses had departed the terminal. We smiled at one another and kept walking.

I began thinking about the policeman. I suppose he tried to talk us out of walking to the train station, but he didn't, in my mind, try hard enough. Had it been the first time an Italian had not mentioned pertinent facts regarding a decision I was making I wouldn't have given it a second thought. However, a similar thing happened six months earlier with a train conductor. I discovered too late that a tobacco shop employee had sold us a ticket that required us to transfer to a bus to reach Rome. We didn't want to do that because of our suitcases. An early morning commuter bus ride into the heart of the city would have been bad enough, but with suitcases it would have been unthinkable. The conductor listened to my explanation and said it would be no problem. "Get off at the next station. You will find a train for Rome."

We were going to do exactly that until I asked what track the train would be on. He said we would need to hike up and over three tracks to get to it. I explained that I was okay with going on to Fiumicino to transfer to a train bound for Rome. I knew from having traveled out of Fiumicino Airport on my first trip that we would not have to lug our suitcases up a bunch of stairs but could instead just wheel our bags to the assigned track. He shrugged his shoulders and with that Italian jutting of the chin said the American equivalent of *Suit yourself.*

We stayed on the train and went on to Fiumicino. As we were wheeling our bags to the train headed for Roma Termini, that same conductor stopped us and told us we needed tickets. Thinking he had forgotten our earlier exchange I showed him our tickets for Rome.

"Tickets no longer good," he said.

"But I just bought them this morning," I protested.

"You go out of zone," he countered.

I was frustrated, but I decided to not let it bother me. The tickets I had purchased to get us from Poggio Mirteto to Rome, a distance of over seventy kilometers, had cost only eight euros for both of us. We were now less than thirty kilometers from Roma Termini, so I figured it would probably cost even less. I pulled out ten euros and asked him for tickets.

"I cannot sell you tickets," he said matter-of-factly. He pointed to the ticket office, the same office where I had bought my first train ticket in Italy—a place for which I had fond memories. Six years earlier I had rehearsed my request numerous times as I flew the last miles to Rome. I had even tried out my *italiano* on an Italian student who was studying in America. She suggested a slight change to my wording. It worked perfectly. The ticket agent responded to me in Italian and gave me the exact ticket I wanted—to the first train station in Tuscany. I was elated that my first use of Italian in Italy had gone so well.

This time the conversation at the ticket office went well again—no misunderstandings in language but plenty of other misunderstandings. It was then that I learned that the conductor had failed to tell us that by choosing to transfer at Fiumicino we were breaking the law—we had traveled to a station for which we didn't have tickets. We would have to pay a penalty for that. We would also have to pay for a ticket from Poggio Mirteto to Fiumicino, which was much more expensive than the ticket from Poggio Mirteto to Rome. And now, because we wanted to get back to Roma Termini, we were going to have to buy a ticket on the high-speed train, which was six times more expensive than the local train we had ridden to Fiumicino.

The total cost to us for not climbing those stairs was a whopping sixty-five euros plus the eight euros we had paid for our original commuter tickets to Rome. Had the conductor mentioned even one of the problems we'd encounter if we didn't get off at the next stop, I would have done exactly what he suggested—no matter how many flights of stairs we had to climb.

I have yet to fathom why the conductor didn't mention all the problems we were creating for ourselves by staying on his train. Maybe at the time he didn't realize that what we were doing was technically illegal. Or maybe he assumed we knew that what we were doing was going to cost us a bunch of money yet we were doing it anyway, so why argue with us. Which is odd, because Italians have absolutely no compunction about arguing with other Italians. I look forward to the day when I know Italian well enough, and have enough chutzpah, that I can get into a vigorous point-counterpoint encounter with an Italian—the kind where we're waving our arms and maybe even yelling, yet when we're done, we respect each other and remain friends. That's the Italian way to argue.

But the policeman in Civitavecchia and I had no such discussion. I didn't know what he knew about what lay between the port and the train station. I knew only that others had told me it was possible to walk from one to the other. But the memories of that walk will stay with us the rest of our lives—each of us trailing suitcases. It's already become a metaphor for the journey of marriage—a reminder that marriage has its ups and downs, and even arguments and disappointments, but can still be a good marriage. I'm glad

Mardi and I were exposed at a very young age to the idea that life is indeed a journey and marriage no less so.

I thought again about *Two for the Road*. I can't say when I first saw it, but it came out when I was a college sophomore, which was two years before I saw Mardi across that crowded room. I was a bit of a film buff in those days. I *do* remember the first time Mardi and I saw the movie together. We were with our new friends, Roger and Bev, who had already journeyed down the road of marriage a couple of years, having wed soon after high school. They understood better than we did what a journey marriage is. They had a child by the time we met them. They may even have called each other *b-words* by that time. Mardi and I had not yet journeyed that far.

Mardi and I traveled down the marriage road for seven years before we hit tough times. Mark and Joanna were looking back on ten years of marriage, which now seems like such a short time. I think of all I've learned about life and marriage since our ten-year anniversary. We have children who have been married longer than Joanna and Mark. Now that I'm counting, I realize that my parents' marriage, ended by the death of my father, did not reach the forty-six-year mark. Death ended the marriage of Mardi's parents as well. Her father died quite young. Her parents were allowed only twenty-five years together.

The bus driver pulled me out of my nostalgic journey when he let us off at a roundabout near Forte Michelangelo and pointed us toward the train station. With each transition we were feeling like we were more truly in Italy. We looked like tourists, but we no longer felt like it. We were in an Italian town—a town that was preparing for a festival. Workmen were setting up barriers along the wide streets. We asked them why and they told us it was for a bike race that would soon be coming through town. Young parents were pushing strollers through the park. Joggers were scurrying past us in both directions, and lots of people were walking their dogs. This did not have the feel of a tourist town. As we walked along, I noticed that the sidewalk was not of concrete but rather of individual blocks laid with a craftsman's expertise and eye. We soon came to what I have come to regard as one of my favorite features of Italian towns—a free-flowing water fountain—we stopped, rinsed our hands, and filled our water bottles.

Despite the hiccup of hiking a mile or so along a road with cars whizzing by, the morning was working out fine. The challenge of getting to the train station added to our sense of adventure. We were thrilled to be walking through the colorful streets of the old port of Civitavecchia greeting the gathering townspeople. I was especially energized by the brightly clad cyclists on sleek bikes as they made their way to the starting line. We knew we had to be getting close to the train station, but we weren't certain when this portion of our journey was going to end. Even when folks pointed at the station and told us we were only a few blocks away, we couldn't figure out which building they were pointing at. Eventually we got to it—even up close it didn't look like a train station—not as grand as we expected in one of the oldest towns in Italy.

Inside we discovered other surprises. The *Oosterdam* carries almost two thousand passengers, but only a few people were milling about and very few looked like tourists. The ship's travel aide had told us we'd need to catch a train from Civitavecchia to Roma Termini and then transfer to a train to Naples. But the timetable showed, and the ticket agent confirmed, that we could go directly from Civitavecchia to Naples. The train, which would be leaving in about twenty minutes, would arrive in Naples about the same time we had expected to be boarding a train in Rome for the two-hour ride to Naples. Even though we'd still have at least one train ride and one bus ride after Naples, it now looked certain that we would get to see the beauty of the Amalfi Coast— we'd arrive long before dark.

Tickets in hand, I turned around and was surprised to once again see the woman who had smiled at us at breakfast—the same woman who had saved us a bunch of time by urging us to squeeze onto the elevator. She was near the front of what was suddenly a rather long line. We exchanged stories. She told me that she and her friend had suffered through two extremely crowded bus rides that still left them with a bit of a hike to get to the train station.

That made me feel even better about our decision to walk. We got to the train station before the crowds and early enough to ride the InterCity train directly to Napoli. We checked the timetable again and moved our luggage out to the track. Lots of folks were nervous—asking questions, trying to figure out where they should be waiting. I remembered the feeling. The first time I boarded a train in Italy I made the rookie mistake of getting on the car that stopped in front of me. I should have found my *carozza*, whose number is marked on the ticket, by walking along the station platform. I didn't know that moving from car to car on an Italian train is not easy—the aisles are narrow and often crowded with people.

A woman who mentioned she was from Bologna struck up a conversation with me. I was flattered that she spoke to me in Italian. She wanted to know if I would help her load her luggage when the train arrived. I checked her ticket and noticed that she was assigned to a different car. As I was explaining to Mardi that I was going to help this woman, a track change was announced. Amazingly though, it didn't require using either a tunnel or stairs to get to the new track—instead of track two, the train would be arriving on *binario tre*.

The friendly woman who had made room for us on the elevator, came up and introduced herself. Donna had noticed me looking at the Italian woman's ticket and asked me to look at hers. I showed her where the number was printed and encouraged her to find her car before she boarded. A few moments later the train pulled into the station. I threw our bags into our car and ran down the platform to help the woman from Bologna. But I couldn't find her. I ran back to our car, hopped on, and was surprised to see Donna talking to Mardi. She had panicked she said, and threw her bags into the first open door. I told her I'd help her. I found our seats, stowed our bags, got Mardi settled in, then returned to help Donna.

What had proved to be extremely difficult for me six years earlier turned out to be quite simple this time—this train was modern and very few people were in the aisles. Donna grabbed a small carry-on. I grabbed her largest suitcase. Her traveling companion stayed with their other bags in the luggage compartment area. When we got to her car we discovered, much to her surprise and mine, that she and her friend had booked a private compartment.

"Wow. Is all this just for us?" she asked.

"For now, it looks like it's all yours," I said as I maneuvered her suitcase into the room.

"It's so nice of you to take the time to do this," she said.

I smiled and told her I was happy to help. I didn't tell her about all the people on three different cars I had to squeeze past with my huge suitcase on my first trip to Italy. Donna had helped me. I was glad to return the favor. My curiosity about how it was that she didn't know she had first class tickets overwhelmed good manners, and I asked her how much she had paid for the first class ticket from Civitavecchia to Napoli. I was surprised that it wasn't that much more than we had paid for our second class tickets. I made a mental note to consider traveling first class next time. Their personal compartment was not only spacious; it was quiet as well. A person could get a lot of work done traveling from Civitavecchia to Naples.

By the time I got back to Mardi she had our space set up for both work and pleasure—the tables between the two sets of facing seats were folded out, she had her computer plugged in, our maps spread out, and she was tracing our progress with a highlighter as we hugged the shore on our way toward Naples. The efficiency of the space reminded me why I love Italian trains. I like all train travel, but especially in Italy—the attention to detail makes getting there much more pleasant.

I settled into the window seat opposite Mardi. I was looking backward at where we had been, Mardi could see forward. On the other side of the half-empty train I caught glimpses of the Mediterranean as we sped south past low-lying hills. A few kilometers south of Ladíspoli I looked out the wall of windows beside me and noticed an Alitalia jet low in the sky flying at a converging angle. It was flying at approach speed—faster than the planes I had flown in my days as a commercial pilot, but still most likely not that much faster than our train as it sped through the Italian countryside at close to one hundred miles an hour. I should have thought to check the wind speed. On a very brisk day, the winds coming off the Mediterranean could slow the speed of the plane over the ground to a point where an ultra-high-speed train could win this race. But on this day we tied—at the exact moment the jet crossed our path we made a rather sharp turn inland toward Rome.

I checked the map and discovered that when we made that turn we were less than a mile from the end of the northwest/southeast runway of Leonardo da Vinci International Airport—and right on its extended centerline. The airliner would have been no more than a few hundred feet above us. Rarely do we get to see planes that low. That close to the ground, jumbo jets look so big and so slow you expect them to fall out of the sky. It was a sight I don't think I will ever forget, and perfectly timed—like the coordination necessary to position a flight of F-16s over a football stadium for a flyover at the exact moment the national anthem ends.

We continued speeding southwest into the heart of Rome. Some of the station stops were familiar. We passed by Trastevere at 1014 and Roma Ostiense at 1017. I had been through them on my first trip to Italy as I made my way to Roma Termini, where I transferred to a high-speed train that whisked me up to Chiusi in Tuscany. Mardi and I had spent a delightful afternoon in the neighborhoods of Trastevere when we lived for a brief time in Rome during our adventure as volunteer olive pickers the previous fall. I loved the feeling of knowing where we were—of what lay beyond the railway corridors we were passing through—that only blocks away people would soon be pulling up chairs on the eclectic streets of Trastevere and the Jewish Ghetto to dine *al fresco*.

At some of the stations we stopped, others we sped through. I highlighted our progress on the map and noted we were now in parts of Italy neither of us had seen. It hit me how fortunate we were to be able to be exploring yet another region of this country while getting to know her people. Italy is divided into twenty regions. On this journey, we hoped at a minimum to add the regions of Campania and Basilicata to the half dozen we already knew between us.

I took photographs. None of them were great—taking a good picture from a train is difficult. The land was gentle and productive, with a backdrop of tall mountains, but it didn't strike me that it was as lovingly cared for or as artistically rendered as the Tuscan landscapes I'd grown to love on my first sojourn in Italy. I hoped that I was making a fair comparison even though it was being made at high speed and not at ground level among the people who lived there.

I also noted that the villages were not at the *tops* of hills as they often are in Tuscany, but were, like the village of Monte San Biagio, on the *sides* of the hills instead. We once again were catching glimpses of the Mediterranean as we sped toward Formia, and across the bay we could see Gaeta jutting out into the Tyrrhenian Sea. I was beginning to realize that this was going to be a very different look at Italy. The sea now dominated, but it did so briefly. By the time we got to Céllole, fields and farms once again stretched to the horizon on both sides of the train.

Soon after Céllole we entered a tunnel and stayed in the dark for a long time. When at last we emerged into the light, we were treated to scenes of colorful shirts and sheets flapping in the breeze on clotheslines stretched high above the ground. Down below, horses grazed in orchards. Pastel-colored houses climbed the steep hillsides, and in the distance, mountains rose on both sides of the train—taller and more rugged on the inland side. By the time we got to Casapesenna we could see the Mediterranean again in the distance on the right side of the train. The farming did not seem as intense as I was used to seeing in Italy. We were in what I would describe as coastal plains—the sandy soil most likely not nearly as productive as the dark, rich topsoil of central Tuscany. A half hour later it felt as if we were coming to the outskirts of a major city. I checked the map and was surprised to discover that we were entering Naples. A few minutes later Napoli Centrale was announced. We packed up our maps and computers and grabbed our suitcases. Our adventure was about to begin in earnest—our Italian language skills and travel smarts would soon be tested.

We had been warned about the pickpockets in Napoli, but then in what city aren't you warned about pickpockets? To be fair to Naples, we had been told that Neapolitans are simply the best at a lot of things. We were cautious entering the station. On board the *Oosterdam* we had been told to book passage on a local train called the *Circumvesuviana*. We were having trouble getting our tongues around all the vowels as we asked people where to find the ticket office. Eventually we did manage to do both and discovered that it was in a different station, Garibaldi, which is conveniently located below Napoli Centrale. But before we bought the tickets we wanted to find a SIM card for my phone. For that we were told to find a tobacco shop. We made note of the location of the stairs leading to Garibaldi and headed out through the crowded station, being careful to keep as much distance as possible from people.

We didn't find a tobacco shop that sold SIM cards, but wonder of wonders we found a cellular phone store that was empty except for the manager. We wheeled our bags into the shop and explained that we were going to be in Italy at least a month, that we wanted to make some phone calls, all within Italy, that we wanted lots of data available to us, that we wanted to stay in touch with our family, and that I wanted to stay in touch with my readers and Facebook followers by posting daily photographs. We were expecting to pay a lot for all these services.

"*Si, si, no problema,*" he said and asked for my phone.

He took it, deftly opened it, took my SIM card out, handed it to me, and inserted a new one.

"*Quanta costa?*" I asked expecting something close to a hundred euros.

"*Trentatre,*" he responded with no emphasis whatsoever.

I was shocked. Had I heard him wrong? It sounded like he had said thirty-three—or was it three hundred thirty?

"Thirty-three euros?"

"*Si,*" he responded.

"And I'll be able to make phone calls?" I had reflexively switched to English when he confirmed the cost in English, but numbers were about the only words of English he understood, so I had to switch back to Italian to ask him to demonstrate how to make a call in Italy. He promptly entered the digits, without the country code, and wonder of wonders, Villa Annalara B&B was on the phone—on my very own iPhone 6s Plus. I was thrilled. What a difference this was going to make from my previous Italian sojourns, when I desperately needed to reach out and had to pay dearly to do it—or worse yet, found it impossible to make a call.

"*Mi chiamo James Ernest Shaw...*" I began.

"*Si.* Oh yes. We're expecting you tonight. My name is Salvatore," he responded in English.

I was relieved. First that there had been no mix-up in the reservations I had made many weeks ago and second that he spoke English. I had failed to put anything in my calendar other than the name of the B&B and its phone number—I didn't even have the address. I had a lot of questions for Salvatore—questions that I would have struggled to ask in Italian. He didn't know the answer to all of them—like how best to get to his place from Naples, but he did know that his bed and breakfast was located in Amalfi and not Positano. Until that moment I hadn't even known there was a town on the Amalfi Coast named Amalfi. Photographs of Positano had drawn me to the Amalfi Coast, and *Positano* was what I had typed in the *Hotels.com* search engine. The views from Villa Annalara's balcony were stunning—that's what had sold me. The description on the website sounded like a perfect match for my desire for a late-in-life honeymoon. To someone whose knowledge of the Amalfi Coast was limited to photographs of its beauty, the photographs taken from Salvatore's terrace looked to my undiscerning eye to be shots of Positano.

To say that I was shocked when Salvatore told me his B&B was not in Positano was a huge understatement. I felt foolish, but I tried to not let Mardi know how disappointed I was in myself. My job in the army was to film in locations throughout the Pacific and Alaska, including Korea and Vietnam. We were taught to pay attention to the minutest details to make sure we arrived where we were supposed to be, on time, and ready to produce for every assignment. Excuses were not allowed. Booking a room in the wrong town would have gotten me in trouble with my commanding officer, and I would have felt the same way if one of my employees had done something similar when, later in life, I was producing films throughout Europe and South America. If I was expecting to be filming in Cusco, Peru, I wouldn't want to discover that my assistant had booked a room in Chincheros.

The good news was that Salvatore sounded delightful. He was excited that we were already in Naples. He assured me that we would have plenty of daylight for our journey along the Amalfi Coast, whether we began it in Salerno or Sorrento. He suggested we stop by a tourist office to check on the schedules. As I said goodbye to Salvatore I was thinking that we could salvage the situation by taking day trips to Positano or that we might even be able to hike along the Amalfi Coast to reach that most romantic of Italian port towns.

I paid for the SIM card and was delighted to find there were no hidden charges—no per-minute add-ons. We now had access to every phone number in Italy and all of the Internet right on my phone. Our next task was to figure out whether we were buying tickets on the *Circumvesuviana* to Sorrento or Salerno. I couldn't keep the two straight. We checked our Touring Club Italiano book and discovered that Salerno was more distant from Naples, but it was closer to Amalfi by far. Before heading to the ticket office, we followed Salvatore's advice and began looking for that simple blue sign with a lowercase *i* that signifies a tourist office in Italy. Sometimes you find them right away. Other times you have to look hard and ask a lot of people. This was one of those other times. While we were looking we happened upon a man playing a grand piano. We would have loved to join the gathering crowd to listen to the jaunty Italian tunes, but we were uneasy, knowing that at any time our train might be leaving.

We eventually found a tourist office tucked in a deep recess of the train station. The place was packed. When we reached the head of the queue, we began our inquiry in Italian but switched to English to make sure we were understanding what seemed to be confusing directions. Another agent overheard our conversation and reminded the first that today was Sunday. They both consulted their timetable and assured us that only through *Sorrento* would we be able to get to Amalfi on a late Sunday afternoon. They agreed that it would be a much longer bus ride around the Sorrentine Peninsula but assured us that it would be *bella, bella.* Armed with that information, we headed back toward the Garibaldi station to catch the *Circumvesuviana.*

We had by then grown comfortable with Napoli Centrale. The energy of the people pulled us in. The piano music drifting through the corridors made us feel relaxed and welcomed. We forgot the advice that we should be forever vigilant for pickpockets. We queued up to buy our tickets to Sorrento. I was again surprised at how cheap they were—just over five euros for both tickets. The area in front of the turnstiles was very crowded, so we stood to the side for a moment to watch how people with luggage moved through them. The commuters and people traveling light had no problem, but people with suitcases had to get both themselves and their luggage through the turnstile with one swipe of the ticket.

I noted that seasoned travelers hefted their bags over the turnstile first, and only then did they insert their ticket to let themselves through. Once we learned the steps to the dance, Mardi and I sashayed our way through the barriers. I looked back as we were making our way to the platform. Some folks I recognized from the *Oosterdam* didn't do the steps in the right sequence. They got their suitcase through but not themselves—and now the turnstile arm wasn't budging. I felt sorry for them and wished I could have helped, but the mass of people was moving in one direction only—toward the platform.

As our personal space shrunk to zero thoughts of pickpockets returned. Mardi and I worked our way to the edge of the throng as it descended the stairs like the Blob and oozed its way onto the platform along the track. A few uncomfortable minutes later the train pulled into the station. The doors opened. We let the crowd surge in. We should have been concerned that we wouldn't be able to get on the train, but hanging back seemed the right thing to do.

The train absorbed all the people. We wheeled our suitcases into the standing-room-only section, tucked them behind us so they wouldn't roll around, and grabbed the overhead bars as the train pulled from the station. I looked around as I always do at our fellow passengers. The first one I noticed was a fiftysomething well-dressed, well-groomed man who was patting his thigh. I thought maybe he had hurt his leg when the train lurched out of the station.

But as I watched I noticed that he wasn't confining his patting to just one spot on his leg. Then it hit me that he was feeling the pockets on his cargo pants. His hands moved up to his jacket. He was now patting every pocket. He was looking for his billfold. I looked around on the floor, hoping I would see it wedged behind a partition or under someone's suitcase. He noticed me looking and said quite calmly, "My wallet's gone."

He continued patting his pockets, now without energy. Color was draining from his face. He seemed to be talking to himself, and his wife, who was seated near him, as much as he was talking to me. "Two guys bumped me when we were getting on—that had to be when they slipped it out of my pocket."

"Have you checked your bags? Maybe you put it somewhere you don't normally carry it," I said, recalling all the times Mardi has coached me through the panic I was sure this man was feeling—helping me recall that I had put my billfold in my backpack, not my pants pocket.

"No, it was right here," he said and touched his leg in the exact spot I had first observed him patting, first gently and then with quick, jerky motions as he realized he was encountering an empty pocket.

"I hope you didn't have much in it," I said.

Again he answered calmly, "Five hundred euros, all my credit cards, and my driver's license."

"Oh my," I groaned, thinking what an awful way this was to begin a holiday. I looked at his wife. She seemed subdued as well. Only then did it hit me that they were English. Brits don't get as excited as Italians or Americans. But he was right to remain calm. We were rolling down the tracks when he first patted his leg. What could he do at that point?

"I'm James, this is my wife Martha," I said. "I'm so sorry. That's awful."

He nodded his head slowly in resigned agreement, then added, "I'm Ian. This is my wife Linda."

The tone of his voice told me he was embarrassed more than angry at having lost his billfold. I also noticed that he had not yet given up all hope—his hands, as we commiserated with him, were still checking and rechecking his pockets. I knew the feeling—the panic of realizing your money, your ID, your credit cards, are not where you expect them to be—and the hope that you carry that if you look just one more time you will find your billfold in a pocket you've failed to check. I had watched his face take on an ashen pallor and his eyes glaze over in disgust as he realized he had been violated. But my lasting impression was that he was not going to let this ruin his trip to Italy. He blamed himself for not securing his wallet deep within his pack, but he didn't dwell on it. He and his wife began talking of their love of Italy—they had lost count of how many times they had visited. We were amazed and jealous when they mentioned they could fly from their London home to Rome in just a little over two hours. On this journey they were touring the Sorrentine Peninsula by sightseeing bus. They too were headed for Sorrento.

Our conversation waned as Ian began looking through his backpack. I turned my attention to the other passengers. Very few appeared to be tourists. More than likely they were locals who had been to Naples for the day or the weekend. At Torre del Greco a young man with a *bandoneon* got on board. A bandoneon is a small accordion-like musical instrument that for its size puts out a very big sound. He began playing a lively rendition of "Mamma Mia" that soon had people tapping their toes and moving to the beat. I looked around our car and discovered the reason for the big sound. At the other end of our car I caught a glimpse of a wisp of a young girl beating out a rhythm on a little drum. In the middle of the car an older man, wizened yet still overflowing with passion, was playing a guitar. He might well have been a grandfather of the other two, so similar was their infectious enthusiasm.

The lively music brought smiles to many of the faces. Some of the passengers were even singing along. Others seemed to react not at all, as though live music accompanied all their train trips. I was thrilled to be rolling through the undulating countryside shoulder to shoulder with exuberant Italians tapping their toes to traditional music in that crowded train. It felt right that festive music should welcome us to Italy. I wish I could have shown how much I appreciated it, but when the bandoneon player passed his hat, I had nothing. I was disappointed with myself that I hadn't kept a few euros easily accessible. My wallet was tucked deep in my backpack, and that is exactly where I wanted to leave it—in no way did I want to draw attention to where I carried my money. But I very much regretted not being able to express, with more than a *thank you,* my appreciation to those musicians for making our train ride to Sorrento so lively—even passionate.

The *Circumvesuviana* contrasted greatly with the Civitavecchia-to-Naples run. That had been like a business trip. We were able to map out our journey, read some of the articles in our guidebooks about the Amalfi Coast, and even do a little work. This ride was like a celebration. We were among fun-loving Italians, and from time to time fellow passengers, both male and female, offered

Mardi a seat. The convivial character of Italian life was on full display as we slid down the coast toward Sorrento.

The music helped shorten the hour-long ride, and soon we found ourselves faced with the decision of whether to take a sightseeing bus or the regular bus to Amalfi. We chose the regular bus—less expensive and we presumed quicker. We made our way down the hill from the station to the bus stop and discovered we had missed the bus by a few minutes. Knowing we had an hour until the next one, I set off in search of a bank with an ATM where I could pull out some euros at a good exchange rate while at the same time incurring only a small transaction fee. I couldn't remember exactly how much we had been charged six months earlier when we spent the fall picking olives on a farm not far from Rome, but I knew that getting money using plastic was a much better option that handing over dollars to a bank teller.

I had tried the bank-teller method the first time I was in Italy and came face-to-face with Italian bureaucracy. The paperwork necessary for a couple-hundred-dollar transaction was stunning. The time it took to get those euros was equally annoying. I began to wonder if my name had mistakenly been put a terror watch list. When I asked my hosts about the procedure they said, "That's just the way it's done." Time and for that matter paperwork is viewed a bit differently in Italy. My hosts concluded the matter by saying, "If you're in a bit of a hurry, use a *bancomat.*"

And that is exactly what I went in search of that Sunday afternoon in Sorrento—a major bank with an ATM out front. I could have exchanged money in the train station, with no searching and no walking, but even the employees of the station exchange recommended against it when I asked them about rates. They make their money from people who are in a hurry or place a high premium on convenience, and are not concerned at all with what it costs them.

I felt smug as I walked out of the ancient train station, down the granite steps, and into the heart of what looked to be a very interesting city. I was a seasoned traveler and I was going to save myself a bunch of money. Even though I had been told the bank was only a couple blocks away I couldn't find it—at least not one with a *bancomat.* When at last I did find an ATM I discovered my pin didn't work. In the fog of travel I didn't realize I was inserting my bank's credit card, not my debit card. I was miffed at the time, but if I'd been able to get my credit card to work, I would have incurred cash advance fees as well.

I returned to the bus stop with no cash and feeling a lot less smug. I had taken so long that the once-empty bus was now almost full. The luggage bins on the near side of the bus *were* full—the driver told us to maneuver our bags to the far side, the traffic side, to load up. We wheeled them around only to discover that those compartments were full as well. So it was back to the loading side, to the back door, which had room for bags and standing—and that is where we stayed for every *tornante,* every sharp turn, on the Amalfi Coast.

When you travel a route for the first time, even the smallest details take on enormous importance. On this trip I had hoped to see the beautiful views of the rugged coast that I knew were there. I could feel how gorgeous it was just by the reactions of the people who were seated and therefore able to see out the windows. But I was standing, and I'm rather tall, so what I could see out the windows was quite limited. Every once in a while the rock walls would disappear and I could see that we were traversing very high cliffs. I could see a deep blue ocean a dizzying distance below, but almost nothing else except the tops of the heads of the people around me.

The ride along the Amalfi Coast was hot, crowded, and disturbing at times. We were worried that our bags might get stolen, but there was a positive side to the trip—we got a good workout as we rounded corner after corner. It took a lot of strength and a tight grip on the overhead bars to keep ourselves upright in the tight turns. We also discovered that you have to be ready for unannounced and very abrupt stops. I wasn't ready for that first one. As I fought to regain my balance I could see out the front of our bus a line of cars backing up—the drivers looking in their rearview mirrors while inching their cars along the mountain wall to create enough space for our bus to pass. The wonder of it all is that there are any cars on the roads of the Amalfi Coast whose sides aren't covered with scratches and gouges by drivers misjudging how close they were to the rock outcroppings.

As I watched this drama play out mile after mile, I gained a huge amount of respect for the drivers of the Sorrentine Peninsula—especially the bus drivers. I wished that instead of clinging for dear life in the back of the bus I was upfront, near the driver, so that his skills were on full display. Each time we met another bus, both stopped. The drivers then danced. One bus would move forward six inches or so, and stop. Then the other would inch forward to a bit of a wide spot—which would allow the other bus enough room to move. They often worked forward and backward three or four times, each bus creeping just a bit at a time. I realized during the dance that I was as close to the passengers on the other bus as I was to those on my own.

The beauty we were driving through was not mine to see. I did, however, catch sight of ladders twenty to thirty feet tall propped against the sides of the highway. At first I thought they were being used for construction, but I saw so many of them that I finally realized that the people living on the farms in the ravines below climb them to reach the road to walk to town or access their cars parked along the highway.

As we traveled along the coast I tried to catch glimpses of road signs to discover how many kilometers we were from Amalfi. Some of the stops were extremely short, and I wanted to be prepared, the moment the bus stopped, to work my way through the people to our bags, grab them, and get off before the door closed. I feared that one of us would get off and the other wouldn't or that we'd get off and discover to our horror that we didn't have all of our bags.

And that is how we arrived in Positano—fearful and fretting—but we didn't see it, not really. I knew we were in Positano only because I saw a sign. I caught a glimpse of some of its beautiful pastel houses and hotels, but I didn't get to experience the expansive views of the hillsides and the beautiful Mediterranean beyond that had lured me to this area.

When the ride began, Mardi and I were the only people standing, but each mile we traveled along the coast our bus became more crowded. Just beyond Positano, a large group of hikers climbed aboard and forced us so far back I could no longer see our suitcases. I began fearing a fate similar to Ian's in Napoli—my backpack, with computer inside, might get off the bus before I did and I wouldn't even know it until we reached Amalfi.

I was certain from the description on the Annalara B&B website that we would want to get off at the main stop in Amalfi, but I began worrying that we might not even know we were in Amalfi. The bus was far too crowded to pull out a map, and stops were not announced, so I had no idea where we were. None of the hikers jammed around me knew where Amalfi was. I was kicking myself for not asking the driver whether the bus went beyond Amalfi—that bit of knowledge would have saved me a considerable amount of fretting. I was no longer the smug traveler—more like a newbie venturing about in a foreign country for the first time.

It was with those thoughts that our bus ride came to an end. I had no idea what Mardi was thinking. She and I were separated as well. We had pulled into what looked like a transportation hub—a man was marshalling us into a space that looked much too small for our big bus. I sure hoped this was Amalfi.

I watched the people disembarking, still worried that one of our bags would get off the bus without us. But when the passengers had cleared, our bags were right where we had left them. We thanked God, stepped off the bus, and let out a long-pent-up sigh of relief—we were in Amalfi. When I began dreaming of this journey, I didn't know whether traveling from Civitavecchia to the Amalfi Coast in one day, especially on a Sunday, was wise. I was sure the beauty would be overwhelming, but we had arrived having seen very little of it.

But now we could see it unobstructed—and it was glorious. Stunning beauty cascading down from on high—and every square inch of those impossibly steep rock walls had a pink or a blue or a white or a yellow house or hotel attached to it—the effect of that jumbled but somehow sublime combination of colors and architecture made me gasp. I thought I would be prepared.

"That's beautiful," Mardi said as she looked up at the homes and hotels high above us. "This is all beautiful," she added as she scanned the harbor filled with brightly colored boats.

"It is, isn't it," I said and pulled her close to thank her. She looked up at me and I kissed her. It was a kiss that lasted longer than generally expected in a public place, at least in America, where a peck is the preferred display of public affection—but we were in Italy, and I was feeling both grateful and romantic. Italy has the power to do that to a person.

When at last I let go of the kiss, Mardi looked at me as if to say, *What has come over you?* but I think she knew, and she, like me, was beginning to feel the power of Italy to transform.

The harbor walkways and roads were teeming with people—so many that I wasn't sure how to get from the bus to the heart of the town. I noticed a flow of people snaking through the parking lot that looked like it would carry us toward the tall, narrow, palm-tree-flanked city gate. The road we had arrived on, the only road through Amalfi, was filled with cars and buses and motor scooters. We waited for local folks to step out into the crosswalk to stop the flow of traffic, then we ventured forth with our load, wheeling our suitcases across the roadway and under the arch, feeling the march of centuries as we passed through a thick wall that looked a thousand years old. When at last we emerged from the gate, we found ourselves in a *piazza* that literally sucked our breath away—the beauty that lay before us was both unexpected and overwhelming—leading our eyes ever upward was a staircase—*a stairway to heaven*. At the very top of the stairs lay an exquisitely detailed church—an edifice whose green doors were capped with a golden semicircle glowing with the reflected light of a Mediterranean sunset.

I was stunned. Despite having seen literally thousands of photos of Italy's most gorgeous locations, I'd never seen a photo of Amalfi—this spot that looked like paradise on earth. We were standing transfixed in a swirling sea of people, trying to take in beauty beyond belief. Adding to our sense of awe was a *piazza* filled with laughter, conversations, music, and the sound of water flowing from an ornate fountain. The fountain filling the foreground of this magnificent scene was also filling the water bottles of tourists and locals alike—the whole incredible place was overflowing with life, motion, and color.

I searched for comparisons. Even our first sight of the gorgeous and recently refurbished Trevi Fountain in Rome, though memorable, had not caused us to stop and gasp. I suppose surprise was the biggest factor in our reaction, but I don't think it totally explains what happened to us that evening in Amalfi.

I am a sucker for Italy's fountains, and I'm a sucker for a town that has a fountain in its central *piazza*. In one instant I fell in love with Amalfi. I had been attracted to the Amalfi Coast by the beautiful photographs I had seen of the pastel hotels of Positano, but here before me looked like a town to live in—a town that was not only beautiful but one that seemed to have been built for the express purpose of bringing people together in one spot. I liked this even better than the Campo in Siena—and that *piazza* kept me enthralled for hours.

I knew I wouldn't be able to do justice to the moment, but I wanted to try to capture my feelings. I searched for the right foreground to convey the grandeur of the scene and took a photograph. I was intrigued by Amalfi's beauty, but I was even more drawn to the sense of community in the *piazza*. Everywhere we looked people were engaged in what looked to be intense, heartfelt discussions of life. These weren't *Hi, good to see you, catch you later* discussions. The business of living was being discussed as it seems only Italians can do.

Mardi and I were astounded with the immensity of the moment. To go from the interior of a crowded bus from which we could see almost nothing to this stunning magnificence in a matter of moments seemed incomprehensible. It was as though we had been led to the *piazza* and when we were told to remove our blindfolds we could not process quickly enough the glory before us. The suffering we had endured getting to the town became part of our reward. A feeling of gratitude surged through my body as I realized a parallel in my relationship with Mardi. I've traveled much of the road of our marriage wearing a blindfold that prevented me from seeing the true beauty of the woman I was married to. That is part of the joy of falling deeply in love again with a woman you've been married to for forty-some years.

Still tingling with the emotion of being in the center of so much life-affirming activity I began filling our water bottles from the ornate fountain. There were at least a half dozen spigots, some quite sensual. While the bottles filled I eavesdropped. I am always fascinated by the depth of discussions that Italians share in public. Matters of heart and consequence are freely deliberated. We were now without a doubt in the heart of Italy; life itself was flowing in the *piazza* like the water cascading in the fountain. With full bottles we made our way across the crowded square to the steps, where we sat down to let Italian life cascade over us.

I love the way Italians engage each other. They are all in. Conversation in Italy is a contact sport. My eyes were drawn to a fashionably dressed young man with a sweater tied around his neck walking through the *piazza* talking Italian style to a friend ambling beside him as they made their way slowly up the main street of Amalfi. The thirtysomething man by a subtle sweep of his hand let his companion know that he was breaking off for a moment. He then walked straight up to a young man sitting just a few feet from us enjoying a *gelato*. The man stood immediately to greet him. They exchanged hearty shoulder hugs and quick kisses to each cheek—and huge smiles and promises to see each other soon. The exchange was genuine, loving, and full of affection—a life well spent regarding the needs of the other, it seemed. Maybe I was reading too much into the short conversation, but I think not. There was nothing affected in the greeting, only genuine concern for the other's well being. I was quite certain that is what they had been doing their whole lives. There is a connection among Italian men that is quite heartwarming. You see it in the way elderly men walk arm in arm up the street talking and gesturing to each other—or in the way they gather on benches in the *piazza* to pass the time. They are extremely comfortable—glad to be in the other's presence. This is a feature of Italian life I very much like. In this, the Piazza Duomo, on a late Sunday afternoon in April, it was on full display.

I was overwhelmed with thankfulness for the improbable way we had fallen into the beauty, intensity, and passion of Amalfi. I was certain we could have sat there enjoying our fortunate find for the rest of the evening, but we needed to find our B&B and get settled in. I called Salvatore and told him we were sitting on the steps of Saint Andrew's Cathedral. He told me I had only a little way to go. My GPS indicated that the B&B was more than the few hundred meters he was promising. I asked if he could pick us up, but he suggested it would be no problem for us to find the hotel. I wasn't so sure. Remembering the problems we had finding our hotel in Rome the previous fall, I suggested to Mardi that she find a comfortable place to wait with the luggage while I searched for the place with just my backpack and a carry-on.

"I like it right here," she said. "I could sit here for hours."

"You sure you'll be okay?" I asked, remembering her reluctance to be left alone in Rome.

"Don't worry about me, I'll be fine."

Still feeling a little uneasy about leaving her I asked if she preferred to wait in the outdoor café amidst the umbrellas and tables that graced the foreground of the first photo I took of the Duomo di Sant'Andrea. But she said she preferred the steps with their high angle view of the sea of humanity flowing through the *piazza*.

She was probably happy to wait because she was remembering the disaster of last fall's search for our hotel in Rome. We went together, dragging our luggage. I lost my sense of direction and headed the wrong way out of Roma Termini. We had good maps, but we misread one street sign, which convinced us we were heading the right direction. For too long we ignored other clues telling us we were getting farther away from the Hotel Fiamma and managed to turn what is at most a six-block walk into a two-mile trek on the most tortuously rough streets and walkways of Rome.

I wanted to avoid such a start to this journey, so I set out alone with lots of aids that we didn't have on that trip. I now had phone contact and a GPS guiding me, but still I moved with uncertainty. The GPS was leading me much farther into the town and higher up the valley than I expected from the description on *Hotels.com* and from my phone call to Salvatore. Despite my uncertainty, though, I was enjoying the hike. The town was vibrant with the sounds of shoppers in the small stores lining the streets. I noted especially all the restaurants and *trattorias*—and glanced at their menus—although I knew that I'd leave the decision of where to eat to Mardi.

At every opportunity I asked for directions to the Villa Annalara and was disheartened to discover that not one of the half dozen people I questioned had heard of it. I was getting nervous despite the assurance of the GPS that it was nearby. The address was Via Delle Cartiere 1—and I had yet to see that street name. I stopped a woman passing by and asked the question I should have been asking all along: *"Scusi, dove Via Delle Cartiere?"*

She thought for a moment and then said, *"Qui"* and then pointed to an inscription in stone on the wall high above us. I could just make out the words *Via Delle Cartiere* in the late evening light.

"Ah grazie," I said and then as an afterthought, I returned to my original question, *"Dove Villa Annalara?"*

She turned, pointed a short distance up the street, and said, *"Eccolo."* And there, just above a wrought iron gate, was a tastefully executed ceramic sign. We were too far away to read it, but I thought I could see what looked like the letters *B&B*.

"Grazie mille," I said and gave her a large smile tinged with relief. I glanced at the GPS. It had led me close enough to get directions the old fashioned way.

I suppose I could have turned around at that point and walked back to Mardi, but I didn't know what I didn't know, so I went on up the hill to the sign and was confronted with a locked gate. I pushed the call button and was immediately greeted with a resounding click. I pulled on the handle and the big gate swung open with a slight but romantic creak. I felt as if I were being ushered into a very private enclave, none of which I could yet see. Five steps confronted me. I climbed the steps, set down my carry-on, and began pulling it up the slightly inclined vine-covered walkway—to where I didn't know. I could see in the fading light that I was walking through an orchard. At the end of the walkway a sign indicated a choice of stairs or lift. I headed right toward the elevator on another vine-covered walkway. Another thirty yards brought me to a sign in both Italian and English that informed me that patience would be rewarded—that sixty seconds after summoning it, the lift would arrive. Without that sign I would have been tempted to believe that pushing the button had done nothing—not even a click was heard when I punched it. I would have turned around, retraced my steps, and climbed the stairs. I suddenly became aware that even the smallest details were capturing my attention. It was as though the sight of all that passion in the *piazza* had kicked my senses into overdrive—it was taking very little energy to notice everything.

While waiting I began wondering why, beyond the beautiful photographs, I had chosen Villa Annalara. I feared that it might be a total disappointment. I recalled that one reviewer had mentioned that getting to the B&B was not an easy task. I hoped, but could not remember, whether he had reported that it was worth the effort. After the requisite sixty seconds the elevator silently appeared. I opened the ancient doors and wheeled my suitcase inside. It was a slow ride to the first and only stop. When the door opened I was thrilled to see Salvatore standing there to greet me. He grabbed my suitcase and bounded up another flight of stairs to a huge vine-covered terrace. No wonder so many of the reviews mentioned all the stairs—but the reward for all the climbing was more than worth it—the lights of Amalfi now spread out below us. He led me up two more flights of stairs to a delightful room, set somewhat apart from the rest of the B&B—a room reached by walking across a small terrace looking out over Amalfi with a view extending all the way to the Mediterranean Sea. I was thrilled. The reason the views on the website were so spectacular was because of the inn's lofty perch—the land the Villa Annalara sits on climbs the rock wall of the deep ravine in which Amalfi is situated and its rooms sit high above the ancient maritime city-state. Not only was all of Amalfi spread out below us, it also felt as if centuries of history of the *Costiera Amalfitana* was there for our eyes to absorb. I was certain that this B&B was going to get our journey off to an even more fantastic start than I had imagined. I took my backpack off, threw it on the bed, grabbed my credit card and passport, and went to check in. As I bounded down the stairs, I kept repeating, *I love this place, I love this place, I love this place.*

Salvatore was not a disappointment either. His English was tinged with a heavy accent, so heavy that even when he pronounced an English word correctly it often had the sound of Italian instead of English. He also spoke very quickly even when talking in English, which he only occasionally did. I guess maybe I had, in speaking some Italian, given him the impression that I could handle Italian at full speed, which I rarely can. It takes me a few days to develop my ear for the language.

Salvatore did not fully understand my decision to leave Mardi in the *piazza.* To him it seemed like such a short distance. And he was right—if every step is in the right direction. I tried to convey to him what I had learned in Rome, but I don't think my story convinced him. I left a somewhat bewildered Salvatore and made my way back to the Piazza Duomo where I found Mardi photographing the stories unfolding around her. The *passeggiata,* the Italian custom of taking a leisurely evening stroll to see and be seen, was in full swing. Mardi looked engaged and beautiful—her eyes vibrant and her smile wide. She too appeared to be in love with Amalfi. I was relieved she wasn't upset with me for leaving her alone. With a satisfied smile she told me she had been hit on only a couple of times. For a woman in her late sixties, that is a very good thing. She pointed out one of the men who had struck up a conversation with her. No wonder she was flattered. He was at least twenty years younger, very good-looking, and of course, sharply dressed.

The energy of the *piazza* was contagious. I initially attributed it to the water flowing from the fountain, but now I was feeling that *the stairway to heaven* is responsible for the special feeling that sweeps over you in Amalfi. We sat on the steps taking in the life flowing around us. It's no wonder Americans fall in love with Italy and Italians. Life in America is nothing like what we were experiencing, especially for those of us living in suburbs or spending our evenings watching television. Thanks to the tradition of the *passeggiata,* the people of this town were out on the streets, catching up on the lives of their neighbors. The feeling of community in the *piazza* was overwhelming, so much so that I was sure that I had found my Italian town—the place where I wanted to come to the rest of my life to write the words that have been swirling around in my mind forever. This seemed to be the perfect town to find a quiet writing room perched high above the city with views of the sea—and then each day when words are no longer flowing, walk down the hill and sit on my favorite chair in the *piazza* sipping a *cappuccino,* visiting with old friends, and making new ones.

I had by then been in many Italian towns, but nowhere had I felt so comfortable, so enthusiastic, so certain I wanted to spend many of my remaining days on earth in this one spot. Walking through the city gate had stunned me. We had entered into a world I have for years been dreaming about. I was thrilled that the *piazza* had more locals than tourists—but what I really liked was that the locals seemed just as pleased as the tourists to be in that *piazza*—and judging by the smile on Mardi's face she too could not have been happier.

Mardi noticed me looking at her and pulled me out of my reverie by reminding me that we had not eaten a true meal since breakfast. We each grabbed a suitcase and began walking up the narrow main street, overcoming the temptation to peek into the delightful shops we were passing. We did however stop occasionally to glance at the menus of the restaurants. I could tell that Mardi was no longer sorry we had bypassed Rome. I had been carrying a romantic vision for months that I wanted to celebrate her birthday on the Amalfi Coast. She had seemed a little impatient with that desire—four days in one town not named Rome seemed excessive to her. She soon gets bored and wants new experiences, but I hoped that we would slide into the rhythm of the town and be content right here in Amalfi—I knew I could. I had no idea what we'd be doing until her birthday on the sixth, but I knew I'd be content to do as Italians do—take pleasure in the moment. Italians even have an expression for it—*il dolce far niente*—the sweetness of doing nothing.

But at the moment we couldn't do nothing—we had to decide where to eat. We usually choose someplace crowded, but on this night we chose La Galea, which was empty except for us. We were convinced by the menu posted near the door that the restaurant catered to locals, but we had little to back up our belief since the only people in the place were waiters.

We decided to dine lightly. It had been a long day and we wanted to go to bed early. We ordered a margherita pizza, a mixed salad and *vino rosso della casa*. We sat near the front window where we could watch the world go by. Our meal did not disappoint—simple, fresh food perfectly prepared. And as usual we were not rushed. This perfect table was ours as long as we wanted to linger. So we lingered, talking about our good fortune and taking advantage of their very fast Internet connection to correspond with friends and family. I'm not sure how our first meal in Italy could have been better, and it cost only fourteen euros—we would have plenty of the time later for four- and five-course meals when getting to bed early was not a high priority.

I don't think either of us had expected to make love after such a long, exciting day of travel and decision-making, especially since we had commemorated our last night aboard the *Oosterdam* making love. The bells may have had something to do with it. As we were putting out the light to go to sleep the bells of Saint Andrew's began ringing. That lovely sound put us in a romantic mood by reminding us of the magical moment when we walked through the gate and looked up at the beautiful stairway. I kissed Mardi and held it, just as I had done in the harbor and in the *piazza*. The chiming stopped at ten bells.

When Mardi and I hear our friends and classmates talk of sex, or I should say their lack of it, or that they're keeping their sex drive alive with drugs, risking their heart, health, and even their lives, we pause and thank God that we are making love at all. But when we realized that night we were enjoying the best sex of our lives, we got a little giddy. Maybe we could blame it on the Italian music playing on the radio—it was full of passion and energy and emotion. Or it could have been the realization that yes, indeed, after almost forty-six years of marriage we were taking what could only be described as the journey of our lifetime—a honeymoon tailor-made not to the budget of our youth but to the passions of our mature years—a journey among people who have taught us and are forever teaching us how to live just by the privilege of walking the same streets where they go about their daily lives.

The memory of those two guys greeting each other in the *piazza* came to mind. To me it was truly a celebration of the very gift of life. Mardi and I were hoping that by spending time with everyday Italians we would return to America with a better sense of how to live life more fully. We wanted a *passeggiata* mentality to permeate our lives back home. What we had felt earlier in the *piazza* we wanted, not just on holiday, but every day of our lives.

At the moment we drifted off to sleep we had been on the Amalfi Coast less than twelve hours. Was it naive to think we had so quickly and easily found that special place where we hoped to return year after year—a place where we felt welcomed—and vibrantly, even passionately, alive.

CHAPTER FOUR

Amalfi ~ Monday April 4 ~ 67 & Sunny

Making the Transition to Italian Time

> *To my mind, the greatest reward and luxury of travel*
> *is to be able to experience everyday things*
> *as if for the first time, to be in a position*
> *in which almost nothing is so familiar*
> *that it can be taken for granted.*
> BILL BRYSON

■

> *Love is that condition in which the happiness of another person*
> *is essential to your own.*
> ROBERT HEINLEIN

Waking up for the first time in a foreign land is exhilarating—more than likely the sounds you hear will make you realize *I'm not in Kansas anymore.* The distinctive high-pitched *putt-putt* of the little engine that powers the three-wheeled Piaggio Ape, reverberating off the ancient walls of the narrow streets below, transported me from my dreams to Italy. Mingled that morning with the sound of those little trucks scurrying here and there were the insistent cock-a-doodle-doos of competing roosters echoing across the valley. Throw in the laughter of playful children, and we had the perfect soundtrack for our first morning in Amalfi—a town coming to life at a slow, peaceful pace. To my ear they were all good sounds.

I slipped quietly out of bed and tiptoed onto our terrace to see if I could locate the children whose voices sounded so joyful. I was delighted to discover that the boys and girls were not waiting at a bus stop to be transported to school but rather walking up the same street Mardi and I had climbed the night before to get to our B&B. Kids of all ages were making their way from the heart of Amalfi to the school, which presumably was farther up the valley. As I watched their playful antics I thought that the only sound missing was the quiet pealing of the church bells that had lulled us to sleep—an oversight that was taken care of a few minutes later while I was taking a photograph of the captivating village stretched out below me all the way to the Mediterranean Sea.

I was thrilled by our good fortune. Here we were in what seemed like paradise, and until yesterday I didn't even know this delightful town existed. The bells chimed two high and eight low, telling me that it was eight-thirty at the moment the sun peeked over the mountains southeast of Amalfi and bathed the green and gold spire—the cupola of Duomo di Amalfi—in warm sunshine. I wanted to share the moment with Mardi, but I also wanted her to sleep, so I tiptoed back into the room, grabbed my journal, and returned to the beautifully crafted ceramic table at the edge of our terrace to jot down my impressions of this idyllic morning on the Amalfi Coast. I wanted none of these magical moments to have a chance to disappear from my memory.

When traveling you are exposed to so many new and wonderful impressions that unless you write them down your brain doesn't have a chance to preserve them all. The stories you tell your friends when you return home will help you keep those special moments alive, but you can't tell a story about everything, and that is where journaling comes in. I have pulled out journals from twenty and thirty years ago and read about experiences that had completely disappeared from my memory, but after reading a note or two, scenes came flooding back, firing the synapses of my brain with sensations of sounds, smells, and even tastes that color in the details of forgotten chapters of our lives.

Sitting at that table, taking note of my surroundings, I became aware of the smell of fresh-cut branches drifting up the hillside. As I looked for the source of the pungent aroma my eyes were drawn to the rock walls defining the colorful courtyards below. It was easy to imagine that these flower-covered walls had been standing for hundreds, if not thousands, of years. Thinking about such antiquity ushered over me a deep sense of awe for the craftsmanship that has made possible the building of the many homes clinging to the steep hillsides of the narrow valley that defines the village of Amalfi. The feeling of compactness in this tight-knit community was bolstered by the sounds of conversations from people both seen and unseen. I could see workmen gathering their tools in the streets below, people pausing on street corners to chat with friends and neighbors, and women hanging the morning wash on clotheslines, giving the streets a colorful, festive feel as though the shirts and dresses were flags draped along a parade route. The sights and sounds blended together to paint the scene of a town I was falling more deeply in love with every minute. Sometimes a feeling sweeps over you, and this morning, on this rooftop, with all this beauty and life spread out below me, I no longer had any doubt—Mardi and I had found our Camelot.

As I was finishing my note-taking I became aware that Mardi was not only awake but deep into her morning routine. A few minutes later she joined me, gave me a good-morning hug, and reminded me that we had told Salvatore we were early risers and would be down first thing in the morning for breakfast. I checked my phone and discovered it was too late for that—it was almost too late for breakfast. The American in me was embarrassed that we had not kept our word. The Italian in me was certain that Salvatore would understand. We grabbed our guidebooks and bounded down the vine-covered stairway to the breakfast terrace to shower Salvatore with questions about our plans for the day.

In the past seven years I've spent enough time in Italy that I should no longer be surprised by the gracious hospitality of its people. This was my third trip; I've spent a total of over three months living and working with Italian families, and almost every year of my life I've read about, thought about, and/ or written about Italians, but Salvatore's thoughtfulness that morning still caught me by surprise. Maybe I was thinking that because we weren't helping him pick olives, or tending his sheep, but were instead paying him for a place to stay, we wouldn't be treated like family. But before we had finished our first *cappuccino* I was persuaded that the gift of hospitality is embedded so deeply into the strains of an Italian's DNA that nothing will ever dislodge it.

Salvatore fielded our questions, assessed our passions, and suggested we wander the streets of the town, letting our interests tell us what to do next and where to turn, and when we were tired of looking, make our way to the steps of Saint Andrew's, sit down, and let the heartbeat of the town entertain us. That seemed like perfect advice. At the moment we were letting the pulse of the terrace entertain us. A mother and father and their two playful young girls were also eating breakfast—the delightful sisters reminded us of two of our granddaughters, about the same ages as these girls.

While we were eating breakfast, Salvatore's phone rang. Instead of taking the call in his office, he walked to the edge of the terrace and sat on top of the wide wall where he could observe, just as I had, the daily drama of Amalfi coming to life below him. Only moments before I had told Mardi that I didn't think I would ever get bored watching this town wake up. Apparently the feeling is universal. I began dreaming of multitasking, just as Salvatore was doing—sitting down to write, day after day, in a comfortable chair overlooking Amalfi as I searched for the ideas and words to convey to my readers the journeys, challenges, and blessings of life.

It was a small thing, but one of the girls whose playful antics we were enjoying conferred upon me one of my favorite compliments—a blessing you might say. I had gone to the breakfast buffet to get another of Salvatore's delicious croissants to enjoy with my second *cappuccino*. She came in and directed a question at me. I was getting ready to say, *Non parlo italiano*, but a young man appeared with a stack of dishes and the word *piatti* suddenly registered—she had asked me if I knew where the plates were. The exchange was a gentle reminder to carry a bit more confidence in my Italian. I returned to our table with a croissant and a story and found Mardi chatting with a young couple who had sat down near us. They looked familiar.

"Good morning. I'm James. You've met Mardi?"

"Oh yes, yes we have. I'm Simon, and this is my wife Luciana. I can't believe we all ended up here."

"Ah, yes. I remember—you were on the bus," I said. I had noticed them because I wasn't certain they were a couple at first—they looked so different. He had light skin, dark hair, and very refined features. I had guessed that he might be English, and now that he had introduced himself I had no doubt—his accent was undoubtedly British.

But Luciana was still a mystery to me. She had an Italian name, but I was certain she wasn't Italian. Even though her accent had touches of Merrie Olde England, I didn't think she had been born there. My guess was that she was Samoan; she had the relaxed manner and look of Polynesians I had met. The one thing I was sure of, even though we had spent less than a minute together, was that the four of us were going to get along great. I also had a strong feeling they might be very much in love.

We shared a bit of our stories. My hunch was confirmed when I told them how we got to Italy—and that we would definitely recommend traveling by boat, especially for people in love.

"That's for us then," they said simultaneously while looking into each other's eyes. Salvatore noted how well we were getting along and decided to pitch a boat cruise to Capri. I had heard of it, from the hit song if nothing else, but it sounded crowded. However, Simon and Luciana showed a strong interest so Mardi and I decided that spending a day on the Isle of Capri with our new friends would be a great thing to do.

We showed them our guidebooks and talked about our plans for the day. They were interested in our hike to Pontone and Scala, but weren't sure they were up for it just yet. Simon mentioned that walking up the hill from the *piazza* had winded them. When our stories of the difficulty of finding Salvatore's place revealed that I had walked up the hill twice pulling luggage each time, they both uttered a heartfelt *Bravo*—praise that I sent right back at them when I learned how little luggage they were traveling with.

"But we're only going to be here a week, and it sounds like you folks might be staying longer," Simon said.

"If Salvatore's not booked up, we're moving in," I joked.

"And what about our grandkids?" Mardi said.

"You have grandkids?" Luciana asked. "You don't look like grandparents. You seem more like newlyweds."

"Oh, wow. I like you," I said to Luciana, and then looked at Mardi and winked.

"Jim sometimes forgets we have grandkids," she joked. "Ten to be exact."

"I haven't forgotten. We'll go back and visit them twice a year." I smiled as I began picturing what life would be like living here.

Simon returned my smile and asked, "Well, *how long* have you been married?"

"Not very long. We're on our honeymoon," I deadpanned.

"I thought so," Luciana said.

"Jim, tell them the truth," Mardi chided.

"Well, we *are* on our honeymoon," I countered.

"No, I mean about how long we've been married."

"Okay. The honeymoon part is true. We didn't get to go on a honeymoon when we got married. We're also celebrating Mardi's birthday in a couple of days, and I'm hoping we can stay here—I mean Italy—until May 6th when we celebrate our forty-sixth anniversary."

"No—no way." Luciana seemed shocked but went on to say, "That sounds so nice."

"Forty-six years?" Simon asked.

I nodded my head *yes* to both of them. I'm always proud and happy when someone we've just met expresses surprise about how long we've been married. First because of vanity—they frequently add that we don't seem old enough to have been married that long—but mostly I feel good because they are acknowledging that we are bucking the trend sweeping America, and maybe the world, of dissolving a commitment when difficulties arise. I'm proud, and at the same time grateful, that Mardi and I didn't do that.

"Are you on your honeymoon too?" I asked.

"No, this isn't our honeymoon. We've been married thirteen years," Simon said and smiled again at Luciana. That look alone convinced me I had not been hasty in my assessment that they would be good hiking companions.

"Mardi, can you show them the walk Rick Steves recommended from Amalfi to Atrani?"

They weren't familiar with Rick Steves. While we talked they took turns reading about the hikes recommended in his Amalfi Coast guidebook. When Salvatore stopped by to see if we wanted another *cappuccino*, I asked him about the recommendations. He glanced at the book and told us we shouldn't stop at Atrani. "You should definitely hike up to Pontone. You can see the town from right over here." He led me to the edge of the terrace and pointed to a ridge high above and a collection of houses that had to have spectacular views of the Amalfi Coast. My enthusiasm for Salvatore's recommendation, which was presented as two separate day hikes by Rick Steves, convinced Simon and Luciana that they had just met a couple whose interest in trekking was a bit more pronounced than theirs. In typical understated British fashion, Simon said, "I don't think we'll be heading that far afield today."

Salvatore smiled. He was clearing the table of the young family and was probably eager to clear ours as well. It seemed like a good time to excuse ourselves.

"We're so happy to have met you. Looking forward to tomorrow. I think Mardi and I are going to have to come down to breakfast a little earlier to get to the boat by eight," I said.

"*Domani.* Breakfast an hour earlier," Salvatore said. He also suggested we take jackets.

On the hike down to street level, we found the source of the pungent aroma we had enjoyed from our terrace. A gardener was pruning the bushes lining the steps of what once must have been the mansion of an aristocrat. We talked briefly about the beauty of the day, the peacefulness of the morning, and then, as I was about to step over the branches in the pathway, he said, "Piano, piano." I looked closer and noticed the branches had long, thin, very sharp thorns. Mardi, wearing light hiking boots, had already negotiated the pile, but I didn't want to risk it in my sandals. I turned around, climbed back up the steps, and took the slow elevator ride down to the garden level.

As I walked through the orchard I glanced up and saw the gardener high above adding branches to the pile. I waved to him, and wondered whether he had mentioned the thorns. I glanced at my pocket dictionary and noted that the Italian word for thorn is *spina*. If he used that word, I didn't catch it, but when he said *Piano, piano* I knew he was telling me to step slowly and gently through the brush. I was grateful that the knowledge of a little Italian had kept me from ramming a thorn deep into my foot.

Maybe it's learning something new at my advanced age—or maybe it's that I'm a writer and love words, but exchanges like that—in a foreign country, in a language I hope one day to master—thrill me. We clicked our way through the gate and stepped onto the street to join the flow of the people. We soon walked by a small, neighborhood water fountain. Folks were filling water bottles and catching up on the news of the day.

Just beyond the fountain a middle-aged, well-dressed man, leaning against a sleek silver roadster, was idly watching school kids make their way up the hill. A couple of teachers were following along, as though supervising a field trip, but no one was in a rush. Not far behind, a gentle soul in his eighties, shuffling along with the aid of a cane, seemed amused by the antics of the schoolchildren, as though he were reliving the days when he too walked with his friends up this very street to school.

A Cinquecento, an old FIAT 500 from the fifties, parked in front of an ancient paper mill, ushered my thoughts  as well back a half century to a less hurried time. The gentle sound of flowing water completed the transition. I looked for the source and found it below my feet. Amalfi's main street is built over a streambed running down the center of the narrow canyon. Space on that street is so precious that you have to step to the side when you meet a car. If you meet a delivery van, you actually have to duck into the doorway of one of the shops. We sought the safety of an open door and found ourselves in an antique shop with an amazing display of toys from the early twentieth century and an eclectic collection of ancient weapons. I took a few pictures of the guns, while Mardi photographed old letter openers, as well as a ceramic donkey, before turning her attention to a beautiful icon of Mary.

While we were browsing and photographing, I heard the faint sound of a siren. The shopkeeper apparently heard it too and headed toward the street. I thought it odd that he would take time from his customers to watch an ambulance pass, but he didn't stop at the doorway. He stepped quickly into the street, grabbed a small folding sign advertising his business, and leaned it against the building. Once the ambulance had passed, he went outside again, opened the sign, and placed it back in front of his shop. That's how narrow the main street of Amalfi is.

Everywhere I looked I saw scenes worthy of a photograph. I composed a still shot of red chili peppers hanging in the bright sun that were touted as *Viagra Naturale* at five euros a bundle. Juxtaposed beside this natural aphrodisiac were well-endowed ceramic mermaids adding to the colorful scene, as did the lingerie flapping in the breeze just above our heads.

Mardi and I moved with the flow of people onto the cathedral steps. We sat down and began listing the things we loved about Amalfi. We had been in the town less than twenty-four hours, but already we were planning to return many times. Amalfi was crowded, but not oppressive; *vibrant* would be a better description. We also sensed a respectful attitude between vendors and shoppers. The shopkeepers seemed to understand that tourism was essential to their well-being, but they neither pandered nor begged. Drivers seemed respectful as well—neither impatient nor rude—and no one seemed to be in a hurry. The traffic was one lane, one-way. The possibility for a five-minute wait for it to flow the direction you were going was the price paid by those needing to drive a car up the main street of Amalfi.

We were intrigued by the verticality of the town. The steps to the cathedral led our eyes upward the moment we first stepped into the *piazza,* and that introduction kept us focused on the lives lived above street level. We were acutely aware that people's homes were up just a few flights of steps. I tried to imagine what it would be like to wake up each morning and see below me people living in such close proximity—amidst so much vitality.

We sat on the steps for over an hour, enjoying a picnic of yogurt and nuts, noting that residents loved the *piazza* too. We found ourselves playing a game—not simply trying to distinguish who was local and who was not, but trying to figure out the nationalities of the tourists. We came to realize that many of the tourists were Italians. The Amalfi Coast, we decided, has a lot to offer everyone.

Some people, as they approached the doors of the cathedral, sought to present a more respectful mien by covering their arms and legs. I was reminded of my reaction in India, when for the first time in a week I saw a tourist. The sight of bare arms, legs, and midriff in public can be rather off-putting, especially in a country where the local population wears flowing dresses and long sleeved shirts. Mardi and I liked the way the Italians were dressed. I made fun of myself for yesterday's ball cap and decided to buy a hat that was decidedly more Italian—a hat that would also do a better job of protecting my face and neck from the strong sun. We observed clothing, and backpacks, and water bottles, and walking sticks, and man-purses, and neck scarves, and ways to dress more like an Italian. We decided that as soon as we could find a hat I liked we were going to set off on foot for Atrani, and that we might do as Salvatore had suggested—just keep climbing.

But before we got going, some workers on the other side of the *piazza* caught our attention. We noted the lack of mechanical aids—no tractors or cranes. They were employing physical effort to accomplish their task—using shovels and working together to lift objects that were too heavy for one man. These men, working to the tune of good-natured banter, brought to mind the words of a song from my childhood, "Whistle While You Work" from *Snow White and the Seven Dwarfs*. They were working right next to dozens of people enjoying their morning *caffè*, but I don't think any of them were bothered in the least by the workers. Some might argue that the work could be done faster with a tractor, but the Italian mindset seems to be that more local people had jobs and that these men were adding to the ambience of the morning rather than destroying it with the roar of an engine.

We could also see that the fountain in the Piazza Duomo is a gathering place for those who aren't lounging about on the cathedral's magnificent steps. I'll never forget looking up from that fountain to see this whole glorious space filled with people and beauty—totally unexpected, and all of it topped with a shimmering gold cross at the peak of the cathedral. The effect of these perfectly uniform steps ascending in one unbroken flight to a height that seemed beyond belief—and then to have it all topped by the glowing facade of the cathedral, with its twelve arches reaching even higher—was truly stunning.

Completing this perfect public square are the hundreds of tables and umbrellas framing the *piazza*, filled with people enjoying the day and each other. Comfortable chairs, white tablecloths topped with freshly cut flowers, and traditionally attired waiters delivering drinks to tourists and locals alike add to the ambience and so do the beautiful frescoes adorning the walls of the covered entrance to the church. Our favorite was of Saint Andrew the fisherman and Christ asleep in the boat while all around him the storm raged. I don't know whether that scene affected our choice, but before heading toward Atrani we walked to the beach to absorb the maritime beginnings of this village and contemplate the serendipitous flipping of our pinball that had landed us in Amalfi. Maybe someday we will find out, but we couldn't imagine that Positano, where we thought we were headed, would have fit our personalities so perfectly.

From the harbor, we saw another entrance to Amalfi, which gave us a slow reveal of the Piazza Duomo. We were glad that for our first sight of the *piazza* we had entered through the old city gate, and got the full effect all at once. We circled around and walked in the old gate again—and again the light at the end of the arch pulled us onward. And just as before, the flow of the people turned us to the right as we stepped into the light, and then the whole *piazza*, in all of its glory, came at us in an instant. And there we stood, drawn ever upward in a marvelous ascension of our spirit—happy to stand in that spot forever. It was only slightly less mesmerizing this time.

We had planned to stay in Amalfi for four days. Why, we were wondering, as we stood there transfixed, shouldn't we stay right where we were. We could explore the Amalfi Coast and more—as much of southern Italy as possible in the next four or five weeks, but do it from our *new home*. While we were considering that possibility we worked on a new look for me. I must have tried on at least a dozen hats in almost as many stores until we found one that fit my personality yet said *Italian*, not tourist. The friendly shopkeeper who sold it to me dashed that presumption forever—calling out *Ciao James Bond* as I was walking out of his store—so much for blending into the Italian tapestry of Amalfi.

It was well after one o'clock when we finally tore ourselves away from Piazza Duomo to begin our trek to Atrani. The benches lining the promenade were filled with people passing the day in conversation and reading newspapers. I took a few photos hoping I could capture the ambience of the waterfront, but I didn't linger, convinced that I would have plenty of opportunities in the next few weeks.

As we left Amalfi we asked a woman carrying her *bicicletta* down the flight of steps we intended to walk up if we had found *il sentiero correto,* the right path to Atrani. She said that we had and then set her bike down and began pedaling along the Amalfi Coast Highway. If we had followed her we would have arrived in Atrani much quicker. But we weren't looking for the *fastest* way to Atrani or we would have hired a taxi to get us there in a couple of minutes—we were more interested in the journey than the destination.

The hike was quiet. The locals were taking a nap, *un pisolino*, and we were the only tourists climbing the steep steps to Atrani. I took very few photographs. The passageways were narrow, and the buildings tall—we were in shadow most of the way—sunlight could shine on the colorful doorways for only an hour or so each day. We climbed over the top of the ridge and were on our way down looking out at an astonishing view of the little storybook town that is Atrani before we saw anyone. A young family was hiking up.

The woman was carrying a few groceries and a baby. The man, his shoulders laden with bags of food, held a baby stroller high over his head to negotiate the steep and winding steps. Living in these houses we were blissfully walking past requires a reliance on personal mobility that suburbanites who park their cars in attached garages cannot come close to fathoming.

We didn't stay in Atrani long. It was a little after three and the townspeople were still sleeping. We wanted elevation—to feel even greater heights than we had attained on our hike up and over the ridge. Our legs felt good, and so did our lungs. The miles we had walked and the stairs we had climbed aboard the *Oosterdam* were paying dividends. We consulted our map occasionally, but mostly we followed the hand-painted signs on the steps pointing the way to Ravello. We were heading straight up past churches and homes—and beautiful flowing clusters of wisteria framing gorgeous views of the Amalfi Coast as well as gardens of perfectly spaced vegetables and orange trees. The stone-walled gardens overflowing with fruits and vegetables were testimonies to the resourcefulness of the people. A vigorous agricultural economy was thriving on these terraced hillsides and looked like it had for centuries, maybe even thousands of years.

We saw no other hikers, but a couple of times, when our route crossed roads we saw cyclists, legs churning as they climbed up the valley. After two or three kilometers we came to an ancient wall embedded with two colorful ceramic signs; one pointed to Pontone, the other to Ravello. We chose Pontone, the village Salvatore had pointed to at breakfast—it looked wilder and more remote—more like a trek. The pathway led us into the bush. The sounds of traffic disappeared and were replaced with the relaxing gurgle of a small creek. We imagined we'd eventually find a rustic wooden bridge to get us to the other side. We were surprised to find instead a beautifully executed stone structure spanning the flowing water. Just upstream a dam held back a pond. It was so delightfully built that I fully expected to find a castle nearby, but instead of a king and queen's home we found a waterfall flowing over the dam and down a granite streambed. We paused in our hike. Our joy was palpable—our faces were glowing. We were thankful for everything. Just the fact that we were able to make the trek was reason enough to celebrate, but to find ourselves in the midst of such unexpected beauty was truly humbling. I was wishing that a local would come by who could tell us why such a grand bridge had been built in this remote spot, but no one appeared. So we just thanked the Italian propensity to make ordinary things beautiful and finished eating our apples and cheese.

Beyond the bridge the path rose sharply. The sound of the water flowing over the dam was replaced by the crowing of roosters high above. The steps carved into the rock of the hillsides reminded me of the ancient pathway leading to Machu Picchu in Peru—steep and long. At some forks in the path hand-painted signs pointed the way, but not always. We met no one on the climb which heightened our sense of adventure. A few dogs noted our passing, letting us know they were vigilantly protecting their masters' property. The only other sound we heard on our long trek to Pontone was the gentle sound of the wind blowing through the trees. We didn't even hear any church bells.

The first shop we saw open was a *gelateria* with the official sounding name of *Laboratorio Artigianale*. We were certain we had burned quite a few calories on the climb, so we rewarded ourselves with a *gelato*. With cones in hand, and a bit of pride as well for having survived the trek, we walked to the heart of the town. A couple of locals were chatting in the shade of the church, and a rather athletic man in his mid-forties who I took to be an American tourist, possibly from California, was taking a photograph from the vantage point of a rather prosaic overlook. It commanded a breathtaking view of the surrounding mountains and of course the Amalfi Coast in the distance, but in construction and design it was nothing remarkable—a large square with concrete seating on three sides. The only distinguishing feature was a ceramic tile pointing the way to Amalfi, which was of course almost straight down. I walked over to the far edge to see if I could find the trail that would lead us back to the Villa Annalara. I could see Amalfi in the distance and a road straight below us with a bus parked on it, but what route we were going to follow to get from this overlook to Amalfi was not clear.

I asked the *American*, who was wearing an O'Neal t-shirt, if he had hiked to Pontone. He looked at me as if to say *I wish*.

"My wife gets mad at me if I wander off to take a picture that doesn't have a dozen people in it," he said. I learned a lot about the man from that one answer. I learned that he definitely wasn't from America—here was another Brit on holiday. I guessed that he had probably arrived via the bus down below—and that he and his wife didn't share the same passions.

"You a surfer?" I asked.

"No, I ride dirt bikes. O'Neal makes boots and helmets and jackets. I think you're thinking of O'Neill wetsuits. Different spelling."

"Oh, yes. Where you from?" I asked.

"Oxford. We came here a couple of years ago and loved it. My wife and I both work in the schools. It's Easter break," he explained.

He was very talkative, very open. In the span of a few minutes I learned that the last time they were here the weather was much colder, that he grew up on a farm near Galway, that they got milk from their cows, and that his mum still lives in the house she grew up in. "You're very lucky," he said.

"Why is that?" I asked.

"That you're here when it's so warm—and because you can wander." That last part he seemed to add for the benefit of the woman who was at that moment joining us. She grabbed his shoulders and acted as if she was going to shove him over the edge of the overlook when she heard the word *wander*. She looked at me as he regained his balance and said, "He's always wandering off. I look around and straight away he's gone."

"Why don't you bail out on the bus and walk to Amalfi with us?" I kiddingly asked her, but I was really directing the thought toward her husband.

"We can't. We're not staying in Amalfi, we're staying in Sorrento," she said and went on to tell us that they were visiting all the towns up and down the Amalfi Coast in one day. I looked to her husband to get his reaction as she was finishing her description of the day's whirlwind of activities.

"When we get back, I'm going to get a massively big beer," he said.

She grimaced and grabbed his hand. He reluctantly followed. I watched them walk across the *piazza* to join their group. He turned and waved to us just before he disappeared from sight. She didn't look back. I tried to imagine what he was thinking—and what she was thinking. They seemed to be accepting of each other, but they obviously had different philosophies of travel.

They were, it seemed to me, doing the typical tourist thing—cramming too much into too little time—putting as many marks on their checklist as possible. They knew where they were going and when they were going to get there. Our new friend probably even knew what time he would be taking that first sip of that massively big beer. We, on the other hand, knew almost nothing about what we would encounter in what remained of the day.

We were, to use Coach Phil Jackson's favorite advice to Michael Jordan, letting the game come to us. From our vantage point on that overlook we were very high on the mountain, but we weren't at its highest point. Above us I could see the ruins of a large church, and I was intrigued. Mardi was not. She was reluctant to climb higher. She thought it looked like a long hike to the ruins—I thought we could make the climb in ten or fifteen minutes. We compromised. I asked her if she would be willing to climb for five minutes—then we would stop and discuss whether we wanted to go on.

We never had that discussion. We began the climb up the carefully crafted steps, met a couple of well-dressed Italian women heading toward Pontone, and soon after two big white dogs. They checked us out, barked a few times, turned around and climbed back up the steps and out of view. Mardi and I kept climbing. I was curious about the dogs. I didn't fear them even though one bite from their massive jaws could have done tremendous damage. They seemed to be on a mission, not just wandering around. I suspected they were working dogs—that they belonged to a shepherd.

That hunch was confirmed a few minutes later when we got to the top of the steps—to a fork in the pathway. We became aware of bells jingling—the sound getting closer and closer. I pulled my phone out of my pocket and slid it into video mode. We were on a level section—terraced walls climbing above us on either side. I looked to the left and saw the two white dogs we had met on the stairs, acting as scouts, clearing the way. We had climbed high enough that we were now at the same elevation as the ruins. To the right, where the sound of the bells was coming from, a tan dog, similar in size to the white ones, was standing still on the pathway just looking at us. I was certain that he didn't perceive us as a threat—he knew that his two companions had just passed us and had not sounded an alarm, but nevertheless he was still cautious.

I looked beyond the lone dog and saw a single goat the same color as the dog. He too was standing still, waiting for me to make my move. Twenty yards beyond were more goats—all of them just looking at me. I couldn't get off the path. A wall rose straight above me for ten or twelve feet. I pressed my back into the stones, made myself as thin as possible, and slowly brought my iPhone up to chest height and started recording. I hoped that by making myself as small as possible the herd would move forward. But neither the dog nor the goats moved.

One of the two white lead dogs noticed the standoff and jogged past me and Mardi back to the herd. That was all it took for the tan dog and the lead goat to feel comfortable enough to begin moving down the path toward us. We were soon swallowed up in sea of swirling goats. Some of the goats leapt up on the terraces to eat tufts of grass, others jogged quickly past. The goats were followed by dozens of sheep. In the midst of the sheep a shepherd was making his way along the ancient path, his shirt draped over one shoulder, a jaunty blue cap on his head, and a shepherd's crook in his right hand.

He didn't seem alarmed or irritated by our presence. I quietly said *Buongiorno* as he passed. He nodded his head and tipped his hat. I turned my attention to the antics of the goats. As usual they were being goats and making a nuisance of themselves by climbing straight up the walls instead of walking down the path with the sheep. I too had once been a goat herder. I had just over a hundred goats. I didn't count how many were in this flock,

but I guessed there were at least a hundred—maybe more like a hundred fifty—sheep and goats, all moving in a somewhat orderly manner down the path, thanks to the two scout dogs out front, the tan one in the middle of the herd, and two more faithful dogs following along behind, nipping at the heels of the more recalcitrant animals.

Mardi and I joined in the procession after the last animal passed. We became shepherds again, shouting *Andiamo* at the goats standing on their hind legs to reach the grass growing out of the time-worn walls. The goats seemed to understand our Italian and quickly scurried off to join the herd each time we urged them to get going. The dogs who had been nipping at the heels of the laggards thought we were doing such a good job they ran ahead to join the scout dogs.

I would have been happy to follow the herd to its new pasture, but I sensed that Mardi didn't feel the same way. As we were passing the ruins of the church, I quit recording video and took a photograph of the flock heading down the hill. I climbed back up the stairs to the entrance to the church and found Mardi sucking on a sweet lemon drop the kind hostesses of the Basilica di Sant'Eustachio had offered her. They also offered maps of the area and an invitation to walk to the edge of the property, where, they told us, the best views could be found. They were so delightful that I asked if they would pose for a photograph with Mardi. Mardi is only five foot eight, but standing next to these two petite Italian women framed by an ancient arch she looked like a mythical Amazon.

They shared with us some of the church's history—that the materials used to construct it had been carried up the mountain by donkey and the same was true for the roads, and that the church had been sacked in the 1500s. They had questions for us, too. They had assumed we walked up from Pontone. When we shared that we had begun our day in Amalfi, had walked to Atrani, and were now on our way back to Amalfi, they were shocked. They offered more lemon drops and a lemon as well for our hike back to Amalfi.

We didn't retrace our steps to Pontone but chose the route of the shepherd, which was in the general direction of Amalfi. We soon came to a fork in the path—two equally traveled ways. We went to the right for a reason that neither of us felt strongly about. Within a few minutes we met a *contadina*, a farmer. He looked as if he could have been a brother of the shepherd, but I didn't mention getting swallowed up in the flock—I just asked if we could get to Amalfi on this path. He assured us that we could, but if we wanted to get there quicker and easier, it would be better if we turned around and went back a half kilometer—then he described the fork in the road where we had made our lukewarm choice.

We thanked him and set off on what Mardi hoped was going to be a significantly shorter route. Her ankle was a little tender. We slowed our pace and began talking of the many farmers we had met in Italy. That brought to mind our own days as shepherds in the north of Italy, near Bolzano—it was Mardi's second Italian farm—she felt very much at home in the Alps, living her childhood dream of being a *Heidi*. Our first duty each morning was to hike up to the barn, snap a rope onto the alpha sheep's collar, and lead her and her friends from their nightly shelter to their paddock on the high mountain slopes. It turned out to be our favorite chore. Getting to know the personalities of each sheep delighted us.

As we made our way down the cobbled path the couple from Oxford also came to mind. I wondered if he was already hoisting his massively big beer or whether he was still riding the bus. Talking with them made me realize how different their experience of the Amalfi Coast will be from ours. They will obviously see more towns than we will—at least in a shorter span of time— but my hope is that by hiking the Amalfi Coast we will spend more time in each village and may have some unique experiences not open to the person traveling in a large group.

I found out at a very young age that when you travel about using your own power, whether on foot or bicycle, people are much more open, more willing to engage you in conversation or share their day. When I was fifteen years old I set off on a long-distance solo bike trip to the mountains of Colorado that set in motion my love of making myself vulnerable when traveling—open to the lives of the people I meet. I don't know what prompted me to want to make the climb to the ruins of the church, but the desire was there, I followed it, and we were rewarded by being swallowed up by a herd of goats. A church that had been existing as ruins for five hundred years was very interesting, but I'm sure my memories of this day ten years from now will be dominated by the personal connections we made—like the conversations with the two women at the ruins and the bond I felt in greeting a shepherd who appeared not to be walking but rather being borne along the path by the swirling movement of the sheep and goats surrounding him.

On the hike down we were awed by the size and width of the steps leading to Amalfi; large enough that a medieval army could have passed this way. In one section the steps appeared to have been cut right out of a rock wall. It was like walking in an amphitheater with a curved roof overhead. We saw very few hikers, but we did encounter a couple of workers who were finishing up their day and putting away their tools, none of which had engines attached to them. They greeted us with a *Buonasera*. They were repairing a section of the path that was broken up, using, as we say in America, old world craftsmanship. Encountering those workmen made me wish it were possible to do a bit of time traveling, to see this walkway back through the centuries.

We were feeling the tug of history—with each step it seemed we saw something that reminded us that this path had been in use for thousands of years. Amalfi became an independent republic in the seventh century and an unequaled maritime power in the eighth and ninth centuries—much of maritime law emanated from this magnificent spot on the Amalfi Coast. The Cattedrale di Sant'Andrea, which had completely captivated Mardi and me has been doing that to people since the eleventh century—that's a thousand years—a length of time that is hard for Americans to deal with. The pull of Amalfi's history was so strong that when we made it down off the mountain to the main street we kept walking, right on past the Annalara B&B. We couldn't

resist the tug of the Piazza Duomo. It was time for the daily *passeggiata,* and we wanted to be a part of it again even though we'd been walking almost nonstop since lunchtime. It turned out to be another good choice.

We were treated to a photo shoot with a gorgeous red FIAT convertible—a classic from the thirties or forties—parked at the base of the steps to the Cathedral of Saint Andrew. Mardi admired the beauty of the scene—she also liked the looks of the man directing the photo shoot, who was trying to keep the steps clear of tourists and locals long enough for his photographer to get the shot they were envisioning. He was very busy and also very sharply dressed. Mardi was so inspired by his sartorial splendor that she left me journaling in the *piazza.* A half hour later she returned with another attempt to refine my Italian look—an Italian scarf to go with my Italian hat.

I was now certain that we would not leave on Thursday. Amalfi was showing us a pretty good life. No wonder Fellini could title a film *La Dolce Vita* and convince the whole world that the sweet life was to be found in Italy—once you experience the *passeggiata* you know that the Italians have life pretty well figured out. To set aside time every day for your neighbors, to catch up on their lives and share yours, is a pretty good way to live. And even though we were visitors who had been in this town less than two days, we felt very much a part of the daily ritual. We were already seeing people we'd seen yesterday, and that gave us a peculiar sense of belonging.

We could have spent hours in the *piazza*, but we had told Salvatore to expect us for dinner. He most likely had spent the day shopping the local markets to get the fresh food for our meal with Simon and Luciana. We pulled ourselves away from the evening ritual about six. We knew that would give us enough time to get to the B&B, freshen up, change clothes, and be ready to sit down for dinner at seven-thirty.

We all showed up on time. Salvatore served the first course and wished us a hearty *Buon appetito*.

"This is lovely," Luciana said. She was referring to the food, of course, but I could sense by the way she looked around that she also meant the setting on the terrace with the town of Amalfi spread out below us. If she was including the fact that she was dining with new friends as well I would have heartily concurred. We had spent the day hiking in hills that we could envision ourselves hiking for the rest of our lives, and now we were sitting down to a meal unlike any that we were used to eating in America. With such personal attention it is easy to see why people who travel a lot say that Italy provides some of the best dining experiences in the world.

"Is Italy popular in England?" I asked.

"We *are* a bit closer," Simon said, then added, with very little emphasis, as though Luciana completely agreed with him, "I plan to retire in Tuscany."

And with that I discovered that it isn't only Americans who dream of living happily ever after in Italy. That led me to wonder how it was that Luciana ended up living in London.

"I must have been British in another life. I went to London to study and met Simon..."

"And that's all she wrote," interjected Simon.

And our conversation, as conversations are wont to do, took off in an unexpected direction—not toward their improbable romance but rather to a discussion of idioms.

"I thought that was an American saying," I said. "I would have expected you to say, *And Bob's your uncle.*"

"And Fannie's your aunt," Simon said.

And that brought to mind the many delightful weeks we spent with Gianrico, our host farmer in the mountains near Bolzano. I began sharing with them Gianrico's fascination with the idioms I was unwittingly using as we labored together putting in a new wooden floor in his *agriturismo.* The experience of beginning to think in two languages made me realize just how improbable idioms are to a person not yet fluent in a language. My idioms meant nothing to Gianrico because he was translating the literal meaning of the words.

I shared with Simon and Luciana one of my favorite Italian idioms, *Siamo alla frutta,* which literally translates *We are at the fruit* but figuratively means *We are at the end.* Italians tend to eat fruit as the last course of their meals, hence the figurative meaning of *eating fruit.* My feeling is that the day I have a good command of the idioms of the Italian language is the day that I can say that I am fluent in Italian. I don't think it would be possible to write in a language not your own until your command of the language was such that you truly knew the nuances of all the words. Until that time, you'd stand a good chance of writing what you didn't mean.

I admire someone who makes the attempt to write in a language not learned in childhood, but I see it more as an exercise for the benefit of the writer—an attempt to gain control of the language—and not so much for the pleasure of the reader. It is similar to the exercise you go through when someone who is not familiar with your language asks you to explain the idiom you've just used. Only then do you realize when you say that you're going to *hit the books,* or *hit the sack,* you have no intention of doing either. The same is true when you say *You're going to let the cat out of the bag.* One of Gianrico's favorites, which I happened to use when he described a task he wanted me to do was, *That'll be a piece of cake.* He broke out laughing at that one.

Simon shared some his favorite English idioms, a few of which we already knew because of our experience thirty years ago in Greece of learning to captain a sailboat under the tutelage of a very British sailor who salted our language with some choice idioms by telling us *We were in a bit of a pickle* when gale force winds were bearing down and disaster was surrounding us on all sides. The British seem to very much enjoy understating situations—no need to get too excited. That thought of course reminded me of the British man who had lost his wallet on the train to Naples. Some stereotypes are stereotypes because, like clichés, they tend to be backed up by a whole lot of truth.

Salvatore did his part to reinforce the stereotype of Italian hospitality. He stopped by our table and asked, "Was the food okay?"

"Oh, it was delicious," Simon said.

"Mardi was surprised. She doesn't like anchovies," I said.

"I bought them this morning. Fresh makes all the difference," Salvatore said.

"They were nothing like I've had before," Mardi said.

"I'm glad you enjoyed them. Everybody always tells me that they don't like anchovies. And I always ask them, 'Have you had fresh anchovies?' Most of the time people tell me they haven't." With that Salvatore translated the American expression *Duh!* into an Italian shrug and hand gesture. "We love our anchovies," he said as he gathered a few plates and turned toward the kitchen.

Salvatore was proving to be just like the Italians I had met on my previous trips to Italy, especially those I got to know well when I worked with them on their farms. They not only love their local food, they are also proud of their ability to prepare it to perfection. But what seems to make them happiest is knowing that their guests are enjoying their food as much as they do. Italians love sharing their passion for life.

That triggered in Luciana the memory of hearing kids say the word *pomodoro*. "They say the word with such love in their voice. I just adore hearing that word roll off their tongues."

Almost on cue Salvatore brought out a huge salad for all of us to share, which of course featured fresh, delicious tomatoes. I began gushing about my love for Italian food in general and the salads of Italy in particular. "Italians somehow take fresh and delicious to a level that seems to be attained nowhere else," I said. Suddenly the conversation took what I thought to be a rather weird turn.

"That reminds me. Have you guys ever seen *The Fall and Rise of Reginald Perrin?*" Luciana asked.

"We love British shows, but I don't think we've seen that one," Mardi said.

"It's a British sitcom from the seventies," Simon said.

"He loved everything Italian," Luciana said. I now understood Luciana's leap.

She continued, "In one episode he and his wife are out dining with friends and he orders ravioli for his starter. The waitress came and asked, 'And what would you like for your *secondi*?' 'Ravioli,' he answered. Her eyebrows shot up, but she brought him ravioli. Then the scene jumped ahead and the waitress came again, 'And what would you folks like for dessert?' 'Ravioli,' Reginald said."

Luciana laughed at the memory.

Simon took over. "The waitress said to him, 'But sir, ravioli is not a dessert.' Reginald shot back, 'I don't care, I like ravioli.' "

"Oh that's funny," I said and realized that maybe I *had* been a little over the top in my praise of Italian food. But then Luciana let me off the hook.

"Simon and I say that is going to be us soon," she admitted.

Luciana and Simon, in that wonderful British mold of self-deprecating humor, were reminding me that I was not the only one who had been bitten by the Italian bug. It happens often enough that sitcom writers can make fun of exaggerated praise of all things Italian.

And from there our conversation followed a somewhat rational pinball trajectory, jumping from one British television show to another until Mardi and I had exhausted our list of favorites. It began with *Good Neighbors*, then veered to *Agatha Christie* and *Father Brown*, from there to *Midsomer Murders*, and ended with *Doc Martin*. Luciana and Simon carried the ball across the pond and told us that they loved to watch *Cheers*, *Home Improvement*, and *Everybody Loves Raymond*. I was already feeling that meeting them had been a stroke of good fortune, and sharing our favorite moments of those shows made me realize without a doubt that we were with folks who would become good friends. Every one of those shows had been a favorite in our household over the years, and talking about them made me realize how much I missed such shows. No wonder reruns are so popular. By the time we had exhausted stories of our favorite television shows we had heard four different chimings of the bells from Saint Andrews. The fourth brought Simon back to Italy.

"I'd like to do more hiking. I prefer hiking to going about by bus," Simon said.

That was a natural segue for a story about the guy from Oxford in the O'Neal t-shirt, but our conversation never got there. We talked about our hike to Scala—and their hike to Atrani, which brought the conversation, as it always seems to in Italy, back to food—Simon and Luciana's delicious meal in Atrani and our tasty *gelatos* in Pontone. This time, however, it was a short conversation. While we were talking about the delicious meal that Salvatore had prepared for us, the bells chimed again—one high and ten low and we knew it was time to let go of a wonderful day in Italy—our first full day in Amalfi—a day celebrating food and new friends, friends who like us seemed to be in love with each other and with Italy. We were settling into Italian time. There would be plenty of time *domani* for more stories.

CHAPTER FIVE

Amalfi ~ Tuesday April 5 ~ 67 & Sunny

The Essence of Italian Life

One's destination is never a place,
but a new way of seeing things.
HENRY MILLER

■

The more you know the more you love,
and by loving more, the more you enjoy.
CATHERINE OF SIENA

Our third day in Italy began as all days in Italy seem to begin—with a feeling of rightness and serenity. Is it the gentle light, or as is often the case, the sound of roosters crowing, birds chirping, and people gathering? Surely not every day in Italy begins beautifully. So why do so many that I've experienced begin that way? It must be a mental thing. Think and it shall be. I know that in relationships that wise saying applies—love your wife and she will love you. If you want your wife to be beautiful, see her as beautiful, treat her as beautiful.

The birds were right—it was indeed a morning worth singing about, but I didn't want to jostle the bed or take Mardi in my arms until I was certain she had woken up of her own accord so I stayed in bed and began scrolling through my memories of our last few weeks. In almost every aspect my memories topped my dreams. The first two weeks were especially surprising—it was like simultaneously taking a dozen cram courses in how to improve my marriage—and then getting off the ship with a lifetime of wonderful memories for a diploma.

Our marriage, as we made our way to the train station in Civitavecchia, was functioning in a realm that a few years ago I didn't know anyone's marriage operated in—certainly not ours. Apparently, it didn't go unnoticed. On the nights formal attire was required for dinner, photographers would appear at each table and take portraits. The photographer, hoping for pictures that people would buy, encouraged the couples to snuggle up close. As the photographer was turning to us I heard one of our tablemates say, "No need to tell those two to squeeze together, they always look like they're in love." But it wasn't always that way and that gives me hope when we see our kids struggling with their relationships.

The memories of the way we were brought to mind the Oxford couple. We were them not that long ago—not quite on the same page—and not knowing how to get there. As I thought about their differing philosophies of travel the irony hit me. Yesterday they were worried about missing the bus, today we were going to be in their shoes—worrying about missing the boat. Life is funny that way. Yesterday Mardi and I had all the freedom in the world, today we would be on someone else's schedule.

The sun was climbing higher and higher and Mardi was doing such a good job of sleeping that I had to gently kiss her and remind her that Salvatore had promised us an early breakfast—on a terrace with a view of the spectacular Amalfi Coast for our enjoyment—just in case in her dream world she had lost track of the dream we were living.

Salvatore had everything set up for us. We sipped our *cappuccinos* and shared with Simon and Luciana more stories of our hike to Atrani and Pontone. They had their own stories to tell—about encountering donkeys on the trail delivering building materials to a house high in the hills—and their leisurely lunch served by the owner in a little restaurant they happened upon in Atrani. They had done the see-the-Amalfi Coast-by-bus routine, in fact that is why they were on the Sorrento bus the day we first saw them. Now they were exploring it by foot, at a much slower pace, and enjoying it more, they said.

We shared and compared—and ate our breakfast of fruit, croissants, and yogurt as though we had the whole day until we noticed the time. That's when my day took on a decidedly different tone. I patted my pocket just as Ian had done on the train, and just like him I found it empty. I excused myself and raced up the stairs to our room. I hoped I had left my wallet in the pants I was wearing the day before. But it wasn't there. I felt as if I'd been kicked in the gut. I began thinking again of Ian and all that he went through.

What had I bought? The only thing I could remember was a *gelato*. I had the cone in my hand. Putting my wallet in my velcro pocket would have required two hands. A pickpocket must have noticed me drop it into my open pocket—I could think of nothing else that could have happened.

Mardi came into the room and saw that I was still looking for my billfold. "It's eight ten," she said. "We've got to be there by eight thirty."

"We've got a few minutes. Can you think of where my billfold might be?" I had regained a bit of hope and now had a vague memory of having it in the room last night.

"Did you put it in the safe?" Mardi asked.

It was a good question. I had forgotten about putting our important papers, passports, and extra money in the safe. Maybe I had absentmindedly stuck my billfold in there too. I've discovered more often than I like to admit, that I've done just what I'm certain I would never do. But this time, it wasn't there.

"This is crazy." I said as I began rummaging through everything.

"I'm going to go tell Simon and Luciana not to wait for us," Mardi said.

I looked again in the pants I had worn the day before, my jacket, even clothes I didn't think I had worn for days. I tore the sheets off the bed. Mardi came back and joined me in the search. She grabbed a flashlight and looked under the bed and behind the furniture.

I began thinking of all the calls I was going to have to make—to cancel cards, to get identification, and on and on. Mardi remained calm, trying to think of what I could have possibly done with my billfold. We looked in the bathroom. We looked in every unlikely place while keeping an eye on the time, trying to figure out what was the latest we could run from our room and still get to the dock in time to catch the boat.

We began wondering whether we should even be going to Capri. This was going to take a lot of time to deal with. I couldn't imagine calling the police, what good would that do? Plus we'd have to fill out a bunch of forms. Putting holds on our cards was going to be enough of a hassle. I wondered if we had enough money to live on until we got it all sorted out. I asked Mardi if she had any idea how much money I had in my wallet. That apparently triggered a memory. She went to the desk, opened the drawer, and wonder of wonders pulled out my wallet.

What an idiot. I had forgotten about cleaning out my billfold—filing the receipts that had accumulated from three weeks of traveling. I felt so stupid—so like Mark in *Two for the Road* with Joanna always coming to the rescue whenever he panicked.

"Do you think we can still make it? It's eight seventeen," Mardi asked as she grabbed her coat and purse and ran. I stuffed my backpack with a jacket, grabbed my new Italian hat and scarf, made sure I had my phone, and began running down the stairs. I caught Mardi at the front gate. It felt good to be on the street, among the people, but not so good to be running.

"*Buongiorno,*" I yelled to anyone who might step out in front of us to let them know we were coming. We felt foolish running past people ambling along the street at an Italian pace but we didn't want to miss the boat. We were *brutta figura* that morning—presenting a bad appearance—a definite no-no in Italy.

I was certain Simon and Luciana would get to the harbor before us. Mardi disagreed. She thought we could catch them if we jogged. As usual she was right. We spotted them before we got to the Piazza Duomo, walking along as though they didn't have a care in the world. I kept jogging, pretending I hadn't seen them. As I was passing I said, "Top of the mornin' to ya."

"Oh cheerio," Simon shot back. "I take it you found your billfold."

"Mardi did," I admitted. "She's going to keep me on a pretty short leash today."

"Good on ya," Simon said.

We slowed our pace and walked through the *piazza* with them. As we passed by the water fountain I glanced at my phone and noted we had only two minutes to get to the harbor—and we still had the gate to pass through and the main road to cross, which we were able to do rather quickly thanks to a policeman who saw us running and stopped the traffic. Once we were across the highway we had a clear view of the harbor—we were relieved to see our boat at the dock with a line of people waiting to board. I hopped in line to buy our tickets and tried, albeit unsuccessfully, to switch gears to Italian time.

As the captain welcomed me aboard he asked me who the other ticket was for and I responded, "*Mio marito.*" I turned to point to Mardi and realized I had called her my husband. "Oops, *Mia moglie,* Mardi."

He laughed, gave us a big smile, and graciously welcomed us aboard. So much for impressing anyone today with my command of the Italian language.

I could feel my heart rate rising. I love being around people who make their living on the water. Watching the captain maneuver the boat out of the harbor was thrilling. And so was the view we had of Amalfi as we pulled out past the breakwater into the open sea. I imagined the relief of seafaring captains catching sight of Amalfi after many months at sea. It looks like a many-layered wedding cake of pastel colors that begins at the water's edge—and rising out of the cake is the *campanile* that stands next to the Duomo di Sant'Andrea. The town's beauty makes you feel like you're turning the pages of a fairy tale about kings and queens, princes and princesses.

To commemorate the moment I took a photo of Simon, Luciana, and Mardi smiling at the camera with Amalfi hugging the rugged coastline in the background. The deep-throated throbbing of the diesel engine added to the sense of adventure as the boat rose up out of the water and began speeding west toward Capri. I was glad I had a jacket. The boat was creating a stiff breeze in the cool morning air. We were on the upper deck, exposed to the wind and the sea spray. We were only a few feet from the captain. He was scanning the horizon, on the watch for conflicting traffic. We also had an unobstructed view of the Amalfi Coast—no wonder it's been attracting romantics for thousands of years—thrusting up out of the sea with such power and beauty. The rise and fall of the boat, and the wind whipping our hair, added to the feeling that we were setting off on an adventure that we would be talking about the rest of our lives.

As I was looking at the magnificence surrounding us I became aware of a tall, sharply dressed, young man in a leather coat making his way around the boat talking to the passengers. I couldn't hear what he was saying over the noise of the wind and the engine, but it appeared he was acting as a guide, answering questions, and doing it in a way that was totally engaging judging by everyone's response. When he got to us I asked about the yellow buoys we were passing—he told us that they were marking the nets of fisherman—that was why we were giving them a wide berth. He was confirming what I was hoping—that fishermen were still making a living from all this beauty we were passing through.

Vincenzo was offering a guided tour of Capri—his fee, however, was more than the cost of getting there. I thought back to the man from Oxford who wished he was not stuck on a bus with a bunch of tourists. Vincenzo noted my reluctance and played more cards—explaining that the buses were extremely crowded and that it was not uncommon to wait more than a half hour. He was offering minibuses that would be at our disposal—no waiting. But what really sold me was the personable way he imparted his knowledge of the island.

Before moving on he pointed to a village just coming into view, and told us it was Positano, and that we would be stopping to take aboard more passengers. Mardi and I were thrilled. This time we had an unobstructed view of the town. We noticed that it too looked like a wedding cake climbing the cliffs—but it was bigger and had more colors. Mardi and I decided we liked Amalfi just fine. Positano is far more popular and well known so I attributed our partiality to feeling that Amalfi was *our town*—no one had suggested it—our pinball had flung us there and we had fallen in love.

The journey from Positano to Capri reminded me of sailing the Ionian Islands of Greece as we passed by mansions set off by themselves high on the cliffs on the starboard side of the boat. We also saw lighthouses on some of the points, reminding us of the dangers of sailing these waters. Numerous small islands also dotted the route—some of them appearing to be huge ragged teeth jutting out of the sea, others larger, and more inviting with impressive homes hugging the shoreline. As we surged through the swells, with spray flying, I was imagining what a romantic cruise it would be sailing these waters in your own boat and pulling into these ports to pass the night. But when we got to Capri I changed my mind. Only a knowledgeable and experienced captain could have guided our boat in such tight quarters—his finesse had the appearance of a miracle—unseen forces seemed to draw our boat gently to the dock.

Capri was the quintessential vision of a bustling seaport—nothing except the overturned boats on shore remained in the same place for long. Every color of the spectrum lit up the waterfront. Boats of every size were either jockeying for position or were tied up along the seawalls and docks. I could not imagine more people, but Vincenzo told us that what we were seeing was not even close to being crowded.

I looked again. I hadn't noticed we were passing by docks that had not one boat tied up to them. Within thirty days Vincenzo told us that every inch of space would be occupied by a private boat that was at this moment sailing toward Capri for a summer of bliss on the island. I was thankful it was April. Most of the boats were like ours, capable of carrying approximately fifty people. But one boat dominated the harbor. It looked capable of carrying at least a hundred passengers and maybe fifty cars from port to port.

The sight of that large ship made me realize that loving things to death is a real danger. Capri looked vulnerable. Three other sightseeing boats were also unloading passengers. Standing behind the yellow line painted on the ancient cobblestones was a queue a half dozen people wide and fifty people deep. The colorful shops behind them lent a festive atmosphere to the harbor, as did the streets filled with people. The crowds left no doubt—this was a place to see and be seen.

If the harbor looks familiar, yet you've never been to Capri, it may be because you've seen the movie *It Started in Naples*. Sophia Loren's home in the film is now a souvenir shop, but the bewildering bustle that greeted us is exactly what Clark Gable saw when he stepped off the ferry from Naples fifty-some years ago. Vincenzo kept us from being swallowed up in the crowd and gave us a quick overview of the island—pointing out that Capri's popularity stretched back thousands of years. He noted that it is so popular that almost nothing comes up for sale. He continued the history lesson as we hopped onto the minibus and began climbing up the winding roads. The skill of our driver was on full display as he negotiated the incredibly narrow roads, often passing within inches of other buses and cars, barely slowing even though the margin for error was nonexistent.

On an extremely steep section we swung wide around a slow-moving mini tractor carrying a fifty-five gallon barrel on its three-point hitch. We ducked back into our lane at the last millisecond to avoid a bus speeding down the road. I involuntarily sucked my gut in—certain we were going to clip each other. But our driver didn't release the pressure on the accelerator an iota. Neither did the bus speeding down the hill. As we shot past Vincenzo calmly said, "See how we drive here. Now you understand why you shouldn't walk up this road."

Ten minutes later we pulled into a crowded parking lot near the shops in Capri where Vincenzo announced that we had an hour and fifty minutes to see the sights. "But I have a personal request. Come with me for twenty minutes. I will show you something that is really nice. You will then have over an hour to look around on your own."

We hopped off the bus and began following him through the crowded streets. Construction workers were moving tools and materials up the hill. Shopkeepers were setting up their displays. Tourists were milling about, fingering the goods. Walking in a straight line was impossible. Conversations were breaking out everywhere. Defensive maneuvering was required of both pedestrians and drivers—not that there were any cars—the streets of Capri were much too congested with people for anything but carts, both electric and human powered.

For those who were able to stay on his heels Vincenzo continued a running commentary of Capri—those who had been slowed by cross traffic or a conversation breaking out in front of us were hoping that he would find an open area and stop so that we could catch up. It was good that he was tall—shorter guides were flying flags over their heads. Each time I stopped to take a photo I ran the risk of having to run through the throng of people to catch up. Whenever I lost sight of Vincenzo I looked for others in our group, trusting that because they were farther up the road they could see him.

I had no trouble identifying one young woman in our group. From behind she looked exactly like Mardi the summer of '69 when I first laid eyes on her. She was also about the same age as Mardi that summer—and her dress was just as short as Mardi's in those miniskirt days. She had Mardi's gorgeous legs and that vibrant, in love with life movement as she walked up the street taking in the energy of Capri—the sight of her took me back to that August day. It really was love at first sight. My instant assessment had been accurate—Mardi has always has been the most energetic person in the room. The downside is that she doesn't like to let any grass grow in her presence so she sometimes has to be slowed down a bit, but we both have learned to appreciate the less positive aspects of each other's good qualities.

We were walking by shops with exclusive names known all over the world—Gucci, Giorgio Armani, Dior—but Vincenzo was on a mission, to lead us to one of the most beautiful spots on the island of Capri—the Gardens of Augustus. On the way to the garden the roads became walkways, and eventually wisteria-lined paths passing through exquisitely manicured gardens until at last we were on top of the cliffs—stretched out below us were the most beautiful views of islands I have ever seen. My photographer's eye looked for some foreground treatment that might make it possible for a photograph to come close to capturing the experience of seeing such exquisite beauty in person. I found a perfectly manicured tree whose limbs mimicked the shape of the cliffs and then waited for a sailboat motoring in the bay to get to a position that would draw the viewer's eye to the light blue color of the waters near the

shore. It was the one photo I took that day that I felt was going to say in a beautiful but subtle way, *This Is Capri.*

I could now understand why Vincenzo was so enthusiastic about leading us to this spot. I envisioned myself watching the weather roll in from this lofty perch day after day. There is a visceral attraction to observing both people and the world from on high. I continued watching that sailboat motor across the bay—seeing where it had been and where it was going gave me a sense of being with it. I could see the crew moving about on deck. I imagined they were hoping the wind would pick up so they could hoist their sails.

Perched on this high hill overlooking the magnificent beauty that Vincenzo had led us to, I felt the irony of yesterday's smugness as I talked with the Oxford man who envied our free-form touring. Today *I* was the one trailing lockstep behind a guide, inching closer so that I could hear his tales. Vincenzo's knowledge was captivating me. He mentioned that Winston Churchill and Dwight Eisenhower had met on Capri during World War II. It was interesting to contemplate that this historic meeting took place not in halls of power but against a backdrop of incredible beauty. Surreal it seemed. I found myself wondering whether they too were stunned by the glorious beauty that God and man had created here—or did the terrible burdens of war prevent them from appreciating Capri's wonders?

I was pulled out of my musings when I heard Vincenzo mention Lucky Luciano, a mobster often in the news when I was a kid. What, I wondered, could *he* have to do with this gorgeous spot? Turns out that America made a deal with Mr. Luciano—asking him to make sure that word about America's imminent invasion of southern Italy was kept from the Germans. Somehow he had enough influence to pull off that feat. *I help you to win the war, you help me with my business,* was the way Vincenzo put it.

After Vincenzo delivered the punchline in English, he seamlessly transitioned to the same story in German and then Italian. Each time he switched languages, I learned a bit of German and tested my comprehension of Italian. The translations also gave me more time to absorb the beauty. I loved watching the seagulls cavort in the updrafts while I listened to Vincenzo. *My God this place is beautiful!* I was singing the praises of everyone who had anything to do with us being on the island of Capri—not just Vincenzo, but Salvatore, Simon and Luciana as well. I doubted very much that Mardi and I would have done something quite as touristy without their encouragement.

Vincenzo switched back to English and said "I leave you here. You walk back to Piazza Europa on your own. You don't need me to point out how beautiful this is. You go and enjoy it for yourself without having to listen to me."

"But I *want* to listen to him—I just love him," I whispered to Mardi.

Vincenzo walked off, but he didn't get far—some German tourists had more questions. Before he answered them, he turned to those of us who were obediently shuffling off and warned, "You go on your own—just don't go to any touristy places." As we walked around the gardens we heard other guides proclaiming the beauty of Capri in Chinese, French, and Japanese. Vincenzo, who was still being besieged with questions, yelled one more piece of advice to those of us who had wandered off: "Wait until Anacapri to eat!"

"Isn't this amazing?" Luciana said as she and Simon walked up to join Mardi and me. The look on her face told me that she was as enthusiastic about the beauty of this spot as I was. She held out her phone to show us a photo someone had taken of her and Simon.

"Would you take a photo of Mardi and me standing in that same spot?" I asked Simon.

He did, and our portrait turned out great too. It would have been difficult to take a bad photo—everywhere we looked there was overwhelming beauty to behold. The blue of the water was almost otherworldly. I wanted to walk down the serpentine pathway we could see far below that would lead us right to the water's edge, and Mardi and I probably would have, had we been on our own. Instead we wandered the grounds atop the cliffs, took photos of the Modigliani-like statues in the beautifully manicured gardens, checked out the luxuriant perfumes of Capri, and wondered whether we would ever return to this beautiful isle to explore it on our own.

As we made our way down the wisteria-lined paths to the Piazza Europa, we also became aware of the beautiful sounds of Capri—the delightful songs of the birds that seemed as happy as we were to be in paradise. As we were boarding the bus for our trip to Anacapri, a man asked Vincenzo if he had time to go to the Blue Grotto. Vincenzo told him he did but warned him that he would spend a lot of money and time waiting in line for a two-minute look at the blue water of the cave.

"It is beautiful, but if you are here only one day, it is better I think to wander about Capri on your own."

When we hopped off the bus in Anacapri we noticed that the man, like everyone else in the group, took Vincenzo's advice. "This is where we will meet at three-thirty," Vincenzo announced. "You have two and a half hours. I will take you to another *piazza* and then on to a breathtaking view of Capri—it will take ten minutes. Follow me."

While Vincenzo was making his announcement and telling us more about the island a young boy began crying. The father tried to distract the child, but nothing he did worked—the boy had had enough touring. As Vincenzo was finishing his announcement, he walked over to the boy and began talking to him. The boy immediately quit crying. I wasn't close enough to hear what Vincenzo was saying, nor would I have understood since he was talking in German, but his body language told the story of one person feeling another's pain and doing what he could to relieve it. In an instant he had made both the father and the son feel better.

"This guy is Italy personified," I said to Mardi.

"What do you mean?"

"It's just what Italians do. They put themselves in the shoes of another." I was thinking about Italian farmers all over Italy during World War II risking their lives to shelter Allies from certain demise at the hands of the German death squads—heroism I had learned about watching the films of Roberto Rossellini. The Italians who saw these films thought nothing of what the farmers had done. Only when the movies were shown outside of Italy did the world take notice of the Golden Rule attitude of the Italian farmers.

In the *piazza* I happened to catch Vincenzo alone. I complimented him for comforting the boy, and like a true Italian he acted as if it were nothing.

"My family is precious to me. You must take care of the kids," he said and shrugged as if to say that anyone would have done it. Mardi told Vincenzo that as a mother who has had to deal with tired kids in public situations, she was impressed with what he had done. Vincenzo took the praise in stride and reminded us that we had plenty of time for a leisurely lunch, advice we didn't fully take.

We dined with Simon and Luciana, enjoying our meal while again exchanging idioms and peculiarities of our shared language. We may call it English, but oh my, are our idioms different. When we finished our pizza, *insalata mista*, and *limonata*, Mardi and I excused ourselves. We wanted to see more of Anacapri, but Simon and Luciana wanted to linger over their meal, eat some dessert, and have a drink or two. They were taking Vincenzo's advice—we were trying to cram more in.

"We're just going to hang around here until it's time to get on the bus. If you get tired, come back. We'll be here," Luciana said.

After paying our bill, I stopped back by our table to let Simon know that we had not accepted his gracious offer to buy our lunch.

"Mardi wanted me to pay, so I paid," I said.

"Happy wife, happy life," he said.

"You are a smart man," I replied. As I said it I wondered when I had come to fully absorb that bit of wisdom. Was I that smart when Mardi and I were celebrating thirteen years of marriage? I doubt it. At that point I was in over my head getting my business established, and I'm certain many of the decisions I made did not fully address Mardi's concerns. I rallied to my defense in this internal conversation by pointing out that thirteen years into our marriage was 1983—by then we had three children and I was flying all over the middle of America trying to earn a living making industrial films. It makes me sad to remember the squabbles we had over money and raising kids, but back then she and I had a lot more on our minds than the happiness of our spouse. It's a lot easier now for us to look as if we have it all together.

As we were walking the streets of Anacapri a restaurateur overheard us discussing our marriage and invited us to join him for lunch. Even though we knew it was his job to attract customers, his playful invitation was so witty and seemingly personal that we wished we would have had time to join him. We spent less than a minute in witty repartee with him, but that exchange went a long way in coloring my memory of Capri. We expressed our regret saying *forse un giorno ci ritorneremo*—maybe someday we will return—a sentiment that sounds so much better, so much more musical in Italian.

Before we had walked another fifty yards I was again singing the praises of Italy. Our eyes had been drawn to some slender sculptures adorning Chiesa di San Sofia. Their grace and upward-flowing movement made the figures of the saints look absolutely angelic.

"These are beautiful," I said to Mardi. "Shall we go in?"

"Yes," she whispered in reverent awe.

As we entered, our humbling was made complete by the glorious beauty of the church and its masterpieces of painting and sculpture. Mardi and I walked the naves in stunned silence. Adding to the heavenly ambience of the cathedral was a woman, a pregnant woman with long flaxen hair, dressed in a flowing, shimmering gown. So subtle were her movements she appeared to be floating around the church in reverent submission. I prayed for a while, but mostly I praised—thanking God for the grace of this place and the chance to have happened on this little cathedral—for we had not read or heard of it, nor were we guided to it except by the providence of going in search of a *gelato* to savor while we waited for Vincenzo.

And that is what we found soon after pulling ourselves from the serenity of the church. We had some time to people-watch, and I wanted plenty of *gelato* to flavor the experience so I went for a *grande*, even though the price was quite *grande* as well—three fifty. Mardi normally orders the smallest available, but even she got in the mood and stepped up one size. We were indulging—celebrating big time.

We found a bench facing the *piazza*. We could see Vincenzo on the far side of the square fielding questions. Normally I would have wanted to hear what he was saying, but I had reached information overload and wanted to absorb only the festive atmosphere of the afternoon. It seems that in every Italian *piazza* a musician is playing, but on this day a singer had joined in.

"Look at that bus, Mardi. It was crowded when it pulled up, yet they're shoving more people on." As we watched the antics and saw how few of the people were able to board, I said a silent prayer of thanksgiving to Vincenzo for being such a good salesman. Fifteen minutes later he gave a wave as though he were a cowboy rounding up cattle. We followed him to the parking lot. I glanced at the people standing in line for the public buses and realized they were the same people we had seen when we sat down a half hour earlier—and it looked as if most of them would still be waiting long after we were delivered to the harbor for our cruise back to Amalfi.

"I'm going to sit up by the driver," I told Mardi when I realized our bus was too crowded for us to sit together. Vincenzo was checking the other two buses to make sure that everyone in our group was accounted for. A moment later he hopped back on, said *"Andiamo,"* and we were off down the hill.

Before we had reached the first corner I heard Mardi yell out, "Oh no, I left my purse in the restroom." Vincenzo heard her too, and without hesitating instructed the driver, *"Girarsi, tornare indietro."* Vincenzo's words didn't register until I realized the driver was executing a U-turn in middle of the busy road.

When I got to Mardi I asked, "Are you sure? Did you put it in your bag?"

"No, no, I don't have it," she replied, fear rising in her throat.

I dropped to my knees and began looking on the floor of the bus. Mardi carries a white purse with a long strap that she usually puts around her neck. The purse had fallen far back under her seat, but because it was white I immediately saw it.

"I found it," I yelled.

As I stood up I saw that our bus was just about ready to pull back into the traffic and head toward the *piazza*, but when Vincenzo saw that I had the purse, he told the driver to keep turning, and just like that we were headed back toward the harbor—no harm, no foul—a perfectly executed three-sixty in the roadway.

And Vincenzo, true to form, realizing that Mardi was probably embarrassed, addressed everyone on the bus. "I hope you all enjoyed your time in Anacapri," he said as though nothing had happened. Everyone erupted in happy assent. As he began collecting his fees he warned, "You have forty-five minutes before the boat arrives. Don't be late."

We weren't ready when he got to us. We had searched our pockets, purses, and billfolds for folding money but found little. We were down to counting coins and about to be embarrassed again. "Can you go around and collect from someone else?" I asked. "We're just about there, Vincenzo. We have a few more pockets to check."

"Good. They won't let you on the boat…" he said—partly in jest, I hoped.

As we hopped off the bus, we gave Vincenzo a handful of coins and small notes and told him how much we had enjoyed seeing Capri through his eyes. "If I have helped you," he said, "I go home with a big smile."

"You have," I said thinking of all he had done to make our day memorable.

"I think that is why people come to Italy. And keep coming," Vincenzo said. I could tell by his body language that he attributed much of the Italy's appeal to the warmth of its people. But he knew that the country's beauty also attracted us, so he concluded by saying, "Go to the beach and look at the color of the water, and the boats, but be back here by four-thirty."

We began wandering in the direction he had indicated and immediately fell into another exchange with a waiter. He wanted us to have a drink in his bar before getting on the boat. We didn't accept his kind offer but it was another chance to practice my Italian and another confirmation of Vincenzo's assertion that we tourists keep coming back to Italy because of how we're treated.

Vincenzo also said we would find beauty and we did. The wooden boats on shore provided a colorful foreground as seagulls soared above the huge ships in the harbor. I showed the photo to Mardi and said, "Wouldn't this make a great puzzle to put together next Christmas—when we're deep in the middle of Wisconsin winter?"

"Oh—fancy finding you folks here." It was Simon's distinct and familiar voice.

"Can you imagine how crowded this must be in the summer?" Luciana asked.

The bustle of the port was fascinating—ferries being loaded with trucks, cars, and freight—hundreds of people waiting in lines to board cruise boats, and shops lining the harbor displaying their colorful wares. But in summer this scene could turn from bustling to stifling—especially if heat and humidity were added. We were enjoying gentle breezes and cool temperatures. While I photographed I listened to the repartee of the longshoremen as they loaded a large truck onto the ferry—they were discussing how and where to position the vehicle—one of the witticisms made the men laugh so hard they had to temporarily suspend the loading of the truck. The number of words Italians use when they're accomplishing a task amazes me. Americans use far fewer—*left, right, forward, back*. Italians tell stories—Americans grunt.

"Look at our boat. Look at the way he's maneuvering it," I said to Mardi as we joined the queue lining the harbor. With differential power, our captain was making the boat perform intricate twists and turns through traffic on the way to the dock. While I was engrossed in his virtuoso performance Mardi was sharing with Luciana and Simon the benefits of not having children. I thought that was kind of strange considering how much we love our children, until I realized that maybe Simon and Luciana had told her that they didn't plan to have kids. She was doing for them what Vincenzo had done for her—making them feel good about the situation they were in. Every day I think Mardi is becoming more and more Italian, but maybe she's always been Italian, always been a servant—a Martha, even though I call her Mardi. In the story that Matthew told about Jesus, Mary, and Martha, it was Martha who gave herself the task of serving others while Mary sat at the feet of Jesus listening. I married a woman with beautiful legs. I also married a Martha.

"Are we in line for the right boat?" I asked, realizing that four-thirty had come and gone.

"We're in line with the right people," Mardi answered. She was right. The girl with the long legs was queued up right in front of us.

Eventually our line started moving. We shuffled onto the boat, and within a few minutes we were motoring slowly past the breakwater looking back at one of the most gorgeous harbors I've ever seen.

"I miss my Amalfi," Mardi said as we reached open water and the captain punched the throttle. The big diesel roared, and we were soon at cruise speed. I guessed Mardi missed Amalfi because it was much less touristy than Capri. We had enjoyed a very good day on a beautiful island, but I too was glad to be heading home. It was odd to call Amalfi home, but that was how I was feeling. As we sat on the top deck of that boat speeding past the islands between Capri and Positano, watching our captain make minor corrections in his course, we knew that life was good.

"I like our captain's style—his shaved head looks good—like a man in command," I commented.

"I've always liked the clean look," Mardi agreed with a smile.

I gave her a hug for affirming the look God gave me.

In the moist air we could make out the lines of a sleek luxury boat maneuvering toward the dock in Positano as brightly painted fishing boats headed out to sea. The closer we got the more color we saw in the pastel hotels and houses climbing the hills surrounding the town and the more the scene looked like the hundreds of beautiful photographs I had seen of Positano. I vowed that we'd come back another day to walk the streets of this very vertical village that lured me to the Amalfi Coast.

We stayed in Positano only long enough to allow a few passengers to disembark, then our captain hit the throttle once more and the big diesel began purring again. The throaty sound reminded me of my childhood spent driving tractors on my father's farm. As I reminisced, Mardi developed a rapport with a woman sitting just behind her who was staying in Ravello. They talked of their love of Ravello and Amalfi and their affinity for the agricultural flavor of the area and its laid-back atmosphere.

Amalfi's harbor, while beautiful, is a world apart from Capri—much less busy, more of a working town, still home to fishermen. The captain backed toward the dock as the bells of Saint Andrews resonated above the sound of the anchor line playing out. Amalfi was doing its best to welcome us home.

As we stepped off the boat I said, *"Buon compleanno,"* to the woman staying in Ravello. Mardi had discovered that she too was celebrating her birthday the next day. They exchanged warm goodbyes on the dock, but I doubt we'll ever see her again. Some friendships exist only as good memories—others like our friendship with Simon and Luciana, you carry forward. We thanked them for making our day on Capri special and told them we'd see them back at Salvatore's place. We didn't want to make them wait while we shopped.

"This just feels like home," I said to Mardi as we walked into the *piazza*. I grabbed my water bottle and filled it at the fountain—a ritual I'm sure I will never tire of. The sound of the flowing water mixing with dozens of conversations and the pealing of the bells resonating off the buildings gave me a feeling of incredible belonging—as though I'd lived such a life before. It's another mystery I will never, on this side of death, be able to understand.

To celebrate our sense of belonging we did the very hometown thing of stopping at the market to pick up food for the night. The butcher noticed us trying to make up our minds and offered some samples. We took a little of everything he suggested. We especially loved the very thinly sliced *prosciutto.* We then turned our attention to the cheeses. My brain wasn't working very well. I was having trouble translating the words for the various kinds of cheeses as well as the word for "half." I was thinking of ordering a half pound of each, but then I remembered we weren't in Kansas anymore. Cheese in Italy is purchased by the kilogram—two point two pounds. A half of a kilogram is a lot of cheese.

I conveyed to the man selling the cheeses that I wanted a half of a half of a kilogram each of havarti and gouda, as well as some sheep cheese—*pecorino.* I was afraid to order a quarter of a kilogram fearing that I would instead receive four kilograms. He laughed at my pronunciations and my skewed grammar and repeated the word half to me—*mezza*. He emphasized the "zz." I followed his pronunciation and he said, "*Bravo,* very good."

But we weren't done. We discovered there were two floors to the market. We climbed the steep stairs and found our favorite crackers—*Mulino Bianco—Sfoglia di grano.* We took a photograph of the package to make sure we'd never forget the name. We had discovered them in Bolzano when we were shepherds for Gianrico and were delighted to find them here as well.

Back on the main floor we chose a substantial loaf of bread and a couple of bottles of cheap local wine and headed to the checkout, where we picked up a little chocolate. That led to some enjoyable repartee with the cashier—she used a couple of Italian words with which I was unfamiliar, but I understood enough of what she was saying to know that she was quite certain we were getting prepared for a very romantic evening.

"Oh, that was fun," Mardi said as we stepped into the street—a lane just barely wide enough for us to walk side by side with our aphrodisiacs—which, now that I had time to think about it, was probably one of the Italian words I hadn't understood.

"We have cheese. We have crackers. We have *prosciutto.* We have bread. And we have *vino.* What am I forgetting?" I asked.

"You're forgetting chocolate—and that we have a beautiful terrace where we can eat all this," Mardi said as she offered her lips for a kiss.

On the way to Villa Annalara we window-shopped. I was checking out the *ceramica* shops, looking for a set of salt and pepper shakers small enough to carry with us on hikes when behind me I heard Mardi say *domani.* I walked back to see what she was considering for tomorrow. She was looking at a display of sandwiches and rice balls a couple of young men were encouraging her to buy. I took one look at the prices and said *domani* as well. We were planning on a major hike on her birthday, and this food looked perfect to carry in my backpack in case we found ourselves needing lunch while still on the trail.

"That's a meal, look at that," I said to Mardi. "And it's less than three euros."

I doubted the guys in the shop believed us when we again assured them we'd return, but we believed it.

When we stepped back into the street we heard the delightful sound of kids playing. Their excited voices were bouncing off the walls of the shops and houses and even the hills above us, creating an echo canyon effect. We were overwhelmed with a feeling of rightness at the sounds. Here we were on *la strada principale* of Amalfi that leads ever deeper into the canyon in which Amalfi lies—the street that would soon drop us at the front gate of the Villa Annalara Bed & Breakfast—and on this busy evening during the *passeggiata* we could hear no traffic whatsoever—just the sounds of people enjoying themselves. I'm sure that somewhere in Amalfi there had to be televisions playing at that moment, but it didn't seem as if anyone was watching them—they all seemed to be out walking. These people weren't in a hurry to get anywhere, nor were they walking for exercise—they were just seeing and being seen, chatting and listening, finding out what was going on in the lives of their friends and neighbors.

We loved the sounds of the *passeggiata* so much that we considered turning around, walking back through town with our wine and cheese to the Piazza Duomo, and then climbing partway up the steps to enjoy our food while listening and watching the nightly ritual. It was tempting, but the thought of just the two of us dining together on Salvatore's terrace, with the sounds of the town for background music, seemed a bit more romantic.

We saw no one and heard no one when we reached the terrace. We chose a table lit only by the night sky, so far from the lights of the reception area that we could barely read the label of our wine bottle. We toasted each other and began reliving our day on Capri as we delved into the delicious food we had bought at the market. I am always amazed at how good simple food, simply prepared, can taste. We could see the lights of boats in the harbor coming and going, and we tried to imagine where they had been or where they were going and who was on board. The sight of a sailboat always sets me dreaming.

So intent were we on our imaginings that we didn't hear Salvatore approach.

"Is everything okay?" he asked.

"More than okay—it is *molto* okay," I said.

We offered Salvatore some wine and cheese, but he declined and wished us well. We toasted each other again and snuggled closer.

"This is just magnificent," Mardi said to me.

I'm not used to Mardi saying something is "magnificent"—*wonderful* would be more her style. But I couldn't argue with her. What we were experiencing that night and what we had been experiencing for the previous couple of weeks truly *had* been magnificent. However, I came back at Mardi with a smaller, more emotional word.

"I am so happy," I said as I stirred a little sugar into the wine.

"This is the best wine you've ever made," she said, playfully reminding me of the year we had such a bumper crop of raspberries on the farm that I corked almost fifty bottles of wine—a wine I was very proud of—that people really enjoyed. That was the year I developed a liking for sweeter wines.

"Am I winning your heart?" I said as I poured another glass of wine for her.

She didn't say anything, but the look in her eyes said a lot. I was looking so deeply into them that I didn't see Salvatore set a couple of lit candles on our table. He came and went so quietly and quickly that we had to send our thanks to him halfway across the terrace.

Mardi began laughing. It was a laughter of joy. Salvatore had set just the right mood for us—an exclamation point as it were.

"Have you ever had a better marriage?" I asked.

"No. This is the best marriage I've ever had."

Extending her wine glass and offering a silent toast to its powers, she added, "This is the best cheese I've ever had too. It's fantastic."

"You want some *prosciutto* to go with it?" I asked.

"A little, yes."

"A little is all we have."

"Can you believe it?" she said. "This is so perfect."

She was right again. I was reminded of what Rick Steves had written in his guidebook: *If you like Italy as far south as Rome, go farther south—it gets better. If Italy is getting on your nerves, don't go farther. Italy intensifies as you plunge deeper.*

By that I was certain he meant that the characteristics of the Italian people—passion, warmth, hospitality, expressiveness—grow stronger the farther south you go.

I was, of course, comparing our current view of Italy to the Italy I had grown to know and love in Tuscany. Tuscany is without a doubt beautiful, but I was feeling even more at home on the Amalfi Coast—something I wouldn't have thought possible seven years ago. I was trying to explain this to myself and began attributing it to the openness of the people here—they seemed to speak even more expressively with their hands and were even more attuned to each other when they talked. I had felt the camaraderie watching the men load the ferry in Capri—so much emotion was invested in getting those trucks aboard that it was like watching an opera.

As if to underscore our thoughts about hospitality, Salvatore appeared again at our table—he must have noticed that our wine bottle was almost empty when he brought the candles.

"Yesterday you forgot your wine. It is for you and not for us," he said graciously.

We had ordered wine with our meal, but we had left some in the bottles. I had not expected to see it again, but he had saved it for us.

"I love him," I said to Mardi after he had gone.

"I'd like to get a job here in Amalfi," Mardi said. She was thinking my thoughts after me, or maybe before me. I was in love with this town and these people. I couldn't help repeating myself: "I don't think I even knew of Amalfi. It never registered in my mind that there was a town named Amalfi."

"Out of ignorance, I wasn't confused," Mardi said. I wasn't exactly sure what she meant by that, but I could tell by her voice that she was forgiving me for belaboring the point about being so thrilled that I had fallen in love with a town I had never heard of.

"It will be good to go to Maiori and compare," Mardi said.

She was referring to another town I'd never heard of—a few kilometers away where we had found an incredibly low rate for what looked like a very nice hotel.

"Do you want to go to Maiori tomorrow?" I asked.

"We might as well stay here and enjoy Amalfi."

Again, she was thinking clearly. Maiori could wait.

As I started refilling her wine glass again she warned, "Not too much—you don't want a dysfunctional wife."

"I don't think wine hurts our lovemaking," I said.

She lifted her glass, offering another silent toast as the smell of smoke from a wood-fired pizza oven drifted our way.

"The rich do have more fun," Mardi said.

"The Brits have more fun?" I asked wondering why she was thinking of Simon and Luciana.

"No, the RICH," she said. "We're living like we're rich."

I had to agree with her. This was so very different from my first trip to Italy, when I picked olives and grapes and spent almost no time being a tourist. On my second trip, Mardi's first, we gave volunteer farming another try. But either WWOOF (World Wide Opportunities on Organic Farms) had changed or I had. I wanted to share the wonderful time I had volunteering as an olive picker with Mardi, but our first experience together had its share of problems—the most glaring being that for over a week we had no heating oil on the farm—no way to heat water, only camping stoves to prepare meals. We went for a full week without showering. We made the best of a difficult situation, learned a lot, and enjoyed our hosts, but we cut that stay short and headed to Rome to shower and play at being tourists. We booked a room for four days but it took us only one to fall in love with the Eternal City.

Our second WWOOF farm, as shepherds, turned out much better, so much so that we turned a one-week stay into two weeks and almost extended our visit right through Thanksgiving. In fact, I think our hosts, Gianrico and

Annika, would have liked it if we had stayed for Christmas too. We worked hard with them, but we also found lots of time for hiking the high mountains of the Italian Alps.

I had thought that our journey of a lifetime would also include some volunteering, but Mardi was right. We were indeed living like the rich. We had lined up no farms with which to trade our labor. I had wanted to volunteer not just to save money, but to feel more connected to the Italian people, but so far I wasn't feeling any deficit in that department. I didn't know whether that could be blamed on my improved skills speaking Italian, our increasing comfort with Italy because of previous trips, or the hospitality of southern Italians, but I felt almost as connected to the southern Italians as I did to the Tuscan farmers I'd worked side by side with for days on end.

"I see two stars now," Mardi said pulling me out of my thoughts.

"Even barking dogs sound better in Italy," I said not yet fully engaged with Mardi's thinking.

"Oh—four stars...five...they're coming out." She continued to search the black sky, but my eyes had not yet adjusted. I had been staring at the flickering candle flame as I thought back over the three sojourns I had enjoyed in Italy.

"I would love to know more about the history of this place," Mardi said.

Except for the occasional sound of an Ape, we were hearing the sounds this town has been producing for thousands of years. We both reveled in that realization.

"I bet you never thought I could sit down like this," Mardi said.

She was referring to the very un-Martha like behavior she was exhibiting. She had not had to prepare the meal or do much more than enjoy it.

"This *is* a bit different," I admitted.

"You need to change a person's circumstances. I feel more like the person I was when I was a child. I'm not racing around taking care of grandmothers who are yelling, *Mardi, Mardi, Mardi.*"

"Are you as happy now as when you were young?" I asked.

"Yeah, I was a dreamer. I feel now like I did as a child. I didn't want to take care of anything, I didn't serve people. I was not very ambitious."

"But your name is Martha," I pointed out.

"I think deep down a person is probably more the person they were as a child—the way they were meant to be," she said. "That's how I feel now."

"So you're back to normal—the kind of person you were as a child?" I asked.

"Yeah. We've been outside all day, and I still don't want to go in. We're out here having a picnic on the terrace, and I'm in heaven," she said. "I don't want to let go of this day."

I didn't know what to say. I didn't want to break the reverie she was in. She looked completely at ease.

"Look at how that rock face is lit up by the lights of the town," I pointed out.

"Italy has elements of heaven," she responded.

I looked at her, trying to get a good look at her eyes in the dim light to see whether she was mocking me for my over-the-top praise of all things Italian.

"This is a foretaste of heaven. I dreamed that heaven was like this, just like this."

I knew the dream she was talking about, a dream she'd had about heaven but hadn't mentioned for years.

"What did Jesus say—*In my Father's house are many mansions: if it were not so, I would have told you. I go to prepare a place for you.*" I said referring to the verse in John that refers to rooms as mansions in the King James Version I grew up with.

"In my dream, heaven was so material, so real. Gretchen was above us—it was like these houses, but it was also like a dollhouse because I could see into each room. I had never been to Italy. I had never seen people living on top of each other like this, but this is exactly what my dream was like."

"When did you have this dream?" I asked.

"It was twenty-five or thirty years ago. It was material like this. We weren't sitting on clouds—it was quality furniture."

"Of course Gretchen was on top of us," I said referring to our daughter who maintains that she, not we, raised her younger brothers, who are five and seven years younger than she is.

"Each of the boys had his own place. It was just like this—no one had their doors closed."

"Is that what you mean by dollhouse?"

"Yes. I'm realizing after seeing this that it might have been that people just had their doors open—no need to be closed off from everyone."

"I love this more than any town I've seen in Italy," I said. It was easy to say now that Mardi had compared this place to heaven.

"Hey, you two." We turned and saw Luciana walking toward us. Simon was just behind her, moving somewhat unsteadily.

"We fell asleep," he said.

"We're getting plastered. There's another idiom for you," I said stepping back into our lunch conversation.

"Yeah, that's another good one," he said.

"I didn't realize we were so close to your room. Were we bothering you?" Mardi asked Luciana.

"No, we were out of it," Luciana said.

"I didn't know you had a mansion. I thought you just had a room like ours," I said to Simon.

They had left their terrace doors open. I could see that their room was large and had very high ceilings—just the way Mardi had been describing heaven to me.

"Now that we know where you live, you'll never have another moment of privacy," I said.

They laughed and sat down to enjoy some wine with us. We reminisced about our day on Capri and made plans to celebrate Mardi's birthday by eating dinner with them—exactly where we didn't know, but our day on Capri together had turned out so well that the thought of not including them didn't even occur to us.

And yes, the store clerk was right. I don't know what she had envisioned when she noted the food we were buying, but the romantic evening Mardi and I enjoyed in our little room high above the beauty of Amalfi more than fulfilled the fantasies I'd been carrying since I began dreaming many years ago of this once-in-a-lifetime journey—and we were just getting started—the next day we had a birthday to celebrate.

CHAPTER SIX

Amalfi ~ Wednesday April 6 ~ 68 & Sunny

An Orange for Mardi's Birthday

We can do no great things; only small things with great love.
MOTHER TERESA

■

What will survive of us is love.
PHILLIP LARKIN

I gave Mardi a gentle early morning birthday kiss without waking her and slipped quietly out of bed to head toward town to photograph. I saw no one as I left Villa Annalara. The first people I met were some teenagers on the way to school. First the girls, then the boys—totally separated—very different energy from that first morning I'd seen them when they were teasing each other as they walked up the hill.

When I reached town, few shops were open and no tourists were on the street—only a few workmen gathering tools. Even the coast highway was quiet. A few fishermen were casting lines, and a lone tour boat was pulling away from the dock. The bells of Saint Andrew were chiming the quarter hours; otherwise I heard only the waves and the occasional whine of an Ape or a motor scooter echoing off the walls of the hotels lining the waterfront. I walked to the end of the dock and stayed there photographing and journaling long enough that the sounds of the high-pitched engines became more frequent, more insistent—a sure sign that the town would soon be full of life.

When I felt I had done the morning justice with my camera and my pen, I moved back across the now busy Amalfi Coast Highway and into what I had come to consider the most beautiful *piazza* in all of Italy. My eyes immediately

fell upon a policeman in full resplendent uniform with his hand on a man's shoulder—he wasn't arresting him—I doubt the men were even discussing anything of an official nature—they were just doing what Italian men do, catching up on each other's world, and they were doing it in each other's personal space. I sat down on the fountain wall only a few feet from the two men to fill my water bottle and absorb the morning. The scene took me back. I have fond memories of the men of my hometown gathering each morning to sip coffee and talk sports and grain prices and weather. I wonder if one of the reasons I love Italy so deeply is because the camaraderie I see everywhere connects me to my smalltown childhood.

Italians are natural born storytellers, and the people of Amalfi were starting their day telling each other stories. The wonderful tale of Pinocchio didn't originate from the studios of Walt Disney, as many in America might think—this classic story about telling the truth came from the pen of the great Italian writer Carlo Collodi. And it wasn't written in 1940, when Americans first met Jiminy Cricket in the theaters—it was originally published as a serial, beginning in 1881, under the very literal title *La storia di un burattino*—"The tale of a puppet."

The town Collodi described in his book reminds me very much of Amalfi. The life of the village took place in the streets, just as it was this chilly, but sunny morning. As I made my way back to Annalara I passed a woman walking slowly up the hill weighted down with two bags of groceries, one in each hand. She had stopped for a moment to catch her breath. As we exchanged polite *buongiornos* I wondered if this was still a world where I could have offered to help her without her fearing for her safety. I wished that it were, but I didn't want to frighten her so I moved on and continued to take pictures.

Everywhere I looked I saw beautiful scenes to capture. It is difficult to walk anywhere in Italy without finding something that stimulates the photographer in me—it may be something as simple as a colorful doorway graced by flowers—but these scenes speak volumes to me about the character of Italians. I soon met a city worker carrying a push broom in his hand. He was framed perfectly in a tunnel—beautifully backlit by the morning sun—a classic shot of a working man.

When I arrived back at the B&B I discovered that Salvatore had learned that it was Mardi's birthday and had offered to prepare a celebration dinner for her. We discussed the menu with Simon and Luciana and chose fresh sea bass for the main course. My photographer's eye was still engaged. I noticed that Salvatore was wearing white-rimmed glasses, the rims rather thick. They did a great job of complementing his angular face and framing his intense but friendly eyes. Like most Italians he wanted to look good while making us feel great.

Mardi and I enjoyed what had quickly become our standard breakfast— fruit juice, croissants and jam, yogurt and nuts, accompanied by our now customary *cappuccinos*—one to get our *colazione* off to a good start and one to bring breakfast to a very civilized conclusion. We had quickly come to love the routine established by Salvatore's hospitality. On this morning, though, we didn't linger. To celebrate Mardi's birthday, we planned to walk to Ravello via Atrani and possibly farther if our legs felt strong and we were enjoying ourselves.

We stopped by the fountain in the upper part of Amalfi, only a few steps from the gate to Annalara, to fill our water bottles. As we waited our turn I tried to imagine all the conversations that had taken place at this very spot over the centuries. A few doors beyond the fountain we stepped into the shop where we had seen the rice balls and sandwiches that we thought would make an excellent lunch for our hike. I pulled a five-euro note out of my pocket, handed it to one of the guys we'd seen the night before, and said, *"Te l'avevo detto che saremmo tornati."* His smile told me he both understood and remembered us, but just in case I added, "I told you we'd be back."

We left the shop with a sandwich and a rice ball and a bit of change as well, plus the goodwill of these shopkeepers, who were surprised that we had indeed returned. My photographer's eye was still engaged—I was noticing the old men of Amalfi, their faces filled with character and patient wisdom. At the bottom of a long flight of steps a man with a cane and a purple beret was sitting alone, as though waiting for a friend to join him to watch beautiful women walk by. A few doors down the street another old man, dressed in a comfortable white jacket, didn't appear to be waiting, only watching. When we got to the harbor I was still noticing old men, my age and older, sitting on benches along the promenade reading newspapers. Some would glance up when a pretty woman walked by—others seemed not to notice.

A man in his late seventies, on a fine road bike, a Colnago, was waiting at a stop light. But he wasn't at one with the bike. He was dressed more like a jogger. Without a helmet he looked naked and vulnerable. A man about the same age as the cyclist, but not nearly so fit, was making his way gingerly down the steep steps leading into Amalfi—the steps we were planning to climb to reach Atrani. His left foot was the first to descend each time. Then his right foot would join the left and the left would start the process again. As we waited for him to make his way down the narrow stairway, we noticed he was flicking ashes from his cigarette onto the steps.

As we began climbing, an ambulance led by a police car passed noisily below us. The first assumption is always that the narrow, winding road that connects the beautiful villages of the Sorrentine Peninsula has claimed another victim, but even so, if I'd had my bicycle with me, I would have wanted to bike the Amalfi Coast Highway—although I am certain that for my first ride I would choose a quiet Sunday morning with little or no traffic.

As we continued up the steps we saw laundry hanging high above us, taking advantage of the midday sun, which because of the closeness of the buildings would soon disappear. In much less time than it takes to eat lunch in Italy, the shadows would creep slowly up the wall, and no sun would fall on this stretch of cobblestones for another twenty-three or so hours. Even in these darkened walkways, the doors of the homes were brightly painted and always flanked by pots of vibrant flowers. Italians have a knack for making their homes look inviting, both in appearance and by the welcome you get when the door is flung open.

When at last we got to the highest point of the climb and began descending, we were treated to glimpses of the beauty of Atrani. I was once again surprised that I had never seen a photo of this idyllic seaside town clinging to the cliffs, its tightly packed homes and hotels and churches lit by flecks of sunlight reflecting off the breaking waves. Straight under us, the Amalfi Coast Highway was stark and graceful, set off from the deep blue sea below. I loved watching the

buses and cars negotiate the winding road from our eagle's nest vantage point. What at first looked so intimidating had now fully captured my imagination. From where we stood in the bright midday sun, that wild piece of highway engineering now looked like the ultimate challenge of eye-hand coordination. However, once again the distant sound of an ambulance echoing off the cliffs reminded me of my first impressions of that narrow, winding road.

We met few people on our hike. Midday is a better time for sleeping than climbing. But each time we met someone, energetic and enthusiastic *buongiornos* were exchanged. Amalfi Coast is lived vertically, and to adequately appreciate, understand, and enjoy it, you have to climb these ancient steps, one at a time, all the way to the top and then back down. Negotiating these steps ushered us into an honorary society and we were rewarded with admiration and conversation. If you know some *italiano*, so much the better.

The folks we were meeting were excited to see us. By their enthusiasm they were conveying to us that the tourists in the crowded buses below weren't seeing the best that the Amalfi Coast has to offer. As we made our way slowly through Atrani and began the climb to Ravello, we realized that we may have chosen the perfect day for our hike. The wisteria lining the ancient stone path was in full flower—perfectly formed and luxuriously scented. The purple blossoms splendidly framed the village of Atrani.

My photographer's eye kicked into overdrive. I knew a great picture was there for the capturing if I could find the right composition—the perfect blend of wisteria, cliffs, and hillside homes, with the deep blue of the Tyrrhenian Sea as a backdrop. The light was just right—the sky blue—the air dry. Everything was sparkling. The wisteria blossoms provided the foreground, the ancient walls of the path from Atrani to Ravello became the middleground, and Atrani clinging to the cliffs and framed by the sea provided the perfect background. I knew I had a great photo the second I snapped it. That judgment was borne out over the next few months as hundreds of thousands of people *liked* it on Facebook prompting me to choose that shot as the quintessential representative of our once in a lifetime journey. It's the cover shot of this book.

I doubt that Mardi will long remember what I gave her for that birthday, but I'll bet she will never forget what an old man named Raffaele gave her a few moments after I took the *Wisteria of Atrani* photo. We were climbing up, up, up, and he was making his way slowly down. He didn't hide his surprise at seeing us. I commented on the beauty of his walking sticks, and he told me he needed them because his knees were succumbing to a lifetime of wear—climbing and descending the very steps we were on.

Despite the pain in his legs, his face glowed, projecting the effects of a life well-lived and a countenance that was contagious. I immediately felt I was in the presence of a generous man—he looked like a man accustomed to giving of his time and his good fortune as well as his material goods. On that day he was carrying oranges, one of which he promptly presented to Mardi upon learning that she was celebrating *sua sessanta nono compleanno*, her sixty-ninth birthday.

Raffaele thought he had misunderstood my Italian when I told him Mardi's age—he was certain we were much younger than he was. That made us feel quite good, but what really made us feel great was sharing our lives with this humble man along that path on a beautiful spring day with a gentle breeze caressing the slopes. Raffaele told us he lived in Atrani, had been to Ravello that morning, and was making his way back home. It seemed to be a trek he made often. He proudly pointed out his church far below and said that he lived nearby. He also blessed us by pointing out where he had picked the orange he had just given Mardi.

We suspected that it was from his farm but didn't ask—the conversation quickly moved on to the beauty of the day and the panoramas spread out below us—it seemed that even after a lifetime of looking at such magnificence Raffaele was not immune to its allure. That has always been a trait of Italians I have admired—they seem to never tire of beauty—or of giving thanks for

it. Raffaele was the beneficiary of grace and he knew it—and by sharing his grace with us, he made our day—and Mardi's birthday. His thoughtfulness perfectly exemplified an aphorism that I have often heard attributed to Mother Teresa—*We can do no great things; only small things with great love.*

It seemed fitting in the presence of this gentle farmer that a rooster should crow at the exact moment we said goodbye to him. He sent us on our way with assurances that we were indeed on the right path to Ravello. We discovered that the route was well marked but on that morning not well traveled. Raffaele was the only person we encountered until we saw workmen raking brush and burning leaves a half hour later. Recalling Raffaele's problems with his knees, Mardi and I ventured off the path to grab a couple of long, straight branches. I pulled out my Leatherman, flipped out the saw blade and file, and fashioned a couple of walking sticks—not nearly as beautifully crafted as Raffaele's, but nonetheless functional in negotiating what we hoped was the final pitch to Ravello.

We were quite relieved to find a hand-painted sign at the top of the stairs pointing to Ravello Centro. Piazza Centrale looked inviting, so we sat on a bench to delight in the antics of a young girl chasing pigeons in the square. We didn't want to be inside on such a gorgeous day, so we probably missed much of what Ravello has to offer, but we were quite content just to enjoy the outdoor delights of the *piazza*. We watched the tourists and a few locals and absorbed the warmth of the sun while dining on our rice ball and sandwich as well as the cheese, crackers, *prosciutto,* apples, and wine that we invariably carry in my backpack—and of course the orange that Raffaele had given Mardi.

As we sat there, we were reminded of the woman we'd met on the boat from Capri—the one who shared Mardi's birthday. She had told us she very much enjoyed the peace and quiet of Ravello, and that was exactly what we found as we began walking around the town—it was quite serene. We were overwhelmed with the beauty of the Villa Rufolo gardens. We were not surprised to discover that others—numerous artists, musicians, and movie stars such as D. H. Lawrence, Giovanni Boccaccio, Salvador Dali, Greta Garbo, and Humphrey Bogart—had succumbed to their beauty.

Once satisfied that we had seen a good portion of what Ravello had to offer, we headed out of town looking for the path that had brought us to this delightful village and its magnificent view of the Amalfi Coast so favored by the composer Richard Wagner. We made a mental note to return when Ravello was hosting one of its many music festivals so that we could hear beautiful classical compositions while gazing out at the Amalfi Hills rising out of the Tyrrhenian Sea.

We missed the path, and staying true to our pinball philosophy of travel, decided we were being led to chose a gentler descent. We left Ravello following the roadway. We met few cars, but we did meet one very strong cyclist who was beating out a steady rhythm as he climbed the steep hill. I praised him for his powerful cadence. He returned an appreciative smile, but said nothing. I knew the feeling. Once when I had been climbing a steep hill in Tuscany, a couple of teenagers yelled out *Bella bicicletta* and *Molto forte* to me. I was so winded that even uttering *Grazie* was too much. I wished that I had only smiled.

When we reached the spot where we'd seen the workmen burning leaves, we left the road and rejoined the path that had led us to Ravello. Again we saw no one walking the path—only three stonemasons repairing ramps built into the steps that make it possible for a wheelbarrow or other one-wheeled cart to negotiate the steep hill. The workmen were surprised to see us as well. They greeted us with *buonaseras,* a good indication that they felt that their work day was about to end.

"I hope you're enjoying your birthday," I said as we paused to look at a farm on the other side of the valley—the fields, orchards, and vineyards so perfectly laid out as to be a work of art.

"Oh, I am. I so enjoy just being out here with you," Mardi said.

Her sentiment was my sentiment. We stood for a while absorbing the perfection of the moment and the beauty all around us. No matter where we looked, the scene was gorgeous—and it was accompanied by a delightful chorus of birds that convinced us that everything was right in the world. I am amazed at how often I get that feeling in Italy.

We were also catching snippets of conversations of unseen people on the other side of the valley. We wondered if they could hear us as well as we could hear them. As we neared Atrani, our ears became attuned to the sounds of the village. We heard voices of children long before we saw them. We discovered them playing in a beautifully designed park at the edge of town. Life looked festive as we made our way into the village. In the heart of town we were delighted to see a table set for a dozen people in a small *piazza*. Eleven women and a lone man were seated around the table—we would have loved to know the rest of that story, but they didn't invite us to join them, so we kept walking.

We chose a different route through Atrani this time. We let the bell tower of the church be our guide, and that led us to a wide open *piazza* where a photographer was taking wedding pictures. We found a comfortable wall to sit on, well out of his way, to watch him work. He was quite creative in using the beauty of the rugged Amalfi Coast as a backdrop for dramatic photos of the happy bride and groom.

We were joined by a family of hikers—a husband, wife, and two young daughters—who also seemed happy to take a break and watch the beautiful bride and groom. Our attention turned to two men who were repairing some broken pavers near the entrance to the *piazza*. I was surprised to note how many tools they had spread around them. The men finished their work and began picking up—making a heavy load even heavier. I thought they had it to down to two trips, but then the younger of the two, using strength and ingenuity, hoisted a very heavy bucket filled with hand tools and stones onto his shoulder. With his free hand he grabbed the last of the shovels and pickaxes, and off they went—job done.

You would never see such a thing in America. Some sort of mechanical conveyance would have carried the men and their tools to the worksite, but not in Italy. The streets are often too narrow—or as in this case the *piazza* had too many steps—for anything but walking and donkeys. People who value efficiency must be driven nuts in Italy. I cherish beauty, especially beauty handed down through the ages, and the sight of those men walking off with all their tools and supplies on their backs told me that the beauty of Italy will never fall victim to the gods of efficiencies and time-motion studies.

When at last it felt right to leave the *piazza* and Atrani, we noticed some people walking along the highway and decided it would be safe to follow them. We passed the steps that had brought us to Atrani and were surprised to see, far ahead of us and also walking on the highway, the family that had been with us in the *piazza*. I felt better about our decision to follow the coast back to Amalfi knowing that this family felt comfortable walking along the highway with their young girls.

But just as I feeling the relief of not having to climb the steps to get to Amalfi, the family turned into what appeared to be a parking garage. I was bummed. They weren't walking to Amalfi, they were heading to their car. We reached the entrance and were again surprised to see them, still walking, not turning off toward the hundreds of cars parked inside the mountain. We looked for a sign stating that this was a walkway to Amalfi, but saw nothing. Yet we could clearly see that the family of trekkers had not turned off, so we kept following them, but always with the fear that they had parked deep inside the mountain, and we would have to turn back.

Eventually we saw a couple of bright blue arrows on the wall of the passageway—one labeled *Atrani* pointing to where we had come from, and the other, wonder of wonders, labeled *Amalfi* and pointing in the direction we were walking. We wondered why no one had mentioned it, why we had seen nothing about it in the guidebooks, and why the girl carrying her bicycle down the steps didn't direct us to it—in fact, why hadn't she biked through the tunnel to Atrani instead of following the much more dangerous route along the Amalfi Coast Highway?

We kept walking where the arrows pointed and were thrilled to emerge from the mountain at the point where our adventure had begun—the base of the steps leading up to the Duomo Saint Andrew. The thrill of this discovery was intensified because we had not discovered this route in a guidebook, from talking with a local, or at a tourist office. We had found it the old fashioned way by being curious. This was now *our* route to Atrani. It was another affirmation of my love for the adventure of pinball traveling.

When we emerged into the light, we immediately felt as if we were back home, back where we felt extremely comfortable. The *piazza* was beginning to fill with folks on their evening *passeggiata*. The beauty of the steps and the perfect symmetry of their ascending order had a wonderfully calming effect on us. I was convinced that I could take a photograph of these steps every day for the rest of my life and never tire of the unfolding drama in this lovely *piazza*.

We noticed a beautiful young girl being held by her grandfather as a wedding party made its way down the stairs and wondered if the photographer we had seen in Atrani was connected to this wedding. We didn't have to wait long to find out—within minutes he appeared, arranged the wedding party at the bottom of the steps, and took what I'm sure must be the classic wedding photo—the people in three rows at the bottom, with all of the steps and the church edifice rising above, all the way to the deep blue sky above.

When the grandfather set his little princess down, every person within fifty yards saw the possibility for a great photo. Suddenly she was standing by herself—a precious little angel in white at the base of the stairway—with every phone and camera in the whole *piazza* pointed toward her. Whoever was in charge of the chiming of the bells must have been watching for the bells immediately began ringing, proclaiming the sacredness of the moment.

Italians love families, and they especially love weddings. The essence of Italian family life was on full display in the *piazza*. There are a lot of beautiful places to get married in Italy, but the bride and groom couldn't have wished for a more perfect moment than was given to them that evening. The whole town was celebrating with them—every eye in the *piazza* taking in the glory of the moment—and I'm sure that everyone was wishing them well.

We could have stayed there the whole evening, but we had a birthday to celebrate at the Annalara with Simon and Luciana. When we stepped onto the terrace we discovered that a festive atmosphere had been created—balloons adorned the chairs and hung from the trellis above. The tables were beautifully set, and Simon and Luciana had gone all out for the occasion, both dressing in white. Josef, whom we had met on the Capri excursion, joined us as well, bringing a fine Amalfi Coast wine. Ours was an eclectic collection indeed. The conversation went immediately to our shared adventure—and once again we talked about Vincenzo more than the beauty of the island. Josef, who was from Bavaria, praised another facet of Vincenzo's repertoire—his command of German.

Everyone had something good to say about Vincenzo. I mentioned complimenting him about how he had handled the crying boy and how his response had been, *I love kids—family is what it's all about.* "You can't get much more Italian than that," I concluded.

On cue, Salvatore, who is Italian to the core, appeared laden with plates of food balanced on his arm, the quintessential waiter as well. If you've seen *A Farewell to Arms* or have read Ernest Hemingway's book, Salvatore reminds me of Frederick Henry's Italian friend Rinaldi, who is forever saying, *I love you baby, I love you baby.*

"Who ordered the sea bass, and who ordered the lemon wrap?" Salvatore asked in his delightfully energetic accent.

And with that we were treated to a fine meal. I am always amazed at how universal the aptitude for cooking seems to be in Italy. I knew only one Italian family when I was growing up. I now understand why their restaurant was the most popular place in town. Other establishments seemed to come and go, but their café remained. On almost every farm in Italy where I've worked, the food has been outstanding. The pride Italians take in serving and eating great food must be deeply embedded in their DNA—which in itself is another of life's mysteries.

Salvatore stopped by to ask as he always did, *Is everything okay?* I told him that it was fantastic and then asked where he bought the fresh ingredients. I wondered whether he had chosen the same market where we had shopped.

"I pick a lot of it from the garden downstairs," he explained. "That's where a good meal starts."

That reminded me that Italians didn't just start restaurants when they emigrated to America. They became distributors and grocers. Many of the best known in Milwaukee are owned by families with very Italian-sounding names, like Balistreri, Bartolotta, Marchese, and Machi. As Mardi and I were enjoying the personal attention Salvatore was lavishing on us—we were feeling a deep connection to the Italian people, but I wondered whether Simon and Luciana valued this type of holiday as much as we did. They had traveled to more regions of Italy in the previous half dozen years than we had.

"Would you and Luciana come back to Amalfi?" I asked.

They looked at each other. Simon answered the question: "I believe we would, but I think we would come a little earlier next time, before the tourists. How about you guys?"

"I think we will just move here. Seems like a good town for a writer," I said.

"We could come to visit," Simon said.

"We would *definitely* come visit," Luciana confirmed emphatically.

And that is how people fall in love with Italy—a little hospitality here, a little hospitality there—and soon much of the world is dreaming about living somewhere in Italy—at least a few months every year.

CHAPTER SEVEN

Amalfi ~ Thursday April 7 ~ 73 & Sunny

What to Do?

There is no remedy for love but to love more.
HENRY DAVID THOREAU

■

We shall not cease from exploration,
and the end of all our exploring
will be to arrive where we started
and know the place for the first time.
T. S. ELIOT

Mardi and I woke up feeling conflicted. On Tuesday I had found a room in Maiori that would cost half of what we were paying Salvatore. Knowing that special prices often disappear, I booked it. But that was before our wonderful day celebrating Mardi's birthday—a lot of what made yesterday so memorable flowed directly from Salvatore's hospitality.

What we were enjoying in Amalfi was the epitome of what I had told myself we were searching for on this journey. *Find a place that feels good to you, then really get to know the place. Stay long enough that the locals get to know you.* I felt we'd already found what I had come to Italy to find, so why move on?

Incredibly, Mardi agreed. Feeling the thrill of knowing we'd be staying longer in this dream we were living, I walked down to the breakfast terrace to talk to Salvatore. The dreamer in me was satisfied, but the pragmatist wanted to see if he'd be willing to meet the Maiori price.

Salvatore didn't have to think very long.

"I'm sorry James. I cannot do that. I cannot match the prices in Maiori. I also do not have room for you this weekend. We are full," he said as he set down a pitcher of orange juice on the buffet bar. "Amalfi will always cost more than Maiori. Maiori is a sleepy village."

And with that our course was set.

I poured two glasses of juice and returned to our room to share the disappointing news with Mardi. Our love affair with Amalfi would have to be put on hold—our pinball had been flung down the road a half dozen kilometers. I suppose we could have fought harder to remain in Amalfi by trying to find a hotel that wasn't booked up for the weekend, but we decided to go with the flow. For years I've carried a dream of finding an inexpensive place that would make it possible to spend months at a time living and writing in Italy. Maybe Maiori was that place. And who knows, we might like a sleepy little village. With our spirits brightened a bit, we kept our reservation at the unbelievably low price of forty-four euros a night. But even as we were giving ourselves a pep talk, we were thinking, *You get what you pay for.*

With a sense of sadness, we began packing our bags. Life had been good here—really good. I loved waking up each morning knowing that waiting on our terrace was a fabulous view to kick-start our day. A very productive writing session had accompanied the sounds of the town awakening each morning.

I slowly became aware that unlike all the other mornings, the joyful sound of children playing was not coming from the street but from directly below us on the breakfast terrace. We took a break from packing to see what was going on and quickly discovered that the two young girls we had met were playing with the balloons Luciana had bought to decorate the balcony the night before. We also discovered that Simon and Luciana were already eating. As we sat down at the table next to theirs, Salvatore stopped by to see if we wanted our usual.

"*Due cappuccino?*" he asked.

"*Grazie. Si,*" I responded. I was going to miss this routine. I was going to miss joining Simon and Luciana for breakfast on the terrace. It's amazing how quickly you can fall into a pleasant routine—and regret that you'll no longer be able to enjoy it.

"Do you guys go on a holiday every year?" I asked.

"Yes," Simon answered. "We try to."

"Where did you go last year?" Mardi asked.

"We went to Sicily. We loved it. I think you guys would love it too," Luciana added.

"We stayed in Ortigia, a small island off the east coast of Sicily. It's an old town. You get there from Siracusa," Simon said.

"I'm sure we'd like it if you guys liked it," I said convinced that we were *simpatico* travelers.

"The people are very friendly, even more friendly than in Sicily," Luciana said.

"Would you go back?" I asked.

"We definitely would. I'd love to have more time to explore and get to know the people. We've enjoyed all of our holidays in Italy," Simon said. Luciana enthusiastically nodded her agreement.

"Of all the places you've been in Italy, which town do you think Mardi and I would most enjoy?" I asked, putting them on the spot.

"I think you would like Ortigia," Simon said. "The people there are fantastic. So friendly."

I was intrigued. I'd never heard of Ortigia. "Could you excuse me?" I said. "I want to get a guidebook so I can get Ortigia's location firmly planted in my mind."

A few moments later I returned to the table with a couple of guidebooks and a copy of *Christ Stopped at Eboli*. "From the way you're talking about the people you're meeting, I think you would enjoy this book. It's a great story about the people of southern Italy." I handed the book to Simon. He began looking through it. "We're hoping to go to Eboli next week," I added.

I opened one of our guidebooks, found Sicily, and noted that Ortigia was literally a stone's throw from Siracusa, if you had a good arm. We now had another destination for our ever-growing list of Italian towns we hoped to someday see. But that wasn't the only recommendation they had for us.

"Do you guys like to eat meat?" Luciana asked.

I looked toward Mardi. I was sure this had caught her attention. "Yes we do," she answered. "Sometimes I can't even find meat on the menu."

"We noticed that too. We asked Salvatore's brother, Manuel, about it. He recommended a restaurant in Tramonti if we want to find good meat," Luciana said.

"Where's Tramonti?" I asked.

"It's up in the mountains. They raise cows up there," Simon said.

"Would you guys like to go with us? We're going there tomorrow," Luciana said.

I assumed that it was a long way from the Amalfi Coast if farmers had enough pasture for cows. Even though I loved being with Simon and Luciana, my first inclination was to beg off. I didn't want to go on a long bus trip just to eat a good steak. Italian food suits me just fine, and I was hoping Mardi would come around to feeling the same way. I decided this might be a good time to tell them that Salvatore didn't have a room for us and we were moving to Maiori—that would give me an excuse to graciously decline their invitation.

"That's where Manuel says we have to go to catch a bus to Tramonti!" Simon said.

Not yet ready to say yes and not wanting to say no to our new friends, I turned to my guidebook again. "How do you spell Tramonti?" I asked.

I quickly discovered that Tramonti wasn't even in the index. That intrigued me—going to a place recommended by a local that wasn't mentioned in the guidebooks. When Simon explained that Tramonti was less than an hour's drive from Maiori, I was sold. Mardi had long ago jumped aboard—she'd been sold at the word *meat*.

"Do you have scissors, Mardi?" I asked.

She gave me a quizzical look as she reached into her purse. She pulled out a small pair and handed them to me. I walked over to the balloons and cut four of them from the trellis and gave them to the girls. They were delighted.

The girls' parents were pleased too, and immediately opened up to us. They too had been to Italy many times, but this was their first visit to Amalfi. Like us, they had been in the *piazza* the evening the photographer was taking pictures of the wedding party, and it had impressed them as much as it had impressed us. Also like us they were having a love affair with Amalfi.

I'd been double-tasking—talking to them while trying to catch a conversation Salvatore was having with his brother, Manuel. I thought I'd heard him say something about driving to Maiori, so when he stopped by our table to ask if we'd enjoyed our breakfast, I asked, "Excuse me for eavesdropping, but did you tell Manuel that you were driving to Maiori?" I wasn't totally comfortable asking such a personal question, but the thought of being dropped off in Maiori instead of having to hike with suitcases to the bus stop made me a bit bolder than usual.

"Yes you did. I am driving to Maiori this morning," Salvatore said.

"Could we catch a ride with you?" I asked rather bluntly.

"Sure, if you can be ready in thirty minutes," Salvatore said.

We had been thoroughly enjoying our conversation with Simon and Luciana, but this seemed like an opportunity that shouldn't be passed up—a ride right to our new B&B. We were going to spend all of tomorrow with Simon and Luciana. Who could pass up such serendipity?

"Yes, yes. We can be ready. You are wonderful," I said.

"Half hour, you go with me in the car," Salvatore repeated to make sure we were all on the same page.

"*Si, andiamo*. We go," I assured him.

He smiled at my enthusiasm, and possibly at my *italiano*, as he picked up our plates.

"Can I pay you now?" I asked Salvatore.

"*Certo*," he said and turned to go.

I apologized to Simon and Luciana. They told me to think nothing of it and that they'd get in touch to let us know what time in the morning they would meet us in Maiori.

Mardi headed to our room to finish packing and I went to settle up. I could hardly believe our good fortune—what incredible timing.

A half hour later we were at the front gate with all of our luggage when Salvatore pulled up in a mid-sized FIAT. I was glad it wasn't a Cinquecento. I hadn't even thought to ask if his car was big enough to handle the two of us and our luggage. I was even more grateful a few minutes later when he stopped the car suddenly in the street and a woman hopped in.

"This is my wife, Francesca," Salvatore said. "She has a doctor appointment in Maiori."

"I'm James and this is Martha. I hope we aren't going to make you late," I said trying to conceal my shock. My Italian had not been good enough to catch the reason Salvatore was going to Maiori. If I had known he was taking his wife to the doctor I wouldn't have considered asking him to give us a lift.

"It is not necessary to be on time. If you are within a few minutes. That is fine," she said.

"Ah, that is good," I said, relieved she was being so pleasant about the inconvenience.

I switched the subject to Tramonti.

"It is full of sheep," Salvatore said.

"You should get some nice lamb," Francesca added.

"Sounds like it is off the beaten track," Mardi said.

"Definitely," Salvatore added.

I was beginning to think that Salvatore preferred a faster pace to life. From the way he had talked about Maiori I felt like he thought we would soon be bored with it. It was, after all, Salvatore's brother, and not Salvatore, who had recommended Tramonti.

The drive to Maiori became thrilling the moment we pulled into traffic—squeezing into what seemed like an incredibly small gap between cars. I was in the front seat, getting an in-the-cockpit demonstration by a seasoned driver of how to negotiate an impossibly narrow road at a speed more fitting a wide open Wyoming highway. I already knew from our bus ride that driving on the Amalfi Coast is not for the timid—a certain level of panache is required. The margin for error is phenomenally small, but thank heaven most of the cars are also small—if they weren't, traffic would come to an abrupt halt even more often than it does.

As we swung quickly around a corner I was shocked to see a couple of very fit, professional-looking cyclists riding without helmets. That brought to mind an Italian cyclist who defied Mussolini. I knew of him because of my love of cycling and the book *Road to Valor*. The book's cover shows a helmetless Gino Bartali riding past a cordoned-off row of spectators that included men in uniform—it is a very iconic photograph of pre-World War II Europe. Bartoli was the 1938 winner of the Tour de France. He was also deeply distressed by what was happening to the Jews in Italy. Because of his fame and his daily long-distance training rides, he was able to smuggle forged documents to Jewish families that made it possible for them to escape persecution. He hid the documents inside the tubes of his bicycle and traveled from his hometown of Florence at will—although at considerable risk to his life if his exploits had been discovered. I was extremely surprised that Salvatore had not only heard of him but knew the details of his heroics. Salvatore left no doubt that he was very proud of Gino Bartali.

Italians, I have discovered, are all about service—taking care of the people whose paths cross theirs. Salvatore was doing exactly that for us. He called ahead to let the folks at the Casa Raffaele Conforti know that we were on the way. He told them where he'd drop us off and asked if someone could be there to meet us. I shouldn't have been surprised—it's just what Italians do.

A few moments later we were driving along the beach promenade in Maiori. Suddenly Salvatore made a quick left turn onto a narrow street and pulled to a stop near a crosswalk. We hopped out. I handed Salvatore twenty euros and apologized for making him late. He said, "*No problema*, we are close to being on time. That is all that is required."

"Ah, good. We will see you again," I replied, and with that Salvatore was gone.

We looked around and saw a young woman across the street waving at us. I was relieved. I could see no sign for our B&B. With Lidia leading the way and pulling one of our carry-on bags, the journey to our new home was a piece of cake. We walked across the street and into a passageway only a few feet wide. Of all the directions we could have walked from where Salvatore had dropped us off, that would have been my last choice. It didn't look inviting. It did look ancient though. We walked past walls that had to be at least five hundred years old and maybe a thousand judging by the stonework. She led us down a street that was closed off except to foot traffic, but as quickly as the street had closed down it opened up again and was wide enough for a car. We began walking past shops—a hardware, a bakery, a clothing store. I immediately liked the feel of the street. It was old and lively at the same time, with an element of mystery. Lidia opened a door that gave no indication it led to anything—certainly not a hotel or even a B&B. Faded paint was all I noticed.

I stepped in and saw a dimly lit stairway. Lidia bounded up the steps, the sound of her shoes echoing off the bare walls. I picked up the two suitcases I'd been pulling. Mardi did the same with her carry-on. I didn't bound up the stairs. I wondered, as I got more and more winded climbing them, what I had gotten us into.

I was trying to maintain a pace that would keep me within a few steps of Lidia. I slowed slightly as we approached the second landing, thinking the B&B must be on the first floor, which in Italy is the second floor, but she kept going up. We had at least two more flights to go, and I was already breathing hard. I still had seen nothing to indicate we were in a hotel or even any hint that anyone lived here. I now had no doubt I had made a mistake. This was not looking good. But when we reached the fourth flight of stairs I quit kicking myself. Color invaded our drab world. At the top of the staircase I could see an intricate design etched into the glass of a beautiful wooden door, and above the door an elegant crest rendered on the transom.

Casa Raffaele Conforti, the design proclaimed. The gorgeous finish on the doorway also proclaimed that we were entering another era—a time of regal splendor. Lidia led us through two grand rooms and down a hallway lined with historical photographs and documents. At the end of the hallway we walked through an ancient wooden door and were greeted by light spilling into the room through two huge, mostly glass doors. Lidia handed us a map of Maiori and a huge key befitting our regal surroundings and left us to get settled. We stood in the middle of the room with our mouths hanging open and watched her go. We had not expected such luxury. This undoubtedly had once been a bedroom in a very posh home. I was surprised that the description on the Internet hadn't alerted me to the splendor that awaited us—or maybe I had read no further than the incredibly cheap price.

We plopped down on the bed, tried out the couch, checked out the bathroom, and discovered we had a bidet. We had no doubt we were going to be staying a while, so we put everything away. The room quickly took on a homey atmosphere. It had a rolltop desk to help us get organized, but mostly it

had an ambience of permanence. The incredibly high ceilings didn't hurt that feeling. I swear they reached a height of fourteen feet, which would account for the long staircases we climbed.

Suitcases emptied, we stepped onto our balcony and discovered another world of surprises. We were in heart of the village and just below us was a street filled not with cars, but with people, against a backdrop of a huge, colorful cathedral climbing high above us on the hill—not nearly as magnificent as Amalfi's Saint Andrew, but it appeared to be just as large and was right outside our window. I quickly let go of my fears that I'd made a mistake. Four flights of stairs was a small price to pay for such an elegant room in such a glorious setting.

We had promised ourselves a nap but we were too excited. We wanted to get to know our new town. We grabbed that huge key, dropped it off at the desk, and went exploring. We found a laundry across the street and discovered that the street that we had been looking down on was indeed the town's main promenade. We wandered along it toward the beach and found another promenade, the longest along the Amalfi Coast, we were told, where we saw kids playing soccer and a grandfather roughhousing with his young grandson. We settled down on a concrete bench that was cool and built at the perfect angle for taking a nap.

We enjoyed a picnic of cheese, bread, and crackers, as well as an apple and a pear. Pigeons gathered by our bench to beg. We delighted in trying to fling our leftovers far enough away from the seagulls and dominant pigeons so that the meeker birds could get to the food first. A few moments later a well-dressed man walked up carrying a plastic *supermercato* bag. He stopped at a railing and was immediately surrounded by seagulls—a flock so large that their squawking drowned out the sound of the crashing waves. The gulls knew what was coming. We didn't. The man set down the bag, and pulled out a loaf of bread, and began tearing off chunks to fling into the air. We had great seats for the entertaining display of aerial acrobatics as the gulls swooped in to pluck the bits of bread out of the air.

Comfortably full from our picnic lunch, we looked over the excellent map Lidia had given us, trying to decide what to explore next. But before we reached a decision, the soothing sound of the waves crashing on the beach lulled Mardi into such a deep sleep that she didn't wake up when two teenagers sat down on a nearby bench to eat lunch and be boys.

One threw a wadded-up juice carton at the pigeons. A few minutes later the boys got up to put their trash in a receptacle, all but the juice carton, which was left where it had come to rest among the pigeons. The boys moved to another bench and were replaced by other teenagers eating lunch. In fact, we were soon surrounded by kids eating lunch, and all of them took care of their trash when they had finished eating. But still I found myself hoping the kid who had thrown the carton would come back to pick it up. While I was busy hoping, a pigeon flew over and deposited reconstituted cheese on the screen of my iPhone. On the way to the fountain to clean it off I picked up the crumpled carton—I didn't want to let one kid who had not yet developed civic pride take away from the beauty of the promenade or mar my positive impression of the teenagers we had encountered in Italy.

While Mardi slept, I was able to write a couple of pages of notes about this town I had quickly fallen in love with. When Mardi woke up, we walked along the beach promenade and saw so many families hanging out in the park with their young children that we thought a festival must be taking place, but after chatting with a few folks we realized that what we were seeing was normal for this town. We could have spent several more hours watching the kids play and the waves crash but decided to go back to the B&B to see if the Internet was now working, and check in with our own family.

We were walking arm in arm up Via Corso Reginna, a block from Casa Raffaele Conforti, when a personable young man greeted us and encouraged us to give a pleasant looking place called Le Suite a try, assuring us that the Internet connection was working and fast. We looked at each other, shrugged our shoulders and decided to accept his enthusiastic invitation. Inside we found a very friendly young *barista* named Luigi. He knew very little English and had a hard time comprehending my Italian but had a welcoming smile. We quickly established a bond with him while we were ordering a couple of hot teas and a croissant. We chose a corner table where we could spread our things out and still see the passing parade on Corso Reginna. The music was terrific—a mix of current Italian hits and American classics. The Internet was, as promised, lightning quick. We settled in and began working through correspondence that had been neglected since Malaga.

We were surprised and delighted to discover that everyone who came into the bar greeted us. The sense of camaraderie was overwhelming. We had quickly fallen in love with Amalfi, but now our loyalty was being tested. As Salvatore had said, Maiori was *a sleepy village*. Now that we had experienced a bit of the town we translated what he'd said to mean that Maiori was not a tourist town—at least not at the moment. On the promenade, we'd seen photos of Maiori's beachfront in summer. It was so packed with visitors that I'm not sure one more body could have been squeezed onto the sand. But on this afternoon the only folks we saw were locals. I'm sure everyone we met recognized us as strangers.

The fact that we were strangers didn't keep people from acknowledging us. Earlier in the day I'd been walking along Corso Reginna and stopped midstride to write a note on my phone. Before I had typed three words I heard a man call out to me from the outdoor patio of the very bar where we were now sitting, asking if I needed help. I glanced up at him and shook my head. He looked like a man who could be trusted—so I typed a couple more words to help jog my memory and then walked toward him.

"I thought maybe you were looking for directions," he explained. "We love foreigners. We love taking care of them."

"No, I was just jotting down some notes," I replied.

"That's what we do here. If we see someone in need we help them."

"Thanks for asking. Next time I probably *will* be lost."

He asked where I lived, but I didn't immediately answer. Why hadn't he asked *Where are you staying?* which I wouldn't have answered either, or the more innocuous *Where are you from?* which I would have answered. In the split second it took me to ponder those thoughts he apologized for asking.

I could tell his questions were making Mardi a bit leery, but I was intrigued. His English was good. I suspected he'd spent some time in America. My hunch was correct. As we continued talking he told us that he had lived for two years in New York City. But the stress of living in America had gotten to him and he had returned to Italy. His name was Antonio and he asked if we wanted to join him for a beer, but I declined, sensing that Mardi was uncomfortable. I wanted to hear more of his story, but as Simon had so rightly observed, *A happy wife makes for a happy life,* so I told him we'd drink a beer together another day if fortune smiled on us.

And indeed fortune was smiling on us in ways we had not yet fully comprehended. As we were walking around town we had noticed still shots from some of my favorite Italian movies. While I was catching up on correspondence, Mardi searched Wikipedia and discovered that Roberto Rossellini had shot part of the World War II neorealist film *Paisan* here as well as the 1953 *Viaggio in Italia (Journey to Italy)* with Ingrid Bergman, which I had bought only two weeks before we had begun this trip.

Journey to Italy had intrigued me because it was the story of the renewal of a marriage, and now Mardi and I were in the very town where Rossellini had made this touching film about a redeemed relationship. Ingrid Bergman was, of course, Roberto Rossellini's wife, and I'm sure the story told on film was personal. She certainly gave a performance as Katherine Joyce that made it real to Mardi and me. And now serendipity had brought us to the town where it was filmed while we were on our own journey of a lifetime. It seemed but one more example of the weirdness—the improbability—of the lives we all live and wonder about.

Less than twenty-four hours earlier we had been convinced that Amalfi was the town we'd return to year after year, but now Maiori had captured our hearts—not just because of its connection to one of my favorite filmmakers but because it seemed to be a town perfect for raising kids. Not that we would be raising kids again, but we certainly enjoyed being in a family-friendly town—a fine town to grow old in.

We were thrilled to be sitting in an outdoor cafe absorbing the lifeblood of Maiori. Via Corso Reginna is wide. It's designed for people, not cars. From where we were sitting in Le Suite we felt as if we were in the heart of the village. Each time I glanced up from reading emails, I saw a new gathering of people. I loved watching the conversations. I could make out some of the words, but what most intrigued me were the body and hand motions of folks as they gathered. There was much touching and gesturing, some so dramatic I felt as if I was observing a stage production with the "actors" playing to the folks in the back of the auditorium.

But there were tender moments too—a look, a smile, a pat on the hand in parting. Italians touch. Italians kiss. Italians express themselves. Italians walk away and then remember something else they wanted to say, so the goodbye that was expressed is forgotten and a new conversation begun, with the same fervor that they had originally greeted each other. I could have watched this show for hours—in fact *did* watch it for hours—but when six o'clock rolled around we decided to walk until sundown or maybe even until dark, exploring the town. The sun was a couple of handwidths above the horizon, so we figured we had an hour, or maybe an hour and a half, before that big orange ball would slip below the sea's shimmering surface. Our plan was to absorb the delicate beauty of the town and the friendliness of the people while at the same time checking out the menus, atmosphere, and views of all the restaurants in town.

We began by walking up Via Corso Reginna toward the cathedral that loomed over our balcony. We met Mario before we got there. He saw us strolling up the center of the promenade holding hands. He knew we were new to town. He told us as much and then introduced himself and his wife, who wasn't with him: *Oh, my Maria, she's the best cook in town.* He then handed us a small card and pointed toward his café, which did not have a view of the ocean—did not in fact have a view of much of anything—but the place was full, and from what we could see at first glance, the reason had to be because of the food. It certainly wasn't because of the ambience—at least to a tourist's eye.

We enjoyed our repartee with Mario, partly in tourist English, partly in *italiano*, as we each shared a bit of our lives. Mario wanted us to eat with him at once but as we parted company I committed only to coming to eat with him before we left town.

"But when you leave?" Mario implored.

"*Forse un mese,*" I said and smiled at Mardi.

"But of course. You will come many times to eat the best food in town," Mario called as we walked away.

Mardi pulled me closer and asked, "What did you tell him?"

"I told him perhaps we will stay a month."

"Jim, you know we can't stay that long," Mardi said.

"We have to. Our anniversary is on the fifth, and today is only the seventh," I answered, only half kidding. I was beginning to like this place enough that

I could imagine staying here a full month. We noticed another still shot from *Journey to Italy*. It was taken from the very spot we were standing in the middle of the street, which was now the promenade, and showed all of Corso Reginna filled with revelers—the climactic scene of the Virgin Mary being carried aloft by a sea of people that swept around Alexander (George Sanders) and Katherine's car, forcing them to abandon it. But in the confusion they got separated—and that feeling of loss, of separation, made them feel vulnerable. In that panic, they felt the anguish of not having each other. That realization of their absolute need for each other tore down the silly defenses they had set up. In that moment they finally became honest with each other, admitting their feelings of loss, and just as in our marriage, they let go of their separate selves and saw the miracle of two becoming one.

That is what had happened to Mardi and me some eighteen months earlier, and here we were standing at the very spot where a film telling that same story had been made some sixty-three years ago, when we were but six or seven years old. This was a film we didn't even know about when I made reservations for our cruise to Italy. I'm sure that if I had somehow chosen instead to celebrate Mardi's birthday in Portofino, we would have enjoyed ourselves very much, but the significance of being in the one town in all of Italy where Roberto Rossellini filmed the final scene of his movie about the renewal of a marriage, the very thing we had come to Italy to celebrate, was just a bit over the top on the serendipity scale.

Rossellini figured prominently in the revelations of my first book; in fact, his name is in the book's subtitle. He helped me to understand Italy seven years ago, and now, through his art, I had come to see my own marriage more clearly. What a gift. It was all too much for me to comprehend, too wonderful for me to know. We had gone for a walk to enjoy the sunset and find a good place to eat, and here we were trying to get our minds around the unfathomable complexities of this universe that somehow make the impossible possible.

We did the only thing that you can do in such situations—we hugged each other and continued walking—still shaking our heads over the odds of it all. On the other side of the street we saw a billboard in a small *piazza* noting that a margherita pizza was but five euros—four euros for takeout. We strongly considered the offer, but like Mario's place, Masaniello's had no view of the ocean.

"I bet that at least once within the next month we'll eat one of these five-buck pizzas," I said, winking at Mardi.

"I'll bet we eat one of these pizzas before the weekend is over," Mardi shot back.

I was quite certain she was right. Masaniello's looked very popular—filled with lively music and conversation. But we had a romantic notion that we wanted to be by the ocean on our first night in Maiori, so we turned back toward Lungomare Giovanni Amendola—literally the *long sea*—but linguistically *seafront*. Whether poetry or description, those three Italian words have a beautiful sound—a sound befitting the beauty of the location.

When we reached the main road we still had no destination in mind other than to enjoy the beautiful evening. The sun was still at least a half hour from setting. A policeman was monitoring the crosswalk. When he felt a sufficient number of pedestrians had shown up, he held his hand up and brought the traffic to a halt. I nodded toward him in appreciation and reached for Mardi's hand as we moved across the street *in massa*. With traffic at a standstill, the sound of the ocean replaced the sounds of cars, trucks, buses, and motor scooters. By the time the traffic began moving again we were close enough to the ocean that the sound of waves crashing and gulls crying drowned to insignificance the sound of the traffic.

We walked across the promenade, down the stairs, and all the way to the beach, stopping just short of the wet sand. We were surprised to see, despite the cool temperature and the lateness of the day, one very hardy young man high-stepping out of the surf and onto the beach. We wondered what sort of a person would swim in such cold water at temperatures that were struggling to get into the seventies during the day and at the moment could not be much more than sixty, so we turned east to walk along the water's edge in his direction. By the time we reached him, he was lying on a beach mat totally covered by a large towel. We discovered nothing about him we didn't already know, but we did feel the power of the ocean as the waves crashed around us and the seagulls, despite carrying a heavy load of bread crusts, soared gracefully in the shifting air currents.

To the southwest, a sailboat was silhouetted against the setting sun, which, at that moment, was a flattened ball, sitting perfectly on the edge of the rolling ocean. To the northeast we saw hotels and businesses lining the Amalfi Coast Highway. The contrast was stunning. One the beauty of raw nature, the other beautiful as well, but man's part clearly evident. The beachfront looked surreal against its backdrop of mountains, all of it glowing with the reflected light of the sun. We could see the traffic moving along the road and people walking up and down the promenade, but from our perspective, with our feet almost in the ocean, it was a silent movie—a world somehow separate from ours.

As the sun slipped below the horizon we began retracing our steps. Some of them were still clearly imprinted in the sand, the others had been washed away by the crashing surf. We followed the ever-changing boundary between wet sand and dry, always searching for the consistency that made walking easy. Sunlight was reflecting off low-lying clouds, painting a kaleidoscope of colors. The beach was empty. The swimmer, as well as his beach mat and towel, had disappeared. We were truly alone with all this magnificence.

The perfection of the moment was not lost on us. We recognized how truly blessed we were. Less than two years before, we had been nowhere near the state of joy and contentment with each other and with our marriage that we were at that moment enjoying. The improbability of it all was not lost on us either. As I walked along with my arm around Mardi, the memories of good times and bad times in our almost forty-six years of marriage flooded my mind. Crashing waves have that effect on me. I thought of the times I felt Mardi had treated me with disrespect, and I contrasted them with how I felt now. Five years ago I thought we would never be able to get back to the way we were—back when we were young and in love.

I began counting the years as we walked along. Our first three years were spent mostly in Hawaii. They were good years, but they were, at times, lonely years. We knew we were in love, though, and we have the daily letters we wrote whenever we were separated to prove it. Occasionally I'd been away on assignment to places like Vietnam, Korea, and Alaska, but when I was home we were really together. We did everything as a couple. It was just the two of us.

It was the same for a year and a half after I got out of the army. And then Matthew, our first child, came along when we'd been married just over four years. Looking back, I can now see how we slowly drifted away from each other. At the time the movement was imperceptible, but the demands of child-rearing, making a living, and figuring out priorities took a toll on our togetherness, both literally and figuratively. Now that we are totally together again I can recognize the little ways we lost trust in each other.

"Why were we so stubborn—too stubborn to let go of our hurts and be vulnerable with each other?" Mardi asked. She had obviously been thinking some of the same things I had been thinking.

I stopped walking. Mardi turned to look at me. "Thank you for coming back," I said.

The look on her face told me that she too was feeling grateful for this moment, for this life that we now had together. She too had felt the weight of thinking that our life together might have ended. "Thank *you*, for coming back," she said.

It's ironic that we both attribute our renewed relationship to a change that took place in the other. I can pinpoint the resurrection of our marriage to one exact moment—a discussion in our car while we were in the parking lot of the YMCA where I taught spinning.

Mardi remembers it too, as well as the respect and love she began showing for me. But she attributes the change to her realization that she could trust me, and she attributed that to a change in *my* attitude toward her. That was all it took—for both of us to change our attitudes—to begin treating each other with kindness, as we did when we were kids just getting to know each other. I began putting Mardi's needs first. I began asking questions about her life—what she was like before she met me—and that shocked her. She frequently mentions another special moment—a late afternoon on our lakeside dock, a couple of weeks before the YMCA parking lot discussion, as the time she began to think that her husband truly was interested in her.

That was all it took? I frequently ask Mardi. It's the same point Roberto Rossellini made in *Journey to Italy*. And now Mardi and I were in the very town Rossellini chose as a backdrop to make this subtle yet profound point. Life is absolutely too mysterious to comprehend, but here we were enjoying it almost to the point of giddiness. As we reached the steps leading up to the promenade, we embraced. What we were sharing in the fading light was glorious. When we let go, we looked into one another's eyes and kissed.

"So this is why honeymoons are such a big deal," I said.

"Maybe we should have gotten around to this a little earlier," Mardi said with a smile and a wink.

"I don't think we would have appreciated it as much as we do now."

As we walked up the steps and began hearing less of the sea less and more of the sounds of civilization, I swore I could hear the strains of an Andrea Bocelli song I was very familiar with but couldn't name. As we got closer to the promenade I recognized it—"Somos Novios," which happens to be in Spanish, not Italian—but is to my ear one of the most beautiful romantic songs I've ever heard, especially when sung by Bocelli.

Mardi and I were at that moment living an Andrea Bocelli fantasy of love and romance. And we weren't the only lovers on that promenade. Strolling arm in arm and snuggling on the benches were couples who showed every sign of having enjoyed as much as we did the glorious sunset that had brought us to tears of loving gratitude. Only the silhouettes of the denuded eucalyptus trees made the moment seem less than perfect, but even those severely pruned branches spoke of beauty—like the stark trees of a child artist waiting to be covered with the softening lines of shimmering leaves in the moonlight. We followed the line of trees west, toward Atrani and Amalfi, which we knew were on the other side of a magnificent castle, which because of its height on the cliffs above Porto di Maiori, was still catching the last rays of the setting sun.

We didn't know where we were going, just that we wanted a restaurant befitting the mood we were in. We didn't want to leave the beachfront, even though the last vestiges of color in the sky would be gone by the time we'd made our choice and were seated at a table. The song we should have been hearing at that moment was Dean Martin's "That's Amore," romantic and delightfully fun at the same time—singing of *gay tarantellas, when the moon hits your eye like a big pizza pie, bells will ring ting-a-ling, and you'll sing vita bella, when you walk in a dream but you know you're not dreaming, that's amore.* And that is exactly what Mardi and I were suffering from: a severe case of walking in a dream that makes all of life look beautiful—*vita bella,* as Dean Martin crooned in his 1956 hit.

We looked across the street and saw La Vela, a brightly colored restaurant that matched our mood—it looked festive and featured a nautical theme and name, the sail—blue and white and inviting. It reminded us of the sailboat that had passed in front of the setting sun at exactly the right moment. We stopped to check out the menu and were immediately treated as though we were movie stars. Maybe the three waiters who greeted us and the one who showed us to our table—which had an unobstructed view of the ocean—had sensed the aura of lovers in love.

We ordered a light meal—*prosciutto e funghi pizza, insalata pomodorini,* plus *vino rosso della casa.* What we got was a lot more. The staff started us off with *bruschetta* that was almost as good as the *bruschetta* that Pietro had prepared for me a half dozen years earlier seasoned with the oil from the olives we'd picked on his farm. It might be that my personal connection to that *bruschetta* is why it will always hold a special place in my heart, or maybe it will remain there because Pietro assured me, with the confidence that only an Italian chef can muster—that this would be, without a doubt, the best *bruschetta* I had ever eaten. He wanted to tempt me to remain on his farm picking olives and not go, as I had planned, to work on another farm fifty kilometers down the road.

I did nevertheless go the next day, as I had planned. But to tell the rest of the story I came back after only one day. What I had experienced on his farm—his mother's farm—was something I desperately missed once it was no longer mine to enjoy—his good cooking and the camaraderie with him and his mother. I cannot eat a piece of *bruschetta* without thinking of them. Food in Italy is like that—so many associations, and all of them good. And now we were creating more associations. The warmth we felt from everyone in that restaurant was extraordinary, and it wasn't just because they were bringing us food we didn't order—they were also friendly, courteous, and efficient without being obsequious. We felt that the chef wanted to show off his skills, hoping that we would soon return. We were also treated to a delicious cheese and rice ball as well as orange spritzers to brighten our table. Their generosity led to a rather humorous situation.

Our meal, as is the custom in Italy, turned into a long affair, during which we became quite comfortable with our waiter, Donato, enjoying numerous small moments of fun and gentle joking. We had not planned to eat quite so much or stay so long. But we had enjoyed the *bruschetta*, rice balls, and salad so much that at the two-hour mark we still had food on our plates. We were picking at the pizza. I was sharing with Mardi that in Italy it is considered *brutta figura* to ask to have your food boxed up.

At that moment Donato stopped by. "Box it up?" he asked.

"*Certo,*" I said, feeling somewhat embarrassed that I'd just spent three minutes explaining to Mardi why we didn't want to risk looking like foolish tourists by asking for a doggie bag. As he picked up the serving dish he said, "I don't like to take plates back to kitchen with food on them." Mardi and I smiled at each other.

"*Grazie,*" I said, thinking he was heading to a serving area where he'd box up our pizza and then take the empty plate to the kitchen.

"*Prego*," he said as he deftly put half of what was left on Mardi's plate and half on mine, then turned with a flourish toward the kitchen with the now-empty plate.

Mardi and I looked at each other with stunned embarrassment. We tried to suppress our laughter but didn't succeed. Donato must have said something that sounded like *Box it up*, but I could think of nothing in either English or Italian that had the sound or the cadence of those words. Whatever he'd said, we now had the pizza on *our* plates. We had to get to work. But the work we did was mostly drinking and talking.

Twenty minutes later the pizza was still on our plates. We had been absentmindedly picking at the *prosciutto* and mushrooms while we talked about all the wonderful people we had met since stepping off the boat in Civitavecchia. Donato walked by and saw how little progress we had made.

"You no like the pizza?" he asked.

"*Mi piace la pizza, ma—piano, piano*," I said.

"Yes, yes—*Esattamente*," he said as he backed up, bringing his fingertips together and bowing at the same time—showing the essence of gratitude, even respect, for what I had said—that we wanted to eat our food slowly, enjoying our time with him. That I had expressed the sentiment in Italian while using body language was all the more reason to show his pleasure.

With time, a bit more wine, and a lot of intimate conversation, we slowly ate enough pizza that everyone in the kitchen was able to hold their heads high when Donato walked in with our plates. As an expression of gratitude, Donato returned with a delicious pastry—*una torta dolce*—for Mardi and me to share. As with everything else we had been served, it was *delizioso*, and I let Donato know how much we appreciated everything. He had made sure that we enjoyed our food as well as the time we'd spent in his restaurant, under his care.

When our bill came, it listed only three items—the three we had ordered. Everything else had been *è offerto dalla casa*—on the house. Even though a cover charge, *un prezzo del coperto*, was included, I felt that Donato and all the waitstaff, as well as the chef, had gone to exceptional lengths to make us feel welcomed and cared for, so I added a generous tip.

We left La Vela feeling *pieno sazio*, as I told Donato. I hoped it meant something like *fully satisfied*—in terms of both food and experience. We had eaten far more than we expected, but we had also enjoyed ourselves far more than we expected, and we had entered the restaurant with high expectations. That's the thing about eating in Italy—it always puts your dreams to shame.

We crossed back over the Amalfi Coast Highway to walk along the beachfront promenade to let the beauty of our situation sink in and walk in the glow of the moon, which had just appeared over the mountaintops to the southeast. As we walked, the silhouettes of the recently trimmed eucalyptus trees cast strange stick-like shadows on the perfectly placed stones lining our path. The promenade that night was a lovers' lane of couples walking arm in arm and cuddling along the railings. Our love for Maiori was growing with each new experience, and it felt good to share the promenade with other like-minded people.

We found an empty bench and sat down to cuddle and watch lovers and joggers, as well as folks out walking their dogs. We felt an incredible sense of belonging—totally disproportionate to the amount of time we'd spent in Maiori. But then I thought back to my reaction to the first time I saw Mardi across that crowded room. I was certain I was crazy about that girl without having spoken one word to her—just the way she moved and looked around the room with a level of energy that spoke of a person in love with life made me fall for her to an extent totally unjustified if you're of a sensible mind. But some things can't be defended with logic or science. Allowance for mystery needs to be made. The same was proving true of Maiori. The place just felt right. It was a town I could fall in love with—in fact, *had* fallen in love with.

We should have been tired, or at least a little sleepy, but we didn't want to let go of the day. We began walking toward the castle we could see on a point at the east end of the bay. Maiori, we realized, has castles on promontories at both ends of the bay—the ancient one we were walking toward, and the more modern one that had looked so beautiful reflecting the light of the setting sun.

"I think it's the improbability of seeing castles and homes built on such inaccessible and inhospitable walls of rock that makes me feel we are in a world where dreams come true," I said.

The mention of castles brought to mind a Mercer Mayer story about a princess that I read to our kids and was now reading to our grandkids, and that made me feel a little guilty. I'm aware of the adage that we're supposed to bloom where we're planted, but lately I've been thinking that I sure would like to do some flowering in Italy. Seven years before, when I'd spent that marvelous two months picking grapes and olives in Tuscany, I'd told myself that I wanted to take a bit of the Tuscan lifestyle back to my farm in western Wisconsin. But I no longer have that farm. I'm in a different season of life. We had kids in college back then; now we don't. We've married off all our children. We no longer own a home. I love the sense of freedom that gives me, and I think Mardi feels it too.

I don't think her sense of freedom makes her want to move to Italy. Mine doesn't either. But it extends far enough that I could see heading to Italy a couple of times a year and staying as long as our tourist visas allow. Not having a home and a mortgage back in the States makes such a thought almost plausible—at least that's what I was dropping hints about as we walked in the moonlight, trying to convince not only Mardi but myself as well.

When we got to the east end of the promenade we turned around and headed back toward the Casa Raffaele Conforti, but still I didn't want to let go of the evening.

"Let's stop off at Le Suite," I suggested. "I love that place. It felt like we were in Cheers." That thought reminded me that the sale of my farm had not been as painful as I'd thought it would be. Even though I loved that land, I was beginning to realize that I love community as well. I grew up in a small town where everybody knew your name, and I could see living in such a place again—not necessarily as small as my hometown, but in a neighborhood where everyone knows your name—and that's not going to happen in the suburbs. It's only going to happen in a community where people walk to and from their work and their shopping and their recreation. In other words, a place like Maiori.

"Okay, but only one drink," Mardi said.

"I'm going to ask Luigi to choose it for me."

"What if he isn't there?"

"*Ma,*" I said jutting my chin out and opening my palms in the best imitation I could muster of an Italian using his whole body to communicate. I think I was successful. I could tell she had understood that I'd said the American equivalent of *We'll cross that bridge when we come to it.* But Luigi *was* there, and he greeted us as though we'd been friends for a very long time.

"Good evening, my friends. Tea for two?" he asked and smiled.

"No, not tonight," I said and then switched to Italian and tried to ask him to prepare a drink that he would recommend, that would remind us of Maiori. But the word *recommend* in Italian is *raccomandare*—and there was something about the way I was saying the word that was not registering. I switched back to English, but that didn't get us anywhere either. I was just about to give up, worried that I was taking too much of his time, when he reached for his phone and asked me to type in what I was asking.

I typed in *recommend.* The app translated it and he said, "Me? You want me?" And then he switched to Italian, *Vuoi che mi consiglia?*

"*Si,*" I said. Realizing that he had not used the word I was trying so hard to say, but had used a synonym I had forgotten about—*consigliare.* Such moments make me wonder if I'll ever have a command of Italian, but we had worked through it thanks to the smartphone world we now live in.

"*E per voi?* And for you," he said to Mardi, showing off his English and helping us with our Italian at the same time.

"I will try what you make for him first," Mardi said.

Luigi didn't quite understand what she had said, so I gave a very loose interpretation using Italian words I felt I had command of.

"*Lei aspetterà*," I said and just in case my tense was off I added the root word, "*Aspetta*," which has the disadvantage of sounding more like a command—*Wait*—but such a lack in manners, when you are learning a language, is easily forgiven, and Luigi set about cheerfully preparing a drink for me while Mardi and I headed to our favorite table in the corner, which was waiting patiently for us like Norm's spot at the end of the bar in *Cheers*.

Quite a few people were gathered both inside and out on the sidewalk. American jazz was playing. As we moved to our table we were greeted by the people who had not yet said hello when we first walked in. Some spoke, others just tipped their heads slightly in acknowledgment of our presence. The feeling was good—similar to the reception we had received earlier in the afternoon when we'd spent almost two hours catching up on our emails.

We sat by the window, which because of the pleasant evening temperature was open. Three men were sitting outside, leaning against the building, passing time and watching the world go by. Two were smoking, and even though it bothered me a little I hoped Luigi would not close the window—I liked the feeling of being near to what was going on. A father and his son were kicking a soccer ball on the far side of the street. Three women, who had stopped to talk to two other women as we walked into the bar, were still chatting. A girl about seven years old was riding her bicycle back and forth on our side of the street. Suddenly she stopped right in front of the three men and began talking to them as though it were a conversation that had been going on forever. This struck me as odd. The men appeared to be in their fifties and sixties, and the tone of the conversation was comfortable familiarity, almost to the point of teasing. The girl, whose voice was resonant and self-assured, seemed to be very much enjoying talking to the men. And then, just like that, she was off, heading up the street again. But this time she crossed over to the other side and parked her bike in front of a shop.

That's when I recalled that I'd seen her earlier in the day playing catch with her father in front of that same shop. That took me back to my childhood, back when I had waited uptown with my dad on nights when his farm equipment store was open. I too rode my bike up and down the street. I too stopped and talked with men as old or older than my father. Those were the days when there was contact between generations—when young people knew old people they weren't related to.

The street where Mardi and I were sitting was that girl's home, and she must know the people who hang out here, just as I knew the butcher, the banker, the grocer, and everyone who sat on the liars' bench in front of the grocery store in our town. Everyone knew I was Ernie Shaw's boy—and if something bad were to happen to me, my dad would hear about it. I was safe riding up and down the main street of Hayes Center just as this girl was safe riding up and down the main street of Maiori, and she was even safe stopping to talk to men drinking at a bar. Easygoing banter among the generations in this town was no problem. I loved that.

I turned and saw Luigi setting my drink on the table. "*Amaro del capo*," he said. "I hope you like it." He had also given us *una torta dolce* for our sweet tooth. He'd probably noticed how many bags of sugar we had added to our tea earlier in the day.

"I'm sure I will," I said.

"*Salute*," he said as he returned to the bar.

I tasted the drink. It was a liqueur, and I liked it. We took advantage of our smartphones and looked it up. We had said we wanted something to remind us of Maiori. We were informed that *Amaro del Capo is a Calabrian herb-based liqueur that has been developed over four generations of the Caffo family.* Calabria, I explained to Mardi, is the toe of Italy—a place I hoped someday to visit, but it was not likely that it would be on this journey.

We turned our attention back to the street and saw that the little girl had abandoned her bike and was now trying to get her small dog to chase a plastic bottle, but the dog wasn't interested. Another little girl, five or six years old, came running up to join the fun, but she tripped and skinned her knee. This was typical small town life that I'd grown up with but was not used to seeing anymore. In America you usually don't see young children outside of their homes—they're inside playing or watching something electronic. I'm sure Italian kids do that too, but if Maiori is typical, it certainly seemed to be happening a bit less than in America. The playground that afternoon had been awash in kids, perhaps as many as one hundred if you counted the whole of the promenade. And now we were still seeing kids outside even though it was getting close to bedtime or maybe even past except for the kids of shopkeepers. It was also getting close to bedtime for Mardi and me. We told Luigi that we had definitely enjoyed the drink but were eager to get to bed. That caused his eyebrows to rise up and a knowing smile to cross his face. Luigi was onto us. We left him a moderate tip—we didn't want to set an expectation that we couldn't keep up.

"*Ciao*, my friends," he said.

"*Ciao. Domani—Ci vediamo domani,*" I said.

"Tomorrow? You come tomorrow?" Luigi asked.

"*Si,*" I said.

"I will be here." And with that farewell I felt that a pattern had been set for our days in Maiori.

A half hour later I sensed another pattern developing. I was certain I could easily get used to preparing for bed to the accompaniment of what I had begun calling the bells of Saint Mary—the Cathedral of Santa Maria a Mare—that stood majestically outside of our almost-as-majestic bedroom doors. I walked out onto our balcony at the sound of one high and ten low pealings and took a photo of the church shining in the moonlight. I stayed there for a long time—the bells rang two more times at fifteen minute intervals while I absorbed the beauty of the night. The last time I'd experienced such mind-blowing beauty was when we lived for a season surrounded by white-capped fourteen-thousand-foot peaks in the abandoned mining town of Ashcroft, Colorado, the Rocky Mountains in all their glorious essence just beyond our bedroom windows.

The magnificence of that memory reminded me that mountains reach for the heavens and so do cathedrals. Both create in me the desire to humbly pause to give thanks for the beauty of this world and this life. Mardi joined me just as the bells began the count to eleven. We kissed—a kiss we didn't let go of until the bells quit ringing.

CHAPTER EIGHT

Maiori ~ Friday April 8 ~ 67 & Partly Cloudy

A Day in the Country

*A mind that is stretched by a new experience
can never go back to its old dimensions.*
OLIVER WENDELL HOLMES

■

Life without love is like a tree without blossoms or fruit.
KAHLIL GIBRAN

I didn't immediately know where I was as I made the uncertain transition from dreams to consciousness. In the dim light I could see that the ceiling was far above me. As my mind searched for an explanation to make sense of such expansiveness, the feeling I'd had yesterday when I first walked into this room swept over me and I was suddenly ushered into the world where Mardi and I were living in luxury in Italy.

I knew that close to me, most likely only a slight roll of my body away, I would encounter the warmth of Mardi. I tucked my chin into the gentle curve of the back of her neck and held her. After a few seconds she softly asked, "What time is it?"

"I have no idea. I only know I love you," I whispered into her ear.

She purred, and with a slight shift of her hips encouraged me to move closer.

"I thought I was in love with you in America...and on the *Oosterdam*...and in Amalfi, but that was only a foreshadowing of the love I'm feeling for you now."

She was not yet awake. She was floating in that fuzzy world where it is easier to fall back to sleep than it is to wake up.

"Mmmmmm…" she purred again, shifting her body to face me.…

In between the time Mardi had asked *What time is it?* and when the bells of Santa Maria a Mare began ringing, we made sweet, gentle love, but at the sound of the bells we broke out laughing. They were the first pealings we had heard all night, and their heavenly sound made it seem like God had answered Mardi's question.

We had fallen asleep in each other's arms thinking the bells would fall silent once they'd rung out the eleventh hour so that the townspeople could sleep. But now that we were awake, we knew of course that they'd been ringing all night—we just hadn't heard them. We laughed at ourselves as we counted out the high rings and the low. I held her closer to let her know how much I loved her for this journey we were taking together—as well as the journey we had been taking for so many years.

We were enjoying our laugh so much that one of us missed the switch from the high-pitched to the low-pitched bell. We couldn't agree on whether it was three forty-five or four thirty. We were certain, though, that it was too early to start the day and that neither of us was going to look at a phone or open a computer to find out for sure.

As I was falling back to sleep, bits and pieces of my dreams came to me, giving me a deep sense of gratitude, as though the Holy Spirit were filling my mind with thoughts that made me realize what a fortunate man I was—memories of our incredible dinner at La Vela—and our love for each other that keeps growing. I also began thinking that we may have found our home in Italy—at forty-four euros a night we might be able to spend a lot of days in Maiori.

Questions flooded my mind. *Do we travel by train to other parts of Italy, or do we stay here and find a cheap car rental to drive to Eboli, Aliano, and other towns? And do we stay in Maiori or move back to Amalfi on Sunday?* I fell asleep with all these things on my mind. I don't think Mardi had nearly as much on her's. She fell quickly back to sleep—long before five soft bells sounded.

A few hours later I awakened again, still feeling like the most fortunate man in the world. The sun was now lighting our room, our floor-to-ceiling window coverings were fluttering in the breeze. The sounds of the town slowly waking up resounded in the *piazza* below. The bells began ringing again, but this time they didn't stop at seven or eight or nine—they kept ringing as though they too were celebrating the incredible love that Mardi and I were feeling for each other. And they kept pealing. We eventually decided that though the timing and the sentiments expressed were perfect these bells had nothing to do with us—they were the IT'S TIME TO GET UP bells of Maiori. We began laughing again. This town was feeling more like our home with every unexpected peal of Saint Maria's bells.

My phone, too, began ringing. It was a text from Roger informing me that he'd had a heart attack on Easter Sunday, his cancer was spreading, and he was resuming treatments on Monday. He also mentioned that I shouldn't be alarmed—that he was feeling "quite well."

I doubted that very much. He had added that because he didn't want us to come home early. I'm sure that's also why he'd waited so long to inform me of his heart attack. If he had sent a text Easter morning telling me he was in the hospital, we would have gotten off the boat at Civitavecchia and headed straight for Leonardo da Vinci airport to fly home. But now the worst of it had passed and he could tell me to stay where I was. That's the kind of friend he is.

I made no attempt to get out of bed. Roger's news had stunned me. Finally the bells fell silent. I lay there thinking back over my life with Roger while Mardi went to check out the breakfast. I was still in bed reminiscing about all the places we'd traveled together—Greece, Machu Picchu, Alaska, England, New Zealand, even my hometown of Hayes Center—when the bells began ringing again. The last of eight bells rang as Mardi came into the room with a glass of orange juice and the information that a nice young man was waiting for us at the breakfast bar.

"He wants to know how we want our eggs prepared—I told him we'd like omelettes. Bring your camera—you're going to want a picture of all this food." She returned to the breakfast room. I got up, pulled on my jogging pants and jacket, grabbed my phone, and headed down the hall to join her.

"*Buongiorno,*" I said to the smiling young man standing near the breakfast buffet. He was wearing black slacks, black shoes, a black sweater, and heavy-framed black glasses.

"Good morning," he said. "*Cappuccino?*"

"Yes please," I said and then added, " *Due, per favore.*"

"*Certo.*"

"*Mi chiamo James.*"

"My name is Maximiliano," he responded with a shy smile. He emphasized the second and fourth syllables, making it one of the most poetic and musical names I'd ever heard.

"Oh, what a beautiful name." I was familiar with Maximilian Schell, the actor, but this was Maximiliano, and I had trouble getting my tongue around all the syllables. I'd had the same problem seven years earlier when I first heard the word *Montepulciano*, the name of a town famous for its grapes and wine, not far from the first farm I worked on in Tuscany. It was a word I loved hearing—his name rhymed with Montepulciano and had that same beautiful cadence.

"*Scrivi Maximiliano, per favore?*" I asked, but he didn't understand my pronunciation—I had to ask Mardi for a pen and paper before he understood that I was asking him to write his name. I wanted the spelling to help me nail down the beautiful cadence and the rhythmic way Maximiliano said his name.

He wrote it down and handed me the paper proudly. I pronounced it, but each time he would say his name again, letting me know that I did not yet have it. I felt like continuing to say it wrong just so I could keep hearing him say his name, but eventually I did manage to say it right, with the proper emphasis on the second and fourth syllables, emphasizing *eee* and *lee*—letting my tongue roll with the sounds.

"Maximiliano, this pretty young lady's name is Mardi," I said turning to her.

"Mar-ta?" he asked.

"Or Martha. That's her real name."

He had as much trouble pronouncing Mardi's name as I did pronouncing his, but he had no trouble with my name.

"James," he said with a deep resonance. "Bond, James Bond," he repeated with a long and drawn out OH sound.

He walked out of the room to get our *cappuccinos* repeating *Bond, James Bond,* and I turned to the breakfast laid out before us and kept repeating *MAX EE MEE LEE ON OH.*

I was certain we were the only folks staying in the B&B, but Maximiliano had put out a spread capable of feeding two dozen people. I didn't understand it, but I wasn't complaining—croissants, tomatoes, *prosciutto*, cheeses galore, pastries, orange juice, eggs, yogurts, apples, bananas, oranges—there was no end to the feast.

"This is crazy," I said as I took several photographs, trying to find an angle that did justice to the variety and composition of all the food. As I took the last photo, Maximiliano appeared with our *cappuccinos.*

"Ah, beautiful," I said and then complimented him on the food and the layout. He was surprised by my gratitude. I had no idea how long he had been working as a host, but he certainly was not jaded. He was enthusiastic, and slightly naive, or maybe he was just very new to his job. He was obviously enjoying pleasing us.

"Can I give you a hug?" I asked. He was taken aback but he let me put an arm around his shoulder. I wasn't sure what he said in response, but I think it was *I am here to serve.*

The bells rang out—two high and eight low. Time is measured so beautifully in Maiori. I was certain I would never tire of hearing those bells.

While Maximiliano was in the kitchen preparing our omelettes, Lidia appeared at the door of the dining room and asked, "Is he doing okay?" which confirmed my assessment that he was new at this game. But we couldn't have been more delighted with Maximiliano. He was perfect, and we assured her that he was doing a great job of taking care of us. Maiori, Maximiliano, and the Casa Raffaele Conforti—everything was coming together to make us feel as if we were living a dream.

"Is everything okay?" Maximiliano asked as he returned with fried eggs. We were expecting omelettes, but we didn't miss a beat responding that everything looked *perfetto.*

Maximiliano smiled, walked toward the serving table, and rearranged the juice pitchers.

"You like it here?" Mardi asked me, knowing full well what my answer would be.

"No, no, not at all," I joked.

Maximiliano returned to our table and filled our water glasses. It was obvious he loved his job.

"Is it okay if we take our time?" I asked.

He smiled again, and I realized that he probably knew very little English and didn't understand what I'd asked. I also noticed that he and Mardi were dressed similarly—both in black with only a touch of white showing at the collar. They didn't look exactly like priests, but pretty close to it. I asked them to stand beside each other so I could take a picture. Maximiliano beamed with appreciation.

"*Domani lavoro?*" I asked and realized as the words were leaving my mouth that I should have reversed the order, and said *lavori* instead of *lavoro.* That would have changed my question from *Tomorrow work?* to the much more linguistically sophisticated *Are you working tomorrow?*

The endings of Italian words can make an amazing difference in their meanings. But Maximiliano understood what I was asking.

"*Si, domani,*" Maximiliano said using words, hands, and body language to assure us that he would be here tomorrow to take care of us.

"Oh, this is good," I said after tasting my *cappuccino.* "*Mi piace.*"

"Maximiliano, *mi piace* is 'I like it,' but how you say in *italiano*, 'I love it?' I asked. "Is it *Io amore esso?*"

Maximiliano jutted out his chin, raised his eyebrows, and laughed. "Maybe better to say, *Lo adoro.*"

He was enjoying sharing his language with us. He pronounced the words slowly and distinctly—always with a smile.

The bells began ringing again. "Seven, eight, nine...it's nine o'clock," I said.

"*Nove in punto,*" Maximiliano said as he picked up our empty plates, leaving the many that still had food on them, and headed for the kitchen. *In punto* I was not familiar with, but *nove* is nine, so I was certain he was just repeating the time, which must have reminded him that he had other work to do.

"Mardi, I love this," I said using my best Italian hand gestures to help her understand that I was referring to the whole of the experience—to Maximiliano, to this gorgeously grand home in which we were now living, and this wondrous town we had found because we were willing to gamble on a ridiculously low price for a B&B on the Amalfi Coast.

"Can I give you another piece of *prosciutto?*" Mardi asked and then added, "*Io pieno,*" using a word that Maximiliano had helped us pronounce correctly, so that it wouldn't sound like the word *piano*. Mardi was not telling me she was slow, but rather that she was full—stuffed to the max by Maximiliano.

I too was getting full, but I was not in a hurry. I had my eye on a beautiful piece of pie Maximiliano had set out a few minutes earlier, so when he returned and asked *Cappuccinos?*

I said again, "*Due, grazie.*"

"*Prego,*" he said as he turned quickly to head back to the kitchen to get us another round.

We had already been enjoying breakfast for over an hour and had the bells to prove it, but I was not yet ready to let go of this experience. While we waited for our *cappuccinos* I walked around the room looking at memorabilia. This had been an aristocrat's home from the nineteenth century, and I loved looking at the family photographs—the stiff clothing and arrested smiles and gestures of the early days of photography. The ceiling frescoes were worthy of a museum exhibit—chubby cherubs dancing on the clouds of heaven. If only the room had had a harp instead of a second piano, Mardi could have provided the music to go with the setting. She played a harp in high school, and for years I have carried the dream of someday having a bank account and a room large enough to house a harp. But for now the life we were living that morning was about as close to perfection as I could imagine. The harp would have to wait.

Maximiliano returned with the *cappuccinos*. Mardi and I continued contemplating our good fortune. I had dreamt big when I imagined our journey of a lifetime, but I didn't get anywhere near where we were that morning. It seemed that almost every day I'd comment, *This can't get any better,* but each day topped the one before it. What could be next, I wondered.

"A bit of pragmatism," Mardi answered. "We need to pick up our laundry."

That brought me back to earth, but only partway. We said goodbye to Maximiliano and headed across the street to continue our luxurious life—picking up laundry that someone else had slaved over. I could definitely get used to this, and I was certain Mardi could too. In three weeks, the closest she'd come to preparing a meal was opening a yogurt container and slicing some cheese and apples. This without a doubt was what living the good life was all about—and to be able to do it with someone you loved was out-of-this-world blessed.

"*Ecco qua,*" the laundress said as she handed me our shirts and pants on hangers and pointed to our bag of folded laundry. She told me what we owed, but she said it so fast I wasn't certain how much money to give her, so I handed her a credit card.

"We do cash," she said. Trying to pay with a credit card signified I wasn't local, so she'd switched to English. Instead of showing my ignorance by asking her to repeat the amount, I handed her a twenty, hoping that would cover it. It didn't.

"*Un euro si prega,*" she said.

I was glad she'd switched back to Italian.

Mardi handed her a one euro coin.

"*Aperto domani?*" I asked.

She told me she was, but that led to some confusion regarding the hours on Saturday. And that led to her asking where we were from. And that led to her telling us that her son lives in the states, *il Stati Uniti*. Normally I would have asked where he lived in America, but the shop was quite small and four other customers had come in since we began our bilingual transaction. She knew hardly any English and I was having trouble understanding her Italian—so in the interest of efficiency and the goodwill of those waiting in line, it seemed best to just smile and say, "*Torneremo domani,* we'll be back tomorrow." But even that I got wrong. In Italian the construction is, *Tomorrow, we'll be back.*

Lidia was not at her desk, nor was she in the breakfast room, which was now spotlessly clean, as though the breakfast we'd just eaten had been only in our dreams. We seemed to be alone in our new home. I called it home, for

I was quite certain I had found my Italian hideaway. I asked Mardi whether she preferred to stay here or return to Amalfi at the end of the week.

"I think we should stay here. We can take a bus to Amalfi. It's a lot cheaper here."

Mardi's pragmatism gave the nod to Maiori, and that was good enough for me. She didn't have to be as crazy for the town as I was in order for us to have a good time, even a great time.

"Then I should find Lidia to tell her we're staying longer?" I asked, hoping she'd agree.

"Let's wait. Let's see how things go today."

I couldn't argue, but I also couldn't imagine what would happen that would make us change our minds about Maiori. At the end of the hall I opened the door, heard the welcoming creak of ancient hinges, and stepped into our huge room. I loved seeing those white billowing curtains, knowing that just beyond those tall windows our balcony beckoned, where we could sit every day and look out over the heart of the town. Life in Italy, much more than in America, is lived on the streets, and I loved the sense of being in the middle of it all. I felt a bit like a voyeur, but I was looking forward to getting to know the habits of the people of Maiori from our little perch on the world. And if I could do a little reading and writing each morning while sitting on our balcony so much the better.

Mardi reminded me that not everything was perfect here at Casa Raffaele Conforti. If it were, she would have let me hang out on the balcony indulging my voyeuristic tendencies as long as I wanted. But, as Lidia had informed us when we'd checked in, the B&B's Internet was not working—and it still wasn't working. That less-than-perfect situation had, happily, led us to Le Suite the day before. Life is funny that way.

We stopped by the fruit and vegetable shop on our block-and-a-half walk to Le Suite and found just about everything except what we were looking for. Vegetables in Italy are as beautiful as any in the world. They are without a doubt the best tasting. Mardi thinks there may be no cure for what I've got. She's convinced that I'm hopelessly in love with everything Italian—so much so that it has impaired my judgment. I tried to convince her that my childhood spent eating vegetables and fruit grown by my mom and dad created in me the capability to discern the superior quality of Italian fruit and vegetables. I'm not sure I was successful.

"*Hai ravanelli?*" I asked the shopkeeper.

She didn't immediately respond, so I said, "*Avete* radishes?" I'm never sure of my pronunciation of the various words for *have* or even which word I should use in a given situation, but that phrase worked. Whether it was the way I pronounced *hai* or *ravanelli* I will never know, but she jumped up, disappeared into a back room, and quickly reappeared with a small bunch of radishes.

"*È questo che vuoi?*" she asked.

"*Si,* yes, that's what we want," I said, then added, "How you say radishes in *italiano?*"

"*Ravanelli,*" she said, but of course she rolled her *r* and put emphasis on the third syllable that I had not, and made the word much more beautiful than I probably ever will. But I tried again, and she rewarded me with a *Bravo*.

Italians love it when you roll your *r's*, even if you badly mangle them. I handed her a one euro coin and got change in return and a nice smile as well.

"*Vieni di nuovo.*"

"We will," I said. "*Certamente.*"

As we walked out of the shop Mardi asked, "What did she say?"

"She told us to come new."

"What?"

"It's the Italian equivalent of *Come again.*"

"Oh, I like that," she said. "I'm going to take these back and put them in the refrigerator. Our table is empty—why don't you grab it."

I looked toward Le Suite. The outdoor chairs were well occupied. A bunch of local men were comfortably situated and looked as if they'd been there for quite some time. But our corner table, on the other side of the wall from where the men were sitting, was empty. I nodded to the men and said *Buongiorno* as I walked into the bar. A trio of *Buongiornos* greeted me back, each said with a slightly different cadence and emphasis. *Buongiorno* is the universal morning greeting, but each man gave it his own unique, and to my ear, musical interpretation.

Luigi was behind the bar. He smiled when he saw me.

"We are back."

"Ah, good, my friend," he said, and I was certain he meant it.

"*Americano?*"

"*Si.*"

I was surprised he asked. We had spoken at length the day before and I'd assumed he knew from my accent that I was from the United States. But the obvious difference to me between an American and a British accent must not be as clear to an Italian's ear. Luigi was probably having the same difficulty I have differentiating between a Kiwi and an Aussie accent.

"Where you from?" Luigi asked.

He had never heard of Wisconsin, so I asked him if had heard of Chicago. That helped him place us. I told him we were *nord di* Chicago, *vicino al* Canada.

"*Freddo?*" he asked

"*Certo,* it's cold. Hockey is big in Wisconsin." I knew from the day before that he spoke some English, but maybe I was assuming too much, because he didn't seem to understand me.

"*Parli inglese?*"

At that Luigi stuck out his hand toward me, and shook it.

"A little?" I asked.

He shrugged and said, "Maybe a leettle."

"Do you speak French?"

"Me? No?" he said and laughed.

"*Parli italiano?*"

"*Italiano?*" He gave me a big smile and said, "*Si!*"

The look in his eyes told me we were going to have a good time in this bar.

"*Aqua caldo due, per favore.*"

"*Per il té?*" he asked.

"*Si,* we have our own bags," and then realized I should try to say it in Italian, but I couldn't think of the word for tea bags, so I said, "*Solamente aqua caldo.*"

"Only hot water?" Luigi asked.

"*Bravo,*" I said.

Luigi smiled again and turned to his *espresso* machine.

Our corner table was still available, so I laid claim to it by setting up my computer. I turned back toward the bar to grab our cups, but Luigi said, "You sit. I bring."

I sat down with a strong feeling of already being part of the town. The learning of Italian and the teaching of English in this bar were going to be two sides of the same coin. I pulled out my Italian-English dictionary and discovered that in Italian the word for tea bag is *bustina di té*. I didn't have to wait long to impress Mardi with my newfound knowledge.

"*Hai bustine di tè nella vostra borsa?*" I asked her. She probably understood at most three words in the sentence, but often that's all that's required. If you can decipher just a few words of Italian in any sentence you have a good chance of understanding it. I'm sure she heard the word *tè,* and even though it's pronounced *tay* in Italian she knew I was asking if she had tea bags in her purse.

As promised, Luigi delivered our hot water. Not as promised was a selection of sweets delivered by a young woman who introduced herself as Jessica. "*E alcune torte dolci per voi,"* which she translated for us into English with one of the most delightful accents I'd ever heard, *"And some sweet cakes for you."*

"Grazie," I said.

"Prego," Luigi said as he moved on to the table of a pretty young woman who had just come into the bar. Jessica stayed and talked. She was friendly, energetic, and very interested in polishing her considerable language skills. I sensed immediately the beginning of a beautiful friendship—her curiosity and delightful personality captured both Mardi and me. As she excused herself to wait on others, I found myself imagining that a few years had passed and we were still enjoying our routine of stopping in each morning for tea and sweets with Luigi and Jessica. In my dream, I was polishing the final drafts of another book, and each day after I'd written for five or six hours, Mardi would meet me here so that we could catch up on each other's day and practice our Italian.

"I could see living here," I said to Mardi.

"I thought that's what I was seeing in your eyes," she said. "You looked like you'd floated off somewhere."

"Yeah. I was imagining that we did this every day. We both had bikes. And after I finished writing for the day I went for a long bike ride."

"Sounds a lot like your life back home."

"You're right. The only difference is that I'm learning Italian here. And instead of drinking tea at home we're going out."

"You could do that in Wisconsin," Mardi said, ever the pragmatist.

"Getting in the car and driving five miles through the suburbs to Panera is not quite the same as walking out your door and in less than two minutes sitting down in your favorite chair in your favorite bar where Luigi knows exactly what you want—and at home you need a clock to know what time it is," I added.

"Okay. The part about the clock did it. I'm convinced."

I knew she was kidding, but I hoped a seed had been planted that someday might take root. As if God were helping me sell her on the idea, the bells of Santa Maria began ringing again. I counted them out, as I did every time I heard them—what a reassuring ritual it had become—three high...and eight, nine, ten, but thankfully no eleventh bell. I was certain that if Simon and Luciana didn't show up at Le Suite we'd be able to find them along the promenade somewhere. Meanwhile I had a good hour to continue jotting down my impressions of Maiori.

After a half hour of pleasant writing, of feeling the pace of the town quicken, I noticed a young man of thirty or so, impeccably dressed, pull up and park his bicycle. His technique was eye-catching, even elegant, and so was the bike—the color was striking—a subtle shade of sand I'd describe as ripe wheat. He didn't park it in a bike rack or drop down a kickstand; he slowly pedaled to a stop along the promenade, placed the inside pedal atop the curb, stepped off the bike, and walked into the shop next door where we had bought our radishes. I looked back at his bike, wondering what was keeping it standing.

I looked closer. It was a direct-drive single-speed—the pedal and the two wheels formed a tripod. The pedal could not move unless the wheels were turning, so the bike stood like a faithful steed waiting for its master to return. I loved that the rider had not had to perform the inelegant task of tying his mount up with a lock and chain. I'm sure everyone in town knew who belonged to that elegant piece of sculpture, and anyone attempting to ride away with that bike would not have been able to get far.

"Mardi, I want to rent a bike like that and ride around Maiori. Isn't it beautiful? That's just how I'd park it, too."

"I don't think I have any hope of getting you out of here."

"What do you mean?"

"I think you're ready to die here," she went on. "You're drooling over an Italian bike, in an Italian town, in an Italian *espresso* bar. You've got your computer, you've got a pitcher of Earl Grey tea, and you've got a window seat with a promenade view."

"It *is* pretty good isn't it?"

I was feeling perfectly situated as we waited for our friends. The morning sun was lighting up the street, people were gathering on the benches along Corso Reginna, the sounds of *Buongiornos* and *Ciaos* were resounding off the buildings. We felt like regulars at Le Suite. We had already claimed our territory. The Internet was fast, the service great, the music the kind I could write to. The conversations were not distracting—more like beautiful music to channel my creativity.

"People are so slender here," Mardi said. "Maybe they walk more. The food is so rich I don't see how they stay so thin."

"It's the wine that goes with every meal," I said, only half joking.

"Look at that girl over there—she's really cute."

I was glad to oblige. Normally she gets jealous if she thinks I've noticed a woman who's good looking and within fifty years of my age. I thanked Mardi for pointing her out. The young woman was indeed good looking. We had a great window on the world.

"Jim, I don't see many tourists. You know what? I don't see ANY tourists."

She was probably right. That morning we were probably the only people out and about who had not been out and about on that street just about every day of their lives. The three men seated next to us had been involved in a nonstop conversation since we'd arrived. I loved the feeling of being next to them, even though I'd understood very little of what they'd said. It takes tremendous concentration for me to follow Italians talking at Italian speed, but still I like to try.

"I love it," Mardi said followed a few seconds later by a contented *Mmmm* that lets me know she's appreciating something. I followed her gaze—she was watching a young girl curl up on a bench by her mother—they were positioning themselves to catch the warmth of the early morning sun. We were looking at everything with fresh eyes.

"You see that man over there? He was in the bar last night," she said.

"Yeah, I noticed him. We made eye contact when he walked in. He gave me a silent *Buongiorno* and dipped his head slightly. I gave him a Hayes Center nod—just like I saw my dad do whenever he saw someone he knew but not well enough to go up and greet them."

At that moment a Vespa flashed by. The girl riding it was holding her billowing dress with her knees, a short scarf fluttering like a flag from her slender neck. She looked fresh and vibrant, like a young Audrey Hepburn holding onto Gregory Peck as they circled the Colosseum in *Roman Holiday*. But this girl was riding solo. She wasn't sightseeing either. She knew exactly where she was going, her scooter's little engine playing a slightly discordant high note.

"Mardi, I love this. Even horn honks and scooter engines sound good echoing back and forth between the buildings—I could start every day right here."

"I now know it's hopeless—back home you go crazy if you have to listen to a weed whacker or lawn mower for thirty seconds."

"*Touché.*"

I realized that these sounds weren't bothering me because I was associating them with people living a good life. I could hear the mechanical sounds, but I could also hear the sound of kids playing soccer and jumping rope. The sounds blended together to make beautiful music that resurrected pleasant memories of my childhood. I grew up knowing everybody in town—all the shopkeepers and the people from twenty or thirty miles around who came to shop and play cards and catch up on their neighbors' lives. This was before television had come to our small, isolated town on the high plains. Maiori was feeling just like my pre-1955 hometown.

"I think we've found our place, Mardi."

She smiled with the same expression she'd used for our oldest son when he was five and said he was going to become a fighter pilot—a gentle *It's Great to Have a Dream* smile. The amazing thing is that our oldest son *did* become a fighter pilot—and a darned good one.

"I'm going to quit wearing shorts," I said.

"Why?" she asked, wondering what had prompted that thought.

"Look at that," I said, pointing out two couples walking up the street. We had finally seen some tourists—way too much skin was showing. I turned away, looking for something kinder to my eyes. They landed on a group of five men chatting in the center of the street—three seated and two standing like bookends. "The guy on the right sure is good looking."

Mardi quickly agreed. "I suppose now it's my turn to point out another good-looking woman to you."

"Yeah, if you want."

"What did Cathy look like?" she asked.

"Besides beautiful?"

"Yeah."

"She had dark hair, almond eyes, flawless olive skin, and she was thin and tall."

"Okay, that's enough. I get the idea."

"I suppose a bit like Audrey Hepburn, but very Italian looking—southern Italian, I'm beginning to realize," I said.

Cathy was the only Italian girl I knew when I was a kid. Her brother, Rossy, was a good friend. Cathy and my cousin, who were a few years older, taught me to kiss. I had a huge crush on Cathy for years. Every once in awhile Mardi asks me if this or that girl looks like Cathy. She has a few jealous bones in her body, as my mother was fond of saying. I suppose my mother would also add that I had a little something to do with Mardi's jealous bones.

My thoughts returned to Maiori. I was beginning to realize that fast Internet service is the key to living my dream. As long as I could stay in touch with my readers and promote my books we could live anywhere in Italy. Sitting in this sidewalk café, I realized that I'd been carrying this dream since high school, when I'd read Hemingway's autobiographical story *A Moveable Feast.* I vividly recalled fantasizing about living the literary life—hanging out in sidewalk cafés, playing chess, journaling notes, and talking with friends, just as the men next to us were doing. This was exactly what I imagined I'd have done if I'd lived in Paris as Hemingway did or in Rome as I dreamed of doing. I now had that one special spot in that one special café where I felt I belonged.

Maybe that's why I'd fallen so quickly, so deeply in love with Maiori. I'd been imagining this place my whole life.

"Jim, look." Mardi was directing me with her eyes to look at an older man struggling along Corso Reginna with two large plastic bags most likely filled with groceries. "Do you think it would be okay to go help him?" she asked. "It reminds me of walking home from Sendik's with thirty pounds of meat, milk, and apples. My arms were killing me."

I got up from the table, trying to decide what to say to the man—I didn't want to offend him. He appeared to be about my age, but was a bit frail.

"They're too heavy for him," Mardi said as if she knew I was having second thoughts about the appropriateness of a foreigner stepping in when the man was surrounded by younger Italian men who could help him.

At the very moment I decided to risk offending him, I noticed a thirtysomething man walking briskly toward him. I was closer than the younger man was, so I slowed my step to see if he was indeed coming to help. The young man held out his hands in that universal expression of *Let me help you.* So little was said between the two men that I guessed the younger man was a bit late getting to the *alimentari* and the old man had taken off on his own. If so, that would explain why no one else offered to help—everyone knew that help was on its way. Only the recently arrived foreigner did not yet know the patterns of the day.

"Oh, that's nice," Mardi said when I got back to our table. "Did you see the way they looked at each other?"

"Yeah, and did you notice how little was said between them? It was as though they were expecting each other."

"No, I didn't think about that. I just loved how they looked at each other."

Mardi and I would have been content to stay right where we were the rest of the morning but on this day we were directing our pinball's flight.

"I don't think Simon and Luciana are coming here. We'd better go find them," I said as I started packing up my computer and journal.

Mardi glanced at her watch and quickly began gathering her things too.

"*Arrivederci,* Luigi," I said. I looked for Jessica but didn't see her.

"*Alla prossima,*" Luigi responded.

I had not heard the expression before, but I was sure that it must be the equivalent of *Until the next time.*

"*Domani,*" I said.

"*Sì.* See you tomorrow," Luigi said.

And with that simple exchange a momentous morning came to an end for me. So little and yet so much, but if you've been waiting a lifetime for such a morning, you take note of it.

"I think the money was well spent," I said as we walked past the boxes of vegetables and fruit lining the street. "He only charged us two euros."

"Didn't he charge us for the sweets?"

"I don't really know. Maybe he didn't charge anything for the hot water," I said and then added, "Mardi, this is just marvelous."

We left our cozy nook and began walking around town looking for our friends in all the cafés. We found them sipping *cappuccinos* on Via Capone, the name of the street that the Amalfi Coast Highway follows along the beach through town. "It's nice to see you again," I said before they had noticed us.

"Oh, hi. How you finding Maiori?" Simon asked.

"We love it," I said. "Not many tourists here."

"It does seem pretty laid-back," Luciana said.

We shared with them our impressions of Maiori. They had been here before, but they hadn't been as impressed as we were. When they'd visited, the place was crowded, a festival was going on complete with marching bands, and they'd felt a bit overwhelmed by all the bustle. As we talked we walked to the tobacco shop where we'd been told we could buy bus tickets. But the shop had none, so we walked back to the magazine store across the street from Le Suite where we had been assured that we would find tickets.

"*Scusi, biglietti? Tramonti, per favore, quattro biglietti,*" I said. "Four tickets, up back *ritorno,*" I added just in case he understood English better than I pronounced Italian.

He handed me four tickets that I was certain wouldn't get us as far as Tramonti.

I searched my mind for the words to ask him why the tickets were so cheap. All I could come up with was *"Perché economico?"*

"Amalfi vicino," he said.

"But we want to go to Tramonti, to the mountains."

Apparently I'd mispronounced Tramonti. I had said *tra-MAWN-tee*. What I should have said, I realized, after hearing him say it was, *tra-MOAN-tee*. The syllables and cadence were the same as if I had said *Amalfi*, so Amalfi is what he heard. I also think he was used to tourists asking for tickets to Amalfi—not so used to them asking for tickets to places not even mentioned in the guidebooks.

In any case, he didn't have tickets for getting beyond the local zone, so he directed us to another shop, a bit more out of the way, where we found the tickets we were looking for. I'm not sure why the system is such that the ticket-sellers don't have adequate inventory, but this experience convinced me to buy eight tickets and stash the extras in my billfold.

Since we had plenty of time, I suggested that we walk past Le Suite on the way to the bus stop. As if on cue, as I was telling Simon and Luciana how friendly Maiori was, Luigi appeared and greeted us warmly. He seemed to be walking to the restaurant on the other side of the street. I asked him about it.

"Is owned by same family," Luigi said.

"Ah, now I understand why I saw you come and go many times last night."

"*Si*, we help," he said.

"Luigi, these are our friends from England, Simon and Luciana."

"*Piacere*," he said. "Pleased to meet you." And then he turned to me as he continued across the street. "Will we see you tonight?"

"*Certo, Luigi, certo*. Will you save our table?"

Luigi smiled and turned to indicate with his hands and body, *Who knows what will happen tonight?*

But his demeanor and smile told me that we would definitely be welcome.

"So you like it here?" Simon asked, knowing the answer.

Of course I told him that we did. But I would have said the same thing about Salvatore's in Amalfi, and had he had a room for us we would not have been unhappy at all. But would we have found a bar that felt so much like Cheers, where everybody already knew our name?

As we continued to the bus stop we told Simon and Luciana about our meal at *La Vela*—about the food they kept serving us that we hadn't ordered. And we of course told them about Maximiliano and his many *cappuccinos* and his *egg-za*. We already had lots of stories to share, and we'd been living separate lives for only a little over twenty-four hours.

"Do we need to be on the other side of the street to catch the bus?" Mardi asked.

It was a good question. We were alone on the beachfront side of the street, but on the city side of the highway we saw several folks waiting at the *Fermata* sign.

We walked across the street. I chose an older woman reading a newspaper to bother.

"*Parli inglese?*"

"*No*," she said.

"*L'autobus e Tramonti*," I said being sure to emphasize the long *o* on Tramonti and saying *Lout ta boose*, not *Low ta bus*. I had discovered that Maximiliano had no idea what I was talking about when I made that slight mispronunciation of the Italian word for bus.

"*Si, Tramonti, qui.*" she said without so much as a slight pause to decipher what I'd said.

"*Grazie,*" I said, tipping my head to emphasize my appreciation. I was thrilled she had understood me.

"*Prego,*" she replied.

I love the word *prego* and the many ways Italians say it and use it. It's used in many situations. It can mean *You are welcome* or *Please* or *After you* or *Not at all* or *Don't mention it* or *Please come in* or *Pleased to be of service.* Shopkeepers use it when they see you lingering at their door looking at something. A host at a restaurant will say *Prego* as he pulls out a chair for you. It's a universal word like *Ciao* that conveys a meaning that depends on the situation and the body language that accompanies it.

After that simple, precise, and very quick exchange we put aside our fear that we were waiting at the wrong bus stop on the wrong side of the street. Moments later the bus arrived.

"This is exciting," Luciana said as we settled into our seats.

"Did you miss us last night?" I asked.

"Luckily we had Josef," Luciana said reminding me of the fun we had had at Salvatore's—two Americans, a Brit, a Brazilian, and a German getting together to celebrate a birthday hosted by an Italian.

"I'm still upset about those dried beans," I said, remembering the one negative aspect about the night—the fresh beans I thought I was getting that weren't.

"Stodgy, they were?" Simon asked using a word an American would never think to use, and a sentence construction that caught my ear as well.

I laughed. Simon had a way of surprising me with his line of thinking, and that reminded me of Salvatore's surprise. I wanted to tell them what a good thing Salvatore had done for us.

"Not only did he drop us off near the hotel, he called ahead and had someone waiting to lead us to our room," I said.

Simon and Luciana told us that Salvatore and Manual had gotten into an argument. I told them I thought that was just the way Italians were, full of passion and emotion with a large measure of desire to serve and please. That led to stories of Antonio, the man who told us Italians love to help foreigners, and the breakfast Maximiliano set out for us, as well as further details of the previous night's three-hour meal at La Vela.

"I'm beginning to wonder whether they thought we were critics writing a review of their restaurant. Remember, Mardi, I took a photo of the bottle of wine they brought us," I said.

I wasn't sure why I had brought it up. I didn't really believe they thought we were critics. They had poured the wine we ordered, the cheapest on the menu, as though it was the most expensive wine ever purchased in their restaurant—and that was before I'd taken the first of many photos. Maybe I was feeling that I was being a little too over the top again in my praise of all things Italian and wanted to temper it with a bit of snarkiness.

We were enjoying our bus ride in the country but soon realized we didn't know where to get off. We had thought Tramonti was a town, but were beginning to realize it designated an area. While we were trying to decide whether to get off, the bus slowed and then stopped—in the middle of a river of sheep that flowed around the bus like a boulder parting the waters of a fast-flowing mountain stream. Toward the back of the flow was a big white Maremma and a shepherd encouraging the stragglers to keep moving.

We were definitely in farm country. Even though we had not yet seen any cows, the sight of the sheep was enough to convince us that we'd ridden far enough to get some meat with our meal. We were certain the restaurant that Manuel had recommended must be nearby.

"That was very rustic, wasn't it?" Simon said as we stepped off the bus at the next bus stop. We were near a little shop at the intersection of three roads. Simon took the lead.

"May I help you?" the young man behind the counter asked as we approached.

"We're looking for the Osteria Reale."

"It's the other side of town. For dinner or lunch. They close at three o'clock."

"We'd like to join them for lunch," Luciana said.

"If you wait thirty minutes, I can drive you."

Here was the love of foreigners shining through again. We needed only to wait until his replacement showed up and he'd give us a ride. All of us were cheered by his kindness to strangers, but it occurred to me that he might be able to serve us in another way that would not require him to allow two Americans, a Brazilian, and a Brit to overwhelm what was most likely a small car as well as his schedule, so I asked if there was a restaurant or an *agriturismo* within walking distance.

"*Si*—yes. One thousand meters, follow this road for ten minutes." He pointed toward where we had come from—where the bus driver had let us off. "It is a farm. You will see signs." He pointed again, this time to a pole with a dozen or so signs climbing up it. "Il Raduno is very, very good."

"*Ah, va bene. Mi chiamo James.*"

I wanted to be able to tell the folks at Il Raduno the name of the young man who had sent us their way.

"I am Marco. It is in Capitignano, you will find a bus stop in front of Il Raduno."

Good fortune was smiling on us again. We began walking up the mountain in the direction Marco had pointed. It was easy to imagine that we might encounter another flock of sheep as we walked. The air was brisk, the sounds of people working on the distant mountains could be clearly heard in the thin air, even the sound of our shoes sliding across the grains of gravel on the road seemed heightened.

"That is beautiful, James," said Luciana as I stopped to take a photo of the rugged peaks, using a picturesque grapevine winding around a trellis as foreground.

A few hundred yards down the road we passed the Capitignano sign, and a bit beyond we found a colorful ceramic sign with the name "Il Raduno." If I had not previously biked around Tuscany looking for *agriturismo* after *agriturismo*, I might have thought the beautiful house along the road was Il Raduno, but I looked around and saw a more rustic collection of buildings high above us. Roosters were crowing and birds were singing—everything felt right. We had to lean into the hill to walk up it. I was confident that somewhere up this steep road we would find Il Raduno. Unlike the first *agriturismo* I journeyed to a half dozen years before, this one left no doubt which door I was to enter. However, it was locked.

On the climb we'd passed by a couple of men sitting in a truck warming up its engine, so I walked back and asked the driver, *"Parli inglese?"*

I got in return a fluttering hand held out the window, just like Luigi had offered when I asked him the same question.

"We were hoping to eat lunch—*pranzo per quattro?*" I asked.

"Sì, quattro, for four? *Un momento,"* he said as he reached for his cell phone.

Some very quickly spoken *italiano* flowed into that phone, only about half of it I understood. But I could tell things were looking good. He put down his phone and said, *"Un momento,"* and with gestures and an emphatically uttered, *"Aspettare lì,"* we understood that we were to wait by the locked door. He backed the truck down the path a short way, turned it around, and proceeded carefully down the very steep hill we had just walked up.

A moment later the lock clicked, the door opened, and a woman appeared.

"Allo, would you be able to serve four for lunch?" I asked. *"Mi chiamo* James. Marco recommended you."

"Ah Marco *a negozio.* Yes. Where would you like to eat?"

While we were looking at each other she said, "Maybe rain. Inside?"

We were so thrilled that she was accommodating us we took her recommendation immediately, even though the deck looked very inviting. We chose a table by the window with a view of the mountains that was almost as good as the view from the deck. While we were deciding who got to look at which mountains, Brigida brought menus. We were stunned by the selections— and the prices.

"You can get a mixed grill for ten euros," Simon said. "Four different meats."

"I like the sound of that," Mardi said.

We liked the sound of everything. It took us a long time to order. Brigida was patient with us as we tried to make sure we didn't duplicate our selections. When we had made our choices, we were left with great anticipation and Il Raduno's *vino di casa* to toast each other.

"To good friends," I said.

"And good holidays," Simon said.

"And good marriages," Luciana said.

"And good meat," Mardi said.

"Cheers," we all said.

"This is cool," Luciana said as she looked around at the tastefully decorated room.

"I can't believe she opened the restaurant just for us," Mardi said.

"I think this has worked out quite well," Simon said as Brigida served the *bruschetta*.

He was referring to the fact that we had not made it to the restaurant we were aiming at but had ended up at Il Raduno. The game was definitely coming to us—in the form of wild boar—*il cinghiale* was on the menu. We were all intrigued.

The conversation flowed on pace with the house wine. We were enjoying a delightful time getting to know one another even better. We talked about games we enjoyed playing, movies we liked, even the way to pronounce my last name. I tend to get lazy and say *shah*, like the Shah of Iran. Simon pronounced my name correctly to rhyme with *saw*, emphasizing the vowel sound by opening his mouth and dropping his jaw the way a proper Englishman like Robert Shaw would pronounce his name.

"I liked him best in *Jaws*," Simon said.

"He was in *The Sting* too, wasn't he?" I asked and the conversation veered off in the direction of other English actors and their roles in our favorite movies. We were enjoying a very Italian lunch at Brigida's pace. She brought more food for us as it was ready from the kitchen—neither rushing nor apologizing. We felt very much as if she had invited us into her home and was thoroughly committed to giving us the best of Italian hospitality—and food.

"It would be nice to live here," Simon said, obviously feeling very comfortable in this rural setting. The contrast with the Amalfi Coast was stunning. Even though it was less than a half hour away by car, farming dominated the landscape in the valley.

"Are you enjoying this?" I asked.

"I'm loving it," Simon said.

"More food coming," Mardi noted.

"Don't you love it how Italians bring out a little bit at a time?" I asked.

I don't think Italian kitchens have warming lights—when the food is ready, it is served. When the mixed meats, the *carne mista*, were put on the table, we were amazed by the generous portions. We were even more pleasantly surprised when we sampled the selections—the lamb was especially tasty. The wild boar was, as I remembered it from my first visit to Italy, very flavorful. We were running out of superlatives to express our admiration for the meal. The salad was off-the-charts delicious. We studied it, trying to figure out what set it apart and were left attributing the delicious flavor to freshness—or maybe there's something in the soil in this valley. In any case, Brigida's salad became the benchmark by which I now judge all salads.

"I'm in heaven," I said.

"*Grazie mille,*" Simon said.

"*Prego,*" I said even though I had no idea why he was thanking me. He and Luciana had invited us to head into the mountains to get meat. Maybe he was thanking me for our pinball approach to travel—for asking for Marco's recommendation—rather than waiting for him to drive us to the restaurant Manuel had recommended. The hike to Il Raduno had turned out quite nice as well. Walking along that road, we were treated to the full effect of being in the country. We saw people working in the fields, tractors passing us on the road. We heard the sound of chainsaws echoing off the hills and roosters crowing. We felt the crispness of the air of a high mountain valley and the fragrant smell of freshly-turned earth. Walking allowed us to make a slow transition to a different lifestyle.

Great food served at a slow pace promotes conversation, a chance to really share your lives. Luciana surprised us, as we returned to the story of her courtship with Simon, by telling us she was considered the black sheep of her family. She said she was headstrong and her parents sent her away to boarding school.

"I broke my mom's heart in so many ways. Ways that I didn't understand then, but I do now."

We were enjoying the kind of conversation that seems so common in Italy. We had time for more than a CliffsNotes version of the story of how a girl from Brazil and a boy from England got together. Their story had elements of our story as well. They had noticed each other across a crowded room.

"This guy turned my world upside down. You see a face you just want to keep seeing," Luciana said looking at Simon with deep affection.

I glanced at Simon. He was looking at Luciana with the same loving regard.

"He is my treasure. I feel really bad when people say marriage is a life sentence," Luciana added.

"We are grateful for each other," Simon said.

"We're looking to you guys for inspiration," Luciana added.

They were inspiring us as well. It had been obvious from the first time we met them that they appreciated each other.

Brigida appeared and offered us sweets and coffee.

We had been sharing everything else, so we shared dessert too—a *tiramisu,* which was especially tasty. We didn't share coffees. We each got a *cappuccino.* We continued talking and tasting. It was a meal that you want never to end, but you know that it must.

"Wasn't that a lovely meal?" I said.

"We eat like that all the time," Luciana dead-panned.

"We don't," Mardi said and mentioned our fondness for soups, for one-course meals.

"I want a photo of you two," Luciana said impulsively.

I'd been taking photos of everything—the food, the menu, the rustic decor, the view. The photo I wish I'd taken would have included Brigida with the four of us.

"I want to come and work on this farm," I said to Mardi, but I wasn't really sure I meant it. I'd wanted to volunteer to work on farms so that we'd be involved with the Italian people, but I was feeling that our adventure so far was affording us plenty of opportunities. Even though we were doing touristy things, we still seemed to be getting to know a lot of Italian people.

Brigida overheard us and brought us a brochure for the farm. I quickly realized I didn't want to work on this farm—I wanted to *honeymoon* on this farm, especially if we could eat like this every day. We made no promises to Brigida, but I sure was hoping our pinball would get flung back to Il Raduno. I think Simon was thinking the same thing. He talked of using this farm as a base camp for treks into the mountains.

"Maybe there is a time we could come up here and stay," Mardi said. She was looking out at the sheep grazing on the hillsides and probably thinking that this would be a marvelous view to wake up to each morning.

Luciana was feeling the pull of the food and the mountains as well. "You guys are so lucky. You don't have any arrangements. You don't have a ticket back. You don't know where you are going."

"If we'd been on a tight schedule or even *any* schedule, we wouldn't have been able to come up here with you guys," I said, feeling very thankful that I had not followed my first inclination, which was to avoid a bus ride. We had just enjoyed one of my favorite meals ever—not only was it fabulously tasty, it was so unexpected, and the conversation we had shared had been deep and meaningful. We'd shared our lives and our thoughts about marriage and relationships, and we did it in a setting that seemed to have only us in mind. We were certainly the only folks Brigida was serving. Our angels were taking very good care of us.

We all in our own way said a very grateful goodbye to Brigida. She knew what we knew—that the four of us had enjoyed a once-in-a-lifetime dining experience. Her meal represented for me the very best of Italy—the beauty of the countryside, the hospitality of Italians, and of course their insistence on eating the best food possible—and doing it at a pace that celebrates with gratitude the life we have been given.

When you think about it, such hospitality shouldn't be such a surprise, but it is, and that is why I think Italy is in a class by itself. And if it is not, I hope that in my remaining time on this earth I will be given the opportunity to spend time in those countries where, like Italy, hospitality is the national pastime.

I asked Simon to pose for a photograph with Luciana on one side and Mardi on the other. I knew I'd never forget this meal, but I wanted to capture their happiness. As we began walking down the hill, we noted that even the birds seemed to be singing their praise of our meal. We were all undoubtedly a little heavier, but we were walking down the steep hill with very light steps. Great meals are capable of turning the ordinary into the extraordinary.

Our good feelings must have been infectious. A family working in a vineyard greeted us with a chorus of musical *Buonaseras*. The scene was old world. I asked if I might take a photo. The grandmother, who was quite good looking, struck a fetching pose, very excited that her photograph would be going back to Wisconsin with us. I told her that we had just enjoyed a great meal at Il Raduno. She agreed that their meals were *delizioso*. It made me feel even better about our experience to know that Brigida's reputation was solid among her neighbors.

Marco had told us we could catch the bus at Il Raduno but we wanted to stop by to thank him or to ask whoever was on duty to pass on our gratitude. It also seemed right that we should end the meal the way it began—with a walk down a country lane absorbing the smells, sounds, and sights of the very productive valley that had produced our meal. The Slow Food movement, which touts the consumption of local food, was founded in Italy in 1986 by Carlo Petrini, and we had just enjoyed the fruits of what he had set out to preserve.

When we got to the shop we were thrilled to discover that Marco would be back at five o'clock, five minutes before our bus was scheduled to depart for Maiori. We had a little over a half hour to wait, so we felt comfortable walking fifteen minutes down a road that looked like it led toward a church and some shops. But mostly we saw more farms—more evidence that small farms are still producing food in Italy. At the fifteen-minute mark near a butcher shop where we turned around, Simon made a new friend. He and a dog became *simpatico*. The pup provided us company for much of our walk back to the little store by the bus stop.

"Marco, we love you. That meal was *fantastico*," I said.

"Did you try the cheesecake?" Marco asked.

"No, we missed that. We'll have to go back," I said and meant it. It had been a meal unlike any other I had ever eaten—a serendipitous joy-filled experience to treasure for a lifetime.

"There's a blue bus coming down the mountain," Mardi said.

"I bet that's our bus," I responded.

Marco confirmed my bet and off we scurried to the bus stop.

We weren't exactly silent on the bus ride down the mountain, but we weren't nearly as talkative as we had been on the ride up or during the meal. I think we may all have been, in our own way, reliving the meal and the experiences of the day. What we had enjoyed was extraordinary. It takes a while to process such goodness. Mardi noticed.

"Too bad you're not enjoying yourself," she joked, bringing me out of my reverie.

"I sure liked that wine we had for lunch," I said. My description of it would be earthy, flavorful, and robust. I especially liked that we had probably walked past the very vines that had produced that wine. While talking about the meal, I became aware that the bus was beeping as we approached each hairpin turn and the tight spots near buildings. I suppose it might be possible to someday become so nonchalant about driving these roads that you'd need a warning to pay attention, but I couldn't imagine it. It's amazing that these buses can maneuver up and down these tortuously crooked little roads, but every day they do—and apparently without incident—unless you count coming to a sometimes rather abrupt stop. But this time we were delivered to the streets of Maiori without stopping once—not even for a herd of sheep.

Immediately upon stepping off the bus we were greeted with the sounds of children playing. As we made our way to Casa Raffaele Conforti, we showed our friends places we had come to know, like our laundry. When we reached the B&B and showed off our room, they were as shocked as we had been by the grandeur of the place. As we stepped onto the balcony to show them our view of the street life of Maiori the church bells began chiming. The photo I took of them out there will always be a treasure. The playful way they held each other and smiled into the camera will forever remind me of the truly remarkable day we had shared.

"You have found a lovely spot," Simon said.

"This *is* lovely," Luciana said. "Thanks for showing us."

"And now we must introduce you to the rest of our friends at Le Suite," I said.

Before we reached the bar we were greeted by Mario. He of course told Simon and Luciana that Maria was the best cook in all of Maiori. I promised again that I would come and find out if she truly was the best cook in all of Maiori. As if to confirm my claim that Maiori was a very friendly town, several people greeted us during the very short walk to Le Suite. I of course pointed out the shop where we'd found radishes. When I turned from saying hello to the shopkeeper, I saw Jessica standing in the street in front of Le Suite, watching us walk toward her. She was still wearing this morning's playful smile, but now she was also wearing something that made *me* smile—Converse shoes, just like the ones I wore when I played basketball in high school—but on her they looked great.

If Simon and Luciana had been wondering why we felt so comfortable in Maiori, Jessica removed all doubt. Her greeting was filled with warmth and familiarity. We introduced our friends and told her we'd be back after a short walk down to the beach. I didn't ask her to save our table, but I suspected it might be available when we returned.

"Nice to be among the locals just going about their day," Luciana said as we crossed the Amalfi Coast Highway along with several families on the way to the park. A couple of soccer games were in progress. One in particular caught our eye—a mom was playing goalie. Simon and Luciana seemed to be enjoying the family aspect of Maiori as much as Mardi and I had the first time we spent time in the park. The four of us stayed on the promenade much longer than I had expected.

"I think you just missed your bus," I said.

"I guess we will have to sleep on your couch," Simon retorted.

"I don't know why we couldn't live here six months a year," I said as we began walking back toward Le Suite past all the families still enjoying the park. As I had hoped and maybe even expected, our table in the corner near the street was available. Jessica was at our table before we had sat down. The music was by Al Jarreau, the earthy sexiness by Jessica.

"What you want?" she asked in her delightful accent.

"Would you choose for me?" I asked.

"*Amaro del capo*," she suggested and smiled.

"Ah yes, that is wonderful," I said.

Simon and Luciana ordered double *espressos*. Mardi, fearing that she'd be up all night, ordered decaf.

"This is really nice—not very touristy at all," Luciana said.

"The café life," I said.

An hour passed quickly as we talked about what seems to be a very common dream—the desire to return to Italy year after year. I could easily imagine that we would see Simon and Luciana again—if not in Maiori or Amalfi—then next year in Sicily or the Italian Alps.

"We've got to go now, but would you come visit us in Amalfi?" Luciana asked.

"We will," I said.

And with that our marvelous day with Simon and Luciana ended. Mardi and I stayed at Le Suite, letting the day linger—the feelings of rightness washing over us. We loved watching Luigi and Jessica as they moved among their guests, interacting with them. It was a dance I didn't think we'd ever tire of watching. The place was small enough that you could easily remain aware of the comings and goings of all the patrons. A curious voyeur on a good night could imagine many stories. We had our own stories to think about, though. The marvelous day we'd just enjoyed with new friends turned our thoughts to old friends.

"What if we find out Roger isn't doing well?" Mardi asked.

"Then we will have to go back," I said.

For many reasons I didn't want to have to face that decision. Roger obviously didn't want us making that decision either. He'd suffered a heart attack but didn't tell us about it until he felt well enough to reassure us that he was doing fine. Roger had waited too long to begin his journey of a lifetime—he wanted nothing to do with interrupting ours.

"Do you want to go?" I asked.

"But we're having such a great time," Mardi said.

I should have told her that my thoughts were still with Roger, who was missing out on what we were enjoying, but I wanted her thoughts to return to what had been one of the most enjoyable days of our life, so I told a little lie and said I was tired. Everything about the evening had been perfect. I could tell by the way she lingered as she said goodbye that Jessica had been hoping we'd stay longer to share more Italian/English lessons and stories of each other's lives. The music too had perfectly matched our mood. The evening was relatively young. I wasn't sleepy—it was just that all of a sudden I had begun greatly missing Roger and Bev—maybe I was feeling guilty for enjoying life so much.

"Each day has its own flavor," I said.

"Thanks to you," Mardi said. I didn't know exactly what she meant, but I didn't want to go into it. I wanted to stay with the thoughts of my friend, so I smiled and pulled her close as we walked arm in arm to our new home. Mardi grew silent too. Maybe Roger was on her mind as well.

CHAPTER NINE

Maiori ~ Saturday April 9 ~ 60 & Sunny

Are We There Yet?

All journeys have secret destinations of which the traveler is unaware.
MARTIN BUBER

.

*There is no more lovely, friendly, and charming relationship,
communion or company than a good marriage.*
MARTIN LUTHER

$\mathcal{A}$s seven soft pealings of the bells of Santa Maria brought me out of a gentle dream, I slowly realized why I feel so at home in Maiori: I once lived vicariously in the Sicilian town of Adano through the pages of a book written by John Hersey. So compelling was *A Bell for Adano* that I have been subconsciously carrying the dream of one day living in a village where the ringing of a bell draws the people of the town together. I am convinced that Maiori, and Amalfi as well, would suffer, as Adano suffered from the loss of the bell that measured its day in such a civilized and comforting way.

If you've had the pleasure of reading Hersey's heartwarming story or seeing the 1945 film, you may recall that Major Joppolo recognized that Adano was not the same after the Nazis melted down the town's bell to make rifle barrels. As the Allied commander in charge of the region, he set himself the goal of restoring the community by finding a way to get a bell, a bell with a beautiful, clear, pleasing tone, back in the town's bell tower. Almost everyone thought it was a fool's mission. The book was a gentle reminder of the power of shared experiences: *This bell was the center of the town. All life revolved around it. The farmers in the country were wakened by it, the drivers of the carts knew when to start by it, the bakers baked by it...*

Even though we had spent much of the previous day high above Maiori in the mountains of Tramonti, which I was delighted to discover means *sunsets*, that wonderful day was made better because we knew we'd be coming home to Maiori and the bells that make me feel as if I could live in this town for much of the rest of my life. That's the way it is when you've found a place you love. You venture out with confidence knowing you have security awaiting you when you return. I'm convinced that we've found in Maiori a home base to which we'll return to recharge our batteries after each adventure.

"Mardi, I think I've figured out why I feel so at home here," I said as I joined her in the dining room, eager to share my philosophical musings. She was eager to share more immediate and tangible concerns. Maximiliano had already brought her a *cappuccino*.

She smiled and said, "You have to try one of these croissants. The taste is out of this world."

She offered me a bite. It was incredible. How something as simple as a croissant could be made to taste so delicious seemed incomprehensible.

As I was filling my plate with my own croissants, *marmellata,* and fresh strawberries and deciding what other delights to try, Maximiliano came into the room.

"*Buongiorno, James,*" he said.

"*Buongiorno, Maximiliano.*"

"*Bravo,*" Maximiliano said. He was congratulating me on the pronunciation of his name, which I had emphasized.

"*Cappuccino?*" he asked.

I could foresee such a routine beginning my days for the rest of our time in Italy—at least until something better came along, although at the moment I couldn't imagine what that could be. We were sitting in a grand dining room with the morning sun streaming in, with a delicious breakfast awaiting us the moment we woke up and the pleasant demeanor of Maximiliano getting our day off to a good start. What could be better than a perfectly brewed *cappuccino* and a moist, sweet croissant?

"*Mi piace,*" I said to Maximiliano, indicating with an Italian gesture that I was referring to everything, but most especially the croissants.

"But I am not the chef," he protested earnestly.

"You are wonderful, Maximiliano," I said, overcome by his forthright delivery, his willingness to be completely open to us.

My words embarrassed him, but he smiled and asked if I wanted juice. As he poured me a glass of orange juice, he uttered a deep and resonant *Bond, James, Bond.* Then he gave me an even bigger smile.

"*Bravissimo, Maximiliano,*" I said in appreciation of his excellent Sean Connery impersonation.

"Thank you," he said as he headed to the kitchen to get my *cappuccino.*

Mardi and I had in front of us a day with no plans other than to get to know Maiori better—to see if we'd been hasty in declaring our love so indiscriminately. Was it really possible to fall in love so quickly? Or maybe the more important question: Is it dangerous to be so easily manipulated by emotions that one can fall in love and declare that love at the drop of a hat (to use another rather strange idiom)?

As I've mentioned before, this was not the first time I'd been overwhelmed by my emotions. I was crazy about Mardi the instant I set eyes on her in the student union that August morning in 1969, and I'd been totally enamored when I walked through the gates of old Amalfi and suddenly found myself in what must be the most beautiful *piazza* in all of Italy—the essence of the perfect gathering place.

But now I'd fallen in love with the family life being lived in Maiori—the interconnectedness of the townspeople—and the part that architecture played in creating this very liveable town. I'd fallen so hard for Maiori that I was envisioning living here. I don't know whether Mardi was just humoring my enthusiasm or whether she too had been smitten, but she threw no cold water on my passions.

Nor did Maximiliano. I took delight in everything I saw him do. The way he smiled when he brought my *cappuccino,* his interest in making sure we had everything we wanted, and his patience teaching us *italiano.*

"Will we see you *domani?*" I asked.

"*Lunedì,*" he replied.

"*Quando si lavora?*" I asked to make sure he understood that I was asking him when he worked again.

"No work Sunday," he said.

What I wanted to say at that point I didn't have the words to say smoothly in Italian, so I pulled out my phrasebook to let him know that we might not see him again, but before I finished, Lidia called for him. I didn't know, as he headed off to see what she wanted, how much I'd managed to convey to Maximiliano. One thing I've learned about communication is that it's not perfect, even between husbands and wives who have lived together forty-six years. So how could I hope to accurately convey our intentions, especially when they were, at that moment, highly uncertain?

After breakfast, on our way to Le Suite to enjoy yet another Italian coffee, we noticed there was no line in the laundry so we stopped to pick up our clothes. This life was feeling very good—everything we needed was within a few doors of where we lived. We'd already decided that on future Italian journeys we'd take one less suitcase and help the local economy by looking for the laundry when we check into a town.

We also decided that it's fun to buy clothing locally.

"It's twenty euros," I said, wrapping a beautiful scarf around my neck to get Mardi's opinion. "Does it make me look at least a little bit Italian?"

"It does," she lied.

That bit of humoring was all it took for me to want that scarf. I gave the clerk a twenty euro note and walked out of the shop with a bit more swagger. A half block later I was showing off my new look at Le Suite. Luigi, as usual, was behind the bar.

"*Buongiorno,* my friend," he said.

"*Come va?*" I asked.

"Good," he answered. "*E tu?*"

"We are *fantastico.* I think we are in love," I said.

"*Con tua moglie?*" Luigi asked.

"No. With Maiori. I think we are in love with Maiori."

"But not your wife, my friend?" he asked, surprised.

"*Si,* Luigi. I KNOW I am in love with my wife. I THINK we are in love with Maiori," I said with a smile.

"Ah, but we shall see. You do not yet know Maiori," he cautioned.

"But what I know I like, *mio amico,*" I said.

He gave me the subtle Italian equivalent of the body language for *Touché* and said, "*Vuoi l'acqua calda?*"

"Two please," I answered.

"*Prego,*" Luigi said as he gestured that I should join Mardi at our usual corner table. "I bring to you."

The Italian music playing sounded like a love song. It was also a good song for spinning—a great driving beat—one I'd love to listen to while riding my stationary bicycle. I tried to pick out the words—I'd already heard *amore*— love—as well as *Ti amo,* which means *I love you.* When Luigi brought our cups of hot water I asked him about some words I couldn't find in our little phrasebook.

ARE WE THERE YET?

"I teach you *italiano*. You teach me English," Luigi said. We now had two offers.

We taught each other words common to ordering in a bar. He explained that his value as a *barista* is linked to his command of English because English is the universal language of tourism. For us it was a good deal. Every word of Italian we learn seems to open up more adventures for us.

Mardi and I began talking of our plans, checking out prices and availability on *Hotels.com*. We thought again of returning to Amalfi, but forty-some bucks for Maiori and Maximiliano was an offer we couldn't refuse. Swearing allegiance to pinball traveling, we decided to stay right where we were if we could continue to get the same fabulous rate. I was so excited that Mardi was willing to let some grass grow under her feet that I left her sitting at Le Suite to run back to Casa Raffaele Conforti to confirm with Lidia that we could stay longer.

I was no more than a dozen steps from Le Suite when I saw her walking down Corso Reginna toward me.

"*Buongiorno, Lidia,*" I said.

"Hello," she said.

"*Scusi*, can we stay longer?"

"No problem." She said it so quickly that I thought maybe she hadn't understood that I was asking to reserve a longer stay at Casa Raffaele.

"Same price, we stay more days?"

"*Si, no problema,*" she said again as though it was the most natural request in the world.

"Can stay in same room? We like that room," I said.

"*Certo,*" she said as she pulled out her phone and called someone. I caught enough of the conversation to know that she was confirming our request. She hung up and said, "*Va bene.*"

"We stay there forever?" I asked with a hint of a smile.

"It is possible," she said, smiling back.

"Forever?"

"*Si.* I see you later," Lidia said and continued down the street.

"Bye bye, *grazie mille*," I said thinking that the exchange had been a God thing—the timing was weird.

I turned to head back into Le Suite and noticed that Mardi had been watching me talk with Lidia. I flashed a thumbs up and joined her, "We can stay as long as we want," I said.

"Still at forty-four a night?" Mardi asked.

"That's what she said, but I'm going to go pay her to make sure there's no misunderstanding. If you see her heading back to the hotel, let me know." Mardi had a good view of the street. I had a good view of all that was happening in the bar. I loved watching Luigi greet customers—loved hearing the sound of the cash register opening and closing and the enthusiastic *arrivedercis*, *buongiornos*, *ciaos*, *grazies*, and *pregos* that followed.

A man I had yet to meet walked in and sent a hearty *Buongiorno* toward us. It didn't take long to figure out that he was Luigi's boss—the owner of the bar—and Jessica's brother. Jessica had told me that I'd see the family resemblance. He was, as she said he would be, handsome.

While trying to pick out the Italian words from another love song I begin researching *A Bell for Adano*. The fictional Adano is the factual Licata, a seaside town on the north coast of Sicily. By driving eight hours we could get to Licata, but that may have to wait until next year. I returned to researching, turning my attention to another favorite book, *Christ Stopped at Eboli*.

I discovered that from the exact spot where we were sitting, we were only an hour's drive from Eboli. When Carlo Levi passed through Eboli, if he'd had a modern FIAT and today's roads, he would have been only two hours from where Mussolini had banned him. But back then it was another world and a very long trip.

As I studied the maps I discovered that many of the towns I wanted to visit were within a few of hours of Eboli. It was amazing to compare the geography I remembered from reading Levi's book with what I now knew about the region. His descriptions of the land had brought me to southern Italy—*to this Godforsaken land*—now I had a strong desire to make this geography mine.

"What else do I need to look up?" I asked Mardi. I was enjoying using Le Suite as my office. I felt that this routine could be good for my writing. It would keep me from staring at the computer screen too long. Something was always happening to capture my attention. At that moment I heard the familiar whirring sound of a *peloton*. I turned around just in time to see a dozen bikers sweep past clad in sleek racing jerseys, many in Italy's national colors. I hoped someday to ride with such a group, heading out for a morning of biking the twisting roads of the Amalfi Coast, pushing my heart rate to its maximum on the climbs, then recovering on the thrilling descents. The hook was being set ever deeper—Maiori and the Amalfi Coast were reeling me in.

"It's almost noon, Jim." I'm sure Mardi knew what was going through my mind, what goes through my mind every time I see someone fly by on a beautiful bike pedaling at a high cadence. I knew what was on her mind, too.

As much as she was loving our morning in Le Suite, she wanted to be out *living* a good life—not *observing* a good life.

We packed up our office, the computer and books, told Luigi we'd be back, stopped to see Lidia to confirm with money our intention to live a while longer in Maiori, grabbed our jackets and a little food, and set off on what we thought would be a hike on the Path of Lemons to nearby Minori. But we didn't get out of town—at least not right away.

"Let's stop by L'Angolo del Gusto," I said. That was the shop owned by the man whose daughter we'd seen biking around town, stopping by Le Suite to chat with the patrons—the little girl who lived on Corso Reginna just as I'd lived on the main street of Hayes Center as a child. We weren't even sure what he sold—we just knew we wanted to buy something from him.

"*Buongiorno,*" the girl's father said to us the moment we stepped into his shop. "Would you like to try some *limoncello?*"

At that point in our education of Italian matters we had not been introduced to the wonders of Amalfi Coast *limoncello*. I gave him the best Italian gesture I knew to indicate that we might be willing to give it a try.

"Good or the best?" he asked.

"*Migliore,*" I said.

"Ah the best. The green lemon, not the yellow," he explained as he poured me a small glass. The smell revealed that it could have a kick to it—a bit of an alcoholic kick. I raised the glass slowly to my lips.

"Mmm, *mi piace,*" I said, suddenly realizing why *limoncello* was such a big deal on the Amalfi Coast.

"This is the best," he said, proudly showing me the bottle.

"May I try the good?" I said, wondering if I'd be able to tell the difference.

He opened a second bottle, grabbed a fresh glass, and poured me a little. It felt different on my tongue. It tasted different as well. I didn't tell him I preferred the best. I didn't yet know the prices.

"Yes, the difference," he said. I noted how different the word sounded when he said it. He probably could have closed the sale at that point, but he turned his attention to Mardi. She was looking at a particularly appealing bottle of red wine.

"Is it sweet?" Mardi asked.

"It is somewhat sweet. It is from Tramonti."

That was all it took.

"I would like to buy," she said.

"Is it a present?" he asked.

"No, just for us," she said.

"It should be a present," he said with much certainty as he put it in what looked very much like a gift bag.

I was surprised that Mardi had made up her mind so quickly. I was sure she'd chosen it to remind us of our wonderful time at Il Raduno the day before, but I wondered whether she might also have thought it was a good way to keep her rather impulsive husband from buying something he knew so little about—a hunch that was confirmed as we walked back to our hotel room to lighten our load by one bottle of wine. That purchase changed the course of our day. Instead of climbing to the high country on the Path of Lemons, we dropped down to the beach to warm up and see if we might find a shortcut to Minori—a low-altitude shortcut like the tunnel from Atrani to Amalfi.

Instead of turning right when we got to Corso Reginna, we turned left toward the promenade. When we reached the promenade we turned right toward Minori. This also led us toward the harbor. Within a block we had passed La Vela, where we'd eaten our first meal in Maiori, but the territory to the west was new to us. The look of the promenade was similar—a wide boulevard for strolling featuring severely trimmed eucalyptus trees forming a line leading all the way to the cliffs at the far end of the bay.

It was there that we discovered the beautiful and perfectly protected harbor of Maiori—a discovery that would further strengthen our bond to the town. We found working fishing boats—not charter boats for tourists, but get-up-and-go-out-very-early-to-make-a-living-off-the-sea boats—the kind a man spends every day of his life on—the kind we'd seen in Greece thirty years before. We began seeing the Amalfi Coast through the lens of history. People survived here because they fished here, not because it was beautiful.

I knew the answer, but I asked Mardi anyway: "Do you still like it here?"

"I love it," she answered quickly.

There was no people-watching to do, no fishermen about, and no shortcut to Minori so we headed back to Corso Reginna. The street looked much as it had an hour earlier, but with more energy now—more women with shopping bags who had stopped to talk, more men walking two by two with their arms behind their backs, more benches filled to overflowing, and more kids playing soccer in the street. The sounds of the town almost brought tears to my eyes. I didn't know a village could sound so good.

Del Gusto was playing soccer with his daughter and some other kids— maybe they were all his. We were sure that wasn't the shop owner's name, but it fit his personality—he was energetic and athletic and looked like a great father.

"I am going to go get another *cappuccino*." I could see that our table was available. I had a few thoughts I wanted to jot down. Mardi had a few shops she wanted to check out.

"*Ciao, Luigi,*" I said. A beautiful jazz selection was playing—nothing I knew the name of, but I did know I liked it.

"What do you recommend?" I said.

"What you feel like?"

"Something cool, *freddo.*"

"Ah, very good."

I settled in, connected my computer, and began typing. I had a half page filled by the time Luigi arrived at my table with a tall orange drink sporting a British flag. He also brought some cheese and a selection of meats, crackers, and biscuits—what Americans call cookies.

Luigi was busy, or I would have asked him if this truly was a British drink. I suspected he may have forgotten that I was American. The place was a hubbub of activity, even young children were in the bar. This was a Cheers for all ages, and all nationalities, and they had the flags behind the bar to prove it.

"I thought you were going to have another *cappuccino,*" Mardi said as she joined me.

"No, I decided to live adventurously. I asked Luigi to choose a drink for me again."

"And you got lunch too, it looks like."

"Yeah, that was a bit of a surprise," I said, offering her a taste. "Did you find some salt and pepper shakers?"

"No, couldn't find any I liked. But I did discover that the path to Minori starts right at the church, and it's only a kilometer."

I couldn't imagine that Minori was that close, especially since we were going to have to hike up and over the ridge separating the two towns, but I was ready for an adventure. I was also thinking that we might find the doors of Santa Maria unlocked and sneak a look inside.

Just getting to the church doors was a bit of a climb. The central part of Maiori is quite level, but when you start going up in Maiori you go up really fast. Mardi and I have always felt that health and fitness are their own reward, but in Italy, especially on the Amalfi Coast, health and fitness pay unique rewards.

"Wow, beautiful," Mardi said as we paused to look out over the rooftops of Maiori to the beautiful deep blue of the Tyrrhenian Sea. While we were still catching our breath the bells began ringing. The sound was still lovely, but it had a different timbre because the sounds weren't bouncing off anything before they reached our ears. It was almost as if they had a different personality. Up close the ringing was more a call to worship than a way to mark the passage of time.

We walked up to the church doors and pushed one slowly inward with some trepidation—not being Catholic, I'm always afraid I'll commit an indiscretion or interrupt a service. When my eyes had adjusted to the dim light I saw a man near the front of the church talking with an older woman. I announced our presence by giving him a small wave. The church was beautiful but dark. We began walking toward the altar. Just as we reached the front of the nave the man excused himself from the woman and began walking toward us.

"Are you English?" he asked.

"American," I said.

I wondered why he'd asked, but I didn't say anything. He indicated that we should follow him. He led us to a door, unlocked it, and handed us a brochure. I said *Thank you* and he said *Prego*. I thought he was just acknowledging my thanking him for the brochure, but then realized that he was welcoming us to his church, and that we should continue following him. He led us down a very long hall to another locked door leading to what I still didn't know.

I felt unworthy of such attention. We had just popped in to admire the church, hoping to see its windows from the inside, and here we were apparently being led into its inner sanctum. Once inside that second door he gestured that we were free to look around. We were in a hall filled with artifacts dating back at least a thousand years. We introduced ourselves and learned that his name was Josef.

He gave no indication why we were being accorded such privilege. It seemed extraordinary that he would give us so much of his time. As always in the churches of Italy, Mardi and I were overwhelmed with the beauty, but this time we were overcome with surprise.

"A movie set? What was the film?" I asked Mardi who was intently studying a display.

"Rossellini shot *Festa, The Miracle, Paese, Amore,* and *Journey to Italy* here."

My mind was reeling—Rossellini had used this little town as though it were his personal studio. He had seen something in Maiori that helped him tell his stories, and now I too had fallen for its charms.

We also learned of Maiori's deep connection to the sea. The full name of the church is *Santa Maria a Mare* (Saint Maria of the Sea). Oh, how I would have loved seeing Maiori in the years before World War II, when I'm sure the harbor would have come vibrantly alive in the predawn hours each day as fishermen made their way out to sea.

We could imagine various eras as we walked around the museum observing the changes in art over the centuries that this church had been standing on this spot looking out to sea and calling the families of Maiori to walk through its doors and worship God. I was so overwhelmed by all that we had seen that it wouldn't have surprised me to find original works of art by the masters deep within this church. I risked showing my ignorance as we walked past what I was sure was a painting by Caravaggio. Josef had rejoined us and was showing us the way back to the central nave.

"*Originale quadro*?" I asked.

"No, copy," he said.

I smiled and thanked him profusely for allowing us such a privileged look at the church. He seemed to think nothing of it. That is the way it is with Italians. They give you the shirt off their back and act as if it has been to their honor that you have allowed them the privilege of serving you. And then, just as we stepped back out into the sunshine, the bells began ringing as though the church itself was thanking us for stopping in. These were insistent chimings, having nothing to do with time-telling. They continued ringing at a high pitch and then low-pitched and slower paced. Then two by two. Then single beats. Then double beats. Ending with small bells, very quietly. From the first insistent pealings to the very last tingle of the final small bells, the beautiful composition had lasted over four minutes. The last flicks of the bell were ever so subtle, sending chills down my back.

"Isn't it fun, getting to know just one place," I asked, "rather than wandering all over Italy?"

"Like getting to know one woman," Mardi said with a sly smile. She rarely misses an opportunity to remind me of the benefits of a long-lasting marriage.

I kissed her. We walked arm in arm up the steps as we resumed our climb to Minori. Our view of Maiori was changing quickly. Soon we were looking down at our hotel, down at Corso Reginna from a small *piazza* surrounding the upper part of the cathedral. As I was filling my water bottle from *la fontana di piazza* I noticed the walls were adorned with more stills from Rossellini's films.

"It looks like this may have been where the final scene of *Journey to Italy* was filmed." It would be fitting that here, where Mardi pointed out the beauty of getting to know just one woman, Rossellini's film about coming to realize the value of committing your life to one woman should have been filmed. Too perfect, but sometimes life is like that. This day—in fact, this whole journey— was proving every day to be too good to be true.

"Look, at night this little *piazza* is lit up," Mardi said pointing out lights embedded in the stonework.

"Oh, that would be pretty. We should climb up here some evening," I said.

On the far side of the *piazza* I noticed a colorful ceramic sign reading *Limone Sentiero. Sentiero* confused me for a moment. I was translating it as something like *knowledge*, before recalling it means *pathway*. This trail to Minori is called *Pathway of Lemons*. I wondered if this was a recent market-driven name paying homage to Amalfi Coast *limoncello*. Or maybe the Amalfi Coast has been a tourist destination for thousands of years. In this age of smartphones, I suppose I could have looked it up on the spot, but I didn't want to break the mood.

I was also enjoying letting Mardi lead the way. It gave me plenty of time to take photos—and catch my breath. I was wearing a backpack holding extra clothes and food, just in case—as well as water. The steps and pathways above the church were taking us high quickly. Fortunately the path seemed designed for dawdlers like me—a bench here, a fountain there, an overlook from which to photograph. The impressive green and yellow dome of the church was soon below us. The people on the beach, the few who were there, looked incredibly small. We were so high above the church that the sounds of the village and beach were being replaced by the sounds of birds and farm animals.

"If this is a walk, I wonder how tough a trek would be," I commented. A tourist pamphlet described this journey to Minori as a " short walk," but it seemed to be neither short nor a walk. We had been on the path for quite some time. I was beginning to sweat. I had taken off my sweater. I was considering stripping down to my T-shirt.

"This path still has lights," Mardi noted. "Even way up here."

"We could have walked this at night," I said. And I wished we had. As cool as it was, it would have been cooler at night. We were looking for a walk, and like the one from Amalfi to Atrani, it was up and over the mountain—except we still weren't to the *over* part. We were still climbing and still looking down at Maiori. Minori was still someplace over there, beyond the mountain still in front of us.

"Being fit adds a lot to a journey," I said. I was trying to see the positive side. If we hadn't been fit we wouldn't be up here and wouldn't be seeing Maiori from this perspective. We'd seen the church because we'd been willing to climb the steps, but we had long ago left the church.

"I can't wait until we meet a donkey on a path," I said. I was continuing my quest to find positive things about our climb. But instead of *asini* we met *gatti*. They were sitting along the edge of the path, sometimes as many as a half dozen cats gathered on one rooftop, watching us climb. The homes they were sitting on were looking less and less substantial.

"I keep thinking we should be done going up. Shouldn't we?" I asked, but Mardi said nothing. Instead she asked if I wanted to wash my hands and eat something. We had stopped at what must have been the twelfth fountain we'd seen. I was beginning to feel a water bottle in this part of Italy was not necessary.

We rinsed our hands and began sharing an apple while looking out at sailboats crisscrossing the sea. The Amalfi Coast was absolutely beautiful from that spot—I quit complaining. This trek or walk or whatever was worth all the sweating. We finished off the apple and decided we had time for an orange, too. *Why doesn't America have fountains everywhere?* I wondered. It's so civilized.

After we finished eating the orange we rinsed our hands again and resumed walking. "I wonder if all this had to come in by donkey," I asked. We were walking past farm after farm, but we had seen no tractors, only animals. "I can't imagine you can get a car or a truck anywhere near here," I said.

Now that we were so high, so far away from roads, utilitarian seemed to be the yardstick by which things were measured—no longer did beauty dominate—bed frames were gates. It may have looked presentable when it was first hung on hinges, but now it just looked rusty and junky.

"Mardi, I've found a place for us. *Vendesi* means *For Sale*. It might need a little work, but we'd have a great view of all the storms blowing in."

She looked. The sky, the sea, the hills—it was breathtaking, but the farmer in her was not enamored. It was going to take more than one of the most beautiful views she had seen in her life to make her think she wanted to live way up here, at least an hour's walk from Le Suite. The farmer in me, however, was impressed.

"Oh, look at the lemons. I wonder if they grow anything else there," I said.

The earth was perfectly and beautifully tilled under every tree. The lemons were the size of large oranges. Nearby a field of lettuce caught our eye—perfection personified. Nothing was out of place, the soil had not one weed. "They have different stages of lettuce. I bet this is for a restaurant. I can't imagine a field being more beautiful," I said. The many shades of green set off by the deep rich color of the earth looked glorious to this farmer's eyes.

Twenty minutes later we were traversing the ridge we had for so long been looking up at. The fields were a little larger. I was wondering if we had taken a wrong path.

"I think Minori is that way," I said, pointing back toward the ocean.

I turned on Strava, the bicycle mapping app I use back home. It confirmed what I suspected. We had climbed far higher than necessary and had bypassed at least one much shorter route to Minori.

"Did you pull a fast one on me? Is this the park you wanted to see?" I asked, pointing to a large green spot on the Strava map we seemed to be heading toward.

"No, it's on the other side," she said.

She may have been as confused as I was at that moment. It sure seemed like we were heading right toward what looked like a large nature preserve. The beauty surrounding us certainly deserved to be preserved.

"When we get around that corner up there I think we're going to get hit by a pretty strong wind off the ocean," I warned.

And we were. We looked for a route that would get us off the ridge as quickly as possible, but we didn't find one. "Look at that big ship," I said, gesturing toward the sea. The whole world seemed spread out below us. We were feeling euphoric—it was like a mountain climber's high—our legs and lungs had carried us to an incredible height. We paused to take it all in and heard waves crashing on shore. It was weird.

"This was worth the price of admission," I joked as we resumed walking.

"Convento San Nicola," Mardi said, reading a sign near a fork in the path. "I think we should go up there—we've climbed this far."

"We have time," I replied and continued following my adventurous wife.

At the top of the path we saw a beautifully crafted walking stick leaning against a gate. I'm not sure why the sight of that walking stick made us turn back, but it did—or maybe it was the gate. We didn't even check to see if it was locked—we just spun around and wondered why this magnificent vista wasn't mentioned in every guidebook written about the Amalfi Coast.

Mardi stopped to study the sign again.

"It says Convento San Nicola is still that way," she said and pointed in the general direction we were now walking. It was a good thing we'd turned around when we got to that gate. We were most likely on the path to someone's farm. No wonder the owner felt comfortable leaving his walking stick leaning against his gate.

"So we're still not heading toward Minori?" I asked.

"I wasn't going to Minori. I was going to the convent."

"I wish I'd known that. I might have argued with you a bit."

She didn't say anything but kept studying the sign. She looked again at her map and then turned to read the sign again.

"I had a feeling we weren't on the Path of Lemons anymore," I said.

"Wow. This is confusing," she murmured, still engrossed in the map.

"Did you miss the sign back there a little ways that said eight kilometers to the convent?" I asked.

That did it—her need for adventure blew right off the ridge with that piece of news. Something wasn't making sense to her, but no way did we have the time or energy to hike another eight kilometers and then back again.

"Surely there's a way down from here," she said.

We were heading away from Minori—going deeper into the hills. I didn't want to go back to rejoin the Path of Lemons, I wanted to forge a new route to Minori. I was beginning to enjoy the trailblazing now that we were no longer climbing. We were actually losing an inch or two with every step instead of gaining a foot. What had been a sufferfest was now a walk in the park, or so it seemed in comparison.

"Oh my, look at those steps," I said.

We had come upon a long, narrow staircase heading straight down the mountain. But I saw no indication that it was a public path, no sign indicating that Minori was down at the bottom of this seemingly endless staircase. I wondered if it could be like the path that took us to the walking stick leaning against the gate—leading only to someone's home.

"They wouldn't put up a railing unless it was a public path," Mardi said.

I hoped she was right, but even if she wasn't, we were going to walk down these stairs even if they led us to someone's farm—surely a farmer would forgive some hopelessly lost Americans for trespassing.

Normally when I've encountered stairs in the backcountry they are steps laid on the surface of the land, but these were different. This was an actual staircase cut deep into the earth and getting deeper—so deep that the surrounding walls were at times over ten feet high. It was also very long. I could see no end to it. The wind carried the wail of an ambulance to our ears, its ominous sound echoing against the walls.

"Hope we don't have to turn around and go back up," Mardi said.

"Oh, I'm not climbing back up this. A helicopter will have to come and get us," I said, only half jokingly.

Mardi began to apologize for leading me on such a difficult climb, which was a rather strange reversal. Usually I'm the one who bites off more than we can chew. I began to focus on the weirdness of the day's adventure.

"Do you suppose *any* tourist has ever been on this path?" I asked.

It was difficult to imagine that anyone but a very seasoned hiker or someone who lived up here would attempt this trail. It was like walking through a tunnel that was going almost straight down except that we could see a sliver of sky over our heads.

"Isn't this incredible? This has to be an ancient path."

Mardi was getting so far ahead of me that she had to stop walking to hear me.

"This would be a great workout for an athlete to run all the way to the top," I said as I knelt down to try to emphasize the depth of the cut for a photo. Mardi kept going. I fiddled a bit, took a few more photos, and moved on. I wasn't happy with any of the shots—they weren't nearly as dramatic as the real thing. I kept walking down. The walls got shorter and eventually the steps were once again on the hillside, giving us another dramatic view of the Amalfi Coast.

"Probably the last sixty-nine-year-old who climbed these steps lived up here somewhere," I shouted. "And probably died soon after."

I couldn't tell whether Mardi couldn't hear me or whether she was just ignoring my attempts at witty repartee.

"Allo—are you alone?" I heard a woman ask, but I could see no one except Mardi.

"No—*mio marito* is up the hill," Mardi said and pointed toward me.

"You are much faster than he is," the woman said with a laugh as she came into my view. She was attractive, quite fit, and dressed in colorful clothes.

"He is taking photos," Mardi explained.

I hopped off the path and bent down in front of a pot of red geraniums to take a picture—one that turned out quite well—that gave a sense of how high we were. I was too far away to hear everything, but I heard her tell Mardi that she did not often see tourists this high and that she and her husband operated an *agriturismo*.

"He has worked so hard—I like to show it off," she said as I reached the landing where they were standing. I introduced myself, and learned that her name was Ornella.

"Our apartment is up there," she said, pointing high above us. "With kitchen I can cook for my guests. We opened about ten years ago." She was doing a good job selling us on the idea of spending time with her. She described great breakfasts, the red and white wines she served with dinner, and the after-dinner *limoncellos*. She didn't have to sell us on the view, but she did anyway, saying we could see the music festival in Ravello from her apartments. The views were so spectacular that had we been able to stay for a few days I think we would have tried to work it into our schedule, but her minimum was a week. The amount of work that had been done was amazing, most of it involving terracing the very steep hillside. She told us that her husband had been raised on this land and that soon it would be a three-generation farm.

"Do you have a donkey?" I asked.

"No. All the groceries must come in on my arm," Ornella said.

I looked toward Minori, still far below us, and tried to imagine climbing this high several times a week with my arms weighted down with bags of groceries. I then realized Ornella probably grows a lot of what she feeds her guests. It then occurred to me that she probably didn't have to climb all the way from sea level up to her farm—I noticed a road below us.

"Do you have a car?" I asked her.

"Yes. You can see it there." She pointed to a car parked far below along the edge of a narrow road. But between the car and her front gate were an awful lot of steps. In exchange for the inconvenience of carrying groceries up here, and everything else, she had a glorious place to live on this earth. The glow in her eyes revealed that she realized how fortunate she was.

"You remember me, a present for you," she said as she handed Mardi a small bag. It contained a brochure and some lemon soaps. I had not until that moment noticed that we were standing beside what could best be described as a small store, with lots of products, most of them associated in one way or another with lemons.

"How much is your *limoncello*?" I asked.

"A bottle? Ten euros."

I didn't ask if it was the best or better. Her price was considerably cheaper than Del Gusto's. At that point I didn't care that his *limoncello* might be a better quality than hers. I just wanted to let her know in a small way that we appreciated her showing us her farm. Farming on this steep land has to be mind-blowingly difficult, and Ornella had been kind enough to give us a great tour. It was good advertising for her, but she made it feel as if she had given us a personal tour because we were friends. How she was able to do that even though she had just met us is one of the mysteries of Italian hospitality—it's just what Italians do.

"You come back with your friends," she said as we reached her gate and began walking down the steep steps. It was tempting, but I sincerely doubted we would be back during this journey. We were growing very fond of the convenience of Maiori—the feeling of being in the middle of each evening's *passeggiata*.

"Can I take a look at your map?" I asked. I suddenly had the desire to get back to the streets of Maiori by the shortest route possible—by a route that didn't drop us all the way down to the streets of Minori. We had worked hard to gain this elevation and I wanted to lose as little of it as possible reconnecting with the Path of Lemons.

"Wouldn't it be funny if it really *was* just a short walk from Maiori to Minori?" I said as I found a path that looked like it would take us toward Minori's church but keep us high above it on a ridge, and that ridge just might connect with the Path of Lemons.

After a few hundred yards the path became relatively flat. I could hear the wind blowing through the pines high above and the waves crashing on the beach far below. It was a good walk. We were getting a very different look at Minori. We passed by the church still looking down at it and soon found ourselves on a well-worn path—on what almost certainly had to be the Path of Lemons. We could have gone either way. I gave the choice to Mardi. She turned toward Maiori.

"Thank you for not making me walk down into Minori," I said. We were on a gentle climb, having lost very little of our elevation. We soon came to a small church with an adjoining *piazza* that commanded a view of the whole coast. We were now most certainly at the highest point of the Path of Lemons. It would be downhill all the way to Maiori.

"I've been looking for this all day," I joked. I was getting snarky again. Mardi defended herself.

"If we hadn't climbed all the way up there, we would never have met Ornella and we wouldn't have the *limoncello*."

We didn't yet know it, but we were about to meet someone who was going to more than make up for all our climbing, as well as all my complaining. After a short, but delightful pause in the *piazza* looking out at the sailboats still crisscrossing the blue waters below, Mardi set out for Maiori. As usual I was lagging behind photographing.

"That's not it—it's a dead end," I heard Mardi say. She was walking back toward me.

"Somewhere around here is where I think you led me wrong," I yelled to her as she reached a fork in the path and turned toward what I hoped was Maiori. I stopped to take a photo. I was composing a shot that included a couple of cats near a beautiful gate flanked by a colorful and well-designed ceramic sign bearing the address. As I knelt down looking for a good angle I became aware of a man of thirty or so on the other side of the wall watering his garden.

"Allo," I said.

"Allo," he returned.

"Did you do this?" I asked pointing at the sign next to the gate.

"No, the artist is my uncle," he said. "He has a shop in Minori, right next to the church."

The ceramic sang Amalfi Coast to me. It spoke of sun, and sand, and sky and somehow evoked hospitality as well. If I commissioned one with our house number on it, people would know they were welcome when they arrived at our door.

"*Mi chiamo James.*"

"My name is Giovanni."

We fell into an easy conversation. I learned that he was taking care of the place for his uncle, that he had just been to England, that his brother was a restaurant manager, and that he had been in New York City, Washington, DC, and Miami. I had already fallen in love with his uncle's work, and now Giovanni had spoken so glowingly of his uncle I had no doubt that on our first free day we would head to Minori again. Giovanni gave me permission to take a photo of his cats that included him.

I found Mardi waiting for me at the fork in the path where she'd led me astray. We shared a fig bar and I told her about Giovanni. She promised we'd take the shortcut to Minori next time.

A family passed by while we were snacking. We enjoyed a pleasant conversation with them. Soon a man walked by. We also chatted with him. Just as he started to tell us he was walking to work, his phone rang and he answered it. Mardi and I were in no hurry. We could see Maiori below us. We decided that if everyone who came by wanted to chat, we would be happy to visit as long as they wanted. When the man got off the phone, he told us he worked in a bar, one I hadn't seen in Maiori. He asked us where we were coming from, and when I told him we were coming from Maiori and going to Maiori, the look on his face told me he didn't understand.

I explained that we left Maiori after lunch, got to this point and then went up, up, and up, across the ridge, and then took some steep steps down to Minori. He was certain we couldn't have done that. He pointed to where Minori was, and where Maiori was, and I said, "Yes, I know"—and then went on to explain that Mardi had led me on a very long hike to the high country, and now we were almost back home.

"Ooh, la la," he said. His voice and expression told us he was impressed with how far we had walked and how high we had climbed. The conversation definitely picked up our spirits, especially since the man was a bit of a walker himself, commuting to work on foot every day.

He checked the time and realized he had to get going. No one else came by, so we packed up and continued walking on the now-familiar path, the one that had led us to this delightful spot three hours earlier. Fifty yards down the path I took a picture of a wisteria arbor I had photographed midday. This shot was not nearly as good. The colors were muted. The scene was in shade. Time of day can be crucial in photography, as in life. A few minutes one way or the other and Giovanni would probably not have been watering his garden. We did not yet realize the good fortune that was coming our way because of that chance meeting—that bounce of the pinball.

Even though we were still high above Maiori, we were meeting so many people on the path it felt like the *passeggiata* had already begun. Often we were the first to say *Buonasera,* unless we were meeting older folks, and then they were usually the first to offer a greeting.

"Oh, what a fun day this has been," Mardi said after one such exchange with another family we'd met on the path and with whom we'd enjoyed a brief but interesting conversation.

"Remember the first time we went by this garden, how high we thought we had climbed? It was nothing compared to where we ended up. Now it seems so low, so close to town," I said.

"Yes, it is—we can hear the waves again."

"Should we go down and eat at the beach?" I asked.

My mind was still focused on the chance meetings we'd had, and I wondered if there was more to come on the beach. I guessed this game could be played all day. You never know what is going to happen or whom we might have met had we not climbed so high up into the hills, but as we walked back toward Maiori I was extremely thankful for the way the day had turned out. I guess that's why Saint Paul told us to be thankful in all situations—and why my bit of complaining was quite unnecessary.

"This low angle light is beautiful. Look at the way it's lighting up the church tower," I said. The sun's rays were bouncing off low-hanging clouds and giving the town an even stronger fairy tale appearance. If we had met a donkey train on this ancient trail, my day would really have been off-the-charts good. I was convinced it might yet happen. Simon and Luciana had met donkeys on the trail above Amalfi. We often heard donkeys on our hikes. Surely the chances of meeting a donkey were good in an area where the donkey is revered. Adding to my certainty was the sight of straw on the ground as though bales had recently been hauled along this path.

But no beasts of burden of any kind did we meet on the trail. We were beside the green and yellow tiles of the church by the time two bells and five chimed out. I was still lagging behind, taking photos. A couple sitting on a bench just a few steps off the path facing the setting sun had caught my eye, but I wasn't able to make the photograph as beautiful as it appeared to me.

It was also impossible to convey with a photograph my feelings as I walked down the steps from the Cathedral of Santa Maria. It was again like coming home. As I stepped onto Corso Reginna a family greeted me—a family I had no memory of seeing before, yet they greeted me as though we were friends. Kids were playing soccer on the promenade just as they had been when we left town. The sounds of people greeting each other contributed to my feeling of belonging, because that is how they were greeting me as well. Mario biked by, recognized me, and sang out a hearty *Ciao, my friend*. I mean no disrespect, but Mario reminds me of Kermit the Frog as he rides his bike around town sharing with folks who somehow might not yet know that his wife is the best cook in town. His friendliness makes me feel good. His wit makes me smile. His sincerity convinced us that we should soon try his wife's cooking.

I found Mardi sitting on a bench on Corso Reginna not far from L'Angolo del Gusto, where we'd been given a taste of *limoncello* five hours earlier. The proprietor's daughter was again riding her bike up and down the street greeting people. Everywhere I looked I saw something that made me feel connected to the town.

The sight of Mardi sitting there also made me laugh. She was eating. We had hiked all afternoon, and now that we were back within one hundred yards of Casa Raffaele Conforti, she'd settled in for a picnic on the *corso*.

"Would you like some cheese to go with that?" I asked.

"That would be nice."

I couldn't have agreed more. Even though we could have lightened our load by eating this food before we'd carried it to the top of the mountain and back, it felt right to eat it while sitting next to Mardi on that bench and absorbing the sounds and sights of the town. Life was being lived out here on the street, and it felt good to be a part of it. What I dearly loved was that even teenagers seem to enjoy themselves on this street. As we sat there, people of every age could be seen—the *passeggiata* was represented by kids in their single digits, and of course babies, all the way up to a couple of folks who must have been in their nineties. It wouldn't surprise me if someone who has topped one hundred might occasionally show up given the propensity of Italians to live very long lives.

A gentle rain began, more like a mist, but it didn't dampen the spirits of the party, so we stayed until we'd finished most of the food we'd carried with us. Very few people who passed by failed to acknowledge our presence with either a nod or a polite *Buonasera*. The cumulative effect of receiving a gentle greeting from everyone made us feel completely welcomed.

The mist became rain, and we rushed to the B&B. Some young girls had also been sent scurrying inside. They were playing in the stairwell. As a kid I did such things too, playing marbles or jacks while waiting out a rain shower. In a small town you know the places where you can seek shelter—where the owners will not tell you to get lost.

Maximiliano was waiting at the top of the stairs to greet us. I had a feeling he'd been watching us run toward the hotel.

"*Ciao, Maximiliano*—you look very sharp," I said.

He asked about our day. We asked about his. He offered *cappuccinos* and we accepted.

While he prepared them we headed to our room to get into dry clothes. A few minutes later Maximiliano delivered the *cappuccinos* to our door. No wonder we were in love with this town. We made the coffees last longer than Italians typically do as we recounted our day—mostly discussing the people we'd met, the ones we exchanged names with, like Josef and Ornella and Giovanni, and the people whose names we hadn't learned, like the man walking to work who couldn't believe that we'd walked so far and the dozens of people who shared just a few moments with us on the trail.

Remembering our promise to Mario, we chose to eat at Mario and Maria's. We were surprised to find it empty. If Maria was as good a cook as Mario said, we figured we'd have to wait in line to get in. I don't think a line ever formed, but it wasn't long before the place began filling up. The food flowed, and so did the excitement over a soccer game.

The young boy who waited on us was very inexperienced and didn't understand English at all, which definitely made us feel as if we were in a family restaurant. It turned out to be another of those situations that strengthen my resolve to become fluent in Italian. Stories were flowing around that room far faster than I could keep up with. We understood when to laugh, when to smile, and when to cheer, but the nuances of the tales I couldn't follow.

"This is a comfortable place," Mardi said.

"I knew you'd like it."

"Any place where the husband says that his wife is the best cook in all of Maiori has to be good," she said.

We changed our routine by ordering lasagna along with our usual mixed salad. Both were great, especially the tomatoes. The bread and wine were terrific, too. Add in the extremely fast Internet, and we had another place we knew we could grow to love.

"When we show up, things start happening," Mardi said.

"It just may be that we tend to go to dinner a little earlier than most Italians."

"So we're not the catalyst after all," she shot back.

"Look at me and smile."

I took a picture of her, but mostly I wanted a photo of the men behind her, who had showed up not long after we arrived. They were hard-working men who ordered a lot of food that just kept coming. They were deeply into the soccer game and jeered loudly when things didn't go well for their team, which I think was Napoli.

"Do you think the bread is homemade?" Mardi asked.

"Yes. I'm sure it is."

To confirm this, I asked our waiter, who had grown more comfortable in his role in a very short time. He told us the bread was from a local baker, and then he asked about us. My Italian was not grammatically correct, but I was able to tell him where we had walked today. The young man was so surprised that he announced our feat to the men next to us. They were so impressed that for a moment the soccer game was forgotten. They offered a salute to our accomplishment, praising us loudly enough that everyone in the restaurant learned how we had spent our day. The feeling in the room was one of belonging, as though we were in someone's house among friends.

"NO, NO, NO," one of the men shouted at the television. I turned just in time to see the ball hit the back of the net. I was happy a goal had been scored. All that attention focused on us was making me a little uncomfortable.

"They have a pizza oven," Mardi announced.

"Well then, I think we should come here and get a pizza sometime," I said, feeling that we'd found an easy-going restaurant where we'd always be welcome. As we were paying our bill, we enjoyed some good laughs with Mario. Italians have a knack for making mundane chores and daily occurrences pleasant.

"Shall we go over to Le Suite and have tea?" I asked as we left Mario and Maria's.

"And some dessert."

"It would be a good night for a Bailey's Irish Cream. This is so darned much fun."

We crossed the street and walked the short distance to Le Suite where, quite miraculously, our table was the only one not occupied. Next to our table was a good-looking bunch of thirtysomethings, one of whom, an attractive brunette, inexplicably took notice of us. I felt as if it had been announced that we'd soon be arriving and that our table must be kept clear.

Saturday night soccer was the focus here as well. Enthusiasm for the game was not lacking. A young woman in her twenties, sitting with three others about her age got up from her table and ran across Corso Reginna straight up to four young men walking by. She kissed one of them on each cheek, smiled, and then walked back across the boulevard to join another group of young women standing in front of Le Suite. The scene had caught my eye because it seemed so exuberant, so playful, so inexplicable—a boyfriend, a brother, a *former* boyfriend? So many scenes caught my eye in Le Suite—so many stories I'd love to know more about.

We again let Le Suite choose our drink for us. Jessica asked about our day, what we'd eaten, and what kind of mood we were in. She took it all in and served us a fabulous dessert drink—Kahlúa with a thick coating of chocolate on the rim of the glass. When the soccer game ended, energetic music kept the place rocking—great songs for spinning, many new ones, and many of the old standards I teach to. We felt so comfortable, so at home, that it seemed that our pre-Italy life had blended into our post-Italy life and we were now leading a seamless life—a life in which I was imagining that I would soon be fluent in Italian. Maybe it was the Kahlúa.

CHAPTER TEN

Casa Raffaele Conforti ~ Sunday April 10 ~ 42 & Fog

Sunday in Maiori

Though we travel the world over to find the beautiful,
we must carry it with us or we find it not.
RALPH WALDO EMERSON

■

I soon realized that no journey carries one far unless,
as it extends into the world around us,
it goes an equal distance into the world within.
LILLIAN SMITH

Sleepily and with a bit of pain in my lower back from writing too long, I eased back into bed, hoping not to wake Mardi. But she either felt me jostle the bed or heard me and began to apply pressure to my lower back. "You're the most wonderful person in the world," I murmured through the delicious pain—the therapeutic pain—that her hands were sending through my body.

"I'm trying to be," she whispered.

"Well, you're succeeding remarkably well," I assured her. As soon as I said it I recalled her pledge to try to be a better person, kinder to all. She was trying to emulate Marco, the young man we'd met in Tramonti who offered to drive us to our restaurant if we could wait a half hour until he got off work. He was willing to help us for no other reason than he could be of service to someone in need. Italians, I keep discovering, are like that.

The night before, Mario had walked with us as we left his restaurant, asking if we had enjoyed the cooking of his wife, who, he had assured us numerous times, was the best cook in all of Maiori. *"Delizioso,"* I said and assured him that we would come back for pizza. He explained that pizza was *his* specialty and not his wife's. We told him we'd be willing to try it even if she hadn't baked it. He got a kick out of that.

Life had been very good to us during the week we'd been in Italy. As I thought back over the things we'd done and the people we'd met, I was amazed that so much could happen in so little time. I was also amazed that I been so lost in thought as Mardi rubbed me that I hadn't realized the bells had not quit ringing after informing us of the time.

"Those are the Get-up-and-go-to-church-you-lazy-bum bells" Mardi slurred and fell back to sleep. She can fall asleep faster than anyone I've ever met—a necessary survival skill, I suppose, for getting up at night all her life to take care of children, a mother, and a mother-in-law. She continued sleeping as I slipped out of bed and stepped onto the balcony to get the full effect of the call to worship. As the sound of the bells began to fade, I could just barely hear other bells ringing, possibly from Ravello high above us. The effect was glorious. The very last chimes of Santa Maria's bells were again ever so subtle—a gentle flicking—and very musical.

We had no specific plans for the day. We were looking no farther than breakfast, and even that was only penciled in because Maximiliano wouldn't be there.

But Maximiliano *was* there, and so were a lot of other people. Maximiliano was in his element, scurrying about the room taking his short, quick steps—caring for the needs of nearly a dozen guests. Mardi noticed that most of the people were wearing coats when they came in and deduced that they were coming from the Hotel Miramare to have breakfast at the Casa Raffaele. Something must have happened at the Miramare—that would account for all the people as well as the presence of Maximiliano on this day that he wasn't scheduled to work.

We were joined that morning by trekkers from France, an Italian family with young children, two young lovers, and a couple we'd talked with the day before. The wife had been to America, the husband hadn't. He said *Buongiorno* upon leaving. She said *Bye*.

Since we didn't have Maximiliano's undivided attention, we didn't linger over breakfast nearly as long. We decided to go to where the people were coming from. Nadia had told us that we were welcome to use the Miramare's Internet.

The journey should have been simple, but it didn't turn out that way. When I asked Maximiliano for directions he pointed as though it was just across the street. But after fifteen minutes of wandering, we ended up back at Le Suite, without seeing a hint of the Hotel Miramare.

But we had noticed the *pescheria*, where fishermen bring their catch to be sold, so we abandoned our search and headed toward the harbor to be among people who make a living from the sea. Watching the fishermen cast their nets reminded us of the original economy of the Amalfi Coast—the reason this rugged coastline had homes and now hotels clinging to the stark beauty of its hills. As we turned to look back at Maiori from this long distance view, we saw what had to be the Hotel Miramare—it appeared to be less than two blocks from the Casa Raffaele Conforti, and we now knew exactly which direction to walk.

At the Miramare we found a fast Internet and a comfortable lobby, but in no way was Le Suite in danger of losing our business. The purchase of a *cappuccino* or two was a small price to pay for the good life Le Suite was giving us.

"Do you think we're making a big mistake staying in one town?" I asked Mardi.

"No, not at all."

Her enthusiastic response gave me the courage to check *Hotels.com* to see if other hotels in Maiori were affordable as well. I discovered that Casa Mannini was less expensive and even closer to Le Suite. But Mardi was a step ahead of me. She had discovered a convent in Maiori that welcomed guests. I was intrigued by its location—down by the harbor where the fishing boats docked.

As we stepped out of the hotel we were overwhelmed again by the delightful sounds of Maiori—people talking and kids playing soccer—happy sounds echoing off the buildings.

"This town is so alive," I said as I eavesdropped on a gathering of men enjoying an animated conversation, apparently about someone's sister. We were still within earshot when they began laughing, and I realized they'd been telling jokes. It was but another reminder of why I deeply desire to become fluent—I want to be a part of everyday conversations—the bits and pieces of this beautiful language that sing on the streets of Italy.

We were soon at the door of Casa Mannini. It too was up a few flights. We chose to take the elevator and were greeted by a woman who showed us a room. It was delightful and colorful—as modern as our room at Casa Raffaele Conforti was ancient. The cost was less than we were paying, but I wasn't sure it was a big enough difference to forgo our great view of the church and, of course, the good times we were enjoying with Maximiliano.

We were again surprised to find a Rossellini connection—many of the paintings and photographs in the hallways paid homage to my favorite Italian director. We left without making a commitment, but it was nice to know that the low price we were paying was not a fluke—if Casa Raffaele was booked up we'd have a good option. We stepped back onto the street with an even greater love and appreciation for the town knowing how affordable it was.

"I'm sure Rossellini could have chosen any town in Italy for his films, yet he chose Maiori," I said.

I don't think Mardi was as convinced as I was that we should be judging Maiori through Roberto Rossellini's prism, so I added, "Any man who choses Ingrid Bergman for his wife has to be able to figure out what town he likes to be in, right?"

She humored me with a smile so I kept going.

"Any man who chooses Martha Dieterich for his wife has to know the best town in Italy to stay in, right?"

She rolled her eyes at that one. She could see I was a hopeless case.

"Or should we move to Salerno," Mardi asked, crushing my spirit, "where we could travel cheaply to all the places we want to go?"

I countered that suggestion; "Maybe we should try the Rosie Bar." It was only a couple of doors from Le Suite and also seemed to be a hangout for locals. We walked in, noticed that we'd be closed off from the *passeggiata*, and walked out. We had taken all of ten seconds for our evaluation.

"There's our girl," Mardi said as we stepped back into the expansiveness of Corso Reginna. She was, of course, referring to Jessica, and confirming that we had already found our hangout. Jessica greeted us warmly and made me wonder why I had given even a second's thought to trying another bar. We thanked her for the Kahlúa and told her we'd be back after we checked out the convent. A half block later Mario rode by on his bicycle and waved.

"Don't you think I need to get a bicycle so I can ride around town with Mario?"

She ignored me on that one, too. I took it as a sign she was tired of hearing me whine about buying an Italian bike. I changed the subject, sort of.

"This town is just a little bit of all right."

She continued to ignore me.

"There's another set of Cathy eyes." She didn't ignore *that* sally.

"Should you have married Cathy?"

"Oh, we didn't hit it off that well. She was too old—it was puppy love for me. I doubt she ever had any romantic interest. I was more like a little brother."

"You're in good hands with me," she said.

"You've got that right. It's fun discovering Italy with you."

We were almost to the harbor. The sea was roaring. Carpenters were erecting the little shops that pop up along the promenade each spring. The feeling was one of anticipation—of what the summer crowds would bring. We too were filled with anticipation—wondering what we would discover when we walked across the street and through the ancient doors of the convent.

The first thing we discovered was that we had chosen the wrong door—we found ourselves in a large hallway leading to lots of rooms. On the walls were photographs of towns in the area—many of them scenes from various Rossellini movies. In one room we discovered what looked like a birthday party for a young girl. Our presence was noted by one of the mothers. I asked if she knew whether the convent rented rooms. As Italians are wont to do, she immediately set out to help this stranger who had fallen into her world. She told me I'd find someone who could help me on the first or second floor and then began to describe how to get there.

She realized as she began describing the route how complicated it was, so she turned to a young girl—her daughter, I presumed—and asked her to lead us. But the girl was too shy, so the woman passed off her birthday party duties to another parent and asked us to follow her.

I quickly discovered I might have been presumptuous about the young girl being shy—she just may not have known how to get where we needed to go—the route was extremely complicated. We were led through a labyrinth of hallways and up twisting staircases to what appeared to be a reception area, but no one was there. Her job still wasn't done. She asked us to wait and went off to find someone.

The willingness of Italians to help strangers often makes me slightly uncomfortable. As I waited for her to return, my mind was flooded with memories of people who had gone out of their way to help me during my bicycle tour of Tuscany. I was given water, food, directions, recommendations, and even on one occasion a place to sleep by Italians who knew me not at all.

After a few minutes she returned with Andrea. I'm sure the task had taken much more of her time than she expected, but she made us feel that it had been her privilege to serve us. Andrea was soon joined by Gerardo. Neither did anything to detract from our favorable impression of Italians—nor our conviction that within the Italian psyche is a deep seated propensity for being kind to strangers.

Apparently our helpful guide had told Andrea that we wanted a room beginning immediately, so when I asked for a room beginning Thursday, he assumed I'd misspoken and that I wanted a room *until* Thursday, at which time we would be checking out, not in. It took a bit of time—and a switch to English which Gerardo understood better than I spoke Italian—to get that sorted out. But the misunderstanding provided some good laughs, and by the time we had it straightened out Gerardo seemed like an old friend.

We invited him to come to Wisconsin and he immediately accepted *to see the cows.* He knew Wisconsin culture—cheese and Green Bay Packers. He was built like a football player and made me think of the French actor Gerard Depardieu—similar names and outgoing, larger-than-life personalities. He was, in short, a presence who would be noticed the moment he entered any room. He led us down a very convent-like corridor. We expected the room to be just as spartan.

But it was filled with light and very spacious. We'd already fallen in love with the convent—the art gracing the walkways, the quiet spaces for contemplation, and the sense of history flowing from the ancient walls. Now he was showing us a room that had all that we wanted, plus a great vantage point on the beauty of the Amalfi Coast. The price, which we at first thought was comparable to what we were paying at Casa Raffaele Conforti, turned out to be twice that—the rate we'd noted on a brochure while we were waiting was per person, not per room, so staying at the convent would cost double what we'd been paying.

When we got back to the reception area we explained our misunderstanding to Andrea and Gerardo. Andrea offered to discount the room ten euros a day, which brought the cost down to what we had paid Salvatore in Amalfi. We quickly accepted Andrea's offer. The thought of waking up to the sound of the ocean right outside our door convinced us we'd be making a good investment. It also seemed crazy that we'd meet but not spend more time with Gerardo, a jolly Santa Claus of a man who had begun, like Maximiliano, to call me James Bond.

"What do you do here?" I asked Gerardo.

"I take care of everything," he said, not boasting but matter-of-fact. It was only then that I noted he had paint on his clothes. He did seem like a jack of all trades—a man capable of keeping a huge place like this operating smoothly. He showed us the breakfast room and some beautiful spots in the garden that seemed like perfect places to write or contemplate, much as the monks and nuns had done over the centuries. As he was walking us to the main gate, Gerardo shared with us that the convent was also known as *Amici di San Francesco*, The Friends of Saint Francis. It was easy to imagine Saint Francis walking quietly down one of the many flower-graced pathways and out the large gate to the beach just as we were now doing.

"Mardi, I kind of like this town," I said, stating the obvious, as we walked across the highway to the harbor *piazza*. Maiori, we were discovering, seemed to have an unending supply of surprises for us. We had walked in this area a couple of nights earlier and had noticed a little church with walls on either side, but gave no thought to what might lay on the other side of those walls. There was a world of beauty back there, and beginning Thursday we'd get to know it even better, and maybe even learn some of its secrets. We sat down on the steps in the *piazza* and watched the rowers we'd seen earlier from the balcony of the room Gerardo had shown us. Mardi was reading the brochures she'd picked up.

"I wonder if the convent has chickens?" she asked.

"I heard a rooster when we were walking in the gardens. I bet they do," I said as I watched the coordinated efforts of the rowers, who were now lifting their boats, that looked to be over twenty feet long, out of the water. We were struck by their good-natured camaraderie—at least twenty men and women working together to lift the sculls onto a double-deck trailer—and each time the group erupted into a big cheer as they settled the boat into its cradles.

Buoyed by the enthusiasm of the rowers I suddenly felt giddy at our good fortune. I thanked Mardi again for discovering the convent. We too make a good team. I'm more inclined to let events unfold. She's more likely to affect and even occasionally effect their outcome.

"I've spent at least a part of almost every day of my life for the past fifteen years learning something about Italy, but somehow I never heard of this town," I said. That made me realize that wonders were spread throughout this country that remain undetected on the radar screen of tourism—towns all over this beautiful land for people to fall in love with and want to move to, hoping to capture for themselves a little of the sweet life of Italy.

But Maiori was becoming our town. We began walking up the promenade thinking about eating, trying to decide which restaurant to choose. We had walked no more than fifty yards when we saw Mario again. The genius of his advertising struck me. Sometimes all it takes is a little nudging.

He saw us and called out, "Pizza?"

"*Domani, Mario,*" I said.

"Tomorrow," he confirmed.

He had nudged us toward pizza, but we were thinking about saving money so we could afford to stay at the convent. We recalled seeing again a billboard announcing an incredibly low price for pizza while looking for the Hotel Miramare a few hours earlier. A few euros here and a few euros there each day, and we'd have the cost difference covered. On the way to the pizza shop the beauty of Italian women became the subject of our conversation— thankfully the subject was brought up by Mardi. "Italian women are pretty fine, aren't they?"

I thought that was an interesting way to put it. She was forever telling me that women were at least as aware of beautiful women as men are and she just may be right. I hadn't noticed the woman that had started this ball rolling, but when Mardi pointed her out I agreed wholeheartedly. I just wouldn't have used the word *fine*—I would have said *gorgeous* if it were my friend Roger who had pointed her out—but since it was Mardi I merely agreed that the woman in question was *good-looking*.

I was thankful that we made it up Corso Reginna and past Le Suite without seeing Jessica. Mardi might have asked me if I thought Jessica was good-looking, too. I didn't want to create any jealous bones in Mardi's body about Jessica, who was like a daughter or a niece to me—witty, playful, and energetic—she also had that delightful accent. That she was pretty was obvious, but I preferred to leave that unsaid.

"Is this the street?" I asked.

"Yes, it's right here," Mardi said and led me to an entrance that couldn't be seen from Corso Reginna. Masaniello truly looked like a locals' hangout. We stepped inside and were immediately greeted as though we were friends.

"This is good?" the young man asked pointing toward the only table available, one with a great view of the wood-fired oven. We knew we wanted a mixed salad and a pizza but decided to be adventurous. The pizza menu was very long, some were familiar but many were not. We asked the waiter to recommend his favorite. It didn't take me long to accept his choice, especially when he mentioned Italian sausage. The only problem I had was with the name of the pizza—*Ricchezza*. I always fail to give double zz's enough emphasis— *ree kate za* was the phonetic interpretation that garnered a *Bravo* from our waiter, Roberto.

"This would have been a lovely place to see in the forties and fifties," I said to Mardi after returning from the restroom. On the way I'd seen some photographs of Maiori taken during the war and just after that showed a town that was strongly agricultural. "The streets would have been lined with huge-wheeled carts being pulled by oxen."

I also told her she'd see more photos from Roberto Rossellini films as well as a beautiful interior of the church whose bells we'd fallen in love with. By the time she'd finished looking at the photographs, Roberto was serving our pizza with a hearty *Buon appetito*. It looked as good as his description of it. I was, for a multitude of reasons, feeling especially grateful. I concluded my prayer, *Thank you Lord for everything, especially this beautiful woman you have given me.*

She smiled at me, but turned her attention to the pizza. "This doesn't have tomato sauce. It has pesto," she said, somewhat surprised. She and I attacked the pizza very differently. I had picked up the Italian way of eating and she had not. She moved her fork from her left hand when cutting to her right hand when eating, whereas I left the fork in my left hand.

"They don't make forks very sharp."

"Eat like this," I said. "Use both hands. Keep your fork in your left hand, the knife in your right."

"That works," she said as she gave it a try.

"Instead of cutting the crust, you kind of pull it apart."

But on the next piece she almost flipped the pizza onto the floor as she pulled. We broke out laughing.

"This is your first time," I said. "You can't expect to learn to eat pizza on your first trip to Italy."

"But this isn't my first time. Remember the margherita pizza we ate on the plaza in Bolzano—and the wonderful time we had watching the kids go through the Christmas bazaar."

She was reminding me of one of the last days of our first trip together to Italy. We'd rarely eaten out because we had been exchanging labor for room and board, but this was our last Sunday in Italy and we were Christmas shopping on the Walther Square within sight of the beautiful Bolzano Cathedral. The beauty of that afternoon may have been the genesis of the idea that our next trip to Italy should be more of a honeymoon and less of a working vacation. We had felt a special closeness that afternoon as the sun dropped behind the spire of the cathedral and the temperature dropped what felt like an immediate ten degrees.

"You like the pizza?" the owner asked, pulling us out of our memories of Bolzano and back to Maiori.

"Very much, thank you, we love it," we said almost in unison.

In an Italian restaurant you will never *not* be asked if you are enjoying your meal—at least once. Enjoying your food is a national necessity.

"This pizza is fabulous," I said to Mardi, realizing I could have been more effusive in my praise to the owner.

"You didn't even salt and pepper it," she remarked.

"No, it's perfect just the way it is. And so are you. I'm in love. With you—with this town—and everything about it. This is the best pizza I've ever had."

Now it was Roberto's turn to check on us. "You like the pizza." With him though, it was more of a statement. He must have overheard my enthusiastic praise to Mardi, and of course he also had recommended it. When I explained that it was now my favorite pizza in all of Italy he said that next time I must try it the way he likes it. I asked him to show it to me on the menu.

"Oh, no. It is not on the menu. You just tell me to add a little tomato sauce to the *ricchezza*."

That led to an exchange of the short stories of our lives. Roberto had spent time in England, and that led to some Italian lessons and yet another person calling me James Bond. Even though the room remained quite busy, Roberto stopped by numerous times to chat and expand our Italian vocabulary. It was of course for him a chance to hone his command of English. We left with the promise that we would return to try the *ricchezza* Roberto-style.

When we stepped onto Corso Reginna we were surprised that the sun had moved so far during lunch. A few moments later the bells of Santa Maria confirmed that we'd taken over two hours eating a simple meal of pizza and salad, chatting with Roberto, and enjoying the camaraderie of people enjoying a game of football Italian-style—*calcio*.

We were in no hurry to change the pace established by our meal. We strolled down the street arm in arm past Le Suite and into Mama Mia's *gelateria*, where we discovered the secret of the Kahlúa that Jessica had served the night before—a thick chocolate concoction that was the perfect topping for the *stracciatella* that was quickly becoming my favorite *gelato*. Mardi ordered her favorite, pistachio, and we sat down on one of the benches lining Corso Reginna, close enough to Le Suite to listen to its music and watch the passing parade, which included a surprising number of people we knew, some of them well enough to talk to, others we just waved to.

"I may have found two favorites today," I said.

I was thinking of the *ricchezza* and the chocolate-covered *stracciatella*, but I quickly realized my list of favorites was much longer than two.

"Why don't we just live in Maiori?" I blurted out.

As Mardi began enumerating the reasons we couldn't and shouldn't, Michael Bublé began singing of possible reasons we could and should.

It's a new dawn,
It's a new day
It's a new life

Jessica appeared and pulled me out of my reverie, "Is that Michael Bublé?"

I told her that indeed it was. She seemed pleased. I had thought her comment was a preamble to a longer discussion, but she turned and walked into Le Suite at a rather quick pace. I went right back into dreams borne by Bublé's smooth voice.

And this old world is a new world
And a bold world
It's a new life for me
Fish in the sea you know how I feel
Birds flying high you know how I feel
Butterflies all havin' fun, you know what I mean
Sleep in peace when the day is done, that's what I mean

Before the song ended Jessica had returned, offering each of us a glass of water. The chocolate topping was extremely rich—a *piccolo* scoop might be the size to ask for next time.

"That was nice of Jessica to bring us water," I said, now realizing why she had left us so quickly.

"She thinks we're cute," Mardi said. "She likes the way you touch me."

"How do you know?"

"I've noticed her watching us. Women can tell what other women are thinking. Her eyes give her thoughts away."

As we joined the *passeggiata* towards the promenade, I thought of a Michael Bublé song that would have blown my mind had I suddenly heard it—his song *Someday*, begins *I love seeing you happy* and features the line:

Someday maybe when we're old and gray
We could be in love once more.

It's a jaunty tune that would have matched our feelings perfectly. Instead we heard the inimitable voice of Pavarotti when we reached the promenade. His voice always reminds me of love.

"Attractive lady walking our way," I said.

"She was in the pizza place, and so was that little boy over there," Mardi pointed out.

She was convincing me that she was more observant than I was when it comes to women.

"I kinda like ya," I said. "Are you wearing enough clothes to walk down by the water?"

"The radiance of your soul warms me," she replied with a sly smile.

"Aren't you the poetic one this afternoon," I said.

It was not the sort of thing she would typically say to me. Maybe Maiori was getting to her, too. She must have realized it was a little over the top and came back with a question she must have hoped would yield some insight into her husband.

"How do you see yourself as different from other tourists?" she asked.

I wasn't sure what to say so I sidestepped the question.

"Maybe I'm a little more curious. By the way, I finally heard from that farm in Salerno. They said they could handle only one person at a time, and that person needed to speak excellent Italian."

Our path didn't seem to be leading us to volunteering on farms for our journey of a lifetime—but what had bothered us before our trip, we were now seeing as a Godsend. Every one of our days had turned out better than we had hoped.

"I see why Rossellini liked it here," Mardi said.

"You mean you like it better than Amalfi?" I asked, surprised by her enthusiasm.

"I think this is prettier."

"Is it because the sea is so accessible—that we have such a good beach?" I asked.

Her smile seemed to indicate the beach had more than a little to do with her assessment. Her desire to keep walking along the coast, once we reached the end of the promenade, confirmed it. The Torre Norman Castle was beckoning,

poised as though it was a lighthouse out on the point of the bay. It looked like an unforgettable dining experience. But to get there we'd have to abandon our stroll along the beach and risk our lives along the Amalfi Coast Highway.

Trucks, buses, and cars were whizzing by. The only way we mustered up the courage was by drawing on the faith of those already walking along the highway. We were surprised that it took only a few minutes of vigilant walking. And we were relieved that the speed of the traffic was being slowed by cars stopping to drop off and pick up customers at the restaurant. A Jeep Cherokee was waiting halfway on the highway, halfway off, when we reached the castle. We asked the folks inside the Jeep about the food.

"We just ate there—they take really good care of you," the driver said. I noted he didn't mention the food. His accent was familiar. I asked where he was from. He must have recognized my accent as well, for few outside of the Upper Midwest would have understood his answer.

"We're from the People's Republic of Madison," he quipped.

"We're from Brookfield. We're big fans of Wisconsin basketball," I said.

While he waited for his passengers we talked of Bo Ryan, Sam Dekker, and Frank Kaminsky as well as the new coach at Wisconsin, Greg Gard—and a little bit about how much we each loved Italy.

Once his passengers were aboard he drove off, and his spot was taken by a parking attendant. We hoped this young man would know of a road—a path possibly—called Via Monte Corso that we had noticed on our detailed maps of Italy that morning. He was very familiar with it—assuring us that the stairs to a safe route back to Maiori were just across the road and that ten minutes of easy walking would get us back on the promenade.

The route into town showed us another facet of Maiori—that it was also a farming community—and that its farmers were very fastidious. The plants on the farms were perfectly aligned, forming an intricate tapestry of greens and golds on earth-colored canvases framed by well-built terraces that had not one stone out of place. Occasional splotches of brilliant flowers and brightly colored doors beckoned and made us wonder what kind of people lived on the other side of those ancient walls bordering their farms. Surely their lives couldn't be as perfect as their walls—they had to have a stone or two out of place.

As we worked our way around the face of the mountain and closer to the heart of Maiori we became aware of music drifting up from the promenade. We could also see that a lot more people were in the park than when we walked through an hour earlier. From our lofty vantage point, Sunday in Maiori looked very special. The music, which at first I couldn't identify, matched the mood of the gathering—a festive celebration for kids. When we reached the promenade I realized that the music was from a Walt Disney film I'd seen. Mardi helped me pinpoint it—"Under the Sea" from *The Little Mermaid*.

Kids of all ages were in the park—smiling, laughing, running, jumping, and playing on the swings, seesaws, and climbing bars. Parents were sitting on benches, chatting with other parents while watching their children. Even teenagers were hanging around, some playing soccer, others just talking. The whole town seemed to be there—babies to grandparents, maybe even great-grandparents.

As we made our way along the promenade the music changed, but only slightly. It was again "Under the Sea," but this time the lyrics were Italian. "Do you think these kids have any idea how doggone good they have it?" I asked. I wondered if every Sunday night was like this—thinking what fun it must be for grandparents to gather here every week with their grandkids.

Some of my favorite memories from childhood were playing with the country kids who came to town on Wednesday and Saturday nights when the stores were open. This scene was that memory romanticized, then doubled, and quadrupled. I had no idea that a town this small could have so many children.

"What a wonderful play place for kids," Mardi said.

We were repeating ourselves, but we didn't mind. If the scene had been in a movie, you would have said the director had gone over the top. Too many kids having too much fun at one time. It was too perfect. Mardi and I had been celebrating the day Italian-style—drinking *limoncello*. But we hid the fact by drinking it from an insulated tea mug.

"I'm starting to get a little tipsy," she said.

"It has a kick to it, doesn't it?" I said rolling the sharp taste on my tongue.

"That's what you need—a man purse," Mardi said pointing to a young man walking by with a sleek bag that was just big enough for a small laptop. I was still carrying my computer in the backpack I'd purchased for my journey around Italy by bicycle. My computer was now about half the size and three or four pounds lighter, and it was time, she felt, for a more fashionable way to transport it. I had to admit that at least on that man a purse looked good. It certainly looked more practical than my now-oversized backpack. But it was not something we were going to be able to deal with at that moment.

"Hey, our bench is open—the one you took a nap on," I said.

It was in the sun and would be a perfect place to rest from our hike and watch the changing colors of the sunset. The sound of the waves crashing on the shore mingled with the happy voices of the children and the playful tunes from the sound system, adding to the atmosphere. Maybe for the Italians present it wasn't quite as idyllic as it was for us. They'd understand the words of what most likely were political speeches being broadcast a bit farther down the promenade, but to us the voices were like musical accompaniment to a festive party.

"Let's just stay right here the rest of the night," I said even though I doubted we had the clothes to last much past sunset, which was probably about an hour away. Until then this beach, this promenade, this view were ours to enjoy.

"I didn't want you to see her," Mardi said, realizing that I'd already seen the beautiful woman she hoped I wouldn't notice.

"She's not as pretty as you," I whispered in her ear.

"Yeah, right," she said as she watched the fashionably dressed *bella donna* glide down the boardwalk, an equally beautiful dog leading the way.

"I thought it would take me ten years to find this town," I said.

I'm not sure where Mardi's thoughts went. Maybe she was still thinking about the beautiful woman, but as I sat looking at the waves crashing on shore I began thinking of my dreams for Italy and our future in this country and couldn't imagine how life could be improved. Here was everything I'd hoped for, at a price that was about half of what I thought we'd have to pay, and it was in a town I'd never heard of. I liked that. That was probably one of the things John Steinbeck had liked about Positano—he'd never heard of the town when a friend invited him to visit in the 1950s. In a way it became his town. I lived with those good thoughts for a long time as I watched the sun settle gently toward the horizon. Mardi napped and must have been thinking good thoughts too—I could tell by the contented look on her face each time she was startled awake by a child's exuberant shout. After a wild cheer for a goal scored in a soccer game being played near us, she woke up and asked if I'd like a few slices of apple with peanut butter.

"You okay with not eating dinner tonight?" I asked.

"Yeah, that's what we said we were going to do to save money so we could stay at the convent," she said.

"Then I'd love an apple with peanut butter."

As we dined we were treated to some delightful examples of the universality of parenthood.

"Listen to the noise that mom is making—*Choo, choo*—do parents all over the world say *Choo, choo* when they put their kids on a train?" Mardi wondered.

We were also hearing parents say *Andiamo*, which translates to *Let's go* in English, and just like at the parks in America the kids were saying *No, no, no*. And just like in America we saw a father play his ace card—*Okay—if you're not going to come with us, Ciao—see you later*.

Mom and dad walked away, pretending they were going to leave the small boy. *"Aspettare!"* he said and ran off to join them.

Despite the large number of families that had left, the sound of children playing still dominated the promenade.

"Even the fishermen are heading home," I said as I looked out to sea and saw that three boats had recently turned toward the harbor.

"You should be happy that I'm so content," Mardi said. What she didn't say but I knew she was implying was that she didn't feel like going shopping.

Not all the kids were willing to let go of their beautiful day—one little girl was led away sobbing.

"Shall we go? I'm getting cold," I said.

The promenade party was ending—one family at a time. The sun had slid below the horizon just after six thirty, and by seven most of the parents had rounded up their kids and headed home for the universal bedtime of eight or nine o'clock on a school night. Even the fishermen on shore were collapsing their super-long poles and heading home for dinner. Only the most headstrong kids were still playing, having convinced their parents they'd throw a temper tantrum if forced to head for home while other kids were still in the park.

As the air continued to chill, stocking caps came out. The temperature dropped quickly now that the sun's rays were no longer warming the promenade's paving stones. Coats were unfolded, put on, and buttoned up. Whole families, though, were still on the promenade. Mardi was moved, as I was, to take a few photos of the parents struggling to convince their children that they really did have to go.

Like the children, we didn't want to go, but it was too chilly for us now that the sky was turning from the deep rich colors of the sunset to black. We made our way reluctantly the short distance to Le Suite. We looked back and saw that only the most energetic of the kids were still in the park.

"Let's grab our table and check out their selection of teas," I said.

"*Due té?*" Luigi asked.

"*Grazie,*" I said.

We had enjoyed a wonderful day even though we hadn't left the town except to climb high above and look down on its beauty. We'd shared in the daily happenings of our adopted hometown. And we also discovered that Le Suite serves Whittington teas and that their Earl Grey tea was great, as was the croissant Luigi brought us.

"How do they make a croissant taste so good?" I asked. I didn't expect an answer. It tasted like Le Suite and Maximiliano were buying their croissants from the same baker.

"They treat us awfully well here," Mardi said.

"Oh, look, there goes Maximiliano," I said.

"I guess he didn't see us," Mardi said.

"I love you," I said, suddenly overcome with tender regard for her because of the disappointment she was showing that Maximiliano hadn't greeted us.

"How do you say *I love you* in Italian?" she asked.

"I think it's just *ti amo*."

"There he goes again," I said. Maximiliano was now headed back toward Casa Raffaele Conforti.

"Maybe it's not him," she said.

"I don't think it's possible to not recognize Maximiliano."

While we watched people walk by, and greet each other, we worked on our Italian, looking up the various forms of the word the little boy had said to his parents when he thought they were leaving him, *Aspettare!*—Wait! We loved learning that *Wait for me!* required only a slight change to the ending— *Aspettami!* Gentle jazz accompanied our Italian studies.

"Mardi, thank you for coming to Italy with me. Life shouldn't be this good." I'm not sure why I said that—I didn't really mean it. I've always dreamed that someday life would be this good. I guess it was just my clumsy way of trying to express how much I had enjoyed our day together—a day during which nothing much had happened, yet it felt as if everything had.

CHAPTER ELEVEN

Maiori ~ Monday April 11 ~ 64 & Partly Cloudy

Jessica's Gift

The heart has its reasons which reason knows not.
BLAISE PASCAL

■

Love doesn't make the world go round;
love is what makes the ride worthwhile.
ELIZABETH BARRETT BROWNING

$\mathcal{Y}$ou never know what a day in Italy is going to bring. We thought we were just going to Amalfi to say goodbye to Simon and Luciana. I began the day very early—so early that Maximiliano did not yet have the breakfast room prepared. I planned to buy bus tickets, then walk around town to get a feel for Monday mornings in Maiori. I started my professional life as a photographer and I've never tired of trying to capture the essence of a place with a still shot.

A street cleaner was sweeping Corso Reginna with a broom, but I saw no one else. Even the shops along Via Capone that sell bus tickets weren't open. The futile search did lead me to a few nice compositions of the harbor and the beach, but I wanted people in my shots, and they weren't around, so I worked my way back toward Corso Reginna.

After climbing the four long flights of stairs to Casa Raffaele Conforti I discovered I was locked out. I rang the bell, waited, got no response, and decided to try to get in the old-fashioned way—by hiking back down the stairs, going outside, walking down the street to stand below our window, and whistle—and hope that Mardi would recognize my two-handed owl call. I knew I risked irritating everybody within earshot. People are used to the bells of Santa Maria, but my piercingly loud whistle might not be such a welcome sound. Fortunately, I was saved—just as I stepped out onto the street I met Maximiliano heading into the building with a huge cake. We walked together up the first three flights, but on the fourth and final set of stairs he pulled ahead. I was surprised to discover, as I caught up with him while he was unlocking the door, that the hike up had not been as easy for him as his final sprint made it appear—he too was breathing hard. But he recovered quickly, opened the door with a flair and asked, *"Due cappuccino?"*

I was glad Maximiliano wasn't a clock watcher. We were awake, so was he—why not offer us our usual even if the appointed hour for breakfast had not yet arrived. His willingness to bend the rules was working perfectly with our plan, such as it was. We wanted to get to Amalfi early. Our hope, although we hadn't shared it with Simon and Luciana, was to enjoy a bit of breakfast with them on Salvatore's terrace.

With Maximiliano we drank our usual *cappuccino*, ate a few of those incredibly delicious croissants, and enjoyed a couple of laughs about his unwitting snub of us the night before. Except for being in a bit of hurry, it was a very Italian breakfast. We took time for some fruit and nuts, but none for Earl Grey tea. If we were going get to Amalfi while Simon and Luciana were still enjoying Salvatore's breakfast, we couldn't linger over our usual two-hour *colazione* with Maximiliano.

"Un altro cappuccino?" Maximiliano asked.

"Sono pieno," I said.

"Bravo! Maximiliano said, then he added the words *piano, piano* very slowly. He then pushed his tummy out and said, *"Pieno, pieno,"* with a large amount of gusto.

Maximiliano was happy I'd pronounced the Italian word for *full* correctly, but he wasn't so pleased that we were rushing out. I remembered the big cake he had been carrying when I met him coming into the hotel and wondered whether he'd bought it just for us. It was a distinct possibility. No one else had come into the breakfast room. I hated disappointing him. He was working so hard to please us. He looked heartbroken as we walked out of the dining room.

"Do we have anything uniquely American we can give to Simon and Luciana?" Mardi asked as we were trying to decide whether to wear our jackets.

"That's a good thought. Anything that says Wisconsin?" I asked.

"Are you going to give them a copy of *An Italian Journey*?"

"Yeah, I've written the inscription. I have one for them and one for Vincenzo," I said and grabbed the last two copies as we left the room. I wished

I'd had the foresight to pack a few more as well as a bunch of postcards of Wisconsin cows and cheeseheads to give away.

The shops were now open, but still we had trouble finding bus tickets. The first tobacco shop only had the 1.6 euro tickets—just the opposite of the problem we'd encountered when we were heading to Tramonti. We finally found a shop that had a couple of 1.2 euro tickets, which was all we needed to get to Amalfi. We also bought a couple of twenty-four-hour tickets just in case. By this time we'd walked so far down Via Capone that we decided to just keep going to the last stop in Maiori—the one at the Convento di San Francesco, the Friends of Saint Francis. Even a simple thing like catching a bus can be an adventure in a foreign country—we kept glancing over our shoulders to make sure the bus that we could see making its way up the coast highway wasn't going to get to the bus stop before we did.

As I was validating our tickets aboard the bus I wondered why I had not thought to use the extra, more expensive, tickets I had in my billfold—it would have cost only forty cents more for each of us and would have saved us a worried walk/jog half the length of Maiori. When a woman with a stroller and a young child stepped up to the door but didn't get on, I wondered whether the driver had informed her that he didn't sell tickets onboard. That is but one more reason to always have extra tickets stashed. If I'd been close enough to the front to have heard the conversation I could have given the woman the tickets she needed—who knows how much trouble she was going to have finding tickets.

Even though we had traveled this section of the Amalfi Coast Highway before, it was as though it were the first time. On our first journey we were enjoying our conversation with Salvatore and his wife so much we didn't look closely at the spectacular beauty. Or maybe I was so focused on the road and hoping we stayed on it that I couldn't take my eyes off the cars I feared were going to crash into us.

"I have such great respect for these bus drivers. They're so calm," I said.

Mardi's eyes were focused on what was coming at us—our way forward looked impossible—this time we weren't blocked by a car, it was another large SITA bus. The driver was maneuvering his bus into a cranny so tight I swear he was leaving paint on the rock walls. Our driver inched forward until the mirrors of the two buses were all but touching, then he swung just wide enough to clear the mirrors and stopped. It was now the other driver's turn to inch forward. Two more dances like that and we were on our way.

Most of our fellow passengers were reading newspapers, not watching the dance or looking at the scenery, only a couple of people glanced at Atrani as we drove through. We seemed to be the only non-Italians aboard. "I don't think we'll have to hit the stop button," I said as we came around the corner and saw the spectacular harbor of Amalfi shining like a jewel in front of us. "At least twenty-nine people will be getting off."

I hadn't resorted to hyperbole. The bus all but emptied at the first stop, the one near the entrance to the tunnel that leads to Atrani. We weren't as jaded the other riders, but we were feeling a bit of familiarity with Amalfi. We knew exactly where we were heading. Even though the bells weren't ringing, Amalfi has a unique sound and we once again felt welcomed. We followed the flow of people to the main gate, then walked across the busy highway to the bus stop where we'd caught our first glimpse of Amalfi exactly eight days ago. As we looked for Simon and Luciana, I was amazed to think of all that had happened since we first stepped off that crowded bus from Sorrento. In just one week we'd fallen in love twice—once with Amalfi and once with Maiori.

"How we doing? Do we have time to drop the book off for Vincenzo?" I asked Mardi.

She didn't feel we did so she stayed among the buses while I headed over to the harbor. I didn't find Vincenzo, but he had apparently told the young man selling tickets for the cruise that I'd be dropping a book off, so I felt confident that Vincenzo would get it the next time he hopped on the boat to lead a group of tourists around Capri.

With that taken care of, we turned our attention back to finding Simon and Luciana. Mardi wanted to wait at the bus stop to make sure we didn't miss them, but I felt we had plenty of time to get to the Annalara before they left, so we compromised—we split up and walked the two possible routes from the bus stop to Annalara. Mardi went through the ancient gate we'd first walked through a week and a day ago, while I chose the longer route through the less spectacular entrance to the Piazza Duomo.

I would have hated to miss saying goodbye to Simon and Luciana. We had known them only a week, but sometimes friends can be made very quickly— friends who will impact the rest of your life. Roger had been like that. One day he was not in my life, the next, a lifetime friendship had been formed. Life is like that, full of beautiful surprises—*Belle Sorprese*.

Both entrances into Amalfi lead to the steps of Saint Andrew's Cathedral. We looked around the Piazza Duomo thinking that Luciana and Simon might be enjoying one last moment of reflection in this most beautiful of Italian squares. Lots of people were basking in the sun of a glorious morning, but we didn't see our British friends so we started up the street, glancing in all the *ceramica* shops in case they had stopped to pick up a last minute souvenir. I still liked the feeling of the town, but now that we had Maiori to compare it to, I realized Amalfi is more touristy than we had first thought. But to be fair, we weren't looking in the shops where Mardi and I had found so many tasty meats and cheeses and wines—shops where the locals hang out.

We got all the way to the gate of the Annalara without seeing Simon and Luciana. Salvatore buzzed us in. Mardi took the lift. I walked up. Even though the chances of finding our friends on the stairs with all their bags was almost nil, I've traveled long enough to know that strange things are often the order of the day. We climbed up the final steps together and walked onto Salvatore's delightful vine-shrouded terrace. As we'd envisioned, there sat Simon and Luciana, enjoying their last breakfast in Amalfi, and just as I had hoped, there sat Simon's jaunty straw hat beside him. I'm sure I'll always associate that wide, flat circular brim with Simon. He wore it with flair. I swear kids in Britain must grow up going to a flair fair where they're taught how to comport themselves with a bit of dignity.

Simon and Luciana were surprised to see us. Salvatore was not. He immediately said, *"Due cappuccino?"* It was as though we'd never left.

Mardi started to refuse, not wanting to trouble him, but I, not wanting to refuse his hospitality—and also remembering that we'd enjoyed only one round of *cappuccinos* with Maximiliano—gave Salvatore an Italian dip of my head and uttered my best rendition of *"Prego,"* making certain to roll my *r* just right. And then, just to make sure I was using *Prego* in the right sense, for it is a bit of an all-purpose word, I added, *"Grazie,"* which in English I hoped would be the equivalent *Please and thank you.*

"What are you doing here...a bit of slumming in Amalfi?" Simon asked.

"Yeah, we had to see how it was again, having to suffer through another of Salvatore's breakfasts on this beautiful balcony," I said. "Sad day, is it?"

"We hate to go," Luciana said.

"What time do you have to be at the bus?" I asked.

"I think it's just a bit after ten," Simon said.

I glanced at the time and realized we wouldn't have had to cut our breakfast with Maximiliano short, but it was nice to realize that we had over an hour to spend with our friends.

"This is really cool to see you," Luciana said.

"People are moving into our room today. We shouldn't really let them," Simon said.

"We came to be your porters, to help you with your bags—and we wanted to give you a copy of our first story about Italy—and to ask, if we happen to mention you in our second book, would you want us to change your names?"

Simon looked toward Luciana as he always did to make sure they were in agreement before answering. "I don't think we have anything to hide?" He did, however, end the sentence as though he were asking a question.

I handed the book to Simon.

"But isn't that your only copy, James?" Luciana said. "We could buy a copy from Amazon." Apparently she remembered Mardi reminding me that I only had two books left the day I promised Vincenzo a copy.

"I've already inscribed it to you. I hope you have room in your suitcase for it," I said.

"That's very nice of you," Simon said.

"Not to get all mushy and over-the-top on you, but we're very glad we met you. That meal we enjoyed in Tramonti is going to be a story we will be telling people the rest of our lives. Marco offering to drive us is a good story by itself, but then you add in the great meal Brigida served us... well, you know," I said.

I was amazed at how comfortable we felt with them that morning sitting in the sun on Salvatore's terrace. Moments like that are what you take away from a holiday. Seeing the beauty of Capri was great, and we did that with Simon and Luciana, too, but it was sitting around that table, just talking again about our favorite British and American sitcoms, that will probably linger longest and dearest in my memory. We shared our favorite things, and in that sharing Simon and Luciana were added to our list of favorite things. I will never forget the delightful lilt to Luciana's voice each time she said my wife's name. We never corrected her slight mispronunciation. She savored the syllables so lovingly—rendering them as a classical singer would, making the word *Marti* sing—an interpretation that I shall always hear.

We got so carried away with our leisurely breakfast that it put Simon and Luciana in a time crunch. They had even less luggage than I thought and didn't need our help, so they scurried off to the bus while we went to say goodbye to Salvatore and tell him we had decided to stay at the convent in Maori. "Until next time," he said.

I was sure he was right—there definitely would be a next time. "Come in the off-season—I won't have to charge you so much," he yelled as we hurried across the terrace to catch up with Simon and Luciana so that we could say a proper goodbye.

We bypassed the elevator, knowing we'd have to wait at least a minute for it to appear. We ran down the steps, hoping we might even get there before Simon and Luciana reached the gate. But they weren't there. We were surprised again when we didn't see them the moment we stepped onto the street—how could they have gotten so far ahead of us? Mardi was convinced we'd passed them on the elevator and decided to wait for them. I ran ahead, telling her I'd send out the two-handed owl call—the one that I hadn't used in Maiori—if I saw them.

Once I was through the tunnel—where I'd framed the photograph of the workman the week before—and had a clear shot of the street ahead, I saw them walking cheerfully along as though they had not a care in the world, the same way it had been the morning I thought my missing wallet was going to make us late for the boat to Capri. I stopped mid-stride and put everything I could into my whistle, hoping Mardi would hear me over the morning bustle.

Then I fast-walked and caught Simon and Luciana right at the base of the *Stairway to Heaven*. I ran up a few steps and took a short burst of video as they walked along. They noticed they were being filmed and laughed. Mardi caught up to us as we paused to soak up a bit of the energy of the Piazza Duomo.

"Did you hear my whistle?" I asked.

"Oh, yes. It echoed off the buildings," Mardi said.

"Kind of like the call of Wind in His Hair bouncing off the mountain cliffs in that final scene in *Dances with Wolves* when Lt. Dunbar is leaving," I said, comparing situations, as I often do, to scenes in my favorite movies. And that led to talk of other movies as we walked together through the ancient gate and across the street to the bus stop. Their bus was not ready to board, so we asked a man walking by if he would take a photo of the four of us. He made a nice composition, framing the harbor behind us—a great reminder of our time together.

"Love you guys," I said as we studied the photo of the four of us.

We hugged and exchanged Italian kisses as we said goodbye.

"Take care of this guy," I said to Luciana.

"Look after Marti—she's a keeper," Luciana said.

"Come see us," Mardi said.

"This time next year," Simon said with only a slight rise to his voice as though it were more of a suggestion than a question—and I'm quite sure he meant they would be coming to see us in Amalfi and not Wisconsin.

They disappeared into the surge getting on the bus and I thought *Why not*? Why shouldn't we make a yearly trek to the Amalfi Coast? We stepped back and waited for the bus to pull out before setting our minds to the task of deciding what to do with our day. We had so many options that we decided to return to the Piazza Duomo for inspiration. We climbed halfway up the steps and sat down to take in the grand spectacle.

It would have been easy to spend the whole morning watching people come and go. People-watching anywhere is enjoyable, but Italy raises the bar because the Italian language is so visible—you don't have to hear conversations to get a good sense of what people are talking about. You can watch unobtrusively from a great distance. We dined on what was left of the yogurt, apples, and nuts Maximiliano had given us and played again at being detectives by trying to figure out who was from Italy, who was not, who was on holiday, and who was not.

As we guessed, we also discussed possibilities for our free day on the Amalfi Coast. Minori kept coming up. On Saturday's hike we had not dropped all the way down into the town, fearing we'd be tempted to take the bus back to Maiori instead of hiking the beautiful Path of Lemons. Because of that decision, we'd met the nephew of a ceramicist whose work I was admiring. It was another of those strange pinball rebounds, and today seemed like a good day to see where it would lead us. Giovanni had told us we'd find Vittorio at his shop near the church in the heart of Minori. That seemed to be a bit of serendipity that should be honored. We checked the schedule and discovered that the bus to Minori would depart in ten minutes. We planned to be on it.

We jumped aboard a blue bus labeled "Salerno" in big bold letters. A minute later it pulled out. Like every journey on the Amalfi Coast, this ride was an adventure. My admiration for the drivers of these buses is immense. They are patient. They are skilled. They are diplomatic. They have most likely seen it all. We weren't surprised that the beauty we drove past was stunning— the sheer cliffs, the otherworldly blue of the water far below, the audacity of the visionaries who put homes in the most impossible places commanding views that must surely rival those of heaven, but it was the precision of the drivers on that defiantly audacious road that overwhelmed me during our short journey to Minori.

This was the first time we'd been on an uncrowded bus. We sat on the right side toward the front so that we could observe the driver's facial expressions as he performed his incredible feats. We were disappointed. There were none. His virtuoso performance was completed with quiet aplomb and in fifteen decidedly entertaining minutes we were in Minori. We knew that Vittorio's shop was in the heart of the town, next to the church, and that the beach lay just across the street. We probably could have ridden the bus almost to his doorstep, but we wanted to wander the back streets and alleys to get a feel for his town before meeting him.

On the other hand, we didn't want to get off so early that we'd be forced to walk along the highway to get to the village. The drivers on the Amalfi Coast are skilled, and I was sure they would avoid us, but we didn't want to put their abilities to a test. Once we saw side streets, we pulled the cord and stood up. The bus stopped, but the driver didn't open the back door to let us off. We began walking toward the front. The bus began moving again. We were well underway before the driver noticed us. He stopped the bus at once, but we were nowhere near a bus stop. We hopped off in the middle of the block. That too may have been part of the pinball bounce that led us to Vittorio with a good story to tell.

Across the street we saw the Santa Lucia Hotel and a little farther on down we spied a sharply diagonal pedestrian walkway, but we couldn't get to it, at least not safely. Cars were parked on what should have been sidewalks, and in other places the edge of the highway was the wall of a hotel. So we looked quickly both ways, saw an opening in the flow of traffic, and jumped across the street—literally. Some might accuse me of a bit of hyperbole in that description, but I think it's justified. The Amalfi Coast Highway, as it winds through Minori, is at times about as wide as a tight alleyway.

We ducked down a street beside the Hotel Caporal that was so tight even Cinquecentos were barred—a solid post divided the narrow gap between two buildings into two narrow slivers. The town took on a medieval atmosphere as we stepped carefully on uneven paving stones set millennia ago. I was certain we were nowhere near Vittorio's shop, but some exquisitely colored ceramic bowls displayed in a window drew us in even though we saw no signs proclaiming the pieces were for sale.

A young woman welcomed us with a cheerful *Prego*. As I looked around, I saw that we'd stepped into a workshop. I started to apologize, but the woman offered and we gladly accepted a tour. She showed us many beautiful finished works of art and then picked up a piece that had not yet been fired. She pointed out a section that was gray and said that after the firing it would be green. She explained firings, getting the heat just right, and the thrill of unloading kilns to see what beautiful colors the flames had created.

The colors and the designs on the ceramics bore a strong resemblance to the *numero di casa ceramica* we'd seen on the Path of Lemons. We wondered whether everyone in this region created similar work—whether tourists liked a particular look and that was all the local artists created. We were tempted to buy some pieces, but we wanted to see Giovanni's uncle's shop first. We made no promises to return but we let her know we were impressed.

We continued wandering, letting our interests dictate which street to choose. The window displays attracted our attention, but none tempted us enough to enter the shops. Most of the souvenirs I've brought home from my travels around the world are in storage, so I'm reluctant to buy more. What we found most interesting were the dozens of old photographs displayed throughout the town showing what a very different world the Amalfi Coast was one hundred years ago—dominated by donkeys and people on foot—much of this land was so rugged that it was impassable even by carts. No wonder the streets are so tight.

Eventually our nose for historical photographs led us to the Basilica Santa Trofimena adorned with statues of Matthew, Mark, Luke, and John on the exterior of the church. Our curiosity led us inside. As we fully expected, the church was beautiful and inspiring. The sense of worship the moment we entered was overwhelming. Even without an organ or a choir, I felt I was hearing beautiful music praising God. Fashioning beautiful spaces is in itself a worshipful activity—in the churches of Italy that worship is on full display. Even in a town like Minori, whose very name means *small*, the cathedral was stunningly gorgeous.

Once outside we entered another world worthy of praise—a bright, colorful vista with the Mediterranean Sea stretched out to the horizon. Giovanni had told us that from the steps of the church we'd be able to see his uncle's shop. I figured the best way to introduce ourselves would be show his uncle the *numero di casa ceramica* I had taken a picture of and ask if it was his.

"*É tuo?*" I asked.

"*Si,*" he said. "Yes, that is mine."

He was surprised we had discovered his work so high up in the hills. He was even more surprised when I mentioned his nephew.

"*Sei zio di Giovanni?*"

With a very quizzical look, he said that Giovanni was indeed his nephew. He began asking me questions I couldn't quite understand and probably couldn't have answered in Italian. He tried, I tried, but we weren't getting as far as we wanted to go as fast as we wanted to get there.

"*Scusi,*" he said and went to the door of his shop and shouted, "*Sergio, vieni qui.*"

A few moments later a ponytailed, artistic-looking soul about our age walked through the door. I wasn't surprised when he introduced himself in English. Vittorio turned to me and I told our story in English and Sergio translated. We quickly settled into a comfortable three-way exchange. We learned that Sergio was a graduate of the Rhode Island School of Design in Architecture and that Vittorio, in addition to being a talented ceramicist, was also a farmer, as well as the most respected man in town, according to Sergio, whose opinion I was beginning to trust.

Sergio explained, after Vittorio excused himself to help a customer, that Vittorio often starts his day at four in the morning—walking in the dark to his farm high above Minori—so high that by the time he gets to it he is within a stone's throw of Ravello. After Vittorio completed the sale of what I couldn't help noticing were some gorgeous plates, he rejoined us. I was so moved by what Sergio had told us about Vittorio and his farm that I had the urge to offer our skills as farmers and WWOOFers, not in exchange for a place to stay or a seat at his kitchen table, but just to help him. I pulled enough Italian words together like *work* and *walk* and *farm* and *four* and *morning,* as well as maybe a touch of passion, that Vittorio understood what I was saying.

"*No problemo. Domenica*—Sunday—at nine, not four. You meet me here?" Vittorio asked. "And Sergio too. He can interpret. We work some, then we eat."

I could hardly believe what Vittorio was suggesting—and Sergio and Mardi were agreeing as well. We were all on board. Sunday is of course a day of rest, and my dad had always told me that the work you do on Sunday as a farmer will be lost on Monday. But Dad also told me that you should respect the ways of others—if Vittorio works on Sunday, work alongside him—help him out.

In my excitement I shook Vittorio's hand much too vigorously and discovered why he may have been willing to accept an overly enthusiastic foreigner's help—he was recovering from a broken wrist suffered when he'd fallen off a ladder while pruning trees a few weeks earlier.

When he excused himself again to help people browsing in his show room, I began walking around looking at his work but not really concentrating—I was in a daze, unable to believe our good fortune. Mardi and I were going to prune trees, fix a fence, mend a wall—I wasn't sure—he hadn't been specific— and then sit down to an Italian Sunday dinner. Vittorio had not said it that way—he'd just said we'd eat together, but I know what it means to eat together on Sunday in Italy. And to eat together on a farm on the Amalfi Coast high above Minori—oh my, what must the view from up there be? I couldn't even imagine. I was beyond excited. I was loving the adventure that Mardi and I were on—our honeymoon—but now we were going to connect with an Italian family, just like I'd done on my first sojourn in Italy—Mardi and I were going to get to do it together, and with an affable interpreter—a bit of an independent soul like ourselves—at our side. Our broken record was playing again—this was way too good to be true.

A small car pulled up to the store, so close that it all but blocked the entrance. Vittorio walked to the door and began talking to the driver. She didn't appear to be a customer. It was more like a conversation husbands and wives have—cryptic utterances, most of which I couldn't understand. I did understand enough to know that he'd told her he'd invited a couple of strangers to the farm the next Sunday and that he'd promised them a meal. I also understood enough Italian and enough body language and hand gestures to know that she wasn't excited as I was.

After his wife left and while Vittorio was helping another customer, I interrupted Sergio's conversation with Mardi—they were talking about Colorado, where Sergio apparently had also lived—to ask him about Vittorio's wife's reaction to the news that she was to expect guests next Sunday. He assured me that we were still invited—that she was just being a little dramatic. Just in case Sergio had misread her body language, I told him that we'd understand if Vittorio had to cancel.

I gave Sergio my phone number and email address and let him know I was serious about not being the cause of trouble between Vittorio and his wife. He thanked me and said it was all settled—he would meet us on Sunday right here at the shop. He then excused himself and went about the morning he'd been enjoying before Vittorio called on his skills as an interpreter.

Mardi and I stayed in the shop. We had some choosing to do. We'd fallen in love with Vittorio's work and his bright color palette. We bought small plates and saucers and cups as well as a little turquoise donkey. He told us that because of the area's rough terrain the donkey had become the iconic symbol of the Amalfi Coast. Without *l'asino* to carry materials, the rugged terrain of the Amalfi Coast would still be just that—nature untamed and gorgeous. As a reminder of the beauty of the Amalfi Coast we wanted to take a donkey home with us.

As Vittorio wrapped our pieces we told him about the first shop we had stopped in.

"*Questo è il mio negozio,*" Vittorio said with a touch of pride. No wonder the pieces had looked so much like his—they *were* his. I wanted to offer to help him with his next firing, but I decided that enough good fortune had come our way for one day. I had once made a film about a potter and was familiar with the hard work of firing a wood kiln, but for now lending my back and my experience as a farmer had gotten us more than I had hoped—an invitation to his table. *Don't push your luck, James* my angels, otherwise known as conscience, were telling me.

We paid for our ceramics, said goodbye to Vittorio, and walked as if on a cloud to the beach to bask in our good fortune and wonder what other good things might come our way on this glorious day. For it really was one of those perfect Amalfi Coast spring days—a day for sitting in the sun absorbing the beauty and the sense of history surrounding us. We still had a croissant in my backpack, a couple of sweets, and an apple, which we enjoyed while sitting on a bench watching the day go by. We were surrounded by local people doing exactly what we were doing—appreciating the unique environment where they live. I love that aspect of Italian life. I rarely get the sense that Italians are bored with life. They make each day special—at least that's how it looks to me when I see them talking with such enthusiasm and animation with their neighbors and friends. It is how I've always felt life was meant to be.

We sat there long enough being entertained by the passing parade that we felt it was time for another *cappuccino*. Italian ways are infectious. We crossed back over the Amalfi Coast Highway to the *piazza* in front of the church. Just across the street from Vittorio's I had noticed a little coffee bar with a couple of tables out front. It wasn't quaint or touristy, just well used. While we were looking around Vittorio's shop I had occasionally glanced across the street and saw folks coming and going—stopping by that bar seemed to be a natural part of their day.

While we were checking out places to get a bite to eat, Mardi also looked for a shoulder bag for my laptop—she had grown tired of seeing me wearing a backpack just to carry my computer and a few snacks. I think she was also influenced by the sharp way Italian men dress. She had already bought me a couple of scarves and was insisting that I wrap my sweater around my neck and shoulders rather than carry it in my backpack when it got too warm to wear it. I didn't think she was ever going to succeed in making me look Italian, but she was doing her best to make me look less like a tourist.

She found no man purse for me nor did she find a restaurant that pleased her. I mentioned the coffee bar again and suggested we check it out. "They might have sandwiches or something," I said as we began walking toward it. When we rounded the corner of Vittorio's shop we could see that the tables were no longer overflowing with conversation.

"I don't like it—too dark," Mardi said. "And there's no one in there. Must not be very good."

Actually, one person was inside, and he turned out to be the owner. When he saw us out in the street looking in, obviously trying to make up our minds, he came to the door and said, "Welcome, please come in."

"*Grazie,*" I said and then gave him my best Italian shoulder shrug and said, "It's up to her."

"She's the boss?" he asked.

"She's the boss," I confirmed.

"I know the situation," he said.

"You've been there?" I asked.

"I have three bosses," he said.

"*Three bosses?*"

"One wife—and two daughters."

Mardi laughed.

"Believe me, I UNDERSTAND," he said as he slowly bowed his head toward Mardi and turned his palms up as if to say, *What are you going to do.*

I immediately liked him. He was very quick on his feet. He hadn't missed a beat when I told him his place didn't appear to be making the cut. He also had a warm, enigmatic smile, and there was a playfulness, even orneriness about him.

"But maybe we be back," I said as I hurried to catch up with Mardi, who had already begun walking toward what I presumed was a rather expensive restaurant with dozens of tables directly across the street from Vittorio's. It certainly was prime real estate, commanding a view of the beach from its dozens of awning-covered tables. I was hoping that one glance at the menu would make her reconsider. I also had not yet made my case that a picnic on the boardwalk or the beach would be more in keeping with the character of the day.

"I'm sure he has sandwiches or something," I repeated as Mardi checked out the menu of what we now saw was a pastry shop—a *pasticceria.* I had enjoyed the repartee with the owner of the coffee bar so I made my best pitch. "How about we just grab something from that guy's bar and go listen to the waves crash for a while—maybe even take a nap. It's gotta be cheaper than this place. Look at this—look at the view."

I couldn't help pointing out that there was no one here either. Our rule of choosing places by how popular they appeared was, at that moment, not working.

"Oh, okay. As usual, you win," she said, only half joking.

I pulled her close and gave her a light kiss on her forehead as we began walking back toward the church and the little hole-in-the-wall coffee bar that I could now see was named, of all things, the Bambi Bar.

"Ah, you have come back. *Prego,*" the owner said as he swept his arm in a generous expression of hospitality. He was tall and slender—dark hair, sly smile, twinkling eyes. We introduced ourselves. His name was Michele.

"Would you like the *Welcome to Minori?*" he asked mischievously as he pulled out a jug.

"Is it strong?" I asked.

"No, no—it is from the priest," he said.

"Ah, the priest," I said. I looked around the bar and realized he was not alone. A young woman was also behind the bar. She too was smiling. She probably knew what was about to happen. We didn't.

"This *grappa*—ninety percent—maybe is powerful," he said, pulling the words apart and emphasizing each of them. He then poured me a spoonful.

I put it to my lips. The smell took my breath away. The taste sent shock waves through my body.

Mardi refused the spoonful he poured for her. So he pulled out a match and lit it, then slowly tipped the spoon on its side, letting the flames fall to the countertop, where they quickly spread. The *grappa* continued to burn. He dabbed some on his finger, licked it, and suggested we do the same. I stuck my finger in the flame, quickly got a little on the tip, and tasted it.

"Oh, that's good," I said.

Michele motioned with his whole body for Mardi to do the same.

Reluctantly she reached out her hand toward the edge of the fire, got a little *grappa* on the tip of her finger, then apprehensively licked it.

"It tastes like licorice," she said, relieved.

"No, it is anise," Michele said and smiled. He quickly added, "I'm glad you came back."

"Me too," I said.

"Welcome. What can I get you?"

"You have sandwiches?" I asked.

"No, sorry. Not for another two weeks. No one here," he shrugged.

"Maybe you have hot water for tea?" I asked.

Mardi pulled our insulated drinking cups out of her shoulder bag.

"Yes. I fill for you," he said.

As he heated the water he asked where we were from. And we asked about his family.

"I have two daughters. One who is fourteen, and one who is eight," he said. "So three bosses."

"I have only one daughter. She used to be my boss…"

"Ah, so you know the troubles I have," Michele said as he handed us our insulated mugs filled with steaming water.

"But now that she's married I have only one boss," I said.

"I'm not the boss!" Mardi protested.

"You know Collodi?" Michele asked Mardi.

Mardi had no idea what he was talking about. I did and thought, *This is going to be fun.*

Michele put his thumb and index finger to his nose and pulled them away as though forming a long Pinocchio nose—a playful way for him to let Mardi know he wasn't buying her story—he knew that in the end the women in his life were his bosses. And he could imagine the same thing in mine.

"That's my wife—she's the boss," Michele said, motioning toward the woman I'd noticed earlier who looked almost young enough to be his daughter, but then I remembered he'd said his daughters were eight and fourteen. She didn't look that young.

"She runs things?" I asked.

"She's the first boss," Michele said.

Mardi shook her head. She didn't like where this story had been or where it was going.

"I have a hard life," he continued.

"You don't have a hard life," I said making the judgment call that his first boss looked quite amiable, as well as pretty.

"Believe me, I have a hard life. I am Italian. I live in Italy. I have three bosses—believe me, believe me," he said as he wiped off the countertop now that the *grappa* had burned itself out. "I am a son. I have a mother who wanted me to be a priest—she sent me to *seminario*," he continued.

"What about your brother?" I asked. "Surely you had a brother."

"My brother? Like me—he has a war in his head," Michele said.

I laughed at that, knowing the desire of Italian mothers to have a least one priest in the family.

"I started in seminary," Michele said.

"How long did you study?" I asked.

"Not too much before I escaped," Michele quipped.

"You escaped before they got you?"

"*Si,* I escaped to this."

I was having a great time, but Mardi not so much. She grabbed some black pepper sea salt chips and a couple of Ritter bars and set them on the counter. I gave Michele a ten euro note and got far more in change than I expected. We chose a table outside near the front door. We discovered the water was so hot we needed cups so we could sip the tea. I walked back in and asked if we could get a couple of cups, however I did it in Italian.

"No, my friend. I do not think you need a couple of taxis," he said.

I squinted my eyes at him and cocked my head, wondering what was coming next. He obviously delighted in perplexing me. I'd been right in guessing that he had a bit of an ornery streak, as my mom used to say of people she didn't quite trust.

"*Tazze,*" he said putting a huge emphasis on the double zz's and changing my "ee" to "eh." I knew that *tazza* was cup, and *tazze* was cups, but I had made it sound more like *tazzi,* which is very close to *taxi* in English.

Michele put in front of me three cups. "A baby bear cup, a mama bear cup, and a papa bear *tazza,*" he said.

I chose the two he had called *cups*—the baby bear and the mama bear.

"Grazie mille," I said. I gave him my best ornery smile and turned to take the cups to Mardi and tell her what I'd learned about Italian, and the need to get every syllable and every sound just right, as though I were Goldilocks looking for the *just right* bed.

I was in heaven relaxing outside the Bambi Bar, watching the townspeople come and go, sipping tea, nibbling on chocolate bars and knowing that on Sunday we'd be sitting down at the table of the person Sergio said was the most interesting, most beloved man in all of Minori.

"You got a little too excited, Jim. You almost broke Vittorio's wrist again when you were shaking his hand."

She was right. I'd given Vittorio a solid farmer's handshake, I suppose partly out of exuberance and partly to convince him that I was strong enough to be of some help on his farm, but apparently I'd overdone it. Sergio later assured me that no damage had been done—at least no *permanent* damage.

But Mardi was not done. She had another bone to pick with me.

"You also got a little crazy in there with Michele," she said.

"I wanted him to know I appreciated his *grappa*," I said.

"Well you certainly did that," she said.

But maybe she wasn't referring to the *grappa* as much as to the storytelling—to the painting of her as a domineering type, which she of course is not.

I had loved the exchange. It seemed so typically—stereotypically—Italian. The hospitality was there, the sharing of a drink, the husband as a macho man who is in reality dominated by the women in his life—and a mother who wanted him to be a priest. It was all there, even a reference to Italy's beloved author Collodi, who wrote perhaps the most insightful book ever about the nature of Italian people.

All Americans know the character he created, but not many Americans know the name of the man who wrote the story about the puppeteer, Giuseppe, who created the puppet who came to life. They think Walt Disney was responsible for the beloved Pinocchio, but it was Carlos Collodi who created the mischievous puppet, who has delighted Italian readers in the four-hundred-seventy-five-page edition—not the thirty-five-page Golden Books version that has been read to American children for seventy-five years or the movie we've been watching for fifty-five years. In the original Italian the reader is subtly made aware of the passion of Italian people for openness, sincerity, and honesty.

"This is pleasant," I said surveying our surroundings. We could see the ocean from where we were sitting. We could see Vittorio's shop. The sun was shining. Like Michele had said, we were the only tourists around, and we were getting to know the character and characters of another Italian town. The music

Michele was playing matched the feeling of the day. It may have had the same effect as the music I choose for my spinning classes at the YMCA—it gets the class ready to commit to exercising. Maybe the music Michele plays pumps him up for his daily exchanges with his customers.

"*Grazie Dio*, thank you, God, for this day," I said, acutely aware of the grace that had flowed our way as I watched Vittorio close up his shop, walk across the *piazza*, and presumably head off for his afternoon nap, *il suo sonnellino*.

"And thanks for the tea," Mardi said showing appreciation for the pragmatic pleasures of our days. We were in no hurry. We were where we wanted to be. Mardi pulled out a sandwich and an apple she had packed and we enjoyed a light lunch on Minori's main square. Michele, after helping a woman with a broken arm get into her car, stopped by our table to chat. We asked him how to find the Path of Lemons to Maiori.

"You must go behind the church, it is long steps—very hard," he cautioned.

We told him the story of our first hike on the Path of Lemons—that we had hiked round-trip between Maiori and Minori, but we had not dropped down into the streets of Minori. He immediately became less concerned that we were biting off more than we could chew.

"Ah very good—*perfetto*," he said.

We told him we'd see him again, although we didn't tell him why.

"When you come back, I will be very happy to see you again," he said.

We left Michele, walked behind the church, found the stairs, and were on the way to Maiori accompanied by the sounds of a high school band practicing, sounding much like I remembered mine sounding—slightly out of tune, even discordant at times.

"What a wonderful story. Finally we find a piece of art that we like, and it's by someone who is also a farmer..." Mardi said.

"The most beloved man in town," I added, remembering again what Sergio had said about Vittorio.

"Someone we're going to work for," she added.

We were reeling from all the good fortune coming our way. I was no longer disappointed that all my months of searching for a farm had yielded nothing.

"I love you so much—can I give you a kiss?" I asked.

"No, I just put on lipstick," Mardi said, then gave me a big kiss.

We gained elevation quickly and were soon where we'd been before. I turned and looked toward the sea. "Look at those fishing boats. See the blue one sitting there? Isn't that beautiful?" I said, thrilled to be walking once again high above the Amalfi Coast.

"Two days ago when we went by here, I was really tired. I was ready to take a break," Mardi said.

"Did we?" I asked.

"Yes, we sat right over there on that wall and studied the map while we looked out at the beautiful view," she replied.

"Oh yeah. We got a drink here, too. I remember the handle on that spigot—it sprayed me."

"Vittorio's place is just up there around the corner. I was waiting just beyond, wondering what had happened to you," she went on.

"Up around this corner—right?" I asked, the details of that long walk beginning to come back to me.

"Here we are," I said a few minutes later when I saw Vittorio's gate, but this time there was no Giovanni and there were no cats to photograph, but I stopped to see if I could improve on the photo I'd taken of the *numero di casa ceramica*.

Mardi walked ahead to sit down where she had waited before. That is the lot of a wife married to a photographer who likes his compositions to have just the right elements in the right positions. She has learned to live with my idiosyncrasies as I have with hers.

I joined her and offered her a fig bar, in case she, like me, was beginning to run short of energy. While we were sharing it I realized we were hearing the faint sound of donkeys braying far off in the distance. We had heard them before when we were out hiking but unlike Simon and Luciana, we'd never met a donkey train or even a lone donkey on the trail.

"Maybe today will be *our* day," I said.

Unlike Saturday, when we rested in this same spot and talked to at least a dozen people, on this day no one came by. Intrigued by the braying of the donkeys echoing off the hills, we began walking toward where we thought the sounds were coming from.

We were passing by familiar scenes—places I'd photographed on our first hike, framed by the beautiful purple blossoms of wisteria plants.

"Those donkeys have to be right over there, but I don't see them," Mardi said.

We couldn't figure out why we couldn't see the animals that were making a sound so loud we were feeling it, not just hearing it.

"In these hills, the sound could be bouncing off anything," I rationalized.

And indeed it was. We broadened our search to where the sound *didn't* seem to be coming from and saw in a pasture just below us, four *asine* that were as excited as we were by the sound of donkeys on the trail. Donkeys, like horses, especially those that are confined, get a little bit crazy when they see some of their own kind running free.

I stopped to study the penned-up donkeys. I looked where they were looking and finally saw what we had been hoping to see since we had first set foot on the trails of the Amalfi Coast: donkeys doing what they've been doing for thousands of years—carrying the supplies and food that make it possible to live in these very beautiful but extremely remote, even treacherous hills. These sure-footed animals made possible the house Vittorio enjoys high on the hills above the Amalfi Coast. No wonder he celebrates the *asino* in his ceramics. I was glad I had one of Vittorio's donkeys in my backpack.

"There they are, Mardi, can you see them?" I asked and pointed across the valley.

Their colors were blending almost perfectly into the hillside. When she finally saw them she began worrying that they were on a different path. I had been studying their movements as they worked their way across the hill and was certain we'd soon encounter them. I followed the contour of the path with my eyes and saw a wide spot in the trail at a corner. But the donkeys were closer to it than we were. Mardi and I began jogging. My plan was to get there before the donkeys, step off the trail, and turn on my phone's video recorder. I knew I'd never forget this moment, but I wanted film, to use the old-fashioned term, to cut into promotional videos for my books. I was also feeling the thrill that I experienced for so many decades as a documentary filmmaker when I was able to come home with a scene that told the quintessential story of a location.

I was certain the donkeys were used to encountering people on the trail, so I didn't think our presence would bother them if they were able to get by us. As we got closer to the wide spot we could see a slightly elevated ledge off to the side. That would be perfect—we could step up and off the trail, and neither the donkeys nor the teamster would even have to break stride as they passed by.

But we now had another problem—I couldn't tell who was winning this race. The donkeys were approaching a corner—and we were approaching a corner. We couldn't see around it, but we could see where the penned-up animals were looking. We felt we still had a chance if we kept jogging. The path had become even tighter—a wall on one side, a drop-off on the other. This was going to be an Amalfi Coast Highway–like dance of the buses if we didn't get to that wide spot in time.

The braying suddenly became piercingly loud, the rock walls around us apparently creating an echo chamber. I was afraid to look toward the donkeys, afraid I'd see that they had won the race. But I got to the ledge first and stepped up. As I turned slowly to look, it hit me why the sound was so loud—the donkeys *were in* an echo chamber—they were just emerging from a tunnel created by the wall of a three story house on one side, and the sheer rock wall of the mountain on the other. I cautiously raised my phone to chest height and began recording.

One donkey, two donkeys, three donkeys…the teamster saw us, and in one graceful motion hopped up on the back of the lead animal to ride sidesaddle, his legs pointing to the inside, where we were. The lead animal showed no fear, barely looking at us as he walked by. I wasn't so blasé. The back of my neck was tingling. These weren't donkeys taking tourists to the bottom of the Grand Canyon—they were most likely the progeny of animals who had for thousands of years been walking along these trails delivering the necessities of life. I liked that.

"*Buongiorno*," the teamster said as he passed.

"*Buongiorno*," I replied quietly. He was riding comfortably, an enigmatic smile on his face as though he was surprised by the deference we were according him. The moment reminded me of people spreading their cloaks on the road as Jesus rode into Jerusalem on the back of a donkey.

I panned the camera with the last donkey as it walked past—I was surprised there were only three. Their loads were securely lashed with rope and covered with burlap and leather. I couldn't tell exactly what they were carrying but it looked like building materials and one extremely heavy piece of metal.

"Perfect—wow," I whispered to Mardi, and then to God I said, "Thank you, Lord."

"That was on my bucket list," Mardi said as we breathlessly watched the donkeys climbing high above us.

"Oh, look, he's making a delivery to that guy up there," I said. "He just dropped the last burrow off and kept going. I bet he'll stop by on the way back to pick him up. That's efficient."

"We'll have to let Simon and Luciana know we got to see donkeys on the trail," Mardi said.

"You said we had to buy a donkey from Vittorio for luck. I'd say it worked," I said. "That couldn't have been better."

We stood and watched until they disappeared from sight and the penned-up animals settled down. But *we* couldn't settle down—we were still gushing about what we'd just seen. Except for the sound of the wind and the birds, we could hear nothing. The silence seemed to intensify our elation. The moment was ours alone.

I uttered a heartfelt *Wow!*

"What a day!" Mardi added.

She was right. It wasn't just the donkey sighting. This day was going to color our whole impression of the Amalfi Coast—of Italy, for that matter. Our pinball had bounced us to an invitation to a Sunday celebration with an Italian family. We stayed on our high and so did the trail as we worked our way across the hillside. For the longest time we were looking down at the green and yellow dome that dominates Maiori. In the intense afternoon light I took some photos of the church and then began descending quickly. The first person I saw gave me a big wave as I was walking down the steps of Santa Maria. *"Bella giornata,"* he yelled as he rode by on a bicycle. It was Mirko, Jessica's brother.

"Beautiful day, indeed," I yelled back as I stepped onto Corso Reginna. Mardi, as usual, was a bit ahead of me.

"Nice to be welcomed back to town by the manager of our favorite bar," I said to Mardi when I reached her side—she was waiting on the bench where we'd eaten lunch a couple of days earlier.

"Did you say hello to Josef?" Mardi asked.

"I didn't see him."

"He was carrying a ladder up the steps." He was the man who had ushered us into the inner sanctum of the church on our first hike on the Path of Lemons.

"Bummer. Missed him," I said, remembering that the beautiful photo I'd taken of the back of his church was the reason I hadn't seen him.

Just as I said that, Mario bicycled past. He gave us an extra-hearty wave. He should have asked if we were going to join him for pizza, but he didn't.

"Wow, what an incredible day," I said as we watched him ride by in his inimitable style toward the promenade. He was quickly becoming one of my favorite characters in Maiori—a larger-than-life personality I was certain I would never forget.

A moment later one high-pitched bell rang followed by three low-pitched pealings, telling us that if we wanted to find a man purse we had best get looking. We walked toward the promenade where that morning we'd noticed, just across the street from Le Suite, a shop that looked like it sold suitcases. We'd start our search there.

We didn't have to go any farther. We walked in, and Antonio greeted us. We told him what we were looking for. He showed us a few shoulder bags he had on display, but none of them seemed right. I pulled out my computer, and his face lit up.

"*Scusi, un momento,*" he said and disappeared into the basement. A minute later he returned with what he felt would be the *borsa da uomo perfetta* for me. And was he ever right. It was just big enough for my MacBook to fit horizontally. Antonio was pleased that it pleased me. We were amazed that we had found the perfect computer bag, but it was more than that. It was, of course, Italian-designed, and as we studied it we realized it could serve as my office on the go—carrying my MacBook as well as my Italian phrasebook, billfold, journal, pens, highlighters, and iPhone—everything I needed to write, film, photograph, and research.

"You want to walk along the beach?" Mardi asked as we walked out of the store with her attempt to make me look a little less like a tourist. She insisted I sling it over my shoulder, Italian-style. I did and she was right, it did feel good. However, I also had on the backpack I wore as I biked around Tuscany, so I probably didn't look that much different. Seven years before I thought I looked like an adventurer. Actually, I didn't care what I looked like. It was the most practical backpack I had ever owned, it had a protected sleeve for my computer—it was perfect for providing an office to live out of while biking. But I was no longer biking, and Mardi was right to want me to have a different office—one that was smaller and more stylish. And as Michele had noted, I had learned that Mardi is the boss—clear evidence that I am at least a little smarter than I was a half dozen or so years ago.

I didn't say anything to Mardi about all this—I just told her I wanted to fill my mug with cold water. That would put us on the other side of the Amalfi Coast Highway—into a very different world—a world where my strongest desire was to walk along the beach. And that is exactly what we did until one of the promenade's comfortable benches, a bench in full sun, called our name.

"My feet hurt," Mardi said as we sat down.

"Let me massage them," I said, kneeling in front of her.

"Oh, that's perfect. Rub my ankle—that's what hurts," she said.

Immediately we attracted a feathered crowd. One pigeon was strutting around as if to say *Look at me, ain't I pretty.* But we didn't share any food. A man nearby did, so we quickly lost our admirers.

"Okay, that's all the fun you get to have with my feet," Mardi said.

She never lets me massage her as long as I let her massage me. It isn't even close. I don't know whether she doesn't enjoy it as much as I do or whether she feels guilty having all the attention. I never feel guilty. That's the difference between us. Well, that's not entirely true that I *never* feel guilty, but rarely do I let guilt keep me from enjoying one of Mardi's fantastic massages.

"People think we're so cute together, so lovey-dovey," she said.

At first I thought Jessica had come to mind, but maybe someone had walked by who had seen me rubbing her feet, and she felt self-conscious. As I reluctantly quit, she confirmed my suspicions.

"Thank you. I get uncomfortable with so much attention," she explained.

I got up, sat down beside her, and gave her a hug.

"Look at that," she said, her face aglow with the evening light.

"You mean that boat dancing on sparkling water?" I asked.

It was one of those moments when the interplay between water and the angle of the sun's rays turns the surface of the ocean into thousands of points of light.

"You like it here?" I asked.

She smiled.

"A one-block walk to the beach, people all over town waving to us, and donkeys," I said, reciting a few of the things I knew were making her feel good about Maiori.

"It's a lot prettier than Rome—palm trees, beach…" Mardi said.

I was surprised she'd brought up Rome. She loved it there. We'd seen Trevi Fountain, the Pantheon, the Spanish Steps, the Colosseum, the Roman Forum, Piazza Navona, and St. Peter's Basilica, but the memory of all the people we'd met and the waves crashing on the shore were giving the edge to the Amalfi Coast. All of a sudden her thoughts turned from the beauty of Maiori to feelings that were miles away from where mine were.

"I'm just not much good for you. I don't write anything, I can't speak Italian. How can I be more helpful? I will try to be some earthly good," Mardi said.

It's funny how in sync our thoughts are at times. She'll mention a letter I should write to a relative or friend whose name has not come up for months, and I'll realize that I had, only moments before, been feeling guilty for not having written that person. I had been sitting there thinking how good life is with Mardi—how much more I was enjoying Italy on this journey because she was at my side.

I did my best to assure her of my appreciation for all that she brings to our partnership, to our marriage. I was able to bring her attention back to the beauty of the day and our love of the Amalfi Coast. We began listing all the people we had met. That list confirmed that we liked it here because of the welcome we received from the people. Not once had I ever felt they welcomed us to encourage us to buy something—it always seemed as if they truly enjoyed having us among them. So many exchanges backed up that feeling, whether it was Salvatore, Vincenzo, Luigi, Jessica, Michele, or Vittorio.

The *passeggiata* reached full flower while we were reminiscing. I jotted notes on my phone and took the occasional photo. Groups of four, six, and sometimes eight or more strolled along the Via G Capone boulevard. I loved the sounds of their animated conversations punctuated by the roar of the surf. We stayed on the promenade enjoying the parade until the chill air persuaded us to switch to the other routine that had come to define the end of each of our days in Maiori. We walked to Le Suite and asked Jessica about eating across the street, at Dedalo, but she asked us to dine with her, offering to serve us. We agreed. The jazz music matched our mood, and we'd have the comfort of *our table*—the food would come from Dedalo, the service from Jessica—that was an offer we couldn't refuse.

We ordered our usual—a margherita pizza and a mixed salad—a meal we never seemed to tire of. The place was full of life and good music that night as always. We loved the feeling of belonging that always came over us the moment we sat down in Le Suite. That is probably why we didn't keep yesterday's promise to Mario to eat his pizza.

"I'm so happy," Mardi said.

"I can tell. It's written all over your face," I said.

"*La vostra pizza,*" said a woman we'd seen in the bar but not met as she served our pizza. We had expected Jessica to deliver it, but she had suddenly become extremely busy. Every table was filled. Someone we didn't know shouted "*Buonasera*" to us.

"I love you," Mardi said. She was paying forward the good feelings we had received.

"I'd say we've had another good day," I said as we toasted each other and our day.

Luigi walked by and I told him he looked like a million bucks. He didn't understand the idiom, so I looked it up online. It didn't translate well—the website translated the phrase literally—no wonder he looked so confused.

"What are you still smiling about?" Mardi asked.

"I'm writing Luciana and Simon—telling them about seeing the donkeys on the trail."

Jessica also noticed me smiling and stopped to ask why I was so happy. I told her about our day and then asked her who had delivered our pizza. That's when I had to bring out a pad and pencil—names of relatives began flying so fast I couldn't keep up. Siandra had brought us the pizza. I had seen her around the bar before but had no inkling that she and Mirko were married, or that Jessica was engaged to Giovanni, who also worked at Le Suite, but was of course *not* Giovanni the nephew of Vittorio. Jessica's parents were still alive and living in Maiori, and she had a another brother named Jonathan.

"He is my *tween*," she informed us. "His English is very good. He is very beautiful."

I smiled, thinking she was also complimenting herself, until I realized that it's impossible for twins of the opposite sex to be identical. Even if she had been declaring herself beautiful I wouldn't have argued, but I would have kidded her about it—and then I would have wondered whether she would understand the word *kidding.*

"*Sorella?* Do you have a sister?" I asked.

"*Si,* Anna. She works here, too. At Dedalo's, she's the boss there. Mirko's the boss here," she said and motioned toward her brother, who had just come into the bar.

"He stands like a boss, you know what I mean?" I said, noticing the confidence he exuded.

"Very handsome," Mardi said.

"I think *she's* the boss," Jessica said, indicating with an Italian shift of her eyes that she was referring to Mardi.

"Funny you should say that. I told someone that very thing just today—that I work for Mardi—that my job is to keep my boss happy."

"You and her are *simpatico*," Jessica said.

"We are in love," I said.

"*Quanti anni matrimonio?*"

"*Quarantasei anni*," I said.

"Oooh," she said, her eyes widening in surprise.

"Just forty-six years—we are newlyweds," I said.

Jessica looked at us in wide-eyed amazement tinged with tender regard. She wasn't certain she'd heard me right—she didn't think we were old enough to have been married that long. I suddenly realized that the music was matching her observations about us.

You'll never find, as long as you live
Someone who loves you tender like I do.
You'll never find, no matter where you search
Someone who cares about you the way I do
You'll never find someone to understand you like I do—
You'll never find the rhythm, the rhyme, all the magic we shared, just us two.

The sexy, dreamy voice of Lou Rawls was filling the room.

"We are on our honeymoon—do you know the word *honeymoon*?" I asked.

"Very difficult," she said.

"It's when you first get married you go..." I started.

"Ah—*luna di miele*," Jessica and Siandra, who had joined our discussion, spoke as one, telling us that the Italian translation is very literal—*the moon of honey.*

"Two days after we were married I was in the army—no time for *luna di miele*. Then we were too busy making babies," I joked.

"How many?" Jessica asked.

"*Cinque bambinos,*" I said.

"*Allora,*" Jessica said.

It's a word that I love hearing Italians say because it can carry so much meaning. Her face told me that again she was surprised. She asked about our kids, and I did the best I could to describe them while sticking to Italian. She was especially interested to know that we too had a Jonathan. After my somewhat embarrassing attempt to tell them about our family in *italiano*, a discussion that I didn't fully understand began. Jessica either said that I spoke Italian well or that she hopes to speak English good. We began discussing the differences between well and good—the conversation turned technical—about adjectives and adverbs. It seemed that she had paid me a compliment rather than patting herself on the back, but who knows. It was a delightfully fun conversation no matter what she had meant or said.

Jessica ran to the bar and brought out her language book—a thick tome on English. Our conversation had piqued her curiosity. We made promises that night to teach each other two words each day. Mardi and I planned to try to teach her idioms—things she might not find in her big, heavy book. When Jessica had switched from being a student to once again being a *barista*, I said to Mardi, "Isn't it amazing how much fun it is knowing a little bit of Italian?" Our extended conversations about family, and Italian/English lessons, and idioms had drawn a large crowd around our table as one person after another became curious about our animated discussion and joined in.

"What time is it?" I asked, wondering how long we'd been talking family and language. I guessed we'd been at it the better part of an hour.

"Eight-fifteen" Mardi said, confirming my hunch.

"We could go to bed early tonight," I suggested.

"I don't know—it rarely happens. Something always keeps us up."

Ten minutes later we found out what that something was.

"*Marmellata* and *crema*," Siandra said as she placed a croissant with marmalade and cream cheese in front of us. I didn't know whether Mardi had ordered it or whether it had just appeared, and I didn't ask. I was getting used to food appearing at just the right time. We knew the croissants were delicious and would perfectly complement the Earl Grey tea—the *Whittington's* Earl Grey tea that she also had just served. We thanked her and began to *count the ways* à la Elizabeth Barrett Browning.

And that is how another glorious day on the Amalfi Coast ended. We didn't get to bed early. We stayed at our table counting and chatting with Jessica about love and marriage, munching again on the best-tasting croissants we'd ever eaten, enjoying easy-listening music like that of Michael Bublé singing "Haven't Met You Yet." The lyrics resonated with me that night even if the title of the song didn't, for I *have* met her, and that someday for me has come.

> And I know someday that it'll all turn out
> You'll make me work so we can work to work it out
> And I promise you kid, that I'll give so much more than I get

That is certainly what I felt Maiori and the Amalfi Coast were giving us— more than we were giving. We were leaving some money in these delightful towns, but we were getting in return things money can't buy. We were being given the chance to look at ourselves, and our marriage, through the eyes of a young woman whose own romantic fantasies had been piqued by the relationship she observed between Mardi and me.

What a gift!

CHAPTER TWELVE

Casa Raffaele Conforti ~ Tuesday April 12 ~ 46 & Partly Cloudy

Steinbeck Fell in Love Too

Tourists don't know where they've been,
travelers don't know where they're going.
PAUL THEROUX

∎

Positano bites deep. It is a dream place that isn't quite real
when you are there and becomes beckoningly real after you have gone.
JOHN STEINBECK

*E*ven on days when we left our room thinking we knew where we were going, we often didn't get there. The pinball deflection this morning came from a rather frail but friendly-looking woman in dark clothes waiting for a bus. I confirmed with her that this was the correct stop for *l'autobus* Sorrento. She was interested in where we were from and where we were staying and where we were going. I shared all of it with her as best as I could in Italian. She shared thoughts with us about where we should sit on various legs of the ride and then suggested something that ended up changing our day. She recommended that instead of getting off in Positano on the way to Sorrento, we should save Positano for the return trip. She told me—with a twinkle in her eye—that the light would be much better that time of day. Italians revere beauty. Even the quintessential little old Italian *vedova* has a photographer's eye for the best light.

We took her advice about where to sit, and the best time of the day to photograph Positano, and decided that riding a bus all the way to Sorrento and back was risky—we might miss the good light. So we got off *before* we reached Positano—in the little village of Praiano, another town we had never heard of.

We thought we might find a walking path to Positano, but if we didn't, we had our ride-all-you-want tickets—we'd just hop back on the bus. But wherever our pinball got flipped, we hoped to arrive in Positano mid-afternoon and wander its up-and-down streets as the sun inched its way toward the horizon. We planned to take advantage of the beautiful light reflecting off the Tyrrhenian Sea that our delightful guardian angel had promised us.

No one got off the bus with us—no one to flip our pinball so we began walking toward the tallest building, which in an Italian village is invariably the cathedral. Next to it we found a small *piazza* with a graceful statue of Padre Pio and a place to sit down while we got acquainted with Praiano via guidebook.

"There's a beach down there somewhere," Mardi said.

"Do you want to eat first or walk down?" I asked, feeling that the hike could be significant considering how high we were. We were looking down at Positano, which we could see across the bay, its pastel colors painting the hills.

"I feel like walking," she said.

"Me, too. I've been sitting long enough."

I topped off our bottles in the water fountain. It was not even noon yet, but the day was already uncomfortably warm—our first taste of humidity on the Amalfi Coast.

"I think we'll find a restaurant down there," Mardi said.

"Think it will be open? Michele said no tourists yet."

We certainly weren't seeing any tourists in Praiano, but we saw plenty of evidence they were coming. The hike to the beach, following *Alla Spiaggia* signs, was well marked at every place where a tourist might be tempted to wander the wrong direction.

Mardi was soon ahead of me. Not only was I taking pictures, I was also pausing each time I felt a cooling breeze blow through the trees. As usual, she wondered why I was so slow.

"I'm trying to not sweat, but I don't think it's possible. These jeans are too hot." While she was listening to my excuses, I caught up with her and lightened my load by placing my Italian hat on her head.

"That looks better on you than it does on me," I said. She looked stunningly stylish, her long dark hair set off by the soft white of the wide brim. I also pulled off my long-sleeved shirt, which I had worn to keep from getting sunburned, but sunlight was hitting us only in flickering patches as the wind jostled the branches high above us.

We were in what could best be described as a tropical forest complete with the songs of many birds. Their brilliant plumage and full-throated songs captivated me. I suddenly understood the drive of birdwatchers to categorize their sightings as I watched what I presumed were warblers flitting about.

When we got to the beach, which wasn't so much a beach as a place to swim, we discovered that there were tourists in Praiano—three to be exact. A young girl of seven or eight was swimming in the cool water. We opened a conversation with her parents in Italian. They spoke to us in French. Mardi and I were delighted to discover that we had retained a bit of conversational French from our high school studies.

The setting was dramatic—reminding me of a quarry—huge blocks of stone to sun on. An overturned rowboat provided a colorful foreground for a shot of Positano in the distance and reminded me of my own wooden boat at home and how much I would love to take it out each morning on these beautiful waters to watch the sun rise—just as I used to do on Phantom Lake back in Wisconsin. I was really dreaming. Not only was I envisioning myself living in Italy, but my bicycle and my 14-foot Lyman wooden boat were with me as well.

Even though we stopped often, the hike back up to the heart of Praiano was a good workout. Just before reaching the church we stopped to talk to some workmen. They told us the tourists were coming—they had less than a week to finish their work.

The *trattoria* we chose for lunch definitely wasn't crowded, but I'm sure it's extremely popular in the summer, with its view of the islands dotting the bay and boats small and large creating silver streaks in the deep blue water, and all of it framed by lemons hanging down from the awnings. But on this day we shared the striking vista with only one other couple.

We chose our usual fare, recalling our promise to cut back in order to afford our stay in the convent, which turned our conversation to the interiors of the churches we'd seen on this trip and how beautiful each had been, even in small towns like Minori and Anacapri. We began wondering how impressed we will be when we finally see the interior of Saint Peter's Basilica. During our four days in Rome we saw almost everything we wanted, but we didn't want to stand in line, so Saint Peter's and the Sistine Chapel are still on our must-see list.

We walked all over Rome—not once did we take a taxi or a bus. Ours was an intimate look at the city, talking to the residents of Trastevere, the Ghetto, the Quirinale. We also learned that it's very easy to get turned around in Rome. We never felt lost, but rarely did we take the shortest route from one attraction to another. We left the Spanish Steps thinking we were heading toward the Trevi Fountain, but we ended up in Piazza Navona. We didn't much care, though. We knew we could see it another day. Good thing, too—had we found it that first day it would still have been shrouded in the scaffolding of an almost two-year, two-million-euro restoration.

Our pinball got flipped there a couple of days later, just in time for the fountain's grand reopening, but we knew nothing of it. We happened on it while wandering the city and thought the place was always that crowded. We didn't know that for two years tourists hadn't been able to throw coins into the fountain, which of course left them wondering whether they would ever return to the Eternal City. We could have made certain *our* return by tossing coins over our shoulders, but instead we spent our money at a nearby *gelateria*. A great tasting *gelato* has, I'm sure, brought a lot of people back to Roma over the years.

As we finished reliving our Rome adventure—and a few minutes later our meal, I said, *"Sono pieno"* and immediately thought of Maximiliano pushing out his tummy. We'd eaten everything we'd been served, but it had taken a lot of time—exactly how much I didn't know. I knew only that the other diners had left long ago.

"We have ten minutes to get to the bus," Mardi said. I suppose we could have taken the next one and continued talking about Rome, but we had promised our guardian angel that we'd arrive in Positano with the good light, so we paid for our meal and crossed the street to the bus stop. The town was busier now. Folks of all ages were approaching the bus stop. Most of the younger people went right on by, presumably heading home—many of them riding skateboards.

The ride to Positano was quick and uneventful, if you can consider any trip on the Amalfi Coast Highway uneventful. We were almost getting used to the stunning beauty, the narrow misses—cars coming to a complete stop to let us pass. We decided to ride through Positano and get out high on the Sorrento side, just as we'd done in Minori, and walk down to the beach. We took a look at the map before we got off the bus, then packed it away—planning to follow our interests to the seashore, heading down whichever streets looked interesting.

The first thing that captured our attention was a very colorful, very narrow park that appeared to be cantilevered out over the steep cliffs of Positano. It was surrounded by a tall iron fence to keep children from tumbling out. A couple of moms were chatting while watching their kids scurry from the slide to the rocking frog to the swimming fish, each painted in a different primary color. The scene was made even more vibrant because the women were wearing colors even brighter than the play equipment—an orchid pullover for one and a bright blue blouse for the other—and all of it set off against the pastel hues of the houses and hotels climbing the steep ravine on the other side of Positano.

We kept walking, kept working our way downward, choosing the smallest, most interesting street at every corner. Not far from the park we discovered a stairway that seemed public, even though it was barely wider than the stairs leading to a typical American basement. We followed it down the

hill and were delighted to turn a corner and see before us a bright yellow door surrounded by pots of flowers equally as vivid as the scene we had just encountered in the park—reds, yellows, whites, blues, and that bright rich purple of orchid again. Above the door was a bit of a portico and a half moon window with a welcoming light beyond. The photo I took of that home's front door looked so inviting that it soon became one of the most viewed and admired photos I've ever put on *An Italian Journey*'s Facebook page. Within a couple of months it had been *liked* by a half million people, and its popularity shows no sign of tapering off.

We kept working our way down until we came to a street wide enough for cars and began following it as it contoured slowly downward. We stopped to talk with an elderly man sitting in front of a grocery store. I think he said his name was Alessandro, but we were having as much trouble understanding him as he was understanding us. However, the expressions of his body, hands, and face, as well as his demeanor, told us we were speaking with a warm and loving man. We eventually developed a bit of an ear for the way he spoke and came to understand that this *alimentari* had been here for a very long time and that he had retired but still loved sitting in front of his shop greeting his customers every day.

We were enjoying chatting with him, but we didn't want to keep him from his regulars so we moved on. Everywhere I looked I saw another colorful scene to photograph, many with flowers in the foreground. Even the bright yellow signs of the Agip gas station made a pretty picture when composed with the saffron yellow of a flower box of daisies in the foreground. I've never seen a town so in love with colors, and so proud of them—yet somehow they blend into a harmonious whole. The town is without a doubt, a photographer's delight.

I suppose many would say it's a shopper's delight as well, and a diner's delight. We can't speak with authority on dining other than to say that our *gelato* was as good as any we had tasted. Mostly we just walked and browsed. The art fair along a vine-covered promenade was particularly appealing, as were the *ceramica* shops, full of color and cheerful designs. The Cathedral of Santa Maria Assunta was more gorgeous inside than out—stunningly beautiful. The light pouring in the windows was, as one would hope, heavenly.

We left the church and headed for the beach, which was colorful too. Bright yellow kayaks and the hulls of overturned boats made us think of summer even though only a few people were sitting on the shore and even fewer were in the water. I offered to take a portrait of a Chinese couple struggling to compose a selfie that included their hotel in the background.

"Perfect—we like it—thank you." They gave me huge smiles. It seems everyone can speak at least a little English.

A couple from Denmark heard them praise the photo and asked me to do the same for them. Instead of a selfie of Mardi and me I chose to commemorate the beach in Positano by composing a dog sleeping in the foreground near the water's edge and the iconic green and gold cupola of Santa Maria in the background. I should have shot the selfie.

As we made our way back into town, past all the artists with their easels painting portraits of Positano, I noticed John Steinbeck's name on a ceramic attached to the wall of the Hotel Buca di Bacco. I was thrilled—I had been hoping to find the apartment where the author had stayed in 1952 when, as he described, Positano was *a sleepy fishing village*. Steinbeck found in that

little room on the beach, what I have been dreaming about finding for much of my life.

It was terribly hot in Rome the summer of '52—a friend, Alberto Moravia, tempted Steinbeck with stories of cool breezes blowing along the beaches of the Amalfi Coast, telling him it was *one of the fine places of Italy*. Steinbeck was drawn to the fishermen of the town, but he also, on his many walks, found shoemakers, carpenters, and a few entrepreneurs dabbling in arts and crafts. Steinbeck felt *it would be difficult to consider tourists an industry because there are not enough of them*. He noted that the occasional tourist was significant only as *a bit of luxury for the villagers*—those few who happened to sell a pair of sandals or were hired as a guide.

When Steinbeck's essay was published in the May 1953 issue of *Harper's Bazaar* Positano *was* a little-known fishing village on the Amalfi Coast. A hundred years earlier it had been home to over eight thousand people, but that was before hard times and the wars. The summer Steinbeck lived in that little apartment only two thousand people called Positano home. In his essay he turned his attention first to Italian traffic. Like many Americans, he thought it *down-right nonsense. It seems hysterical, it follow no rules.*

He felt differently about his adopted town though. He wrote *Positano bites deep... a dream place that isn't quite real. When you find a place as beautiful as Positano, your impulse is to conceal it... If I tell, it will be crowded with tourists and they will ruin it...* but he had a second impulse and wrote: *There isn't the slightest chance of this in Positano. In the first place there is no room.*

Oh how wrong Steinbeck was. He thought Positano had room for *five hundred visitors, no more*. He didn't account for Italian ingenuity fueled by insatiable demand. Steinbeck would probably have considered the number of tourists in town the evening Mardi and I were visiting overwhelming, but we were told that in two weeks the pace and character of the town would be much different. But that evening the feel of the town was ideal, and so was the light as the sun worked its way toward the horizon, changing the hues of the hotels with subtle shifts on the color wheel. As the bright orange disc flattened briefly before sinking slowly into the ocean, Mardi and I began climbing the steps toward the Amalfi Coast Highway that we could see winding its way across the face of Positano's seemingly haphazard, yet delightful, wall of hotels and houses.

"You can see how someone would fall in love with this place," I said.

I could tell Mardi agreed, but I could also sense that she would have been more comfortable with the Positano of 1952—Steinbeck's Positano. The harbor would have been full of fishing boats. But over the years, most of them have been converted to tour boats—the tourists providing a more comfortable living than the fish. But the rambunctious Positano, full of characters, that Steinbeck described had not disappeared. As we were making our way up the steep hill toward the bus stop a motor scooter suddenly zipped past us—one, two, three, *four* people perched precariously on its two tiny wheels. Once the whine of that little engine carrying those four souls to who knows where faded, we heard first, then saw up a side street, a mom yelling at her kids, at full volume, accompanied by wild waving of her hands. Steinbeck would be happy knowing that the passion for life that he fell in love with, still resounds in the streets and stairways of Positano.

It seemed fitting that in this town Steinbeck described as a *dream place that isn't quite real* that we would find a restaurant whose outdoor seating was on the other side of a road. The waiters, balancing plates, had to cross the roadway to serve their guests. It was tempting to take a table, next to the beautifully formed wrought iron fence that keeps diners from tumbling off the cliff. It would have been a memorable place to absorb the beauty of Positano, as the sinking sun painted the hillside with a golden hue, making everything, as our guardian angel *nonna* promised it would be, *molto bello*. But we were not yet hungry, and we had promised ourselves that we wanted to ride most of the way home to Maiori in what remained of the daylight. Instead of eating, we added that improbable restaurant to our growing list of things to do on our next visit to the Amalfi Coast.

While waiting for the bus we struck up a conversation with a young couple from Germany. They were going to Amalfi and from there to Agerola, where they had left their car while they hiked the Path of the Gods. When we asked them what they thought of Italy, they summed up their feelings succinctly.

"The food is great," the husband said.

"The driving is crazy," the wife reported. "Scooters pop around you on either side."

I soon gathered from our conversation that they were not interacting with Italians. They showed little appreciation for the differences in culture between Germany and Italy. Their comments made it seem they wished Italians were more like Germans, except for the food.

They asked how long we planned to stay in Italy. I gave them what had become my stock answer: *two or three months*. As usual, Mardi immediately set them straight.

"We've been on holiday for a month, but that includes our two-week cruise getting here," I said.

"Really—you came all the way across the Atlantic!" the husband exclaimed.

We were getting used to that response. They couldn't imagine doing such a thing—*Why take two weeks doing something you can accomplish in a day*? I might have pointed out, had I been bolder, that they themselves had just spent a day hiking from Agerola to Positano on the *Il Sentiero degli Dei*—a trip that could be accomplished in less than an hour by car.

That's one of the beauties of travel. You constantly open yourself up to new ideas—new ways of looking at things. In talking with this couple, we learned about the geography of Germany, a bit about the German mindset, and the reactions of these particular Germans to Italians. It would be unfair or unwise to project their feelings upon all Germans, but if you travel enough and interact with enough people from a certain country, you invariably come away convinced that a semblance of a national conscience exists. A Brit is different from a German, who is different from an Italian. As the French say, *Vive la difference*—Long live difference.

They asked us what we thought of Maiori. Mardi told them about the bigger, nicer beach and the cheaper prices. I told them about the town's people. "Each one of these little towns along the Amalfi Coast has its own personality," I said. "We've loved getting to know the people."

The bus arrived, interrupting what had been an engaging conversation. I thought again of the advantages to the citizens of countries that insist that their students learn foreign languages. Most of the Germans we'd met on this trip, and there had been a lot, both on the ship and since arriving in Italy, knew at least enough English to get along, and many had been close to fluent.

While getting on the bus we lost track of the couple and never saw them again, but I didn't forget them. They set in motion a pinball shot that has not yet struck its target—another item for our Amalfi Coast to-do list—hiking the Path of the Gods so that we can see the beauty of Positano from another angle. I'd also love to get to know a family from a long line of fishermen stretching back hundreds of years. The beauty of Positano is overwhelming, but I regretted that we developed no deep personal connections while we were there. Relationships take time. People need to see you a few times to feel that you'll be back—that their investment in you will yield a return. Next time we're in Positano we might develop such a relationship, but it was to Maiori that our pinball bounced from Amalfi, and it was to Maiori that we were returning.

The bus was crowded. Italians were yelling back and forth. It sounded like a family, but I couldn't figure out what they were arguing about or even, I should admit, whether they were arguing at all. The passion with which Italians express themselves often causes me to jump to the wrong conclusion.

On the bus ride I found a few other items to add to my Amalfi Coast list. Just before Smeralda I noticed, from high above, what looked like an ancient fishing village down below in what can only be described as a crevice in the rocks. Oh, how I'd love to row my little boat into that harbor and listen to the stories of the old fishermen. Maybe when I become fluent in Italian I'll do just that—choosing a morning when the waters are gentle and row from Positano along the coast to this improbable location for a village. Italians have a flair for the dramatic—what else can explain a village being built where it looked like a donkey could not even get to. If I'm wrong about that, and there's a walking path to that town, I want that on my to-do list as well. The Amalfi Coast was becoming one never-ending bucket list for me. Fortunate indeed is the person who has the general classification checked off, but few could go to the Amalfi Coast and not come away with a whole slew of subheadings on his to-do list.

Beyond Smeralda I saw two other villages that looked worthy of our list—Vetica, which appeared to be a lemon growers' paradise high on the cliffs above—and also a little town called Lone, which most likely would be pronounced as two syllables, *low nay*. The engineering marvel that is the Amalfi Coast Highway took on an added touch of the dramatic as we drew close to Amalfi. The lights of the approaching cars and buses snaking around the cliffs, appeared suspended in mid-air since we could not see, in the fading light, the roadway beneath them.

As we came around the headland and saw the lights of Amalfi's harbor, it looked as if we would arrive right on schedule, which meant we could, if we wanted, switch buses and be on the way to Maiori in a matter of minutes. We were eager to see our friends at Le Suite, but we were in Amalfi—why not walk into Piazza Duomo and be mesmerized again?

But first we wanted to use the restrooms in the tourist office near the tunnel to Atrani. Knowing exactly where to find restrooms in each town is invaluable, and so is having the necessary change available.

"*Buonasera. Come va?*" the tourist agent said as I scurried in.

"*Bene,*" I answered quickly.

"Would you pay for me?" I yelled back to Mardi as I rushed into *il bagno*.

This was only the second time we'd used a public toilet—the first was on Anacapri, when Mardi thought she had left her purse behind. As I sat there, I became aware of a conversation taking place in the hallway and realized that the folks operating the tourist office were ready to head home and we, or maybe I should say *I*, was delaying them. Mardi gave me a rather enigmatic smile as I walked out of the restroom and thanked our hosts, but our conversation soon turned to the Piazza Duomo and I failed to ask her why she had been smiling.

We walked into the *piazza* and were once again overcome by its beauty. The late evening light allowed me to create one of my favorite photographs of Saint Andrew. Surprisingly few people were on the steps, and the lights of the *limoncello* shop on the right of the staircase and the pizzeria on the left produced a warm golden pool of light leading the viewer's eye to the cross at the peak of the church façade high above.

"Oh, look there's a cross up there," I said. "No, not that one on the church. Higher up."

"Oh, that's a cemetery," Mardi said.

"Those arches are beautiful," I said.

The late evening light was reflecting off their white surface, painting a kaleidoscope of color to further convince me that there could not possibly be a more glorious *piazza* in all of Italy—maybe the Piazza San Marco is more grand, but this was intimately beautiful, and until a visit to Venice convinces me otherwise, I will continue to proclaim this *piazza* the most beautiful in all of Italy.

"Do you want to stay longer?" I asked as the last of the color in the sky disappeared.

"We don't know where to find Wi-Fi, and we would just spend money."

"Let's go home then."

Mardi had attributed her desire to get back to Maiori to the inconvenience of having to log on to a new Internet address—and to the fact that we had no idea how much it would cost—but I think the real reason was that she, like me, wanted familiarity. We were winding down after a long day of walking and riding the bus, and we wanted to be among friends.

So we walked through the ancient gate, across the highway to the harbor as the sky turned deep black, climbed onto the bus, and settled into our favorite seats. Mardi realized, as we were waiting that we had not made certain we were on the right bus, so she hopped off and approached a group of drivers chatting nearby. I saw her point to the bus we had boarded, but I couldn't hear the conversation. While it appeared we had chosen the right bus, the conversation with one of the men lasted a bit longer than I would have expected for such a simple question. Mardi, it seemed, was becoming more and more Italian every day.

"What did he say to you?" I asked after she climbed on the bus and settled in next to me.

"I asked him, *Is this the bus to May Or Ee* and he said *My Or Ee—Yes. In five minutes.*"

"I bet he'll get on and announce, *Is that woman who said May Or Ee on here?*" I said.

"He thought I was cute. He said everybody says it wrong," Mardi said.

"He didn't say that—you're making that up."

But that is probably exactly what he *had* said. It also looked like he might have been flirting a bit with her—he had given her a pretty big smile.

"You've got to keep your eye on those Italian men," I said and thought of our discussion with the German couple and the stereotyping that inevitably follows.

"Did you know you were in the women's bathroom?" Mardi asked, shifting the spotlight.

"No, I wasn't in the women's room," I said thinking she was trying to get back at me for teasing her.

"Yes you were," she insisted.

"Oh no—I can't believe I did that," I said and realized that was what that conversation I overheard was about—that stupid *Americano* who doesn't know the difference between *Uomini* and *Donne*. I laughed at the memory of my desperate dash.

The drive to Maiori was uneventful. In what seemed like a very short time, most likely because there was no traffic, we came around the final curve, the one below the castle, and found ourselves looking down at the lights of Maiori.

"I'd say we get off the first time the door opens," I suggested. We both felt like walking along the promenade instead of going directly to Le Suite. We wanted to feel our town, to hear its sounds—the waves crashing on the shore, the high pitch of Vespa engines bouncing off the hotels, and of course the bells, always the bells. We were thrilled that the door opened at the harbor, just across the street from the Friends of San Francesco Convent. The circular drive of the park was filled, as it often was, with teenagers and young adults. We had no worries about walking past them. We had seen no disrespect shown by anyone since we arrived in town. We felt safe.

"We should bring a blanket down here some night, head out to the breakwater, and listen to the waves breaking on the rocks," Mardi said.

I liked the idea. We'd get a different perspective on Maiori—looking back at the changing colors of the buildings and the rocks rather than out at the setting sun.

"This is heaven to me—a beautiful beach, a wide promenade, and a coffee bar where everyone knows our name. Why didn't we find a place like Le Suite in Amalfi?" I asked.

"We had everything we needed at Salvatore's—we didn't need a Le Suite."

She was right. Le Suite was a gift given to us because the Internet at Casa Raffaele Conforti wasn't working. If ever we needed a reminder to give thanks in all situations—the good, the supposedly bad, as well as the mildly inconvenient—this was it.

We now had Internet service in our room, but we stopped by Le Suite as always and met another Giovanni. He told us that he had lived for several years in Boston and had worked at Le Suite for nine years. I loved hearing that. I think it is part of the attraction of the bars and restaurants of Italy. The people serving you seem proud of their jobs.

"It's great the way people keep their jobs," I told him.

Giovanni didn't reveal whether he agreed that it was a good thing that he had been at the same job for almost ten years but I got the sense that he enjoyed his work, and that certainly seemed like a good thing to me.

Once again we didn't get to bed early. We spent the evening getting to know Boston Giovanni, chatting with Jessica, and trying to figure out where to go the next day with what was left of our twenty-four-hour bus pass. We were making a very big deal out of our ride-all-you-want ticket.

"Our choices are Ravello, Amalfi, and Tramonti," Mardi said. She'd been studying the local brochures. We'd already been to all three towns.

"I'm a local kind of guy. I want to stay around Maiori," I said.

"What about taking a bus to someplace close by—then we could walk back to Maiori and lie on the beach," Mardi suggested.

"Works for me, Beautiful," I answered.

"Are you trying to get on my good side?"

"Tell me which side is your good side, and I'll try to get on it," I said.

She ignored my attempt at humor and returned to the question at hand: what to do about tomorrow. I was willing to let tomorrow take care of tomorrow. This day had shown us just how good life feels to us in Maiori. I didn't feel like leaving even if we *did* have a free ticket to ride. We had enjoyed an interesting day, but we'd had little close contact with Italians. The feeling of finally being back home that evening overwhelmed me. I felt relaxed, protected, and welcomed. I knew without a doubt, *This is where I belong.* As Mardi and I sat in Le Suite discussing our day and watching people come and go we saw more clearly that our love affair is not so much with Italy as it is with the Italian people. We decided we didn't much care where tomorrow's guardian angel, or flip of our pinball, would send us—we were more curious to find out *who* we would meet and what uniquely Italian experience would come our way.

CHAPTER THIRTEEN

Raffaele Conforti ~ Wednesday April 13 ~ 52 & Sunny

I Want to Go Back to Maiori

In dreams and in love there are no impossibilities.
JANOS ARNAY

■

A happy marriage is a long conversation
which always seems too short.
ANDRE MAROIS

Seven bells sounded and just kept ringing—the call to worship in Maiori. The bells brought me out of a state of semi-wakefulness with a desire to cuddle. I also woke up with the desire to get serious about learning Italian, and the only way to make it happen, it seemed to me, would be if Mardi and I forced ourselves to speak Italian to each other.

"*Voglio attenzione,*" I said to Mardi, who was already well on her way to starting her day.

"*Voglio* I don't know—*attenzione* I do—I assume that means you want some attention," she said as she began massaging my tender legs.

"I'm going to make Jessica an offer she can't refuse," I said.

"What's that?"

"We'll teach her English if she'll teach us Italian."

"She's already said she would teach us a couple of words a day. She probably doesn't have time for more."

"Good point. Still, it won't hurt to ask if she'd have a hour, or even a half hour, just for language," I said.

"Oh, there's a wind today," Mardi said, looking out the window.

"A what?" I said hoping she'd recall our pledge to speak to each other in Italian.

"A wind," she repeated.

"*Vento.*"

"I thought *vento* was twenty."

"*Venti* is twenty, *vento* is wind."

"What is window?" she asked.

"*Finestra.*"

"Impressive," she said.

"I know a lot of Italian words, but I stumble when I put them together in sentences. Instead of just saying *hot water, please*, I need to say, *Mi piacerebbe acqua calda per il tè, per favore.*"

"Oh, I see what you mean. That's hard."

"It would force me to think about feelings, not just things. Just adding *I would like* requires a lot of thought, and so does remembering that it is *water hot* instead of *hot water.*"

I continued practicing the ordering of tea, adding the *barista's* name to the exchange and then adding—*Come va?*, the equivalent of *How's it going?*—and trying to make it all sound smooth and unpracticed, with perfect pronunciation—until Mardi reminded me that the buffet would soon be closing.

"I love you," I said and then quickly changed it to "*Ti amo.*"

"What is *I* in Italian?"

"*Io,*" I said. "*Sono* is *I'm.*"

"Then how is *Ti amo* I love you?"

"I don't know. *Non lo so* in Italian," I said. "That's why we need Jessica and Maximiliano to help us."

The dining room was ours alone. Maximiliano was waiting. I ordered our eggs in Italian. He had not heard me use the word *frittata* before. That garnered a *bravo.* Omelette works in Italian as well, but *frittata* impressed him, and he did a little dance for us. Even when you don't get the language exactly right, Italians let you know they appreciate you trying, and Maximiliano was no exception. He always encouraged us even when he had to pronounce a phrase or word repeatedly until we had said it perfectly. It was comical. He'd say a phrase like *l'autobus*, and we'd repeat it, sure we'd said it to perfection, but he would say it again and we'd have to try again. I don't think we ever satisfied him on *l'autobus*—he just gave up.

"We're being treated like we're spending a fortune here," Mardi remarked as Maximiliano returned to the kitchen.

"It's the Italian way," I said.

Maximiliano arrived with our eggs. My omelette tasted great, and I let him know it. I also raved about the bread. A few minutes later he brought our *due cappuccinos* perfectly prepared. I tasted mine and said *Bravo,* and then added *Ti amo Maximiliano.* That garnered an exuberant display of dancing.

"*Pazzo, Maximiliano, pazzo,*" I said.

"What does *pazzo* mean?" Mardi asked as she watched his feet fly around the floor.

"*Pazzo* is "crazy, wild, loony," I said.

"That's a good word to know," she said as he finished his dance and gave a quick bow.

I told him I was so happy I was going to give Mardi a kiss, but he didn't understand my pronunciation of *bacio,* so I just went ahead and kissed her. That surprised as well as delighted him, and he broke out laughing.

A few moments later Lidia walked by. I couldn't tell whether it was just happenstance or whether she was checking on Maximiliano.

"The very beautiful Lidia," Maximilliano said as we watched her walk down the hall.

"What is the word for *trouble,* Maximiliano? Are we getting you in trouble?" I asked.

"*Non lo so,*" he said.

"You don't know the word for trouble? Or you don't know if we've gotten you in trouble?" I asked.

"Ah, *problema,*" Maximiliano said. "*Nessun problema.*" He seemed not to be concerned. We were still his only guests.

He responded to our repeated phrase *Cos'è questo?* giving us the words for things we could see in the room—plate, saucer, cup, glass, shirt, sweater—*piatto, piattino, tazza, bicchiere, camicia, maglione.* He was a good teacher. He was precise in his pronunciations and demanded the same of us. I tried *l'autobus* again but he still did not like the way I was saying it. I tend to gravitate toward *lotto bus*—and he wanted me closer to *lout ta boose,* rhyming with moose.

"Max you *are* in trouble," I said. "Lidia is calling you."

He had been so intent on getting me to pronounce *l'autobus* correctly that he had broken out laughing at my attempt and had not heard Lidia calling him.

"*Domani, Maximiliano,*" I said as he scurried off to see what Lidia wanted and we hurried off to catch the *lout ta boose.* Maximiliano had convinced us that we really should see Salerno, describing it as *una bella città.* We'd also be able to check out the train station we would most likely be using when at last the day came when we had to leave Italy and go back to the lives we used to live in America—lives that were beginning to seem foreign to us.

"What time is it?" I asked Mardi as we stepped onto the street and then realized I was already breaking my pledge to speak in Italian.

"Nine oh eight," she said.

"So we have ten minutes?"

"Yes, but it came early yesterday," she said.

We turned the corner onto Corso Reginna and saw in front of Le Suite a gathering of people. As we walked by we peered inside to see who was working.

"*Buongiorno, James. Buongiorno, Mardi,*" a young woman's voice called.

We hadn't noticed that Jessica was at the center of that gathering. We chatted briefly, exchanging our Italian/English lesson for the day. When we mentioned we were on our way to the bus stop she sent us on our way with the promise that we would come by in the evening to tell her about our trip to Salerno.

"Where are all these people going?" Mardi asked a few miles outside of Maiori as a large number of people got off the bus in what appeared to be the middle of nowhere. She apparently hadn't noticed that many of them were carrying flowers, and they had gotten off near a sign bearing the word *cimitero*.

"I don't have to be a genius to answer your question," I said with a smile.

My somewhat snarky comment didn't put her off; my voice must have told her I was gently pointing out that she'd missed a clue or two. We both laughed, she at herself for not noticing the flowers and I because I loved her for being a good sport and not taking offense at what I'd said. A few moments later we discovered something that we didn't know existed on the Amalfi Coast Highway: a section of road where two buses could pass by each other with neither bus having to move over. But that wasn't typical; most of the ride was spent lurching along, slowing and sometimes stopping for cars that hadn't moved over far enough to let us by.

We spent much of the ride looking at maps, trying to decide whether we could see all the way to Sicily. It was a George Tice kind of morning, referring to a photographer whose work featured a progressive graying effect on the dark hills of his native Pennsylvania due to morning haze that all but obscured the most distant hilltops.

We grew to appreciate the two-tone horns of the buses—a gentle warning rather than a blaring blast at each corner. We also noticed that some highway signs were in English, the most notable being *STOP*. It has such an onomatopoeic sound. It works for all languages.

"Where are all *these* people going?" Mardi asked in a tone of consternation as we approached the port of Salerno which she had apparently not noticed.

"Again, you don't have to be a genius to answer your question—they're going to work."

It's sometimes possible to lose sight, when you're on holiday, of the fact that not all the world is on holiday with you. In fact, that's the kind of holiday I enjoy the most—a working holiday where I have the opportunity to share in the lives of my hosts. I first experienced this pleasure when I was only twelve years old. A local farmer whose kids weren't old enough to help out during wheat harvest asked my dad if he could borrow me for a couple of weeks. Curly cut his own wheat. My dad hired a big outfit with lots of combines to cut his. Curly could use a young boy to help out. Dad didn't need me. Every morning Curly's dad, who had retired from farming, picked me up in front of my house in his '49 Chevy, and I'd spend the rest of the day helping do whatever was necessary. I don't remember a lot about the work I did except how different their days, including their meals, were from those of my family. Their meals were more structured than ours and always featured an elaborate dessert. I realized at a very young age that working alongside people sure helps you to get to know them.

That realization was the central idea of the first book I wrote about Italy—that I would work as a volunteer for olive growers with the hope that I might learn a bit about them and about Italy as I labored. I had hoped that Mardi and I might do something similar, but the dynamic was slightly different when we worked as a couple. Mardi, I also discovered, is a bit less patient than I am. She does not tolerate tedium as well as I do. I spent an awful lot of my childhood driving a tractor ten, twelve, fourteen hours a day. I probably spent a large part of those days thinking outside of the box and dreaming of adventures to stave off boredom. I found out in Italy that I still didn't mind working long hours, especially when I was working alongside someone and we could talk while we worked. Unfortunately, the first farm where Mardi and I worked together used mechanical shakers to dislodge the olives—conversation was nil or sporadic.

What had been a marvelous experience for me proved not to be as enjoyable for Mardi. We had considered trying it again for this journey, but none of our offers were accepted, so we gave up and decided we would get to know the Italian people by walking alongside them—by doing things the way Italians do them. We even let this idea dictate where we did things like getting off buses; we got off where everyone else did.

But everyone else knew where they were going. We didn't. Within seconds we were standing alone. Across the highway a harbor filled with colorful fishing boats caught our eye. Most of the boats were bright blue—most of the nets were bright orange. I had not expected to see such a traditional scene in a large city. Mardi was struck by how strongly these men repairing their brightly colored nets and cleaning the day's catch reminded her of Greek fishermen. Maybe men of the sea are the same all over the world, or at least all over the Mediterranean.

Salerno was, as Maximiliano promised, a beautiful city, but we didn't feel like sightseeing, and we didn't want to buy anything, or spend the day in a museum, so once we had pinpointed the train station we were ready to move on. But first we needed to do what everyone else was doing—have an *espresso*. We tried to blend in, but I don't think we were successful. We were in a bar frequented by regulars—hardly any words flowed between customer and *barista*—the process was automatic. The coffee appeared, was consumed, then paid for. I tried to pay when I ordered and again when we were served, but the *barista* wasn't interested. I don't know how they keep track—it must be on the honor system. Even though we put a couple of hiccups in the smooth flowing process, we enjoyed standing at the bar, downing our *espressos*, trying to look like we fit in.

After our caffeine fix, we joined the crowd at the bus stop. Mardi fed croissant crumbs to the pigeons. To our right a large group of men were chatting. On our left three young mothers were sharing photos of their children on their iPhones. We got a good feel for the town sitting there eavesdropping. I also got to see some beautiful bikes go by including a top-of-the-line Pinarello—a Dogma just like the bike Chris Froome, the winner of the Tour de France, rides. It also happens to be the bike I'd love to ride, but I'd be happy with a not-quite-top-of-the-line Pinarello—they're good bikes, they're Italian bikes—beautifully designed and crafted.

The bus finally showed up. Whether it was on time we didn't know, we didn't have a schedule, but it delivered us to Vietri sul Mare, to a beautiful park right in the center of town. It was made more delightful by the playful fish planters filled with bright flowers along the wall that keeps passersby from falling onto the farm below. A photo I took of the farm has proved to be extremely popular on Facebook. I think what resonates with so many people is the sight of gorgeously productive green space, a Garden of Eden, right in the heart of town.

We stepped into the first *ceramica* store we came to. Mardi was hesitant. She felt we should be loyal to Vittorio. In slightly broken Italian I asked the shopkeeper if the piece I was holding in my hand was an original, and if so, was she the artist. I learned that it was indeed *un originale*, that she was the *artista*, and that her name was Elena. She added with much pride that *quattro genitori* had sold ceramics from that location—her connection to ceramics and

to that location in Vietri sul Mare stretched back four generations. Mardi and
I both liked what we saw—the colors and especially the depictions of the *asino*,
but her loyalty to Vittorio prevailed and we left without buying.

"*Lei è il capo*," I said to Elena and gave a shrug but quickly added, "*Ci torneremo,*" letting her know that even though Mardi was the boss I hoped we'd be able to return. We stepped outside and saw a couple of shopkeepers spontaneously break into a jig. Other shopkeepers sitting on nearby benches were applauding. In the *piazza* old men were watching the day go by on turquoise benches—they had a lot to watch—life, as always in Italian towns, was being lived on the streets. We settled onto a nearby bench to watch with them. We were surrounded by families. Bells were chiming. The feeling, as it always is in Italian *piazzas,* was good.

"I want to go back to Maiori," Mardi said, surprising me with her bluntness and resolve.

I didn't understand why. Was it because we had a ticket to Maiori that would expire within the next hour, or because she wanted to buy only from Vittorio, or did she just want to be back among our friends?

"Don't you just love how people gather on the streets?" I said hoping she wasn't serious.

She didn't respond. We watched a couple of dogs square off as though they were going to fight, but they didn't. Students were showing up. It was one of the warmest days we'd experienced, eighty degrees and somewhat cloudy. I was busy photographing and journaling about my love of Italian towns, trying to portray how delightful it was to be on the streets with people who were themselves enjoying life. I took a photo of seven men sitting next to me before I moved off to make room for more men to join them. Mardi moved to a nearby bench in the shade, and after a while I joined her. Despite the desire she had expressed to return to Maiori, I think she too was enjoying the *piazza* life. She was jotting notes in her journal as well.

To the right of the old men was a six-place bench filled with younger men— aged thirty to fifty. The sixty-to-eighty crowd was gathered on a corner bench that seated at least a dozen. To our left was a three-generation family doting on a curly-haired toddler—mom, daughter, *nonna e nonno*—apparently they had been waiting for dad to join them on his lunch break. When he arrived they strolled off with the little girl now comfortably seated in a high-tech stroller.

"There goes our bus to Maiori," Mardi said, nodding toward the last bus on which we could have used our twenty-four-hour ticket.

I'd been typing away on my MacBook, eating a pear and a bit of croissant we had saved from breakfast—not thinking of buses, just enjoying the pace of the town. We were sitting on a turquoise bench, the bright color perfectly appropriate in a town that celebrates ceramics. I had first experienced the camaraderie of the *piazza* in the Tuscan villages I got to know on my first trip to Italy, but the pace of these southern towns felt even more comfortable. I wondered if I would enjoy life in Sicilian towns even more. Simon had insisted that I would.

Now that a free ride to Maiori was no longer possible, Mardi turned her attention to *pranzo*. I stayed in the *piazza* taking notes and responding to readers while she strolled about town looking at menus. She ended up choosing a *trattoria* I could see from where I was sitting, which was just fine with me. I was engrossed watching people going about their daily lives. It's probably my small-town upbringing, but I'm not sure anything gives me a greater sense that all is right in the world than townspeople gathering to share what is happening, both the important and the trivial. It all matters.

We chose an outside table, where I could see the men I had moments before been listening to. As usual, we ordered a pizza and a salad. I had gone into the restaurant thinking I'd switch it up a bit and order a plate of pasta, but all it took was one look at a pizza on the way into the restaurant and I changed my mind. We weren't disappointed—in the salad or the pizza.

"Why do the tomatoes taste so much better here?" Mardi asked.

It was a question we often asked ourselves, and a fair one. I grew up eating tomatoes out of my mom's garden, so I know fresh is part of the answer, but I think ultimately it's the pride Italians take in their food. They judge food on taste. Convenience, ease of preparation, price—nothing surpasses the necessity of food tasting good.

"Bachelors don't live as long as married men," Mardi said seeming to change the subject, but then I realized she was probably indicating that food was the primary reason—the tendency of families to eat better than single people.

"Mardi, you picked the perfect restaurant," I said paying tribute to the food as well as the location.

"What a good time you're having—it is just surreal," Mardi said. I thought that was another strange thing to say until I realized she was reading from an email her sister had sent.

"Maximiliano sure gets a kick out of you," Mardi said, again keeping me guessing.

"Yeah, when I helped him understand what I was saying by kissing you, that really broke him up."

"Our broken Italian is what really breaks Maximiliano up," she said.

A man suddenly appeared at our table playing an accordion. I had neither seen nor heard him coming, but his timing was perfect, dovetailing with my comment about kissing Mardi. I couldn't name the song—probably an early Dean Martin ballad. His demeanor was delightful, and he was also a pretty good musician—or maybe anything Italian sounds good in a situation like that—dining with your wife of forty-some years and feeling that life is oh, so very good. He continued playing a medley of Italian classics, standing beside our table, creating in us a feeling that we were blessed. I tipped him and asked him to play more. He stayed and played. The new song wasn't as recognizable as the first but was more energetic—a traditional folk song I could imagine Italians dancing to at a family get-together.

He finished the song and disappeared as quickly and quietly as he had come. We looked around realized that our fellow diners had also disappeared,

and the *piazza* too had emptied. It was time for the afternoon *pausa*, but our waiter showed no impatience with us. We began looking up words and got stuck among s-words—same, sandals, sand, and sauce—which is *salsa*. We also noted other words for siesta—*dormitina* and another s-word, *sonnelino*.

Our waiter noticed what we were doing and complimented us on our commitment to learning Italian. He even pronounced a few words for us—differentiating between *ogni* and *oggi*—the words for *each* and *today*.

"I love how waiters never rush you in Italy," I said as he moved off to clear a table.

But Mardi was ready to be rushed. She wanted to know how to ask for the bill. I think she knew the answer—it was just a gentle reminder that she was still looking forward to getting back to Maiori.

"*Il conto, per favore,*" I said to our waiter as he went by with a tray of plates and glasses.

"*Prego,*" he said and returned a few minutes later with our bill which Mardi immediately studied. She had not yet gotten used to the item on the bill labeled *coperto*. A cover charge seems reasonable to me. We had rented their table for almost two hours, enjoyed an excellent meal, were given access to a very fast Internet, and even received some personalized instruction in Italian—yet we were not expected to tip.

Mardi was willing to let me return to Elena's shop since we had plenty of time before the next bus. Elena was happy to see us again and let us know it. We looked over her extensive inventory but found nothing we admired more than the small cups with donkeys on them that I had fallen in love with on our previous visit.

"These would be for *espresso*—one for you and one for me," I said and chose a small serving tray that matched.

Elena noticed that we were ready to pay and apologized using gestures for keeping us waiting. She was talking with a man who seemed adamant about getting her to reduce her prices on what seemed to be a rather large order.

"We're in no hurry," I said. I wished I had been able to think how to express it in Italian, but nothing came to me. When the man suddenly left the store, she joined us at the counter.

"Beautiful, *bello*," she said, noting our choices.

As she was wrapping our cups and serving tray the man came back. I didn't understand everything he said, but I liked the way Elena conducted herself. He wanted something cheaper than she was willing to sell it for, and even though it was a large order, she stood by her pricing.

"*Grazie*," Elena said, appreciative of our small purchase.

"*Prego*," I said and then, because she had given me such a sincere smile, I asked, "May I take your picture?"

She laughed. She was reluctant or shy, I couldn't tell which.

"But you are so beautiful," I blurted out.

"*Mama mia!*" she said and blushed as she posed for my camera.

I took the photo quickly. She relaxed. The second one, which I didn't announce, was good—her gracious smile would be a beautiful reminder of the fun we had looking for a memento that would remind us, each time we drank Italian coffee, of our happy days on the Amalfi Coast.

Three bells sounded as we walked out of the shop, reminding us that we had only a short time before our bus would be departing. The *gelato* shop was on the same street, just beyond the restaurant where we'd eaten. We were by then quite adept at ordering *gelati*. It was a good thing too. As we were paying for them the place was overrun with high school kids. In an instant the shop became so packed we had to slide through the crowd with our *gelatos* held close to our bodies to get out of the shop.

We chose the same turquoise bench we'd had before as teenagers filtered out of the *gelateria* and joined us, gathering in groups to tease and flirt. The sound of their happy voices was delightful—no harsh arguments or cursing, just lots of laughing, flirting, and good natured roughhousing.

Mardi decided to do a little flirting of her own.

"You are *so* handsome," she said.

"Well, take a picture and prove it," I said.

"I already did," she said and showed me a photo she'd taken at the restaurant just after the accordionist had left our table. I had to admit it was one of the best pictures I had ever seen of myself. She had captured the happiness and contentment I had felt sharing that moment with her. She had also captured my attempt at an Italian look—I had my sweater tied around my neck.

Mardi and I were discovering that we enjoy somewhat of an *Enchanted Cottage* love for each other. If you've seen the 1945 film starring Robert Young and Dorothy McGuire, you'll remember that transcendent love transformed their lives, making each of them see the other as no one else in the world did. She didn't see his disfigured face from a war injury, and his love for her turned her beautiful. Love is blind, they say. They also say that life is a game and love is the prize. We felt that afternoon that we had not only won the prize, we had won the lottery.

"I want to go home," I said.

Mardi understood of course that I meant Maiori, and not Wisconsin. We ate the last of our cones and walked toward the bus stop on streets that had become rather congested. The contrast with the quiet *piazza* we had enjoyed less than an hour earlier was stark—it was now rush hour. Our bus stop was on the main arterial through town—at a busy intersection—with long lines of cars stretched in three directions.

As we were waiting a small car suddenly stopped in traffic. The front passenger hopped out, jumped in the back seat, such as it was, and a woman who had been waiting for the bus hopped in the front seat. It was an impulsive maneuver in a traffic lane, but it was deftly done. The thing that most impressed me was not the precision and timing of the maneuver, but the forgiveness of the inconvenienced drivers. They apparently realized that someday they might want to do the same thing—or maybe they'd done it just the day before. Italians in general are much more tolerant than Americans—not so wedded to the clock but rather to experiences and life. This driver was being a good Samaritan, and he didn't have to suffer the indignity of blaring horns or middle finger salutes to give the woman a lift home. So much for the stereotypical view of Italian drivers as wildly gesticulating maniacs shouting obscenities about mothers and pigs.

Our ride home was pleasant, with only minor moments of panic. I took videos to remind us years from now what it was like to ride a bus on the Amalfi Coast.

"Are we going to make it?" Mardi asked as we inched by another bus.

"Plenty of room—there was at least an inch and a half," I joked as I looked into the eyes of the other bus driver as he crept by us at one mile per hour. A moment later we were at speed again on a sharp corner that jutted out and over the water. I looked down and saw that we were passing within inches of two extremely concerned tourists in a rental car. The eyes of the passenger were popping out of her head with fear—a crash looked imminent, but we somehow cleared each other. I think that's the attraction of the Amalfi Coast Highway—sheer beauty occasionally punctuated by sheer panic.

"Let's get something to drink and sit on the beach," I suggested as we pulled into town. I wanted to experience the subtle beauty of the late afternoon sky again. I was thinking of getting a tea at Le Suite and taking it to the beach, but Mardi had noticed the *supermercato* that morning and wanted to check it out.

"Can I wait for you outside?" I said, not willing to let go of the glorious evening colors.

While I waited I noticed that a lot of customers were parking electric bikes. They looked perfectly suited to daily shopping in Italy—with lights, locks, a small basket for groceries, and power assist to get started and for climbing hills.

"I wonder what a bike like that costs," I said when Mardi rejoined me in front of the store.

She ignored my question, as she often does when the possibility of spending money on bicycles comes up.

"Where do you want to go?" she asked.

"Wherever I can find a comfortable bench," I said.

As we walked along the promenade we had the sense of kids swirling around us—the feeling that had led us to fall in love with Maiori. The sound of the waves crashing on the beach did nothing to dissuade us from our infatuation with the town. I was glad I had listened to Mardi—she knew that if we set foot in Le Suite, we would never leave. The beach was the right place to make the transition back to Amalfi Coast time.

"Which bench do you want?" Mardi asked.

"Let's go a little farther," I said. I had grown fond of the bench where we had first fed pigeons. It faced the setting sun. We settled onto it. I began checking out what she'd purchased. She had bought a picnic—apricot juice, Edam cheese, gummi bears, even a Ritter *espresso* chocolate bar, as well as our favorite crackers.

Once again we attracted a crowd.

"Are you feeding those pigeons my good crackers?" I asked.

"I want to be generous."

"Well throw me some—you can be generous to me, too."

"I can't believe you don't want to feed the birds," she said. "Saint Francis did."

We sat feeding the birds and enjoying the evening so long that we had to put on our sweaters and tie scarves around our necks. Le Suite could wait. We didn't want to leave the beauty of the evening.

"We now know where all these little towns are from Salerno to Sorrento," Mardi said.

She had been checking the map and comparing our current knowledge of the Sorrentine Peninsula to what it had been two weeks ago, when we didn't even know there was a town named Amalfi on the Amalfi Coast or the difference between Salerno and Sorrento.

Mardi surprised me by saying something to me in Italian. She had to repeat it in English—that she was amazed how many kids were out here on a school night. I was paying attention to the fishing boats making their way toward the harbor at the far end of Lungomare. They were, just like the boats we'd seen early that morning in Salerno, brightly painted. Seeing those boats reminded me of Salvatore running down to the fish market to buy fresh anchovies for Mardi's birthday dinner—so many people making a living locally.

As we watched the fishing boats come in, the sun went down and the temperature dropped drastically. We walked to our B&B via a back street so that no one in Le Suite would see us. We wanted to shower, change clothes, and get warmed up before joining our friends. When we arrived at Casa Raffaele Conforti we were surprised and thrilled to find Maximiliano waiting for us. We had feared we might not get a chance to say goodbye.

"Good evening, Maximiliano," I said. "Did we get you in trouble this morning?"

"No problem," he said. "*Nessun problema.*"

We explained, as best as we could, why we were moving to the convent. He was disappointed but cheered up when we told him we'd come back to see him. We headed toward Le Suite feeling good and as usual we saw our friend Mario. It occurred to me that we had never introduced ourselves.

"*Mi chiamo James e questa è la mia moglie, Mardi,*" I said.

"Gianni," he said without fanfare.

"So you're *not* Mario?"

"No, Mario my son."

"Your son?" I asked.

"My bubba."

"We have lots of bubbas too," I said. "Five of them to be exact. One of them is named Jonnie."

Gianni was surprised that we would have a child with an Italian name—he broke out laughing when I spelled *Jonnie.*

To say that we were shocked that Mario was actually Gianni was a huge understatement. Mario and Maria's place was in reality Gianni and Maria's. I can see the reason for the name change—Mario and Maria's rolls off the tongue much better and is certainly more memorable. Still digesting the news, we stepped into another place we had come to love—a *ceramica* shop just across the street from Le Suite.

"Do you have salt and pepper shakers?" I asked. "*Sale e pepe?*" I repeated in Italian. The word *shakers* is unnecessary for some reason.

The shopkeeper showed me a rather large pair.

"Smaller—*piu piccola,*" I said.

"Do you have one with a donkey?" Mardi asked.

"Donkey?" the shopkeeper asked, perplexed.

"*Asino,*" I said.

"No, I am sorry," he said and looked genuinely disappointed. I loved him for his concern.

"*Mi chiamo James,*" I said.

"Ah, Rosario," said the shopkeeper.

"*Piacere,*" I said.

"*Mia moglie Martha.*"

"*Piacere,*" Rosario said and gave that beautiful Italian tilt of the head that is so disarming—so winsome. Rosario began showing Mardi the choices available if we were willing to give up on our desire for shakers with donkeys on them. I turned my attention to looking for *anything* with donkeys and found several possibilities.

"*Ci torneremo,*" I said as we left, convinced that on our last day in Maiori we'd return to buy souvenirs for our grandkids.

Anna, Jessica's sister, was in front of Le Suite. I introduced myself. Jessica had told me that Anna also managed a small hotel. I made the presumption, when I learned that the name of the manager of Casa Mannini was Anna, that it must be the same Anna who managed Dedalo. I also presumed that she would know of our reservations.

"*Arrivando Sabato, alle dodici,*" I said.

"Ah," Anna said.

"We will be at the San Francesco convent two days and then come back here," I said mostly in English.

She seemed a little perplexed, but I thought little about it at the time. I assumed that her manager at the hotel had let her know we were the same folks who frequented Le Suite and that we'd be checking in on Saturday at twelve. We told Anna how much we were enjoying Maiori, excused ourselves, and claimed a table near our favorite spot in Le Suite.

A few minutes later Jessica came to our table and asked, "Is everything okay?"

That too should have been a clue, but I thought nothing of it and gave her a quick synopsis of our journey to Salerno and Vietri sul Mare. The conversation quickly turned to her desire to learn English and of ours to learn Italian.

"I have studied maybe seven years," she said and here is where I lost track of our conversation. I thought she was telling me that she had, for those seven years, studied English for one hour a day. But I finally figured out, after a bit of embarrassment, that she was saying *we* should spend one hour a day studying *bello italiano—un'ora per giorni*.

What followed was a rather intensive discussion of the difficulties associated with the differences between Italian and English. She brought out her workbook. Mardi and I pulled out our phrasebooks and dictionary. I had been trying to differentiate between *work* as a verb and *work* as a noun. As it often went with our Italian lessons with Jessica, there was a lot of miscommunication, but the laughs were good.

"A present for you," Anna said. She had brought us a very rich-looking dessert. Mirko was at her side asking what we would like to drink. They were obviously honoring us, but we weren't sure why. I didn't know what to say, but I didn't want to refuse their hospitality. A few minutes later Anna presented us with an anchovy pizza and a hearty *Buon appetito*.

"I don't understand what's going on," Mardi said.

"I think she just loved that I introduced myself to her," I replied after Anna had left. We never did find out why we were presented with that free meal. As often happened at Le Suite, we couldn't keep up with everything going on.

"Cheers," I said to Mardi as we toasted each other and our hosts. "Where everybody knows your name." I looked around the bar and saw that we really were surrounded by people who knew us.

A family with young kids came in and took a table close by. The music was mostly jazz—plus a bit of Michael Bublé. Conversations were flowing from table to table. Between conversations we tried to do as Jessica had suggested—study

Italian—but it wasn't easy. People were including us in their conversations even more than usual.

"Where are you from?" A young woman at the bar had turned around and addressed us with no preamble. Her English was quite good, but I was sure she wasn't from the States.

"From Wisconsin in the USA," I said.

"Ah, okay," she said as she moved near our table.

"And you?" I asked.

"I am from Uruguay, but I used to live in the USA, in Atlanta," she said. "I did a master's study at the University of Georgia."

"My name is James, and this is my wife, Mardi."

"James?" she asked. Something in the way she said my name prompted my response.

"Bond...James Bond," I said, trying to echo the cadence of Sean Connery and mimic his distinctive accent. I was disappointed in what I heard, but she laughed heartily, obviously aware of the popular films of Ian Fleming's Agent 007.

"My name is Maria. Nice to meet you."

"*Piacere.* Good to meet you as well," I said.

"I saw you here yesterday, and the day before," she said.

"We're here a lot. We like it here. We like Maiori a lot," I said. "How did you end up here?"

"Randomly," Maria said. "I booked a hotel in Maiori and decided to stay. Been here five days."

"We've been here ten days," I said. "Are you going to stay longer?"

"Yes," she said with much conviction.

"Maiori has that effect on people," I noted.

I was getting a little nervous talking to her so long. Mardi had not joined in—and Maria, who was at least twenty-five years younger than we were, was not directing any of her comments toward Mardi.

"Good talking to you," I said.

"Yes—yes," Maria said.

"I am sure we will see you again," I said.

"Yes, sure, sure, yes," she said with a hearty, slightly nervous laugh.

She excused herself and went back to talk to Giovanni at the bar.

As she walked away I said to Mardi, "Now what was I looking up?"

With feigned jealousy, she said, "You were looking up *I will no longer travel alone.*"

I looked at her for an explanation.

"She couldn't take her eyes off you."

"She's interested in Giovanni."

"She'd better not be. Giovanni is Jessica's man."

"Are you sure? I've never noticed anything."

"Yeah, I'm sure. Maybe we could pair her up with *Boston* Giovanni."

"I don't think Giovanni needs our help. He can do his own darn pairing up."

"He might," Mardi said and put a high note on the end of the word *might* that suggested she wanted to make sure Maria had somebody—anybody but her husband—to be interested in.

Jessica stopped by and asked me to repeat today's phrase.

Un'ora per giornale," I said rather proudly.

Jessica laughed and corrected me. "*Giornale* is newspaper. *Giorno* is day."

Un'ora per giorno," I said sheepishly as Jessica moved off to wipe down a table.

"Woman of all ages flirting with you," Mardi said. "It's hopeless."

"What?" I asked. "Surely you don't think Jessica's flirting with me."

"I don't want you to forget about me with all these women paying attention to you."

If thoughts of romance were filling the room, it might have been the fault of the music—it was dreamy and so sexy.

"Shall we go home and have some *limoncello*?" I asked.

"Already?"

"You're right—I still have lots of people to respond to on Facebook."

"Why don't you go ahead," she said.

I moved to a different table to plug in my computer. Mirko saw that I was having difficulty and drew my attention to an outlet near the table we had been occupying.

"*Limoncello*?" Mirko asked.

"*Certo,"* I said.

How had he overheard me mention *limoncello* to Mardi? Once again I shook my head over the skill of Italians at taking care of your desires almost before you realize you have them.

I don't know whether it was to get back at me or not, but Mardi's mind did not go toward hospitality. She mentioned instead how good-looking Mirko was.

I didn't display any jealousy, instead I agreed with her.

"I hit the jackpot with that photograph, didn't I?" I said, looking at my Facebook page.

"Which one?" Mardi asked.

"The one of Atrani with the wisteria in the foreground. I have more than one hundred sixty responses to look through."

"Go ahead. Take your time. I'm enjoying this," she said.

"I'm going to tell on you," I whispered to Mardi. Jessica was heading toward our table.

"My wife thinks your brother is good-looking," I said when she reached us. She smiled at Mardi and then turned to look at Mirko behind the bar. Her body language told me, as she moved on to another table, that she heard that all the time.

"They play good music here, don't they," I said to Maria, who had just showed up at our table again.

"Yeah, I love this place," Maria said. "Yesterday I told Siandra I came here first and have not gone anywhere else. Maiori for me is from here to there," pointing first at the bar and then to the door of Le Suite.

"What is your job now?" I asked.

"I am not currently working," she said. "I am traveling. I started a travel blog."

We talked of all the languages she knows—the list climbed to five.

"If I come to the US I will contact you," she said.

"If you want to find us you will have to come back to Maiori. You might find us in Wisconsin. You will surely find us here," I said as Mirko stopped by to ask if we liked the *limoncello.*

"We are planning to work for you," Maria said to Mirko.

"We wash dishes," Mardi added.

Mirko just smiled. I was right—his lack of response told me he was used to women flirting with him.

"You come here in the mornings?" Maria asked me when Mirko moved on without hiring her.

Nodding toward the corner by the window, I said, "Sometimes we start our day here. Usually we sit at that table, but someone already had it this evening so we sat here."

"You have connections here?" she asked, but she didn't wait for my answer. She had noticed that Giovanni was again on the business side of the bar near where she had been sitting.

Mardi leaned close to me and said playfully, "No, you're not exchanging emails with Maria."

"You're funny," I said.

"No, I'm not. She's too pretty, she's too young, and she's too interested in you," she said with more than a little emphasis.

"She just wanted to practice speaking English."

"I don't *think* so," Mardi countered with a sing-songy lilt to her voice.

To change the subject I mentioned that one of my biking buddies had written to tell me he hoped we were having a good time in Italy and that he was missing our bike rides.

"I bet he does. And Maria is going to have to miss exchanging emails with you as well."

Mardi wasn't about to let it drop. We fell into a bit of silence, checking our emails and Facebook accounts while listening with divided attention to the conversations in the room. I liked that Mardi was jealous and that she thought a much younger, very good-looking, personable, and—did I mention—well-built woman was interested in me. *I* didn't think she was interested, but it was fun to think Mardi was concerned enough to be jealous.

We had a productive, fun-filled evening in Le Suite. I responded to all of my Facebook notifications, learned several new Italian phrases from Jessica, sparked a few jealous streaks in Mardi, and recharged my computer.

"*Grazie, Anna*," I said indicating that I was thanking her for the pizza she had given Mardi and me.

"*Va bene?*" Anna asked.

"The best, the best—*il migliore*," I said relieved that the Italian word for *best* had come to me.

"It's hard to imagine not coming in here every night," Mardi said as I packed my computer and charge cords into my new man purse. Maria was still at the bar, still chatting with Jessica's Giovanni. We bid everyone goodnight and walked arm in arm into the crisp night air. Boston Giovanni was outside. He saw us and broke into the song "Raindrops Keep Falling on My Head."

"B.J. Thomas," I said.

"Burt Bacharach," Giovanni shot back.

"Yes, he wrote it, but B.J. Thomas sang it," I said as I turned to look back into Le Suite, where Maria was still talking to Jessica's Giovanni "…and Maria will be expecting you to sing it to *her*."

He gave a little laugh, smiled, and pointed to his wedding ring—a ring neither Mardi nor I had noticed.

"Never mind," Mardi said as we turned to head to our room. Giovanni resumed singing. He was making us feel like Robert Redford and Katharine Ross sneaking off for an illicit rendezvous in *Butch Cassidy and the Sundance Kid*. It was a film that figured prominently in our courting days. We saw it about a month after our first date. We loved the sexy, steamy, humorous scene when you first see them together—when you think that Butch is forcing himself on Emma at the point of a gun until she utters one of the best lines in movie history—*Can't you just once be on time?*

"You were flirting too much," Mardi said, pulling me close.

"You think so?" I asked. "I thought she was just being friendly."

"And I thought *you* were being *too* friendly," Mardi retorted. Bells were chiming. We counted them as we climbed the stairs to Casa Raffaele Conforti—one and ten.

"Do you still love me?" I asked.

"You told Andy, on the ship, not to make trouble for himself," Mardi said. "Good advice for you too."

"Andy seems like such a long time ago," I said and began thinking of the many things that had happened since we'd walked down that gangplank.

She pulled me close again as we walked down the hall to our room and whispered, "I feel so protective of you."

As we stepped into our room I hugged her and asked, "Do you have enough energy for a massage?"

"What hurts?"

"My feet, my knees, my legs—*attenzione tutto,*" I said as I plopped onto the bed.

We were lying on the bed intertwined, our heads close together. The bells began ringing. This time it was three high—forty-five minutes after something. We began counting the low bells—would they quit ringing at eleven or twelve? We weren't sure how long we had been asleep.

"I love you," Mardi whispered.

"You still love me after all that?"

"I think I do," she said and began mmmm-ing.

"That was something else," I said and kissed her gently on her forehead.

We lost track of the count … it didn't much matter. This day—this beautiful day—was done.

CHAPTER FOURTEEN

Casa Raffaele Conforti ~ Thursday April 14 ~ 63 & Sunny

Living with Saint Francis

Grow old with me! The best is yet to be.
ROBERT BROWNING

■

Travel does what good novelists also do to the life of everyday,
placing it like a picture in a frame or a gem in its setting,
so that the intrinsic qualities are made more clear.
Travel does this with the very stuff that everyday life is made of,
giving to it the sharp contour and meaning of art.
FREYA STARK

I woke up aware that I had been dreaming of a shower shutting off, and a hair dryer turning on. I looked toward the bathroom and saw Mardi wrapping her hair in a towel.

"Wow. I was really sleeping," I said.

"Yeah, you were a good boy, you slept a long time."

"I'm a new man. I had a lot of dreams."

"Were any of them named Maria?" she asked, taking me instantly back to last night.

"No, no," I said reflexively and then began piecing together what I'd been dreaming and realized that my instinctual response might not have been totally truthful. I was picking up a thread of a dream that *did* have a woman in it—a woman I didn't know very well. It wasn't Maria, but it did seem to be a foreign woman in a foreign city. I mentioned none of that to Mardi and moved on to another dream—a delightful, not-quite-in-touch-with-reality vision of me skiing down a very long and very steep hill near my boyhood home on more snow than has ever fallen on the state of Nebraska in its one-hundred-fifty-year history. My attempt to make sense of skiing over the tops of fence posts was interrupted by a gentle tapping on our door and the voice of Maximiliano announcing that breakfast was served.

"*Grazie, Maximiliano,*" I said. "We'll be right there."

But first I had to satisfy my curiosity about the party we were missing. I put on my robe and stepped onto our terrace. The scene was right out of a Roberto Rossellini movie from the forties or fifties except that it was in color. Just below me, the streets were filled with people—a morning *passeggiata.* Widows in black were hugging, young girls were greeting each other, and men, both standing and seated, were talking in small groups. I looked for the young daughter of the man who had given us our first taste of *limoncello,* but I saw neither her nor her bicycle. But it looked like the rest of the town was there—or soon would be. I would have been content to grab my journal and sit there listening to the good times—and probably would have, had I not already told Maximiliano we were coming.

And had I not already told Gerardo we were checking into the convent today I would have been happy to stay right where we were. I had grown to love the feeling of everything about this place—even the creaking of the door. The deep and resonant sound of the massive hinges spoke of more elegant times. The halls were lined with old photographs of the elegant family that once called this architectural gem their home. A portrait of the master of the house graced the top of the grand piano that added a touch of class to the dining room. On this morning Maximiliano was standing beside it waiting for me. I'm sure he had heard the door creak and knew I was coming.

"*Buongiorno,*" he said softly, bowing ever so slightly and tipping his head.

"I am so sorry we are late. Mardi is coming. We decided we wanted to sleep in on our last day. Hope that was okay, Maximiliano," I said trying to match the cadence and deep timbre of the way he said his own name.

"*Bene,*" he said and smiled as he turned toward the display of food adorning the tables on the other side of the dining room.

"Look at that," I said as I walked along tables laden with far more food than Mardi and I would ever eat. I moved past the fruit, the pastries, and the juices and onto the balcony. Maximiliano followed.

"Oh my, Max. You are so fortunate you live in such a beautiful place, Maximiliano," I said emphasizing his full name because I realized that in my reaction to the beauty of the day and the deep blue of the ocean I had shortened his name to Max, but he gave no indication that he had been offended.

"Ah, very good _____" he said but I couldn't make out the last word. It rhymed with Pompeii.

"Also very beautiful," Maximiliano added as I continued to try to figure out what he had said was *very good*.

"Good people, too," I added.

Now it was Maximiliano's turn to be puzzled. I could tell he hadn't quite understood what I had said, so I switched to Italian and said "*buono...*" but I couldn't retrieve the word for "people." I knew it and had used it, but I couldn't pull it out. We were having a heck of a time communicating what should have been simple thoughts. We persisted though. He went through a bunch of "*buona*" words, "*Buona sera, buona mare...*" before switching back to English, "...and the beach."

I switched it back and said, "*buona spiaggia.*" Maximiliano corrected me: "*Bella spiaggia,*" which is of course "beautiful beach" rather than "good beach." Maiori definitely has both, but this morning it was gorgeous. We were looking out over the rooftops to the trees lining the promenade and the glorious ocean beyond as we shared our Italian/English lesson.

"I love it, Maximiliano. You're a good man," I said.

I was referring to both the beauty of the setting and his willingness to correct my Italian. He was slightly embarrassed by my praise and smiled bashfully as he adjusted his black heavy-rimmed glasses. I noticed how sharp he looked. He was wearing new pants and I asked about them.

"*Nuovi pantaloni?*"

"*Si,*" he said, posing so that I could see them better.

"*Bella donna,*" I said as Mardi joined us, making sure I said *doe na*, not *dawn na*.

"I'm sorry we are so late this morning," Mardi said.

"*Uova fritte?*" Maximiliano asked, getting right to the point.

"*Due,* over easy," I said and added. "I've not been able to find a suitable translation for 'over easy,' so I'll stick with the American."

"*Uno, due,*" Maximiliano said pointing first to Mardi and then to me.

"No—*due, due,*" I said pointing first to me and then to Mardi.

"You want two as well, don't you Mardi?" I asked. She nodded yes.

"*Quattro per noi due,*" I said.

"Four egg-za," Maximiliano said succinctly as he turned toward the kitchen. Mardi and I smiled at each other over the beautiful way he had said eggs—with such a strong emphasis on the *s*.

While we waited for the eggs I shared with Mardi the words Maximiliano had just taught me. A gentle breeze billowed the sheer drapes and pulled our thoughts toward the beach. The day outside looked perfect. Our *cappuccinos,* which Maximiliano had just delivered were, as always, incredible.

"Mardi, this is a wonderful life," I said.

"Of course, we live like kings—we've got Maximiliano taking care of our every whim—standing by to serve us breakfast the moment we wake up—why wouldn't we love it?"

"It's more than that. I love *everything* about this—this hotel, Maximiliano, this town, our friends at Le Suite—I don't know how we're going to leave."

"Maybe we can talk Maximiliano into coming to America with us?" she suggested as he walked toward us with our eggs.

"How should I say *I love Maximiliano*?" I asked as he set our plates in front of us.

"*Amo Maximiliano,*" he said somewhat shyly.

"*Amo Maximiliano,*" I repeated with a tip of my head as he stepped back from our table.

"*Bravo,*" he exclaimed and clasped his hands together. His face lit up in a huge smile as he began placing silverware on the table next to ours.

"Oh, is someone else coming?" I asked Maximiliano.

"*No, no*—for a photo," he explained.

"*Panino?*" I asked, pointing to a sandwich he had just placed ever so carefully. I asked if I had the right word and whether I was pronouncing it correctly, but he was concentrating on one task only—he no longer had time for Italian lessons. Suddenly he stopped arranging the table and pulled out his cell phone. "*Pronto,*" he said, and listened. He said nothing else and hung up after a few seconds.

"Manager, Miramare," he said.

"I am going to miss you Maximiliano," I said. "*Io triste, Maximiliano.*"

He didn't react—just kept setting the tables around us.

"Maximiliano, I am sad I am leaving you," I said.

Again he only smiled.

"*Capisce, Maximiliano?*" I said. "*Io triste*—I am sad."

Still he seemed not to understand, so I tried once more. I realized that in Italian I had said *I sad,* not *I am sad.* Maybe he had just not understood.

"*Sono triste, Maximiliano*—I'm sad that we will not see you at breakfast each morning."

"*Cappuccino?*" he asked as he finished setting the tables as though he had heard none of what I had said.

"*Si, due,*" I said.

"No, not for me," Mardi said.

"Oops—*uno cappuccino per me*," I said.

Maximiliano smiled, said *"Bravo,"* and headed toward the kitchen.

"I'm not sure we're going to be able to get him to discuss our leaving," I said.

Mardi watched him walk away. She was smiling. Maximiliano had us both perplexed.

"Let's go out to the terrace," she said.

"Oh, great idea—get out of his way."

Mardi looked beautiful stepping through the doors and onto the terrace. Italy was putting a glow on her face, and it wasn't just from the Mediterranean sun. We felt we were being totally cared for, and not just by Maximiliano.

"When I began thinking of our honeymoon and said I wanted to feel like part of a town—I had no idea my wish would be fulfilled so completely. I didn't even know towns like this still existed. I thought this way of life ended not long after World War II," I said, and thought back to the small-town camaraderie Roberto Rossellini portrayed in his early films. And here we stood, by God's grace, looking out over the very town Rossellini used to tell his stories of the interconnectedness of Italian life.

Some might say that we stood there by coincidence, but to me that's just a meaningless word for things that are too wonderful for us to know—that we use when the odds of something happening seem overwhelming, yet nevertheless they occur. We knew, without a doubt, we were living a blessed life at that moment.

We had been talking at breakfast, while we watched Maximiliano fret over the placement of every piece of silverware, about the uniqueness of each of our days since we set foot on Italian soil, and now we were moving to a convent associated with Saint Francis of Assisi in a town Roberto Rossellini loved. I'd been aware of neither of these things when we decided to come to the Amalfi Coast—to Positano. Strange indeed—yet Rossellini's name is in the subtitle of my first book about Italy and a whole chapter is devoted to Le Celle, the monastery that Saint Francis founded near Cortona. Both Rossellini and Saint Francis were deeply connected to Maiori, and I had known nothing about it. This whole adventure was a beautiful surprise—*bella scoperta*—a phrase that figured prominently in my first book. No wonder we were feeling a little giddy. The beauty of the day and the gorgeous vista stretching out before us weren't helping to quell any of our euphoria either.

The only thing that dampened our spirits that morning was that packing took so long that by the time we left Casa Raffaele Conforti, Maximiliano had gone home. We said a quiet goodbye to Lidia, knowing we'd see her again when we returned to say goodbye to Maximiliano.

The first person we saw when we turned the corner onto Corso Reginna was the beautiful Jessica—the beautiful Aunt Jessica we discovered. She had an equally beautiful niece in her arms. When she noticed that we were trailing suitcases her happy smile turned to a look of concern. "Leaving Maiori?"

We assured her that we were only switching hotels—that we'd be at the convent for a couple of days.

"Amici di San Francesco in Maiori, not Amalfi?" she asked.

"That is right. We are walking," I said.

"Oh, very good," she said. Her joyous personality returned. She turned to Mardi and smiled.

"We will be back Saturday. We will see you then, maybe sooner," I said as we continued toward the promenade. I wasn't certain why I'd said that. Of course we'd see her before Saturday. Just because we were going to be a half mile away instead of a half block, surely that wouldn't prevent us from spending time in Le Suite. As we joined the flow of people toward the promenade I slowly became aware that someone was yelling my name. I turned and saw Jessica rushing toward us, the baby still in her arms.

"Please come meet my parents," she said when she reached our side.

We followed her back to Le Suite. Her mother was elegantly dressed and her father looked like a solid man—a friendly, loving man. Jessica was glowing as we chatted with her parents. I turned to Jessica and told her that we had now met the whole family except Jonathan.

"Dorme," she said playfully. "Mirko e Jonathan, dorme."

The way she said her brothers' names revealed that she loved them. Even though she was teasing them for sleeping late, I had the feeling she felt they deserved it. I don't think there was anything else Jessica could have done that morning that would have made us feel more like part of her family. No matter how far the circle of an Italian family extends, there always seems to be room for more.

Our walk down Corso Reginna was the stuff of movies—perfect movies. The temperature was in the high sixties, the wind calm, the sun bright. We were following two old grandmothers dressed in black walking arm in arm. If one fell the other would go down too. But for the moment they were doing just fine—out for their morning stroll enjoying the day together. It was hard to imagine that a second of silence had ever passed between them.

"That was fun. I'm so glad we got to meet Jessica's papa and momma," I said when we got to the pedestrian walkway crossing the highway.

"I noticed them a couple of nights ago," Mardi said.

"Oh, good catch. I hadn't seen them. I feel honored that Jessica called us back to introduce us." I was surprised they were younger than us, but I wasn't surprised that they were delightful and energetic, warm and loving.

A policeman halted traffic and we crossed over to the promenade. Folks of all ages were floating by on bicycles, men were walking their dogs, a *nonna* was walking along behind her grandchild, parents and their children were beginning to fill the park, and boats were gliding by in the harbor. The only thing marring the morning was a helicopter swinging wide over the water, probably filled with tourists, but it was gone in seconds, and soon afterward so was the whop-whop-whop of its mood-killing noise.

Buongiorno, said a man coming out of the shop where we'd promised to try their *gelatos* and pastries. *Ciao,* said another man walking into the same shop. It felt more like a Sunday than a Thursday.

"I can see coming here every year," I said. "We'll be the harbingers of spring for the residents of Maiori—like the swallows of Capistrano. Le Suite will know it's spring when we arrive."

"Good morning, sir," said an older man strolling slowly with his arms behind his back.

"Buongiorno, signore," I said.

"Funny, he thinks I'm not Italian," I said quietly to Mardi. "Do you suppose it's the suitcase I'm wheeling along behind me that gave me away?"

"That might have tipped him off," she said. "It couldn't have been the way you're dressed. You look totally Italian this morning."

I knew she was kidding. Passing me off as Italian is not going to happen even though I feel perfectly at home with Italian people—with all of Italy. I often wonder if hidden somewhere in my past is an Italian connection. I've come very close to ordering the *Ancestry.com* DNA test, but something always stops me—probably the fear that I would be devastated if the results show that I'm strictly Irish, Scottish, English, and German. If I don't take the test, I can hold out hope that I am a teeny-weeny bit Italian.

On the half mile walk to the convent we leapfrogged three fashionably dressed men several times, one of whom was walking a small dog. They were walking more slowly than we were, but they would amble past each time I stopped to take a photo or watch cyclists go by. A century ride, one hundred kilometers, must have been passing through town. In small groups, a total of at least thirty or forty cyclists rode by—men and women of all ages. I stopped each time to watch them. The riders called out *Buongiorno—Allo—Good morning.* I was curious to see what bikes were favored. I saw lots of Colnagos, a Bottecchia, and a Trek, as well as numerous Scotts, even an Orbea, and one gorgeous black-on-black Pinarello—now firmly at the top of my wish list.

"This would be a wonderful town to bike in—just you and me riding around. Lots of wide streets and the promenade to ride on. There's another Bottecchia—that's an Italian bike too," I said.

The rider yelled out *Hello*.

"Allo," I yelled back.

"Oh, Mardi, what a beautiful morning!" I said. The sight of brightly clad bikers riding at a brisk pace always sets my heart beating wildly.

"I have a wonderful feeling, everything's going my way..." Mardi sang, picking up on my happiness, as we approached Amici di San Francesco. We crossed the Amalfi Coast Highway at the harbor. This time we knew which gate to enter. We walked up the driveway and went in through the garden under the vine-covered trellis. It was like walking back a century.

"Buongiorno," I sang out to Gerardo, who was watering flowers.

Even before he looked up he said, "James... James Bond," and gave a hearty laugh of welcome as he turned toward us. *"Benvenuto,"* he boomed.

"We're happy to be here," I said and turned to Andrea, who was behind the lobby desk. "It's a gorgeous day—*bella giornata.*"

Andrea smiled and said, *"Buongiorno. Passaporti?"*

"Si," I said and reached into my back pocket where I'd placed the passports earlier, knowing we'd need them to check in.

"Lunch today?" Gerardo asked.

"No, we are going to eat lunch in Maiori," I said.

"Breakfast tomorrow?"

"Si, colazione domani."

"And this afternoon, what are you going to do?" Gerardo asked, ever the friendly man, ever the curious.

"As they say in America, just relax," I said.

"James Bond—relax? I don't think so," Gerardo joked.

Andrea handed us our passports and looked toward Gerardo.

"Follow me James, James Bond," he said, leading us toward an ancient caged elevator.

"I do not think that James Bond spends his days relaxing," he said as he held open the folding door. I wished my Sean Connery impression were better, but it would have ruined the beautiful moment Gerardo had created, so I simply smiled and turned my attention to the intricate craftsmanship of the building.

"Did you notice the ironwork, Mardi? It was beautiful," I said as we wheeled our suitcases out of the elevator and down a long hall. Gerardo was smiling.

He knew what was coming. We did not. He opened the door to our room and invited us in. He then pulled back the floor-to-ceiling drapes with a flair, as though he were opening the curtains for a stage play.

"Oh my, my," were the only words I could get out. The view of the beach and the ocean was overwhelming. We were so close it felt as if we were part of the scene—perched perhaps atop the mast of one of the sailboats lining the docks. We could hear the waves clearly and the cries of the seagulls—even the voices of fishermen as they made their way back into port with their morning's catch.

"Oh my, my," echoed Gerardo, getting a kick out of our reaction. I am sure that everyone he shows this room to is stunned the first time they see it. I knew that Gerardo had shown us a room the first day we were at the convent, but it couldn't have been this one—this room made us feel as though the whole of the Amalfi Coast was there just for our enjoyment—or maybe it was that we now knew that this was going to be ours for a few days and the realization was too much to process.

Oh my, MY!" I said again. I was repeating myself, but I could think of no other words except *Oh my God!* to match the impact of what Gerardo was showing us. It would not have been taking the Lord's name in vain, for I was silently praising Him for the beauty that must also have deeply affected Saint Francis the first time he saw this lovely spot.

"*Bella, bella,*" Mardi said.

"*Bello,*" Gerardo said as he stood to the side to let us get the full effect.

The room, if you studied it closely, was not all that special, but it was spacious, filled with light, and had that amazing view. It also had a large terrace with an unobstructed view of everything—people walking along the promenade, sleek sculls slicing through the water, swimmers braving the cool waters of the Mediterranean, lovers camped out on the rocks of the breakwater. It was a celebration of all that is beautiful about the Amalfi Coast and it was so close we felt we could reach out and gather it in.

I was falling in love again—another dream room to live in and write books—another place where we could enjoy the Italian people and Italy. It was perfectly centered on the harbor—I couldn't imagine a better place for a writer. The quiet ambience of a convent married to a million-dollar view with a perfect promenade just a few steps from our door. What could heaven have, besides God, that this didn't?

"He will never leave here," Mardi said as she stepped past Gerardo and onto the terrace.

"*Amo Gerardo,*" I said.

"*Per il mio amico,*" he said.

"You are definitely my friend. This is beautiful."

"Okay, James Bond—you may *now* relax," Gerardo said as he handed me the key and bid us goodbye.

"Mardi, you're a genius for finding this place. I love you," I said, twirling around on the terrace to take it all in.

"Oh yes—this is mine, isn't it?"

"Mio amica," I said as I kissed her and held the kiss for a long time. When I opened my eyes I looked up at the castle sitting high on the hill above us. It felt again as if we had walked into a fairy tale that would have a very happy ending.

Some moments stick in your mind forever. I was sure this would be one of them. We had seen before much of what lay before us, but we hadn't seen it from this perspective, nor with the knowledge that this would be our view of the world for as many days as we rented this room. And if we chose to come in the off-season, this could be our view for a lot of days the rest of our lives.

"No wonder we couldn't get a WWOOF job," I said. "You know how hard I tried, but nothing worked out. Apparently God had other things in mind for us. Maybe this is where we'll come and live."

"Yes," Mardi agreed, which totally surprised me. Apparently she was feeling the power of the room too.

"Seriously, I could write here—we've got the beauty, the inspiration."

"And the convent for quiet, for concentration," she said.

"Especially off-season."

"Can we get out of our reservation at Casa Mannini?" she asked.

"I don't know. I don't think so."

"If we didn't eat out we could afford this," she said.

"Oh look, a little icing on the cake—an old Cinquecento is sitting in front of the convent." I was standing on our balcony trying to take it all in—trying to make sense of our good fortune, how it was that on this morning we were staying in such a beautiful place. I walked back into the room, plopped onto the bed, and began replaying in my mind the highlights of this incredible morning.

"I've been wondering what I'd do if you died before you finished your next book," Mardi said.

"I don't like you," I blurted out and then tried to figure out why she was talking about my death. It seemed like an odd thing to say at that moment. I certainly didn't feel as if I was near my final curtain, but then I'm sure her father didn't feel that way either on a beautiful Father's Day fifty-five years ago, even though a few hours later he would die of a massive heart failure at the age of fifty-one. Mardi had seen what it was like for her mother to live without her husband the rest of her life. She lived almost forty-four years after her husband of twenty-five years died. So I suppose I shouldn't be surprised that Mardi wonders how long I will be around. She knows to the core of her being that you don't have to be old to die. She has lived with that knowledge since she was an eighth grader.

"Don't let anything happen to you, with or without a book," she said. "I want you around."

I suppose God paired me up with the perfect wife. One who, because of what had happened to her father, was willing to allow her husband to do what he felt was necessary to live as long as possible. When I got the bad news back in the Vietnam War years that I had a low number in the draft lottery, I made the commitment that if I were going to give up two or three years of my life in my twenties, I planned to get back more than two or three years of healthy, strong, productive living on the other side of my life. I can still see where I was standing—next to the drafting table in the front room of my apartment at 1201 D Street in Lincoln, Nebraska—when I wrote that promise to myself on one of the blue five-by-seven notecards I used then as my journal. If the U.S. Army was going to take those years away, I was going to keep myself as physically fit as a competitive athlete throughout my life. When I made that promise I had no idea biking would reward me as much it has. My commitment to biking, and it has been considerable, has rewarded me in ways, and in years, that I could never have imagined back then. I had no idea that the present day version of me could have given the 1969 model of me a good challenge in a short bike race and would probably have won a long race.

But that level of fitness would not have been possible if it weren't for Mardi not only allowing me to train all my life, but encouraging my hours of biking each day. She knows that time on the road makes my body stronger, and she also knows that I create better when I'm fit. The hours I spend biking are a good time to listen to my muse.

Mardi also recognizes that there are times when the work of the muse has been done and the words are ready to flow. I had been shown a spot on this earth that fueled my creativity, and I wanted to let my thoughts pour out— and she wanted to explore our new home, leaving me to enjoy the writerly atmosphere of the room.

The sounds of the harbor and the breezes blowing in off the sea, matched perfectly a dream I have been carrying for many years of writing in a lovely seaside Italian town—a village with the sparkling waters of an ocean stretching out to a distant horizon. As I wrote I watched fishing boats make their way into and out of the harbor. I got lost in a productive reverie that was not interrupted until Mardi returned an hour later.

"Did you get tea?" I asked her.

"No, I couldn't find any, but I found a garden with a spring right next to a canopy of wisteria. You could write there every morning. The feeling of this place is totally different from Casa Raffaele Conforti—it's so pastoral."

I could tell by the look on Mardi's face as she told me about the lovely spots she had found that she was as in love with this place as I was. We'd already fallen in love with Maiori, and now we had found what felt like the perfect room—a room that must have been matching Mardi's dream as well. Or maybe for Mardi it was not the room but the convent, the town, everything. An image flashed in my mind of us sitting in on a town meeting in Maiori—it was obviously a dream. I was understanding everything that was being said.

We've lived what some might call a peripatetic life, so we're used to change, to adjusting to new circumstances. The notion of living in Italy long enough to become woven into the fabric of the community was a wild idea for a couple who has had twenty or more addresses in their married life. We were wondering what it would be like to live in a different land, among different people—we were trying on for size a new version of our marriage and our lives—something we'd been doing since we boarded the *Oosterdam*. We were on a honeymoon, but in many ways it was not disconnected from the good life we'd been living. I was still writing, still communicating with my readers, and Mardi was still staying in touch with our kids and grandkids.

"Do you mind if I stay in heaven a little bit longer?" I asked.

She knew what I meant—I wasn't ready to let go of the moment. I sometimes get into reveries when all the world seems perfect. I've been transported to those dreamlike states by a song, or by a breeze blowing through the trees on a blue-sky day, or by choosing the perfect line through the twists and turns of a mountain road on my bike. At those moments I've felt a oneness with God— as though I was meant for that time, that place. I was feeling it that day—a moment of grace made even more special because I was sharing it with Mardi.

"I love the sound of the voices coming from the courtyard below us," I said. "Italians always sound like they're having a good time. I know that can't be true, but the Italian language flows so beautifully it sure sounds that way."

"You could put a desk right by the window. You could hear the people, the wind, and the waves while you write," Mardi suggested.

The joyful sound of kids playing soccer in the little *piazza* in the harbor drew us onto the terrace. The game was the foreground of a peaceful harbor scene with colorful boats in port, and beyond, a huge ship sat on the horizon, barely visible in the moist air. Below us in the circular court leading to the park, a professional photographer was using the scene that was captivating us as a background for a photo shoot of a sleek Jaguar automobile. Mardi chose that moment, which she knew had a hold on her husband, to do a bit of negotiating.

"If you'll get rid of your stuff, I'll come here every year with you," she said, and I could see she meant it. She has for years been trying to get me to be less sentimental. Only recently have I gotten rid of clothes I wore in college. I still have a shirt or two from the days when we first dated, and I have two of the three bikes we bought when we lived in Hawaii and didn't have a car. Her bike was stolen and we replaced it with a VW van. But those other two bikes have been with us through everyone of our twenty-some moves. But if we could spend part of every year in Maiori, I would be willing to keep those bikes only as sweet memories of our first three years of marriage.

We felt as if we were in an amphitheater, in a very special box seat, and the whole of Maiori's coastline was on stage for us to enjoy. We especially enjoyed watching the young and not-so-young lovers heading out to the distant headland projecting into the harbor.

"Would you like to go out on the rocks and cuddle?" I asked Mardi.

The beauty of the day was tempting a fair number of people to do just that—climbing up on huge boulders and snuggling, with the Mediterranean on one side and a romantic view of Maiori on the other. My photographer's eye pulled me out there too. A colorful, traditional boat is hard for me to resist, especially when I can use it in the foreground of an Amalfi Coastline photo. We were fully aware of just how good we had it. But even so, I got a little greedy and prayed for something we *didn't* have—an invitation to go out on a fishing boat.

A few moments later when an opportunity presented itself I didn't even do my part. I was taking photos of some men painting their wooden boats. We were joking with each other as they worked, but I didn't engage them in a meaningful conversation. I was having trouble thinking of the words for things I wanted to say, so rather than risk embarrassment I let the conversation die. As I walked away, disgusted with myself, I offered a different prayer, a prayer I'm still uttering—that someday I'll be fluent enough that I'll always feel comfortable engaging Italians in conversation.

"I love how intensely Italians talk with each other," I said when I rejoined Mardi on the promenade. "The eyes of those guys lit up when they were telling me about their boats. Their expressions were so vivid."

I explained to Mardi how inadequate I'd felt not being able to respond more fully to the men. A smile is good, but better is witty or knowledgeable repartee, and I had neither. I'd gotten some good photographs, and we shared some good laughs, but I would have preferred a meaningful conversation, especially because we shared a love of wooden boats.

The late afternoon light turned my thoughts back to photographing. Evening is perfect for taking a picture of almost anything, but it is especially good for photographing boats—the low angle light makes boats pop out from their background and gives definition to their sensual lines.

From the headland it was easy to see why Saint Francis and his followers had chosen this dramatic spot. On my first visit to Italy, I was told by my host that I could not return to America until I had seen Le Celle, the monastery Saint Francis had founded a few miles outside of Cortona, Tuscany. Straddling a granite gorge, it reminded me of Machu Picchu high in the Andean Mountains of Peru in its otherworldly magnificence. This religious retreat, nestled at the base of a cliff on the Amalfi Coast, while not as remote, nevertheless is inspiring.

I grew up loving architecture. I felt that the homes and spaces we live in affect the lives we lead. I can't help wondering who created these almost perfect outdoor environments that abound in Maiori and Amalfi. Did the love of Saint Francis for dramatic locations start all this? I may someday discover that no one person or group of persons is responsible—it may instead be attributable to the innate love of beauty and sense of heroic scale that Italians possess in spades. The Amalfi Coast, more than any other place I have been in the world seems to have an overwhelming number of splendid spaces where people want to gather to share their love of community.

And that is exactly what the people of Maiori were doing that afternoon. Young families were especially noticeable. I can't say with certainty that the kids of Maiori realize how good they have it—people are rarely afforded that wisdom until they get much older and a bit wiser—but from my vantage point, a kid's life in Maiori is pretty darn good. I know I am an outsider, and the opinion I offer is not born of years of study of this town, but nevertheless, Maiori offers what all parents want for their children—a safe, secure, friendly environment.

Near the playground we joined the queue to get a lemon ice from a colorfully dressed young woman dispensing the delicious treats from her bicycle-powered goody wagon. The sounds of the afternoon were as captivating as its appearance—lively music, conversations of dozens of parents keeping an eye on their kids, and the even livelier voices of the kids playing, along with gulls calling and waves rolling in. It was a good life we were taking part in that afternoon.

We sat down on one of the perfectly designed promenade benches to enjoy the sharp/sweet/cool taste of the lemon ice as well as the passing parade. The first person who recognized us was Mario, aka Gianni, riding by on his bike. We waved and he waved. A man carrying a very long fishing pole—perhaps twenty feet—caught our eye. He walked out to the water's edge and began casting into the surf. Watching the undulating line create graceful curves in the air before finally falling limp on the water was endlessly fascinating,

We were also enjoying watching a soccer game taking place right in front of us on the promenade—a pickup game kids were playing within sight of their parents. It reminded me of the stories I'd read about what Brooklyn was like in the forties and fifties when the Dodgers played in Ebbets Field and the kids of that neighborhood played stickball in the streets.

"I think this is one of the most liveable towns I've ever seen," I said to Mardi.

As if to emphasize that point Antonio walked by. He was the shop clerk who had helped us decide which man purse to buy. The whole day had been like that—a doubling down on our view of Maiori as being community oriented and perfect for families. It was small enough that you knew everyone yet large enough to possess contagious energy.

"Someone is running this town very well—the benches, the trees. I wonder if at one time the highway through town was wider but someone made the call that a wide promenade was just what this town needed," I said.

Mardi and I stayed on that bench enjoying the evening so long that the sun set, the soccer games ended, and most of the kids began heading home. The ones still in the park began putting jackets on. We weren't ready to let go of the day, so we ambled back past the playground and turned up Corso Reginna to stop by Rosario's shop. We planned to dine on our terrace to keep the mood of the day alive as long as possible—to do that we needed more Amalfi Coast pottery—some platters for serving cheese and *prosciutto*. We'd already made our choices, so it was a quick purchase. Rosario's wife, Marguerita, gave me too much change. She got a good laugh out of a foreigner catching her mistake. While pointing it out to her I mentioned that I had been in her store the previous day.

"You must speak *italiano* pretty well if you know the word for yesterday," she said. With that compliment she became one of my favorite people in Maiori, even though I knew she was assuming far too much. Rosario was already one of Mardi's favorites. He had entertained her with stories of the Amalfi Coast the day before and was doing the same today while I paid for our purchases. It was another demonstration of the knack Italians have for making the little things of life pleasant.

The same thing happened at the *supermercato*. We enjoyed, as always, choosing our food. I especially loved squeezing the bread to find the consistency and weight I was looking for. A substantial loaf is how I'd describe what I chose that night. I also chose a cheap local red wine, a brick of edam cheese, and thinly sliced *prosciutto*.

I often feel a bit inadequate when checking out—I'm worried that the clerk will ask me a question I don't understand. But in my more confident moments I know that it will be a good chance to learn more Italian. On this evening I needn't have worried. I commented in Italian about the incredibly low price for the wine—less than two euros a bottle. The young lady responded in English telling me that it was also a very good wine. I complimented her on her English and told her that we'd seen her yesterday and would always try to get in her checkout line.

"I am always here," she responded cheerily.

Why shouldn't checking out be a breeze? Why shouldn't we be treated graciously? It had been that kind of day. Walking home with our dinner was pleasant too. Most of the families on the promenade had headed home to get the kids in bed. The *passeggiata* was now dominated by young lovers, older folks, and always the dog walkers. Oh, what a civilizing influence the *passeggiata* is on society—so much better than watching the evening news walled up in your own home. On your daily walk among friends and neighbors you learn of the matters that are really important in your life and in your community rather than the salacious and sensationalistic stories nightly news broadcasts invariably push.

I had been marveling to Mardi all day about the sights and sounds of Maiori, and as we crossed the road to the convent with our dinner we were suddenly overcome by a scent that seemed unique to the Amalfi Coast and Capri.

"I'm not sure there's a better smell," I said.

I couldn't place it but knew I'd smelled it before. My associations with it were pleasant indeed.

"It smells like wisteria," Mardi said.

Sure enough, as we entered the convent we were suddenly shrouded in wisteria.

"You could build me an arbor like this," she said.

Even though I wasn't looking for any projects, I might be talked into one if I could be convinced that wisteria would thrive in Wisconsin. That's how good it smells. I did, however, offer Mardi an alternative.

"How about I just write a book and we come stay someplace where someone is already growing it?" I suggested as we stepped into the lovely covered walkway leading to the lobby of the convent. I suddenly heard Gerardo's booming voice.

"James, James," he called.

"*Buonasera, Gerardo*," I said and shared a few highlights of our day. He was delighted that we were having a good time—and that we'd done more than just relax.

"Did you explain to Andrea that we are staying two days?" I asked Gerardo.

"Yeah, yeah, yeah," he said with as much energy as though he were cheering for a goal by his favorite soccer player.

"*Va bene*," I said.

"You're quite a man, a good man, James," Gerardo said as he grabbed both my hands and arms in affirmation and gave a hearty laugh. "I have respect for you."

What I had done to deserve such acclamation I didn't know. I think it's just part of the Italian character to affirm people—to make them feel loved and appreciated. He had done it just by warmly calling me *James, James Bond*.

"Do you like the room?" he asked.

"Beautiful, *bella*. You gave us the perfect room. We're going to come back and stay a whole year," I said, smiling to let him know I was only half serious.

He slapped me on the back and said, "Oh, James," and launched into a flurry of Italian that I didn't fully understand, but his gestures told me he loved the way I joked with him. He seemed to understand how much I appreciated his hospitality. If we hadn't been hungry, I think we would have chatted all night with Gerardo, but it had been a long day and we were looking forward to dinner on our terrace before going to bed.

"We're going to call it a night. *Buona notte*," I said.

"*Buona notte*," Gerardo said reluctantly. Italians are really good at making you feel that anything less than a half hour conversation is too short.

"Let's take the lift," Mardi said.

"We didn't use an elevator but once on the boat—and here we're using it to go up one flight?" I teased.

It had been quite a day. We were quitting early enough that the promenade was still filled with people—still walking up and down along the beach. We could hear the waves and the muffled sound of young people having fun as we set up our evening meal on the terrace. It seemed right to eat under the stars. We had begun the day dining with Maximiliano, enjoying his view of the Tyrrhenian Sea, and now we were ending our day with this much more intense and animated view of the coast right at our feet.

With the sounds of the ocean as background music, we enjoyed one of the most memorable meals of our honeymoon right there on our terrace—an inexpensive bottle of wine, delicious bread, edam cheese and *prosciutto*. And later as we gazed at the rising moon—we shared chocolate. Our view of the Amalfi Coast that evening was phenomenal, made especially so by the dancing lights of passing automobiles and boats.

"We're going to get spoiled," Mardi said.

I smiled, blew a kiss her way, and toasted her. We discovered that night that the little *cappuccino* cups we'd bought from Rosario and Marguerita worked equally well for *limoncello*. Every once in awhile a day comes along that you know is special while you've living it. You don't need memory to color it in. This was one of those days.

CHAPTER FIFTEEN

Amici di San Francesco ~ Friday April 15 ~ 49 & Clear

Coming Full Circle

*The real voyage of discovery consists not in seeking new landscapes
but in having new eyes.*
MARCEL PROUST

■

*Love at first sight is easy to understand;
it's when two people have been looking at each other for a lifetime
that it becomes a miracle.*
SAM LEVENSON

"How do you do that—go right to the spot I want you to massage?" I asked, my voice gravelly with sleep.

"Umm, maybe it's a God thing," Mardi said.

"It must be, because I had hardly completed the thought when you began rubbing my shoulder."

"You can ask me, too," she said.

"Yeah, but it's nice to do it by just thinking about it."

I had been lying in the dark thinking—thinking about how blessed we were. I was listening to the gentle *putt-putt* of a fishing boat's diesel engine idling in the harbor. We'd walked among those boats the night before—speculating about which boats belonged to working fishermen and which belonged to sport fishermen.

"Just beautiful, isn't it?" Mardi said.

"Yeah it *is* a beautiful sound. Fishing boats heading out in the early morning, just like in Greece."

Thirty years ago, we sailed the Ionian Islands of Greece for two weeks. The first week we stayed in a villa taking day cruises from our home port in Nidri—the second week, being more seasoned sailors, we sailed from port to port, and slept each night on our boat. The sounds just outside our window in Maiori were the same as we'd heard all that week: engines idling, halyard hardware clinking against masts, and seagulls crying.

But on that trip I was working—filming as many as fifteen hours a day. Rarely was I able to turn my attention exclusively to Mardi. A honeymoon requires more than two weeks in an idyllic location—it requires time together. And that's what was turning *this* vacation into a *luna di miele*—a honeymoon.

"When you thought of staying in a convent, did you imagine it being this wonderful?" I asked.

"I thought it would be quiet and comfortable. I didn't even think about a view," Mardi said as she got out of bed to look for the boat we'd heard. I was glad she was curious. I wanted to see it too.

"Oh, look—the waves are huge—really rocking it around," I said as the boat passed by the breakwater. It was thrilling to know that fishermen were still heading out before dawn to make their living on the Amalfi Coast as they had for hundreds, perhaps thousands of years. We weren't seeing as many fishermen as Steinbeck saw, but it was nice knowing that tourism had not wiped out the fishing industry. People travel the world looking for beauty, but what keeps them coming back is discovering that farmers and fishermen are still making a living stewarding nature in these beautiful places. That was true of Tuscany and seemed true here too.

"It's so quiet that you can hear the waves," Mardi said as we got back into bed to soak up the soft sounds of morning—and that's the last thing I remember. The next time I opened my eyes, the day was well on its way. The sound of fishing boats and seagulls had been replaced by the more insistent sound of school kids and commuters—but not so insistent that they woke Mardi. While she slept I wrote about the sounds of silence and people who make their living from the sea. I hoped someday I'd get to head out to sea with a working fisherman to get a taste of what their lives are like, just as I had working alongside olive farmers. Fishermen are like farmers. Both are at the mercy of nature, which tends to ground them, giving them a firm foundation in the important things of the world.

At breakfast we discovered that there was no *Maximiliano*. Without such help we didn't quite know what to do or where to find things. Fortunately we weren't the only guests—Lars and Astrid knew the routine well and spoke excellent English. We exchanged the usual information fellow travelers share—

numbers of kids and grandkids, where we'd been and where we were going. They had visited Florence and Naples and even this convent on a previous holiday. I'm always envious of how easy it is for Europeans to get to Italy. Our new friends left the dining room promising to see us again the next day.

While we were trying to decide what to do with our day, we heard from behind us the deep, booming voice of Gerardo: "James, James Bond."

"Good morning, Gerardo," I said, turning to see his smiling face.

"It's all right?" Gerardo asked.

"It's all right—everything is very good—*va bene*." I said.

He asked about our plans for the day. When we told him we had none other than to enjoy Maiori, he offered to show us the Rossellini Room and the library. I wasn't prepared for what we discovered—*bella scoperta*. Italy, I am forever learning, is full of beautiful surprises. I have lots of favorite scenes from Rossellini's films. Gerardo led us to a room where one of them was filmed—the priests eating with the soldiers and the chaplain in *Paisa*. I was flabbergasted.

It was because of *Paisa* and other Rossellini films about World War II that I chose to include the filmmaker's name in the subtitle of my first book about Italy: *An Italian Journey: A Harvest of Revelations in the Olive Groves of Tuscany: A Pretty Girl, Seven Tuscan Farmers, and a Roberto Rossellini Film.* The heart and soul of my revelations about Italy came from his films. After seven weeks of picking olives with Italian farmers and a thousand miles of biking the backroads of Tuscany, I had eyes to see and ears to hear what the films of Rossellini had to tell me.

"Beautiful," was all I could say as I stood dumbfounded in front of still shots from many of my favorite films. My mind was reeling from the improbability of it all—that we would end up staying in the very monastery where the soldiers in *Paisa* found hospitality and comfort—and that we would find out about it by admitting we had no plans for our day.

"Good?" Gerardo asked.

"Very good. *Molto, molto bene.* I know this scene. Was it filmed right here?"

"Yes, *si,* in this room," he said proudly.

"Amazing. I had no idea *Paisa* was shot in Maiori—I love that film."

"We'll have to get a copy," Mardi said.

She was right. I should have copies of both *Paisa* and *Era Notte a Roma*, as well as *Rome Open City*—the three films of Roberto Rossellini that helped me gain the insight about Italians that I wrote about in my first book. I had rented them from Netflix, as I had dozens of other films about Italy, in my quest to comprehend the why of the country. Living in the homes of Italian farmers convinced me of the what—the answer to that question is hospitality. But it was Rossellini who opened my eyes to the why.

Another reason I should have Rossellini's films in my collection is that someday I'll be able to watch them without subtitles. Pietro, one of the more memorable characters from my first Italian sojourn, had told me that if I wanted to understand Dante's *Divine Comedy* I must become fluent in Italian. It was advice I took to heart. Pietro would know. He had learned English living in Australia. He understood the limitations faced by a person who does not know *italiano*—no language but Italian is up to the task of conveying Dante's mysterious message about the afterlife.

I am forever trying to understand why I have such a fascination with Italy and Italians, and moments like being in the Rossellini Room of a Renaissance-era convent give me a glimpse of the answer: Italians love the mysteries of life, and they celebrate those mysteries. Dante Alighieri wrote a book seven hundred years ago that Italian schoolchildren still read and memorize. And what is it about? It begins as an encounter with Hell and ends up a journey of the soul toward God. The fact that Italians memorize much of it, and that a man like Roberto Benigni has memorized *all* of it and performs it in *piazzas* all over Italy to overflow crowds gives non-Italians a glimpse into the Italian mindset. And someday, just as Pietro advised, I will get the full effect by learning Italian.

"Is this amazing or what?" I asked Mardi.

She could sense how grateful I was feeling—knowing what Rossellini's films have meant to me. I'm sure Gerardo was a bit mystified by my over-the-top reaction to the news that a seventy-year-old film had been shot in his convent, but he had work to do, so he left us to wander and wonder, telling us to take all the time we wanted.

"Here's a scene of Saint Francis feeding the birds," Mardi said, pointing out a still from *The Flowers of Saint Francis*, another film about the character of Italians that made the cut in my first book about Italy.

"I am amazed that Rossellini was so connected to Maiori, but my research uncovered none of this," I said as I leaned down to look at yet another still shot from *Paisa*. "How did *you* discover this place?"

"I found it in a book about religious pilgrimages," Mardi answered.

That was part of the explanation of how we'd ended up in this convent that was so instrumental in Rossellini's films, but our pinball had to bounce quite a few times before a book about religious pilgrimages became a factor. After all, if Salvatore hadn't been fully booked, we would still be in Amalfi.

"So what are we going to accomplish today?" Mardi asked, ever the gentle persuader. My mind was focused on mysteries and she wanted to get something done. I could have spent all morning examining the room's memorabilia, but a beautiful day was waiting outside. This room I could explore some winter day.

"Maybe nothing more than living the good life," I responded. We had begun the day listening to a fishing boat motor quietly out of the harbor—maybe it would be a good day to eat a little of what the fishermen went out to catch. We had our sights set on a seaside restaurant where we could watch the boats coming and going from the harbor as we ate.

Waves were crashing all around us as we got to our table. We decided that I should sit in the shade of the umbrella and Mardi would get the warmth of the sun. I was dressed fashionably Italian with a sweater around my shoulders to put on if the ocean breeze chilled me.

"Oh, this is so beautiful," Mardi exclaimed, and she was right. We were so far from shore it felt as if we were aboard a boat, but without the rocking motion. As a sailboat motored by, Mardi's thoughts, I was quite sure, joined mine on that sailboat.

"What size boat is that?" she asked.

"I'd say about a twenty-six or twenty-eight-foot—about the same size we sailed in Greece. Wouldn't it be great, sailing from port to port along the Amalfi Coast, sleeping in the harbors or choosing a hotel right on the water?"

We got lost in our dreams. We had always wanted to go cruising again—this time without a film assignment—with our friends Roger and Bev, who had been with us on our first sailing adventure. But for Roger and Bev a journey by sailboat was no longer an option. Roger's health had forced him to sell his pride and joy—a 36-foot Hunter. Even sailing on the lakes of Nebraska was no longer possible.

I had lost count of the number of times we had talked about sailing with Roger and Bev again. On that first excursion we were all in our thirties. We should have repeated it in our forties or fifties, but somehow you always feel you can get to it next year. Unfortunately, next year doesn't always work out. It had been that way with our honeymoon. Heck—it had even been that way with our relationship—we knew things weren't right, but we didn't take the steps to correct a marriage that we knew could be better—and so it languished. But I didn't want to pursue those thoughts.

Mardi was still gazing at the sailboat, probably recalling the wonderful time we had docking each night in a different town, walking a few feet to enjoy a great Greek meal. It seemed like a good time to ask her if she'd be interested in sailing around Italy. But the conversation didn't get there. We began talking about how different this dining experience had been from all of our other meals. The only reason we could come up with was that we had chosen a restaurant for its view. Lunch wasn't truly a disappointment—how could it be when we felt as if we were sitting on the deck of a boat anchored just off the coast, but this truly was a place that only a tourist would choose. While waiting for our check, Mardi turned to her guidebook and I to my Italian dictionary.

"Avoid Italy in August," she reported.

"*Barca* is boat. *Basta* is enough," I said as we turned our thoughts to the rest of our day.

Gerardo had made our morning special—we decided we'd let Jessica color in our afternoon. Even before we got to Le Suite, while we were walking up Corso Reginna, Jessica greeted us. She cited a few possibilities and then pointed to Castello di San Nicola de Thoro-Plano high above, the fortified castle to which the residents of Maiori fled when marauders attacked the city in the Middle Ages. It sounded like a story we wanted to hear the rest of.

Its location ensured that those with evil intentions would be tired by the time they reached the castle walls. The same is true for the merely curious today. The serious part of the hike started at the Church of San Pietro, where steps began claiming elevation quickly. We soon passed through a very old *piazza*. It was easy to imagine the whole neighborhood gathering every day to wash clothes and fill water jugs.

The views were spectacular—we were looking down at the streets of Maiori and out at the deep blue of the Mediterranean. It both energized and calmed us. We rested frequently. Thoughts of Jessica came to mind as we climbed. We often turned and looked back toward Corso Reginna and waved, wondering whether she could see us as we made the slow ascent. We could see the very spot where we'd been standing as she pointed out our route.

The chiming of the bells of Santa Maria let us know our progress in fifteen-minute increments as we passed farm after farm on the terraced slopes—lambs, turkeys, and goats as well as lots of children, plus more churches, *piazzas,* and fountains. Jessica had warned us that the climb would be long and hard. She was surprised when we told her we were going to do it anyway. The higher we climbed, the smaller the people down below became, and the more we understood her concern.

Each time we stopped to rest, we looked out to sea. We were watching boats crossing the bay—comparing their progress to ours, imagining races between us—were we going to get to the castle before they disappeared from sight? These games took our minds off our labored breathing and fast-beating hearts.

The barking of dogs echoed off the ancient walls as we made our way ever upward past houses that must have been along this trail for hundreds—possibly thousands—of years. The stones had been worn smooth with the passing of millions of footsteps. In Italy, you never lose sight of a deep connection to enduring time.

"*Attenzione,*" Mardi said, warning me of yet another pile of dog poop. I was lagging behind as usual, trying not to soak my shirt with sweat and stopping frequently to take photographs of houses built where they shouldn't be. Italians have a knack for making beautiful places even more beautiful with the improbable structures they build. Maybe it's because I'd like to live in such a dramatic place that their houses fascinate me. Most people would think about the difficulty of getting to these homes hanging off cliffs—I tend to focus on the beauty of the location. I guess that makes me more romantic than practical.

"Hello puppy," I said to a small dog passing us. I wondered whether he understood English and whether he had been responsible for the *attenzione* that Mardi had just called out. But he said nothing and kept going as though he had an appointment somewhere and couldn't be bothered with a silly tourist.

I glanced up the hill and saw Mardi sitting on a small wall waiting for me. Her presence was bothering another dog—thankfully this dog was behind bars. He sounded huge. Just as I reached her I heard the owner tell the dog to be quiet.

Mardi handed me a water bottle. I was more than ready to take a break, but I wanted to do it where we weren't disturbing dogs or owners. We soon met a tourist on the way down. I had no doubt we were on the right trail, but it was nice to get confirmation. We had by then been climbing almost an hour and were still looking straight down at Maiori. We could see farms on the other side of the valley perched high on the slopes, and serving as a backdrop for all this grandeur was the magnificent ocean. Agonizingly close above us loomed the castle, but it was still straight up.

"Oh, it's going to be beautiful up there," Mardi said. "I think this is what makes the Amalfi Coast so special."

"Do you mean the combination of mountains and sea?" I asked. She twirled as though she were filming it all in a three-hundred-sixty-degree arc.

"Look there's another mountain range over there," she said, pointing to a distant ridge.

"Beautiful panorama," I said and would have taken one on my phone, but I never know what to do with panoramas after I take them.

"Talk about being on top of the world," she said.

"I wonder if Jessica can see us now?"

"Let's wave to her," Mardi suggested, and we did.

"We're just about there," I said, realizing I'd been saying that for quite some time.

"I feel stronger today."

"Me too," I said, but I wasn't sure I meant it. I think I was just walking slowly and taking lots of breaks to try to keep my shirt dry.

We each took another drink of water and resumed hiking. We were close enough we could imagine the end of the climbing. We could see where we were, where we were going—as well as the trail we'd follow on the open slope beneath the castle—an area that was kept clear of houses so that invaders would be exposed to attack.

"We did it!" Mardi exclaimed when at last we were directly beneath the wall of the castle.

"There's a bench here," I said, breathing hard. I'd given up keeping my shirt dry. "I want to take a picture of you sitting here. I want to remember this."

The view was marvelous, stunning, captivating—I kept searching for words but none seemed adequate, so I kept taking photos—but none of them did the job of capturing the feeling of being perched so high above Maiori.

Jessica had told us it would be absolutely beautiful. She didn't, however, mention that a very personable and entertaining man would be awaiting our arrival. By the time I got to the castle gate, Mardi and Crescenzo were good buddies. He left no doubt that he was delighted to share his good fortune with us. He led us to a turret with an out-of-this-world view. I looked through the little window and said, "This is where I want to write my book about Italy—right from here." Another day, another mind-blowingly gorgeous spot on this earth to set my mind to fantasizing. Italy has a way of doing that to me.

I sat down and began to imagine what it would be like writing by that window day after day with such a stunning view to inspire me. I hadn't forgotten about the view from our room at the convent, but this was even more spectacular. I looked out at the immensity of the sea and at the ridgetops surrounding Maiori, and said a silent prayer of thanksgiving for Jessica for suggesting we climb up here. The ridgetops that had looked so high when we were standing on Corso Reginna were now far below us. I glanced at the seaside restaurant where we'd eaten lunch and then followed with my eyes as best as I could the route we'd climbed to get to this spot. I was amazed.

"Is this where you sit, Crescenzo? Did you see us walking up here?" I asked.

He told us he had many places where he could see those who would soon be invading the quiet of his days, just as the defenders of Maiori were able to watch assailants advance on the castle. I had the feeling he had been the caretaker of Castello di San Nicola de Thoro-Plano for many years. He knew exactly where to step and was able to grab things to show us without even looking to see where they were.

"Is this where you sleep?" I asked as we stepped into a room with a small alcove.

"No, I have an apartment," he answered, dashing my romantic vision of a Renaissance man living in a Middle Ages castle. It certainly looked as if someone lived here—maybe he did everything *except* sleep here.

"Your family crest?" Mardi asked as she stepped up to a commemorative display.

"*Sì*, Martino. My name is Crescenzo di Martino."

He proudly told us, if I understood him correctly, that a member of his family had been taking care of the site for the past two hundred-plus years. He showed us the keys to the castle and described the protection it offered to the villagers and how it was defended. Maybe I *was* correct in holding a romantic vision of Crescenzo. He certainly looked the part. He was a barrel-chested man whose huge hands convinced me that he had done a lot of hard work. He was friendly, engaging, and seemingly the perfect man for this job.

"May I take a picture of you?" I asked.

He loved that. He showed us photos of him posing with visitors over the years and decades. Just as I was trying to figure out how old he was, he proudly told us that he was *settantotto,* seventy-eight.

He was enjoying showing us around. We were enjoying his generous use of Italian as he explained the daily routines—where they watered their animals and ground grain for flour—he wanted us to have a complete picture of what life was like for those who lived behind the fortified walls of the castle. He also wanted us to know that families lived here, not just warriors. He too was growing food here, grinding grain, baking pizzas, reading books.

"Agosto—limoni. Settembre—vino. Ottobre—oliva." Crescenzo explained the harvests and when they occurred. "Baptismal for baby," he said as he told us about the church. Ours was not a linear discussion—it popped all over the place depending upon what caught our eye or what Crescenzo thought would interest us. He was the kind of guy I could spend the whole day with and still want to be with him longer.

"Oliva finito," he said, letting us know that either there were no longer olive trees within the walls of the castle—or maybe that it was the wrong time of the year for making olive oil. I think it was the latter, but I got him off track.

"Look at the walking sticks."

"No, no. For fruit," he said with a hearty laugh at my blunder. He grabbed one and demonstrated how the sticks were used for picking fruit.

"This is a strange-looking axe," I said pointing to a sharp tool with a very wide blade.

"Guillotine," Crescenzo joked—at least I hoped he was joking. He showed us a huge set of pliers and said, "Take your teeth out." Maybe he wasn't joking about the guillotine after all. Mardi and I looked around for something else to talk about and noticed buildings above us, much higher up the hill.

"Bella, bella," Mardi said as we saw what looked like a church above us.

"Let's go up," I said.

"Are we allowed?" Mardi asked Crescenzo. He directed us first to another structure not quite so far up the steep slope.

"Casa Romano," he said, pointing toward the steps we were to climb. It was at that point we realized he wasn't going with us—he wasn't going to climb those steps for the thousandth time. Every time we looked back he motioned for us to keep climbing. The higher we climbed the more enthusiastically he waved.

"We're home," Mardi said when at last we reached the door of the Roman house. As with everything from that site the view was fantastic.

"A Roman house," Mardi said repeating what Crescenzo had said to us as though she couldn't believe she was walking through a house an ancient Roman once lived in—this was something for history books, not for hiking to.

"Molti passi," I shouted to Crescenzo far below as we began climbing the many steps leading ever upward from the house.

"What a beautiful day to be here," Mardi said as she took a moment to catch her breath. I stopped and caught mine as well.

Far below, Crescenzo was still waving, encouraging us to look at everything. We stopped to read every plaque—*Tall window of the ancient church of San Nicola*, I read in both English and Italian. It was a chance to hone our Italian and give our hearts a break.

We read, climbed, and read until we had climbed as high as we could climb.

"Wow. Wouldn't this be a beautiful place to bring a picnic lunch?" I asked.

I hadn't brought a full meal, but I had enough for a snack—a pear, an apple, and a fig bar to share.

"Good idea to come up here."

At first I thought Mardi was speaking of the castle, but then I realized, as she looked around in wonder, that she was referring specifically to this last climb, the climb that Crescenzo didn't make. There are some things on your bucket list that you don't remove once you've done them. You just leave them there, knowing that, God willing, you'll be able to do them again. Jessica had put Castello di Thoro-Plano on our list and that's where it was going to stay. Italy is like that too. It is never going to disappear from our to-do list, no matter how many times we travel to this boot-shaped land. *Paradise* no longer conjures images of beaches graced by palm trees—paradise is the endlessly fascinating people and country of Italy.

"Ohhhh, this is beautiful," I said and looked at Mardi to see if she was thinking what I was thinking. She obviously was. Her face was absolutely glowing. I don't think she had ever looked better to me.

Not that I thought there was any danger of forgetting the moment I nevertheless asked Mardi to turn slightly toward me so that I could create a portrait of her sitting on that ancient wall framed in a doorway capped by a Roman arch—her smile was every bit as glorious as the vista commanded by the castle.

"Isn't this *something!*" she exclaimed.

It wasn't the word she chose that let me know how thrilled she was—it was the emotion in her voice.

"*Bella, bella, bella,*" I said feeling very inadequate as a wordsmith. We were both overwhelmed by the beauty of the site—as well as all the work of people long ago to create what we were now enjoying.

"Are you okay?" Mardi asked.

"Just enjoying the view and the moment," I said. She must have seen something in my face that made her realize that I was overwhelmed to the point of overload.

"This is unfathomable," she said.

I asked her what she meant. She wasn't shy in her answer. She was thinking not just of how spectacular this site was but of all that we were experiencing—not just in Italy, but in our lives together. She was trying to convey that this moment epitomized all that was good about our lives. We had endured hardship to get to this moment, it had been a tough climb to get all the way up here, but oh, my, was the reward worth it. We were feeling a deep sense of accomplishment for hiking so high. We were also feeling a sense of accomplishment for staying with our marriage through so many tough times.

Sometimes a moment sums things up nicely—this moment was doing just that. We were celebrating it together—just the two of us. We knew Crescenzo was far below us somewhere, but we couldn't see him. This castle and all of Italy was ours for the moment. Our life together was ours to enjoy too. We had worked hard for the benefits that we were reaping. Our unconditional love for each other at that moment was overwhelming us. With God's grace we had endured, and this moment, on this mountaintop was confirmation that we had arrived at a special level—with a special understanding of the grace that had delivered us to what felt like the pinnacle of providence. Only a few times in my life have I felt as if I was at the absolute center of God's will. This was one of them.

We stayed in that moment of grace, and blue sky sunshine, until we became aware that Crescenzo had other guests. He was entertaining a young couple who had entered the castle without our noticing. Mardi looked at the time and reminded me that it was a long way back to Maiori. I reluctantly began following her down the steps to say goodbye to Crescenzo and offer a token of our appreciation for not only his hospitality but the knowledge he had shared with us. He was, I was certain, at least partly responsible for how good Mardi and I were feeling. He had certainly rewarded us with his gift of hospitality, and I wanted to make sure he knew we appreciated it. He noticed me making a contribution to the upkeep of the castle and interrupted his comments to the young couple to come over and say goodbye.

I should have told him that we'd be back, but I didn't. I also wanted to ask him if there was a relative waiting to take his place if ever he retired. But the young couple was waiting.

"*Grazie,*" was all I said, and I truly meant it.

Mardi said, "Thank you."

"*Prego,*" Crescenzo said and gave that beautiful little Italian nod of his head as if to say *My pleasure.*

The depth of our feeling for each other at that moment was conveyed not in the number of words we chose to use, but in the manner in which those few words were said. We exchanged hugs and Italian brushings of the cheeks and left.

I was in no hurry to get down from either the literal or figurative heights we had been enjoying. The light was much different than it had been on the climb. I took many of the same shots to compare the difference that the angle of the sun makes in a photograph. Mardi was patient with me. She was enjoying the breaks too, as well as the slow descent.

While photographing the flowing patterns of a wrought iron gate I disturbed the peace of a small dog. It began yapping at me. I moved on. A few moments later I was surprised to see that same little dog walking down the steps beside me as though he had adopted us. Where we were going seemed to be where he was going.

"Oh, look where we are. Not too much farther," I said when at last we reached the ancient *piazza* where we'd filled our water bottles on the way up. A traditionally-dressed woman was washing vegetables in the fountain. When I stopped to take a photograph, the dog kept going—so much for adopting us.

"See that, Mardi?" I asked. "The horizon is finally cutting through the dome of Santa Maria a Mare. Our adventure was almost over. We'd soon be on Corso Reginna.

"Oh good—a railing," Mardi sighed as we began the last few hundred feet of our descent.

Near the bottom of the steps, an older man just beginning the climb greeted us. We turned to watch his slow climb and noticed the castle high above, still glowing in the evening sun. In fading light we stepped onto the level streets of Maiori and relaxed. The first thing that caught our eye, now that we no longer had to watch the placement of our feet with every step, was the name "Martino" on a building we passed. We were amassing a lot of questions for Crescenzo the next time we saw him. We imagined that knowing the history of the Martino family would tell us a lot about the history of Maiori.

I was surprised by how good it felt to be back on Corso Reginna—the easy walking, the familiarity, made me feel great. I will never tire of the sounds of Maiori—kids playing soccer, dozens of conversations, yet hardly any cars. And then the bells began ringing—not the timekeeping bells, but the call-to-worship bells.

"*Buonasera*," said a woman passing by with a small bag of groceries.

"*Buonasera*," I said and nodded to her. I love the friendliness of Italians. It reminds me of the friendliness of my hometown. You would never think of passing someone on the street without saying hello, or in some way acknowledging their presence. The same seemed true here.

"Is she there?" Mardi asked.

Jessica not only was there, she was making her way out of the bar to greet us. She, like Crescenzo, must have been anticipating our arrival.

"You climb to *castello*?" she asked.

"Yes, yes, thank you," I said.

Mardi pantomimed breathing hard.

"*Quanto tempo?*" Jessica asked. "How long take you?"

"We ran up, maybe ten minutes," I said with a smile. *Dieci minuti.*"

"*Teen meenuts*," she laughed and made a gesture of elongating her nose Pinocchio-style.

"Would you believe a half hour, forty-five minutes," I said as though it were nothing.

"I do not believe you," she answered.

"Maybe a little longer," I smiled, acknowledging that she had my number, and told her how much we had enjoyed ourselves—how special the day turned out.

"*Bella panorama?*" she asked.

"*Bellissimo*," I said and pulled out my camera to show her the photo of Mardi framed by the Roman arch.

She kissed her fingers and said, "Beautiful," and then quickly added, "We see you later tonight?"

"I don't know. We want to go sit on the beach and feed the birds—and watch the sunset. I think we are tired," I said. "You wore us out today."

"No, never," she said, lifting our spirits.

Every time we saw her it made us smile just to be in her presence. She was a bit of a romantic. She never failed to let us know in one way or another that she loved seeing old people in love. She never said it that way, but I don't think she would have adopted us so completely had we been a couple in our forties or fifties who openly expressed their love for one another. But maybe I'm wrong about that. Maybe I should just leave it at *Jessica's a romantic.*

We're romantics too, and we wanted to end this day listening to the waves crashing on the beach and the seagulls crying. I'd been carrying bread for the birds all day. We also still had a little food for ourselves. We got to the end of Corso Reginna and waited for *il poliziotto* to stop the traffic. As I waited I thought about how much more I enjoyed this personal touch rather than pushing a button to get a *Walk* signal.

The moment we were on the other side of the traffic the sound of kids playing, waves crashing, and birds in flight took over. No wonder the promenade is filled every evening. It's like entering another world the moment you step across the highway. I love the worlds that exist on either side, but on that night we wanted the ocean to dominate. We had been in the mountains, now we wanted the calming effect of the water lapping on shore.

"I think I can see our bench right now—the one with our name on it," I said.

It's funny how quickly a person becomes attached to certain locations. It was as if we were heading to our favorite pew in church. The bench was the first one we had chosen—where Mardi had fallen asleep. In my mind this was now our bench. On our first day in Maiori we had watched the waves break on shore from that bench as the sun made its journey toward the horizon, and that was exactly where we wanted to end this day, in familiar and comfortable surroundings.

"Isn't this beautiful?" I said as we sat down. It had been a long time since it had felt so good to sit. Mardi reached into my backpack and pulled out a large chocolate bar that I hadn't realized I'd been carrying all day. We came close to devouring the whole thing as we sat there enjoying the sound of kids playing all around us and the antics of the birds as we flicked pieces of bread toward the least aggressive members of the flock. Watching the *passeggiata* was the perfect antidote for our weariness. These contented people were a terrific reminder of all that we love about Italy. And if by chance a few of them weren't contented, they sure weren't showing it. They all looked just like us—happy to be where they were.

"The town seems even more alive tonight," I said.

"It's Friday," Mardi reminded me.

"Maybe that explains why everyone looks so happy. The weekend is here."

The promenade did seem to have an especially enthusiastic feeling, as though the collective presence was expecting something big to happen. But maybe Mardi was right, the joy we were sensing might be attributable to the natural rhythms of the week—to kids who weren't going to school the next day—to parents who weren't going to work.

When we had exhausted the snacks in my backpack our thoughts turned to stopping by the market on the way back to the convent. We wanted to maintain the mood we were in. Our dinner would be light and simple and within sight of the sunset. Simple food, simple surroundings, simply prepared—cheese, *prosciutto*, bread, fruit, and wine were what we wanted.

We had by then fallen in love with the ritual of stopping each evening at the market to buy whatever appealed to us. That night it was Edam cheese again and the same bread we had chosen a couple of days earlier. We had wine—no need to buy more. We hopped in the line of the English-speaking cashier. Her English was good, better than Jessica's, but her personality didn't come close. We rarely got beyond simple pleasantries, but her line was quick and efficient, and we knew we wouldn't be embarrassed by slowing things down because of our lack of fluency in Italian.

We crossed back over the highway to rejoin the *passeggiata*. The west end of the promenade, from Corso Reginna to the harbor where the convent was located, was typically a more diverse lot—young parents with babies in strollers, teenagers wanting to be away from their parents, and old people, as well as the everpresent dog walkers.

We arrived at the convent just as the sun was flattening out on the horizon. By the time we stepped onto our terrace, we had only half of an orange ball to watch disappear into the ocean. We had arrived in time to watch the sky above us light up from the reflected rays of the sun as the sky darkened and the clouds began to glow.

Mardi told me she'd chosen the Edam cheese because it was good for my heart. Certainly the waves pounding the shore and the brilliant display in the heavens were good for my heart as well. Wine, Saint Paul had assured us, was good for our stomachs. On that night it felt like *everything* was good for us. Climbing to the castle had been good for us—so was Crescenzo's commentary on the survival of Maiori because of the fortifications of San Nicola—as was the *passeggiata*. Italy at that moment, and in all moments, seemed good for us.

"Let's take it easy on our legs tomorrow," I said. "I want to be ready for Vittorio Sunday in case he has lots of work for us."

"I can't believe he invited us to his farm," Mardi said.

"And that Sergio is going with us," I added.

We were both pinching ourselves over our good fortune. Each time I got on my computer I feared I'd see an email from Vittorio or Sergio telling me that something had come up and we wouldn't be able to go to the farm on Sunday.

The gentle *putt-putt* of a fishing boat pulling into the harbor reminded me of my desire to spend a day on the water with a real fisherman, one who knew the sea as intimately as I got to know the fields I'd prepared for planting when I was a wheat farmer for my dad and later for myself. If Vittorio did cancel, I would try to salvage the day by spending it with a fisherman.

As we sat on the terrace, we again sang Jessica's praises for suggesting that we climb to the castle. We had a strong feeling of accomplishment and a deep sense of gratitude for having met a stalwart of the community, a member of the di Martino family. We smiled as another stalwart of the community showed up. A policeman in the park interrupted our thoughts and those of many others as well. The first to notice was the driver of the car the kids had been hanging around. He soon drove off. We then saw a man walking quickly toward a car parked on the far side of the circle drive.

"That's funny—all he had to do was show up, pull out his clipboard, and people came running," I said.

"So there are some places in Italy you can't park," Mardi said.

"You'd think those places would be on a blind curve where the road is only one car wide, but no, it's there in the park," I said.

It seemed odd to hear ourselves complaining about some facet of Italian society.

"What can I get you?" Mardi asked.

"A *limoncello?*"

"I can do that," she said.

"Are you vying for woman-of-the-year honors?" I asked, smiling.

She poured a small amount in our donkey cups and handed one to me. We had just enjoyed another wonderful meal on the terrace. It had been very similar to the previous night's feast, and we saw no reason to try to improve on it.

"Aren't we the intrepid travelers?"

"Why do you say that?" Mardi asked.

"I was just thinking about Crescenzo and Jessica—their reaction, I guess, to us climbing all the way up there," I said. "Can you toss me that brochure about the castle?"

"But it's in Italian," she warned.

"Mardi, I can read Italian."

She knew I was joking. But often I could get pretty close to figuring out the thrust of printed pieces that relied heavily on photos and illustrations.

"That was heaven," I said as I looked through the brochure and was reminded of the stories Crescenzo had shared with us.

"Would you like more *limoncello?*" Mardi asked.

"I'm done for the night. It will keep until tomorrow. We've had a good day."

Mardi started massaging me. My legs loved the attention. They *needed* the attention. Walking is one thing. Climbing uneven steps is another. That was the reason I'd jokingly referred to ourselves as intrepid travelers. It's the reason Crescenzo was amazed. It was the reason Jessica was so impressed with what we had done and how quickly we had done it. It was why we were both feeling so blessed. We had just enjoyed a beautiful day, *una bella giornata*, that we never would have experienced had we not been in good shape, had we not been willing to push ourselves outside our comfort zone. And now Mardi's hands were working their healing magic.

"Oh Mardi, you're wonderful," I said and meant it to the core of my being. The relationship we had together, now that we were allowing ourselves to love each other unconditionally, was indeed full of wonder.

We would have loved to go back to Le Suite to spend more time joking with Jessica, but the terrace that Gerardo had given us, with its gorgeous but calming view of the Amalfi Coast, seemed like the perfect place to end our unbelievably good day. Despite Jessica's assertion that she didn't think it was possible to wear us out, the hike up to Crescenzo's castle had done just that. We were content to end the day listening to the soothing sounds of halyard hardware clinking on the masts of the sailboats and the occasional thrum of a diesel engine bringing a fishing boat back to the harbor. We had begun the day with those sounds. Coming full circle seemed the best way to end another surprising day of grace and goodness on the Amalfi Coast.

The Heart of Maiori

*Mystery creates wonder and
wonder is the basis of man's desire to understand.*
NEIL ARMSTRONG

■

*I love you not only for what you are,
but for what I am when I am with you.
I love you not only for what you have made of yourself,
but for what you are making of me.*
ROY CROFT

After our first day at the convent we thought we would never want to leave. The room was perfect for our needs—the view was inspiring, and the feeling of being right on the water was thrilling—but we soon discovered we deeply missed the people we'd gotten to know along Corso Reginna. We had lost our community. They missed us and we missed them, so when a rate under forty euros a night popped up for Casa Mannini I grabbed it.

"Somebody walks by our window whistling every morning at six-thirty," Mardi said as she stepped back into our room carrying her devotionals. Usually I'm the first one up, but she must have gone out on the terrace to read, hoping that if she was quiet I might sleep a bit longer.

"It's probably Gerardo beginning his workday," I said.

I'd been lying in bed listening to the morning. I swear that the world sounds different along the Amalfi Coast—or maybe it's just here at the convent. The cries of the gulls, the beat of the diesel engines, even the waves breaking onshore reverberate with an intensity that seems out of proportion to our distance from the harbor—as though I might step out of our door and find waves breaking on our terrace. It reminded me of the acoustics in the Pantheon. The dome gathers and amplifies sounds, making a whisper uttered on the other side of the huge room sound as though the whisperer were standing at your side. Maybe the cliffs surrounding the convent do the same thing.

Mardi pulled me out of my ponderings and began testing my resolve to stay in Italy until our anniversary. She first mentioned how gorgeous the weather had been in Wisconsin. And then she asked, "Don't you kind of miss biking?" Neither of those jabs did I parry.

"Maybe we need to go to a poorer part of Italy, like Eboli," she said. We had finally connected.

"How about Eboli on Monday," I suggested.

"You mean by car?"

"Yeah. Presuming we don't work ourselves silly at Vittorio's on Sunday and need a rest."

Mardi was getting impatient. Her German was showing—she was feeling too much grass growing under her feet. Dieterich, if I haven't mentioned it, is her maiden name. We were, however, letting a little grass grow that morning, enjoying the ambience of the room as long as possible. Even though luxury was not what came to mind when I thought of staying at a convent, we felt as though we were participating in the lifestyles of the rich and famous. I imagined that I was feeling what John Steinbeck felt when he found himself in a town he had never heard of, living right on the beach—typing away—surrounded by Italians living as they've always lived, making their living from the ocean. The sound from the harbor of fishing boats coming and going was a sound my romantic heart could listen to all day. Mardi fell asleep to the romance of it. I jotted notes.

"I'm going for a little walk," I said when Mardi woke up an hour and a half later.

"Are you going to go photograph?"

"Yes—I can hear fishermen coming back in."

But we snuggled instead and fell asleep again. Photographing fishermen is one thing, but cuddling to the sound of fishermen returning to port is quite another.

"Here comes another boat," I said some time later. I had no idea how long we'd been asleep—I just knew that it had been a good sleep. To show my appreciation I served her breakfast in bed. It wasn't much—orange juice, yogurt and nuts, but it got her attention.

"Have you always been so thoughtful?"

"Apparently not, or you wouldn't have asked the question," I said as I leaned down to kiss the top of her head.

She was right to ask. I had *not* always been so thoughtful. But a switch had been thrown in our marriage, and we were taking a great deal of pleasure in delighting each other. It wasn't just the disappearance of kids from our list of responsibilities, nor, for me, having the best and most fulfilling job of my life—a writer whose first book was well received and was finding more and more readers every year. No, the difference came about when we began trusting each other with our vulnerability—our need for each other; when we accepted that we weren't perfect or even close to it. We came to the realization we had hurt each other in the past, but now we were putting the interests of each other first. As my favorite spinning song, "Wake Me Up," puts it succinctly and perfectly, *Life's a game made for everyone, and love is the prize.* I just wish I'd learned the rules of the game a long time ago.

The photographs I took that morning were not the great images I'd imagined while Mardi slept and I wrote. By the time we got to the harbor, the magical light of morning was gone. We walked along the quay arm in arm, noting the bright colors of the boats and the nets. Fishing boats always conjure happy memories of fishing with my father. Dad bought a 14-foot aluminum boat, a 9-1/2 hp Evinrude motor, and an eight-by-eight-foot canvas tent the summer I was eight and took my brother and me camping for a whole week at Lake McConaughy—the first time I'd slept in a tent. Each morning we got up at first light to go fishing—it's a favorite memory of my childhood. So was the reading of Ernest Hemingway's little masterpiece *The Old Man and the Sea.* That summer of fishing with my father, whose name was also Ernest, inspired me to read Hemingway's book. It was about a young boy and an old man going fishing—and like my father, and Santiago, I caught a boatload that morning in Maiori—a boatload of good memories. We were feeling nostalgic—sad to be leaving the convent but full of anticipation for our return to Corso Reginna and the heart of Maiori.

We wondered as we walked along the promenade what chores we would be doing the next day. We hoped to be able to work alongside Vittorio and Sergio. Seven years earlier, six and a half to be exact, I had volunteered to work on farms in Tuscany so that I might eat with Italians. As I shared with Mardi the great storytelling and witty jokes I'd enjoyed as an olive picker I began worrying that I might be setting her up for a big disappointment. The stories I shared had been condensed from seven weeks of good times in Tuscany—we were going to be on Vittorio's farm for only one day.

We were surprised to discover, when we got to the convent, that our Norwegian friends were still in the breakfast room. Astrid shared with us that they were in a bit of quandary. "We cannot make up our minds whether to stay or go. We are feeling oversaturated."

They were speaking of their experience in Italy using words I often use after I've been at a museum for a few hours and don't want to take in any more information. It is a feeling that is possible when you are observing but not so likely when you're participating. I decided to tell them about our adventure in Tramonti, hoping that a day in the country would make them feel a little less overwrought. I wasn't far into the story when I realized that the uncertainty of our days did not appeal to them.

"Can they really fix the meat properly?" Lars wanted to know.

He obviously felt that Italians didn't know how to cook meat, so I told them that Brigida certainly did, and then steered the conversation toward the enjoyment of the people we had met. Mardi tried to explain Tramonti to them, about how hard it had been to figure out where to get off the bus and how much fun we had because of the mistakes we had made.

"What could we do that is not so complicated?" Astrid asked with a sigh.

Despite their misgivings, we were certain they would enjoy a meal with Brigida, but as I began to think about how they would get to Il Raduno I realized Astrid was right—it would be complicated. I tried to think of something else we might recommend and realized that almost everything we'd done since we arrived on the Amalfi Coast would involve a bit more uncertainty and a bit more walking than they would like.

"What do you plan to do today?" I asked.

"We haven't made our plans for today," Astrid said.

Their plans were so uncertain that among them was the possibility of flying back to Norway. They asked about our plans. We told them that we were mostly resting, getting ready for our day on Vittorio's farm. The thought of helping a farmer overwhelmed them. I was shocked to realize that Vittorio's invitation, something I saw as having the potential of being the highlight of our whole trip, was of little interest to them.

Nevertheless, we enjoyed our chat. Lars told us about skiing in Norway and Astrid spoke of the influence of Christianity on the art of Europe. Apparently they enjoyed talking with us as well; they invited us to visit them in Oslo. Scandinavia had not been on our bucket list, but their description of living in the heart of the city without a car, but with a small boat, intrigued us.

By the time we were packed and ready to leave the convent, it was almost noon. Gerardo was not around to say goodbye, neither did we see Astrid or

Lars. We said a quiet goodbye to Andrea and told him we'd turn in our key when we came back to retrieve a couple of bags we'd left in our room.

Our move to Casa Mannini, strolling along the coast with our rolling suitcases, was a *piece of cake*, to use Gianrico's favorite expression. The day, like all of our days on the Amalfi Coast, was beautiful. The promenade was very busy, so busy that a policeman was again stopping traffic for pedestrians crossing the main highway onto Corso Reginna.

Anna, Jessica's sister, was, as usual, standing in front of Dedalo.

"Where are you going?" she asked.

"We are sorry we're late," I said.

"Are you coming to eat?"

"No, we just want to check into the hotel. Is someone there who can help us?" I asked as we began walking toward Casa Mannini.

"*Si*," Anna responded with a puzzled look on her face.

I was beginning to suspect that Anna might not be the manager of Casa Mannini—or maybe we didn't even have a reservation.

"Allo," Gianni sang out as he biked up to us and stopped.

"Top of the morning to you," I replied.

"Holiday finished?"

"No, no, we are just moving to a different hotel—Casa Mannini."

"Ah, Casa Mannini." He gestured good-naturedly toward it.

"You will have to put up with us for a few more days," I said.

"Ah, very good," he said as he resumed riding.

It might be safe to say that Gianni spends more time on his bike than I do. I don't know whether he rides because he enjoys it or for his health—or because he's found that riding his bike is a good way to promote his restaurant that features the best cook in all of Maiori. Whatever the reason, Maiori wouldn't be the same for me without him. It hadn't escaped my attention that were Mario spelled with two *i*'s it would be an anagram for Maiori. Mario *is* Maiori. The percentage of times we encountered Gianni when we were out walking would represent a respectable free throw average for a high school or college basketball player—somewhere in the seventies or eighties. And now that we were checking into a hotel that was even closer to his restaurant, we'd probably see him even more.

We were certain we'd miss Maximiliano, but Casa Mannini did have one advantage that we noticed right away—we didn't have to climb four flights of stairs. Its ancient elevator was a treasure, although a bit cantankerous. We punched the button and after lots of clicks, clacks, and whirring, the antiquated box appeared. We opened the outer door and the inner cage and looked in. We weren't sure we'd both fit. Even without luggage it looked tight, but we stacked our suitcases and squeezed in. Then we discovered another problem. We'd forgotten which floor we were heading to, but it didn't seem to matter—no matter which button we pushed, the elevator went nowhere.

We translated the posted notices as well as we could and learned nothing that helped. I was ready to give up and hike up the stairs. Mardi wasn't. She asked if the door was completely shut. I opened the cage door first and then pushed open the outer solid door and reclosed it. It shut with a resounding click. I did the same with the cage door, giving it a little nudge at the end. Everything looked the same as it had before, but something must have been different. We took a wild guess and pushed the button for floor three, the cage started rising very slowly—and it stayed slow. When at last we got to floor three, we opened both doors and were surprised to find a very pleasant-looking woman waiting for us.

"Hello—are you expecting us?" I asked.

"*Si,* Mr. and Mrs. Shaw?" she replied.

"Yes, yes." I was relieved that we wouldn't have to deal with the hassle of a misplaced reservation, or worse, a reservation for another hotel. I didn't mention that Anna seemed not to know we had reservations. I was happy that this woman, whose name was Maya, was expecting us. She looked like a Maya too—South American with short brown hair, but for all I knew she was as Italian as Gianni. My ear is not close to being able to pick up the dialects of the different regions of Italy or even the accent of someone for whom Italian is a second, third, or fourth language.

Maya led us to the Amalfi Room, *trentatre,* number thirty-three. If the room at Casa Raffaele Conforti was large, luxurious, and expansive, this room was the opposite, but not in a bad way. It was light and fresh, cozy and clean—a very efficient use of a small space. It had obviously been remodeled recently with the needs of the technological traveler in mind—outlets were conveniently placed on either side of the bed as well as night stands to hold computers, phones, and Kindles.

"*Mi piace,*" I said to Maya as she handed us the key and excused herself.

The room was Mediterranean cheery, with a bright blue floor and a trim of vines that framed our bed perfectly, but what thrilled me most was knowing that a stone's throw away were our friends at Le Suite. It was a great value at less than forty euros a night, and we even had a balcony with a view of the sea at no extra charge. From it we could also see Corso Reginna, but no longer could we see Santa Maria a Mare. I grabbed the bottle of *limoncello* we'd carried from the agriturismo high above Minori, filled the little Amalfi

Coast cups we'd bought from Rosario and Marguerite, and sat on the balcony to toast our return.

Our plans for the day were quite loose. I wanted to rest my knee. Mardi wanted to rest her feet. We had no idea what would be required of us on Vittorio's farm, but we wanted to exceed his expectations.

We made an enjoyable day doing nothing more significant than retrieving our luggage, thanking Gerardo for making our stay so pleasant, promising him we'd be back, and doing what everyone else in town seemed to be doing— basking in the sweet pleasure of doing nothing. We did it so comfortably and so long that by the time we stepped into the *frutta e verdura negozio,* the proper greeting for the shopkeeper was *buonasera.* While she retrieved our radishes we looked over her displays of fruit and vegetables. We walked out of the shop with tomatoes, plums, apples, and grapes as well our beloved *ravanelli.*

"I like going shopping like that," I said.

"Very old world," Mardi replied.

"Do you want to put the food away or just keep walking?"

While we were trying to decide Gianni biked by and waved. As we watched him biking Kermit-the-Frog-like toward the promenade we noticed Boston Giovanni walking toward us.

"Beautiful day," he said and stopped to chat for awhile before heading into Le Suite. Corso Reginna was dotted with groups of people chatting—a surprising number of the gatherings had a child or two in the center, soaking up love and attention.

"It doesn't feel like any of these people drove here," I said. "I don't see enough cars."

The size of the gathering outside the little church by the *supermercato* seemed to confirm our supposition—unless these people had come by tour bus, which seemed highly unlikely. We were in the midst of a town and a people who traveled about the old-fashioned way—on foot.

"Oh, isn't that policeman handsome," Mardi said.

"Italian women are prettier than the men are handsome," I said. I didn't really know what I meant or even why I'd said it, but it didn't change Mardi's opinion of the policemen of Italy. She rarely passed one without commenting on his good looks.

Yet another family doting on a beautiful little girl in a stroller caught my attention. Mardi was still watching the policeman.

"He wants that car moved," she observed. "He whistled, but nobody came to move it, so he's writing a ticket."

I began watching him too. He glanced up occasionally as he wrote, which made me think that if the owner showed up before he finished, all would be forgiven. We were discovering that this town was even more old world—neighbor helping neighbor—on weekends.

When the policeman finished writing the ticket, and had placed it on the car, Mardi turned her attention to the beautiful sunset the sky was promising. "See the angel in that cloud?"

I looked and saw what she saw—the uplifted arms of an ascending spirit. I pulled her close and held her arm as we strolled.

"Who would have thought that we would get along so well," Mardi said. I could tell that she was referring to how much we were enjoying just walking around together, the very thing for which Italians have a beautiful expression—the sweetness of doing nothing—*il dolce far niente*.

"Look at that guy—he's so Fellini-esque," she said drawing my attention to a man who looked exactly like Federico Fellini, the man who made famous another expression that captures Italian spirit—*la dolce vita*. He was an oversized man wearing a flowing white cape, a black hat with a wide brim, and smoking a big cigar. For all I knew it was Fellini himself enjoying *the sweet life* of the Amalfi Coast until I did the math and realized Fellini would be nearing one hundred.

The more we walked, the more engrossed I became in the snippets of conversations we were overhearing as we sauntered along the promenade. I also occasionally noted how beautifully some of the women were dressed.

"She *is* pretty, isn't she?" Mardi said, apparently having noticed where my eyes had lingered.

"She *did look* very Italian, didn't she," I said.

"I definitely think you have some Italian blood in you," Mardi said.

I smiled and said, "I wish I had enough Italian blood to figure out what those people did that they enjoyed so much." I was referring to an animated group of people who had obviously had a very good day together and were now doing the next best thing—telling stories about it as they ambled along.

We were also passing by lots of lovers strolling up and down the promenade. The more lovers we saw, and the more beautiful the sunset became, the more it motivated us to cap off our evening enjoying a romantic dinner on our balcony—another simple meal of fresh, flavor-filled food. We were back in the heart of Maiori, surrounded by beauty, listening to the sounds of people excelling in the sweet art of doing nothing, which seemed the perfect thing for us to do to get ready for our big day.

CHAPTER SEVENTEEN

Casa Mannini ~ Sunday April 17 ~ 53 & Clear

Vittorio's Surprise

I don't know what your destiny will be,
but one thing I do know:
the only ones among you who will be really happy
are those who have sought and found how to serve.
ALBERT SCHWEITZER

■

I love you without knowing how, or when, or from where.
I love you simply, without problems or pride: I love you in this way
because I do not know any other way of loving but this,
in which there is no I or you,
so intimate that your hand upon my chest is my hand,
so intimate that when I fall asleep your eyes close.
PABLO NERUDA, *100 LOVE SONNETS*

Y*ou will not find a more loved man in all of Minori.*

That is what Sergio said of Vittorio, the man who has invited Mardi and me to help him on his farm high in the mountains above his *ceramica* shop in Minori—so high, Sergio told us, that we will have walked almost to Ravello by the time we get to his farm.

We began preparing the night before. We ate well, priming our bodies with plenty of protein. We did sit-ups and stretching exercises and even went to bed early so that we'd be well rested for the chores Vittorio would share with us—we felt like athletes getting ready for the big game. We didn't know what we would be doing; we presumed we would be pruning trees, clearing brush and weeds, or maybe just moving building materials. The only clue Vittorio had given us was that gloves wouldn't be needed, only sturdy walking shoes.

We slept eight hours, ate a breakfast of nuts, fruit, cereal and milk, and left early for the bus stop, having learned that buses in this part of Italy occasionally run early, and sometimes late, but you can't count on late, so early is required. We were early enough to have a quick *cappuccino* at Le Suite. Luigi greeted us enthusiastically as always: "*Ciao, amici*—how are you today?"

"*Va bene*, my friend," I said as Mardi and I bellied up to the bar. It could have been a scene from a 1950s western were the place decorated differently. We were Luigi's only guests.

"Hot water for tea?" he asked.

"No—we have only a moment. *Due cappuccini per favore*," I said and then shared with him our plans for the day. It was a typical start to our Italian days—a start that I deeply miss—a visceral longing that will pull us back to Italy year after year the rest of our lives. We miss everything about Italy, even the bus rides, which on that morning was as uneventful as any bus ride on the Amalfi Coast can be. The traffic was light. We didn't once have to back up or even come to a stop. We met and passed dozens of bicyclists—our driver was calm and patient—it was a pleasant ride for us and a safe ride for the cyclists.

We arrived in Minori so early that I had time to photograph. As I made my way toward the water it hit me again how much I love the sounds of the Amalfi Coast—the wind, the waves crashing on shore, the call of the gulls, and the peculiar sound of Vespas ricocheting off the hotel fronts and cliffs. The beach was empty. A fisherman in a double-ended wooden boat was taking short strokes on his oars, maintaining his position just offshore, waiting for something—a something I had not figured out.

"*Bella giornata*," I said, coloring my voice with emotion to convey my appreciation for the day. He responded with a soft *Buongiorno* and a respectful nod. I wanted to start a conversation that would be as beautiful as the morning, but I knew that wasn't possible for me in Italian and I didn't want to presume that he knew English. I uttered a few words of appreciation for the classic lines of his boat and asked if I might take a few photos. I hoped, as ideas for good shots kept coming, that he might forgive me for taking more than a few.

While I was choosing different angles and backgrounds, the bells of Minori's Saint Trofimena Basilica rang out using the same timekeeping system as the Church of Santa Maria in Maiori. One high-pitched and eight low-pitched tones told me that I had forty-five minutes until Sergio would arrive to guide us to Vittorio's farm.

The blue in the foreground, the cliffs behind, and the rugged good looks of the fisherman would combine for an iconic shot of the Amalfi Coast if I was willing to wade into the surf. I walked back to the bench where Mardi was sitting to take off my shoes, but she didn't want me to get wet. She wanted me to be ready in case Sergio showed up early so I joined her on the bench. She had settled in to the laid-back pace of Minori. The town is aptly named, it's even smaller than Maiori. I too was enjoying the quiet pace of the morning, but I couldn't quit thinking about the fisherman, still rowing calmly in the shallow water.

"Maybe he just needs help," I said and walked back across the highway, across the promenade, and back onto the pebbly beach. As I walked toward the fisherman, I studied the shape of his boat—a perfect form that had evolved over the years just for fishing these waters. The paint scheme was a bright blue topped by a yellow gunwale all the way around what looked to be an 18-foot boat. I had lots of questions about why it was set up as it was, but I didn't have the words, so I asked only what I knew, "*Aiuto?*"

He said that indeed he did. He looked toward town and indicated that his help was on the way. A younger man, not dressed like a traditional fisherman, not even wearing a hat, was walking across the beach toward us. The fisherman took a couple of strong strokes with his long oars propelling the boat toward shore. He threw a coiled rope onto the beach and stepped toward the stern, raising the bow so that the boat would glide as far as possible onto the shore. This is when my offer of help was accepted—it's also when I wished I'd brought the gloves that Vittorio assured me I wouldn't need.

The younger man grabbed the rope and began pulling the boat toward shore, I quit photographing and moved closer. The man, about forty and fit, handed me the end of the rope. He then joined the fisherman, who had jumped into the water. They both began pushing on the back of the boat. I pulled on the rope with all the strength I could gather and immediately wished I had wrapped the rope around my midsection. When we had pulled the boat as far as it would go, I dropped the rope and looked at my hands. I had pulled so hard I got a rope burn.

The fisherman reached into his boat and pulled out four wooden chocks, spacing them out in front of the keel, far enough apart that they could be moved from back to front as the men slid the boat farther onto shore—they didn't quit until they had more than enough for a first down, well over thirty feet from the lapping waterline and out of reach of a rising tide. It was a job that would have been impossible for the fisherman alone. I was thankful they had allowed me to help.

It wasn't quite what I imagined when I had prayed a few days earlier that someday I could go out and spend the day with an Amalfi Coast fisherman, but it was a start. I learned a bit of Amelio's story. He had been a full-time fisherman in his younger days but now goes out only on Sundays and waits for Vincenzo to come help him pull his boat ashore. He looked like a fisherman should look—to my eye he fit the part of Santiago, the old man in Ernest Hemingway's *The Old Man and the Sea,* much better than Spencer Tracy.

When we had finished working and talking I said *Arrivederci.* They responded *Ciao.* I took that as a sign they had valued my help. During my first journey in Italy I'd learned that visitors should not initiate the use of the word *Ciao* when saying goodbye to an Italian—it's too familiar; they should use *Arrivederci* or even *Arrivederla.* I moved a respectful distance away and watched, wondering about the relationship between the two men—were they relatives or friends? They chatted a few minutes, then Vincenzo turned toward the highway. I didn't notice where he went or where he had come from.

Amelio tidied his boat, gathered his oars, his life preserver, and his catch, then hoisted everything onto his shoulders and began walking across the beach—a sturdy man walking tall with the tools and produce of his trade—it was an image to treasure. He crossed the highway, leaned the oars against a second story railing, and unlocked a freshly painted door. I wondered whether he had grown up in that awning-covered house, which looked straight out onto the Mediterranean Sea. Oh, what stories he must have to tell of storms and near misses if he was indeed the fisherman he looked to be. His skin was tanned and weathered—the shade you would expect if it had endured fifty or sixty years on the water.

I spent only a short time with Amelio, but that encounter shines bright in my memories of the Amalfi Coast. Helping someone—sharing emotions and work—that's what I most enjoy about my sojourns in foreign lands. I will never forget a serendipitous invitation to a wedding feast high in the Peruvian Andes. I was hiking with my film crew on the back route into Machu Picchu. We were heading upriver. The wedding party was heading downvalley, but after a few moments of chatting we were invited to join their celebration. We danced with them, ate with them, and laughed with them. It was a week-long party and we shared only a few hours of it, but oh, what a precious few hours they were. I've always wondered if the members of the wedding party remember that day as fondly and as well as I do. My guess is no, for I had the advantage of capturing the good times on film. I've always regretted that I never returned to Peru, never had the chance to show the film we took that day to the bride and groom and the wedding party.

I took photographs and video of Amelio and his friend. Next year when we return like swallows to Capistrano, some Sunday morning I'll go down to the beach in Minori and wait for Amelio to come in from the sea. I'll help bring the boat ashore and then pull out my phone and show him the memories I caught, and ask to see what he has caught that day. I captured what I think is a good portrait of a fisherman returning from a morning at sea, and I'd like Amelio and his family to have it.

"I see you're not standing around collecting dust," Sergio said as I joined him and Mardi in front of Vittorio's shop. I smiled and shook his hand.

"That was fun. He even showed me the squid he caught."

"You definitely aren't lacking interaction with the locals."

"That's the best part of traveling."

"Well, you may like this, then. Vittorio is using you two as an excuse for a party. You'll have a chance to interact with a lot of locals," Sergio said and took a phone call that we soon realized was from Vittorio as they began discussing where to meet. My mind was reeling. I was both disappointed and elated. I had been looking forward to helping on the farm, but the thought of an Italian Sunday dinner with a table overflowing with Vittorio's friends and family...oh my.

"*Va bene, ciao, ciao,*" Sergio said to Vittorio and then switched to English to talk to us. "Okay, let's go. We can start for the farm. We will meet him. He is walking to town."

"Oh, no, we forgot our wine," I said, realizing that Vittorio must be coming to town for more food and drink.

"Don't worry, Vittorio has that covered."

We began climbing and catching up on each other's week. Sergio had been busy getting ready, with Vittorio's help, for an exhibition of his sculptures. I wanted to give Sergio a sense of all that had happened to us but I didn't want to dominate the conversation, so I proceeded with the stories slowly, just as I intended to do with this hike. Sergio seemed happy to do that as well. The day was already quite warm. The views of Minori became more interesting the higher we climbed, the storybook quality of the town more evident—dollhouse compact. Each photograph I took gave me a chance to catch my breath and cool off at the same time.

We met Vittorio while we were still in the upper streets of the village. He must have gotten up very early. He was wearing four layers, including a vest to ward off the morning chill. He introduced us to his dog, Lilo. Vittorio ducked into several homes and shops and each time came out with another delicacy for our feast, including a gallon jug of red wine. At a small stone building he emerged with a bottle of olive oil made from olives picked on·his farm. By the time we were a half hour into our hike, we all had our hands full and Vittorio and I were shedding layers.

On one of our breaks, at a lookout over Minori, Sergio said, "This little town is pretty nice. Everybody sees everyone else several times a day. In order for that not to happen you have to make an appointment *not* to see someone—*avoid the piazza between two and three*—that's the only way you're not going to run into someone."

Vittorio told us about the early days of the town. The first shop Mardi and I had entered on our first day in Minori had once been a pasta-making shop. The north-facing windows were excellent for drying pasta, he explained. He also pointed out a Roman arch and told of Dutch ships that sank offshore, adding to the local economy. He also mentioned that papermaking had once contributed to the wealth of the town, just as it had in Amalfi.

He talked about things that had happened over four hundred years ago as though they were stories handed down from family member to family member instead of historical facts, and I suppose that is the way it should be—the Italian word for story and the Italian word for history is the same, *storia*. His stories had a ring of immediacy because he was pointing to the sites and speaking of families that were still around. He told a story about spoiled boys wanting a Ferrari as though he were speaking of the same families that had plundered the Dutch ships. His stories reminded me of the stories that Aurora had told me a half dozen years ago on her farm as we picked olives. History seems so personal for Italians—they are master storytellers.

I asked whether it was difficult to grow lemons here and was treated to a tale about Chinese traders following the Silk Route who brought lemon seeds to the area. The local farmers learned that the soil and climate here were almost perfect for the production of lemons, and now lemons are synonymous with the Amalfi Coast.

The next thing that piqued my curiosity was the path we were walking on. It was both beautiful and well crafted. I imagined that it had been around forever, but Sergio told us that the Bourbons in the nineteenth century had built these steps—just before the outbreak of the Civil War in America.

"Notice they used no cement," he said, then added, "This path goes on to Ravello, but beyond Vittorio's it is not as nice."

"Why is that?" I asked.

"This is a public road, but it is Vittorio who cleans it."

"*Ogni giorno* he walks this road?"

"*Si*. And every day he takes care of it."

"*Lontano,*" Vittorio said with resignation.

I translated it for Mardi the only way I knew, which was *far*. It was indeed a long hike to his farm. We'd been walking for almost an hour. I'm sure Vittorio does it in much less time, especially when he is not stopping to tell stories about long ago invasions, or pausing under a grape arbor to chat with a neighbor perched high above training his vines to grow exactly where he wants so that they will produce luscious fruit in the Amalfi Coast sunlight. The question about lemons had turned into an interesting story, so I probed again.

"When were cattle introduced in this area?"

Vittorio's answer was personal, detailed, and entertaining. It evolved into a story about survival.

"Each family produced everything it needed," Sergio said, succinctly summarizing what Vittorio had told us.

"How much land did a family need?" I asked.

"Almost two acres," Vittorio said.

I had asked that question in Tuscany as well and was surprised at how many people a few acres of land could sustain one hundred years ago. I was surprised again at the answer on the less easily farmable land of the Amalfi Coast.

"My mother had a little piece of land, and she got a dozen eggs and a half a basket of figs a year as rent."

I didn't ask how little the piece of land was. It was a beautiful story that fit nicely with the tales I had been told in Tuscany and the many books I'd read about farming in Italy in the days before industrialization. To the uninitiated, Vittorio's story might have sounded like hyperbole, but it described the character of a people doing whatever was necessary to survive in an inhospitable but beautiful environment.

Vittorio was carrying the heaviest load—the wine and a large bag filled with what I didn't know, but from the way it hung from his hand I could tell that it was heavy. Mardi and I were keeping up with him well enough, and so was Sergio. "This is what keeps Vittorio in shape."

"This is what keeps all of Italy in shape," I said.

When Vittorio accepted our offer I think he envisioned letting us work alongside him. Even though Sergio had said we were heading to a party, I was still hoping we'd be able to help Vittorio get some work done. But as we picked up more and more food, I began to accept that we'd climbed all this way not to trim bushes or carry rocks or whack weeds—he'd invited us to his farm to do what Italians do best—share the good of their lives with family and friends.

"Oh, this is beautiful, I want to get a picture," I said, sensing that we had finally climbed high enough that we were seeing the view that greets Vittorio every morning from his farm. My photograph couldn't include the sound of the bells chiming from Ravello, which added to the ambience of the morning, but I was able to include in the photograph the silver arrowheads pointing at the backs of the sleek boats going this way and that way below us on the dark blue of the water. The feeling of being on a cliff high above an ocean resonates deeply with me—it always has. It conveys that a whole world is out there just beyond the curve of the horizon, although at that moment I wanted to explore no farther than the bit of paradise on which we were standing—I didn't know blue sky, blue water, green grass, and sunshine could be so gorgeous.

Vittorio opened a gate and motioned for us to enter.

"*E qui,* it is here..." Vittorio began before switching back to Italian to tell the story of breaking his wrist while pruning branches. We were passing by a small tree with a ladder still propped against its trunk, climbing steep stairs to Vittorio's house, which we could see above us, terraces stepping up the hill on either side of us all the way to his beautiful home.

"Oh my. Look at this. Can you imagine waking up to this every day?" I asked as we emerged onto a wide terrace just below the house, the whole of the Amalfi Coast spread out below, framed by low-hanging branches of various trees, only one of which I could identify—a lemon tree. We could see all the way down the coast to Salerno, and even farther.

"*Bella giornata,*" Vittorio said.

He was right. We had not enjoyed a more glorious day since arriving on the Amalfi Coast exactly two weeks earlier. The days had all been beautiful, but this was a cut above.

"A blue sky day," I said.

"*Cielo bleu,*" Vittorio translated for me.

"*Bella,*" Mardi said breathlessly, not from exertion, but from admiration.

Words are not adequate when you find yourself suddenly in the midst of indescribable beauty, but a word like *Bella* is almost worthy—the human voice can layer that sumptuous word with the necessary nuances of emotion. When Mardi said *Bella* as we turned to look out at the deep blue of the Mediterranean Sea far below stretching out to a distant horizon, I heard in her voice—in those two syllables—a deep, reverent awe, as though heaven were stretched out before our eyes. Adding to our feelings of reverence was the realization of how much work, effort, and time had been required to get us to this spot. Also at play was the grace of it all—the circumstances that had led to us stepping into Vittorio's shop on a morning when Sergio happened to be about—for I am not sure the invitation to Vittorio's farm would have been so enthusiastically conveyed to us if Sergio had not been around to translate our offer to help. And of course, had I not spent seven weeks working on Tuscan farms, I might not have had the confidence to volunteer to help Vittorio. A lot of angels had been working overtime to bring us to this special moment.

When you are already head over heels crazy in love with a country, how do you fall even more deeply in love? You get together on a perfect, not-a-cloud-in-the-sky day with a bunch of passionate Italians and set the whole scene to music. This seemed like a movie set, so why not have the perfect soundtrack—an energetic collection of the traditional and modern songs of Italy. The music came from somewhere inside the work in progress that was Vittorio's home. As befitting a house looking out on one of the most beautiful views in the world, the wrap-around deck was its most prominent feature—that and large windows.

Mardi and I took in as much beauty as we could absorb and then reached for each other. When you're overwhelmed, a hug is often necessary to regain a sense of equilibrium. We held each other close and looked out at the incredibly nuanced view of the coast—layer upon layer of subtle gradations of color, form, and even movement—waves and boats moving across the surface of the water. Our good fortune and our love for each other were again rendering us giddy.

"What is the Italian word for thankful?" I asked when I'd recovered a bit of decorum.

"*Grati,*" Sergio said.

"Ah, gratitude," I said. "And what about *shade?*"

"*Ombra.*"

"*Sono grati per ombra?*" I said more as a question than a statement. I'd soaked my shirt during the climb, and now the cooling breezes and shade of the trees gracing Vittorio's patio were cooling me off.

"Close enough."

"*Grazie, grazie, Sergio,*" I said, emotion coloring my voice.

I was overflowing with gratitude to Sergio and Vittorio for showing us this stunning view of the Amalfi Coast. If you've seen the delightful movie *Il Postino,* you'll remember the cliff-top home of Pablo Neruda, who moved to Italy to write his romantic poetry. When I began sending out queries to farms where Mardi and I might volunteer, I dreamed of finding a small farm on a hilltop overlooking the ocean. Vittorio's location was just as beautiful as Neruda's, but it would never have worked for the film for there is no way to bicycle to this spot, which was a central element of the story—the postman delivering fan letters from all over the world to Pablo Neruda by bicycle.

But in every other way, Vittorio's farm would have conveyed the romance of a poet finding the perfect spot from which to write his paeans to love. My mind again surged into hyperdrive, imagining that I might someday write my books about the uniqueness of Italy and Italians from such a spot. I imagined the thrill of waking each morning to write while looking out at the beauty of God's creation from such a place as this.

"Can you ask Vittorio to point out the boundaries of his property?" I asked Sergio.

Vittorio pointed and told stories as he described his farm of about twenty acres.

"The house once was a stable. They've totally rebuilt it," Sergio said making sure I had understood Vittorio's story.

"*Quanti anni hai lavorato qui?*" I asked, curious how many years he had been working on this land, refurbishing these buildings.

Vittorio answered my question in Italian, much of which I understood, because I had heard such stories before. The dining room of the first farm in Italy I ever worked on had once been a large barn—that family had described in detail after frustrating detail the costly bureaucratic roadblocks they had encountered in transforming it.

"He began this work fifteen years ago," Sergio interpreted. "It is very difficult to build because of the restrictions and also because of the view. What you do inside, not so much of a problem, but if it can be seen, then it is a major problem."

I asked again if there was any work I could help him do, but Vittorio shook his head.

"*Domani, un altro giorno, forse?*" I asked. "Tomorrow or another day?"

He smiled and asked whether I preferred *limonata o caffé*. I chose lemonade and got my wish. Vittorio put my hands to work squeezing the biggest, most pungent lemons I'd ever seen. He also put my mind to work by introducing me to Serena and his son Francesco.

"Vittorio just told me there are about twenty people coming," Sergio said as he walked into the kitchen to watch me work.

"Wow," I said and began trying to associate memory prompters. I imagined Francesco as a young Saint Francis.

"Serena looks like our friend Melissa, *noi sorella*," I said, then quickly corrected myself. "*Intendo, un amico di nostra figlia.*" I had said she looked like our sister, then realizing my mistake, I said she looked like a friend of our daughter.

"Bravo," Vittorio said. He was always appreciative of our attempts at Italian, especially when we managed to get it right. I had four names taken care of—Vittorio, Sergio, Francesco, and Serena—only a dozen or so more to go.

"Vittorio was going to invite about forty people, but he decided to cut it down," Sergio said. I tried to imagine forty people gathered around one table and failed. Twenty would be plenty. While my hands squeezed lemons to the rhythms of the music, Mardi took a picture, claiming she now had proof that I had set foot in a kitchen. The party was gathering momentum—the music demanded it. More people were showing up, each carrying something to eat or drink. My job was not done. The squeezing was a lot easier than the remembering.

"Zucchero?" Vittorio asked as I squeezed the last of the lemons.

"Si," I said. *"Molti zucchero."*

Italians take their coffee sweet. I hoped they took their lemonade sweet as well. My work done for the moment, I joined Sergio on a low rock wall in the shade of a lemon tree and mentioned again our offer to drive him down the coast to see his grandfather's hunting lodge.

"Would you like to go on Tuesday?"

"Tuesday I'm going to Naples, but Wednesday would be perfect."

"We'd love that," I said.

"There is a river nearby—we used to go fishing and duck hunting—it's near Paestum."

My mind was reeling again—to go on a personal quest, to a special place that Sergio went to as a child—a place on the coast near the ruins of Paestum, an ancient Greek settlement I read about in grade school. What an adventure—and with an Italian for a guide. Our pinball was doing some mind-boggling bouncing.

Vittorio came by with a very Italian appetizer—thorns from lemon trees, the longest I'd ever seen, were the skewers holding tasty bits of *prosciutto* and fava beans together. We kept a thorn and smuggled it back to Wisconsin. I am surprised at how often that incredibly strong, extremely sharp, slowly tapering thorn has been a great help in completing a task around my home or shop—and of course using it brings to mind our unbelievable day at Vittorio's.

Sergio said what I was calling *prosciutto* was actually a special kind of bacon—raw bacon. While Vittorio served appetizers we got to know Sergio better. We learned that he had a showing of Venetian mirrors coming up in September and that his connection to China was because of a girlfriend.

"Wouldn't you know," I said. "It's always a woman."

He smiled sheepishly and went on to tell us that he had never been married. He asked about us. We mentioned first our son who is an artist. His interests most closely match those of Sergio and Vittorio, who had rejoined us. We then told them about our son who is a farmer. Vittorio was very interested—asking a lot of questions about what he sold at the farmers markets.

Mardi quickly described the rest of our kids. She was trying to not dominate the conversation by talking about our family, especially with Sergio, who had none. She and I were relieved when the conversation took a weird pinball bounce when Sergio noted, "All dogs speak English, did you ever notice that?"

"Everyone, including dogs, seems to know what *stop* means," I said thrilled to be on another subject.

"English is taught universally around the world. You can't be part of the international community unless you can speak English," Sergio said.

We mentioned Jessica and her desire to learn English, but the conversation soon went back to food as Serena served a plate of *bruschetta*.

"*Buon appetito,*" Vittorio declared.

"*Delizioso,*" I said and it truly was.

"They don't have this in Minnesota," Sergio said.

He enjoyed chiding me about neighboring Minnesota as though that was where we lived, and doing it with a Canadian twang.

"I don't think I've ever been in *Min nee sow ta* or Wisconsin," he admitted.

Vittorio saved me from having to come up with a clever retort to Sergio's jabs by asking if we'd like an archaeological tour of the farm. It turned out to be archaeology and more. Sergio first pointed out the nets covering the lemon trees.

"This is to prevent hail damage," he explained. "At the end of May they take them off so that the bees can pollinate."

I mentioned that we'd been told that the nets never came off.

"Well, not everyone is as careful as Vittorio," Sergio asserted.

"Ah, very good point. Cherry trees?" I asked as we walked along the carefully manicured walkways between terraced plots of trees.

"*Ciliegia?*" Sergio asked Vittorio.

"*Un albero di fico,*" he said and went on to explain that this was a new transplant—he was hoping for a much improved fig.

"This kind of farming is why the Greeks called Southern Italy *Magna Grecia*, the Great Greece," Sergio explained, "because they couldn't grow anything in Greece, but here they could grow everything."

Mardi and I were, to put it mildly, astounded by the productivity of Vittorio's terraces—so much food being produced on so little land.

"Vittorio has invented a system of tying the branches together so they don't need support," Sergio said as he pointed to some trees along the way.

"Impressive," I said, noting how efficiently they were tied and how little support each plant required.

"He wakes up at four, comes here and works all morning, and then he goes and produces ceramics," Sergio went on.

The farmer in me appreciated all that I was seeing and also what I was not seeing. The place was clean, neat, and orderly. Sure there was a lot to do, but on what farm are there not projects waiting to be completed.

"He just broke his arm, yet he still maintains this schedule."

I wanted with every fiber of my being to help him—this was just the kind of farm I had been hoping for with every query I sent out, and Vittorio was just the man I could spend weeks working beside, learning from.

"This tree is one hundred fifty years old," Vittorio said, gesturing toward a very productive tree.

"These are all orange trees that Vittorio has transformed into lemon trees. The knowledge may disappear with Vittorio, though. Francesco is probably not going to be doing this." I hoped Sergio was wrong. I know that my kids' interests have changed over the years. One of Vittorio's children may undergo a similar transformation. It would be a shame for all of Vittorio's hard-earned knowledge to be lost.

As we neared a small building, the tour turned from agriculture to archeology. Vittorio showed us a leather-curing shop that had been on the land for a thousand years.

"It was a very smelly industry, that is why it was way out here," Sergio interpreted for us to make sure we had understood Vittorio's story.

"Look, *guarda*," Vittorio said, doing his own interpreting.

"Oh my, my! *Bella*," I said. We were looking at a particularly beautiful view of the coast framed by the bricks of a very ancient arched doorway. I had learned in architecture school that the Romans had perfected the use of arches in construction, and here Mardi and I were, posing for a photograph under a Roman arch on Vittorio's land.

Vittorio explained that not long ago, this building had been used as a *frantoio*, where olives are pressed to make oil. I loved the passion with which Vittorio told his story of spending much of his childhood on this land playing in these buildings.

"Grandfather bought this farm in the forties," Vittorio said. "He bought it after the war when property was really cheap." Sometimes he spoke directly to us, and miraculously we'd understand him. We loved those moments. But we also loved that Sergio was there to help when we didn't understand something Vittorio had said.

Sergio helped us understand that the ceiling had collapsed in 1968 and thirty years was all it took for the land to turn back into a forest. He also told us that in the 1700s a small chapel had been on this land. Our minds reeled as we tried to grapple with the history of this beautiful spot.

"*Sono felice,* I am happy," I said. "This is fun."

"There is no one like Vittorio…" Sergio said.

"In all of Italy," I said.

"In the whole world," Sergio added. "He's a very special guy."

"He's a very energetic man, a very friendly man—a very hospitable man," I said.

"He helped me move from my place up there…" Sergio pointed toward Ravello, high on the mountain above us, "…to Minori. He put a case on his shoulder and just headed down."

"He's like a burro," I said.

"He's very strong. Look, it is one month since he broke his arm and it's practically healed. He's in really good shape."

"He's a good man." I said.

"He's young," Sergio added with a wry smile.

"How did you get to know Vittorio?" I asked.

"I asked him if he would help me make a sculpture," Sergio said. "Then I helped him with his lighting and his graphics."

"How long ago was that?"

"Two or three years."

"And you just happened to be near his shop the day we met?"

"Yes. I was just walking by."

"And Vittorio asked you for a little help interpreting English?"

"Something like that."

"That was our lucky day," I said watching Vittorio graft a branch onto a tree. Sergio explained that Vittorio had developed a new fruit. It was the size of a large grapefruit.

"I think he speaks with the plants."

"A plant whisperer he is," I said.

"Yes, yes, that's Vittorio."

"*Ecco qua,*" Vittorio said and handed each of us a section of a huge orange he'd just deftly peeled with his grafting knife.

Mardi took a bite. Her eyes widened. "*Dolce,*" she said and gestured for me to try it.

I did and my eyes went wide too. "Wow—very good."

I had just bitten into the sweetest orange I'd ever tasted. Vittorio was telling us about the oranges, but I was understanding very little of it except the part about them being very sweet.

Sergio explained, "These don't exist in commerce anymore. Vittorio is keeping the line going."

"*Questa clementino*," Vittorio said.

"Oh, clementines—we eat them all the time," Mardi said.

"But they never tasted this good," I said, taking another bite.

"Half orange, half mandarin," Sergio said.

"*Questa mandarino*," Vittorio said, confirming what Sergio had said—that we were eating a hybrid. But these oranges were off the high end of the flavor scale. They didn't look like either clementines or mandarins, but more like the fruit I had grown up calling by its color. Vittorio offered us another orange, which he quickly peeled and sectioned. This was becoming more like heaven all the time—delicious food just for the picking and peeling.

Vittorio also pointed out his grapes and told us that he had another farm where he raised grapes for making wine. Sergio showed us pink grapefruit and then almonds.

"He has everything here."

"Oh, there are more potatoes," I said. I was already carrying pocketfuls of new potatoes we'd dug earlier in our tour.

"*Domani*," Vittorio said.

I had to laugh at myself. I was ready to dig them up, but when I looked closer I saw that they were indeed small. It would be quite a few tomorrows before they were ready for the table.

"This is the wild version of that sweet orange we just ate," Sergio said, pointing out a tree as we walked by. "Used to make chutney, marmalade. His mother used to make these wonderful condiments with them."

We were getting what I assumed was the full tour—we kept climbing higher and higher on ancient terraces. The tilled ground was at times no more than a few feet wide before the next terrace started. Most of the walls were in great repair. Others could have used a little work. I recalled the ancient Etruscan terrace wall I'd rebuilt for Pietro on his farm near Cortona. I began imagining doing the same work for Vittorio.

"Watch your step, Mardi," I warned. Her foot was near a lizard sunning itself on a stone.

"Finish *mia terra*," Vittorio said.

"Right there—*finito?*" I asked.

"*Si,*" he responded, but then he said, "*Carruba?*"

"Carob," Mardi said.

We were standing near huge *carruba* plants, and beyond were olive trees he had planted.

"Mardi, he's not done, he's planting olive trees for five hundred years from now—for Matteo's *bambinos*—and Matteo's *bambino's bambinos*, and on and on."

Vittorio laughed.

Mardi pointed out asparagus and orchids. Vittorio had said we were finished but we weren't, not quite. He saw that we were willing so he took us higher, climbing a very narrow staircase of a rock wall with no sides or railings.

"Oh look—a cistern," I pointed out as we kept climbing.

"To irrigate all these terraces," Sergio said.

"This is good soil."

"Good Minnesota soil," Sergio chided.

The farmer in me was impressed with the productivity on such steep land. These walls had been in existence for a thousand years, maybe more. It didn't take a lot of imagination to deduce that Vittorio was not the first to have farmed this land. Everywhere we looked we saw evidence of antiquity.

"Look at those hills over there, Mardi. When we saw them from Tramonti, we thought they were so high—now we're higher than they are."

She was impressed, but her interest at that moment was not in the view but where she was going to place her foot. We had reached a rather precarious point in our journey to the top. Sergio was still touting the productivity of the volcanic soil, not recognizing her concern.

"Watch your step, Mardi. *Attenzione.*"

This time I wasn't pointing out a lizard or a pile of dog poop—it was a very risky and very narrow walkway with a precarious turn at the top. We had climbed step after step with nothing to hold onto. It was straight out of one of my favorite stories of Peru. Roger Morgan and I were inching our way along a narrow path high in the Andes, fearing that even the slightest misstep would plunge us off the mountainside. I was hugging the sheer wall, convinced that my heavy camera would bump into a rock, knocking me off balance, and I would topple off that narrow ledge. Roger was inching along in front of me, leading the way. All of a sudden I heard him whimper, "This is no place for Mrs. Morgan's baby boy!"

Never in my life have I laughed as hard as I did that afternoon clinging to a rock on the side of that mountain. His timing and delivery were perfect and totally unexpected.

"I think we've found a job for ourselves, Mardi. We will have to put up a railing."

Vittorio and Sergio laughed at the idea of code-dictated railings on ancient terraced walls.

We made it safely to the top, and two of us for certain, and maybe three, let out a noticeable sigh of relief. Vittorio began pointing out edible plants growing wild, including anise.

"You found chicory too?" I asked Mardi.

"Yes, smell it," she said. We had found all the ingredients we needed for a great salad.

"Il tour é finito," Vittorio said.

"The tour is finished?" I asked.

"Si," he said, and this time he meant it. He had taken us higher and higher, and now he led us back past all his plants to the house, back to his guests and the feast.

"Hey, popolo," Vittorio announced, greeting his guests with great enthusiasm. Their response told me that Sergio had been right in his assertion. Vittorio was truly adored.

He introduced us to everyone. I wanted to remember all the names, but there were far too many. I delivered my load of new potatoes to the kitchen and then headed to the bathroom to wash my hands. The place was alive with conversation. I made my way to the balcony where I could observe the guests settling in for an afternoon of absorbing Vittorio's hospitality.

"The Italian way of life is alive and well at Vittorio's, wouldn't you say?" I remarked to Mardi. "Did you see that table?"

"I did. I feel so indebted to Vittorio—to all of them."

As we made our way down to the main courtyard where the people were gathering, our minds were overloaded attempting to interpret all the Italian that was swirling around us.

"This is going to be an all-day affair. It will be five o'clock before we're done eating."

"James, come and sit down," Sergio said. "They want to know about your farm."

"We used to raise goats, and cattle, and before that *grano*—we raised wheat," I said.

"What is your land like?"

"Big fields, *grande* fields like a *tavola*—a table."

"No limone?" Vittorio asked.

"We grew apples—*mele*—but no lemons or oranges," I explained. "And lots of vegetables, potatoes, and corn."

"Do you still have a farm?" Sergio asked.

"No."

"Or we wouldn't be here," Mardi quickly added.

"We sold it about six years ago," I said.

Those seven words described what was a very difficult decision for me. I loved that land, but Mardi didn't. That is not quite accurate. She loved the land but she didn't love all the old buildings, nor did she like the isolation. We lived about ten miles from the nearest town of a substantial size—and most of our kids were no longer living with us. A lot of reasons contributed to our decision to sell the farm, not the least of which was the success of my first book about Italy. We began envisioning a life that would allow us more freedom—more time traveling and writing and being with our kids, grandkids, and friends. The farm was good for us in many ways, but we had a vision of a fuller life. And so we sold my dream and moved on to another dream—the dream we were now living.

It seemed like a good time to ask Vittorio about his childhood memories of the farm. He told us that his family used to export lemons to New York City, but times were different now. This was similar to stories I'd heard while picking olives on Tuscan farms.

"A laborer earns seventy euros a day. Selling lemons you can make only twenty euros a day, so you lose fifty euros a day growing them." Sergio translated and I was reminded of Lorenzo, the farmer who sold his wine and olive oil at the farmers market in Florence—*On some days*, he said, *a farmer would make more money if he just stayed in bed all day.*

Vittorio began a story about his great-grandmother that turned into a very entertaining tale of the war and the landing of the Americans at Salerno, less than twenty miles up the coast—a place on the beach that Sergio reminded us we could see from where we were sitting.

Vittorio continued, "They were bombing the other side of the peninsula."

"Where were you during the war?" I asked. Vittorio was telling the story with such compassion and familiarity that I lost track of the fact that he was much too young to have witnessed the war—Vittorio certainly wasn't around in 1943 when the Americans were landing on the beaches of Salerno and Anzio. That is the power of storytelling. He was telling the story with such conviction I thought that he had witnessed it all.

"Where was your papa during World War II?" I said, recovering a semblance of the time frame involved in the story.

"*Si, allora,*" began Vittorio with a sigh. The stories that Italians tell of the war are deeply personal. For Americans the fighting was *over there*. For Italians *over there* was *here*.

"His father was stationed in Northern Italy in 1943," Sergio interpreted, making sure we understood the story Vittorio was telling us. His parents knew each other, in fact lived right next door to each other, but did not marry until six years after the war ended. Vittorio told of Germans hiding in caves when the Americans came, of his family's country home being bombed, of their city home becoming the Canadian headquarters.

"When I was a kid my grandfather's front door was still painted khaki green," he told us.

Jessica arrived and Vittorio introduced us. She was not the Jessica who was teaching us Italian, but she was just as pretty. As I planted that association in my memory bank I looked high above us and saw an energetic young man coming down the steps with a wheelbarrow that he filled with kindling and hardwood—transforming it instantly into a fire pit with the striking of a match. His name was Marco, and that brought to mind another Marco associated with meat—the kind young man who had directed us to our *pasto pieno di carne* at Il Raduno. As conversations often do, ours jumped around—from the war years to present day Minori.

"I am sure Vittorio knows all two thousand people who live here." He then went on to describe the village, "It doesn't have any real attractions—just a pleasant town to live in."

"What could be better?" I said and meant it. "Any Americans in Minori?" Imagining what it would be like to someday let my kids and grandkids experience the Italian lifestyle.

"Americans have married locals. They come for a vacation, fall in love, and stay."

"We won't be the first?"

"Italy has been overrun before. Everybody wants to live here," Sergio said. "It's the most beautiful country in the world, just about."

I happen to agree. I was surprised he added "just about." I think he was just being gracious.

"Why do you think Italy was so favored?" I asked.

"Because it's fertile, and Rome has one of the most amazing weather patterns in the world. If you had all of the world to make your capital, where would you go? You would go to best place—and the same thing if you needed food—you'd go where the land was most fertile."

"Is that what the popes did?" I asked.

"Well, when Saint Peter went to Rome it was already the capital," Sergio said.

Such a statement puts Italy and Rome into a perspective that truly set them apart. It helped me start to get a grip on just how ancient Ancient Rome is. We were talking Biblical references here. Its physical attributes are no less stunning.

"The sunlight is beautiful here," I said. Mardi reminded me that I had made a similar comment thirty years ago when I first visited Greece.

Vittorio excused himself to answer his phone. I commented about how often it rang. Sergio maintained that Vittorio's phone had actually been rather quiet. He attributed it to the fact that it was Sunday.

"If you walk down the street with him, people stop him every two steps—he has time for everyone."

"Do they ask about ceramics?" Mardi wanted to know.

"About everything."

"*Va bene. Ciao,*" Vittorio said, ending one call and taking another.

I asked Sergio if he knew when Vittorio would next be firing ceramics.

"He is unloading his current firing tomorrow."

I tried to figure out what day we could help, but before I could offer, Sergio was prompted by the sightseeing boats that we could see and hear below to tell us that this spot was not far from where Ulysses had himself tied to his mast to keep from succumbing to the songs of the sirens.

That's a story I associate with the Ionian Islands of Greece, having sailed there and produced a film about our experience. But Sergio assured me that it was along the Amalfi Coast that Ulysses was tempted. I didn't argue, because the story was good, and it sounded like the tour guide on the boat below was regaling his passengers with a similar story as we caught bits and pieces of the wind-tossed commentary because of the Pantheon effect of the Amalfi Coast.

"The tourists are beginning to arrive on the Amalfi Coast," I said.

"Not just tourists—locals too—it's a beautiful day to be out on the water."

"Aren't we fortunate that this is one of the most beautiful days of the spring so far?" I said.

"Yes we are, especially to be up here. The coast is beautiful from down there, but you can appreciate it so much more from up here," Sergio said.

I've always loved the Italian propensity for appreciating beauty. They never seem to tire of viewing it or creating it. I could see three tour boats along the cliffs below, and Sergio was right. Mardi and I had passed these cliffs on the morning we took the boat to Capri, quite impressed with the beauty we saw but never imagining how many orders of magnitude more beautiful it was from on top of the cliffs we were looking at. What Sergio had said was a good reminder that we can pass near beauty, and happiness, yet fail to truly see it or appreciate it. Mardi and I had for years been content with the view from the boat of our marriage, not realizing how much better it would look from high above, if only we would start loving each other unconditionally—holding nothing back.

That makes the salvation of our relationship sound simple, but looking back over the past few years I can say that the metaphor of spending the morning climbing up to Vittorio's farm to gain this view of the Amalfi Coast is apt. The climb took only a few hours, but the grace of this moment took a lifetime to accept—to be the people to whom such an invitation would be offered.

Surrounded by this profound beauty, my mind flirted around the edges of some of life's most perplexing questions, but I was able to get no farther than to attribute our good fortune to God's grace—an answer that is satisfying only to those who are aware of their need of God's grace. Unable to penetrate further into the mysteries of life, I asked Vittorio a very practical question. In all of our hiking and touring of the farm, I had seen nothing resembling a road since we had left the streets of Minori. We had arrived at his farm using the only conveyance possible, our feet.

"No animale?"

"Only Lilo," Vittorio answered.

"No asino?"

"Vittorio asino," he said with no emotion.

"Vittorio is the beast of burden around here," Sergio said to make sure we had understood Vittorio's quip.

"Animale troppo lavoro—too much work. I can't take care of them properly," Vittorio explained.

It was odd to hear him say that anything was too much work, but he was right. Animals take a lot of care, and it is constant, daily care. Plant schedules are not so demanding.

We were sitting on rock walls in the shade of a large tree—the wine was flowing as freely as the jokes. Francesco, one of Vittorio's sons, appeared to be the main chef. He was wearing a white apron. Sergio leaned toward us and said, "What started as just a work morning has changed into this—a celebration."

Even though he had of course seen other such celebrations, he, like us, was impressed with what Vittorio had put together. Mardi and I weren't the only ones taking photos and videos. This was enough of a special occasion that others wanted to capture it as well. I was pleased about that. I wanted as much as possible to be just part of the party.

"*Al tavola,*" Vittorio said as he got up and moved toward the covered terrace.

"To the table," I translated. Vittorio smiled in appreciation.

"James, sit down," said Rosario, the young man who would eventually begin wearing my hat. I didn't yet know his connection to the others. I also suspected that he wouldn't have described himself as young, but he was a heck of a lot younger than me.

"Right here?" I asked.

"*Si,* right in the center of the table," Rosario said.

Buon appetito rang out from a dozen folks at once. The feast had begun. Everyone was cheering and clapping. The food and drink began flowing.

"Today is Anna's birthday," Vittorio announced as he put his arm around his wife. She smiled at Vittorio. She looked slightly uncomfortable with all the attention.

"*Buon compleanno,*" I said.

"*Salute,*" said Sergio.

Vittorio gave a an elegant toast in flowing Italian, ending with *Tomorrow we work, today we enjoy.*

"These are mostly from Italy," Sergio said as he passed me a platter laden with cheeses.

"We love the cheeses of Italy," I said.

"We love the *prosciutto* of Italy too," Mardi added.

"We love the food of Italy—that just about covers it," I said.

"James, do you like wine?" Rosario asked as he began pouring me a glass.

"*Mi piace vino,*" I said.

A beautiful tribute to wine ensued. Some of the words I didn't understand, but the sentiments were unmistakable because of the flowing hands and shining eyes. I interpreted part of it as *The wine is so good that peaches peel themselves.*

I asked Sergio if he would translate. He said it was difficult but that I had come close to the essence of it. Jessica took a stab at it. Her voice, cadence, and accent made the poetry sound even more beautiful.

Matteo, another of Vittorio's sons, broke out in song. His voice was very good. The singing, the cheering, and the clapping for the food intensified. It was not raucous—rather it was spirited. Italians celebrate eating like no other people I have ever been among. The feelings of grace and celebration for what we were about to eat were unmistakable.

"*Cinghiale,*" someone announced—another of my favorite Italian words— it rolls off the tongue, and is a delightful taste treat as well. The wild boar appetizers made their way around the huge table.

"Is this speaking to you?" Sergio asked.

"Oh my, is this speaking to me," I said.

"We're just getting started—we're still working on appetizers," he warned.

"*Bravo*," I said and realized, as I stood to receive yet another platter of *cinghiale* appetizers, that I was already feeling the effects of the wine.

"*Mangiare*," said somebody, but nobody needed to be told. We were all eating and we were all enjoying the *cinghiale*.

"James Bond, the sauce was made by Anna," Rosario said. "And Francesco cooked the boar."

"*Perfetto*," I said, kissing my fingertips.

"This is a Neapolitan tradition. Three hours, you go walk the neighborhood and it will be done when you return," Rosario said.

"*Sergio, io morto e vada paradiso*," I said.

"*No capito*," Sergio said.

"Okay, I'm trying to say, *I've died and gone to heaven*."

"Oh," he said and gave me an understanding smile as well as the correct translation—*Sono morto e andato in paradiso*.

"Ah, *sono morto e andato in paradiso. Grazie*. That's exactly what this feels like—heaven.

"This is a little bit of old Italy, a little bit of country-style Italy," Sergio said.

"Who knew when we walked into that shop what was going to happen a week later," I said to Sergio and Mardi.

"You like?" Francesco asked. Italians love knowing that their efforts in the *cucina* have succeeded.

"*Sono felice*," I said.

"Leave a little bit of room for the next three courses," Sergio cautioned.

"I'm trying to, but without much success. What a celebration—help me understand who's who."

"The parents of Francesco's girlfriend, Serena are here. Some of these people get together all the time. Others I'm not sure who they are. Remember, I've known Vittorio only three years."

As Sergio filled me in as best he could we got up from the table to watch the meat cook. An essential tool was missing—a garden trowel had been pressed into service to flip the meat, sizzling on a grate perched atop a mound of embers, piled so high it was overflowing the wheelbarrow.

"Italian barbeque," I said.

"Napoli barbeque," Francesco corrected.

I was sensing a rhythm to the gathering—an ebb and flow. The meal was organic—more like a game or an athletic contest than the typical American meal, where all the food comes out at once and is consumed in the next few minutes. It had been over thirty minutes since Vittorio had invited us to the table, and it felt like the meal was gathering momentum as we watched and participated in the preparation of another course.

"Oh, you're having wine?" I said to Mardi.

"Yes, and it knocked me out."

"*Allora,*" I said feeling very Italian watching smoke curl as another dozen steaks sizzled and popped as they encountered the heat of the Napoli barbeque.

"*Grazie,*" I said, tipping my wine glass toward Vittorio.

"*Bella giornata.*" he said.

"*Sono felice,*" I said.

"And so am I," said Vittorio. "Very happy."

"I still want to come and work for you."

He didn't understand so I switched to Italian—*lavoro per te.*

I tried to convey to him that we wanted to help him, no matter how menial or hard the task—the view of the Amalfi Coast would be more than enough to keep us happy. I promised him we wouldn't be bored. Vittorio laughed and thanked me. Whether he realized I was serious I couldn't say, but I was certain he knew that Mardi and I were very grateful to him for including us. He had done more than that—he and everyone else at the party were making us feel like honored guests. The more I get to know Italy and Italians the more convinced I am that the assertion I made the first time I came to Italy, that Italy's national pastime is hospitality, was fully justified. It is not soccer or any other sport—it is making the stranger among them feel welcome.

"*Prego, prego,*" an older woman was asking those of us who had left the table to return.

"*Grazie, Lucia,*" I heard a younger woman say and thought how beautifully those words flowed off her tongue. The music had been replaced by the melodious hum of conversation from the kitchen, the table, and the courtyard where people of at least four generations had gathered to watch the meat being grilled while they talked. I began thanking God for this meal—this day—in every way I knew how. Sergio seemed to again be firmly in tune with my thoughts.

"It's good that you didn't have to go back to America," he said.

Vittorio heaped a huge helping of meat onto my plate. "This is like it was before the Second World War," Sergio said as Vittorio piled his own plate high as well.

"And Vittorio is keeping the tradition alive," I said.

Laughter had overtaken conversation as the background music. I watched Vittorio watch his guests. He had the look of a man who enjoys making sure they enjoy themselves. Suddenly he too began laughing. His platter was empty. He returned to the *bar-b Napoli* to fill it.

I let out a big *Ahhhh* and the woman whose voice I loved, the one who reminded me of Jessica, said very slowly in English and with great emphasis, "Oh—my—God."

Her sense of timing, delivery, and sentiments were right on. She was, like Sergio, perfectly in tune with my feelings.

"*Oh mon Dieu—Dio mio,*" I said and tipped my wine glass to her in appreciation.

"*Ruocco vino,*" someone said as the wine Vittorio had made and had carried up the mountain was passed around the table again.

"Mardi, more lamb," I said reaching for the *piatto di carne* that followed closely on the heels of the *vino bottiglia*.

"This is a dinner fit for a Fellini movie," I said as I put a small piece of *agnello* on her plate. She acted as if she wouldn't be able to eat it all. "*Cane fortunata,*" I said glancing toward Lilo, who was looking up at me. "It is a fortunate dog who eats scraps from this table."

The lamb and beef were followed by a platter of sausage.

"Mardi, you have to try this," I said. "This *salsiccia* is as good as I've ever eaten."

She accepted a small morsel. Even though we had been pacing ourselves, we both knew we were in trouble.

"I see why Italians say *Mangia, mangia, mangia*—you have to eat, eat, eat to keep up," I said, looking at the meat piled high on my plate.

"*Aiuto,*" I called out.

That plea caught the ear of everyone. They understood why I was crying for help. They too were on the verge of eating too much.

"This is just a normal lunch," Sergio said to me.

"Yeah—a normal lunch in which you eat slabs and slabs of lamb, beef, pork, and sausage," I said. "The three-hour siesta makes sense now. What else can you do?"

I looked around at all the people enjoying themselves and realized that celebrations such as this *were* the norm, not the exception. And while it seemed that no one could possibly be having a better time than Mardi and me; this beautiful Sunday afternoon was playing host to family get-togethers all over this boot-shaped country where the food, fun, and *vino* were flowing just as freely as here.

"We'll have to carry each other down the hill," I said to Sergio, who was still with me at the table.

"*Dolce,*" Francesco announced.

The return to the table began slowly.

"This is just the appetizer, the *aperitivo,*" Sergio said.

"I've been in Italy enough times to know that's not true," I said.

"Would you believe this is the appetizer for the final course?"

I shook my head.

"You don't believe me?"

"Not yet," I said.

"James—James Bond, how are you?" Rosario was calling me from the end of the table where he was seated. He had begun wearing my hat and looked very good in it.

"*Va bene,*" I assured him.

"*Mangia, mangia,*" he said and gestured toward the platter being passed.

I took some cantaloupe and recalled what I had learned on my first visit to Italy: *siamo alla frutta* means *we are at the last*—fruit is often the final course for Italian meals.

"Mmm—this is very good. Very sweet." I said, tipping my head toward him. "You're looking good, Rosario." My hat really did suit his square face, strong jaw, and penetrating eyes.

Rosario began singing "Happy Birthday" to Anna in English, and everyone joined in. I expected them to switch to Italian, but they never did. I think I may have been the only one who said *Buon Compleanno.* Everyone else said *Happy Birthday.*

"Rosario looks pretty good in that hat, doesn't he?" I said as I asked for a photo of him and Anna. He threw an arm around Anna and I snapped the picture. Then he asked for a photo of Mardi and me. As Rosario was taking our photo the *grappa* came out.

"That hat's made for you. You should keep it," I said.

"Very well, thank you," Rosario said.

"*Una bellissima giornata,*" I said and realized that I didn't know the relationship between Anna and Rosario. I wondered whether they might be brother and sister. Sergio began to fill me in but Serena took over.

"I am in love with Francesco," she began.

"Love?" I said, surprised that she had not said *boyfriend* or that she was engaged to Francesco.

"*Sì,*" she answered. "And Rosario is my father and Anna is Francesco's mother, Vittorio's wife."

"James, *grappa*?" Rosario asked.

"I'm still working on the *vino*," I said as I envisioned the family trees that would soon be growing together. This party was definitely not over yet, even if we were at the fruit.

"*Domenica normale*," Sergio quipped.

He was making fun of the Italian stereotype that this was just the typical Sunday get-together in Italy—nothing special.

"*Sono pieno*," I said. "Is that how you would say it?"

"Don't say it, pretend it doesn't exist."

"Just keep eating? Pretend I'm not full?"

"That's the idea. It is a concept that is not allowed at an Italian meal. There is always room for more."

There certainly was room for more fun. If laughter is good for the soul, these people were being well cared for.

"Water wars," yelled someone. A friendly battle had broken out with water pistols, but none of us at the table had been sprayed despite a serious escalation in the conflict when a water hose was requisitioned to serve as a cannon.

"Mardi, have some artichokes," I said ducking out of harm's way. Even though I knew she was full I was certain that she would do as Sergio had said and ignore that fact.

"*Matteo basta*," Vittorio said with more than a little emphasis. He wanted the water fight to come to an end.

"Do you smoke, James?" Rosario wondered.

"*No, grazie*," I said. "Are we at the end now?"

"No. Now is the time for coffee," Sergio said as he watched coffee being poured from a traditional Italian coffee maker.

"Every family reunion has to have a water fight," I said thinking back to the huge family reunions of my childhood. I tried to paint a picture for Anna and Sergio what our gatherings were like. "We may have had more people, but we didn't have as many courses. And all the food came out at once."

"Thanksgiving is like that," Sergio said.

"*Esattamente*," I said and took a sip of the coffee. It, like everything else that day, was *perfetto*. I sat back to enjoy the last moments of what had been a most incredible experience. I eavesdropped as best I could on the many conversations. I heard the words *mother, sister, brother,* and sometimes *father*. I also heard smatterings of English. I didn't know whether it was for our benefit or whether English words just naturally show up in Italian conversations.

"Last man sitting," I said of Sergio alone at the table. He was putting the cap on the *grappa*. There could be no doubt, the meal had ended. But the laughter had not. Cleaning up was a celebration too. Sergio marveled at the work that Mardi had done clearing the table.

"Vittorio, contento," an older woman said, and gestured toward Vittorio, who was sitting comfortably in a chair in the shade of the lemon tree. Now that the work was done the pace of the conversation and the activity had slowed. People had gone off to sit under trees or on the walls. We were all feeling the effect of a joyous afternoon. Mardi and I were sitting together on the stone wall taking it all in. "All I have to say is, *Wow.*" She gave me a hug and kissed me lightly on the cheek.

"I think we have definitely found that the Italian Sunday meal is alive and well. Was that fun or what?"

"Oh, it was," Mardi said.

"I love you. Thank you for experiencing this with me."

"I got some ideas for our own meals," she said.

"It takes everybody chipping in to make something like this happen," I said.

"James, for you. Thank you," Rosario said as he walked up and handed me my hat.

"Prego," I said and thanked him for making us feel so welcome, so much a part of the celebration.

Mardi and I looked over at Sergio, sitting nearby. I didn't want the day to end, but it was. The ladies began a line dance. And while that didn't necessarily mean the party was over, it seemed like a good note to end on—a good time for us to begin our trek down the hill.

"You ready?" I said to Sergio.

"Yes," he answered with a sigh, as though he had just run the mealtime equivalent of a marathon.

"What a day," I said. Sergio heartily concurred.

We walked into the kitchen to say goodbye.

"Vittorio, do you want us to carry garbage down?" I asked.

"No, no," Vittorio said as he twirled a plastic bag closed. "These are some lemons for you."

"Grazie," I said. "Will you live here when you retire?"

He didn't understand the question, so I switched to Italian and asked, *When you are sixty, will you live here?*

"Si, yes," Vittorio said with much enthusiasm.

"Lots of work," I said as I looked toward the tools lining the far end of the room. There was no end to the work that I could help him do, just like there is no end to the work that I could help my son with on his ranch. It's that way with every farm. The good thing about helping with work on an Italian farm is the way eating is celebrated.

Sergio turned to us and said, "Vittorio wants you to know that you will always be welcome to stop by."

"Oh, that's wonderful. We will, we definitely will," I said.

"*Quando parti?*" Vittorio asked.

"We don't yet know when we are leaving," I answered. I explained that we were renting a car until Friday and that on Wednesday we would drive Sergio to his grandfather's place—and that we would definitely stop by the shop before we left.

"*Amore,*" Vittorio said.

"*Ciao,*" Anna said.

"Thank you so much. We had a wonderful time," I said.

"*Ciao, ciao,*" Vittorio said.

"Bye-bye, James," Rosario yelled from the terrace above.

"*Ciao,* and thank you. See you soon, Rosario," I yelled back.

To Vittorio I said, "I love Rosario. I think he should have kept my hat."

"I love James," Rosario shouted. My voice must have carried all the way to Rosario up on the terrace.

"Bye-bye, James," shouted Serena.

"Bye, Serena. See you next time. Thank you, thank you, thank you," I said.

"*Ciao, ciao, ciao,*" Vittorio said.

We began walking slowly down the steps and out the gate. When we were down the path fifty yards or so, I looked back up at the house. Rosario was waving.

"*Yahweh, Yahweh,*" he yelled. I couldn't imagine that was actually what he was saying, but it had the rhythm and cadence of *Yahweh,* the Jewish word for God, being repeated.

The sound and our relative positions reminded me again of the climactic scene in *Dancing with Wolves* when the brave warrior Wind in His Hair yells down to Dances with Wolves. Just as it did in the movie, the sound reverberated off the hills, capturing the feeling of that moment perfectly. We felt loved by our new friends—all the world seemed right. I waved one last time to Rosario, tipped my hat, the hat I had wanted him to keep, and smiled.

We walked down to Minori mostly in silence. We were lost in our thoughts. I stopped to take a lot of photos—I wanted to forget nothing about the day.

"Do you want me to carry more?" Mardi called back to me.

"No. Everywhere I look I see a picture."

As we were coming to the streets of Minori Sergio slowed to allow me to catch up. We exchanged phone numbers. "What time do you want us to pick you up on Wednesday?" I asked.

"As early as you want. Let's touch base on Tuesday night."

"I will wait for your call," I said. "*Ciao*. Thank you for everything."

"*Ciao*," he said and began walking slowly toward his home.

"If anything changes, let us know. We can go another day," I called out to Sergio.

"*Certo,*" he said and resumed walking.

I sat down to check the bus schedule.

"Mardi, there's no bus until nine-fifteen. We've missed the five-fifteen."

"Oh, no."

"I feel like walking home. It feels right that we should end this day by walking home from Vittorio's farm all the way to Maiori," I said.

"I agree. It's a good way to end a day such as this."

"We could have some tea before we leave town—lighten our loads a little."

We chose the first bench we came to on the promenade.

"*Buonasera,*" I said to a man walking by with his hands behind his back. He greeted me politely, even enthusiastically.

"See how happy that little girl is," I said. I was watching her and her father kick a soccer ball back and forth. I couldn't take my eyes off them. He had the delicate touch of a professional and she returned many balls that I was sure were going to get past her.

I shouldn't have been, but I was surprised that the promenade was soon filled with dozens of people enjoying a beautiful Sunday evening. "So if this is what April in Italy is like. How many more people would be out enjoying the *passeggiata* in May?" I wondered. Mardi didn't bite.

"It will probably take us an hour to walk home," she said. I couldn't tell whether she was looking forward to walking home or regretting that her husband was so impractical as to want to walk home just because it felt like the right way to end the day.

"Are you sorry you married me?" I asked.

That got her attention. She looked at me, trying to figure out whether it had been a serious question.

"How many years did you spend regretting that you married me?" I asked.

"About thirty. I thought we were incompatible—that you hated me."

"And what do you think now?"

"I wasted an awful lot of good years."

It was a good answer. I gave her a hug and we began walking toward Maiori. On the other side of the highway Michele greeted us—he was standing in the doorway of the Bambi Café. It seemed only right that on this perfect day we should be reminded by a cheerful hello from a new friend just how good life was for us now.

"*Ciao, Michele,*" I said.

"Everything okay?" he asked.

"*Perfetto,*" I answered. "We are walking home. *Ciao.*"

"*Ciao.* See you soon."

"What a life. What a life," I said to Mardi as we turned at the school.

"Some people would probably say that this is hell, walking over the mountain to Maiori."

I could tell by the way she said it that she was not one of those people.

"You didn't like that today, did you—hanging out with a bunch of people you don't know?" I asked.

"And you didn't like having a gorgeous view, probably one of the most beautiful views on the Amalfi Coast—maybe the world," she asked.

"Good evening. Have a nice walk," said a lady passing us on the trail.

"*Buonasera,*" I called out to her.

A minute later we met another family walking toward Minori. We greeted each other warmly. By the time we got to the little *piazza* near the highest point of the walk, we'd been greeted almost a dozen times—families, couples, and folks walking by themselves. As we started down I began recalling our first hike on The Path of Lemons.

"This is where we went wrong, you dastardly person—you made us hike straight up from here," I chided. "We were so close to Minori, yet you turned a fifteen-minute walk into a two-hour hike."

At that fork in the path where Mardi had led me into the high country, we took a break and began recalling our other hikes on the *Limone Sentiero*. A large family came by and stopped to talk. They too were headed to Maiori. They were surprised to see us up there. We didn't tell them of the other walking we had done that day—that we were on our way home from Ravello.

While we sat talking, another family stopped to talk. Clearly, the Sunday *passeggiata* was going to be well attended in Maiori. The family wandered on, and a few minutes later a lone, tall man greeted us. He was going up. He was about our age and dressed traditionally, wearing a jacket and a hat.

"Hi," he said.

"Hello," I said.

"Very nice to go down," the man said as he walked past.

"I think both up and down are good," I said.

After a slight delay to consider what I had said, he replied, "Yes, it is true." He then stopped suddenly, turned to look back as if to assess us, but said nothing. He dipped his head slightly before continuing on up the trail.

"Bye," he said when he had resumed walking.

"*Ciao*," I said, feeling that under the circumstances the familiarity of *Ciao* was acceptable. We had looked into each other's eyes during that brief moment of assessment.

I would have loved to know why he stopped to look back at us—and what his assessment had been—but I didn't ask, nor did his body language offer any clue beyond his sudden stop and the steady warmth of his gaze.

When we resumed walking, we began discussing the number of courses Vittorio and his friends had served.

"We had the appetizers on the lemon thorns, then the lemon salad, then the bread, and the *bruschetta*," Mardi recalled, describing only the first half hour of the meal. I didn't correct her when she said *broo chetta*, I had mispronounced it the first two dozen times I said it to Pietro a half dozen years ago. I can still hear his voice saying over and over, *Brew skate tah, James, brew skate tah.*

"There were three or four courses of meat. We started with *prosciutto.*"

"*Buonasera*," a woman walking by greeted us. She too was climbing.

"*Buonasera*," I echoed.

As we neared the cathedral, the pathway became congested with people. Music played throughout the neighborhood, including a classical Italian love song sung by a tenor coming from a radio on a terrace just above our heads.

"Vittorio invited us back. Next time I want to be able to talk to him without an interpreter," I said.

"Oh, my."

"It was amazing how much we were able to understand though, wasn't it?"

"Even before Sergio translated it for us," Mardi said.

The bells of Maiori began to ring. I stopped to count—one high and eight low.

"I love my bells."

"Can you hear the waves?" she asked.

"Yes, and I hear the birds too."

The sounds of Maiori were welcoming us back. I stopped to drink from the fountain just above the church that had a photo from the movie *Amore* hanging next to it.

"What a fantastic day—*Che giornata fantastica*," I said feeling the need to speak of the day using Italian words.

"Isn't it amazing that we're staying in the town where *Amore* was filmed and then we meet Vittorio—can you think of anyone you've ever met who is more passionate than he is?" I asked.

"No," she said and I could tell she really meant it.

"*Love, Passion, and Italy.* It's all here," I said. "That would be a great title for our story."

I was speaking of both stories—the story of our sojourn in Italy and the journey of our marriage. I pulled Mardi close, wanting to thank her for the incredible day we had spent together.

"You're even beginning to look like an Italian. Your skin is getting dark," I said. "I think we'd better check *your* DNA—there's Italian blood flowing somewhere in there."

"You're the passionate one. You act more Italian than I do."

"You and I are one. *Tu e mi sono uno.*"

We could see Corso Reginna clearly—kids playing soccer, parents greeting their friends—older folks sitting on the benches. The scene was timeless. A not quite full moon hung low in the sky gathering light and would soon be shining bright. We were in no hurry to finish the day's journey. The church *piazza* seemed like a good place to pause and reflect, to thank God for the day. The sounds of children's voices, mingled with the songs of the birds, echoed off the walls of the church.

"Mardi, I love you."

"That was the goal for my life."

"To have a husband who loved you?" I asked, surprised by her response.

"That and adventure—I wanted to be a medical missionary."

"You didn't dream about having a feast with a bunch of passionate Italians on the side of a mountain?"

She smiled at that and continued. "And if I couldn't be a medical missionary like Albert Schweitzer, I wanted to be a forest ranger. You, a loving husband, were somewhere down the list, but you were on there."

I smiled at that and gave her a hug. I too had dreamed of being other things—a clarinet player like Benny Goodman, a baseball player like Duke Snider, a basketball player like Jerry West, an architect like Frank Lloyd Wright, even a writer like John Steinbeck or Ernest Hemingway, but always on the list would be a woman who loved me and whom I loved—and we would share adventures. Did I ever dream that such a day as this would be possible when I was a kid? Not that I recall, but the closeness and the friendship I felt toward Mardi, that I did dream about—that I wanted.

The bells began ringing again. I didn't have to count. I knew they would stop at two and eight. We'd been absorbing the mysterious attraction that we feel toward Maiori for fifteen minutes—listening to the sounds, watching the people move about below us—knowing that we too would soon be down there among them, down there where someone else could be up high observing us making our way across Corso Reginna and into the doorway leading up to Casa Mannini. They might wonder about us just as we were wondering about the lives of the people we saw on the streets below. We expected to see *Mario* riding about on his bicycle, but on this evening we did not see him. But we knew Gianni was there, somewhere.

"I'm in love with you," I said.

"My Italian lover," she said, pulling me closer and stroking my hair. "Where have you been all my life?"

She was right to ask the question and right to call me an Italian lover, for it is true I am a lover of all things Italian, but I am also an Italian lover in the usual sense in which those two words are combined. My sojourns in Italy have taught me much about love and loving, and about serving.

Where have I been all of Mardi's life? Why wasn't I always there for her—and why has she discovered me only late in life? All good questions, and there's one more. *What part has Italy played in turning me into an Italian lover—a lover who is concerned not just about my needs but about the needs of my wife as well?*

We didn't end our day at the church. We waited until it was almost dark, until the moon was shining bright, to walk down the steps of the Cathedral of Santa Maria and make the short journey hand-in-hand across Corso Reginna to our hotel, where we climbed the steps to our room to end our perfect day making love—*finire la nostra giornata perfetta facendo l'amore.*

CHAPTER EIGHTEEN

Maiori ~ Monday April 18 ~ 58 & Partly Cloudy

A Transformational Act

*Love is of all passions the strongest,
for it attacks simultaneously the head,
the heart and the senses.*
LAO TZU

■

*I went to the woods because I wished to live deliberately,
to front only the essential facts of life
and see if I could not learn what it has to teach, and not,
when I came to die, discover that I had not lived.*
HENRY DAVID THOREAU

Mardi didn't want to rent a car. She was okay with riding a bus on the Amalfi Coast—they were big and the drivers most likely had been negotiating these roads that only Italians could dream up all their lives. Our rental car would be small, and the mountain roads I'd driven much of my life were superhighways compared to the Amalfi Coast roads that at times looked as if they were designed for donkey carts, which of course they were. She couldn't imagine driving on a road perched high on the cliffs above the ocean—a road so narrow that at times even cars have to slow to a crawl to squeeze past each other. Why I wanted to subject myself to such a challenge was beyond her. She was certain we'd come around a hairpin turn, see an out-of-control semi careening toward us, and have to choose between being flattened by the truck or flying off the road, over the cliffs, and into the ocean a thousand feet below.

For the first two weeks I agreed with her, but I wanted to experience the out-of-the-way towns of Basilicata, which was known as Lucania in 1935 when Mussolini forced Carlo Levi to live in its barrenness and poverty. Trains did not deliver Levi to Aliano eighty-some years ago. Buses got him close, but it was only by car that he was delivered to this Godforsaken land, and the same would be true for us.

I believe that traveling, especially *living* in a foreign land, accomplishes what Thoreau went to the woods to do. A foreign culture, if you will let it, allows you to confront what may have become tediums in your life. You may discover better ways of living, especially in the everyday patterns of life—eating, moving about, greeting your friends, and living among your neighbors. The multicourse meal, the evening *passeggiata*, and making time for those who live nearby—all these Italian traditions have greatly influenced our lives.

Not that life was getting boring on the Amalfi Coast—far from it. Each day had brought its own rewards, its own surprises. Yesterday was off-the-charts unique, as if that word needed a qualifier. We had been treated to a seven-course meal, or was it eight or nine—a long lost relative returning from America could not have been accorded more gracious hospitality than Mardi and I were shown.

This day too showed promise of being in a class by itself. I was controlling the flippers, and I'd have to face the consequences—a displeased spouse—if things didn't go well. Mardi, even after discussing the merits, still wasn't sure she wanted to be in a car I was driving on the Amalfi Coast Highway. I wasn't so sure I wanted that either, but I rationalized that if I could just get out of Salerno and onto an *autostrada,* I'd have time to get used to Italian drivers, Italian police, and Italian road signs in a situation that couldn't be too much different from driving on an interstate back home. The timing also seemed right. We must have tallied at least fifteen miles, maybe more, hiking to Vittorio's farm and back. Surely our feet and legs could use a rest.

But even with all these sensible reasons for renting a car, I still wasn't certain I was going to go through with it. I hemmed and hawed while we ate a light breakfast in our bright and cheery room at Casa Mannini. Even though I missed Maximiliano, I was glad I didn't have to explain why we were again rushing off and not basking in the luxury of a one- to two-hour breakfast. We had chosen, since moving to Casa Mannini, to go without a breakfast plan, and so far it had been a wise move. We were definitely saving euros.

We were also saving euros by taking the bus to Salerno to pick up our car. I had reserved a FIAT 500 for the very reasonable price of one hundred twenty euros for four days—at least that's what I thought as I read and reread the fine print on the website. I have no idea how much time I spent researching Italian car rentals—let's just say it was a lot. I'd also gone to the trouble of getting an international driver's license just in case I got up the nerve to mix it up with Italian drivers.

But even with all this foresight, planning, and worrying, I wasn't boarding the bus to Salerno with any semblance of confidence, which is unusual for me. I've been an adventurer all my life—a guy willing not only to think outside the box, but live outside the box as well. Among the riskier things I've done is to fly an airplane on a daily schedule, which means that every morning at the very same time I took off from one airport and flew to another. The thing about a daily schedule is that weather is not so consistent. The other thing about this daily schedule was that in between the first stop and the second and last stop was a range of high mountains. Getting to that second stop sometimes required some out-of-the box flying. I wasn't reckless. I always left myself plenty of outs, but it wasn't always a joyride in severe clear air. I had to rely on my experience, my talent, and my preparations to make sure that whether I was dodging blue sky as I lifted off from Rock Hill, South Carolina or thunderstorms over the rugged Blue Ridge Mountains, I would arrive safely back on the ground in Knoxville, Tennessee.

So you'd think that the prospect of driving in Italy wouldn't cause me much concern, but it was. I noticed very little of the beauty that lay outside the bus window that morning. It might have been because the bus was so crowded with commuters that I could hardly see out, or it might have been that Mardi and I had ridden on an uncrowded mid-morning bus to Salerno a few days earlier, or it might have been that the only thing I could think about was what I was about to do. My stomach was churning.

I had brought my GPS just in case, the one I'd purchased seven years earlier for my journey around Tuscany by bicycle, hoping that its familiarity would relieve some of my anxiety. It had been my trusted guide then and I was going to rely on it to get me out of Salerno and onto the A3 Superstrada. We were even using it to guide us to the Hertz office. I had wanted to pick the car up at the train station. We knew exactly where that was from our exploratory trip a few days earlier. But car rentals were either unavailable or much more expensive from the station so I chose a location that seemed nearby.

I love the adventure of traveling, but on some days you want familiarity, and this was one of those days. I feared I was going to get my fill of adventure as soon as I got behind the wheel of the FIAT 500. I had ridden in FIAT Pandas. I had test-driven a MINI Cooper, but as I had discovered on my first trip to Italy, a MINI Cooper is a large car compared to the FIAT 500.

And now I was going into battle with Italian drivers in one of the smallest cars ever produced—a car I had never driven. Would I be too timid? Would I overcompensate and be too aggressive? Surely not. Is it possible to be more aggressive than the typical Italian driver?

I've ridden in the backseats of never-use-your-brakes drivers in taxis all over the world—New Delhi, Saigon, London—but as we were walking the final few blocks to the Hertz office, I suddenly realized that this would be only the third time I had driven a car in a foreign land. The first was on a sleepy Greek island where auto traffic did not exist, only the occasional pickup or donkey cart. The second was in New Zealand, where they drive on the wrong side of the road and there are more sheep than people. Neither experience would help me negotiate Salerno's crowded streets.

As we walked along and the streets became more and more crowded, and I got more and more nervous, I wondered why the GPS was leading us toward the train station, instead of the cheaper location, and what I hoped would also be a less congested location. Then I realized I must have entered the address of the train station in the GPS instead of the rental office. While I was kicking myself, Mardi noticed that the GPS wasn't directing us to the train station but rather to take a right turn at the next corner. We got to the Piazza Vittorio Veneto, looked right, and there was a Hertz sign. With a strong arm I could have flung a baseball to the front portico of the train station.

We walked in the door of the Hertz office expecting a hassle. We had discovered too late that my regular driver's license was required *as well as* my international license. We promptly informed the young man that I'd left my Wisconsin license at our hotel. He didn't even look up from his typing. "*No problemo*—don't worry." Italians have a tendency to ignore rules and regulations if it is to their advantage—and most of the time it is.

I had heard horror stories about surcharges, so I asked whether there were any hidden charges. He assured me that the total cost would be exactly what I was expecting—and that we did indeed have unlimited miles. I asked about getting to Eboli. He didn't have a map, but he said it would be no problem. *No problem for him* I'm thinking but for me—*maybe*. In rapid-fire English/Italian he described the turns to take to get on A3 to Eboli. He then slowed his delivery and told me that there was one problem—he was not able to fulfill my request for a FIAT 500. I told him I was disappointed—that I'd been looking forward to driving an Italian car on Italian highways.

"*No problemo*," he said. "You weel be driving an Eetalian car. You weel be driving a FIAT Punta. I theenk you will love it. It is beeger than a Cinquecento. You weel have more room for your luggage."

"*Va bene,*" I said mirroring his enthusiasm as I folded the contract, although inwardly I was disappointed. I lost that disappointment when I stepped into the street and saw the car, a sleek beauty parked in the Piazza Vittorio Veneto traffic circle, which loops in front of the train station. So far this adventure that I had been fearing was turning out to be another *Gianrico piece of cake.*

We settled into the car, connected the GPS, and punched in Eboli, where, according to Carlo Levi, Christ had stopped. Levi's book had mentioned very little of Eboli beyond proclaiming it in the title, but it was such an intriguing name for a book that I felt I had to journey to Eboli—to see if there was indeed a demarcation between where Christ had journeyed and where He had not—to determine whether the south of Italy was as Godforsaken as Carlo Levi said it was. We were about to get a lesson in geography as well as the power of metaphor.

I started the car, checked my mirrors, and eased into the traffic circle feeling like a sixteen-year-old taking his driver's test. I hoped Mardi would be as kind as that examiner who gave me the most memorable birthday present of my life—a freedom-bestowing license to drive. That was a day to remember. My thumping heart was telling me that this day was going to make a deep impression too.

I was relieved that in my first venture into Italian traffic there was none. I was alone in the circle looking for the second right. I didn't encounter any cross-traffic in the first intersection either, but I was not so fortunate at the next. I could see, as I looked through the traffic streaming past, that the one-way street I was on turned into a one-way street coming right at me. Every car and scooter at that incredibly busy intersection was going to have to turn one way or the other. The intersection had a traffic light, but right turns on red are legal in Italy, so the folks behind me would expect me to jump into the flow. I was hoping the light would turn green before I got to the head of the queue. I didn't want to have to be watching for folks stepping off the curb and cars speeding by as I made my first turn into Italian traffic. But I wasn't that lucky. All of a sudden I was at the corner—up to bat. The traffic was flying by. The two cars before me had gotten to the front of the line and darted into the traffic, and I wanted to do the same. I was nervous, but I said nothing to Mardi. I had to appear confident—otherwise she'd sense my fear, and her nervousness would make me even more nervous.

I asked, and hoped she wouldn't hear the fear in my voice, whether we turned right, not that I had much of a choice. We were on the right side of the street and we were going to get carried right whether we wanted to go that direction or not.

"Yes, right turn," Mardi said, sounding anxious.

For some reason my GPS, *Dorothy,* had gone silent. I needed aural cues, and she had chosen the worst possible moment to clam up. I punched her buttons, but she wouldn't even say *ouch.* I inched forward, got a look at the cars streaming at me from the left, and saw a gap just big enough to slip into the flow of traffic if no one stepped off the curb and walked against the blinking "NO WALK" sign. Just as I let out the clutch the light turned green. Now instead of coming from the left I suddenly had a car coming at me from the other side of the intersection. But it had to turn and so did I. That driver had a lane to turn into and so did I, so I kept going and so did he. We turned into our lanes with such precision and speed that it felt as if we'd been practicing the maneuver. That gave me a bit of confidence. That and the fact that I'd also avoided turning into the buses-only lane.

American drivers would not have made the quick, almost go-kart like turn made by that driver, who was now beside me. Driving in Italy was definitely going to be a unique experience. I was super focused, my eyes darting this way and that. I quickly shifted up through second gear and into third to stay with the flow of traffic the man beside me was establishing. I held back slightly so that if he wanted my lane he could have it. But he didn't. I was cueing my speed off his. I planned to do that a lot—watching how Italians drove to figure out how I should drive. We were on Corso Giuseppe Garibaldi, named after the father of modern Italy, the man who unified what had been an unruly collection of city states. I liked that. I was hoping for some order.

"When do we turn again?" I asked Mardi, not wanting to take my eyes off the cars around me for even a millisecond. From what I remembered of the agent's instructions, I was certain we had another right turn to negotiate, but I wasn't sure how far it was. I gave Dorothy a gentle punch but still she said nothing. I was afraid to look at her, afraid to take my eyes off the scooters that would appear in my rearview mirror, and then quickly dart around, just as that German couple in Positano had warned me they would.

Mardi wasn't responding either. I mustered a shot of courage and stole a quick glance at the GPS and saw that Dorothy was asking for a right turn, but I was afraid to stare at her long enough to figure out where—I had far too many scooters scooting this way and that.

"Can you call out the turn for me, Mardi?" I asked again.

"Two more blocks. See where those cars are turning? Take a right there."

I worked my way to the right through the buses and turned. I was surprised that we were now on a much tighter, narrower street, but Dorothy didn't recalculate, so it must have been the correct turn. I was trying to be cool for

Mardi's benefit but I was sweating like crazy. I glanced at a street sign. We were on Via Dalmazia, moving briskly along, I was gaining enough confidence that I took my eyes off the road long enough to look at Dorothy. We were approaching a roundabout—or maybe just an intersection with a lot of streets coming into it, but I couldn't take my eyes off the road long enough to figure out which exit to take—there were so many at odd angles. I longed to hear Dorothy's obnoxious voice, but again, nothing.

"I can't tell you which turn it is, there are too many of them," Mardi said confirming what I already feared.

I bypassed the first exit. I figured that if we were getting on Italy's version of an interstate, at least one other car would have taken that turn. The car in front of me took the next turn, and I followed. I immediately realized I shouldn't have, but I didn't want to jerk back to catch the next exit even though I had plenty of time. The driver next to me might have been about ready to jump into that space too, so I went with the flow.

I'd made my first wrong turn in Italian traffic, but I hadn't hit anyone or even incurred the wrath of an Italian driver. I was just going to have to figure out how to get back on the roundabout for a take two. I ignored Dorothy and went for a cruise around the block, as we say in America, but in Italy it's not as straightforward as making three right turns. However, I possessed enough situational awareness, to use another aviation term, that within a few moments I was lined up for a do-over.

This time I darted through the crowded intersection with a touch of panache and was soon speeding along the *Autostrada* following the Reggio Calabria signs at one hundred kilometers per hour. It not only sounded fast, it felt fast, but I wanted to keep up with the traffic. Dorothy still was not talking but Mardi told me she wanted us to exit left. I worked my way across the lanes to be ready. I was pegging the speed limit. but it wasn't fast enough for a guy on a big motorcycle. He came right up on my tail, encouraging me to move over. Normally I would have been happy to relinquish the lane, but I didn't know whether it was a one lane exit or two, so I stayed put. I wanted to get back to America without a driving, parking, or speeding ticket. A disapproving glance of a young man on a hot bike I could accept.

I made the exit, matched the speed of the cars around me, and settled into one of the center lanes. After so many days spent either walking or riding a bus at the start-and-stop pace of the hairpin turns on the Amalfi Coast, it felt bizarre to be moving so fast. I still wasn't comfortable looking at Dorothy for very long.

"Okay, in fifteen miles we do something," I said.

"That's probably the Eboli exit," Mardi said.

"Oh, it can't be already."

"Well the speed limit is one hundred."

I looked at the speedometer for the first time. "Oh no, I'm going a hundred and twenty," I said as I glanced in the rearview mirror. "Uh-oh, somebody's coming." My chest tightened. Just what I didn't want—a ticket.

"Good grief. It's a Maserati or..." Before I could finish the sentence, it swooshed by on my left—a black Ferrari at full roar—its vortex rocking our little Punto.

"Look at that thing go!" I shouted as it shot up the road. It looked like it was on rails as it leaped from lane to lane, shooting through gaps between cars moving at less than half its speed. The show didn't last very long—that sweet piece of Italian art and engineering was soon a black dot far up the road pulling back a distant memory of another black Ferrari—it was *déjà vu all over again,* as that wordsmith Yogi Berra is said to have quipped.

I had managed to get tickets for a Bulls playoff game at the United Center—a big deal. I was obsessed with Michael Jordan and Scottie Pippen. We were early for the game—the skyline of Chicago was just coming into view. I was driving my son Matt's car, a red Audi. I noticed in my rearview mirror, a black car maneuvering through traffic. In an instant it was on my tail, blocked by cars spread across the freeway. Matt had been watching it too, and told me it was a Ferrari. I looked hard at the driver and realized it was Michael Jordan. My heart raced. He had probably chosen our red Audi, figuring we'd be most likely to let a fast car through the logjam.

Feeling the headiness of the moment, I punched the accelerator and just like that Jordan's Ferrari was free to run. We watched him fly by and that's when I lost my head. I decided to follow him. He was going to the United Center and so were we—why not let him show us the best way through Chicago traffic. Matt's Audi 100 was up to it. We jumped on his tail. Jordan wasn't pushing his Ferrari anywhere near its limit, but we were flying down the freeway faster than I could afford. The intoxicating speed brought me to my senses. If we got pulled over, Jordan would have a great excuse and I would have none. The Bulls were playing Miami and Matt's car happened to be registered in Florida, where he was going to college. The headline in the next day's Tribune flashed in my mind: *Crazed Heat Fan Arrested Chasing Michael Jordan.*

I let him go. Jordan's Ferrari quickly disappeared just as this one had. Jordan got to the United Center long before Matt and I did, just as the driver of that black Ferrari got to Eboli long before we did—but we got there, and we met no *polizia* on the way.

"I hope Eboli doesn't turn out to be too disappointing," Mardi said.

"Oh, I don't think it will be disappointing. We will have gone as far as Christ went."

She gave a soft laugh.

"And then, once we've had lunch, we'll go farther than Christ did."

We asked Dorothy to direct us to the train station, figuring that would get us close to *il centro della citta*, the center of town. Next we had to figure out where to park. I feared I would misread a sign and we'd return from lunch and find that our car had been towed. I looked for a street that wasn't busy, wasn't metered, and was near a bar. I parked, walked in and asked the *barista* if my car would still be parked on his street when I returned in a couple of hours. "*Ma certo,*" he said as though he were speaking of the sun rising tomorrow.

That fear calmed, I set out to quell another one—of getting lost, or forgetting where we had parked. We were near the train station, but I used technology to further pinpoint the car. I marked it on the GPS, turned on Strava, and took a photo of the street. I was determined to do all I could to make sure I wouldn't regret renting a car in Italy. Our car wasn't very distinctive looking, at least in Italy—it was a silver hatchback. I took a photograph of it and its license plate. If the worst happened, I was going to be able to identify that car.

As we walked away from the car a surge of relief swept over me. I was thrilled to have made it to Eboli without incident. It seemed like a good time to confess.

"I was nervous this morning. *Do I really want to rent a car?*"

"I didn't know that. I thought you were pretty sure of it."

"No, not at all, but I must say now I'm glad I went through with it."

I was happy to be walking the streets of Eboli, which were nothing like I had imagined. Instead of a backwater town, it was a rather large city. The streets were filled with cars and the sidewalks with people. What I loved most, though, was that lots of kids were playing. It felt like a family town—not quite like Maiori, but still friendly. As in every Italian city that I've grown to love, the sound of water flowing from a fountain was a prominent feature. Eboli's fountain was made for getting your feet wet, and little boys especially were having a great time. We felt at home. Our oldest kids had grown up in Aspen, which featured a fountain at the end of Hyman Avenue Mall with dozens of shooting jets of water programmed in a sequence that kids loved to try to guess. And if they got it wrong they got wet, but that was part of the fun. These kids were enjoying this fountain too, and they too were getting wet.

We liked the feel of the area, so we chose a coffee bar that looked as if it was frequented by neighborhood regulars—it also happened to have a good selection of *gelatos*. I ordered a *medio stracciatella* and Mardi chose a medium mint *gelato*. I handed the *barista* a five euro note and asked, *Possiamo anche ottenere acqua calda?*"

I was afraid he might ask for more money, but he handed me back two fifty in change.

"*Due cinquanta* for two *gelatos* and two cups of hot water?" I asked.

"*Si, grazie*," the man said.

We chose a sidewalk table not far from a man reading a newspaper. He took no notice of us. He looked so comfortable that it was easy to imagine he'd been enjoying his coffee and his newspaper in that same chair for most of his rather long life. A few minutes later a man with a hoarse voice joined him. Their perfunctory greeting confirmed my supposition that the two saw each other every day of the week at these same tables. I was also certain that a third man who would normally have been there, wasn't—and that was because of a certain *signorina* he had recently met. The men were enjoying a good tale at their friend's expense. Their facial expressions and hand gestures and my limited understanding of Italian helped me enjoy the story too. But the punchline that sent them into fits of laughter—I completely missed.

"That was quite an exchange. What was it about?" Mardi asked as she finished her *gelato*. I had long ago finished mine and was now sipping my tea.

"It was about a man, a regular, who didn't show up this morning—a man who fancied himself to be quite a ladies' man, but they lost me right at the end," I said.

"They sure were having a good time with it."

"I've *got to* learn Italian so I can do a better job of eavesdropping."

As I said the word *eavesdropping*, I pulled it apart and realized what a strange word it is—*dropping eaves* means listening secretly to a private conversation—and that made me realize that technically I wasn't eavesdropping. I wasn't listening secretly, and they weren't having a private conversation, far from it. Maybe good manners dictated that I should have ignored the story, but I couldn't resist trying to stretch my Italian vocabulary.

After watching people and sipping tea for a half hour, Mardi turned to me and said, "People are heavier here. I saw hardly anyone, except tourists, who were heavy in Maiori."

I looked and noticed the man with the hoarse voice was definitely big, as were many of the people walking by.

"Yeah—even though we're in the mountains, it's really quite flat here in town," I said.

"All those steps on the Amalfi Coast keep people thin."

We were doing what people love to do in sidewalk cafés—nothing—and neither of us felt the need to do anything else. We had found our spot.

"Did you want a *cappuccino?*" Mardi asked. "The prices are so good."

"I'd love a *cappuccino*. This is a very nice place. Lots of living going on."

We could see the kids still playing in the fountain just up the street. Looking the other way, toward where we had parked our car, we could see people coming and going from the *frutta e verdura* shop, and just beyond was a sidewalk vendor offering a huge selection of books. We were in a veritable people-watcher's paradise. The two-man conversation had become a three-way sport, still at the expense of the missing man.

"Everyone seems to know each other. I don't know how they can in such a big town," Mardi said as she returned to our table with two *cappuccinos*.

"My guess is that they frequent the same blocks all the time," I said.

We settled in, sipping our *cappuccinos* and enjoying the atmosphere. I pulled out my computer and pretended I was at a sidewalk café in Hemingway's Paris, the scene he'd captured in *A Moveable Feast,* which may have been the first book that gave me the romantic notion that I would someday be a writer. It was a dream I didn't hold very tightly, though. I knew that few people make a go of it as a writer, and I, in addition to being a bit of a romantic, also had a practical side—I wanted to get married and eventually have a family. So I continued writing but didn't try to make a living at it—at least not until our two youngest kids were almost on their own. On some days I regret not having more confidence at a younger age that I could have made a living as a writer—this was one of those days. It was probably the ambience of Eboli—and not a revelation that I could have succeeded years ago if only I had been willing to try.

We spent more than an hour at the café. Neither of us wanted to move on. I was feeling creative—words were flowing—and Mardi was catching up with family emails. The regulars had come and gone—only the man reading the newspaper was still there. We had found our table. I had no idea whether we would ever see Eboli again, but if we did I was certain we'd make straight away for this spot, with its great views of the patrons and the street in both directions.

We finally felt the pull of unexplored places and began walking toward our car, but we didn't get far. The fruit and vegetable market pulled us in. If we'd been living in Eboli we would have walked out with armloads, but since we were just passing through, not stopping as Christ did, we bought only a few apples and some grapes for our journey deep into Basilicata.

The shopkeeper eagerly initiated a conversation with me as I was paying for the fruit. He wanted to know where we were from. He apparently thought we were European, because he was quite surprised when I told him we were American. He told me he was from Italy, from Eboli. We both smiled at that. He had no idea where Wisconsin was. Chicago he had heard of, so I loosely located Wisconsin as being between Canada and Chicago. By this time not only was the shopkeeper fully engaged, so was almost everyone else in the store. The shopkeeper had an uncle in New Jersey, and a couple of the women in line had relatives on the East Coast as well. As he was counting out my change I suggested that he come to America, to Wisconsin. He reached out, vigorously shook my hand, and told me to come back again.

I enjoyed that exchange so much that when we passed a *supermercato* I suggested picking up some chocolate and a lemon tea drink. But this store was much larger and the cashier was a teenager not yet comfortable with striking up conversations with strangers.

As we walked the final few blocks to our car with plastic bags from the *frutta e verdura* market and the *supermercato,* a car went by and honked at us. It was one of the women who'd been in line behind us at the *frutta e verdura* market who had relatives in America.

"That was quick. We're already known in town," I said.

"Not quite like Cheers yet, but it's a start," Mardi said.

Eboli was treating us well. Just as the *barista* had promised our car was right where we'd parked it and it had no ticket. We hopped in. I punched Castelmezzano in the GPS, a town I'd read about in my research of Basilicata, and headed out of town with Dorothy calling out the turns. We never did figure out why she had abandoned us in Salerno, but it was good to have her back to guide us to the *Autostrada.*

Beyond Eboli the land rose up quickly, making us feel at home. Our two oldest kids' formative years were spent in the mountains, and our only daughter, as well as our son Jon, had been born in Colorado. We feel in tune with mountain people.

"This looks a little more like Tuscany. These towns are on the top of the hill instead of clinging to the side of a mountain," I said.

We were driving through dramatic country on wide roads with sweeping turns through tunnels. As peaks with snow on them came into view my reservations about renting a car vanished, which is to say that my fears disappeared. As we came out of a tunnel and my eyes adjusted to the sunlight

I realized I was about to shoot around a *carabinieri* in the slow lane. I hit the brakes and pulled in behind him. But none of the other cars bothered—they flew quickly around both of us.

"They use speed cameras," Mardi said as I gathered courage from all the examples set by the faster drivers and began inching around the police car. "They don't stop you, you get a ticket in the mail. And you can get a ticket for driving with your brights on."

I was desperately wishing Sergio was with us. I couldn't even figure out whether I had my lights *on*. "Mardi, do we have an owner's manual? I can't find the brights."

"Continue along this road for thirty-two miles…" Dorothy droned as I slowed again to keep pace with the policeman.

Mardi found the owner's manual and began reading it, but I still couldn't figure out whether my brights were on or off. I definitely didn't want to be drawing attention to myself by flashing my lights. I began looking for an exit. Thank heaven the policeman was looking for that same exit. He took it. I kept going. My heart rate dropped thirty beats a minute. I don't think I've ever been so glad to no longer be driving along near a policeman.

I felt I could once again enjoy the drive. The feeling of being on a road trip was palpable. I was reminded again of *Two for the Road*—of the early days of our marriage and the freedom of the open road—a map and enough money to pay for a hotel room wherever we ended up.

"I had no idea southern Italy was so gorgeous. Look at that beautiful bridge," Mardi said.

It was stunning—nothing utilitarian about it. It spanned the road we were on, but was hundreds of feet above us, flowing in a gentle arc from one rock wall to another. A few moments later we passed into Basilicata. I was thrilled realizing that we would soon know another region of Italy. I love filling in maps of Italy with memories of her people. Seven years ago I knew where Rome was and that Tuscany was north of Rome, and I had a vague notion that Venice was north of Tuscany, but the rest of Italy was pretty much a featureless boot. Now, everywhere I look, Italy is colored in with either memories of people or the desire to make memories in its various regions.

Construction barricades shuttled us off the main road and drove Dorothy crazy as she tried to figure out where to send us. We didn't much care. The beauty was overwhelming—we were thrilled just to be on the road.

"That looks like a field of wheat up there," I said.

"And there are some windmills," Mardi said, completing the journey to my Nebraska childhood.

We were passing by fields of every shade of green—alfalfa, wheat, oats—a patchwork quilt of colors. The tractors were getting bigger along with the fields. I had no idea the land would be so productive. Italy constantly surprises me. I suggested that we pull off and have a picnic. But Mardi wanted to get higher before we took a break, out of Nebraska and up to Colorado country, which we could see high above.

"Is that Pietrapertosa that we're looking at way up there?" I asked.

I was feeling a bit more confident in the car *and* my driving abilities. We looked at the map and decided to let the pinball effect take over. We'd been shuttled off the main highway at a point Dorothy didn't like, and it now made more sense to go to Pietrapertosa than Castelmezzano. I had read that both were beautiful. Just then a bicycle whooshed by heading quickly down the road. My curiosity kicked in. I wanted to see where the biker had come from. Dorothy chimed in: *In three point seven miles take Strada Provinciale Thirteen to Pietrapertosa.* Our course was set. The road switchbacked fiercely, climbing quickly in the rocky soil with turn after beautiful turn. I was fantasizing about bicycling these winding roads. We met very few cars and passed none.

After a dozen or so switchbacks I saw a spot where I could get the car completely off the road. I dove into it. The coolness of the air surprised us when we opened the door—so did the silence. "Hear the turkeys?" I asked. It was a familiar sound. The terrain was familiar too. The turkeys reminded us of Wisconsin, the terrain of Colorado. We reveled in the silence. We even considered a picnic, but were unable to find a piece of ground level enough and large enough to spread a blanket, so we hopped in the car to finish the climb to Pietrapertosa.

"This road is amazing—what a great bike ride—this will get me primed for driving on the Amalfi Coast," I said as I negotiated turn after turn, shifting from gear to gear, as I powered through the corners, using skills I'd learned as a driver of sports cars in my younger days. The car was more powerful than I had expected, and it took corners like a go-kart. The final climb to Pietrapertosa was so steep I had to shift down into second gear coming out of the corners.

"This parking spot has our name on it," I said when the rocks we were executing hairpin turns around suddenly had homes on them—we had arrived in Pietrapertosa just like that. We got out of the car and the sharp, clean air enveloped us. We stepped to the railing that kept our car from plunging over the edge of the cliff and looked out at an incredible, vertigo-inducing view of the mountain valley far below.

"Wow!" Mardi said.

We'd been saying that word a lot as we approached Pietrapertosa. No other word expresses wonder quite so well. Except maybe "Oh my God," which is what I said when I looked out at the view. *God done good here.*

A young man stopped his car on the road, leaned out the window, and asked a question in full-speed Italian. I responded, *Sono un turista.* I didn't like admitting it, but that is exactly what I was for his purposes. He had asked the question so quickly that I hadn't even been able to come close to understanding what he had asked and even if I had, the possibility of me knowing the answer to his question was nil. He thanked me and drove on. But he had paid me a compliment for which I was grateful: he had presumed I spoke *italiano* and that I looked enough like a local that I could help him get to where he wanted to go.

The sound of his car pulling quickly away was replaced by the crowing of roosters, which in a village built on the top of a mountain ridge sounds very different—it echoed off the sheer rock walls with crystal clarity. Pietrapertosa was revealing itself to be a village unlike any I had ever seen. The town is perched on the top of monstrous boulders and tilted slabs of rock pointing toward the sky. The effect is staggering—the beauty overwhelming.

Across the road two men were working on the roof of a patio, getting their *ristorante* ready for the season. It would have been a delightful place to eat, with its spectacular view of the surrounding valleys, but it obviously wasn't open. We read some of the promotional literature posted nearby and wondered how it was that I'd heard of this town only by reading an obscure book that I'd discovered quite by chance. No one's trying to keep Pietrapertosa a secret—it's on the list of *I Borghi più Belli d'Italia*—The Most Beautiful Villages of Italy—but somehow I'd missed it. We also discovered, as we read, that Pietrapertosa had one very interesting claim to fame—it was the lifelong home of Lucia Lauria Vigna, one of Italy's oldest citizens. She had slipped to number ten on the all-time list, but for two and a half years she was the oldest verified living Italian until she died at the age of one hundred thirteen years, one hundred sixteen days.

Admiring her longevity, I was inspired to look further and discovered that Emma Moreno, currently the oldest living Italian, was born in 1899—five years before my father, who died in 1976, forty years ago. She was also born in Italy, up north in Piedmont. Life expectancy in Italy is much greater than in the US. Italy ranks number eight and the United States thirty or so—82.7 years versus 79.3 years. That confirmed what I felt the first time I journeyed to Italy—not only do Italians live longer, they seem more vibrant in their old age than do Americans. How our last years on this earth are spent is becoming of greater and greater importance to me with every passing day.

Whether this town had anything to do with Lucia Vigna's long life I didn't know, but it certainly was a unique town to grow old in. The best word to describe it is *fanciful*, built as it is on sheer rock faces. Even if the town hadn't been beautiful, we would have loved being there. The air was crisp, the sun was shining bright, and the temperature was refreshing. Maybe a few hours breathing this clear mountain air would add a few days to *our* lifespans.

We had no destination in mind other than to experience the full effect of this unique town by walking its steep streets. Everywhere I pointed my camera I captured a shot that spoke of the pride of the residents—the doors were gorgeously finished and always flanked by bright flowers. The homes, as they stair-stepped up and down the sides of the huge boulders, made for dramatic and colorful photographs. I imagined that growing up in this town must have been like living in a fairytale. Just then, two young kids ran by holding hands, a boy and a girl about seven years old, with all the freshness of youth displayed in the carefree insouciance with which they were bounding up the hill, smiles of glee lighting their faces, expressing the exuberance of living in a small town, the freedom and joy of it.

Mardi and I were thrilled to be in a town whose existence we couldn't have imagined in our wildest dreams. Who but Italians would build a town on such an inhospitable site? I wondered what it must have been like to have lived here before World War II when it was even more isolated than it is now—in that unique period of time when Mussolini chose to punish Carlo Levi by forcing him to live in this Godforsaken land. It didn't look like a place God had abandoned to me, but as I've mentioned many times, I'm a bit of a romantic.

We heard church bells and began walking toward them, certain we'd find the heart of the town. What we found first were bells hanging around the necks

of sheep grazing in a meadow near a park on the lower side of town, down where there was soil—and trees and lush grass. The flock was in shadow, but the alpha sheep was working its way toward a patch of sunlight. In ten or fifteen minutes, they would be in full sunshine in the clearing, and a beautiful shot of a mountain town with homes and rock faces shining in the background would be a click away.

While waiting, I watched a half dozen teenage boys playing soccer in the park. On the other side of the meadow a couple of older men were whiling away the afternoon near a statue. They looked old enough to tell the story of the town, but I wasn't feeling confident. I had understood almost nothing of what the young man in the car had asked me. Maybe he had used a dialect that I had no chance of understanding, but I didn't want to ask these men about the history of Pietrapertosa and then discover that I couldn't understand a word of their stories.

The photo was worth the wait. I snapped off a half dozen shots, waited for a few moments for more sheep to reach the sunlight, and clicked off another half dozen. I had my Pietrapertosa portrait—an Italian high-country village with sheep trimming the grass in the park—and yet another reason for loving Italy: its never-ending ability to surprise and amaze.

I also discovered that Pietrapertosa seemed to have a fondness for cats. Many of the graceful entrances to the homes featured cats lounging on doorsteps. While I took pictures, Mardi waited on a park bench for *il bagno pubblico* to become unoccupied. When it did, she went in and came right back out.

"I'm not that desperate," she said.

"What do you mean?"

"Take a look."

It appeared to be a unisex toilet so I followed her in. There was neither a urinal nor a toilet, only a ceramic hole in the ground. I laughed at the thought of Mardi seeing one of those for the first time. I had seen my first one in Vietnam.

"You put your feet there, and squat," I said.

"I can wait," she said and quickly walked out. I followed.

"I'd say the first restaurant we find open is the restaurant we're going to choose," I said.

Three boys flew by on bicycles. It sounded like they were repeating *Oliva, oliva, oliva* over and over—*Olive, olive, olive*. Or maybe it was *Libero, libero, libero* which would translate to *Free, free, free* as they coasted down the steep street. The sound of their voices was beautiful. I shouldn't idealize the lives of Italian kids too much, but there is a quality about their activities that takes me back to my own childhood, back before television, when we'd play on the streets for hours. We were free and unencumbered—and that was just how these kids appeared to me in this town hidden away at the top of a mountain in Basilicata. I was sure they had access to the same things our kids in America do, but here in Italy they still get together on the streets and act like kids—and seem not to have a care in the world.

The sound of their happy voices was once again replaced by the melodic sounds of the bells on the necks of the sheep. Everywhere I pointed my camera I captured a photo that spoke of humility—the bare essentials. The church tower was topped by a simple wrought iron cross. A nearby monument to citizens who had moved to America was classically understated.

"This is a beautiful place," Mardi said. "One of my favorite towns."

As quickly as I had fallen in love with Amalfi and Maiori, Mardi was succumbing to the charms of Pietrapertosa. "I can't help it, I prefer mountains," she said. The town was obviously speaking to her—what besides the need to squat was there for her not to like?

Gathering a bit courage I walked up to the two men chatting near the statue. I asked if there was a restaurant open. The first to speak, classically dressed and spinning a cane, suggested we might have to drive to Accettura. The taller, thinner man, after thinking for a moment, suddenly said, "Frantoio."

"*Grazie*," I said, recalling a sign I'd noted earlier for a pensione called Il Frantoio.

"*Prego*," said both of the gentlemen and immediately resumed their conversation.

"This seems like a nice town to stay in—so small, so untouristy," I said as we continued walking.

I was beginning to realize that we might not get back to Maiori unless I was willing to drive at night, and I was quite sure I didn't want to do that.

"*Scusi, dov'è Il Frantoio*," I said to a young man we met a few blocks later walking on the all but empty streets. He pointed the way but said it might not be open.

"If it is, it's getting my business," I said.

The young man smiled. Whether he had understood me I didn't know. I had proclaimed my intent in English.

"It is also a bed and breakfast," Mardi said, after checking our guidebook.

I wondered if she too was considering staying in Basilicata instead of driving back, but I didn't say anything. I wanted to try the idea on for size a bit longer before I made the suggestion. I feared she would balk at the idea of paying for two hotel rooms.

We soon found the restaurant, and as we suspected, it didn't have Wi-Fi. We were the only folks eating—it was an in-between time of the day, too late for lunch and too early for dinner, but the pleasant owner accommodated us and did it with a smile. We ordered a slight variation on our usual—a mixed salad, but this time with a plate of *orecchiette pasta* instead of a pizza. As usual, simple fare made for a great meal.

According to the menu, the owner, Nicola Perticara, had chosen the name *il Frantoio* to honor the olive growing heritage of the area. He and his family had for thirty years been preserving the traditional dishes of Lucania. If the pasta that I ate that afternoon was an example, they were definitely worth preserving.

The brief history on the menu also mentioned that tourism was growing in the region. If our reaction to the town and region was typical, it was easy to see why people were visiting—not just foreign visitors but Italians as well. We didn't hear the rest of the story that day—for that we had to wait a year, when we discovered at the Milwaukee Italian Film Festival that Pietrapertosa, in addition to its other attributes, was also a movie star.

On that day we felt as if *we* had discovered Pietrapertosa. We were there because of a little-known book I had read. We liked the friendly ambience of the town. We noticed what seemed to us a unique idiosyncrasy—folks stopping by said *Ciao* or *Buongiorno* before they stepped into the restaurant. It may have had something to do with the fact that the front door was not really a door but a curtain of plastic beads. They were easily penetrated by people but seemed to provide a barrier to flies—and they were certainly no impediment to greetings shouted from those about to enter as well as people just walking by.

"*Bene?*" the proprietor said as though she were aware of our desire to eat like this back home.

"*Molto bene,*" I said. "We love it."

"I guess if we just ordered a soup and a salad…" Mardi said.

"Yeah, we might keep the tab under ten, but I can guarantee you it wouldn't be this good," I said.

"*Delizioso, mi piace,* very good," I said to our amiable host as she passed our table again on her way to speak to a woman who had just stepped into the restaurant. They chatted as though they knew each other very well.

"How long did it take to get from Eboli to here?" I asked Mardi.

"I think it took only about an hour and a half."

"That means we aren't much more than two hours from Salerno. No wonder they're pushing for tourism."

I did some mental calculations to figure out how much gas we'd burn driving back to Maiori and then returning tomorrow morning to either Castelmezzano or Aliano, both of which I was now certain I wanted to see.

"*Quanto lontano Aliano, sessanta chilometri?*" I asked our host.

"*No meno, quaranta chilometri,*" the woman said.

Even on mountain roads, forty kilometers could be covered in no more than an hour. I didn't want to get this close and not see Aliano. But convincing Mardi to find a room here or in Aliano was going to be tough unless I could convince her that we'd spend as much on gas getting back here as we would just staying here, even though we'd have to pay for two hotel rooms. I wanted Mardi to make the *six of one, half a dozen of the other* proposition.

"Do you like it here?" I asked.

"What's not to like?" she shot back.

She'd just given me the perfect opening to sell my idea. "Here's what I'm thinking. It would be very good if we stayed here for the night even though we didn't bring any clothes. I don't want to drive on the Amalfi Coast in the dark."

"I don't have any medicine. I will get fat. My hair will fall out and I'll get cranky," Mardi said. I knew I had her. She was overselling her case.

"We could go to Aliano tomorrow morning and get back to Maiori before rush hour."

She said nothing, so I jumped back in.

"And we could enjoy this evening here in Pietrapertosa."

"I don't have anything for my contacts," she countered.

"We aren't paying for breakfast back there."

"I don't think I like the idea. I have no coconut oil."

I laughed, knowing what she meant, convinced that I was winning the battle because she had brought up the subject of sex. She was way overplaying her hand.

"How far is Aliano? It might be cheaper than here," Mardi said and I knew we were going to be staying somewhere in Basilicata.

We thanked our host, paid our bill and began hiking back to our car. We allowed our curiosity to dictate which streets to take, which stairs to climb. We eventually found our way, but it was by no means the most direct route. We had seen a lot of the beautiful doors of Pietrapertosa by the time we found the road where we had parked.

Dorothy informed us that Accettura was only twenty kilometers and thirty-six minutes away, and would get us to within an hour or so of Aliano. We reached the isolated town with no difficulties, found a parking place near a mini-market, and began walking toward the center of town, figuring that we'd find a hotel the old-fashioned way, by walking past it. We had arrived in time for the *passeggiata*—the streets and the walkways were filled with people—enough folks out walking that the occasional car had to inch its way around strollers and through clusters of conversations to navigate the three of four blocks of the main street. We were delighted to see that kids were walking around freely in this town too—a girl of not more than seven was walking hand in hand with a boy of three or four. It was like that when I was a kid. Seeing children walking by themselves was an everyday occurrence—I was one of those kids—no one gave it a second thought.

Another thing I saw in Accettura that I hadn't seen since my boyhood was men playing cards while other men watched—card playing as a spectator sport. The game of choice in our pool hall was either pitch or rummy, both played for money. My dad stopped by now and then to watch and to play. Rarely did I see a pot that topped a few dollars. I didn't see any money on the tables in Accettura—another difference was that these tables were outside, a half dozen tables near the *piazza*, a couple of tables across the street, with as many people watching as playing. I watched for awhile, but couldn't figure out what game they were playing—it was like pitch, but the cards were different. I

AN ITALIAN LOVE STORY

could have asked but I didn't. We also could have asked where to find a hotel, but we just kept walking. We were enjoying being among the people of the town, watching them greet each other as though they hadn't seen each other in years, although that seemed highly unlikely in a town as small as Accettura. Though bigger than my hometown of a few hundred, it couldn't have been home to more than a couple of thousand people.

We ambled along the ancient streets enjoying the crisp mountain air and photographing the colorful entrances to the homes. We eventually happened upon a small hotel, but it was closed. We decided to give serendipity a bit of help by checking our map. We needn't have bothered. The map indicated the town had two more hotels and that we would pass by both of them getting back to the card players in the *piazza*. The first one we came to didn't look like it had been open for quite some time. It was starting to seem like a good time to begin worrying—I might have to drive these mountain roads, as well as the Amalfi Coast Highway, in the dark.

We followed the winding streets back toward the heart of town and found the Hotel Sangiuliano only a stone's throw from the card games. It seemed to be very much in business, with flowers flanking the front door, but it too was locked. A woman nearby confirmed what the doors told me, but she didn't offer any further explanation.

We were discouraged that we were having a tough time finding a place to stay. We liked what we had seen very much. It's hard not to fall in love with an Italian town when your first exposure to it is during the *passeggiata*. This was small town life like I had never seen it before. People of all ages gathering on the streets, just like in Maiori, but more so—and in a more compact, more intimate space.

From the front door of the hotel we could see a large group of men watching a card game in front of a café. We joined them. The only person who took his eyes off the cards to notice us was a man holding a small dog in his arms. I greeted the dog in my native tongue, remembering that Sergio had said that all dogs understand English. His master I greeted in Italian. Then I asked him, "*C'é un pensione aperto?*"

I had asked the right man. "Cesare!" the man said with more than a little energy. A young man across the table from us took his eyes off his cards and looked up. "*Vogliono una stanza.*"

"*Un momento,*" Cesare said and then played a card. He handed his remaining cards to a man who had been looking over his shoulder, got up from the table, and came to greet us. "Yes, we can help you. We are normally closed on Monday, but we can take care of you," he said in English with an accent that reminded me strongly of Simon's—a lovely combination of Cockney and Italian—and if not Cockney, surely working class.

"How long you be stayin' with us?"

I explained our situation—told him how much we liked Accettura on first impression, that we had a room in Maiori, but we didn't want to drive back in the dark.

"We can definitely take care of you. We had a busy weekend, but we have no one in the hotel tonight. We'll also give you a wonderful breakfast in the morning—you name the time. Fifty-five euros."

I looked at Mardi. We had decided to pass on the offer of forty-nine in Pietrapertosa, but that was a couple of hours ago. Her glance told me that she was hoping that we wouldn't have to pay much more than we were paying in Maiori.

"We are paying forty in Maiori," I said.

"I can't do that. This is only our second week. But I will tell you what I *will* do. I will give you the honeymoon suite for fifty-five euros. It has the best view in all of Accettura—it has a big, beautiful terrace that looks out over the whole village. You two will love it."

I immediately liked Cesare, equating us with a honeymoon. I wanted to get to know him and his story, and I wanted to get to know his town. I was especially interested in what I thought I had heard him say—that he had just opened this hotel, but I didn't understand. The book I had read about Basilicata mentioned a hotel, and I was now certain that it was named Sangiuliano.

But just to be sure about this room—with the best view in all of Accettura— we asked if we could see it. While we were climbing the curved stone staircase I asked if I had heard him right, that this was a new venture for him. He told me that indeed I had, that he and six other blokes from Accettura were off on the adventure of their lifetime—that none of them had ever run a hotel, but they loved their town, they all needed jobs, and they were gambling that if they could get the word out that there was once again a nice hotel, with great food, they would be able to turn Accettura into a tourist destination.

Cesare's enthusiasm, his wit, and his charm won us over before we had finished the climb to the third floor. He could have shown us a closet with a view of a brick wall and we would have been happy to spend the night in Accettura just to have the chance to chat with him again at breakfast. What he showed us, though, was anything but. The room was pleasant, expansive, and the view was everything he said it would be. I knew exactly where I was going to be the following morning. I'd be up before dawn watching the town come alive from the balcony with the best view in all of Accettura—in fact, a view of almost *all* of Accettura.

We had no difficulty deciding that paying for two hotel rooms was the right thing to do. Our pinball had been flung to Accettura and we were now in the care of Cesare and his six compatriots, two of whom we met that night, Antonio and Domenico. But it was Cesare who took us under his wing. We had interrupted his card game and he was going to make sure we enjoyed ourselves.

We made ourselves comfortable in the lobby to take full advantage of the speed of the Internet. Cesare didn't return to his card game, but stayed busy on the computer. Once he was certain he'd answered all our questions and that we were comfortable, he headed home, promising he'd be back at nine in the morning to serve us breakfast. Domenico offered us orange juice and we gladly accepted as we researched Accettura. I checked my notes and discovered that the author of *Seasons in Basilicata* had ended up in Accettura for a reason similar to ours—he couldn't find a *pensione* in Aliano. And he had indeed stayed at Hotel Sangiuliano, but that was twenty-some years ago.

We also discovered that we were two thousand five hundred thirty feet above sea level, that livestock and cereal crops were the principal source of income, that in the thirteenth century the town was completely destroyed by fire, that tourism was not well developed, and that the population matched the height above sea level: twenty-five hundred people. And the card game we discovered was called *scopa, a game beloved by all of Italy*, our guide book informed us. With that information, we were ready to walk the streets of Accettura again.

But this time we joined the *passeggiata* with a *stracciatella gelato* for me and *tiramisu* for Mardi. They were delicious and cheap. Two dips cost a euro and a half. I was struck by the vibrancy of this isolated agricultural town. We were far from a city, we weren't at the crossroad of a major highway, yet the town seemed robust—or if not robust economically, then energetic in spirit. Pre-teen boys were thumbing through a Lego magazine. Two young mothers were wheeling their baby strollers down the center of the street. Three young girls, around eight or nine, one holding onto a bicycle, had formed a back-to-back-to-back triangle and were comparing their heights. Teenagers were walking with purpose, as though late for a date. And everywhere older men and older women were gathered in small groups talking.

A man strolling along the street stopped to talk to a couple of women. One reached out to clasp his hand in friendship. Close by, a gathering of a half dozen men were chatting. Their relaxed postures conveyed that they'd been talking with each other for a very long time and were nowhere near finished with their conversation. Everyone was moving at a *passeggiata* pace—not really going anywhere—merely out walking, sharing their lives with their neighbors. Farther down the street a half dozen boys had taken over a portion of the wide promenade for an impromptu game of *calcio*, known in America as soccer. The game was relaxed enough that the goalie had time to turn around and say *Ciao* to me and Mardi as we walked behind the park bench that also served as the goal he was guarding.

And of course, the games of *scopa* were still drawing crowds. We had become so mesmerized by the evening ritual and the living of life on the streets that we realized, as we peered through the darkness at a man riding a draft horse through town, that night had fallen. First it was sheep in the heart of Pietrapertosa, now a horse on the main street of Accettura. I couldn't resist. I wanted a photograph of that man and his horse to help tell the story of Basilicata. I thought I would have a hard time catching him, but he stopped frequently to talk to people in their homes, often through the kitchen door. Some conversations were brief, others lasted a few minutes.

I kept a respectful distance, not near enough to hear the conversations, but his body language told me he was just catching up on what his neighbors had been doing while he was out in the fields. It had become far too dark to get a good picture, but I kept following because I wondered why he was no longer heading through town but riding deeper into the heart of the village. Eventually my curiosity was satisfied. He stopped his horse in the middle of a narrow street and dismounted. I watched as he unloaded the supplies he had draped over the horse's shoulders, removed the saddle, and brushed him down. I would have loved to talk with him, but I didn't want to invade his private moment with his horse.

While waiting for him to finish bedding his horse, Mardi and I got into a philosophical discussion. On the drive to Accettura, she had begun talking again about how she felt in high school, but our conversation had been interrupted by the beauty we were driving through.

"You said you were discovering yourself on this trip. What did you mean?" I asked.

"I lost sight of the person I was. This trip has made it possible for me reconnect with the person I was when I was young. I lost it when I got married—trying to solve all the problems of having kids, figuring out where to live, making ends meet, and doing what's best for everyone. You kind of cover yourself up all those years. The tyranny of the urgent," she explained. "Now I'm getting a chance to pay attention to the original person I was."

"Do you feel more alive now?"

"Yes, or maybe I should say I feel more myself. You come to understand yourself better, because you don't have the frustrations of bringing up kids. I don't think it's a matter of having time to lie on the beach—it's more cerebral than that—it's having the time to be who you are."

"There are stages in life, and we're entering a new one," I mused, then shared the thought with Mardi.

"Oh, look at that, first it was moon over Maiori, now it's moon over Accettura," she said as we watched the man lead his horse into the house and not come back out. We had just seen what I thought I'd never experience—a town where a man could still stable his horse on the ground floor and live above. That we had watched it by the light of a big moon made it even more special.

"I love you, Mardi."

"You should," she shot back.

"Not only do I love you, I appreciate you."

"I love you, baby," she said using an oft-repeated line from Ernest Hemingway's *A Farewell to Arms*. It was her way of reminding me why I should love her. She and I tend to like the same movies.

"Do you think my underwear would be dry by morning if I washed it tonight and hung it out on the terrace?" I asked.

"I can see your underwear flying through the *piazza* tomorrow morning when a big scirocco wind, like the one in *Chocolat,* blows in." We'd watched that movie at least a half dozen times together and Accettura reminded us of the ancient village that was the star of that movie—a town that was very provincial—a town where strangers were definitely noticed.

"It was nice of Cesare to give us this room," I said when we arrived back at the hotel.

"Yes, it was sweet."

"So how did we end up here?"

"You asked the guy holding the little dog in his arms if there was a *pensione* in town."

"And we ended up in the hotel mentioned in *Seasons in Basilicata,*" I added, thinking back over the improbable course that had led us to a honeymoon suite in Accettura—*suite di luna di miele,* as Jessica had taught us—with a big silver moon hanging in the sky above a hotel that was showing great promise of becoming Mardi's favorite.

Life is just weird sometimes.

CHAPTER NINETEEN

Accettura ~ Tuesday April 19 ~ 56 & Clear

A Dream Come True

The traveler sees what he sees,
the tourist sees what he has come to see.
GILBERT K. CHESTERTON

∎

The real act of marriage takes place in the heart,
not in the ballroom or church or synagogue.
It's a choice you make–not just on your wedding day,
but over and over again–and that choice is reflected in the way
you treat your husband or wife.
BARBARA DE ANGELIS

𝒜round four-thirty I stepped through the double doors of our room and onto the cool tiles of the terrace to see if anyone was stirring. I heard only silence. Starting on the western horizon, I searched in the early morning light for the slightest movement. Near the end of my sweeping arc of Accettura I saw a young man walking quickly across a small *piazza* a few blocks away. He didn't appear to be a farmer. I guessed he was a commuter working in a distant city. Sure enough, moments later when tail lights appeared on the main road, they were attached to a new-looking white car heading out of town. The sound of his car faded and absolute stillness once again enveloped me. I had forgotten the feeling of high altitude silence. Not even the wind was stirring. The sun, and it's uneven heating of the earth, and the resulting noise of gentle movements of air was still a long way away. I began writing.

Despite the chill, I stayed on the balcony, putting into words my impressions of Accettura and its people. This place was different and I wanted to try to capture that difference. The silence of the town was helping as I wrote page after page, occasionally glancing up, not because I had heard something, but because I had not. I realized I was not used to life being so quiet. After what felt like an hour of writing and sweeping pans of the town looking for other early morning people, but not finding them, I pulled out my phone to check on sunrise. I discovered that the sun would make its appearance in seventeen minutes at six-ten, and so too I presumed would the people of Accettura.

But I didn't have to wait quite that long. A man began singsonging a short phrase containing the word *verdura*, vegetable—his throaty voice echoed off the ancient walls of the buildings. The sound was so loud I was certain he was in the street just below me, but I could not locate him or anyone moving toward him anywhere in the village. His anachronistic call, mingled with the crow of a rooster that had apparently been woken up by the vendor, made me wonder whether Cesare should add time travel to the list of attractions of Accettura. The town looked and sounded like 19th century Italy. The only car I could see was ours, looking oddly out of place in the street below.

At six minutes after six I finally saw movement. A blue Sita bus showed up near the city center, seemingly ushering in other movement. Every minute or so a man would appear somewhere within the village, walking toward what I presumed was a just-opened coffee bar. The chatter of conversations coming from an unseen *piazza* became background music to the vendor's calls. Cesare was right—we had a good window on the world that is Accettura. Fourteen minutes after official sunrise the sun still had not appeared, but halos on the peaks hinted that its warming rays would soon strike the town's red-tiled roofs. I kept writing and watching.

Twenty-two minutes after official sunrise, the sun's rays broke above the rugged horizon and began lighting the faces of the houses stair-stepping up the hills. The sun ushered in more movement. Another Sita bus appeared at the top of the town, and then a few minutes later, a Tito bus. That made three buses within an hour. Tractors trailing large machinery were moving about on the jumbled streets—Cesare had mentioned that this was a farming community, and that was now clearly evident, but still I marveled that a town was ever built in such a remote location, and then rebuilt after a fire.

A gentle breeze began blowing in the valley as the sun heated the rooftop tiles. Every home was topped with the same red clay, giving the town a uniform of-the-earth look. I tried for a photograph to capture the beauty of the morning, but it would have taken a talent on the order of a Van Gogh to capture what

I was feeling as the sun lit the various surfaces and textures of the town and surrounding countryside, turning the scene into a kaleidoscope of color.

Ecco quo vado—Ecco quo vado the vendor now seemed to be yelling—*Here's where I go* or maybe *Here I go.* I had been looking but I still had not caught a glimpse of him. However, his deeply penetrating voice left no doubt he was there somewhere. Mardi joined me on the terrace. She listened for a while and said, "Can you believe this?"

"It's a storybook town," I said. "People going this way and that. Here comes a policeman with a fancy uniform and white hat."

"He's talking to everyone who crosses the street," Mardi marveled as he directed traffic, if you could call an occasional car or tractor traffic.

A woman dressed in black appeared on her balcony about halfway to the crosswalk where the policeman was stopping cars to let the schoolchildren cross. Mardi and I were surprised that she seemed to be doing the same thing we were—watching the people come and go. Even though she had probably seen it every day of her life, her body language told us that she still found the morning routine interesting.

She, like us, was watching a couple of girls who had stopped to chat in front of the bakery just up the street. A moment later a woman parked her stroller near the girls and continued walking, holding the hand of a little boy. It looked as if she had asked the girls to watch her baby for a moment. However, we were just speculating. The stroller could have been empty. But from what we were learning about the town, it would not have been out of character for such a thing to happen.

A little girl wearing a frilly dress and holding her mom's hand caught our eye as she pranced across the street. The policeman was getting busier—an almost steady stream of kids was flowing from the main street toward an unseen school in the labyrinth of streets to the west of us. Traffic was picking up, too. A white van drove into town from the north, a huge truck approached town from the south, and more and more cars simply appeared. Another woman, also dressed in black including a shawl, came out on her balcony not far from where the girls were still chatting. She pinned two dozen table napkins to a clothesline and went back into her house.

Mardi and I began studying body language. "Did you see the way that man walked up to the woman by the statue? His hands were in a posture of submission, as if he was either asking her for something or extremely pleased to see her," I said.

"This is like watching a stage play," Mardi said.

And then, like a spigot being turned off, the flow of children stopped and the policeman began walking our way. We could now see that he had a chest full of medals on his uniform—and just like Carlo Levi's description of the policeman in Aliano, he was walking with an exaggerated sense of self-importance.

We turned our attention to the countryside and saw olive groves and large fields of wheat, but no vineyards. An older tractor pulled out of a field and turned toward town. It was red, the color of a Massey-Ferguson, but it probably wasn't—most likely a FIAT.

It passed by city workers in orange coveralls erecting poles along the main street, which we presumed were for the upcoming festival Cesare had mentioned. An Audi station wagon pulled into town and parked in front of the bar. It probably wouldn't be there long—it was double-parked in the street.

I was surprised by our reaction—we were watching everything as if it were a clue to solving a mystery. A little boy and his mother appeared walking down the main street toward the crosswalk. Mardi and I both reflexively checked the time—quarter to nine. We had presumed school started at half past eight and were surprised they weren't in a hurry.

The widow wearing the shawl came back out onto her balcony. We were convinced that her view wasn't as good as ours, but it seemed good enough that she too was interested in watching everything going on.

In the *piazza* near the statue dedicated to emigrants a little girl in a pink dress and an older woman were waiting at the crosswalk, but they didn't seem interested in getting to the other side, where the school was located. We wondered whether the little girl was with her *nonna,* but what really had us puzzled was why they didn't cross the street. Only when the white delivery truck we'd seen earlier pulled up and the driver hopped out and gave them a package was our curiosity satisfied.

Older men wearing jackets began showing up. Some sat at the *scopa* tables and read newspapers. Most talked. A distinguished gentleman appeared in the *piazza* sporting a walking stick and a jaunty hat that seemed more Irish than Italian.

"Five minutes to nine," Mardi said, interrupting my musing about the man's story. She was giving me a subtle reminder that we had told Cesare we'd be ready for breakfast at nine. I did the math and only then did I realize that Accettura had so captivated me that I had been writing and watching the town wake up for over four hours. As we were getting ready to leave our box seats we looked down and saw a familiar face.

"Isn't that Domenico?" Mardi asked.

"Yes, it certainly is. *Buongiorno, Domenico,*" I sang out.

He looked up, startled to hear his name shouted from above. He waved and said, *"Buongiorno,"* then entered the hotel. His surprise confirmed my hunch that people walking by were not aware that we were watching them from above.

"Shall we go down and see if he has some hot tea for us?" I asked.

By the time we got to the dining room, Cesare and Domenico had breakfast set up—juice, coffee, tea, fruit, and something new—potato pizza.

"How is it? Is it nice?" Cesare asked.

"It's good," I said and meant it. My grandfathers were from Ireland and now that I was eating potato pizza I was certain a potato dish did not exist that I would not like.

"Will you be firing up your pizza oven later this season?" I asked.

"Yes. Thursday, Friday, Saturday, and Sunday. It's a small village. We don't work Monday, Tuesday, Wednesday—not quite that busy yet."

"Too bad we didn't get here Sunday," Mardi said.

"Yes, you missed it. You'd have tasted lovely pizza—we have a great pizza guy. We have a great chef as well. He's from a nearby village. He comes Thursday and returns home Monday morning."

"You have a lot of people come in?" Mardi asked.

"It doesn't seem like it now, but it was full this weekend."

"Town people?" she asked.

"Village people, all the towns around too. Some people came from Pietrapertosa, where you folks had been. This is only our second week in this business."

"Seriously?" I said even though he had already told us that last night. The hotel seemed too big, too polished for novices. It was sinking in that we could be among their first guests if this was only their second week.

I had told Cesare that Carlo Levi's book had brought us to the area. Now it was time to tell him of the book that had led us to Accettura. I was surprised that he'd never heard of it since Hotel Sangiuliano is mentioned frequently—the book is the reason Accettura was highlighted on my map—and why I said *Why not* when Mardi asked me if it was okay to enter Accettura as well as Aliano into the GPS as we were leaving Pietrapertosa. Accettura had also been mentioned by the man with the cane in the park in Pietrapertosa—and that's how we ended up spending the night in Accettura and eating potato pizza with Cesare the next morning. Weird indeed.

"The reason we're interested in the area, as I told you yesterday, is because of Carlo Levi's book about being shipped off to Aliano by Mussolini," I said.

"Do you know the way to Aliano?" Cesare asked, diverting my attention from Accettura.

"I was thinking we'd just head out on the road that goes south. But I'd love your recommendation."

"Straight up, that's right. But then again, there's some short ways that you can cut, but I won't tell you them because you might get confused."

"I've got a very good map, so I might bring it down and have you point out those shortcuts to me."

"Ok, enjoy your breakfast."

"It's too bad we didn't come here this weekend," Mardi said as he walked away. "It would have been so much fun."

Cesare had been talking to us as though we were family. The folks we had met on the streets the night before talked to us as though they expected to see us again. They made us feel like we were part of their town, that they were glad we had come, and that they wanted us not only to see the town in its best light but to understand its traditions as well. They were certain we wouldn't comprehend their town without knowing what made them special. Rick Steves was right—Italy becomes more *Italian* the farther south you go.

"Can I get you folks anything?" Cesare said as he returned to our table.

"May I have some more hot water?" Mardi asked as she handed him our insulated mugs.

"*Certo.*"

I excused myself to get my mapbook. I couldn't help comparing Cesare to Pietro, Aurora's son, the one who had tricked me into rebuilding a stone wall by myself on a day when it was too wet to pick olives. They were similar in stature and appearance. Both had a British influence on their accent—Pietro had an Australian touch to his Italian. Both possessed wit in spades, but Cesare was much more the always-attentive host. In Pietro's defense, though, he boasted that he would cook for me the best meal I'd ever eaten in Tuscany, and he delivered. That night he was the ever-gracious host. However, the next day he was again the caustic, never-quite-pleased Pietro that Annamaria, Aurora's friend, forever complained about. I don't think that will ever be the case with Cesare—he seems a steady man.

When Cesare returned with the hot water I handed him my mapbook opened to the page on which Accettura was highlighted. He consulted his partners and soon returned to our table.

"Straight up, then go for Stigliano," Cesare said, then traced the route with his finger.

"Looks like lots of switchbacks," I said.

"Yes, it is beautiful."

I couldn't help marvel that these young men, who seemed to have no direct experience in managing a hotel, were now doing just that—and doing a very good job of it.

"Weekends are very busy, especially the restaurant. Saturday we've got about thirty people sleeping here as well," Cesare said.

"Did some of you used to work here?" I asked, remembering how much I'd learned about the hotel business working as a bellman and desk clerk in college.

"It's a new experience for all of us," he said, confirming what I was having trouble believing. He told us more about their new venture—they had pooled their money, limited knowhow, and enthusiasm in an attempt to bring life, jobs, and money to their remote village.

I had told Cesare that I was a writer, but it seemed like a good time to make certain that he understood that their story was of great interest to me and that, if it was okay with him and his partners, I would like to mention their venture in my next book.

"Certainly," he said. "Write whatever you would like. We'd love it. The previous managers didn't do a very good job, and there's a bunch of negative reviews out there. We have to overcome those."

"Would you write the names down of all seven of you?"

"Of course."

When he handed me the list, I handed him my card and told him that books are long-term propositions—that he'd have to stay in business for quite a few years if what I might write was going to do him any good.

"That's our plan. We're here for the long haul."

Cesare gave us the quick history of the hotel—that the owner had bought two houses twenty-five years before and turned them into a hotel. That was surprising. The place didn't have the look of a bed and breakfast but rather a hotel designed to impress, complete with a grand staircase.

He gave us a quick history of the festival, too, explaining that the whole town would be filled up in the middle of May—and then he told us the rest of the story.

"We have another hotel, but it's not ready yet. We have enough rooms for seventy."

"You guys are jumping right into the fire, aren't you?" Each new facet of their story surprised me.

"It's a bit risky. Our village has lived on olives. The older generation used to raise grapes. But not the younger generation—it's too hard for them."

"People must be commuting to nearby towns? I saw lots of buses this morning."

"Yes they are traveling to Petrolia."

I could tell by the way Cesare spoke about those who have to commute that he didn't necessarily think it was good to have people living in Accettura only at night.

"This town feels even more community-oriented than I am used to in Italy. I was surprised by how many people were out on the streets."

"It's a small village. They all get together outside the bars to play a game of cards, like you saw last night. They have a *passeggiata*—it's a nice, peaceful village. No violence."

"I loved seeing even young girls, off on their own."

"Yeah, my two boys play in the middle of the street, they play football. This is the old part of the village," he added, reminding me of the many questions I had about his town.

"We saw a man riding his draft horse through the streets."

"A few people still have donkeys and horses."

"It looked like he was keeping his horse right here in town."

"Oh, yes, they've got their own stables—can't do that in America, can you?" he said and winked.

"Not so much."

"I love the peace here. If I want chaos, then I'll go somewhere else to find it."

"This reminds me of America in the fifties," Mardi said.

"Everybody knows everybody," Cesare said.

He proceeded to tell us what he thought was the secret of Accettura. It was a story that sounded as if it was out of the Middle Ages, which it probably was. He pointed out that the reenactment of this tradition, that required the participation of the whole town was what gave the residents a strong sense of community.

"Once a year everyone comes together to mate two trees from different forests. We put together a team of big cows to drag the male tree, *il maggio*, some twenty kilometers from the forest of Montepiano to Accettura, where it is joined with the female tree that we have carried on our backs from Gallipoli— it's a lovely festival. You've got to live it to realize what it's all about."

"I assume you've carried the trees," I said.

"I've been going down every year, but this year I can't because we've got the hotel. It's a pity you weren't here this past weekend—we chose the female tree. You get together. You throw parties. You eat. You drink."

"So what happens this weekend?" I asked.

"This weekend," he started with energy and then said, "Nothing. You missed it."

"In about ten days, we go and cut the male tree down and leave it there. The female you chop down the day you go to pick it up."

I confessed to Cesare that was I having trouble envisioning his story—it sounded more like fantasy.

"You've got to live it—it's a four-day celebration—a lovely experience."

"Do you have a room?" I said and glanced at Mardi. She rolled her eyes.

"Room?" Cesare asked. He noticed Mardi looking hard at me and suddenly understood what I was thinking.

"During the festival?" He asked, passion coloring his voice. "We're booking right now, but we have a couple of empty rooms. You wouldn't be able to have the lovely room you're in now, but we could take care of you."

"No, we're leaving, we're going home," Mardi said.

"But we're so close, Mardi. It's only a couple of weeks. We could celebrate our marriage on May fifth and in another week we could celebrate the tree's marriage, isn't that right Cesare?"

"That's right, the weekend of May fourteenth."

Mardi's eyes flashed daggers.

"If you change your mind, you'll be welcome. You won't regret it."

The phone rang. Cesare answered it. Even though she was whispering, Mardi was emphatically telling me that I was crazy.

"What a blast it would be," I countered.

"Next year."

"I love you," I said.

Cesare got off the phone and realized that Mardi and I were still discussing the festival, Italian style.

"There's a saying—when you come to this village, you cry twice—when you get here and when you leave."

"We definitely didn't cry when we got here, but we may when we leave," I said.

"Don't get me wrong," Mardi said. "I love it. It's my favorite village. I love the mountains, but we're not millionaires." She had directed her comments to Cesare, trying to quell a bit of his enthusiasm, and mine.

I handed Cesare my white flag of surrender, a no-foreign-transaction-fees Visa card. He and I had given it a good shot.

He picked up a pile of papers from his desk.

"Here's the paperwork. We applied two months ago, but we don't have it yet."

"I think I can give you the exact amount in cash."

"When are you flying back?"

"We don't have tickets," Mardi said.

"Well then, you can come back for the festival," he said, giving it yet another shot.

"We have five children and ten grandchildren," she countered.

Cesare recognized that the game was over. Mardi had played the grandchildren card.

"If you need a nice place to eat in Aliano, I can give you a recommendation—it's called Friends of Carlo Levi."

"I can remember that," I said.

"Amici di Carlo Levi. You tell them that the boys from Hotel Sangiuliano sent you."

"Fantastic," I said.

I had mistakenly thought Cesare too had sent up the white flag, but he had more salvos. He began mentioning the tourist attractions in the area. First, the zipline between Pietrapertosa and Castelmezzano called Angel Flight. He then mentioned Matera, "where Mel Gibson did *The Passion of Christ*. It's about an hour from here." And then he started listing famous people from Basilicata. "Francis Ford Coppola is from Bernalda. His grandparents came from a small village near Metaponto. Also the New York mayor is from this region."

"Oh, you mean Giuliani?" I asked.

"Yes, he's from Grassano; it's only an hour away from here."

"He was a great mayor," I said. "He turned New York around."

"What is your town?" Cesare asked.

"Brookfield. It's a suburb of Milwaukee. Milwaukee is on Lake Michigan. Lots of Italians."

"Italians are everywhere."

"The parents of one of my good friends when I was a boy were from Italy. I don't know exactly what town."

"I bet they were from the south. Most of the immigrants were from Calabria or Sicily—all over southern Italy, because there were no jobs. The northern Italians had jobs, so they didn't go anywhere."

"Italians are good workers," I said.

"Yes, strong workers."

"Very family oriented."

"When my grandparents moved to England, they didn't know a word of English."

"What did they do?"

"My father used to make boots and work in a drugstore with medicines and tablets. He also worked steel."

"How many years ago?" I asked, feeling as if I was returning to my former occupation as a filmmaker, interviewing a subject—but the story of the mass exodus of southern Italians fascinates me. I find it hard to imagine leaving such a beautiful land, but as one immigrant so sagely put it, *You can't eat quaint.*

"What was your father doing when he left England?"

"He was managing restaurants and pubs."

"Did he do that when he came back here?" I asked, thinking that maybe Cesare had learned from his father.

"He came back when he was quite old; he was near pension. Now he's passed away."

"And your mom?"

"She was a hairdresser—a pensioner. My mom would have been delighted to meet you, and talk to you—she loves reading—she knows a lot more about Carlo Levi than I do."

"Two of our boys are married to Italian girls," Mardi said.

"I haven't had my DNA tested, but I think I have some Italian blood in me," I said.

Cesare turned to Mardi. "I understand the problem. He loves Italy and you want to get back to your grandkids."

It was a simplification, but it accurately reflected our situation. I missed our grandkids too, but the thought of being part of a centuries-old celebration thrilled me.

"Ah, here comes my sister Teresa—born in Nottingham too."

"You look a little alike," I said.

"A little bit," she said.

"I'm the better-looking one, though," Cesare said.

"Whoa," I said.

"Now get on," Teresa said. "I've not got me makeup on."

We were in the midst of a sister and brother spat. This really was feeling like family.

"She comes and cleans for us," Cesare said.

I asked Teresa what she thought of her brother's venture and discovered that her husband was one of the partners. This was a good story getting better. What a great thing for the town if it worked out. I mentioned again the book that had brought us to Accettura, thinking Cesare should know about it in case it could help attract others to Accettura.

"I don't think I've heard of it. What's it called again?" Cesare asked.

"*Seasons in Basilicata*. It mentioned Hotel Sangiuliano and a tilemaker named Giuliano who sounded like quite a character."

"A tilemaker?" Cesare asked.

"For roofs—and I'd say he must have been quite successful judging by the uniform look of all the houses in Accettura."

"If you'd stay more days, I could arrange for you to meet his son," Cesare said. "Giuliano has died, but his son is related to my wife."

"Oh, no," Mardi said, feeling the pressure of our relentless assault. She had lost another battle and feared she'd soon lose the war.

"You are good, Cesare. You are very good. This town is going to do just fine," I said, impressed by his nimble skills as a negotiator, salesman, and promoter.

"You're going to have to get us a job here if we're going to be able to afford to stay," Mardi said.

"Too bad you weren't here four months ago. I could have got you a job picking olives."

"Believe it or not, we have olive-picking experience in Italy," I said.

"We also have shepherding experience," Mardi said.

"Do you also milk? We have great cheeses here."

At that moment Cesare's chef walked in.

"This is Francesco," Cesare said. "We have two Francescos, so his nickname is Cesco."

"So we have met five of the group?" I asked.

"No, you've met only four," Cesare said.

"Well, Mardi. We've got to stay long enough...or come back so we can meet all seven."

Everyone laughed—except Mardi.

"Come back this weekend. We'll have the pizza oven going," Cesare said.

"Not sure we will still have the rental car," Mardi said.

"You can get to Potenza by train, and then take a bus. But then again, we run a taxi service. We can pick you up in Potenza anytime, no problem."

"They do it all," Teresa said.

"Did you get everything out of the room?" I asked Mardi.

"Yes. We aren't traveling with much."

Another partner walked in.

"This is Antonio," Cesare said.

"So now we're down to two?"

"You stay a bit longer and you will meet us all."

I was tempted, but Mardi was not. I told them we'd be back—just a question of when.

"Now when you leave, go straight down the way you came. But at the bottom you gotta turn right, and then suddenly turn left by the park to go up—because if that man with the uniform and the medals sees you taking a shortcut—going the wrong way on our little street down there, he will give you a nice little ticket. You don't want to hear his whistle."

"No, I don't. I don't want that to be one of my memories of Accettura."

Everyone came to the door to wish us well. We felt as if we were leaving family even though we had been with these people less than twenty-four hours.

As I drove away, Cesare sang out, "Enjoy Aliano."

I couldn't imagine that we'd enjoy Aliano as much as Accettura. But I was thankful for Aliano—for Carlo Levi's writing. I was even thankful for Mussolini. We never would have met these delightful people were it not for Mussolini banishing Levi to the south of Italy.

"Do you realize that if we'd come two weeks ago, they wouldn't have been managing the hotel?" Mardi asked.

I began trying to put together the pieces of this improbable visit. "So we end up at the hotel I'd hoped to find, and one of the managers turns out to be related to this tilemaker Giuliano I had wanted to meet—and Cesare offers to take us to see the oven where his son still makes the tiles. This is too much."

"Don't die before you've written all this down. Don't get Alzheimer's. Don't get hit riding your bike."

"You want to be able to get a return on your investment of being married to a dreamer for forty-six years?" I asked.

"I want to be able to read this story. I'm not sure I even believe it, and I'm living it. We've met so many interesting people."

"Oh, wow, look at that. I've got to take a picture of that little house," I said.

"This should be part of the story too. Every five minutes we stop to take a picture."

"I don't think readers would find that very interesting. You don't, and you're here to see what I'm taking a picture of."

My artistic eye is partial to rural landscapes. A lone house sitting on a hill commanding a vast panorama had captured my attention. Despite numerous attempts, though, I wasn't able to capture the passion of the scene. The church steeple in Accettura was too far away from the house to make them both work in the same composition. A painter with Van Gogh's eye could have pulled that steeple in, but painting that picture would have taken far more than five minutes.

"A jewel of a day for sure," I said when I got back in the car. I could see that Mardi had been reading emails.

"Gretchen is worrying that I'm not having a good time."

"I never did like that girl," I blurted out.

Mardi laughed, knowing how much I adore my only daughter.

"I'm afraid to tell her what a good time I'm having. She'll worry that we'll never come back."

"I don't know why she would think that spending a month in Italy with me would be so bad."

"Maybe she thinks all we do is go around taking photographs."

"Touché."

A few miles later I was braking again. Through the trees I could see a sign with the words: *Cristo de Fermata e Eboli.* I had to stop. I wondered if Carlo Levi had any idea that generations later people would be proudly quoting him. The sign had been erected to let passersby know that these woods, *Bosco di Montepiano,* were mentioned in *Christ Stopped at Eboli.*

"Did you notice how peaceful, how quiet it was?" Mardi asked. "There is something about a forest in the mountains."

"Someone else thought that too. That is exactly what *Montepiano* means— *quiet mountain.*"

"Do you think we will come back Thursday? After we check out of Casa Mannini?"

I was thrilled to hear Mardi ask that question. These woods, these mountains, these people were working their magic.

"There is no telling what will happen with Sergio—who we'll meet—where we'll want to go next," I said, keeping true to my pinball philosophy.

"I would love to come back here," she said.

I was surprised to hear her say that. She and I were now definitely in sync, and I'd found yet another reason for wanting to come back: driving was a blast—zipping through the dense forest on a perfectly smooth road, using the gears of the little car for both braking and accelerating through the corners. The engine was singing. I vowed to buy a FIAT 500 when I got home, but I didn't share the idea with Mardi. It was enough that she had said she wanted to return to Accettura—no need to press my good fortune by asking for too much all at once. I did, however, mention that I hoped one day to be able to bike this route. It would be a thrill on a fast road bike—a Pinarello to keep with my all-Italian theme.

"The woods are deep and dark," I said mimicking the cadence of the Robert Frost poem, but just as I said it an opening appeared through the trees. "But there are some big open fields out there too."

It was turning into one of those mystical days when even the feel of the air is perfect. For me this invariably happens on a crisp day in the mountains when the sun is shining bright and the temperature has a bit of a bite to it. We were alone in the woods. I was dreaming about daily bike rides on this gracefully sinuous road, renting a room from Cesare for weeks on end, even learning how to play *scopa* with the men of the town. In my mind I had made the move to Accettura. How would I break it to Jessica that I had fallen in love again?

"This must be the area Cesare was talking about. Look at those mountains way out there—you can just barely make them out," I said as I stopped the car to shoot another George Tice layered photograph of the mountains disappearing in the distance.

"Would you grab a leaf from that tree?" Mardi asked.

I could easily have plucked it for her, but instead I said, "You have to feel this day for yourself."

She joined me on the side of the road, pulled off a leaf, and pressed it in the mapbook so she could identify it later. I glanced at her. She looked delightfully contented.

"Why is Carlo Levi so popular?" she asked.

Southern Italy was working its charm on her. I was predisposed to like it because of all that I had read, but I sensed that vistas like this and our reception in Accettura had captured Mardi too.

"I think it's because he wrote with compassion about the people. He didn't always understand them, but he was rarely critical."

"Does this make you miss the mountains?" she asked.

"Yes, it does. I often forget how crisp the air is," I said as we got back into the car to continue our backroads journey. Just beyond Stigliano the road dropped into a valley. The feeling of remoteness associated with Accettura disappeared as we crossed over a rather busy highway and the Sáuro River. But we were soon climbing again on switchbacks as we worked our way slowly toward Aliano. We could see the edge of the town high on the ridge. My excitement was building. I had been anticipating this day for many years.

We were crawling up the switchbacks behind a heavily laden Ape, its little engine fully revved. I opened the windows to feel and smell the high altitude air. With each turn the landscape became more alkaline, more desert-like.

"It's perfectly fine that we're following a farmer up this hill. I've been thinking of coming to Aliano for a long time, there's no sense in rushing it."

Standing like a lone sentinel, a recently and rather severely pruned olive tree stood guard at the edge of town. I stopped to take a photo. Photographing olive trees is difficult but that doesn't keep me from trying. They have so much character, but I had yet, in many, many tries, captured what I see in the deeply contoured convolutions of their bark. The results were again disappointing, but the feeling of anticipation was not. I sensed, as I photographed, the barrenness of this landscape that Carlo Levi was at first repulsed by, then grew to love.

"Somebody obviously cares about this tree," Mardi said.

It wasn't part of an olive grove, nor was it apparent that there was a farm anywhere near. The tree looked like an orphan—an ancient but loved orphan. If it could talk it would have had many interesting stories to tell. Perhaps Carlo Levi sought its shade, and had Christ ventured this far, the tree looked old enough to have been around to provide him comfort as well.

"So peaceful here," Mardi said.

"Carlo Levi felt the same way. He used to head out into the countryside to paint."

"I'd love to see his paintings."

"He took his easel and brushes to the cemetery often, and when the heat became too much to bear, he would crawl down into the holes of the gravediggers to cool off." It was a thrill to finally see the brutal landscape that had helped produce one of my favorite books.

We got into the car to drive the last few hundred meters into town. I parked on the first street we came to. Mardi wanted to drive into the heart of town, but I wanted to make my entrance into the village on foot. This was the first of our disagreements in Aliano.

"Do you have the backroads of Italy book?" Mardi asked.

"No. The last time I saw it, it was on the floor next to our bed."

"I didn't see it. Guess we'll have to go back to Accettura," she said.

She was blowing me away. I couldn't believe the number of times she'd mentioned going back to Accettura or liking these mountains. I was beginning to think that we might still be in Italy the weekend of Accettura's big celebration. But at the moment we were looking for the Carlo Levi Museum, and we weren't finding it. What we *were* seeing surprised me.

"I didn't expect the town to be so full of cars," I said and quickly realized how silly that was. Just because there was only one automobile in all of Aliano when Carlo Levi was sent here didn't mean mules and carts would forever be the mode of transportation. The streets were not, however, full of people. We didn't immediately fall in love with Aliano.

When at last we met someone on the street, I asked for directions to the museum. I must have spoken rather fluently, because the answer came back in a torrent of Italian that lasted a full sixty seconds, without a pause—and the gentleman, if he knew any English, uttered not one word of it. And wonder of wonders, we understood enough of the beautifully delivered directions that we were able to make our way through town and find the museum, but alas, it wasn't open. It was nap time—*tempo pisolino*. It also wasn't tourist season.

We contented ourselves with looking at the paintings and books of Carlo Levi that we could see through the windows of various storefronts on main street. It was not hard to imagine Aliano as the town that Carlo Levi built, or at least was keeping alive.

"See the kids' faces?" I said. We were looking at an advertisement promoting a Carlo Levi event. The children's big eyes drew our attention, as I'm sure Levi intended—he felt the eyes of the children conveyed the sadness he saw in the lives of the people.

"Ah, there it is, Carlo Levi," Mardi said, thinking we had found the restaurant, but what we had actually found was a panorama point graced by a stately statue of Levi.

A young man walked by as I was studying the inscription. *"Dov'è il ristorante Amici di Carlo Levi?"* I asked.

He began to explain where it was, then suddenly said he was walking that direction and asked us to follow him. He was soon joined by another young man. After a few blocks he stopped to show us the view and began acting as our guide. He told us that when Carlo Levi lived here, many of the homes were in caves on the hill below us and that at this very spot a church had slid down the hill. It was easy to imagine. The soil was ash-like in composition, easily disturbed.

"I remember him mentioning Piazza Garibaldi," I said. "Where is that?"

He pointed and then told us that Carlo Levi thought the houses of Aliano looked like faces, the windows appearing as eyes, the mouth as a door. He also mentioned that the recent celebration was on the occasion of the fortieth anniversary of Carlo Levi's death.

"Is this where he was confined, up here?" I asked, suddenly feeling as if I had been here before. In effect I had because of Carlo Levi's vivid descriptions of this *piazza*.

"Si, casa sua."

Our guide introduced himself. His name was Michele and his friend was Rocco. He apologized for not being able to speak much English and also explained why he was wearing a neck brace. He was a construction worker and had recently fallen off a scaffold, was knocked unconscious, and woke up to discover he had a broken neck. That may also explain why he had so much time to give us—or it might have just been attributable to the Italian penchant toward hospitality. We obviously had a need, and he was available. As is the Italian custom, he chose not only to lead us to where we wanted to go, but give us a fully guided tour along the way.

He knew a lot about Carlo Levi, as well as the history of the town and clearly enjoyed sharing his knowledge. Even though we were taking a lot of his time, he never made us feel that he was doing anything but what he wanted to be doing. We had walked so far that it felt as if we were leaving town. I noted that we were walking past a very large number of cars.

"*Si, convensione,*" Michele said.

That same convention prevented us from having lunch with the Friends of Carlo Levi—the whole restaurant had been reserved. Michele and Rocco were disappointed, but they didn't let this hurdle stifle their hospitality. They led us back into town, back to where the homes had faces, and suggested that we would find a very good meal at La Locanda con gli Occhi. I am certain we would not have chosen to eat there, hidden as it was, with a sign that could easily be overlooked. When I translated the name I was delighted that Michele had suggested it—The Inn with the Eyes.

Mardi didn't want to eat there. She wanted to sit outside at a restaurant she had noticed when we first walked into town. But I wanted to honor the hospitality of Michele and Rocco—they had just given us a half hour of their time showing us around Aliano. I also felt that our bouncing pinball had landed here and we should enjoy it. Mardi, at that moment, was not as tuned into providence as I was. With the exception of a couple of middle-aged ladies sitting in one corner we were the only people in the restaurant.

"Isn't it amazing that what Mussolini did by sending Levi here is helping the economy of Aliano eighty years later?"

"It's a true story?"

"Absolutely. It reminds me of the story of Joseph. Levi could have said to Mussolini, as Joseph said to his brothers, *As for you, you meant evil against me, but God meant it for good, to bring it about that many people should be kept alive.*

"I thought it was a novel."

"You're right, it reads like a novel. Carlo Levi used his medical training to treat the people of the village. He aroused a bit of jealousy. Many of the villagers came to him instead of the local doctor. When you think about it, that's probably one of the reasons he is still so revered. Many of the folks here today are alive because of Carlo Levi."

"*Insalata mista, il condimento,*" pronounced our waitress.

I would have loved to ask if her family were longtime residents of Aliano and if her parents or grandparents had known Carlo Levi, but because she was busy I just said, "*Va bene,* very good, *grazie.*"

Not once had we been disappointed when we ordered the *insalata mista,* and this was no exception. It was always more than Mardi could eat by herself. We also shared our memories of *Christ Stopped at Eboli.* Mardi had seen the movie two or three times, but she hadn't read the book or researched the background of the story.

"I think this is fun," she said.

I know Mardi well enough to know that the comment was a bit of an apology for not wanting to accept the recommendation of Michele and Rocco, and also an acknowledgment of the wonderful time we were having. Also wrapped up in her assessment was the joy she feels in getting a good deal, and at the same time not being wasteful. We had learned early in our Italian journey that one mixed salad and one entree was just the right amount of food for the two of us.

When my pasta arrived I was amazed by its taste. As on the day before in Pietrapertosa, I had ordered the *orecchiette,* named because it is the shape of a small ear. If I had named the pasta I would have called it *piccolo capelli,* for they remind me of small hats.

I'm sure the friends of Carlo Levi would have served us a fine meal—and someday we will probably find out just how good their food is, but for now I was very happy with our simple meal at the inn with *the eyes, the ears, and the hats.*

"What an experience. Every time we need something it seems to come our way. I wanted an introduction to Aliano—a guided tour if it were available—and we got it by asking for directions to a restaurant from a man with a broken neck."

"*Com'è la pasta?*" our hostess asked as we were getting down to our last few morsels.

"Very good, *mi piace. Il conto, per favore,*" I said knowing that Mardi would soon be eager to get out into the sunshine.

"In so many ways this is similar to my first trip to Italy," I said. "I came into town late at night and a couple of men and a very nice woman took me under their wing and introduced me to a priest who offered me a place to sleep for the night. Here, within minutes of arriving in town we got a fully guided tour."

We stepped outside and found that the day had changed. I had to pull my hat down tight to keep it from blowing down the street.

"Carlo Levi wrote that it was windy here. It reminds me of the wind in *Chocolat* blowing through the town," I said, and then realized Mardi had mentioned *Chocolat* the day before when I hung my underwear on the balcony railing despite her admonition to the contrary. It was funny how often our adventure was reminding us of scenes from our favorite movies.

With the exception of an Ape driving through town, the streets were now empty. That little pickup and a dog in the shade of a very old building were all the movement we saw—and the dog didn't move far. He turned in a circle a few times before lying back down to resume his nap.

Since everyone was sleeping, it seemed like a good time to walk around the town, to see if I recognized anything else from Carlo Levi's descriptions. It was a task I didn't have to be very good at. The points of interest were well documented, complete with quotes from *Christ Stopped at Eboli*. I snapped photos so that Mardi wouldn't have to wait while I read the inscriptions.

"Here's a house built into the hill," I said and told Mardi about Levi's reaction when he first encountered the living conditions of the people of Aliano. It was very different from his life in the north of Italy, where poverty was rarely seen.

By the time we got back to our car an hour and a half later we had seen lots of Carlo Levi inscriptions, dozens of beautiful doors and gorgeous gardens, as well as a fair number of tables that looked as if they would soon be hosting a game of *scopa* or two. Oh yes, we saw more dogs too, but not so many cats—and exactly four Apes had driven noisily through town.

We stepped inside a church and were flabbergasted by the beauty. We saw a date of 1641 but couldn't believe the church could be that old—or that the town could even be that old. As we stepped back into the sunshine the bells began ringing but stopped after only three rings. The town would soon be waking.

We had by then seen enough of the sites pertaining to Carlo Levi that only one remained on my list, and that was the cemetery. He wrote often of all that he could see from up there, and of how lonely it felt, too. Again I was surprised. A lot of people have died since Carlo Levi lived in Aliano. It was not the windswept barren hilltop that I pictured but rather a park-like setting with towering pines whistling in the wind—and it was very crowded. The graves were not spread out as they would have been in the States, but concentrated. As one would suspect in Italy, it was not the individual who was honored but the family. I could have spent days in that cemetery learning the stories of the families who lived in Aliano.

I was surprised to learn that Carlo Levi had chosen to be buried in Aliano. He had lived in the town only a short time, from the summer of 1935 to the summer of 1936. Maybe if I had remembered that he lingered in Aliano for ten days after Mussolini released him, I might not have been quite so surprised. However, I think that even Levi himself would have been shocked if he had been told on the day he left Aliano that he would one day return to be buried.

He had promised the people of Aliano, as he said goodbye, that he would return. But it was a promise that he had not yet kept when he completed *Christ Stopped at Eboli* ten years later. In the final chapter he wrote of his regret. Only in death was he able to keep his promise to his beloved friends.

"The sound of the wind in the pines is just gorgeous," I said as we began walking around the well-kept grounds. Mardi and I soon got separated as we began reading the stories of the families interred there. The pictures those histories painted of life in Aliano was fascinating, but I wanted to find Carlo Levi's tomb. I liked that there weren't a lot of signs pointing the way.

That Levi was Jewish was obvious when I finally found his grave. It commanded a magnificent view of the surrounding hills and was laden with small stones, an ancient Jewish tradition—a sign that many people had paid their respects. But on this day Mardi and I were the only people there. That seemed right. That was the way I had always pictured it when Levi went to the cemetery—he was alone with his thoughts and with God.

It had taken me twenty minutes to find his resting place. It took another ten to find Mardi.

"Did you find his grave?" I asked.

"No," she said. "I got too interested in reading everything. Most of the people died when they were quite old."

"I don't think I've ever seen anything quite like this. It seems like each family has its own room."

"Doesn't take up so much space, stacking the vaults on top of each other," Mardi noted.

She read me a few of the stories she had discovered, then I led her to Carlo Levi's resting place. She was touched. The design of the memorial was beautifully executed. A simple ash-colored marble slab etched with his name and the date of his birth and the date of his death, bordered on either side by free-standing brick walls framing a view of the surrounding olive groves and mountains. A single pot of morning glories provided the only color in the memorial.

We stood for a long time transfixed by the view. The feeling was one of calmness, even serenity. Stark beauty greeted our eyes. The mournful song of the pines intensified the feeling of reverence.

I had no destination in mind when we at last drove away from the cemetery. I felt a deep connection to Aliano, thanks to Levi's evocative writing, and I wanted to remain in the special aura of this windswept town. Mardi didn't have as many associations and would gladly have started for Maiori, but she humored me, and her feet, and allowed me to park the car and wander. The old part of town beckoned. I began walking toward the barren cliffs, but I never got there.

An elderly man, old enough to have been alive when Carlo Levi first came to Aliano, stopped in front of me as we were about to pass by each other. He was carrying a cane and dressed like all the men you see in Italian movies from the forties or fifties—dark slacks, a heavy woolen jacket, and wearing a small hat.

He greeted me very warmly and said *Questa nata*, which is Italian for *this born*. But he also mentioned the beauty surrounding us, so I responded with *Panorama—bella, bella*.

He responded, "*Bellissimo*," in an accent and cadence that reminded me of Mario, the lovestruck postman in *Il Postino*.

Next he said what sounded like *Isoldina,* which I didn't understand, so I repeated it and he added *I soldi arriva di Malta pera*, which sounded to me like *money arriving for pears from Malta*. This of course made no sense, but he said it with such conviction and empathy that I was certain I had misunderstood him.

As we continued talking I realized he was talking about Levi's death. We were not far from the bust of Carlo Levi. Maybe the residents had learned that the only foreigners who come to their town do so for two main reasons—they've read *Christ Stopped at Eboli,* or they have a relative somewhere in their family tree from Aliano. The old man may have asked whether I had a relative who had been born here. My new friend, for that was how he acted toward me, told me that Carlo Levi was intelligent and strong.

A passerby smiled and said, "*Buonasera.*"

"*Buonasera*," I said. My friend dipped his head in response but didn't interrupt his story. He began speaking of communists, and the republic, and the problems of the Mezzogiorno. When I asked whether one of the problems he was referring to was the Mafia, he said *Troppo legato.*

Whenever I didn't fully comprehend his words, I tried to discern from his body language what he was saying. I knew *troppo* meant too much, but whether *legato* referred to literally being bound or being related to someone who binds you, I didn't know; however, when he said it, he contorted his face to such an extent that it made me laugh.

Fearing that my laughter might have been inappropriate, I decided it might be a good time to introduce myself. *"Mi chiamo James. Come si chiama?"*

"Giuseppe," he said and gave me a humble, warm smile.

"Molto vento," he said and gestured toward the hills. The wind was beginning to blow sand particles about. We then began talking about the beauty of the day. He surprised me yet again by asking, *"Contadini?"*

I must have revealed in the way I was talking about the land an affinity for farmers and farming. I told him that indeed, I used to be a farmer. I tried to convey that I was still a farmer at heart—*Un contadino a cuore* were the words I chose. Whether this was the right Italian expression I didn't know, but he smiled.

"Americani?"

"Sì."

"Molti italiani in America," he said and began telling me of all the people who had left Aliano for the United States. *"Fame."*

I knew the word well. It was one of the first words I spoke to Aurora when I arrived on her farm seven years ago to pick olives. She had asked if I was hungry, and I put the word *piccolo* in front of *fame,* hoping it might mean *a little bit hungry.*

But what Giuseppe was talking about was more akin to starvation, because in those days there was no work in southern Italy. Giuseppe did not leave Aliano, but many of his relatives did. I would have loved to keep talking with him about his family and his remembrances of those hard times that Carlo Levi had written about. We had been talking for well over a half hour, and I was certain that Mardi was more than ready to move on.

"Mia moglie mi aspetta—my wife is waiting for me."

"Ciao," Giuseppe quickly said.

"Ciao," I replied and turned to leave but he reached out and put his hand on my forearm.

He started to say something, then paused, as if collecting his words, all the time looking into my eyes. When he began speaking he stressed each word, allowing me to hear each vowel. He mentioned a few of the things we had talked about, and then told me he that he had very much enjoyed our conversation. For me that sentiment was multiplied many times. Giuseppe then said, *"Molto..."* followed by a word I didn't understand. It sounded like *tickets* to my ear, but to my heart he seemed to be saying that he was very thankful. So I chose to say exactly what he had said to me, trying to match his cadence, rhythm, and tone.

He responded, *"Anche me"* which means *Me too.*

I was touched by his heartfelt expression.

"Mi piace," he said.

"Mi piace," I echoed.

"Ciao," he said again.

"Ciao," I repeated.

And with that mirrored exchange Giuseppe put some weight on his cane and shuffled away. Even though I had been the one to say that I had to leave, I didn't want to. I could have talked with him the rest of the day. I hadn't understood everything he had said, but his body language, his hands, his face, and his heart told me what I needed to know. I felt very close to this man I had met less than an hour ago. We had connected because of Carlo Levi. He was old enough to have been a boy when Mr. Levi was under house arrest here. He spoke as though he knew him personally, just as I felt close to Mr. Levi because of the many times I had read his book. I felt I knew this town, knew these people—and now that I had spoken at length with a man who had lived all his life in Aliano I was convinced that Carlo Levi was right about these people who had endured so much—they are indeed the salt of the earth.

Just as Carlo Levi had done when he left Aliano, I vowed to return to these people—and I would, I prayed, get back to this town that had reached almost mythical status, and was now very real, in time to continue the conversation with Giuseppe that I had regretfully drawn to a close before its natural conclusion. The mood I was in as I said goodbye to Giuseppe would not be the mood Mardi would be in—I was certain of that. I attempted to begin our conversation graciously.

"Did you get a nap?"

"No," she snapped.

"Should I move the car?"

"We have to. We've been parked there almost fifty-five minutes."

It seemed odd to be worrying about getting a parking ticket in the town that had only one car when Carlo Levi was imprisoned here in the thirties.

"What took you so long?"

"I'm sorry. I was talking with a man."

"Yes I saw. You talked with him for almost an hour."

I had been hoping to meet just such a man as Giuseppe, and he had initiated the conversation. In my mind he was a Godsend. I wanted Mardi to join us, but she probably didn't want to interrupt our conversation. This is one of the difficulties of traveling with someone, especially a person with strong passions. That bloke from Oxford we had met near Scala on our first day of hiking had encountered the wrath of his wife for wandering off—a foreshadowing of what I had just done.

Our discussion was interrupted by the noise of a small articulated tractor pulling a huge load of kindling through town—I was certain the man driving owned a wood-fired oven. With those sticks he would be able to bake his bread and pizza. The sight of all that wood took me back to the first farm Mardi and I worked on together in Italy. Our first job was to get the wood-fired oven up to the perfect temperature to bake four pizzas, a mess of *chambellinis*, and a month's supply of bread. We were amazed by the work involved—and we hadn't done any of the cutting, hauling, and stacking—we were just grabbing armfuls every few minutes and feeding the voracious fire. We were told that big chunks of wood couldn't get the bricks to the right temperature—it had to be load after load of kindling.

As I watched the man zip through town, I wished Mardi and I could help him unload his precious cargo. We could have shared stories about our love of wood while we worked and I could have gotten to know a little bit more about these people Carlo Levi had grown to care for so deeply. But that would have to wait for another day—it was time to say goodbye to Aliano.

We chose to leave town by a different route—a less tortuous road through a landscape that looked like southwestern Colorado. On our drive to the Sorrentine Peninsula we saw land that reminded us of our cross country journeys from Colorado to Wisconsin—high mountain peaks, desolate deserts, huge reservoirs in fertile valleys, and even huge undulating productive fields that reminded us of Iowa—including huge wind turbines on ridge tops. We saw all that variety in less than two hundred miles.

"I didn't know southern Italy had such dramatic land," I said.

"I take it that this looks nothing like Tuscany."

"So true—much of Tuscany looks manicured, but there's absolutely no sign of man's hand on much of this land."

I was feeling comfortable behind the wheel. I've always loved driving in the mountains, but this was off-the-charts fun because the perfect sweeping curves on the sides of the mountains often led into perfect sweeping curves *through* the mountains.

"Jim. We're not in a race."

I didn't feel like I was speeding. I was going with the flow of the traffic, but Mardi pointed out that this was often faster than the posted speed limit. She was right, I was pushing it a little. I wanted to get to the Amalfi Coast

Highway well before dark. I wanted to see not only the beauty of the sea coast but also every potential hazard on that road long before I got to it.

Getting through Vietri sul Mare wasn't a piece of cake, but because we had walked its streets a few days earlier dodging cars, buses, and turning scooters, I knew exactly where to go and had to divert none of my attention to reading signs, looking at the GPS, or checking maps. I'd discovered that if you appear to know where you're going, and will do it quickly, approaching drivers, in congested areas, will slow to allow you to turn left in front of them—and that's exactly what we did to get on the Amalfi Coast Highway in Vietri sul Mare, which saved us a lot of time.

"That was pretty exciting," I said when we had made it through the heart of town at rush hour and were once again moving along at a quick pace on an open road.

"In nine point three miles arrive at Mary," Dorothy droned.

"Dorothy, it's *My Or Ee*," Mardi said, which reminded me of how often I had corrected Mardi for saying *May Or Ee*, which was as often as Pietro had corrected my pronunciation of *bruschetta* on my first journey to Italy. It's *brew skate tah, James,* not *brew chetta.*

"You can go as slow as you want. Won't bother me at all," Mardi said as I felt the adrenaline rush of finding the perfect line through a series of tight turns.

"We have only eight miles to go to get home without scratching the car," I said.

"Oh, geez."

I had given her one more thing to worry about.

I was driving very fast, the engine was revved high.

"Where is my horn?" I located it and sent out a short toot. I felt like a professional shifting through the turns and was now ready to send out a warning if necessary.

"I'm glad this isn't *our* car we're wearing out," she said.

I was shifting into second and sometimes all the way down to low gear to negotiate the corners and the traffic—far too often for Mardi's comfort. We came around a corner and found a car on our side of the road headed straight at us. I shifted down and moved over a bit, the other car did the same, and we flew past each other. I thought of Vincenzo saying, *See how we drive here.*

"It probably freaks a lot of people out to see a car in their lane," I said.

"It's freaking *me* out. Do you really have to go so fast?"

I didn't feel as if I was driving beyond the car's capability or mine, but I slowed down to make her comfortable.

"Not everybody is sane, or a good driver. Some of them might be tourists."

As she said that the road suddenly widened. We were on a section of the highway that was totally out of character with the rest of the Amalfi Coast Highway.

"Thank you for going slow."

The wider road had greatly increased her comfort level and made it seem as if I was driving slower than I was.

"It's getting really pretty again," I said as the road became narrower and more sinuous—more like the Amalfi Coast Highway we were used to.

"What's *he* doing over here?" Mardi screamed.

A car had swing wide around a corner into our lane, but quickly darted back when the driver saw us.

"At these speeds these cars turn pretty sharp," I said as we flew past each other. I too had moved over to make sure we got home with all of our paint.

Mardi didn't say anything. I don't think she was as convinced as I was that these cars were perfectly designed for the unique demands of the Amalfi Coast.

"Thank heaven for Apes," she said as one brought us to a slow crawl.

"We haven't met one bus, have we?" I asked.

"No. The bus doesn't leave until about now."

"So we might meet one pretty soon?"

"Maybe," she said, worry coloring the word.

"That first car doesn't want to pass the Ape—and I'm not going to go around three vehicles," I said.

"Don't you dare. I'm not in that much of a rush to get home."

"An impatient driver would have gone around him right there and that motorcycle would have had to get way over," I said as a Harley flew past us.

"Did you ever look at these cliffs?" Mardi asked. "They're beautiful."

"I'm a little busy here."

She laughed.

"So this is about where we meet a bus, right?" I asked.

"That guy needs to get over; he's scaring people," Mardi said, referring to the car second in line behind the Ape, whose driver was showing signs of impatience. I didn't like the way he was driving either, so I slowed way down in case he tried to dart around the Ape at the wrong place. We were now driving at less than Ape speed. Mardi was happy. For the moment we were alone on the Amalfi Coast Highway—no cars in front of us and none within sight behind us.

"We can enjoy the sunset," Mardi said.

She may have felt *she* could, but I was still keeping my eyes on the winding road that rarely afforded more than five seconds of straight line driving.

"HERE'S a bus! Are you over far enough?" she shouted as I brought the car to an instant stop a few feet from the nose of the bus and began backing to a wider spot in the road before she had finished her sentence.

"That was amazing," she said.

"Did you like that?"

"I had no idea you could drive that well."

I appreciated her comment. I take pride in my driving, as I do in my flying, but rarely do you get a chance to show off your skills on the road—to drive safely you just have to concentrate and stay awake. But driving the Amalfi Coast is a world apart from driving I-80 or I-94.

"There's a big moon out there," Mardi said as we rounded a wide corner that opened up a view toward Salerno.

"I'm still busy here," I said and she laughed again.

We crested a rise, rounded a gentle turn, and all of Maiori stretched out before us, looking like a jewel in a silver-lined setting of water and mountains.

"*Benvenuti*, Maiori. The sign says we've arrived. I don't know what you were worried about," I said.

Dorothy droned, "In half a mile arrive at Mary."

We laughed again. Happy to be home with no damage to our car. And happy to be back in the town where everyone knows our name, even if Dorothy can't pronounce Maiori correctly. The moon was hanging in a darkening sky, painting a glorious picture. We had paid for two rooms the night before, but we had found another Italian town to love. Paying for a room we didn't sleep in was a small price to pay for such precious knowledge.

The drive home had been thrilling, even exhilarating. I had enjoyed two days of the most challenging driving of my life. During my last year of college I had owned an MGB and had driven it in gymkhanas, but those races were not nearly as demanding as driving on the mountain roads to Accettura and Pietrapertosa, or this evening's drive along the Amalfi Coast. And in less than twelve hours we'd be starting another adventure—this time with an Italian riding shotgun.

Through Sergio's Eyes

Not all those who wander are lost.
J.R.R. TOLKIEN

■

Remember that happiness is a way of travel
—not a destination.
ROY M. GOODMAN

1 called Sergio to tell him we wanted to pick him up at nine. We hoped we would encounter fewer buses—maybe even none—and miss most of the morning rush hour by waiting an hour. The last few miles the night before had turned out to be relatively stress-free thanks to an Ape driver who was pedaling as fast as he could into Maiori, and Mardi wanted to do everything she could to ensure that this morning's ride was just as uneventful.

As Mardi suspected, we found little traffic, but even on empty roads a drive on the Amalfi Coast Highway stimulates the imagination. In places the barriers between you and a flight into the sea are nonexistent—nor is there anything to keep you from crashing into rock walls. You will also find plenty of opportunities for head-on collisions. But we didn't even have a close call or meet any buses. As we were driving along the beach, having reached the safety of Minori, Mardi again praised my driving abilities. I was a touch proud—I enjoy impressing her. Guess I'm still a little boy trying to win her heart.

We turned at Vittorio's showroom and found a place to park across the street from the Bambi Café. We were early. We had already shared a morning *cappuccino* with Jessica, now we'd have time for another. The coffee rituals of Italian mornings suit me quite well. Michele, the man controlled by a wife and two daughters, greeted us as we walked into his coffee bar.

"Ah, you come back again. I see you are not walking today."

"We are picking up a friend. Is it okay to park there?"

"I will tell my friends you are okay. The police park there to come get their coffee. But you will be okay for a little while."

"*Grazie.*"

"*Due cappuccini?*"

"*Si,*" I said.

"You like driving Amalfi Coast?"

"I was nervous at first, but now I'm crazy about it."

"If you can drive here, you can drive anywhere," he said.

We settled into a lively discussion, mostly about Italian drivers and Italian roads and a little about Sergio—a conversation I could have enjoyed for a long time because of Michele's wit. But just as we sucked our cups dry Sergio walked into the *piazza.* I paid for our *cappuccinos* and told Michele we were sorry we had to run.

"Until next time," he said. "*Ciao.*"

"*Ciao* my friend," I said as he came to the door to wish us well.

"*Buongiorno, Sergio,*" I called out in a voice loud enough to carry across the *piazza.*

"Ah, good morning," he said. "I see you are again making friends."

"Yes, we are. Michele said to say *Hello,* by the way."

"Ah, yes. Michele was very nice to me when I moved to town—he helped me move a trunk full of junk. We drove to Rome with his daughter and picked it up at my friend's house."

"Yes, we've heard about her. He calls her his boss," I said.

"Michele is very fast on repartee," Sergio said. "He is quite intelligent."

"Yes he is—very quick," I said.

"I've always suspected he is on something," Sergio said as he buckled his seatbelt.

"Maybe it's just the *espressos.* He told us he's already had three this morning."

As we pulled out of the *piazza* and onto the highway to head back toward Maiori we began telling Sergio the story of meeting Michele.

"We walked into town and were trying to figure out where to eat. Mardi was looking at Michele's menu, so I said to him, *Whatever she decides, that's what we do.* And he said, *So she's the boss?* And I said *You got it.* And with that, Michele and I connected."

"He always says I'm the boss, that his main job in life is to keep me happy, but where did we end up eating?"

"Oh yes, that's the rest of the story. Mardi couldn't find anything she liked so we ended up back at Michele's place."

I was slipping up and down through the gears as we wound our way along the coast, shifting down as I pulled into the corners and powering through them to plant the tires firmly on the road. Even though I felt the car was capable of holding a quicker line, I didn't push it. I wanted Sergio, and Mardi as well, to feel comfortable—as comfortable as you can feel as a passenger in a car on the Amalfi Coast Highway.

"Michele said this was a litmus test—if you can drive here you can drive anywhere."

"Did he tell you he has raced a bit—long distance?" Sergio asked.

"I got the feeling he may have raced Formula One cars."

"But we're not. We don't need to race," Mardi said, letting me know that I was not succeeding in my efforts to keep her comfortable. Searching for the right line through tight corners on a demanding road was overtaking my main job in life.

"Michelle said he now drives an ambulance as well," she added.

I wondered whether Mardi was trying to give me a subtle hint that if I didn't slow down we might be seeing Michele again this morning. To make her comfortable I slowed way down, stuck my hand out the window, and waved a car onto the highway that was having difficulty finding a gap large enough to pull into.

"It's a part-time job," Sergio said, and added, "Unfortunately he has this super-boring job."

"He probably makes it interesting with his repartee with his customers," I said.

"Things were pretty lively this morning—lots of police were in there," Mardi said.

"The police station is right across the street," Sergio said.

"I'm afraid I let a very cautious driver pull in front of us."

"That's okay with me," Mardi said.

I told Sergio the story of following an Ape into Maiori. "None of the cars in front of us passed him, so I settled in and we all came into town as a long freight train being pulled by an Ape."

"I like those little three-wheelers," Sergio said.

"He was moving that thing down the road pretty quickly. I was surprised how fast he was taking the corners," I said. "This is an amazing road."

"Isn't it," Sergio agreed, and that led him to mention a narrow, twisting road over Independence Pass from Leadville to Aspen, and *that* led to us discovering that in a former life Sergio had lived in, of all places, the small town of Hotchkiss, Colorado, not far from where Mardi and I often bought canning peaches each fall in the early days of our marriage when we too lived in Colorado.

Befitting our mode of travel, we had a pinball conversation—it jumped all over the place as we shared our stories. Mardi and I told of our days in the army living in Hawaii. Sergio shared stories of living in Asia. We talked of my flying days, of my son flying F-16s, of stories of Naples during World War II, of America losing a battleship in the port of Naples because of a drunken party. We told our Naples story of a fellow traveler losing his wallet. Sergio defended Naples—he didn't think it had any more pickpockets than other cities. He laughed when I said they were just better.

We talked of all these things before we got to Salerno. Once we got to that port city, Dorothy joined the conversation. She was intent on sending us into a traffic jam, but I ignored her. Sergio had told me we'd hug the coast on the way to his grandfather's place, so I turned toward the water each time the streets ahead were clogged.

"This is the route the bus takes," Sergio said, relieving me of the doubt that was creeping in as we worked our way ever southward on congested streets.

"I think Dorothy has finally given up trying to get us on the *Autostrada*. She is turning us onto Lungomare," I said.

"That's the road we want. It goes along the sea," Sergio said and then added, "I used to like to get out like this and drive long distances when I lived in America. But here I rarely drive far." He went on to tell us about the Italian approach to summer vacations. "Most everyone gets the month of August off—everything shuts down."

"I've heard it's very hot and everyone heads to the sea or the mountains," I said.

Sergio confirmed the stereotype of the Italian holiday—sweltering cities abandoned during the heat of late summer. He was sharing Italian life with us from the inside. We weren't getting the tourist view of Italy, or even the Italian view—we were seeing Italy through the eyes of an Italian who had lived in America, who knew the idiosyncrasies of both countries.

"Do you see a gas station?" Mardi asked. A gas tank within a quarter tank of empty is cause for concern for her. I used to push it farther, but no more. I've discovered, probably too late in life, that a few extra stops at gas stations are worth it if it keeps Mardi happy. I pulled into the first one we came to. An attendant was waiting near the pumps.

"*Comba ito o pie*" is what I heard him say, but that meant nothing to me. I looked at Sergio.

"He wants to know if you want him to fill it."

"*Si,*" I said, thankful that Sergio was with me.

"*Prego,*" the man said as he stretched out the hose to the passenger side of the car.

"*Che bella giornata,*" I said as I got out to stretch my legs. "Let me get a picture of you two standing here."

"At a gas station?" Mardi asked.

"But look at that background—the sea is beautiful."

The Gulf of Salerno and the blue of the Mediterranean stretched out beyond, providing a unique setting. I wanted to commemorate the everyday act of buying gas in a foreign country—to remind me years from now of yet another first in Italy. The photo didn't do a good job of conveying how close the sea felt to me, but it did capture that moment when we were setting off on an adventure with a new friend. It showed possibility and serendipity more than beauty. We were soon back on the road.

"We just keep following the coast, right?" I asked.

"The guy at the gas station said we stay on this road the whole way."

I had never seen a coast like this. The only images that came to mind were certain sections of the south—the coasts of the Carolinas.

"From here south, this is southern Italy. It is like going back two hundred years." That sounded a bit like hyperbole but then I remembered the old guidebooks that warned tourists to avoid the toe of Italy.

"Tell me more about what we're going to see," I said.

"This was my grandfather's hunting lodge. We used to celebrate Christmas there and other holidays. All of us cousins used to play together."

I began imagining the stories they would tell if these cousins were still getting together.

"It's at the delta of a river called the Sele, the Fiume Sele. Birds go there because there's lots of fish. There's a tower on the property—a lighthouse from the Saracen era. It's probably a thousand years old. I think my grandfather bought the land in the late 1800s."

My mind was reeling with images and stories.

"His family owns the spring for the water in Naples."

What have Mardi and I fallen into? I couldn't decide which to ask Sergio about first—lighthouses, Saracen pirates, or the water of Naples.

He continued, "My uncle died three years ago."

"And you're due to inherit this property?" I asked. I'm sure my voice revealed my growing incredulity at such a uniquely Italian story.

"Me and ten other cousins."

"So you grew up in the same town with these cousins?" I asked, remembering my childhood living in a small town with lots of cousins, some only a block away.

"Yeah, but now we're spread out all over Italy."

His story was not unlike what has happened all over America. I no longer live near my cousins, but some of my kids are fighting the trend. My three youngest children have cousins who live within the state, and their kids are going to grow up with cousins living in the same town, going to the same schools. I imagined this was still the norm in Italy.

As we were nearing his grandfather's hunting lodge, Sergio spied a café where he remembered hunters gathering to eat and tell their stories. For old times' sake we pulled in. He also remembered a favorite sweet in the glass-fronted display case. Sergio had sworn off sugar, but I hadn't, so I indulged for him. It wasn't the taste treat I expected, but I loved the story. It made me remember some of my own favorites that are nowhere near as tasty today as they were when I was a child.

"We could drive to my grandfather's place or we could walk from here. It will only take five minutes."

"Let's walk," I said.

Sergio had told us that people from all over Europe visit this area. We were joined by a busload of schoolchildren for part of the walk.

"The property starts here," he said as we turned down a lane that cut through a forest. Acreages had been sold off since he was a kid, and many small houses had been built. It all looked very different to Sergio, but eventually we came to the tower. It definitely sparked my imagination—a thousand years standing on this spot. Sergio had hoped a caretaker might be about who would be able to let us in, but serendipity wasn't yet smiling on us. We snapped a couple of photos of Sergio in front of the tower, but without much else to do, and no keys, we moved on. He talked to some maintenance people and construction workers on nearby properties but learned little.

I however was reminded of the global reach of corporations. One of the men we chatted with was wearing a shirt with the logo of a company headquartered in Milwaukee. He wasn't just doing as I do when I don my FIAT hat, showing brand loyalty and desire—he was a long-time employee of a company that I, for a few years, had produced films for. Small world indeed.

"What would you like to do now?" I asked.

Sergio thought for a moment and suggested Palinuro, a seacoast town that he said was a bit off the tourist track. It sounded lovely, so we put it in the GPS and headed toward the toe of Italy. Dorothy led us first to Paestum, which looked like Greece, with impressive temples that were in even better shape than the Parthenon on the Acropolis in Athens. The setting on a coastal plain was not as dramatic, but the attraction for tourists was similar. We snapped a few photos, but Mardi and I wanted a more intimate look at Italy with Sergio as our guide, so within a few minutes we were heading south again.

"Now this is starting to look like Florida," I said.

"We are well into southern Italy and none of us has lost a wallet yet," Sergio joked. As we followed the coast he kept us entertained with stories, telling us that Ulysses had not only sailed near Vittorio's farm where he encountered the sirens, but these dangerous waters as well.

"This area was called Agropoli—because it was used to feed the Greeks," he said and that reminded him how good the food is the farther south you travel in Italy. "The food is really good in Calabria," he said, and *that* reminded him, "In the north the voice originates near the mouth. As you go farther south so does the voice, until the sound starts originating in the stomach. When you get as far south as Sicily we won't even discuss where the sound comes from—it's way, way down."

We laughed as he tickled our curious linguistic ears, "In the north they would probably say *ah grope o lee*, but in the south they would say *ahhh gerop po leee*." Sergio had rolled his *r*, pushed the volume way up, and the pitch down about three octaves, and uttered the word in a perfect impression of the Sicilian dialect.

"I'm impressed—you do tourism well," I said.

"Thanks. We like to think that we don't do tourism at all," he said, and I had to agree. I had meant to convey to him how blessed we felt to be seeing Italy through his eyes. I had just done it clumsily.

"Half the fun of travel is the unknown," Sergio said, reflecting my philosophy perfectly, then he directed me to turn a different direction than I was signaling. I turned the direction Sergio wanted. Dorothy asked me to execute a U-turn. I didn't know who was right, but I didn't care. Wherever our pinball got flipped was fine with me.

"I read that there are as many Italians outside of Italy as there are inside," Sergio said.

"I bet that's true. Emigration, especially after the world wars, was pretty intense," I said.

"Diaspora," he said.

I had never thought of that word in connection with a people other than the Jews.

"Italians were excellent workers," he said.

"Yeah. Italy exported a bunch of Vittorios. They were excellent entrepreneurs, too. In my hometown we had one Italian family, and they ran the restaurant and the theater and were a very vibrant part of the community."

"Bet they all did quite well, no?"

"Italians did extremely well in America, it seems," I said as I maneuvered through a rather tricky chicane of road closures and redirections.

"How do you like this car?" Sergio asked.

"It's not a Maserati. But it does all right." I said and wondered why I had said Maserati—I certainly had never driven one. But it's an Italian car, as are many of the beautiful cars of the world, including the Ferrari that had zipped around us.

"The pilot in you came out for a moment back there," Sergio said.

I smiled at Sergio and said, "Mardi, I could get used to driving in Italy. I'd forgotten how much fun it is to drive a stick."

"It's safer," Sergio pointed out.

I told him about the braking system FIAT developed—how it holds for a moment to give you time to let the clutch out on hills.

"Good engineers," he said.

Sergio, like most Italians, is proud of his heritage—the prestige of Italy.

I noticed a town at the top of a hill. "That looks like a modern Mussolini town," I said and asked about Mussolini's reputation in Italy.

"Italians never had a major problem with Mussolini. He did some great things for the country. He put some order in the system. But he got in trouble because of his association with Hitler, and he was kind of a peasant—he declared war on the United States standing in front of a camera."

I thought that was unfair to peasants, and overlooked the passionate partisan opposition to Mussolini, but I laughed, and he continued.

"He got the trains running on time. He resettled thousands, if not hundreds of thousands, of Northern Italians by building whole new cities. He reclaimed swamps around Rome."

"I think a lot of Americans don't know of the good things Mussolini attempted to do. We remember instead that Carlo Levi opposed Mussolini's views and Mussolini attempted to silence him by sending him down to Aliano."

"Exactly," Sergio said.

"Do you prefer southern or northern Italy?" I asked.

"I really don't know southern Italy. I've hardly been south of Salerno. There are some very beautiful spots in Calabria and Sicily, but I've never been there. I've travelled more in America than I have in Italy."

"You even know where Woody Creek, Colorado is," I said, referring to a town consisting of little more than a tavern that was on my favorite bike route when we lived in the Roaring Fork Valley.

"But you're right—this is pretty country, isn't it?" Sergio said.

"It's so different from the other parts of Italy we've seen," I said.

"Everyone goes to northern Italy, but southern Italy is beautiful too. It's not *more* beautiful, but it is *as* beautiful."

"Do you consider yourself southern Italian?" I asked.

"Well, I consider myself Italian."

I liked his answer, and I liked what he had said about the beauty of Italy. The countryside was indeed beautiful, villages dotting the hills. He was also right about southern Italy. It did feel like we had driven into another century.

"It's amazing that these little towns survive—probably on olives," I said.

"Not very rich towns, I'm sure," he said, and then had a further thought: "Some of them survive on kidnapping." I looked forward to hearing more of that story. Would it have a personal connection to Sergio or his family?

"This one town, much farther south, has a John Paul Getty Jr. Street. Half the town was built on ransom money from the Getty family. Remember the story of the kidnappers cutting off the ear of one of the grandsons of John Paul Getty."

I didn't remember the story, but I was intrigued. It certainly fit in with my childhood impression that the Mafia ruled southern Italy—and that tourists shouldn't go there.

"So the whole town got some of the money?" I asked, wondering how that could be.

"Who knows, but that's the story," Sergio said.

I couldn't tell whether he thought it was true, but it's a story that *could be* true. Sergio's story piqued my curiosity and I later learned that nine kidnappers were arrested, two were convicted, and the rest, including the Mafia bosses, were let go because of lack of evidence, but little of the almost three million dollars in ransom money was recovered, so that money may well have built a southern town.

A police car sped by going the other direction. I instinctively glanced at my speedometer. I was speeding only a little bit.

"What's the difference between *polizia* and *carabinieri*?" I asked, hoping I wasn't going to gain first-hand knowledge of either.

"I think *polizia* is more local and *carabinieri* is more regional. I don't know some very simple things about Italy. It's been a very long while since I've been in Italy for any length of time. I do know that in the nineteenth century this area was full of brigands. It was very dangerous to travel through."

"Make your money off the travelers?" I asked, as I noticed two cars in the distance driving side by side toward us.

"Italy was invaded by everybody. The invaders had no connection to the local communities, so they did whatever they could to survive."

Sergio didn't say, but I wondered if that mentality had led through the centuries to include kidnapping as a means of survival. But my mind didn't stay on that thought very long. We had our own test of survival in the form of those two cars still coming at us, one in each lane—neither car showing any sign of giving way. But in Italy that is no reason for alarm, or even slowing down. Two-lane roads have enough room for three cars driving side by side by side if the car attempting to pass drives right down the centerline and the outside cars hug the edges of the road—and that is what we did as those two cars, still side by side, whizzed by us. The vision of that bus barreling down the road at us on Capri came to mind—and the words of Vincenzo calmly commenting: *See how we drive here.* And that is exactly what I said to Sergio. He laughed.

"When is the last time you took a road trip in Italy?" I asked.

"Going somewhere, like to Rome, fairly often. But just out driving around like this, hardly ever."

I hoped he was enjoying the day. Mardi and I certainly were.

"Look at the town on top of that hill. It looks like an ice cream cone with a chocolate ribbon road winding around it all the way to the top," I said.

"In the Middle Ages, that was the safest place to be," Sergio said. "And now they have electricity."

Dorothy interrupted our ponderings with a recalculation.

"Did we miss a turn?" Sergio asked.

"I think we must have—I got so wrapped up in what we were talking about. We're ten minutes farther from Palinuro than we were just a bit ago."

"If we were to get a feeling, an intuition, that we wanted to find a little restaurant that tourists never go to, in one of these little towns…"

"Ah, very good, Sergio. How about that little town right up there that we've been looking at, the one with a chocolate ribbon road and electricity?" I asked as I slowed down for the exit.

"It's probably not a tourist town," he continued.

In Italy, a wrong turn—or missing one—is not a problem, but rather an opportunity to be celebrated. Sergio was proving himself to be a pinball traveler of the highest order.

"We all carry that romantic notion that we are going to be able to find that place where the local farmers eat," Sergio said, so we stopped and asked a couple of young men walking along the road if they knew where we could find such a place.

They looked at each other and agreed that we were looking for Rosario's, three kilometers up the road. They gave us some complicated directions that didn't seem to faze Sergio. We thanked them and took off. "There's this place three kilometers up the road run by a little old lady…" he said as I glanced at the odometer "…across from the post office."

"So, it's a restaurant run by a little old lady…," I said.

"And has golden arches in front of it—do you want fries with that?" Sergio quipped.

We all got a good laugh about our romantic notions.

"In your wildest dreams, I'm sure you didn't think you would end up in these hills," Sergio said as we drove slowly into town looking for the turns the men had mentioned.

"We've been way more than three kilometers. Should we go back and tell them that they were off on their directions?"

"Maybe they meant three miles," I said.

"Here's a post office," Sergio said as we were beginning to wonder where we had gone wrong, even whether we were in the right town. We parked a few blocks away near the *piazza*, in the shade of the *campanile* and wandered back down the street looking for pickup trucks and farmers, or a sign for Rosario's, but saw nothing. We did see a place called Marilyn's, not directly across the street—more like a half block beyond the post office.

"Just like in New York, restaurants are called Giovanni's," Sergio said.

It was a witty observation, but there's a reason restaurants in New York are called Giovanni's and Luigi's and Mario's—Italians serve great food. Marilyn was not known for her food. I thought again about the directions the men had given us and noticed directly across the street from the post office a building we had overlooked. While Sergio and Mardi checked out Marilyn's, I went back and peered in the window. This was more like it. Red checked tablecloths, family photographs on the walls, and in the back of the room, a door with *Cucina* spelled out on frosted glass. I saw no sign of people, but I wasn't going to give up easily our dream of eating at a place that would more likely be called Nonna's than Marilyn's.

I tested the door. It was unlocked. I stepped in and cautiously said *Buongiorno* but heard no response. I walked toward the back of the room, calling out every few steps. The place was everything I wanted it to be— photographs and nicely detailed drawings of very Italian-looking families, many from the early 1900s. I was almost to the back of the room before I heard anyone. I walked toward the voices and found three people eating in an adjoining room that looked more like a family dining room than a restaurant. I directed my question to the woman at the head of the table, who was the spitting image of the mother of my best friend in high school. *"Possiamo mangiare il pranzo qui?"*

I'm sure she was surprised to see a big American suddenly appear in what was now feeling more like a home, but she recovered quickly and said, *"Certo. Quanti di voi?"*

I told her there were three of us and that I would be right back. I found Mardi and Sergio still debating the merits of Marilyn's. They were less certain than I was that what I had found was truly a restaurant. There was no sign. But a restaurant without a sign was just what I wanted—a place discovered by word of mouth and a bit of inquisitiveness.

When I introduced Sergio to the owner, whose name was Addolorata, they immediately got into a lively discussion—what a non-Italian might call a heated argument. As best as I could make out it was over Neapolitan dialects. I think

Addolorata was astonished that Sergio claimed to be Italian. She thought he was an English or American hippie.

"She won't allow us to order," Sergio said.

"Great," Mardi said.

I couldn't tell whether she was being sarcastic or pleased we wouldn't have to decide.

"She's going to be in charge of what we're going to eat, right?" I asked.

"Right," Sergio confirmed.

"Va bene," I said.

I was excited. Sergio, however, wasn't sharing my enthusiasm. I loved Addolorata's spunk. The repartee between her and Sergio was a delight to the ear and the eye—words were flying—so were hands and arms. The atmosphere of the place convinced me we were where we were meant to be even if it turned out that a farmer had not eaten here in a dozen years.

"These are the little surprises that sometimes..." and Sergio began searching for the words to complete his sentence.

"This is what travel is all about," seemed to be what he was trying to say, so I said it. But Sergio may have been going in a different direction.

"The last word has not yet been said—who knows?" he concluded.

"Oh, that's true, but it looks perfect so far."

I was, of course, basing my assessment on the feelings of *famiglia* evidenced by all the photographs. Sergio was withholding judgment until he had tasted the food. I was buying the sizzle. Sergio wanted to taste the bacon.

While we were debating the merits of the place and marveling at the odd set of circumstances that had led us to this little hilltop town instead of to the seacoast and Palinuro, a young man appeared at our table and asked if we would like wine. Sergio told him we didn't. But I wanted the full effect of this restaurant that looked more like a home. I wanted to try their *vino della casa*—their house wine. It would be a long time before I got back behind the wheel—I had a lot of questions about the photographs on the wall that I was sure would not get answered until the effect of the wine had worn off. I doubt that Sergio at this point realized that he had unwittingly stepped into a battle, nor how formidable his opponent would prove to be. I certainly didn't.

"Famiglia?" I asked Addolorata, pointing to a photograph of an adorable couple who looked to be in their twenties. I guessed the picture had been taken early in the twentieth century, and it possessed that unique quality of catching a very special moment in time—their wedding perhaps, or maybe the day they were engaged.

"Si, mia nonna e nonno," she said as she served our first course.

I looked closer. The family resemblance was strong.

"Buon appetito," she said and then asked how we had found her. Sergio told her the story of the men who had said, *There's a little old lady who makes everything genuine.*

Addolorata got a kick out of that. As she was heading back to the kitchen Sergio said, "We need to quit talking to her or she will burn our dinner."

"I think this is marvelous—just the place you were looking for—a restaurant where the farmers eat," I said.

"A place where the owner says *I will decide what you are going to eat.*"

Sergio was not as pleased as I was. While I was saying "Mmmm," he was saying, "This was already cooked, she got it to the table too quickly."

I didn't know whether that was true, or not. I thought it tasted fine, but maybe I'm not very discerning, even though I've always thought I was a pretty good judge of food.

"What was she telling you when we first came in?" I asked.

"She said, *Are you all English?* And I said, *No, I'm Italian,* and she looked at me from head to toe and said, *You're not Italian. You don't speak Italian.* I had to start speaking in dialect. I told her where I was born. She finally accepted me because her husband was from that region."

He laughed at the memory and so did we. Addolorata was at least a foot shorter, but she was toe to toe and in his face. You would have thought they'd known each other for years the way they went at it—it was a husband and wife kind of battle, or maybe a brother and a sister.

"I guess I'm not dressed like an Italian," Sergio said softly.

"Well, how do Italians dress?" Mardi asked.

"I don't know, apparently not like me."

"It was probably the company you keep that was confusing her," I said.

"My problem is that I shouldn't be drinking, but what do you do when you're faced with a situation like this—I'm going to order a little more wine— once in a while you just have to…"

"Definitely order some more," I said, which brought a disapproving look from Mardi.

"Are you in a rush?" I asked Sergio.

"I have many appointments…" and he began smiling.

So I added, *"Domani?"*

"Yes, tomorrow I am very busy."

"I was so pleased when you told me I spoke perfect Italian," I said.

He laughed, remembering his response the night before when I'd answered his phone call with a prompt *Pronto* delivered with all the ease and confidence I could muster. I knew he'd be calling and I was ready for him—no *Hellos* from me.

"Get the vowels right and pronounce every syllable and you'll be fluent in no time," he said as I struggled to pronounce Addolorata. However, my tongue-twisted attempts to get all the syllables right couldn't keep his mind off the food.

"This is probably microwaved from last week, but it's the thought that counts."

I didn't think it was so bad; actually it was quite good. I never complain when Mardi serves me food I've had the day before or even last week if it's properly stored—some dishes improve with age—especially Mardi's soups. I was willing to give Addolorata a pass. We had come in quite late for lunch, and she was accommodating us. If the food had been prepared some time ago, I didn't much care. I was having a great time. I tried again to move the conversation away from the food by asking for the password for the Internet. But that didn't work either.

"I don't think this is the place those guys told me about, where only the local farmers come to eat."

"Well maybe the local farmers use the Internet to keep up with prices, the markets. This place just looks right," I said.

"Is it working for you, Mardi?" Sergio asked.

Mardi said she was loving it. I think Sergio was beginning to realize that he was going to have to dial his expectations back a bit for us unsophisticated and undiscerning Americans who were thrilled with the experience. Addolorata was perfectly typecast. She truly did remind me of Sarah, my childhood friend Rossy's mother, who in my memory always wore an apron, always had her hair pulled back, and always served great food. Even the way Addolorata stood as she talked with Sergio reminded me of Sarah, with her arms folded across her stomach. I wanted more than ever to find out what part of Italy Sarah was from. An idea for a book was simmering. The Italian influence on America hit me with tremendous force as I watched Sergio and Addolorata argue. I had childhood memories I wanted to deal with—of Italian singers and Italian film stars I'd grown to love while watching movies in the White Theater that Sarah and her husband Ross operated in my hometown. How had I been shaped by those experiences?

To placate Sergio I said, "We could go to Marilyn's for dessert."

Neither Mardi nor Sergio jumped at that suggestion. I was glad. I liked the feel of Addolorata's place—even the traditional music playing on the radio suited my desire to eat at a place frequented by locals, even if they weren't *all* farmers.

Sergio was not eating as enthusiastically as Mardi and I were. Our conversation was not lagging, though. He had many fond memories of Colorado, and of course so did we, so we had a lot of common ground to cover. We talked of picking cherries in the aptly named town of Fruita, of Sergio eating too many and getting sick, and how tart cherry juice is good for shoulder and joint pain.

A few minutes later Addolorata served us another course, a meat dish, but Sergio refused it—I wasn't sure whether it was because he was certain that it was left over or because he truly didn't want more food.

"You don't want any of this?" I asked.

"I've already had too much. Also the speed at which it is arriving is a little alarming."

"*Signora,*" Sergio said quietly.

"*Prego,*" she said, as she moved nearer to Sergio.

Sergio and Addolorata then began another conversation that seemed to last far too long and to be far too animated for two people whose paths had never crossed until an hour ago. A conversation between an American questioning a hostess or chef about food would have been over in thirty seconds, tops—but if two Italians are discussing food or just about anything else, the conversation may last as long two, three, or even five minutes.

Addolorata offered the dish to me. I said, mostly to Sergio, "I'm an *americano*, I like to try things."

"*Grazie,*" I said to Addolorata.

"*Prego,*" she said as she handed me the platter and I took a healthy portion.

The conversation with Sergio, which I thought had ended, resumed as Addolorata offered the platter to Mardi. Again it was lively, and to my ear, much too long if all they were talking about was food. When at last they quit talking I asked if the conversation was again about food.

"I told her that she was serving us too much food and she said that if we don't eat it, they will eat it."

"I like it, but then I like all Italian food," I said.

"Who knows how many months it will be until the next time you are in Italy?"

"It will probably be a while," Mardi said. "I can hear our kids calling us."

My ears weren't quite as attuned as hers. I turned the conversation back to my palate.

"This is the *gnocchi*?" I asked as I took a photograph of my plate. The food was simple and delicious—a taste very similar to the pasta dishes I had eaten in Pietrapertosa and Aliano.

"And this is ravioli, with ricotta," Sergio said. Then he smiled and added, "They say the Internet is clogged with photographs of half-eaten dishes."

"Do you cook for yourself, or do you go out to eat?" I asked.

As I suspected, Sergio dines out—at a restaurant across the street from where he lives.

"At home I eat arugula, broccoli, and the best bread on the planet."

"Remind us to stop by your bakery when we drop you off this evening," I said. "I want a loaf of the best bread on this planet."

Sergio smiled.

Each time Addolorata brought another course she and Sergio got involved in another discussion, also known as an argument. This time she looked offended.

"That discussion wasn't about food," I said after she walked away.

"She asked again how we ended up here. I told her that I'd told some guys we wanted to eat in a place that had never seen a tourist before and she jumped in and said, *What do you mean? Journalists, tourists, everybody shows up here.*"

"I thought I heard her say *giornalista*—I couldn't figure what you two could be talking about that involved journalists."

"No, you heard her right. She seems quite proud that everybody shows up here. Truckers used to stop here until they diverted the road."

Addolorata soon appeared at our table with *grappa* and *limoncello*. Sergio observed that this meal was reminding him of a Sunday dinner some people had enjoyed a few days ago.

"It's turned out that way, hasn't it?" I said, glad to hear that he was softening.

"Mardi, I'm going to take this big piece of *capra*. Will you eat some of it?" I offered some to Sergio as well.

"Obviously everything is precooked—it's all microwaved. I'm sorry to take the veil away..." and Sergio trailed off again, leaving us to fill in his thought. So much for the softening.

Mardi chose to defend Addolorata. "But she cooked it to begin with."

"Heart, lungs, liver..." and again Sergio left his thought dangling.

"And other unmentionables—what we call Rocky Mountain oysters where I come from."

Mardi puckered her face. She had lived long enough in my hometown in the heart of high plains cattle country to know that I was talking about the greatest euphemism known to man.

"We're getting a healthy dose of protein today, Mardi," I said, driving the point home.

"The first thing she said was, *Don't beat me up*," Sergio said.

"What did she mean by that?" I asked.

"Well, Addolorata put this gigantic plate here—and then when I wasn't looking the European beauty put another plate on our table," he said, emphasizing again the point that she was serving us too much food.

"Why do you call her a European beauty?" I asked, referring to a young woman who had just made her first appearance at our table.

"She's Ukrainian, possibly Polish."

"I think you are probably right. You are definitely right about her being beautiful."

"There's been a giant influx in this area, in all of southern Italy."

Sergio seemed to be softening once again. He took some meat from the platter and offered it again to me.

"Is this as good as the food the Italians in your little three-hundred-people village served you?" Sergio asked.

"Oh, that was a long time ago. By the time I was old enough to remember, the meals were fairly Americanized. They served fish on Friday, of course—

halibut. I loved their meats and sauces too, but the halibut really stuck in my memory. I've wondered, these past few years, as I've gotten to know more about the different regions, what part of Italy they were from. I wouldn't be surprised to find out they were from the south."

"Chances are good they were. Most of the immigrants were from the south of Italy."

He directed our attention to Addolorata, who was talking to a man at a nearby table—the first customer to come in since we had arrived.

"He's being allowed to order," Sergio noted.

"We're tourists," I said.

"This is okay, but that is just so-so," Sergio said, rating each meat on the platter.

"Maybe we can stop at McDonald's on the way back," Mardi said.

Sergio laughed hard. "I'll have a Big Mac," he said, playing along.

"I haven't had liver in a long time. I'm enjoying it," I said.

"I hope you didn't have any repercussions after Sunday—too much food?" Sergio asked.

"Surprisingly, no, even though we hadn't eaten so much meat in a long time," Mardi said as she asked me to pass her the platter. She served herself a small piece of goat. While Mardi and I were enjoying the meat dishes, Addolorata and Sergio began arguing again.

"She's going to bring a little bit of dessert," Sergio reported when at last they had finished their protracted "discussion."

"Oh, no, not more food—I guess you told her," Mardi said.

Sergio laughed heartily again. For the past hour and a half he'd been telling Addolorata that we could eat no more.

"She's very persuasive. She has a way about her."

I agreed, remembering how I felt that it was Sarah, who, despite being half the size of Ross, ran the show back in my hometown. I also realized as I watched them talking that Sergio bore a strong resemblance to Ross—both had high foreheads with their hair swept straight back from strong faces with very Roman noses. It was like looking into my childhood seeing the two of them laughing, smiling, and chiding each other—all the time with a glow in their eyes.

I asked Sergio to fill my glass with the house wine I had forced on him.

"In Italy, you must have noticed that very few people get drunk."

"Yeah, even in the guidebooks from the seventeenth century, British tourists were amazed that two hundred Italians were being served free-flowing wine, yet not one of them got drunk."

"Of all of the people I know in Minori, nobody drinks and if they do, they will drink only a glass or two. Even the other day at Vittorio's, people were drinking *grappa*, but no one was drunk—no one was over the limit. They don't consider it fun. Most of my cousins abstain, they don't find it funny or pleasurable."

"It's not part of the culture," I said.

"To lose control is no fun at all. Italy is a difficult society, and if you lose control you lose everything, because there is somebody behind you that will take your place."

Addolorata brought out three bottles of brightly colored liqueur.

"*Cattiva, cattiva,*" Sergio said to her.

Mardi looked at me for an explanation.

"He's saying she's bad for tempting us."

"You're going to have to try all three of them," Sergio said.

"Oh, no," Mardi said.

"Just a taste. This is a walnut liqueur; you will not find it anywhere else on the planet."

"Is it like amaretto?" Mardi asked.

"This is beyond amaretto. The monks invented this," Sergio said, reminding me of what Michele had said before he lit the spoonful of liquor afire.

"What do you suppose this is?" I asked, passing a bottle to Sergio.

"I will try it first," he said and took a taste. "I have no idea." He looked to Addolorata.

She told us it was laurel. She was very proud of her liqueurs, especially when she saw how much we were enjoying them.

"The world is full of excesses," Sergio said, which was, I guessed, a way of excusing our gluttony. "I would say that the little mountain breeze that we feel blowing in is a cherry on top..." and again he trailed off leaving me to say, "of a great meal."

"Yes," Sergio said, once again surprising me.

I didn't know whether he had changed his mind about the food or whether he was now valuing the hospitality of our hostess, but it was clear that he was enjoying himself. We had been given an extraordinary opportunity by a gracious woman. Addolorata had made her kitchen available to us as well as her liquor cabinet, and we partook.

"Here's to the company," I said.

We toasted each other and our hosts. We had been in the restaurant so long that we were once again the only diners.

"I don't think we are going to get to Sicily this evening," Sergio said.

"What about Palinuro?" I asked.

"It's just another tourist trap."

"Like this one?" I asked.

Sergio laughed hard again.

"No one tried the *limoncello*," he said.

"I'll try it," I said.

"I haven't had this in a very long time," Sergio said.

"It's been at least—five days," I said.

Another hearty laugh. He fought for his honor.

"It's been about fifteen years, until today," he said as he lifted his glass. "What is that?"

"It's water," I answered.

"Well, I'm not going to salute you with water. It's bad luck, you know."

"No, I didn't. Is it okay with *limoncello*?"

Sergio smiled.

"So, do you regret that we took a wrong turn?" he asked, looking first at Mardi.

"No," she said. He then turned to me.

"Not at all. How about you?"

"Not at all, not at all. It leaves another adventure for next time," he said as he raised his glass.

"I can drink to that," I said.

"I'm actually pronouncing everything in English now..."

"From hanging out with us?" I asked.

"No, since..." and he motioned toward all the bottles on the table.

"Oh—since hanging out with the walnuts and lemons and grapes," I said.

"You've driven me to drink." It was my turn to I laugh. We had enjoyed a great meal and a great time together made even more enjoyable by a man who loves wordplay.

"Can I get another picture of you two?" I asked.

"Do I look drunk?" Sergio asked as he and Mardi leaned together for a photo.

"Do you know what the Romans used to do? They made laurel crowns," he said, slightly slurring his words, his English words.

"So, you're crowning your insides with laurel?" I asked as I snapped the photo.

"I'm having a laurel moment."

I poured myself a bit more of the walnut liqueur. I was in no hurry to end what was already approaching a three-hour meal.

"These are all monastery products," Sergio said.

"But the monks didn't drive," Mardi said.

"Donkeys, they drove donkeys," he said.

"But the donkeys knew the way home," Mardi protested.

"We really got taken in by Addolorata," Sergio said, trying again to shift the blame to her for our excesses.

"She really worked us over, didn't she?" I said.

"Yes, and it's not over yet."

"You mean we're going to be sitting here at six, still under the control of Addolorata?"

"Congratulations James. You've got it."

I had said Addolorata's name in a staccato rhythm, accentuating each vowel.

"*Ad-do-lo-ra-ta*—I'm Italian," I said.

"In one afternoon, you've learned how to speak Italian—it's amazing."

"I am *so* proud of myself."

Sergio laughed again, a deep laugh, a Sicilian laugh from way down.

"Every time you take a drink you need to learn a new Italian word," Mardi said.

"This is beyond drinking," Sergio said.

"What is this?" I asked.

"This is radical communication."

"I've been radicalized by an Italian-born, American-educated..." and I began searching for the right word, but failed to find it.

"Dolores thought he was an Englishman," Mardi said using the Americanized version of her name.

"Ah that's it. He's an Italian-born, American-educated, English-looking polyglot," I said.

Addolorata joined us again. I had been admiring a beautiful photo of four girls standing in front of the *campanile* that we had parked in the shade of. It seemed like a good time to ask if she was one of those four smiling girls. She told us the story of the photo and that she was indeed one of the girls. She then asked about us—she wanted to know our birth year and whether we were Catholic. She was surprised that we were almost as old as she was. She was also surprised that we weren't Catholic. I think it was because of how many children we have, but before I could find out she had invited us to see her kitchen.

It was amazing. Not only the layout, and all the pots and pans and utensils, but the stunning view overlooking mountaintops all the way to the sea. *"Bella cucina,"* I kept repeating, for it truly was beautiful.

Addolorata's eyes glowed as Mardi and I told her how much we liked her kitchen. She and Sergio got lost again in another discussion—this one quite amiable—as though a truce had been reached. Mardi and I tried to imagine what it would be like to cook every day in such an environment—the ocean and the mountains accompanying every movement of pot and pan.

"I didn't understand what she just said," I said to Sergio, realizing that Addolorata had said something about kids and grandkids that was directed to us as well.

"She is impressed that you two have five children and ten grandchildren."

"Really? How many does she have?"

"They didn't have enough money to have more than three."

"We didn't either, but our kids didn't know that. They just kept coming," Mardi said.

"They would have made a child every six months, she said, if they'd had..." and again Sergio went searching for his thought.

"Soldi," I offered remembering how worried we were when we found out we were expecting our fourth child right at the height of our money woes.

"Mi piacere," Addolorata said reaching out and shaking my hand with both of hers.

"Good to meet you as well," I said.

She leaned in close and hugged Mardi.

Sergio gave Addolorata an Italian kiss on both cheeks.

While we were saying goodbye to the young man and young woman who had also served us, Addolorata and Sergio kept talking. Again I caught only part of the conversation. It sounded good-natured, but with a twist.

"What now?" I asked. "Are we doing dishes?"

"She offered me a bottle of wine to take back."

A truce and a peace pipe. Leaving that restaurant was hard. I wanted to ask about every photo on the wall—who was in it, and their connection to Addolorata. I tried to imagine what it would be like for a relative who had left Italy to come back and see this place—and wonder what their life would have been like if they or their parent or grandparent had not moved to New York or wherever.

We stepped onto the street and my eye was immediately drawn to the *campanile* Addolorata had posed in front of as a ten-year-old girl.

"I have to get a picture of the tower that was in her photographs and a photo of a drunken Italian walking down the main street of Torre Orsaia…"

That brought another Sicilian laugh from Sergio.

"…with a bottle of wine under his arm. Or should I say Englishman?" I asked.

I was in no hurry and no condition to leave town.

"Why don't we put the wine bottle in the car, lock it up, and go to a café," Sergio said. "And have a couple of *espressos*."

"That's very Italian," I said as we began walking toward Marilyn's. "Why should we rush out of town. Let's savor the experience."

"Oh, I loved her," I said as we passed Addolorata's place again.

"Who's that?" Sergio asked. "Someone you knew a long time ago?"

"No, Dolores—she was a delight—delightful Dolores."

"Almost genuine," Sergio said.

I wasn't sure whether Sergio was referring to Addolorata or her food.

"The kitchen was more beautiful than the restaurant," Mardi said.

"The view from the kitchen *was* amazing," I said.

"We got leftovers from last week," Sergio said.

We were all carrying a different impression of the meal. I knew that for me it would be a special memory years from now. It would be Addolorata that I would remember, not whether the meat dishes had been prepared before we arrived.

"What the heck. We had a good time," Sergio said. "She made us believe."

Again, I wasn't sure what Sergio meant—saying that she made us believe—but I didn't ask. I could see by the expression on his face that he had enjoyed the afternoon. We ended up having *espressos* at Marilyn's while waiting for the effects of the liqueurs to wear off. Had we chosen to eat at Marilyn's, I was certain it would have been a forgettable experience. The place had not one photograph on the walls that wasn't an advertisement.

The drive home in the late afternoon light was gorgeous. We followed little-traveled roads through the mountains. The beauty of southern Italy is overwhelming—or maybe as Sergio hinted—the beauty of *all* of *italia* is overwhelming. All the way to Minori we kept talking about stopping to get a *gelato*, but we never did. We just kept driving—enjoying the countryside and talking about our meal. I had said I wanted to get back to Minori in time to get a loaf of the best bread on the planet, which we did, but that was just an excuse—I didn't want any new experiences to dilute the memory of dining for an afternoon in the sure and capable care of Addolorata.

CHAPTER TWENTY-ONE

Casa Mannini ~ Thursday April 21 ~ 55 & Clear

Moon Over Maiori

Who, being loved, is poor?
OSCAR WILDE

■

The best and most beautiful things in the world cannot be seen or even touched—they must be felt with the heart.
HELEN KELLER

"*Oggi andremo a Tramonti,*" I said to Jessica. "We are going to Tramonti today," I repeated as Mardi and I walked into Le Suite with our insulated mugs, eager to get our tea brewing so we could settle in for the morning routine we'd grown to love.

Jessica responded with a short phrase. The only word I was certain of was *montagna.* She often spoke to us in a combination of Italian and English—in the same sentence—but I couldn't tell whether she was mispronouncing an English word or saying something in Italian I didn't understand, or maybe just didn't recognize because of her intoxicating accent. I knew by her inflection she had asked a question, so I said, "Yes, we like the mountains. *Ci piacciono le montagne.*" I often repeated in Italian what I had said in English, or vice versa—for her understanding and mine, hoping that if I had mispronounced a word or used the wrong verb tense she would correct me as I often did with her when her pronoun choice or sentence structure was wrong.

Le Suite was not yet busy. We loved those mornings when we had Jessica's undivided attention. What was not to love? The temperature was consistently perfect, with either a light breeze or none at all. The sun was shining. The sound of the town coming alive spurred my creativity. The Internet was super fast. And the music seemed to always match my mood—or maybe it created it. On top of all that, day after day we were greeted by a friendly hostess who gave us Italian lessons every time she saw us, who smiled warmly, and treated us like we were royalty. If there was something not to like about the life Mardi and I were living in Maiori we had yet to discover it.

Jessica handed us our mugs filled with hot water and then asked another question in full-speed Italian. I was flattered that she felt my comprehension was up to the task. I played the words through quickly in my mind. I started building the sentence off the one word I was sure of—*chiesa*—and figured out that she had asked if we had visited a church—whose name I didn't catch—that you must hike to.

"Can we drive partway?" I asked.

"No drive. *Piedi.*" She pulled out a map and showed me a detailed route that started at Casa Mannini.

"I want to tell Jessica that we are feeling lazy today, but I don't know the word in Italian," I said to Mardi.

Jessica pulled out her dictionary, and looked at me with her big brown eyes imploring me to say the word again. "Lazy," I said. Then I broke the word into two distinct syllables: "*Lay-zee.*" And then I spelled it.

She found it and showed it to me for confirmation. I nodded.

"You are not lazy."

"Today, we are feeling lazy," I said and gave Mardi a hug.

"Then you say, *Oggi siamo pigri.*"

"*Oggi siamo pigri, corretto?*"

"*Si,*" Jessica said and winked. She never hid her appreciation for the affection that Mardi and I show each other.

We took the mugs to our table, pulled out Earl Grey tea bags, and settled in—Mardi to get in touch with our family and me to begin putting into words the serendipitous, nay, heaven-sent experience of touring Italy with an Italian. My memories of our meal with Addolorata and Sergio were still vivid, and I wanted to transfer the film in my mind into words on the pages of my little MacBook Pro. I had so many things to be thankful for that morning, and the capability of that little marvel was high on my list. Add an iPhone and the high-quality photographs it takes, and I had the perfect tools to create books about the adventure of living in a culture not my own—of reading, as Saint Augustine said, more than one page.

As Mardi and I worked, people came and went. It seemed we had all found a home, a cocoon we liked at Le Suite. Some stayed for only a few minutes, others for hours. We had a rental car and could have been sightseeing, but we were doing what we wanted to be doing among people who let us know they enjoyed having us with them.

While going through my notes, I came across a photograph I had taken in Minori when we were relaxing on the beach promenade listening to the waves crash and watching people. It was time stamped Monday, April 18 at 3:35 p.m., and it showed a couple doing what Mardi and I had been doing much of the time since we had arrived in Italy—taking a break from hiking while the husband journaled. But the body language spoke of a couple who instead of having the time of their life seemed to be in pain and misery. Not long after I snapped the photo they began squabbling, rather bitterly, ostensibly about what to do next, but I think they were fighting because neither felt valued by the other. They were in two different worlds even though they were sitting on the same bench. They were looking toward the same amazing view of the Amalfi Coast that Mardi and I were, but they seemed not to appreciate it, or maybe they couldn't even see it, so consumed were they by bitterness.

I showed the photo to Mardi and asked if she recalled them. She did. She remembered how far apart they were sitting and that their bodies were pointed away from each other—as though if they could they would head off in different directions. We recalled that there had been times in our own marriage when we too had sat as far apart as we could—when we wanted to head off in different directions. That happens in a marriage, in a relationship.

It happened that morning in Le Suite. I was still writing about Addolorata and Sergio when Mardi had finished catching up with everyone. That meant she had time to spend in the shops we had for days been walking past—and I had a chance to work without feeling I was slighting her. For Jessica it was unheard of.

She stopped by to ask if everything was okay. I told her that I would like a glass of water. When she brought it she asked about Mardi with concern. I told her that she was shopping.

"In Maiori?" she said with a look on her face that said *Nobody shops in Maiori.*

But Mardi and I had already bought quite a few things in Maiori. I had found the perfect combination computer/journal bag—my man purse, as well as a scarf that gave me a bit of Italian flair. I tried to convince Jessica that she shouldn't be so dismissive of her hometown. Whether I was successful I don't know, but I think I was able to convey how much we loved Maiori and that Le Suite was a big part of the reason. As if to make sure I never forgot,

Jessica taught me another word. She pointed to the glass of water she had just brought me.

"*Cannuccia?*"

She noted the quizzical look on my face and showed me a drinking straw. When I pronounced the double *c* correctly—similar to the English *ch*—she gave me an appreciative smile and handed me the straw. *Cannuccia* was already a bonus word for the day and it didn't stop there. It was a slow morning at Le Suite. Jessica was able to stop by frequently to teach me new Italian words—and I helped her with the English equivalents. Jessica was visibly relieved when Mardi returned and gave me a hug. She said it made her happy to see us back together.

Our comfortable morning at Le Suite meant a late start on our drive to the high country, but we were in no hurry. Mardi was photographing too, and we enjoyed being able to stop where we wanted, to take pictures of a delightful countryside filled with stone walls, tree-lined lanes, and farms overflowing with animals. I knew without a doubt that if ever I had a bicycle with me in Maiori, this road would quickly become one of my favorite rides, climbing through meandering valleys surrounded by rugged peaks, some so steep that trees cannot take root.

The valleys meandered, and so did the lanes. For the most part, they were wide enough for two small cars to pass, but not always. I soon found myself following a delivery van and wishing the driver would turn off, which he soon did, but a few minutes later we came around a corner and saw a cyclist ahead of us. Fortunately, a roadside stand beckoned—a good time to buy some of the local fruit and let the cyclist climb without me on his wheel. We bought oranges, hoping they would taste as sweet and flavorful as Vittorio's, but they weren't even close. The saving grace was that the pull-off had a great view of Mount Vesuvius, Naples, and Pompeii.

We didn't stay long, but even so, by the time we were back on the road, the cyclist had vanished. He must have crested the pass and flown down the mountain much faster than we were descending. We met at least a dozen cyclists climbing up from Napoli, all were riding solo, attacking the mountain at their own pace. Considering the beauty and the steep ascent, it was little wonder that the road was a favorite of serious bikers. We pulled off at a spot with a panoramic view of the Bay of Naples that tempted us to keep right on going all the way to the port city, but the crisp mountain air, bright sunshine, and gentle breeze tugged at our hearts, so we turned around and climbed back up to Tramonti.

"Here's where we saw that dog that loved Simon so much," I said.

We were back on familiar roads, roads that we had walked both coming and going with Simon and Luciana. Mardi was studying the map.

"Marco's is down at the bottom of the hill," she said.

We looked into the shop as we drove by but didn't see Marco, so we turned at the corner where we had gotten off the bus, and headed toward Il Raduno. Memories flooded our minds on the short drive.

"Somewhere down here is where I stopped to take a picture of the *bella donna*."

No one was working in the vineyard as we drove by. Seconds later we arrived at the sign for Il Raduno, but the hill leading up to the *agriturismo* was so steep and the turn so sharp that despite the small size of the FIAT we couldn't make the corner. We continued down the road looking for a place to turn around. We found a small country church and pulled into a parking lot that was empty save for one car and one Vespa. We were disappointed to find the church locked. Since the walk to Il Raduno with Simon and Luciana had been so enjoyable we decided to walk again. We were certain there was little risk of being ticketed or towed from the church parking lot on a Thursday afternoon, or any afternoon for that matter.

The walk led us over a little stone bridge, past piles of drying logs, and alongside ancient rock walls lining a meandering path. Some of the farms were enclosed by wrought iron fences, and every farm seemed to have dozens of pots of flowers lining the driveway or flanking the front door. The pride of Italians in their homes is always on display. The gardens, vineyards, and fences, whether stone or wooden, were all lovingly cared for. *Meticulous* was the word that kept coming to mind as we walked and photographed our way the half mile or so to Il Raduno's steep driveway. We leaned into the hill and walked up it again just as we had with Simon and Luciana—and just like that first time, the door to the dining room was locked—but this time no one was warming up a truck. I listened for some activity but heard nothing. I walked deeper into the compound and heard water running in a small building. I approached the door.

"Allo?" I said but got no response.

I stuck my head into the open doorway and saw a woman washing pots.

"*Buongiorno*," I called, louder this time, but still she didn't hear me.

"*Scusi, dove Brigida?*" She heard me this time but seemed not to understand, so I added, "*Il Raduno per pranzo*."

"*Mangiare?*" she asked me.

"*Si.*"

"Okay, *un momento*," she said and walked deeper into what I now realized was the backside of the kitchen, so far that I could no longer see her.

A few seconds later she was back and said something I didn't quite catch, but her body language told me she was asking how many people would be eating.

"*Due—io e mia moglie*," I said. That seemed to satisfy her and she disappeared again.

I returned to the spot where I had left Mardi but couldn't find her—she had gone wandering. I sent out my two-handed high-pitched owl whistle.

She popped out from behind a shed. She had been admiring Brigida's vegetable garden—the garden that had produced the delicious salad we had eaten a week earlier and hoped to do a take-two on.

The woman opened the door, said she would serve us, and asked where we wanted to sit.

"You'd like to eat out here on the deck, right, Mardi?" I asked.

"It feels like we are closer to the mountains. I like the wooden tables, too."

"*Mi chiamo James, e questo è Martha*," I said. "*Come ti chiami?*"

"*Un momento*," she said as she set the bread and water on our table. She then extended her hand and said, "Maria—Mary."

"*Piacere*," I said.

She asked where we were from, then guessed what sounded like Greece.

"*No, Americano*," I said.

"*Americano?*" she asked with a quizzical look.

"*Sì.*"

"Ah, okay." She thought for awhile, then added, "*Parli molto bella italiano.*"

I uttered a weak "Ah," and the funny thing was that Mardi, a split second later, said the same thing. Because *bella* had registered before the other words I at first thought she had said that it was beautiful here on the veranda with the view of the mountains, which it indeed was, but after processing the rest of the sentence, I realized she had actually said that I spoke Italian very well—*You speak very beautiful Italian.*

Hallelujah. I was shocked. What Sergio had jokingly said the day before was, at least for this moment, true—I had learned to speak Italian well enough that someone I had just met felt moved to compliment me on my use of her language.

"*Vuoi vino?*" Maria asked.

"*Niente vino oggi—sto guidando una macchina*," I said.

"*Solo un po forse*," Maria said.

She understood that I was driving today but she was asking if maybe we wanted a little bit of wine to go with our meal. It was hard to pass up such a tempting offer, because their wine was very good, but we stuck with water. Had we been walking or catching the bus, we would have enjoyed *il vino.*

"*Una caraffa di acqua per favore,*" I said.

"*Prego,*" Maria said.

After she had left the table I said to Mardi, "It will be okay if it comes in a bottle." We don't like plastic water, but we had found that most of Italy didn't share our concern. However, we never let it affect our enjoyment of our meal or the people who served us.

"No chicken available," Mardi reported, looking up from the menu.

"No *pollo* again, that's okay," I said as Maria returned with our water and asked if we were ready to order.

"*Mista insalata per favore,*" Mardi said.

"*Dopo un tempo Carne Mista,*" I said to Maria but it was obvious by the confused look on her face that what I was saying didn't make any sense. I was trying to tell her that the last time I was here I ordered the mixed meat dish. She probably realized at that point that she had made a hasty judgment in saying that I spoke Italian well. Despite the hiccup, I was able to convey to her that my choice was the mixed meat dish.

I looked up *dopo un tempo* after she left the table and realized that instead of saying *The last time I was here I ordered the Carne Mista*, what I had actually said was that *After a time the Carne Mista*—a big difference.

While waiting for the *bruschetta* that we had ordered to begin our meal I continued looking at our guidebooks and dictionaries and absorbing the beauty of the day. A dog was barking in the distance. A chain saw was buzzing in the woods beyond the church where we had parked—so far away that the sound was pleasant. Birds were singing and a rooster occasionally crowed nearby. We were definitely in the country. I discovered that this land was once known as *Campania Felix* because of its fertility. *Felix* also means *happy,* and that was certainly how Mardi and I felt as the peacefulness of the countryside washed over us.

"We should go hiking," Mardi suggested. Simon had said the same thing when we had eaten lunch with them the previous week. The beauty of the land and the high peaks surrounding this magical valley make a person think of a long trek. The sounds seemed intensified—the crisp air carried the calls of chickadees to our ears unfettered. A half dozen cats lounging in the sun made the point better than anything we could say that this was truly a glorious day. One of them got up, walked over and began talking to us, louder and more insistent with each meow. It seemed like a good time to take a walk in Brigida's vegetable garden. Her skill for beautiful compositions, using the earth as a canvas, was on full display. All of us arrived back at the table at the same time, Maria with our *bruschetta* and Mardi and me armed with compliments on the precise layout of the rows of vegetables.

Maria told us what vegetables they raised and which months they were harvested. A few moments later Brigida arrived with the salad and told us she was happy to see us again. It was definitely good to see her again—and her salad. Before taking a bite I took a photograph to use at home for inspiration. It was as delicious as it was gorgeous.

"How is it possible for salad to taste so good? Is it just the combination—is that why it's so darned good?" I asked Mardi after Brigida and Maria returned to the kitchen.

"Well it's fresh—she probably picked all of it from the garden just this morning. And it's also the olive oil and the spices."

"I'm having an out of body experience, and this is just the salad."

"I could eat this the rest of my life," Mardi said and I believed her.

We decided that we would gladly have spent the rest of the afternoon on Brigida's farm—napping in a hammock and listening to the clear sounds echoing around the valley—the good sounds of work getting done on the neighboring farms.

"I love being in the country like this. It's easy to imagine I'm a farmhand fueling my body for an afternoon of work," I said.

"I bet lots of people go trekking through here in the summer. When it gets hot in August I would guess it's still comfortable up here," Mardi said.

We could also hear the sound of plates clinking through the open door of the kitchen as Maria washed dishes. It was a surprisingly pleasant sound, mingling with the more distant sounds of tractors and roosters and chainsaws.

"I love the sound of a chainsaw," Mardi said. "It reminds me of all our trips into the mountains to gather firewood."

I tried to find the source of the sound. After a couple of pans of the hillside on the other side of the valley I caught a glimpse of movement—men loading logs on wagons—but I couldn't see anyone cutting trees.

"I think they're behind the church," Mardi said.

We began talking about the many good days we'd had cutting firewood and then grilling hot dogs and marshmallows for the kids before making the granny-gear trek down the mountain on abandoned logging roads in our old Ford pickup loaded down with enough wood to heat our house for a month and a half of a Rocky Mountain winter—a reminiscence that would have kept us entertained much longer had Brigida not served the *carne mista*—which switched the conversation to the animals she raises and the meats she buys from neighboring farms. Mardi nudged the conversation toward trekking, and by the time Brigida had left our table we were trying to figure out whether we could come back to stay with her on this trip or add her *agriturismo* to our Italian bucket list. I don't particularly like that expression, but it sure captures the essence of it when you get up there in years. You suddenly realize that your time on earth is getting pretty short, and if you're going to *get 'er done* you need to get to it.

"I suppose we should have ordered something different this time…" I began in light of the *new experiences before you die philosophy* that was bouncing around in my mind.

"No," Mardi blurted out.

"…but when you find something that is this good, it seems like you'd be a fool not to order it again if you get the chance," I said, realizing that some things are good enough to just keep going back to the rest of your life, like Earl Grey tea, early morning bike rides, and the *wife of your youth*.

"What is this?" I asked.

"It's pork."

"Well, what's this then?"

"Probably lamb."

"Whatever it is, it's delicious," I said very much surprised, because I am not often fond of lamb.

"I'm sure it's lamb."

Lamb, pork, beef, or whatever, the cat wanted some.

"Oh, hush up," I said.

"NO!" Mardi shouted, surprising both me and the cat.

The cat whimpered, but didn't leave.

"You know I'll clean it up, don't you," she said. She had noticed that I'd left some meat on the bone. I was, however, licking my fingers, not wanting to waste any of the delicious juices. The cat, overcome by the aroma, forgot Mardi's admonition and got insistent again.

"Do you mind?" I asked.

Channeling her storybook-reading-grandma cat voice, Mardi said to me, *I can't believe you won't share. I like the meals here too.* She's sometimes like that with our kids and grandkids too. She says no, but after they whimper a little, she changes her mind. The cat had her figured out and was applying relentless pressure.

None of this broke my resolve. I recalled the time I fed a cat some of my kabobs in Greece, and that cat told all her friends about the sucker she'd just found and I spent the rest of the meal fending off dozen of felines. This food was too good to share with anyone but Mardi.

"We still have some *bruschetta* left," I said.

"Jack Sprat could eat no fat, his wife could eat no lean, and between the two they licked the platter clean," Mardi said.

But this time we didn't live up to the Sprat legend.

"You're leaving a lot," I said. "The cats are going to love you."

"That was incredible," she said as she pulled some fat off the bones to give to the cat.

For the first time since our food had been served we quit talking. We were content. Maria and Brigida were chatting in the kitchen, but we couldn't hear them well enough to make out what they were saying.

"This is a good way to end our time on the Amalfi Coast—doing one of our favorite things," I finally said.

"We should walk down the road and find a field of flowers to lie down in," Mardi suggested.

"Oh, but it's so peaceful right here. I'd love to find a hammock and let the breeze lull me to sleep."

"I even had it in my calendar today—to see if we could take a nap in the mountains," she said as she gave the cats more fat.

We came close to asking if we could take a take a nap on the deck, but we didn't want to impose. We thanked Brigida and Maria for the wonderful meal and told them we hoped someday to return. Brigida, expressing Italian hospitality with a flourish, left no doubt that she would enjoy seeing us again.

As we started down the hill Mardi snuggled up close.

In a staccato rhythm I said, "I love you" with a strong emphasis on *you*.

"This has been wonderful," she said as we walked along the road arm in arm. As we were passing by the farm where the rooster lived that we had been listening to, we also began hearing the sound of bells on the hillside above us, presumably on sheep, or maybe goats. A woman suddenly appeared on the road walking our way. We had been looking so intently for the sheep that it was as if she had materialized out of the sound.

"*Buongiorno*," I said.

"*Buongiorno*," she responded respectfully.

Meeting that woman walking down a country lane satisfied the romantic in me—my vision of the sweet life of Italy. "Is this why you leave the comfort of your own bed, your own La-Z-Boy, to cross an ocean and sleep on hard mattresses? Is this the point of traveling?" I asked.

I knew the answer. It *was* just for moments like this, when all seems right in the world, when a simple greeting from a stranger makes a beautiful day even more memorable. We continued looking for the sheep whose jingling bells were playing a delightful tune for our attentive ears. Why not add a shepherd and his sheep to the beauty of the day?

"There they are, up in the trees. See them?" I said. "They're coming toward us."

We walked the final few yards to the church and chose a bench in the garden to await their arrival. They were eating their way down the hillside and would soon cross the road on the other side of the small bridge that had brought us back to the church. Mardi chose to sit in the sun to wait. I chose the shade.

The chainsaws were silent, but the roosters and dogs were not. A small tractor pulling a wagon loaded with firewood drove by. No wonder the chainsaws were silent—their work was done. The sheep were getting closer, and so were the lovely sounds of their deeply resonant bells. The sounds took us back to our days in the high mountains of South Tyrol, when we were shepherds for Gianrico. Our bucket list is filled with Italian desires, wonderful moments, and shared memories we want to experience again.

We sat in the courtyard a long time watching the sheep and the shepherd wander down the road. We too wandered when we left the church, choosing roads for no other reason than they looked interesting. We knew we'd eventually wind up on the Amalfi Coast Highway if we kept turning southward and downward. That rubric led us along rustic roads to Ravello. The views of the coast were stunning, but the town was busy and parking was nonexistent, so befitting our quiet mood, we continued downward along a path wide enough in places for only one vehicle. The walls at the sides were sometimes over twenty feet tall and beautifully built of native stone, and looked very old. You are never far from a reminder on the Amalfi Coast that these hills have been trod since ancient times.

I had become quite comfortable driving the winding roads of the Sorrentine Peninsula. It no longer bothered me to come around a corner and see people walking along the side of the road, nor was I shocked to encounter cars heading toward me in my lane. Most of the time there was *no* lane that could be called mine. If these roads had lanes, they would only have been wide enough for two bicycles or two Vespas to pass each other, yet it was not uncommon to encounter large buses. In thinking back, and especially in looking back at our journey around the Amalfi Coast, for we have dashcam video of many of our adventures, I'm amazed by how comfortable we became with the you-never-know-what's-around-the-corner philosophy we adopted.

I was also amazed, as we worked our way ever downward on switchbacks, that there could possibly still be a road below us. It already felt as if we were suspended as far out over the water as we could possibly get. But I was wrong. We came around a one hundred eighty degree turn and there before us was a stop sign and a T-intersection wedged between tall buildings and a wall of rock jutting up from the ocean. We slowly worked our way to the head of the queue, looked both ways, and jumped into the traffic heading along the coast toward Salerno. We were once again on the Amalfi Coast Highway, at the very edge of the sea. Within moments we were in Minori. I was ready for a break. We drove past the Hotel Santa Lucia into the parking lot on the harbor, and parked right next to a gorgeous gray FIAT 500—a car that had climbed to the top of my wish list. The drive down from the mountains had been a blast—no road that I'm aware of in the United States would be as fun or as challenging, but it sure would be nice to drive a car with the turning and stopping ability these cars possess, just in case you ever needed it.

We got out, took in the view of the distant headlands, and walked toward the oldest part of town, concentrating on the historic photos on display in many of the narrow streets. Sleek fishing boats powered by a single graceful sail, captured my imagination. Oh, to be a time traveler as well as a pinball traveler—to experience this coast in the days before John Steinbeck brought it to the attention of the world. We wandered through the maze of streets and eventually found Vittorio's shop, but he wasn't in, so we lingered only long enough to buy more of the cups and saucers we had fallen in love with on our first visit, as well as colorful ceramics of each of our favorite towns on the Amalfi Coast.

We were eager to get back to *our town*, which we knew would be a very short drive, for it is a short walk, even if you climb up and over the headland separating the two towns. One stop light separates Minori and Maiori. It turned red seconds before we got to it and we had to wait for a stream of cars to pass. Much of the road between Minori and Maiori is wide enough for only one vehicle and the occasional person walking along the coast. In less than five minutes we were back in Maiori, back where I was moved to exclaim *I just love this town*. Three men in work clothes, deep into a conversation outside a bar near La Vela, reminded me of the strong feelings of community this town evokes in me.

We stopped by our hotel room but were soon back on the streets, back among the people, just in time for the *passeggiata*. One of the first people I saw was Maximiliano. He was dressed in a sleek jogging suit looking very dapper. I was surprised—I hadn't taken him for a runner. I was a few yards behind Mardi. She had walked by him without noticing. When he saw me he spun around, figuring Mardi was nearby. He began jogging toward her, but instead of saying hello he reached out as he ran by, and grabbed her purse, pretending to steal it. I hadn't taken him for a practical joker either.

As we passed by Le Suite, we saw Mirko and Boston Giovanni. We thanked them for the good times they'd shown us, and said a quiet goodbye. They offered to buy us wine, but we declined. We had our sights on the *ricchezza* pizza that I had loved so much. We planned to order take-out and eat another meal on our balcony listening to the sounds of people enjoying themselves in our favorite town.

"Isn't it amazing that in ten minutes they can have a pizza ready?" I said.

"Well, they have the dough," Mardi said.

"And the oven is hot, always," I said.

"They just have to throw the cheese, meat, and spices on it, pop it in the oven and *ecco*," she said, for that is what they had done within seconds of placing our order—plopping the pizza on the long-handled paddle and placing it just so in the heat of the wood-fired oven.

"Can you put your finger on why I like this town better than Minori?" I asked.

"Um-hmmm."

"You can?" I asked, surprised that she had an answer, for I liked both towns.

"The layout is perfect; so many places for people to gather."

"You're right. The wide street with all the shops on it works for me."

"And the long beach, it's so refreshing," she added. "Minori is a little more closed in."

"So nice to walk down the promenade here and run into someone you know," I said.

Within minutes we had paid for our pizza and were walking toward our hotel—the sounds of the town—the people talking, kids laughing, and the bells, always the bells reminding me of why I love Maiori. I didn't need a list of reasons, I just had to experience again a walk along Corso Reginna.

"I'm starting to understand Italian," I said. "I'm even beginning to think in Italian."

I recalled the conversations of the day, delighting in the musical cadence of remembered voices blending with the sounds of people calling out to friends walking by. Scooters were zipping past us, soccer balls were being kicked, life was being lived right on the street and we were very much a part of it, contributing with our money and our presence to what was good in Maiori that night.

"I think we've discovered we like city life, being in the heart of a town," Mardi said.

"Walking down Corso Reginna, looking forward to our favorite pizza is a good memory for our last night in Maiori," I said.

You have just one friend there—Mardi was channeling her best Jessica impression—*Why you go to Aliano?* doing a good job of conveying Jessica's sweet innocence. "Is that going to be the name of this chapter?" Mardi asked.

"That's a good idea," I said. "She was so cute when she said it. And so sincere. *Why don't you stay here with us?*"

We kept repeating Jessica's question—trying to capture her inimitable accent and rhythm, delighting in the rhyme of it—*Why you go to Aliano?*

I hadn't planned it, but as I uncorked the Tuscan wine from Montepulciano it seemed appropriate to pay homage during this, our last meal in Maiori, to my *first* adventure in Italy—the journey that had led to this belated honeymoon, that had turned out so much better than I had dared imagine.

"Can there be other tourists as happy as we are?" Mardi asked as we walked onto our little patio with our pizza on Amalfi Coast pottery and looked out at Maiori below us and the sea beyond. "This is too beautiful."

No wonder Jessica hadn't bought what I was selling. It's hard to be convincing when you are having the time of your life right where you are, and the young woman wanting to know why you're leaving is a big part of your joy.

"Sometimes land that appears Godforsaken can be beautiful," I said, trying to bolster my courage. I knew we had to move on, wanted to move on, but oh my, was I going to miss this. But we had enjoyed Basilicata, and for Mardi there were the mountains, always the mountains.

"Mardi, I love you. Did you know that?" I asked.

"I did and I do."

I was feeling blessed and I wanted her to know that she was the reason, and that I loved sharing my love of Italy with her. Jessica's question had made me even more introspective, even more aware of our good fortune.

"I love hearing the sound of all the people. You don't get that in the suburbs," I said and wondered whether I had said that with the thought that we would someday live in the heart of a city or village. I couldn't imagine leaving our kids and grandkids, but this life we had been living fit us like a perfectly made soft leather glove.

"Everyone is living their lives right down below us," I said.

"You never feel alone when you hear all the people on the streets," Mardi said.

"Oh, look. The peaks have halos. Let's walk to the beach to watch the moon rise." I wanted to squeeze the last sweet drops out of Maiori.

"Oh, I don't know. I'm pretty comfortable here."

Mardi was right. No sense rushing this delightful meal. The pizza was just as good as I remembered it. The same with the earthy wine of Montepulciano—in no way should Maiori ever be rushed.

"Did she put a *but* in front of it?" We hadn't spoken of Jessica for a while, but Mardi knew her question was still playing like a broken record in my mind.

"No. It was just *Why you go to Aliano?*"

The record kept playing and the memories of Maiori kept flowing.

"There it is. It's beautiful," I said as I looked up and noticed that we were too late—the moon had already risen. Mardi could no longer resist. It was too gorgeous. We toasted Maiori with the last of our wine, kissed each other, and set off for the beach.

"We've already said goodbye to everyone at Le Suite, so we can't walk down Corso Reginna," I said.

"Let's go the back way."

Taking a different route took us past restaurants we hadn't tried, shops we hadn't stepped into, shop owners we hadn't met. Jessica was right to ask why we were leaving. We had much more to experience right where we were.

"I like this town, I don't care what you say," I said as we stopped at a water fountain.

"Look—it's rising again," Mardi said. "Moonrise over Maiori."

We weren't too late after all. We were now lower and closer to the mountain, and the moon was once again just beginning to peek over the top of the ridge, outlining the rocks with a silver glow. We crossed the highway and walked onto the promenade. The closer we got to sea, the higher the moon climbed above the mountain.

"We're not the only old people out walking," Mardi said.

A couple, slightly stooped, near the water had caught her eye. On the promenade, another couple walking arm in arm—folks who appeared to be in their eighties—captured my attention. It was couples night on the beach—not just old people but young as well. The moon had drawn all of us out for a stroll—a chance to enjoy the breeze off the ocean—while walking arm in arm. A few single folks were out too, and always the people whose dogs wanted to walk.

We walked, we reminisced, and we circled back, avoiding Corso Reginna, stopping to look at menus, noting restaurants and *gelaterias* that we want to try the next time we live in Maiori—for we were certain there will be a next time—and a next time—and a next time.

"We should have tried this place. It looks good," I said. "They even serve breakfast."

"Maybe we can come here in the morning," Mardi suggested.

It looked like a friendly place—lots of family photographs on the wall and a simple decor reminding us of Addolorata's restaurant.

"How long have we been here?" I asked as we walked past where our car was parked behind a locked gate.

"Two weeks almost."

"I can't believe I hadn't noticed how old this street was."

We had stopped to read some of the plaques on the walls leading to Casa Raffaele Conforti—the very first street we had walked down in Maiori. But we were following Nadia that day, being careful where we placed our feet on the uneven pavement, and had not noticed that we were walking under a Roman arch. But this evening we were aware of the wonders we were leaving—the massive size of the paving stones on Via Mannini, the old stone walls lining the street that led to our hotel.

"They don't tear things down in Italy, they build around the monuments," I said.

"I'm glad we went out," Mardi said as we stepped into the brightly colored lobby of our hotel and opened the door to number 33 with its quaint ceramic depiction of Amalfi.

We had started in Amalfi, had moved to Maiori, and had spent time in almost every town on the Amalfi Coast. We could probably have fallen in love with each of them, but it was Maiori that welcomed us and became our special place. Jessica had been right to ask why we were leaving. We gave her lots of answers, but the only answer that seemed to satisfy her was our promise that we would be back.

Whether Jessica believed us I didn't know. But we had no doubt. Every memory we had of Maiori was good. We topped off our growing list of reasons to return by falling asleep with moonlight streaming in through our open doors, the sound of waves crashing on the shore, and the chatter of happy voices from the streets below coloring our sweet memories of Maiori.

CHAPTER TWENTY-TWO

Maiori ~ Friday April 22 ~ 62 & Sunny

Why You Go to Accettura?

I love thee to the depth and breadth and height my soul can reach.
ELIZABETH BARRETT BROWNING

■

The greatest mistake you can make in life
is to be continually fearing you will make one.
ELBERT HUBBARD

I woke up with the delightful question Jessica had asked us playing like a song in my head. *Why you go to Aliano? Why you go to Accettura?* Our reasons hadn't satisfied her, but it felt right to go, even though we knew we would deeply miss our friends in Maiori, especially her. I had tried to explain that I had read a book about Basilicata, a book with which she happened to be familiar, *Christ Stopped at Eboli.* I reminded her that Mussolini had exiled the author to Aliano, but she interrupted me. "You have one friend in Accettura and twenty friends in Maiori." The look on her face told me she thought we were making a big mistake heading off to the Godforsaken land of Basilicata.

We had stopped by Le Suite a day early to make sure we had time for a proper goodbye. I wanted her to know how much we appreciated her and her family. She promised she would visit us in Wisconsin and then formed her hands in the shape of a heart. "It is good to see two people who are in love," she cooed.

Jessica creates beautiful moments. She has a confidence and a friendly, outgoing personality that draws people in. She had captured us with her wit, her beauty, and her inquisitive nature. She was also Italian to the core, with a servant's heart. She made our happiness and our comfort her concern. She is the kind of person who will be successful no matter what career she chooses and she was not going to let us head off to the wilds of southern Italy without trying to talk some sense into us.

But that was exactly what we were going to do, but first we had the thrill of one last Amalfi Coast Highway adventure, and it didn't disappoint. On our short drive to Salerno to pick up a different car, we encountered the usual memorable moments—two people walking side by side in the road on a blind corner, three cyclists in a convoy of cars, one of whom was sitting up taking off his jacket while coming around a corner with a car close on his wheel, and of course what had become almost commonplace, suddenly meeting a bus swinging wide on a tight corner into our lane. But once again, the bus and our FIAT Punto were able to come to a stop just in time. I quickly backed up and the bus went on—no harm, no foul. Anticipating more such encounters in southern Italy, I had again requested a FIAT 500, a smaller car, for even more control and maneuverability to negotiate the donkey trails we were expecting in the land that even Christ had not visited.

"*Buongiorno,*" I said as I entered the Hertz office.

"No Cinquecento," the young man behind the counter said. It was Matteo, who had helped us our previous visit. He obviously remembered us.

"Okay, we will keep the Punto. It is a good car. We will return it full in Rome—we couldn't find a gas station."

"No problem. Is same car," Matteo said.

"So we won't get charged, right?" I asked.

"No fuel charge. You return car in Roma full. No problem."

"*Va bene,*" I said.

"You prefer to prepay the gasoline? If not full you not have to pay the extra charge for the service."

"Let's do that. I don't have to worry about finding a gas station when I'm worrying about getting to the airport on time. Right?"

"Yes."

"Can I return it empty?"

"As you wish. You will not be charged. You already paid for full tank," Matteo said.

"*Una questione?*"

"*Sì,*" he said.

"If we decided to keep this car longer, would I be able to extend the contract over the phone?" Mardi and I were still not in agreement about when our journey of a lifetime was going to end. She was ready to get back to her former life. I was ready to continue this life.

"If possible, you call in Salerno, or in Rome, no problem."

"*Grazie,* bye-bye," I said, relieved that we could continue allowing our pinball to bounce where it would.

"*Ciao,*" Matteo said.

The exchange had been short, succinct, and efficient. We had communicated in English and Italian. Many times I go into such an encounter vowing that I will rely fully on Italian, but when I encounter a situation in which a misunderstanding may cost me a lot of money I revert to English. That is what I had done with Matteo. It also had worked better for him. He was more confident in his command of English than I was in my comprehension of Italian.

A tinge of excitement swept over me as I looked at our car sitting in the circular drive of the train station. That silver Punto had already carried us to adventures we had not even dared to dream about, and now we were going to settle into it again and experience Italy unfettered. I felt as I did when I had set out from Chiusi a half dozen years ago on my bicycle to explore Tuscany. But this time Mardi would be with me. I knew I'd miss some of the intimacy of traveling about by bicycle, but the joy of traveling with Mardi would more than offset that loss. I hoped that whenever possible we'd get out of the car and walk so that we would once again be vulnerable to the people of Italy—open to the lives they live—just as I was on my bicycle. We were using the car for point-to-point travel, but once we arrived at each destination we planned to park and walk the streets of the villages—we hoped we had more *Jessicas* and *Maximilianos* to meet.

Before I made my first trip to Italy I was convinced that the country was full of interesting people—E. M. Forster had alerted me to that fact when he wrote that I should *love and understand the Italians, for the people are more marvelous than the land.* Having sojourned in Italy, I now claim that truth for myself. When I think of Italy I remember the beauty of her land and her cities, but the people of Italy draw me back year after year. I do not discount the food of Italy as an attraction, but the warm feelings in my heart for this boot-shaped country are born of my love for the people whose faces I see when I give my memory free rein. Their faces may be framed by stunning landscapes, but the eyes of the Italian people light up the collage of memories that spring forth when I think of this unique country. I have had the good fortune to travel a bit in this world but I have yet to encounter a country that tugs at my heart with such passion as does Italy.

As I was thinking these thoughts and programming my GPS for Accettura and the adventure that surely awaited us, a modestly dressed middle-aged man approached our car and asked for change. We said we had none, but something about his reaction made us reconsider. We told him that if he could wait a moment we would see if we had any coins in our suitcases. We rummaged around and placed a sizable collection into his open hand—the total was well north of ten euros, possibly twenty or more, if, as I suspected, many of them were two euro coins. He thanked us gratefully. In *italiano* he asked where we were from. I told him that we were *americanos* and his face lit up. We asked where he was from and were surprised to find out that he was from the Ukraine. He told us he had left because of the fighting, the death, and the destruction. He was very surprised when we mentioned we had a Ukrainian connection—a niece and a nephew who had been adopted from a Ukrainian family. We talked for several minutes, feeling the pain that reverberates through a nation and the world when war breaks out. We wished him well. I hoped that we had brightened his day as much as he had brightened ours with his positive attitude in the face of so much tragedy.

I returned to the task of programming Accettura into the GPS. Once we had a travel time of two and a half hours instead of a half day I began the process of getting out of what had become a very tight spot—cars had hemmed us in front and back. I noticed in my rearview mirror the hands of someone letting me know I could back a little farther—our Ukrainian friend had hung around to help. As we pulled into the traffic circle I stuck my arm out the window and gave him a hearty wave.

"*Buon viaggio,*" he yelled across the *piazza*, making his voice heard above the noise of the traffic.

"*Ciao,*" I yelled back, choosing the *servant* pledge to the *goodbye* call, because he had just served us—but *God Be with You*, which is the original meaning of *goodbye*, would have been just as appropriate as the pledge to be one another's servant, which was the original meaning of *ciao*.

Our journey to the Godforsaken land of Basilicata was off to a good start—an angel in the form of a Ukrainian immigrant was looking out for us. We were able to get out of Salerno without a hitch. We followed the same route as on our previous journey, but this time I didn't exit the roundabout too soon—and just like that we were speeding along the *Autostrada* as though we were locals. I didn't, however, feel like a local when we stopped to get gas; I quickly missed the convenience of traveling with Sergio. An attendant came to explain how things worked—in Italian. The pump's card reader demanded a pin number, but never having needed a pin before with this card I had no idea what it was. I told him I'd switch to cash, and he left me to go help another motorist. It didn't take long before I needed help again. The machine wouldn't accept my money. I looked toward the attendant.

"*Scusi, aiuto, venti euro,*" I called out.

He came over, took my twenty, inserted it, punched the buttons in a sequence that would have taken me a couple of minutes to figure out, and just like that a twenty euro countdown registered. "It will be better to spend the money in Accettura," I explained to Mardi when she asked me why I had not topped off the tank using a credit card. She also had found herself confounded by a machine. Another attendant came to her rescue, punching the right buttons in the right order, and *ecco,* she had *un espresso per lei, e una cioccolata calda per me.*

With enough fuel in the Punto to get to Accettura, we programmed an intermediate stop in Castelmezzano. We had seen the town from Pietrapertosa and were intrigued by its mountaintop location. Before I had finished my hot chocolate we were surrounded by jagged peaks.

"This so beautiful. Let's park the car, walk up on top of a hill, lie down, and just look at all this," Mardi suggested.

It seemed like a good time to ask, "Sure you don't want to stay another two weeks?"

She liked the idea of returning to Accettura, spending more time with Cesare and his friends, and eating the pizza he had raved about, but she wasn't ready to agree to two more weeks. She was, however, willing to allow our pinball to be flung, especially if it were flung in the mountains.

"The next wide spot in the road, we're parking," I said.

We were climbing fast, switchback after tight switchback—the kind of road that demands your full attention.

"Looks like we could drive right off here," I said. "Nothing to stop us."

"Oh, don't say that. It's a long way down," Mardi said, peering over the edge.

I rolled the windows down to feel the crisp air. Two hairpin turns later a spot just wide enough to accommodate our little Punto appeared. I pulled off the road and stopped.

"Look at the eagle soaring out there," she said as I pulled tight on the parking brake.

We were in a glorious spot—a place so beautiful it was beyond imagining. Again it was a combination of the creation of God and the creation of man. The villages of Pietrapertosa and Castelmezzano, linked by a cable, are also linked by the unlikeliness of their existence—clinging to the sides of massive uplifted rock formations without a level plot of land within miles. Who decided to build even one house in such a remote and inhospitable location, much less two villages? Only monasteries should exist in such dramatic, inaccessible spots—yet here were two of *The Most Beautiful Villages of Italy* within sight of each other.

An old FIAT Cinquecento drove by pulling me out of my reverie, but the sound of its little engine was soon absorbed by the mountain and we were within seconds surrounded by silence.

"You know, we are so much alike. We like the same things. We even think the same things. It's so unusual," Mardi said.

She was right. This impromptu picnic at the side of the road was so like us. Crisp air, soaring eagles and hawks, sheep and goats grazing in the distance, and warm sunshine on our shoulders were giving us another perfect day. My perfect days invariably come in the mountains—days when everything is just right—sunlight, temperature, wind, humidity and the feeling that life could not get any better. The feeling lingered as we drove the last few kilometers to Castelmezzano.

"This is the most fun I've ever had driving. This is a blast," I said.

"More fun than the Amalfi Coast?" Mardi asked, obviously surprised.

"You're right. It's a toss-up. A supercharged FIAT 500 would be fun on this road. Look at how smooth it is."

"You're probably thinking what a beautiful road this would be to bike on."

"Actually I wasn't. But now that you've reminded me, I am."

We entered a tunnel, and when we emerged we were in Castelmezzano. The first spot large enough for our Punto, I squeezed in, even though I wasn't sure it was meant for parking. It was on a very steep hill between a nondescript Hyundai and a mountain goat of a four-wheel-drive workhorse pickup. The Hyundai could have been a rental, but the 4-by-4 looked as if it had lived its whole life—a very long life—in these mountains, so I was quite certain no parking ticket would be waiting for us when we returned from exploring Castelmezzano. I fell out of the car when I opened the door, but Mardi was on the uphill side. I had to pull her from her seat.

"Hear those roosters?" I asked as we looked around trying to decide which way to walk in this town that seemed more fanciful than practical—but then that's why I love Italy. We wondered again, *What kind of people build homes in a place like this?* We were about to find out.

The town was inspiring lots of rhetorical questions. Mardi blurted out, "Oh my gosh. Whose idea was that?" when we walked beneath the zipline and got a feel for what a thrill it would be to ride from one improbable town to another.

Funny thing, though, that question was answered for us less than a year later at the Italian Film Fest in Milwaukee. But that's a story for another day.

"Oh, look, those steps go all the way up there," Mardi said, and pointed to the very top of the what looked like a boulder, but was more like the size of a mountain.

"Did you notice that man stop by that shrine and make the sign of the cross?" I asked.

Our curiosity was working in overdrive. The town was a smorgasbord for the eyes—so many sights that until a few moments ago seemed unimaginable—houses clinging to rocks in ways that seemed even more fanciful than those on the Amalfi Coast on the scale of improbability. The people were small-town friendly. By the time we paused in a little *piazza* to decide where to get a *cappuccino*, we had been greeted a half dozen times. A man who appeared to be about fifty walked by and said *Buongiorno*. When Mardi returned his greeting he stopped to talk.

Door slam, is what it sounded like he said to us, but that came close to no words I knew in Italian.

"*Non capisco,*" I said.

In response he said, *O lan,* which also meant nothing to me, but I answered *No* because his body language seemed to indicate that he was trying to guess where we were from. His next response confirmed my suspicions. "France?" he asked.

"No," I said with conviction and a slight French accent. Once I had the rules figured out, we both began enjoying the game.

"Eengleesh?" he guessed.

"No," I said with an English accent and much conviction. He contorted his face in disappointment. He had been certain he had guessed correctly. I was sure he'd guess *American* next, but he said nothing, so after a beat too long I said, "*Americani.*"

"*Americani,*" he repeated and then added, "*Fratello mio—Vair-geen-ia—quattro ristorante.*"

"*Sei stato a Virginia?*" I asked him.

He responded Richmond, apparently not comprehending that I had asked him if he had been to Virginia—or maybe he had been to Richmond, but I think he was telling me where his brother lived.

"*Andato molto tempo fa?*" I asked, hoping that the words I had chosen meant something like *How long ago did he go?*

"*Trent'anni,*" he responded with some resignation.

"*Sei rimasto in italia*—you stayed in Italy?" I asked.

But I don't think he understood what I was asking, or maybe he considered the answer so obvious that it was not worth responding to. I had hoped to engage him in a conversation that might touch on the subject of why he stayed and why his brother left and whether either of them regretted or particularly celebrated their decision. But my Italian would have been severely tested, and his knowledge of English seemed nonexistent.

He offered me a cigarette.

"*No, grazie*," I said.

"*No fumo?*" he said.

"Neither of us smoke," I answered, and not wanting to appear ungrateful for his generosity I added "*Bella*," indicating with a sweep of my hand the view of the town and the mountains surrounding us.

He nodded but seemed content to enjoy his cigarette. He made no attempt to engage us further in conversation, so we said *Arrivederci* and continued searching for a café. He tipped his hat toward us and turned to look back at the view I'm certain he'd been enjoying since his childhood.

"I'm surprised that he guessed so many countries yet didn't try America," I said as we continued up the ancient street.

"Maybe not many American tourists come up here."

A bit farther up the hill we saw a small church and stepped inside. As always we were overwhelmed by the beauty of the chapel and the paintings.

"Do you think these are originals?" I whispered to Mardi.

From somewhere in the darkened interior we heard, "Shut up, please ah."

We peered into the darkness but saw no one in the pews or at the altar. We didn't stay long, not wanting to disturb whoever was in the church any more than we already had. As we stepped from the church a single bell chimed.

The town was not devoid of people, but they were clustered near cafés and shops except for one man cutting trim with a table saw. The pace of the town was relaxed, as though the *pausa* had begun for many folks but not for all. Fearing that we would not likely find another, we stepped into the next café we saw. Everyone turned to greet us. My initial reaction that this was a friendly town was getting strong confirmation.

"*Buonasera*," the barkeep said.

"*Buonasera*," I responded even though it seemed much too early to be speaking of evening.

While he made our *cappuccinos* we settled in at the bar. I sensed that Mardi was miffed about something. I guessed it was that she wanted to be outside. The place was kind of dark, but I liked the feeling of being where the town gathered—a lot of people were in the café. We slid into a pleasant conversation with the barkeep, whose name was Domenico. He gave us a brief introduction to the town's major attraction.

"Have you flown?" I asked.

"Yes, seven flights," he said quite proudly. He went on to tell us that trekking was popular, that it was a two-hour hike to Pietrapertosa, or a quick flight via the angel's wings. We spent a delightful half hour learning the history of the town. I am always heartened by the pleasure Italians take not only in pleasing their customers, but in sharing their lives.

"What do you want to do now?" Mardi asked.

"I'd like to just wander. Didn't Domenico say this town is over two thousand years old?"

The town certainly felt ancient. It felt like no other town, even though it was close to Pietrapertosa. It was situated among upturned gigantic stones as though God wanted to show off his creativity. And man, spurred on by God's genius, decided to build homes on them just for fun. At least that's how it appeared to me, but research revealed that this location had been chosen for the same reason villages in many parts of Italy are at the very top of hills and mountains—for security against invaders. Townspeople rolled stones down these boulders to repel attackers. Necessity created beauty.

"*Buongiorno,*" I said to an older gentleman who was walking slowly up one of Castlemezzano's beautiful streets weighted down by grocery sacks in each hand. We were in a section of town where a Vespa could still travel, but the roads were too narrow for cars—even a FIAT 500.

"*Buongiorno,*" his voice sang out.

"*Bella giornata,*" I added, for it truly was a beautiful day.

"*Bella,*" he said as I passed him. I'm not sure why I didn't slow down and chat with him as we walked. He had the face of a man who had led a good life, whose story I would have loved to hear. We might even have offered to carry his load for a while.

"How are your legs?" I said to Mardi when she caught up to me a few minutes later. I was photographing the beautiful valley stretched out below the town. We both felt good. We had done little walking since renting the car, so we kept climbing toward what seemed to be the top of the town.

We occasionally met a resident of Castelmezzano. But we saw not one tourist. We were no longer walking on anything that could be called a street. We were climbing stairs that clung to the sides of buildings or were dug into the boulders, and they were carrying us straight up. We climbed so high that we reached a spot where the only thing above us was the top of a huge upthrust boulder. We found a wall to sit on to enjoy the sandwich we'd been carrying. As we took in the glorious beauty from our picnic site we looked more closely at our immediate surroundings and realized that the building next to us was abandoned. It was a home that should come with a burro, for only on the back of a very strong person or a beast of burden would it be possible to carry to this lofty perch the necessities of living—but someone in the not too distant past had done it. The view was out of this world, but so was the effort required to get to it. I wondered who had last lived in this house—and why. It would be a good story but one that I am not yet able to tell. Such stories keep me going back to Italy year after year. Italy is filled with tales that capture the imagination, often because, like Castelmezzano itself, they are so improbable.

"I bet we could buy this place really cheap," I said.

"It would be fun to co-own a house with an Italian."

That was the last thing I expected Mardi to say. I didn't think she would ever consider buying a house that required so much effort just to get to, but then Italy works its magic on a person and somehow the impossible seems not only possible but extremely desirable. We would certainly keep fit living in a home this high above the village.

"I felt a raindrop," she said.

"What is that big red thing out there?" I asked, choosing to ignore the rain clouds building in the near distance. At the moment they were beautiful, not threatening.

"Those are like the balls you see around airports. I bet they mark the zip lines."

I had to laugh at myself. As a pilot I should have known exactly what they were and why they appeared to be floating in the valley. Mardi was right—they were suspended there to keep pilots from flying into the zipline cables stretching between Castelmezzano and Pietrapertosa on the other side of the valley.

"This is romantic. Sitting in the rain having lunch," I said. What had been beautiful, moments before, was now getting us wet.

"I could stay here all day and night." She was falling deep under the spell of Italy's powerful allure. We had earned our way to this moment by climbing every step, and now the place seemed like ours because of the effort. I was beginning to think she'd soon suggest that we head back down and find a real estate agent. She was glowing—no longer noticing that the raindrops were getting fairly large. The sound of a single rooster crowing echoed across the valley. Thunder rumbled in the distance.

"Aren't those beautiful sounds in the mountains?" I said.

"Oh, yes," she replied dreamily. The sounds had obviously taken her somewhere.

"Does it remind you of our days in Greece?" I asked.

"Yes, but it also reminds me of food and farming." She was surprising me again. She had not liked living on our farm in Wisconsin, but maybe it was too isolated. We could see lots of farms below us and they were very close together. Farming in Italy is not isolated. The towns are closer together as well, often within walking distance of each other. Vittorio walks to his farm. We had a ten-mile drive to town from our farm.

Neither one of us wanted to leave that place or that moment, but the big drops were reminding us that we could get drenched. Mardi left first, but she didn't take her purse—the little one that holds her phone. I picked it up and after a few moments caught up to her.

"I think you subconsciously wanted a reason to go back up there," I said as I handed her the purse. She smiled but admitted nothing.

As we worked our way down the mountain we noticed bottles sitting in the doorways. We presumed they were for milk. We liked what that said about the town.

"*Buongiorno,*" a man said to us, breaking stride. He was walking up the hill. We were back in the part of town where the streets were almost wide enough for a Cinquecento, but there were none; not even a Vespa could be heard anywhere in town. Only that rooster.

I didn't make the same mistake this time. I stopped to chat.

The subject of the Volo dell'Angelo soon came up and I discovered that this man had flown across the valley five times. He was very proud. I would not have guessed that he would have done it even once. He was in his fifties or sixties, dressed very traditionally, and didn't strike me as particularly athletic or a thrill seeker.

We introduced ourselves.

"Giovanni," he said.

"*Piacere,*" I said.

"*Mia figlia vende i biglietti per Volo dell'Angelo.*"

"His daughter sells the tickets for the flight," I translated for Mardi.

He was eager for the season to begin—he intended to fly again. He told us the flights were helping a lot of families, including his own. He wanted to know why we were there.

"We are going to Accettura," I said.

"*Paese qui?*"

"*Si,*" I answered even though I wasn't sure what he meant by what I translated as *country here*. *Paese* can also mean village and region. But his body language told me that his question required a positive response.

"*Ritorno*," Giovanni implored, suggesting that we would be very welcome—and then he named all the months from May through October, by which I understood that if we returned in any of those six months we would be able to fly from Castelmezzano to Pietrapertosa.

"*Vai a lavorare*," Giovanni said and added, "*Buona giornata.*"

"*Buona giornata*," I said. And then to Mardi, "He's going to work."

He didn't say what kind of work he did, but I guessed construction. As he walked away I noticed hand protectors—modified gloves—hanging from his belt.

"I can't believe how friendly the people are," I said. I also continued to be amazed at the town's beauty—not just the view from its streets but what it looked like up close as well. "Look at this mailbox. The wood has a gorgeous finish—like a wooden boat." Pride of ownership was evident everywhere on the exteriors of homes. A flower box adorned almost every one, and the paint schemes were delightfully bright.

As we wandered back to the heart of town we passed by the table where earlier we had seen two men playing *scopa* while a third watched. But the three chairs were empty now. The light was better, but the picture was not as good because the men were gone. We continued walking and photographing until we got to the *piazza*. It was empty. We stopped to fill our water bottles.

"Next time— *la prossima volta*," I said, glancing up at the curve of the cable.

"That would be scary," Mardi replied.

"But let's do it—it would be fun," I said, convinced by our conversation with Giovanni that the flight would be the adrenaline rush of a lifetime as well as a story to tell again and again.

We continued walking toward the lower part of Castelmezzano, where we had parked our car. The town was still silent except for the singing of birds and the sound of a tractor working in a field far across the valley. We walked a little farther and the sound of the tractor faded—in the mountains sounds travel along strange paths. We still occasionally heard the rooster, along with a few grackles, but their songs were not very melodious.

"*Scusi, parla inglese?*" I said to a young man walking toward a motorcycle.

"*No,*" he answered.

"*Strada per Pietrapertosa?*"

"*Si,*" he responded.

"*Scendere qui?*" I asked, pointing to what looked like an impossibly steep descent to get to the road leading to the tunnel we could see across the valley— the tunnel that we presumed would take us on a shortcut to Pietrapertosa.

"*Si,*" he said, and then as we were walking away he said, "*Tranquillo,*" which implied that we would encounter few other cars on the road to Pietrapertosa.

"*Piano, piano,*" I said in response.

"*Macchina o piedi?*" he asked.

When I answered "*Macchina,*" he motioned for me to follow him. He led me to a precipice and pointed down to show me where to drive. The road looked even more formidable from this vantage point, but the look on his face told me that we would do fine. Without his calm assurance, I am sure I would have looked for another route to the tunnel, a route that may not exist, thus assuring that the road to Pietrapertosa remains tranquil, for I'm sure few tourists have the nerve to venture on this road without some encouragement.

We left Castelmezzano on that ridiculously steep road vowing to return to be among these friendly people and to fly on angels' wings to Pietrapertosa. We discovered that getting to Pietrapertosa from Castelmezzano is an experience no matter how you go about it. The drive was an adrenaline rush—a serpentine road with huge drop-offs. But much of the road was bounded on both sides by walls of native stone, beautifully laid, adding to the magnificence of the drive. I suppose if you've driven it all your life the drive could be considered *tranquillo*. We met only five cars in the fifteen minutes it took to drive to Pietrapertosa. If we had, as Domenico suggested, tried to do it in ten minutes, it would have been anything but tranquil. Even at fifteen minutes Mardi did not find it relaxing—if for no other reason than around almost every bend in the road there was another *O My God*. God must have been in a playful mood when He created this terrain—strange formations of massive boulders jut out of the mountaintops pointing every which way. The result is fun, dramatic, and extremely beautiful. During much of the journey we could see the zipline cables stretching across the valley high above us. It was not hard to imagine how spectacular it would be to see this bizarre landscape from above while hurtling through the air at seventy miles per hour—on the wings of eagles and angels indeed.

"I love you, baby," I said, feeling the power of the moment as we joined the main road and negotiated the last turns to Pietrapertosa and parked in the same parking place we had chosen a week earlier—an overlook with a spectacular view of the wide valley of checkerboard fields and vineyards.

"Arrived at Pietrapertosa," Dorothy droned, although she pronounced it *Peter Pertosa*.

We stepped from the car, took a deep breath of the cool, refreshing air, and looked around. It was just as stunning as it had been the first time, and just as on our first visit, the restaurant across the way was still being renovated. A woman wearing an apron was leaning from her balcony watching the workmen.

"We don't have to stay," Mardi said.

"We've been here and done this before, haven't we?" I said sensing that we were both eager to get to Accettura to surprise Cesare. "I'll take one picture just to prove we've been here today." I chose to take it of Mardi—of the smile on her face as she contemplated the beauty surrounding us. She was in her element. I was certain that Pietrapertosa would have treated us to another special day just as it had the last time, but we were into shortcuts, and our hearts were into Accettura, so we were soon back in the car taking another backroad ignoring the pleas of Dorothy for us to *make a U-turn,* sounding as though we were about to drive off the side of the mountain.

Sergio's assertion that driving south from Salerno felt like traveling back two hundred years certainly applied to our route from Pietrapertosa. Alongside the road, which was now more like a path, we saw a horse-drawn cart with wheels that must have been at least six feet tall. A mare and her foal were grazing nearby and a donkey just beyond. When I got out to take a photo, a very big dog suddenly appeared and encouraged me to get back into the car. He was quite successful.

"Nothing ever happens up here—what's going on?" Mardi said in her best big-dog voice. I was convinced the dog was saying something considerably more menacing.

A bit farther down the lane I took a shot of some beautiful horses in a wide-open spring green meadow. The scene was idyllic. This time no dog spoke to me and I got a great photo.

"Oh this is just perfect, I love it," I said to Mardi, who had just returned to the car from a short walk. The woods were having an effect on both of us. The calmness was overwhelming me, as though nothing could ever disturb the peace of the place. We reluctantly got into the car and began driving again but didn't get very far. A spring tempted me. I stopped to fill our water bottles. Fountains in the cities—springs in the rural areas—what a delightful country.

We heard cowbells and walked up the road to find the source of the lovely sound. The bells were attached to the huge cows that make up the team that drags the tree to Accettura for the festival Cesare and I had been trying to convince Mardi that we need to stay for. This scene was even more idyllic than the last—upwards of one hundred cows were contentedly grazing on lush green grass in open meadows or beneath canopies of shade trees scattered throughout the pasture. Could these animals possibly know what good lives they lead?

Huge Maremma dogs were standing guard watching for anything that might harm their charges. I photographed the beautiful scene from a safe distance. A Maremma may look lovable and playful, a white teddy bear of a dog, but each one is trained to keep wolves, people, and anything that might harm those gorgeous white cows, far away.

Were it not for the fear of disturbing the dogs, we would gladly have thrown down a picnic blanket and watched those magnificent animals grazing for another hour or two, but we thought we might be perceived as a threat, so under the dogs' watchful gaze, we made our way back to the car and drove slowly away. After a few miles the road once again became a lane, and we passed through a farmyard, so close to the house and the barn that I got a good shot of a strutting rooster without even leaving the car.

We had seen only two cars since leaving Pietrapertosa and the same number of people walking. We'd seen far more dogs, cows, horses, roosters, and my favorite, donkeys. I don't know why I like the donkeys so much—it must be because they are so unglamorous. People have donkeys not for show or for pleasure, but for work.

I stopped again to photograph the beauty of the late afternoon light falling on the spring green carpet of grass bordered by lush trees and a well-made fence. The feeling in that meadow connected me to my childhood through beauty and silence teamed with a light breeze. The verdant forest looked nothing like the stark, monochromatic plains I learned to love as a child, but the feeling was the same—the silence, the warmth of the sun beating back the chill of the air, and the knowledge that there must be no person within ten miles touched me to my very soul.

Anticipation tinted the photographs I took that afternoon. What kind of people must this landscape be growing. I know the kind of people the isolated landscape of western Nebraska grew. I wondered if I would feel that same connection to the people of Lucania, the ancient name for this region. Carlo Levi made me believe that I understood them—that they were like the people I had grown up among in the middle of the twentieth century in the middle of America. I was convinced I would be able to relate to the isolation they felt and the poverty they endured. I was certain that this land I was growing to love because of its starkness was raising the same kind of people who raised me more than a half century ago.

That state of mind accompanied me the final few miles into Accettura. I felt as if I was returning home, which is rather bizarre considering that I had spent only one night in Accettura and less than twenty-four hours wandering its streets. I knew nobody well, only a few people by sight, and even fewer by name. But sometimes you just have a feeling about a person or a place. That's one reason I'm so partial to the word *mystery*—there are so many things about the lives we lead that do not have a rational explanation, yet our gut, our faith, our experience tell us are true nevertheless. I had few rational reasons for my feelings about Accettura, but to say that I felt connected to that town would have missed the full truth by many powers of ten.

A few miles after the serene meadow we came to a T-intersection and turned onto the main road to Accettura. Traffic, such as it was, picked up immediately. I was still in a tranquil mood, so when an Audi appeared in my rearview mirror I pulled over to let it pass and received a short beep of appreciation.

But watching the Audi driver's line through the corners inspired me, and soon we were flying through the forest, testing the FIAT's road handling capabilities against those of the much more expensive Audi A8. I wasn't right on his tail, but I kept the Audi in sight. I loved the feeling of driving a car designed to handle a road such as this. I began imagining a future when I knew the roads surrounding Accettura as well as I know the roads of southeastern Wisconsin—biking thousands of miles on sinuous and sensuous Italian roads every year—and if I were riding an Italian bike, so much the better.

The road was smooth, wide by Italian standards—plenty of room for two cars to pass safely—and was beautiful as well, with stone walls lining the roadway. Mardi was surprising me. She seemed to be enjoying the drive almost as much as I was. The forest soon gave way to a barren ridge, and we began catching glimpses of a rather lonely-looking town in the distance as we swept through turn after turn. The traffic that we thought might pick up didn't. It was just the Audi and us on a low-altitude flight along the ridgetop. We flew by recently constructed apartment complexes and landed in old Accettura, inching along narrow streets, stopping to let a car pass, and a half block later winding slowly around a gathering of men talking in the street. And just like that, we were passing by the little grocery store where we had parked the first time we had come to town.

"Do you want to drive around a little first?" Mardi asked.

"I want to go straight to the hotel."

Straight to the hotel meant negotiating the equivalent of only three city blocks, but we passed by dozens of people already on the streets and in the *piazza*. The *passeggiata* had begun. We drove up the narrow street past the table where we had first met Cesare, the evening we interrupted his game of *scopa*.

"Argh—someone is in our parking space," I groaned.

Fortunately the space next to it was open. I pulled in, hopped out of the car, and walked into the hotel, hoping to find Cesare working. He looked up from his computer, chuckled, and said "ALLO!"—then did a huge double take when he realized he shouldn't be seeing me.

"What are you doing still here?" he asked, his face registering his shock.

"We're not still here. We came back."

"You came back, just to taste the pizza?"

"Just to taste the pizza."

"I don't believe it."

"You don't?"

"It means we treated you so well you couldn't stay away."

"You treated us so well *Mardi* wanted to come back."

"Welcome. Can I offer you a coffee?"

"Well, first, we want to know where to park—someone has a car in our parking place."

"I'll get my car out of the way and you put your car back in its spot."

Cesare was still looking at me as though he couldn't believe I was in his lobby.

"We left a book here. We had to come back and get it."

"Here it is. I just read it today and said *Who left this book 'ere?*" He smiled and winked. "You're good, my friend, you're good—very clever."

"You're on to me. Don't tell Mardi." I was playing along with him. Leaving the book had nothing to do with my cleverness—Mardi had just overlooked it when she checked the room while I was paying the bill.

"Obviously you're going to spend the night with us?"

"Yep. If you'll have us?"

"Of course," he said as we went out to move the cars. He greeted Mardi and said in his heavy accent, "*Ee moast be so good ta convince ya ta coam back.*"

Mardi could have given me credit for my persuasive skills, but she didn't.

"I wanted to come back," she said.

"You're thinking of moving to Italy, aren't you?" Cesare said, winking at me.

"Well, if we can make money here, it's okay with me," Mardi said.

"I think you should say bye to America then," he said.

"We absolutely love it here. Like I said, I'm trying to learn *italiano.*"

Cesare immediately began speaking in Italian. "*Adesso io parli italiano porterà bene.*" He assured us that the only way we were going to learn to speak Italian well was if he, and everyone else, began talking to us in Italian.

"I was telling Mardi the other day that when we get back home we should try to communicate with each other in Italian."

"That's right," he said.

"It will be frustrating for you if you speak to us totally in Italian, but I really appreciate it when you do," I said.

"It's not a problem. Actually, I've got more problems speaking English to Italians."

We all laughed even though I wasn't sure what he meant. However, his delivery of the punch line was superb, and funny. He immediately broke his pledge, though, and told us in English, "Just so you know, we have pizza available, but tonight is Friday. In Italy it's fish night." He kissed his fingers. "Our chef is number one—he's a very good chef, and I'm not just saying that because he works here—he is a *very* good chef."

"So, how have you guys been?" I asked.

"We have a party tomorrow night, we've got about thirty people…"

"Do you have room for us?" Mardi asked.

"It is not a problem. I will make room for you. I can't put you in the same room. It's taken, but I can put you in a bigger room, is that okay?"

"Wherever you want to put us," she said.

"Here's the *espresso* for you."

"*Ah. Grazie,*" I said.

"This is the time we use coffee—to wake up," he said.

"I'm moving here," Mardi said. "This is good coffee."

"She likes it here," I said, then corrected myself. "She loves it here."

"I love the mountains," she said.

"*You 'aven't seen noothing yet,*" Cesare said dropping his voice again into his heavy British accent.

"We have more to see?" I asked.

"The best is yet to *coam*," he said.

"We've had a beautiful drive. We took the high ridge from Pietrapertosa to here."

"You've got to try that flight, the *Volo dell'Angelo*," he said.

Mardi surprised me by sharing with Cesare the story of Jessica's plea, *Why you go to Accettura?*

"Accettura has got lots of lovely scenery—did you say that to her?"

We told him that we had told her how beautiful it was, but we didn't tell him about Jessica's concern that we had only one friend in Accettura. We did explain that she thought there was nothing to see, nothing to do.

"No one knows about Basilicata—it's a region to discover. We've got lovely places here—lovely foods—some of the best in Italy. We use our own products."

"But if you pushed the trekking idea," Mardi said.

"My brother lives in Nottingham, and I said to him, *Look, we've got this hotel*"…and then Cesare's countenance softened and he began speaking very quietly…"I want to speak—you're like my parents—can I speak to you like that?"

"Oh, yes," we said simultaneously and leaned in to hear him better.

"I want to push it that way because I think that the only way to make sure this hotel works is to fill the rooms with…" and he paused before he said, "…trekkers. That's what I told my brother back in Nottingham, and I still believe it."

Mardi nodded enthusiastically.

"Because what can you offer? We've got scenery and we've got peace. People pay for peace," he said with conviction.

"That's true," I said remembering the feeling of contentment that had swept over me as I sought the perfect light and angle to capture the beauty of the meadow.

"Because people are sick of living in cities, they want to relax. Our problem is encouraging people to stay 'ere, eat 'ere, sleep 'ere."

Mardi mentioned Pietrapertosa and the vibrancy of trekking in that area. I latched onto that idea and also took Cesare up on his pledge to speak to us in Italian. "*Camminare a Pietrapertosa. Per quanto?*"

But he wasn't ready for my switch.

"*Due ora?*" I asked.

"To get there? Not even that."

"*No. Piedi.*"

"*Piedi?* Yes. Maybe two hours, but by car thirty-five or forty minutes—the back way you came." He concluded in Italian, "*Quaranta minuti macchina— due ora cammino.*"

"Two hours of trekking through beautiful forests to the Angel Flight. That seems perfect," I said. "People would love to come and do that."

"This is our third week—we're trying to push all this, so the more help we get the better."

"We'll try to do our part. We love it," Mardi said.

"Can't wait to see your other hotel," I added.

"Hotel Croccia? It's not ready yet but I will take you later—it's lovely, it's beautiful."

"High ceilings, big rooms?" I asked.

"You're not from the finance bureau, are you? Are you just pretending you can't speak Italian?" Cesare quipped but I didn't understand where he was going with it.

"I'm trying to get some Italian DNA to rub off on me," I said.

"Are you a copper, checking me out—what I've got, what I 'aven't got, what I'm declaring, and what I'm not? You know the Italian way of doing things, they're very strict…"

"How did the police get into the conversation?" I asked.

"You're not in disguise are you? It's too nice to be true, you coming back— you know what I'm saying?"

We laughed. We liked that Cesare was so touched that he was joking about the reason we came back.

"Are you in a rush to get sorted, because I want to pick my kids up from school, take 'em home, and I'll come back."

"Not at all. We're on Italian time—*tempo italiano.*"

"We're going for a walk," Mardi said.

"Okay, if you take a walk now, and then come back in about an hour, I'll be 'ere for you, and I'll sort a room out for you. Is that okay?" he said popping in and out of his heavy Nottingham accent.

"Whenever you show up will be fine," I said.

"No. I'll be here for you. Otherwise Domenico will be here, but he won't understand a word of English."

"The look on your face was priceless…" I said.

"When I saw you walk in?"

"Yes."

"Lovely. It means a lot to me. It means that we're doing something good."

"Yes. Yes, you are. You're definitely doing something good."

"You're doing something very good," Mardi confirmed.

Cesare led us out the door. "I don't know what room to put you in. I wish I could put you back where you were..."

"Don't worry about it. You go take care of your kids," I said.

Cesare hopped in his car. We watched him drive down the street. We were both smiling.

"That was delightful," I said.

Mardi began laughing, thinking back on the fast-moving pinball conversation we'd just enjoyed.

"I love him," I said and began replaying in my mind the highlights of the last thirty minutes. "I love his passion, his energy." The memory felt like *déjà vu*—Cesare in so many ways reminded me of Pietro, the forty-year-old son of Aurora, whose wit had made my first journey in Italy so remarkable. Like Cesare, Pietro spoke English well, having learned it while he lived in Australia. Both had extremely quick minds and a wicked sense of humor. Even in appearance they were similar. Several times I almost called Cesare Pietro. Pietro had not consistently been the welcoming host Cesare was proving to be, but the memory of that one day of warmth he showed me is the memory of Pietro that persists—of Pietro toasting me as he praised me for the dry stone wall I had rebuilt for him. He was standing in front of the ancient wood-fired oven that he had fired up to prepare me *the best bruschetta you will ever eat.* That is how I remember Pietro, and I was quite certain that the lasting memory of Cesare I'd carry would be the look on his face as I walked through the hotel door and back into his life. It meant a lot to him to see us again, and it meant a lot to me to be welcomed so warmly.

"That was fun, but we can't afford to stay until the festival," Mardi said, apparently fearing that because of Cesare's warm welcome I'd try to figure out how to spend the next two weeks in Italy and come back to Accettura for the festival. She had detected that look I get on my face when I'm becoming convinced that *the stars are aligning—that we can't upset the order of the universe.*

"Do you think our suitcases would fit back there?" I asked. We were peering into the back of a Cinquecento.

"We wouldn't be able to take our bikes," Mardi said, worried that this was a prelude to buying a new car when we got back home to help me keep the memory of Italy alive.

"No. But we could learn to pack better—take less."

She didn't respond, apparently assuming that the best way to combat my impulsiveness was to ignore my enthusiasm.

"We need to start talking Italian to each other," I said. I wanted to keep alive the deep connection to Italy and Italian people I was feeling. As we walked toward the *piazza* people greeted us as though we were members of the community—tipping their hats or offering a sincere *Buonasera.*

"*Nonno e nonna e*... what is granddaughter?" Mardi asked. We were watching a grandfather and grandmother walking on either side of their granddaughter. I couldn't think of the word. We followed them across the street, sat on a low wall in the *piazza,* and began commenting to each other in fractured Italian about the quintessential Italian scene of the nightly *passeggiata* playing out before us. Spontaneous conversations sprang up all around. We were falling more deeply in love with the people of Accettura with every conversation we overheard. There could be no doubt, we had happened upon an extremely close-knit community. These people were bonded. We began thinking of how to spend our Saturday and realized we had no map of the area.

"*Scusi, avete una mappa di Accettura?*" I asked the first person I saw after walking through the door of the tourist office. They gave us a map as well as the news that we were the first tourists of the season. They were young volunteers, and we were giving them the opportunity to practice their spiel and their English, although one young man already seemed quite comfortable with our language.

"Yes, I know English well. My mother is from Nottingham."

"Oh, you must know Cesare," I said.

"He is my brother's mom," he said, but I'm sure he meant *He is my mom's brother.* "She works at the hotel."

"Oh, we've met your mom," I said.

We introduced ourselves. His name was Antonio. He introduced us to Angela and Enrica. We were meeting the ProLoco volunteers Cesare had mentioned who led treks in the area and acted as tour guides to local attractions.

"What is the word for *met?*" Mardi asked as we were leaving the tourist office. "We can tell Teresa that we met her son."

"*Abbiamo incontrato Antonio,*" I said.

The streets were filled almost to overflowing with people walking and talking, going someplace and noplace. Mardi paused to look in a shop window and I began taking photos and talking to people. I sat on a park bench near some kids playing soccer, their voices echoing off the monuments lining the main street. The friendliness of the town extended to the kids. They interrupted their game and gathered around me, wondering where I was from.

"I'm from America," I said.

"*Ah, Americano,*" said the bravest of the group. Before this trip, I had thought it would be necessary to work alongside Italians in order to get to know them. But I now see that Italians invite you to share their lives not because you have done something for them but just because it's what Italians do—who they are—Italians are hospitable. Mardi and I certainly felt that hospitality as we sat in the *piazza* taking in the evening ritual of seeing and being seen. They were sharing the events of the day and the nation not just with their neighbors but also with us simply because we were there. The connectedness in the community was a marvel to behold. Mardi rejoined me, and for a long time we sat watching the kids play soccer, feeling the pulse of the town beating from its heart—for that is precisely what an Italian *piazza* is—the very heart of the town.

Sitting in that *piazza*, we sensed a unique camaraderie among the people. We wondered if we might uncover some of secrets of the community if we did a little research. We walked into the town hall, saw a man stepping out of an office, and introduced ourselves. His name was Michele. He asked if we were English. Mardi must have been right—not many Americans visit this region. He wanted to know how long we would be in Accettura.

"We are staying four days, at Hotel Sangiuliano," I said.

"Why don't you stay a month?" he quickly responded.

"Did you hear that, Mardi?" I said, excited to have another ally in my quest to stay longer. I immediately liked him.

"*Mio figlio é lo chef,*" he proudly informed us.

"Your son is Francesco, the chef?"

The town, we were learning, was very interconnected. We also learned more of the history of the village and the festival. The fervor with which Michele talked about the festival made us think that we might have to look no further to uncover the secret of Accettura. He also took the time to show us the work of local artists hanging on the walls of the chamber rooms. It was a gracious introduction to the inner workings of this isolated, proud, close-knit, yet very friendly town. When we returned to the streets for the *passeggiata* we recognized a fair number of people—many by sight, some by name.

"Okay, who is that walking across the street?" I asked.

"That's Angela," Mardi said.

"And there's Antonio," I said.

We stopped to read a quotation that turned out to be by Carlo Levi. A small group of men noticed us and inquired if we were from England. We met Prospero, Giuseppe, and Domenico.

"Da quanto tempo sei stato qui?" They wanted to know how long we had been in Accettura. They were very surprised—even excited—to learn that we were returning for our second visit.

Prospero also suggested that we stay for a month. The pride the villagers have in the festival runs deep.

"How long you going to stay?" Domenico asked.

"Tre mesi," I said with a smile toward Mardi, knowing that our visas were good for three months.

They loved hearing that we liked Accettura so much that we would joke about staying so long. More men joined the conversation. One whose name I didn't catch said that he and his wife moved to America but found they missed Italy so much they moved back four years ago. I believed I knew why. They were lonely. Nowhere else have I felt such a strong sense of community. Not even in my hometown in the fifties did the camaraderie approach what Mardi and I felt on the streets of Accettura that evening.

Not wanting to let the feeling die I asked Mardi if she would mind if we watched the men play cards for a while. It was a journey back to childhood I wanted to take. My dad didn't play cards on the street as these men were, but many afternoons he would take a short break from his business to play pitch or rummy at the pool hall. I loved the conversations that accompanied those games. You could learn a lot about a man by the stories and jokes he shared while playing cards. We watched long enough to learn a bit about the men—our initial assessment still seemed sound—this was a very friendly town. But we didn't watch long enough to figure out the rules of the game.

When we got back to the hotel, Cesare was there to show us our room.

"Have you made friends yet?"

"We met the whole town," I said.

"This is the best village. Accettura means *accetta tutti,* so it means it accepts everybody." Then Cesare said the word slowly again for us, *Accettura,* helping us to absorb the meaning. "You look like a happy man, being back in Accettura," he said as he handed us the key to a room that once again afforded a fantastic view of the *piazza.*

The good fortune that I was feeling must have been evident for Cesare to see. Each day seemed to be topping the previous day. And now we were feeling loved by a whole town.

"I am amazed how friendly the people are. This is beyond my wildest dreams. What an adventure," I said to Mardi as we settled into our very large room. I felt the need to write about Accettura in longhand—words that would survive even if electricity didn't.

I grabbed my journal and walked onto the terrace. Mardi joined me. The sounds of the *piazza* surrounded us—the laughter, the whistles, the delight of the kids, the chatter of the townspeople. But as close as everyone sounded, I believed it would be possible to set up an office on that balcony and work creatively and productively, the sounds of the town mingling into a beautiful musical background—the symphony of a loving community. The sounds had worked their magic on me. I could eat every meal to the accompaniment of these people, to the harmony of their voices echoing off the ancient walls of this improbable hilltop town. I wondered if my feeling would change if I could understand every word that reached my ear. Would I then no longer consider it beautiful music?

As I settled into a comfortable chair a tractor drove down the street, reminding me of the town's connection to agriculture, yet another reason I felt so comfortable. Tractors drove down the main street of my hometown—in fact it was frequently me driving a tractor down the streets of my hometown. My dad sold tractors, and it was often my job to deliver them to the farmers.

What I was feeling about Accettura was taking me back to my state of mind when I first experienced the lure of Italy. I was reminded of my days in Tuscany when I first learned of Italian community—and now, as I had been warned, I was learning that the experience of community grows stronger as you travel south. Cesare told us that Accettura means "accepts all"—*accetta tutti*—and I could offer no argument.

This town that we had first set foot in less than a week ago had certainly accepted us. Italy was casting a deeper spell than I thought possible. My love for my children and grandchildren would keep me from moving to Italy, but I certainly was thinking that I could spend weeks, even months, on this balcony writing about what I had discovered in this little town and these regions of Campania and Basilicata—telling a story for those who wanted to relive the sweetness of life in Italy and for people who had not yet tasted the luscious fruits of Italy. We are born with an innate sense of what life should be, and each of us has a different picture of paradise on earth, but for me this moment was serving as a springboard to what I pictured as a near-perfect addition to the already good life I was living.

A cynic might say that our acceptance in Accettura—indeed in all the towns we had grown to love this past month—was based at least in part on the fact that we were seen as a source of revenue, and I would not argue strongly against that opinion. I would merely add that I've become good friends with people who came into my life because we were at first sources of money or services to each other. That's the beauty of life. We are interconnected.

It is not how you first meet someone that determines your love for them or your admiration for them, but the relationship that ultimately develops—and that is determined quite often by your respect for the life they are leading. On this balcony, on this night, I was admiring the life playing out before me on the streets of Accettura. I know it also had a lot to do with my childhood—I grew up with a great sense of community—my hometown was isolated and close knit. When I was a kid, people showed up in Hayes Center because either they meant to or they were lost—folks didn't just pass through. We didn't have a paved highway until I was ten years old. It was a dead end road that dropped you off in Hayes Center. I was long gone by the time people had a choice as to which direction to leave town in a rainstorm. Accettura is like that—if you end up in Accettura, you most likely wanted to be there, it takes quite a bit of effort.

Isolated towns have a unique identity. When I was younger, one item on my bucket list was to write and produce a photo essay book entitled *Towns at the End of the Road*. I never checked it off my list even though I still have a deep affinity for the communities that develop when accountability is strong, when everyone is known. Strangers are noticed—they can be welcomed, ignored, or shunned. Accettura welcomed us with a great big hug. And now I was sitting down to share that welcome with readers. That is why I have loved books since the time I was growing up in that isolated village—they whisked me away to somewhere I had never been before in my never-ending quest to discover *How Then Should We Live,* to slightly rearrange the title of a book I discovered later in life by Francis Schaeffer *(How Should We Then Live?).* Its central question was: *What effect should a commitment to Christ have on how we live our lives?* I want to change the focus slightly and ask: *How then should we live once we have discovered a society—a way of living that suits us—that we admire? How do we make our own communities more like the communities we admire?* That is at the heart of what we are doing when we journey to other countries—we go to see the sites, and the sights, but we are also researching, to put it rather crassly, a better way of living. At least that's what I'm often doing, and maybe others do it too. Knowing what I do about the way Italians live, *How then should I live?*

A knock at our open door interrupted my reverie. "Allo."

"Entra," I said.

"Sono..." and then Cesare switched to English, most likely because he was eager to get home to his family and knew how long it would take if he continued in Italian. "Basically I've brought you the menu for your meal tonight to choose."

We chose our entrees and then he asked, *"Tutto apposto?"*

He noticed my puzzled expression. "It means *Is everything okay*?"

Quickly I answered, *"Va bene."*

Cesare smiled and turned to go. "Okay, see you later." As he walked away I realized that the literal meaning of what he had said was simply, *All affixed?*, but language is not limited to the literal meaning of words, and that's why I love learning Italian from a native, especially a native who has also lived among English-speaking people and can therefore teach me the interesting nuances of language, the idioms and metaphors known by language lovers.

Cesare turned back to me as he reached the door. "I might not be here tonight, so I'll leave you to the Italians, okay? It's good for you to rely on your Italian—*va bene*. If there are any problems, call me."

I gave an appreciative laugh.

"Ciao," he said as he closed the door, leaving me to bask in the glow of his hospitality as the sounds of his townspeople once again enveloped me in remembered feelings. I returned to my journal, starting with defining *tutto apposto*—I liked the brevity and ring of the words.

I wrote for a while but was soon drawn back to the streets by the sounds of the village. I walked toward the high-pitched whine of an orbital sander a couple of doors from the hotel. I stopped to watch a man working on a beautiful piece of wood. He noticed me.

"Domenico," he announced as he shut off the sander. Before I had time to introduce myself he asked, "From America?"

"Yes, from America," I said. He was the first person all day to have guessed that I was from the United States.

"Where you live?"

"Near Milwaukee."

"I am born in the U.S.A.—in Queens, New York City."

"Va bene."

"You like Accettura?" he asked, and swept his arms in a broad arc over the town.

I delayed slightly as though considering my answer.

When he heard *"Mi piace"* he was thrilled and his face showed it. My guess is that the overwhelming volume of the *Ahhhh* that came from his throat, and even farther down, as Sergio said it must if you're a southern Italian, was born of his surprise that I spoke to him in Italian of my love for his town. Italians love to hear their language spoken by those who come to their shores. The *Ahhhh* turned into a laugh, a deep guttural laugh, as he slapped me on the shoulder and said *"Bene*, very good, very good."

"Love it, love it, love it," I said. *"Lo adoro."*

"You speak Italian," he said affirmatively.

"I'm working at it. If I spend another three years here I think I will have it."

It means a lot to Italians to know that visitors appreciate and like their towns, their country. That is especially true if that Italian has been to the US or has relatives living in America. The pride of connection was unmistakable. Domenico was very proud to tell me that he was born in America, but he was equally proud that I liked the country and the town that he had come back to—that, in essence, I agreed with his family's decision to return to Italy. Jobs are tough to find in Italy, so there may be little financial incentive to return, but a lot of Italians seem to be discovering that the quality of life their home country offers makes up for what may be lacking in financial security.

When I returned to the hotel I was surprised that Cesare was still there. Mardi was in the lobby too, appearing to be the center of attention of a group of young men.

"Can I offer you an *aperitivo*?" he asked.

"Certo."

"Can I do it my way?"

"Oh, yes, certainly."

"Your wife, the same?"

"Yes, she likes..."

Cesare interrupted, saying, "Sorted." Which I took be British slang telling me to put a sock in it, that he already had it figured out—no need for me to babble on.

"Okay, I'll shut up," I said in such a way as to suggest to the others in the room what *sorted* meant in American English. Everyone in the room started laughing. I laughed the hardest and longest. I loved Cesare's no-nonsense, take-charge manner. When the laughing died down Cesare chimed in, "Don't say a word," confirming my definition of *sorted*. The richness and malleability of language is a mystery, a source of unending joy. While Cesare created our drink the whole town seemed to be spilling in through the front doors and saluting. It felt like family. Apparently family was coming to Cesare's mind as well.

"You could be a mafia person with the large family you got."

"Mezza famiglia," I said, trying to convey that the photo I had shown him earlier included only half my family.

Una figlia—quattro figli. And ten grandchildren—*dieci*... what's the word for grandchildren?"

"Nipoti."

"*Dieci nipoti*," I said and winked at Mardi, remembering that she had earlier asked me the Italian word for grandchildren.

"So when it's Christmas every year, all together, it's a mega party," Cesare said.

"No, we rarely all get together. No one has a big enough place," Mardi said.

"You should bring 'em all here. We'll fill up the place," he said as he brought our drinks.

"I was just thinking the same thing. We should celebrate Christmas here. *Mi piace*," I said as I tasted the drink. It was an orange liqueur, very refreshing.

Mardi and I were sitting in the lobby with a great view of the front door. We could also see the bar where all the men were gathering.

"He's a good-looking guy," I said to Mardi about one of the men who had just come into the bar. She looked but said nothing. Her eyes, however, gave her away.

"You guys look relaxed," Cesare said.

"*Tutto apposto*," I said feeling smug that I'd been able to use the phrase he'd just taught us.

"Are ye 'aving fone? That's the main thing."

"We're having a great time," I said. He knew we were having a wonderful time. He had been keeping an eye on us and all of his other guests at the bar and in the restaurant—making sure everyone was taken care of—but it sure felt like his eyes were focused primarily on us. Maybe he really did feel a special connection. We certainly felt a strong bond with him. After we finished our drinks he led us to our table in the dining room and introduced us to our waiter.

"This is Francesco. He's my main man. He will look after you."

"*Piacere*," I said.

"See you tomorrow. Have a good night," Cesare said.

This time it really did seem that we would not see him again until the next day. It was almost nine when we sat down to dinner. We were not the only folks dining late. At the table next to us a family was having a spirited discussion while we enjoyed our bread, salad, and pasta.

"*Cos'è questo?*" I asked Francesco when he served us a platter of assorted seafood.

"*Pesce spada*," he answered.

"*Pesce spada?*" I asked.

He drew out a long nose—even longer than Pinocchio's.

"Ah, swordfish," I said. "It's delicious."

The angry pasta he served was also delicious. The name had intrigued me, and now so was the taste, it had a bit of a kick to it. Not a wrong note was played in the whole splendid symphony of our meal. It was quintessential Italian—simple, fresh food, perfectly prepared, Francesco assiduously attentive. We sat on solid wooden chairs, the table covered with a red cloth. The meal, as Cesare had promised, was exquisite.

"This place could be a blast when it's busy—with these guys' personalities. They are all so helpful, and they want to do well," I said.

"Do you like the wine?" Mardi asked.

"Mardi, I love you."

"Thank you for loving me."

"Isn't it amazing that we get to fall in love at this late stage? Of course, you're not in love with me. But at least I'm in love with you."

She laughed at the thought.

The family that had been dining when we came in was joined by another family. The greetings of all the family members were especially effusive. We were surprised that even though it was late, the kids were still going strong, still eating and talking, no hint of boredom or meltdowns. It was almost as though their meal was still in its middle stages.

"Isn't it amazing how affectionate Italians are?" I commented. We loved watching the interactions as they told story after story, the kids listening as well.

"Okay, *tutto bene?*" Francesco inquired.

"*Siamo alla frutta,*" I said and wondered whether that phrase, which I had learned in Tuscany—*We are at the end*—translated to southern Italy. He gave me no indication whether I had conveyed to him that we were more than satisfied, that we could eat no more—he just smiled and walked toward the kitchen. We were in no hurry to leave. We were totally engrossed, watching the two families, who had joined tables, enjoy their meal.

"Oh my goodness," Mardi said as Francesco placed a beautiful array of fruit and cheeses on our table. We never found out whether he had understood the Tuscan idiom, but our meal was definitely not at an end just yet. He may have thought I was ordering fruit and he aimed to please. We sat at the table for almost another hour enjoying the fruit and cheese and the conviviality of the other diners.

"We're going to be here until midnight," Mardi said.

One of the mothers at the other table was saying *Mangiare, mangiare, mangiare* to her kids, which is just what we were saying to ourselves about the beautiful food Francesco had just delivered to our table—*Eat, eat, eat.*

"Mardi, this is a fifty-dollar meal at a fine restaurant back home, don't you think?"

We tried comparing it to meals back home and realized it was as though we had dined out at a fine restaurant in Milwaukee and the management had thrown in a beautiful room at a first class downtown hotel as a bonus.

"All topped off with out-of-this-world hospitality and friendship," I said.

"*Buonasera*," the family seated closest to us said as they left the dining room. It was nice of them to acknowledge our presence; it made us feel even more a part of the community, almost like part of the family.

"This is just like at the farm with Sergio and Vittorio," Mardi said.

"We'll have to go for a walk around town. Just like we did after our feast at Vittorio's."

The other family was still eating—their kids still doing fine. The youngest girl was playing peek-a-boo with me by popping out from behind a post.

"This is a good lesson. Don't be afraid to come back to a place when you find something you like. What a celebration!" I said feeling elated, as if I were attending a homecoming.

"Can you believe it? We must have lived here before," Mardi said.

"I can't believe kids sit through a two-hour dinner. Most kids can't sit through a ten-minute meal at McDonald's."

"Gretchen is asking if we will be home by May 9th," Mardi said after responding to a text.

"Tell her no promises."

"If we don't go home pretty soon, I won't be able to fit into any of the clothes I bought," Mardi said.

Francesco noticed that we had done a respectable job on the fruit dish and stopped by to ask if everything was okay.

"*Perfetto.* Everything was to perfection."

"*Caffé?*" he asked.

"No, thank you—we would be up all night," Mardi said.

"Good night," Francesco said and bowed slightly.

"*Va bene.* It was excellent," I said to Francesco as we stood to leave. On the way out we paid our respects to the family still in the dining room.

"I know you're not having a good time, but at least your husband is," I said to Mardi as we walked toward the lobby.

She pulled me close and laughed.

"*Passeggiata?*" one of the guys at the bar asked us as we paused at the front door. Their party was still going strong. We were wearing down but wanted to walk a bit before we let go of our marvelous day. We had no destination in mind other than a bit of distance.

"I have the GPS with me. We can find our way back to the hotel," I said as we stepped into the brisk coolness of the night.

The streets were quiet, so quiet we found ourselves whispering, not wanting to disturb the peace of the town. We began talking again of the families we had dined with, still marveling that the kids had no problem with a meal that had lasted over two hours. As we walked through the town we were surprised to see smoke curling from so many chimneys. We also saw lots of firewood neatly stacked. The architecture was not the steep pitched roofs of the Italian Alps where we had been shepherds for Gianrico, but the sense that we were in a mountain community was strongly evident—cool nights, clear days, and long distance vistas. We felt at home. We had raised our oldest children in such an environment. We walked beyond where we had walked before, down ancient cobblestoned streets to what felt like the edge of town. We stopped near a fountain in the center of a small *piazza*. We hugged each other, slightly giddy at our good fortune.

"Have we walked far enough?" I asked.

"No, I'm still fat," Mardi retorted.

I turned her face toward mine and kissed her. We walked back to the hotel in the moonlight laughing as we recalled our amazing day—imagining the stories we would tell Jessica and wondering whether they would help her understand *Why we go to Accettura.*

CHAPTER TWENTY-THREE

Hotel Sangiuliano ~ Saturday April 23 ~ 54 & Cloudy

A Frank Capra Kind of Day

*You'll have to understand the piazza
if you want to find out what goes on inside an Italian's head.*
BEPPE SEVERGNINI

∎

*A successful marriage requires falling in love many times,
always with the same person.*
MIGNON MCLAUGHLIN

𝐼n the predawn blackness the realization I wasn't in Maiori anymore came slowly. The top of the hour came and went but I didn't hear the gentle chiming of bells. I looked through our window, saw silver-lined clouds billowing over the mountains and realized that we were in Basilicata. Major Joppolo brought a bell to Adano; maybe I could bring a bell to Accettura. A community as close-knit as Accettura should have a bell calling out the time. As I lay there slowly waking up, I realized I was already doing as Cesare had requested—trying to think of ways to help him fill the rooms of his two hotels.

I loved the easy familiarity Cesare and his partners displayed with me. Most of them had at one time or another touched me when they talked— asking how things were going or whether I liked something—and when I would say that everything was going well or that I particularly enjoyed a meat or a sauce, they would squeeze my forearm or give me a quick hug. And it was all so natural—just as I had written about in *An Italian Journey*—the joy I'd felt observing two elderly men walking arm in arm toward the *piazza* in

Montefollonico, as though they had been walking up that hill together, content in each other's company, all their lives.

"Buongiorno. Did you sleep well?" Cesare surprised us, suddenly appearing in the dining room as we were relishing the subtle tastes of a light and flavorful croissant. He asked about last night's dinner. We told him that it was, as promised, delicious.

"We had to go for a walk all over town because we ate a lot more than we normally do," Mardi said.

"You didn't go far then, did you?" he quipped.

"Well, we got to the edge," I said and told him about the little *piazza* we'd discovered in the park near the swimming pool.

"And what are you going to do today? It is quite windy."

"Have you seen the movie *Chocolat?*" I asked.

"I've seen it many times. Johnny Depp's in it."

"It's one of our favorite movies, too. Remember when the mother and her daughter show up in the village as though they had been blown in by the wind? Accettura reminded us of that movie this morning. We're going to let the wind blow us about town and see who we might meet."

Cesare liked the idea. The wind blew us first to the *piazza* near where we had met him. We sat on a low wall near the statue that pays homage to emigrants and watched the town slowly come alive. The heartbeat at first was a bit hard to detect. I had my computer and the desire to capture the morning in words. Mardi brought the desire to not let last night's meal go to her waist. She went for a walk in the narrow streets and alleyways.

I stayed on the square and wrote as the town's pulse slowly quickened—an old man shuffled by using a cane to steady himself, two younger men who had been chatting across the street crossed over to my side and sat on the wall to continue their conversation. An itinerant fruit and vegetable vendor parked his mobile market on the square and cranked up the volume of a toe-tapping tarantella—and just like that, the heartbeat of the town was strong and vibrant, and I had the best seat in the house. Within minutes the vendor's little truck with handwritten aphorisms scrawled on its silver panels was completely surrounded, the people having been drawn to the *piazza* by traditional Italian music emanating from loudspeakers tucked somewhere among the fava beans, bananas, oranges, broccoli, lettuce, and tomatoes. Some of his customers must have had standing orders—he handed bags of vegetables to them as they greeted one another. Other customers delivered torrents of words as they chose from the crates displayed on the bed of his blue-canopied Piaggio. Older men

walked slowly by with their arms folded discreetly behind their backs, fingers interlaced, looking closely at the vegetables but buying nothing.

Before long I was not the only one with a good seat. On either side of me men were talking, grandfathers were counseling young boys, and even some twenty-something-year-old men were already on the street telling stories of last night's adventures. The feeling of being surrounded by a whole town, with everyone telling a story, was unlike anything I had ever experienced. This was community written large, and to my mind, perfect. I've always loved the personal touch—add the entrepreneurial flavor of this vendor and I was sold. The music added to the festive atmosphere—Italian songs with strong beats, catchy tunes. People were not in a rush, and while the vendor moved quickly, he didn't seem to be in a hurry. He had time for his customers, even though many people were waiting at the back, sides, and front of the truck. While they waited they talked. Conversation never seemed to stop or even slow. It was a farmers market of one—and every Saturday morning it shows up, almost on your doorstep.

When his truck was no longer surrounded by villagers, he repositioned it a short distance away, parked, hopped out, and began packaging vegetables again—and within a few moments people gathered and the dance began once more. I regretted that Mardi wasn't with me to see this beautiful example of community. I had hardly completed the thought when she was at my side, her face aglow, with her own story.

"I spoke to her the whole time in Italian, and not once did she ask me if I was American," she said, thrilled by her linguistic conquest.

"I know. Isn't it fun. I'm going to walk over and buy some bananas or something from this guy. It's been a blast watching him."

Once the crowd had thinned, I walked toward him and dipped my head in a gentle greeting.

"*Due banane, per favore,*" I said.

"*Cinquanta,*" he replied.

I pulled coins from my pocket, placed fifty cents in his outstretched hand, and said, "*Grazie.*"

"*Prego,*" he said and gave me a soft smile.

It was a minor linguistic conquest, but still it made me feel good. He completed another transaction, got back in his truck, changed the music from a love song to another lively tarantella, and drove a block away to begin again.

"Mardi, I am in love with this. I'm moving here," I said.

"No, Jim," she protested.

"Mardi, I'm *moving* here," I repeated with an emphasis that surprised me.

"No, no," and she began laughing, knowing she was in trouble. I could tell she was feeling what I was feeling. She was laughing so hard at the impossibility of it all that I couldn't understand what she was saying—but her face had grandkids and kids written all over it.

"It's just absolutely..." I began.

"I know, it's amazing," she said.

"...everything I've ever wanted in a town. I had no idea such towns still existed."

It really was like time travel—as though we had woken up in the 1940s—too many people on the streets having too good of a time. *It's a Wonderful Life* came to mind—Frank Capra's story of the benefits of a close-knit community in America. For the first dozen times I saw the film I didn't know it had an Italian connection—that Frank Capra was born Francesco Rosario Capra in 1897—that the stories he told were through the prism of his childhood in Sicily. Accettura that morning felt like Bedford Falls 1946, the year the movie came out. We looked for Jimmy Stewart/George Bailey and quickly found several men who fit the description.

"Yeah, I was walking down the street and this guy said *Hello* to me as though he knew me," Mardi said. "He looked familiar, but we've met so many people. I finally figured out after we had talked a while that he was the man who took us through the community center."

I too had a story to tell. "Remember the man we met last night, right over there by the statue, who was so talkative? He came up to a boy when the vegetable man first showed up and began talking to him, giving the boy advice. It was beautiful how tenderly he was touching him; you could tell how concerned he was. I assume he was the boy's grandfather."

"You mean that man right there?" Mardi said, pointing across the street.

"Yeah, that's him. And then a grandmother came out of the store where you bought your brush and waved to a car going by. The car immediately pulled over to the side of the road and stopped, and the woman driving hopped out and ran onto the sidewalk and began kissing and hugging her. They were so exuberant in their expressions—nothing was held back."

"The whole town seems to be gathered here," Mardi said.

We sat there, absorbing more of the morning. A few shops were open. People were walking their dogs. A horse showed up in the *piazza*. The rider stopped to talk to a young woman. Two elderly gentlemen were walking arm in arm toward us, talking. Every once in awhile they would stop, turn toward each other to make a particular point. Then they would join arms again and continue walking, oblivious to everything going on around them.

All of a sudden the vegetable vendor was back, but this time he was on the other side of the street. With the return of his music, the energy in the *piazza* soared. It was louder than before, a catchy full-of-energy song. *Sará perché ti amo—It will be because I love you*. And the town responded—even more people came out of their homes. As I sat there thrilled by the sight of so many people on the streets, I thought what a timely tune for the good times Mardi and I were having—*It is all because I love you*. We were on the streets of this town that almost no one had heard of because we were celebrating our love for each other by taking the journey of a lifetime, and taking a few risks at the same time—going where the guidebooks don't.

Ever curious, Mardi headed off to the butcher shop, a few doors down from Hotel Sangiuliano. I continued writing. Kids were now showing up, playing soccer in the park and riding skateboards. Dozens of small groups were clustered around the *piazza*. At the Underground across the street a half dozen men were sitting around talking. The music ended abruptly and I could then hear their words clearly—deep, guttural sounds just as Sergio had described the speech of southern Italy.

The music began again—another traditional Italian dance number—as the vegetable vendor repositioned his truck once more. As the music faded it was replaced by the throaty sound of a tractor pulling a wagonload of hay through town. When the sound of the tractor had faded, the music could be heard in the distance. A Nissan 4x4 pickup pulled into town with a small horse standing in back, his head reaching above the cab. He had a bell around his neck that had been silenced with a wad of rope stuffed inside. The truck stopped briefly in front of me before driving up the street and parking in front of the butcher shop. The horse attracted a lot of attention, mostly young kids wanting to pet it, others afraid to get near.

The sun was shining strong, taking away the chill of the wind. I saw Mardi come out of the butcher shop and stop near the pickup. She was watching the driver drop something off at the butcher shop—something that required quite a few trips. Women were walking through the *piazza* carrying small bags, some filled with food, some with clothes and household goods. Shopping the old-fashioned way was on full display that Saturday morning in Accettura.

This reminded me of the good old days when I was a kid, but far more was happening in this *piazza* than I ever saw on the main street of my hometown. As close-knit as our town was it never rivaled this—especially early in the morning.

At any given moment I was within earshot of a half dozen conversations—it would have been too much to follow even if I were fluent in Italian, but the snatches of conversation I did understand revealed a compassion for fellow citizens that I found extraordinary. Minute by minute I was falling even more deeply in love with Accettura. A simple Saturday morning in a southern Italian town took me back to scenes I thought could be found only in the movies of Frank Capra and Roberto Rossellini—but this time I was a small part of the story.

I looked up from my computer screen and noticed that two mountain bikers had pulled into town. The younger of the two men, a thirty-something-year-old, was checking his phone. I took him to be German. They walked up toward the Hotel Sangiuliano, paused, hopped on their bikes, and rode slowly back toward the *piazza*. They stopped across the street at the Café del Popolo. The proprietor directed them up the hill above the *piazza*.

As they biked past me, the younger one said without preamble, "*Nonno.*"

I thought it was rather cheeky, but I did like that he had spoken to me in Italian, and of course he was right, I am a grandfather. But *Buongiorno* would have sufficed. I said *Good morning* rather than *Guten Morgen* even though I was now certain he was German. I took it as a compliment that he had mistaken me for an Italian. Mardi's attempt to give me an Italian flair had at least fooled a tourist. Across the street, in front of the Underground where last night the twentysomething and thirtysomething crowd was gathered, only five men remained. The conversation had lagged. They were now just watching. The five became four as one wandered off.

I continued writing. A half hour later I looked up and saw the mountain bikers heading down the hill—apparently they had finished their lunch and were moving on—spending only enough time in this town to fill their tummies. What a pity, I would say, but they had different needs and desires. They wanted to see more beautiful country and challenge their legs and lungs and hearts. I want to get to know a people and a village.

The size of the group across the street had slipped to three, undetected by me. Two of the men were standing. I was now certain the *sonnellino* had begun. Two more bikers, a young couple, pedaled slowly through town, leaving on the same street as the two men on mountain bikes. The seated man across the street stood up, got into his Fiorino, and drove away. He must have been the life of the party—when he left, the others did too, walking away together. They stood for a moment talking in front of the Café del Popolo. They were now the only actors on stage. I still had the best seat in the house, but I was the only one in the audience. One of the men climbed into a white Panda and drove slowly away. The other man walked up the street with his hands in his pockets—past the Sangiuliano. The streets that were so full of energy an hour before were empty save for a huge delivery truck with Cash & Carry written on the side that had just pulled into town and was backing up to the café.

I sat alone in the now amazingly quiet streets of Accettura typing and reliving the morning. I wasn't certain where Mardi was, but I was sure she too had noticed that the *sonnellino* had begun and would soon be joining me. I could have written for another hour, but when she showed up fifteen minutes later and asked if I was ready to go for a hike I said *Sure*. She is always concerned by the amount of sitting I do exercising my craft as a writer, especially when we travel without my bike.

"*Buongiorno,*" said a deep-voiced man walking with his hands behind his back as he passed through the *piazza*. He was the first person I had seen in quite some time but he didn't pause when I greeted him. I closed my computer, tucked it in my everpresent man purse, and we headed for the park where we had turned around on our midnight trek. We had more exploring to do, and Mardi had stories to tell of her morning, which were similar to mine but so different from a Saturday morning in suburban America.

"I hear cowbells," she said as we passed the swimming pool where we'd turned back the night before.

"Either that or *sheeps,*" I said, which immediately reminded her of our days working as a shepherd for Gianrico in the Italian Alps. He spoke English quite well, but we became fond of the way he said *sheeps.* We also loved our first chore of the morning, taking his small herd out to pasture from the barn where they had spent the night, protected from predators.

"I hear them way down there," I said, looking deep into the park, but I saw no animals. The feeling of suddenly being in the heart of a forest was good. We were treated to a symphony of sounds by the wind, each tree creating in its leaves and branches a unique tone. Birds were also singing. Suddenly a dog barked, interrupting the concert. The discordant sound came from high above us.

"Mardi, look—there's a shepherd down there. He just leaned back against that tree. See him?"

"Maybe he has dogs," she said, worry creeping into her voice.

"I don't think he has seen us yet. He probably thinks the dogs are just barking at him and the sheep."

"Aren't you worried about the dogs?"

"The dogs aren't his, otherwise he'd be looking around trying to figure out why they're barking."

"Let's not bother him. Let's go back the way we came."

I considered it for a moment, but getting to talk with a modern day *pastore* seemed like too good an opportunity to pass up, even though I knew there was a chance that he was not in the park but on private land.

"I think we should walk down and say hello."

"Are you sure we shouldn't be worried about the dogs?" she asked again. I had probably scared her with my story about the guard dogs for the sheep back in Tuscany—how friendly the dogs looked but how vicious they could be if their charges were threatened.

"If his dogs were barking I'd be worried. But see how relaxed he is. I don't think we need to worry either."

We continued walking down the valley, watching our steps so as not to snap a twig.

When we were within fifty yards of the shepherd I could make out that he was sitting on an upturned tire. When we were twenty yards away and he still hadn't looked toward us I called "Allo," loudly enough to be heard but not loud enough to startle him. He turned slowly, saw us, and responded with a gentle nod of his head. The dogs up on the hill were still barking. He watched us approach, occasionally turning toward his sheep to make sure they were still eating comfortably.

"*Buongiorno,*" I said when I was close enough to hold a quiet conversation.

He seemed shy, or maybe just soft-spoken, as one would expect from a shepherd who didn't want to alarm his sheep. "*Buongiorno,*" he said quietly. He didn't seem bothered at all by our presence.

When I was within a few feet of him I said, "*Piano, piano.*"

I didn't understand every word he said in response but enough to know that he was agreeing that his sheep were moving slowly, taking their time eating. He regarded them for a moment, then said, with strong conviction, using a voice louder than before, "*Fa freddo.*"

I gave myself a hug to show that I understood what he had said, and then I said in English so Mardi would understand too, "It *is* a bit chilly this morning."

"*Quanti pecorino?*" I asked, but as the words left my mouth I realized that I had not used the word for sheep—*pecore*—but the word for the delicious cheese made from the milk of a ewe.

He ignored the faux pas and said somewhat sadly, "*Solo quaranta adesso.*" His choice of words and his demeanor told me that he used to have more—*Only forty now.*

I noted his walking stick and pointed to the rather crooked sticks we were using—our Ravello walking sticks. He smiled. They *were* rather funny looking. I told him that even though they were ugly, they were useful in this hilly terrain, and he agreed as he put his hand on his well-worn stick leaning against the tree behind him.

"*Avete cani?*" I asked.

No dogs, he told us. He seemed to be saying with body language that he could manage this many sheep just fine without dogs.

"Oh, look," I said to Mardi. "*Capre!*" I had just noticed that he had a few goats in with the sheep.

"*Capre?*" I asked him.

"*Si. Quattro capre,*" he said.

I could see only two goats, but I could also see only about two dozen sheep. The rest had most likely moved down the hill and out of sight. I wondered if he was nervous that he could not see the whole flock. I introduced myself just in case he was about to get up to leave.

"*Mi chiami James,*" I said extending my hand. "*Come ti chiami?*"

"Vincenzo," he said quickly and gave me a firm handshake—just what I expected from an old farmer. He was, I guessed, in his late seventies or early eighties, but his grip was solid, his smile warm, his eyes soft and forgiving. He was wearing a tweed cap—a type I used to associate with Ireland but was now beginning to see on many older men in Italy as well. His footwear was very practical—mid-calf galoshes. He had probably left home at dawn, or even before first light, when the dew was still heavy on the grass. His pants were baggy and made of wool. His sweater was thick, gray, and well worn.

"*Piacere*," I said and then introduced Mardi, "*Mia moglie*, Marta." She offered her hand and he received it gently.

Mardi noted that what we had at first thought was another walking stick was instead an umbrella. He knew his weather.

"Uh-oh, it's starting to rain," she said. I wasn't sure how I had not noticed the darkening clouds. I guess the excitement of talking with a real-life *pastore* must have narrowed my vision until all I could see was the idyllic panorama of a shepherd leaning against a pine tree watching his flock eat its way down the mountainside.

"*Piove*," I said to Vincenzo, noting the obvious.

"*Andate*," he announced as he stood up to go.

I responded, "*Buona giornata*."

He immediately and enthusiastically said, "*Ciao, ciao*."

I always love hearing *Ciao, ciao* from Italians, especially if they are older and we have just enjoyed a bit of conversation. He smiled, tipped his hat, and walked slowly toward his flock, which by now had disappeared over the brow of the hill. He did not open his umbrella but tucked it up under his arm, fastening it to a small cloth bag which I assumed had a bit of food and water in it, and who knows, maybe even a book. I've always imagined that if I were a shepherd I would carry a book to read while I watched the sheep.

When he paused halfway to the brow of the hill I noticed again his long, thin walking stick, which he leaned on while he took stock of his flock. It was not as long as a shepherd's crook, and it didn't have a hook on the end either. Satisfied, apparently, he resumed walking. His was a graceful gait. He was comfortable walking on uneven ground. We watched him for a long time. The rain that had begun when he left us stopped falling. Sunlight glistened in the mist. Tufts of grass sparkled.

Only once, just as he reached the brow of the hill, did he look back. We waved. He didn't wave back. He just smiled and tipped his head slightly as he disappeared from our view. We could still hear the bells of the sheep. We stayed where he had left us, absorbing the beauty of the moment. I was sure Mardi was feeling, as I was, that we had just experienced a moment we would never forget. The heavens could have opened with a heavy downpour as we stood there without umbrellas and we would still have been counting our blessings. It was that kind of morning.

We walked to the brow of the hill where Vincenzo had turned to look back at us. Below we saw him making his way with steady steps down the hill. Sometimes it was so steep he had to cut across the mountainside, but always he was working his way lower. Some of the sheep were now within a few feet of him, but the goats were no longer in sight. The deep, resonant tone of the bells, the smell of the fresh, wet earth, the scent of pine needles, the wind blowing through the trees, and the beauty of the morning mesmerized us. I wondered if Vincenzo was aware of the stunning beauty, or had he seen it so many times it no longer captivated his senses as it did ours. Of course the picture unfolding before him lacked a very important element—him. Vincenzo was perfectly dressed, perfectly cast; his mountain-man good looks and rugged profile completed what could have been the opening credits for a mega-million-dollar Hollywood movie set in the mountains of southern Italy about a way of life that many think will disappear forever the day he dies.

The light was perfect, occasionally shining brightly through the threatening clouds, providing a glimmer of hope that just maybe things will change—that in this increasingly fast-paced world dominated by a materialistic mindset there will always be people like Vincenzo who are content with a shepherd's life, who recognize the value of a life well-lived, shepherding the land, animals, and people under his care. I was grateful that Mardi and I had gotten a glimpse of what I thought had already disappeared from our world.

"Are you enjoying your honeymoon?" she asked.

"I am indeed. This is fun," I said and hugged her. "This may not be everybody's idea of heaven on earth, but it works for me."

The wind suddenly started to blow hard. The sound in the long-needled pines was glorious. We stayed right where we were, alone in the woods, protected from the rain by the thick growth of trees. We imagined that Vincenzo was also taking shelter somewhere down the mountain, waiting out the squall. When the rain shower turned to a gentle mist we began walking back the way we had come. At the first picnic table we came to we sat down to share the bread, cheese, and apples that we invariably take on our hikes just in case.

"We thought we were in heaven in Maiori... now we think we are in heaven here," Mardi said.

She was right. Wherever we went, it seemed we were falling deeper in love with each other and with this wonderful, ever-surprising country.

"We're going to have to be more discerning, more critical. We've got to quit falling in love with everything we see in Italy," I said.

Mardi didn't see it as a problem. She seemed content to keep loving everything we saw.

"Is it nap time? *Dormitina? Pisolino? Sonnellino?* " she asked.

We had discovered so many great words for siesta, but we didn't have a blanket, so when the sun started shining again we left the shelter of the woods and began climbing back toward Accettura, back to the streets we had grown to love so deeply.

"*Attenzione.* It's become the most valuable Italian word we've learned," I said.

I was calling out dog poo as we climbed the steps past the park shelters.

"*Belle ragazze,*" I said when we had climbed all the way back to the main street of Accettura—back to a very different world than we had shared with the shepherd.

I was pointing out three beautiful young girls gathered outside the *gelateria* enjoying cones with three colorfully different heapings of *gelato.* Farther down the street, near the *piazza,* we saw what had to be the trekkers Cesare was expecting for the night. They were just entering the town and were quite an imposing group, all clad in heavy walking boots, many carrying walking sticks.

When we reached the *piazza,* I asked one of them if he spoke English. He didn't, so I spoke Italian and learned that they were on a three-day hike, something they did almost every weekend, and their goal for the next day was Grassano, about thirty kilometers away. They appeared to be well-equipped, quite serious trekkers. They wandered about town for a while before heading to the Hotel Sangiuliano to check in. We went to the tourist office to meet with the Pro Loco group. Cesare had introduced us to Ruocco the night before and he had offered us a tour of the town. It would be a shakedown cruise for his army of young volunteers.

Antonio, Teresa's son, had been assigned the task of interpreting Ruocco's story of Accettura whenever our comprehension of Italian faltered. We felt quite special to be given such VIP treatment. We were a rather large contingent; sometimes as many as twenty of us gathered around Ruocco as he told tales that dated back thousands of years. We were surprised at how attentive the young volunteers were—how proud they were of their town. Ruocco told us that in the early days each of the wealthy families had their own church. He showed us a huge palace that one family had built. I couldn't help but realize, as I did a little math, that some of these teenagers might be around in 2070 to join the one-thousand-year celebration of this home, appropriately named Grande Casa.

But the celebration I was most interested in was the one I feared we wouldn't see unless Mardi changed her mind. Ruocco recognized her reticence and did his best to encourage her to stay. He talked of the celebration's connection to Saint Giuliano, the Protector of Accettura. It was a fascinating story with parallels to the story of Jesus. Giuliano wasn't accepted, so he stayed underground.

The statistics behind the celebration were staggering—the size of the trees, the cost of the ropes (almost two thousand euros), the hundreds of people and dozens of animals involved in transporting the trees to the marriage ceremony of the male and female trees from the nearby forests, the amount of food that would be served, the number of people who would fill the streets of Accettura in two weeks. We were even shown a film of a previous Maggio Festival. It was hard to believe that what we were watching had been filmed only a few years ago and not a few centuries ago. I was sold on the idea, but Mardi's body language told me she wasn't. I don't know whether Ruocco recognized that she wasn't going to change her mind, but it seemed he felt he had told the story as best as he could, so he changed the subject. He wanted to know about us.

"We are from Wisconsin," I said.

"Freddo?" he asked. It seems that everyone knew of the Green Bay Packers and the many games they play on the *frozen tundra.*

"Si, con la neve. Lots of snow in Wisconsin."

With Antonio's help and my faltering Italian, I gave them a quick story. They were very surprised when I told them that we had traveled to Italy by boat. They were also shocked that we had ten grandchildren, which led them to ask how long we had been married. I guess in some way we had conveyed that we were in love because one of the girls asked in halting English, "What is the *say-gret,* no, secret, for being happy?"

I repeated the question to give myself some time to formulate an answer, and then Antonio gave us a little more time as he interpreted for those who hadn't understood the question.

"We put up with each other," I said and then realized that the idiom might not translate, so I tried again: "We accept—everyone has faults, how to say, *abbiamo problemi, ma accettiamo,"* I concluded.

Mardi gave a short answer that I didn't understand, but everyone else seemed to, so I didn't ask her to translate it. Apparently she also pantomimed something that I didn't see. The look on the face of the girl who had asked the question told me that Mardi had conveyed to everybody that she was in love.

Antonio moved things along by asking if we wanted to stay in Accettura for the festival.

"Is the Pope Catholic?" I said and quickly realized *that* idiom might not translate either and might even offend, so I quickly added *Certo per me* and then stuck my hand out and fluttered it as I said, *Forse per Marta.*

"Please ask Ruocco if he thinks the festival makes the community *forte,* very strong," I said to Antonio.

"*Bravissimo, bellissima domanda—molto intelligente,*" Ruocco said, without waiting for the translation.

"Very intelligent question," Antonio said.

Antonio's succinct translation brought smiles to the faces of many of his friends. Ruocco told us that he thought the festival was at the heart of Accettura's unique spirit.

"Did you like our story, our town?" another girl asked in English.

I answered the question by telling them how we had come to be in Accettura—that it was because of its proximity to Aliano—but we had come back to their town because of the strong feeling of community we'd observed on our first visit.

"I am writing another book about Italy. I will try to tell Accettura's story," I said.

"If you come again, bring it," Antonio said.

"We will come," I answered.

"*Sei sempre benvenuto,*" Ruocco said to us and smiled.

"Ruocco wants you to know you are welcome anytime," Antonio interpreted.

"We'll be around—how to say that in *italiano?*" I asked.

"*Saremo in giro,*" Antonio answered.

"*Fino a domani,*" I said. "Until tomorrow. *Ciao.*"

We thanked everyone, especially Antonio for the fine job he had done translating Ruocco's narration. We had been given an inside look at the workings of a unique mountain community. If we hadn't already been in love with Accettura, this two-hour exploration of the village in the capable hands of its young would have done the job.

When we walked out of the tourist office we were once again in the midst of what had made us fall in love with the town. The *passeggiata* was in full swing, filling the streets of Accettura again.

We greeted many familiar faces as we made our way to the hotel. A filled-to-capacity establishment was adding to the town's vibrancy. I was beginning to understand Cesare's vision.

"How many people do you think they can they put up here?"

"Feels like hundreds," Mardi said, "but I think it's more like fifty."

We walked into the crowded lobby and immediately saw Cesare.

"Ah, my friends, you have made it in time for dinner."

"We just want to do two pizzas tonight," I said. "If we can't eat it all, can we take it away?"

"No problem," he said and led us to the dining room to introduce us to Renato, the pizza chef. Renato spoke English well and had a brother living in Houston, so we had a lot to talk about. We accepted his and Cesare's recommendation of the Buffalo Doc for me and the Bosco for Mardi. Of course, we also ordered a mixed salad.

"Do you want some wine too?" I asked Mardi.

"*Un po*—a little," she said.

"*Salute, bella donna*," I said. "You are beautiful."

I might have been trying to influence her. I wanted to talk about the long list of people who had invited us to stay until the festival, including Renato, who had just told us that without a doubt we must stay. But I got distracted when I noticed the waiters pushing tables together. The dining room was full and getting fuller. Cesare was right, pizza night in Accettura was worth coming back for.

"Older people are lamenting the loss of community," Mardi said, "but it sure doesn't feel like it here."

"*Ecco qua*," our waiter said and placed the pizzas on our table with a flourish.

"*Buon appetito*," I said and offered a short prayer of thanksgiving for our food and our good fortune before sampling the pizza.

"Do you like it?" Mardi asked.

"How does it keep just getting better?" I said, referring not just to the pizza but to everything. "I like this better than the *ricchezza* from Maiori."

"Let me taste it. I'll try to make it at home." Many of my favorite meals are concoctions inspired by the many meals we've eaten in Italy. I tried her pizza as well.

"I like yours but I like the Buffalo Doc better. I've got a new favorite."

Pizza night in Accettura was everything Cesare told us it would be. Every table was filled at least once—and many of them a couple of times. And once again a little girl sitting next to us began playing peek-a-boo with me, and I played along. Once I even hid behind a pillar separating our tables, then popped out to surprise her when she began looking for me. She retreated to the arms of her dad but gave me a "that was fun" smile. The feeling that family is what life is all about is felt everywhere in Italy.

"What does it cost us to live for a day in the United States?" I asked. My mind was churning with possibilities.

"What do I include?" Mardi asked.

We realized as we began listing our fixed expenses that it was not an easy question to answer, but the more we talked about it the more we realized that because we were sharing our home with our youngest son the idea of spending a lot of time in Italy was in the realm of a good possibility—maybe even a certainty—now that we had fallen unabashedly in love.

"I feel really creative here. It inspired me so much to see way the townspeople greet each other on the street—it's so warm and compassionate."

Mardi knew she was in trouble. I was being way too enthusiastic. The cumulative effect of all that we had experienced in just one day in Accettura was clouding my judgment.

"It would be nice to know that we could come to the Hotel Sangiuliano on a moment's notice and feel like we were coming home. I would much prefer this to having a place in Door County or a Colorado cabin."

I wanted to keep working on Mardi, but the sound of laughter, good times, and lively music coming from upstairs was too much for me to resist. When our two-hour pizza feast was over Mardi joined Cesare and the growing crowd of young men in the lobby. I climbed the winding staircase and was amazed to see that all the tables and chairs had been pushed to the walls, creating a dance floor that was overflowing with people. The trekkers were enjoying what might best be described as an old-fashioned barn dance without the barn. I had been watching the dancers fly around the room for all of fifteen seconds when a woman began motioning for me to join her on the dance floor. I hesitated and she came over and led me into the center of the maelstrom.

I protested that I wasn't a good dancer, but that lessened her enthusiasm not one iota. I was soon flying around the floor, doing my best to follow the lead of my exuberant partner. I've always liked polkas, and as best as I could figure, that was what we were doing. I'm sure I must have been taught to polka and square dance in 4-H when I was a kid, but it's not like riding a bike—you *can* forget how to do it. But that was not going to prevent the woman, who reminded me of an enthusiastic kindergarten teacher, from showing me a good time.

As the third dance ended I told her I needed to go get my wife. I ran down the stairs and found Mardi surrounded by good-looking young men. She listened to my explanation about how much fun I was having, but she too protested: "I don't know the steps."

"I told the woman the same thing, but she made me get out there. I stepped all over her, but it was a blast," I said to a still reluctant Mardi as I led her up the stairs.

Everyone in the alpine club was friendly, open, and inviting, but none more so than the woman who met us when we stepped into the room. She was quite attractive, with vibrant brown eyes. The woman I had been dancing with could be described similarly, but this woman was more intense, a few years younger, spoke English well—and she wanted to dance with me. I looked behind me to see if Mardi thought it would be okay.

I was surprised to see that an equally attentive young man was asking her to dance. Within seconds the four of us were flying around the room. It was flat-out fun. I wondered why Mardi and I didn't dance every Saturday night. When the music stopped my partner asked my name. I responded, "James" and asked her, *"Come ti chiami,"* and she, somewhat surprised, said, "Maria." And then, "Oh you have Italian somewhere in your past," and put her hand behind her ear and fanned it quickly, which I took to mean somewhere in my *hidden* past. As we were dancing I guess I had spoken enough Italian to make her think I knew the language. She didn't realize I was nearing my limit of successive Italian words without resorting to broken English.

I glanced at Mardi. She was having a ball. I could tell she was still protesting that she wasn't very good, but that wasn't stopping *her* partner either.

"You want to dance again?" Maria asked.

"Yeah. I'm no good at it, but if you'll dance with me, sure."

"Where are you from?"

"America—Wisconsin."

"Why you are here?" she asked in a rhythm and cadence that reminded me of Jessica.

"Why are we here?"

"Yeah," Maria said.

"We are on our honeymoon," I said, but I don't think she understood me. She quickly asked, "Would you like tomorrow come with us?"

"Sure, where are you going?"

She told me, and this time I was the one who didn't understand, but it didn't matter.

"What time—*a que ora?*" I asked.

"Eight o'clock," she said, then added, "We leave right on time. We are a large group and we are very regimented."

She started to make fun of the group, so I responded with an I-will-be-a-good-little-soldier march and salute and she did the same. Everyone nearby laughed and I heard someone say, "He understands us."

"When you get tired you can turn around," Maria said.

"We won't get tired. We will wait for you to catch up with us," I said.

"Okay," she said, and smiled an uncertain smile trying to figure out whether she had understood me correctly. I returned her smile, hoping she understood I was joking with her.

"We have prepared a drink for you," Maria said, and somehow a drink appeared magically in her hand. She offered it to me and began introducing me to her friends. "*Questa é James*—James Bond," Maria said using a Sean Connery cadence and timber. The reception was warm and spirited. I glanced toward Mardi, but I needn't have worried—she was being taken care of by another equally attentive man.

Cesare stopped by. "Sorry for ignoring you, but it looks like you're doing just fine."

"We are indeed," I said as I took a sip of the drink Maria had handed me. She smiled. It had a bit of kick to it.

"You've got a good story to tell, Saturday night in this town, the whole hotel full, and hopping," I said to Cesare, feeling that if he could duplicate this every Saturday night their venture would be a huge success.

"You are a party animal," Cesare said.

"They have invited us to hike with them."

"I will have breakfast ready for you at seven," he said, not missing a beat.

Staying Alive had been playing while Cesare and I were talking—it ended abruptly and everyone jeered. Mardi was suddenly at my side.

"This confirms what I was thinking about Italians and their afternoon naps. They can stay out late at night," she said, "but I'm not sure I can."

"But this is so much fun." I was having a great time, but I knew it would be best if I took Mardi's clue to heart.

"*Domani*," I said to the group as I reluctantly left the dance floor.

"Good night," everyone said.

"See you tomorrow, James Bond," Maria said.

"Thank you for inviting us to join you," I said, promising again that I would be on time.

"We should dance once a week," I said to Mardi as we turned to go.

"Where?"

"Guess we'll have to come here. All of our Saturday nights should be like this one."

As we made our way to our room we could hear the familiar tune of "YMCA" echoing through the stairways.

"Do you want to go back down?" I asked.

"No, I think we've packed enough into one day."

She was right. It had been an incredible day. I was concerned about one thing, though.

"I'm sorry about the answer I gave when that girl asked about our secret," I said as I unlocked the door to our room. I had been wondering what Mardi's reaction had been to what I had said. She had given the girl a romantic answer—I had given the answer I thought was responsible for getting our marriage on the right track—that made it possible to love her even when I wasn't crazy about something she might have done or not done—and vice versa—when I've danced too long, too enthusiastically with a young woman I've just met.

"Oh, I thought it was a good answer. Love isn't always the answer. I mean *being* in love doesn't ensure a good marriage, because a person is not always *in love*. But putting up with me, that's what it takes. Even when I don't want to let you stay in Italy forever."

"You forgive me then for letting them know our secret is that we love each other in spite of all our quirks?"

"Yes. In spite of all the times you make me jealous."

The Italian Alpine Club had put a spring in our steps. I couldn't think of a better way to have ended our incredible day in Accettura than dancing and laughing with a bunch of enthusiastic, passionate Italians who quite likely were going to dance the rest of the night away.

What Do You Do with a Girl Like Maria?

The name of Italy has magic in its very syllables.
MARY SHELLEY

■

A journey is a person in itself; no two are alike.
And all plans, safeguards, policing, and coercion are fruitless.
We find that after years of struggle that we do not take a trip; a trip takes us.
JOHN STEINBECK

"*I* have a serious question," Maria said as she walked up to our table. She was ready for hiking. Mardi and I were in the dining room, not far from the lobby where the trekkers were milling about waiting for the appointed hour of eight o'clock. Cesare had set up a delicious, hearty breakfast just for the two of us. The Alpine Club's breakfast had been served upstairs in the same room that was the scene of last night's barn dance.

"First. Did you sleep well, yes?" Maria asked.

"We did sleep well. How about you? *Avete dormito bene?*"

"*Fantastico.*"

She seemed slightly nervous, yet still spunky and energetic, just as she had been the night before.

"You speak American, no English, right?" she asked.

"I can translate either," I said, and smiled.

"*Ah, perfetto.* Why you choose Basilicata?" Maria asked with the same seriousness that Jessica had asked *Why you go to Accettura?* Her question made me smile, just as Jessica's had.

"Why did we choose to come to Basilicata?" I asked, stalling for inspiration or wit.

"*Si,*" she said, obviously sincere.

"We like to be with the people," I said when neither wit nor inspiration showed up.

"But why you are *here?*" Maria asked with more force.

"Have ever read the book *Christ Stopped at Eboli* by Carlo Levi?"

"Ah, Aliano," she said.

"That's how I first became interested in this part of Italy. I'm a writer and..."

"Ah—Oh—Fantastic," she said, each word punctuated with a pause—each word getting louder. Then she laughed enthusiastically, the light of understanding shining in her eyes.

"I've written one book about Italy, and I'm writing a second book—I wanted to experience southern Italy."

"Oh—but when are you leaving?" she asked excitedly.

"Ahhhh, we don't know," I said, surprised again by her question.

"Maybe you can change your life to decide to live *here*," she said and laughed heartily.

"I've already made the decision, we're going to stay with Cesare," I joked.

She laughed again and then told us about the attractions of the area. Mardi surprised me. Instead of being jealous, or telling me to cool my jets about moving to Italy, she asked Maria about wild animals, wondering if there were wolves. Maria told us that we would find no wolves but plenty of wild boars, *cinghiali*. She went on to explain the flora and fauna of the region. My curiosity kicked in.

"Where were you born?" I asked. I wondered if she was a native of one of these little hill towns. She seemed extremely knowledgeable, possibly a farmer's daughter, or a hunter.

"You? Born?" She asked, not understanding my question.

"No, you—*nascita*," I said, pointing at her.

"Ah, birth, born. *Nascita, nato*—I am younger," she said.

"Of course you are," I said.

"1963."

"No. Where," Mardi said.

"*Dove?*" I said.

"Ah, Potenza," she said, finally understanding the question.

"I'm sorry, I wasn't asking your age."

"Ahh, I don't understand very well, this is my problem, not your problem," she said.

"Ah, but you are so young," I said.

"Ah, yes, thank you, you are kind," Maria said.

I smiled. Mardi most likely didn't.

"See you later," Maria said.

To the writer in me Maria was revealing herself to be a curious person. To the woman in Mardi she was revealing herself to be a flirt.

"She's not married. She's not wearing any rings," Mardi leaned over to say to me as Maria walked away.

"I didn't notice."

But I did notice that Maria was wearing her hair down, and it was quite long and closer to black than I had realized last night. She looked more Italian.

"I'm keeping my eyes on you," Mardi said with feigned jealousy.

"*Why you go to Accettura? Why you choose Basilicata?*" I said, reminding Mardi of the similarity of the question that Jessica had asked in sincerity, cadence, and delivery.

"How come you attract women?"

"She just wanted to practice her *American*—her English, I mean. Nothing to do with me. When she was born, we were almost out of high school."

"Do you think she realizes she's flirting with a seventy-year-old man?"

I smiled. Mardi had added a few months to my age for effect. "It's almost eight," I said as I stood up and turned to leave. I was surprised to see Cesare by our table.

"Good morning. Are you going to want what they're having, sandwiches to take away with a bottle of water and an apple?" he asked. I started to say *Certo,* but Mardi took over.

"No, we won't be gone that long."

"*Va bene,*" Cesare said. "Wrap yourself up. It's cold and windy out there."

"You sure you don't want to skip the trekking? We could sit around and drink *cappuccinos* and eat croissants," Mardi asked.

"I don't want to miss this. The light is gorgeous this morning." We walked up to our room to grab our jackets and backpacks. I was thinking, but didn't say, that last night had been fun and this day was getting off to a good start too.

"I don't think they're going to be out there by eight," Mardi said as she packed some apples and cheese. She still wasn't convinced we should be heading out into the hills with these serious hikers, most of whom were, after all, much younger and much more used to hiking long distances than we were.

"I'll see you down there," I said remembering my promise to be a punctual little soldier. "I'll get our walking sticks."

The lobby was packed with trekkers. I made my way through the throng to the front door and retrieved our skinny walking sticks.

"What do you call?" I was surprised to hear Maria's voice close behind me.

"A walking stick," I said as I turned.

"In *italiano* this is a *bastone*," she said. I smiled. She had just given me the evidence that would convince Mardi that Maria's only interest was the desire to learn some new English words.

A call for a photo rang out. I glanced at my phone. It was exactly eight o'clock. We all shuffled outside. I held back and Mardi was soon at my side.

"We can take it," I said to a man who was waiting until everyone was in place.

"James, we want you in the photo," Maria yelled as I pulled out my iPhone and snapped a couple of shots.

"Marta, we want you too," Maria added when I hesitated.

I snapped two more shots, then Mardi and I squeezed into the group. We were posing in front of the wall where I had enjoyed the best seat in the house the day before. A big cheer erupted from the club when the photographer signaled that he had the shot.

With the preliminaries out of the way we took off at a brisk clip. While still on the streets of Accettura we overtook an older woman dressed in black carrying bags in each hand. Had we not been with the club I would have offered to carry the groceries, instead I took a photo of the trekkers greeting her. It was a good picture. She was enjoying the repartee with the hikers as they passed.

The photo I took a few moments later of Mardi was quite good too. She looked marvelous walking along with her walking stick and mine, a stylish pink stocking cap rakishly perched on her head and a matching scarf framing a glowing smile. She has always looked good in the mountains, especially when she is wearing bright-colored clothes. The very first photos I took of Mardi were in the mountains. We met in Lincoln, Nebraska, on the last day of summer classes in 1969. To celebrate, we took off in my MGB to the mountains surrounding Breckenridge, Colorado, where I had been a ski bum the previous semester. She looked like a model then, and she looked like a model that morning on the outskirts of Accettura, walking along in the sunshine, the road behind her filled with hikers. I was relieved that the pace so far was relaxed, that we were having no problem keeping up with the group.

"You look good with two sticks," I said.

"She smiles at you just a little too much."

"She's just being friendly."

"A little too friendly for my taste."

"You know you're beautiful."

"So are Italian women."

We started out together, but as we walked along we began breaking into groups. Mardi walked at a steady pace. I was as usual taking photographs. Suddenly Maria was at my side.

"This is the road to Matera," she said.

"This looks like our Badlands in South Dakota. What is the word for *similar* in *italiano?*"

"*Simile* is similar. A lot of Italian words are similar to English."

I smiled at that and asked, "Who is the leader today?"

She explained their procedures and told me of some of the exploits of their most avid hikers. "We have different ages, different abilities—it is not *omogeneo.*"

"Homogenous as we would say in America," I said as Mardi caught up with us.

"Who is the oldest?" Mardi asked.

"I don't know, maybe Vincenzo," she said. "The man who made my walking stick."

I saw a great photograph coming up. I hurried ahead so that I could include hikers in the photo—a long-distance vista of Accettura. It turned out to be worth the effort. I resumed walking. A few moments later I heard my name.

I turned and saw Maria walking up to me with another woman.

"She wants to know if in Aliano you visited the inside of the house that Carlo Levi mentioned."

"We didn't get inside any of them," I said.

The woman was sorry to hear that. She was also quite knowledgeable. She gave me the names of several people to contact in Aliano. We walked along together for a mile or so as Maria and the other woman told me of many attractions in Aliano that Mardi and I had missed. I appreciated the information but I was also very aware that Mardi was behind us somewhere. I excused myself and stopped to take another photograph.

"You give me white hair," Mardi said when she caught up with me.

"She's was just being helpful—giving me some information about Aliano," I said.

She didn't buy that, so I changed the subject.

"It was a nice shot with Accettura in the background," I said, but that didn't get much response either, so I tried again.

"Are you enjoying this beautiful hike in the woods?"

"Yes, except for my philandering husband."

I smiled at Mardi, gave her a hug, and hurried ahead to take a photo of the trekkers climbing over a fence. We were walking through incredibly diverse landscapes—dense woods one moment, eroded hillsides the next—along trails that I'm sure Mardi and I never would have discovered on our own.

"My friend suggests for you in Matera to visit Casa Nora," Maria said. She had caught up to me again. "There is a film about Basilicata, and Carlo Levi."

"I think we *will* go to Matera," I said. The town had been mentioned by numerous hikers when they discovered that we traveled with an open itinerary.

"The movie *The Passion of the Christ* was filmed in Matera," she said. "Francis Ford Coppola's family comes from Basilicata."

I was enjoying the conversation with Maria, but bothered that Mardi was not by my side. I let the conversation lag but Maria picked it up again.

"You arrived in Bari or Napoli?"

"We arrived in Civitavecchia."

"Ah, you came by boat?"

"*Si, in barca, per nave.*"

"How long trip?"

"*Due settimane.*"

"Two weeks, long time," she said.

"We're on our honeymoon, so it seemed like a good thing to do."

"A long time, twenty-five years, no?"

I now knew with certainty she thought I was at most only a few years older than she was.

"*Quarantasei anni,*" I said.

She took a long time processing that information. I think she thought she had heard me wrong, or that I didn't know Italian numbers. She looked at me in disbelief.

"Forty-six years? That you stay together?" She looked at me again. "Ooooooh—how old *are* you?" she asked breathlessly.

I laughed. "I'm a youngster."

She turned to her friends. "*Sposato quarantasei anni,*" she shouted.

I loved it. I couldn't quit smiling. The expression on her face made me feel very good.

"*Fantastico,*" Maria said.

"Since I know how old you are I will tell you how old I am," I said.

"You must be sixty-eight, sixty-nine," said a man walking nearby who had done the math.

"You are right. I am sixty-nine," I said.

"No, you are *meno*," Maria said, still disbelieving.

"We are both sixty-nine," I said.

She turned to Mardi, who was walking a short distance behind us. "It is good *aria* in America."

"It's not just the air. It's good genes, good food, good life," I said.

"Good food, I don't know," she countered.

"Yes, good food. Mardi is a very good cook."

"This is Italy," said the man who had figured out my age.

"My wife is a very good cook, she has learned a lot from Italy."

"Ah good, no fast food," Maria said.

"No, we eat slow food."

"You live the Italian life."

"Yes, yes we do, as much as we can."

"When did you arrive?" Maria asked.

We told them about some of the highlights, the feast Vittorio had given in our honor, the people we had met, the hikes we had taken. I could tell they were quite impressed with the picture of Italy that we had uncovered. We turned the conversation back to them and the hikes their club takes every weekend. I could imagine joining this group if we lived in Italy. We heard many stories—about relatives in America and their adventures to the Grand Canyon, to New York City.

"You have learned much of the Italian language," said one of the men who had often been walking nearby when Maria was talking to me.

"I love the Italian language—the way it flows, the connections—*scarpe* is shoe, *scarpone* is boot," I said.

"And *stivali*—is higher boot," he gestured and pointed to the difference.

"James," Maria said.

"*Si.*"

"When you are tired, tell me—I don't know."

"We were just talking about heading back. I understand there is a steep section coming up."

"Yes, yes," she said.

"We don't want to go down—no *scarpone*," I said.

"Yes, yes, yes—very good," she said before lapsing into silence. If she was trying to decide how to say something in English, I understood. I sometimes have to practice my sentences in Italian quite a few times before I utter them. But practice doesn't always prevent me from getting things wrong, like saying *nascita* (birth), when I should have said *nata*, (born).

"Is a good day for you?" she asked.

"A very good day, a beautiful day," I said and smiled. I added nothing in Italian, guessing that she wanted to speak English.

She gave a light laugh but added nothing.

"Enjoyable," I said.

She laughed again. But said nothing further.

"*Sono felice,*" I said.

She again said nothing. I was not sure why she was walking beside me. I was certain Mardi was wondering the same.

"I am happy," I said preferring to talk about Italian and English words while we walked.

"I think four *kilometri*..." Maria paused trying to find the right word. When she began speaking again I understood none of what she said, but I kept the conversation going.

"Yes, they just showed me on the map that we have walked four, four and a half kilometers," I said.

"In miles," she said. This time I understood. She pronounced more of an "L" sound this time; earlier the word had sounded like *mize* or *mice*.

"Oh, you want to know how far four kilometers is in miles?"

"Yes," she said. "I have forgotten."

"Point six—*punto sei.*"

"So four kilometers is two point four miles, more or less."

"Exactly—*esatto,*" I said.

"*Esatto,*" she said and pronounced it exactly as I'd pronounced it. I love it when Italians either repeat a word or say *Bravo* when a foreigner pronounces an Italian word correctly.

We had shared a nice moment but we fell into silence again. I knew Mardi was watching me. She was again somewhere behind us, but I didn't know how far back. I didn't want to turn around, though. I had enjoyed working on my Italian, but I was hoping that Maria would strike up a conversation with a woman who was only a couple of steps ahead of us. Then I could slow my pace and rejoin Mardi.

We walked in silence for thirty seconds or so.

"*Zaino* in English is ah..." Maria said.

"Backpack" I said quickly, thrilled that she had chosen a word I knew.

"We have a small backpack with all the necessary ah..." Maria said and began searching again for the right word.

"You never know what you're going to get—you may get rain, you may get fog, you may get snow—*pioggia, nebbia, neve...*" I said.

"No, no, not so much snow here. This winter for example, no snow whatsoever," she said as we crested the top of the slope we'd been climbing since she had begun walking beside me.

"*Bella panorama,*" I said upon seeing the view from the top of the mountain.

"*Bello,*" a man said. I assumed he was correcting me. If so, I was grateful. I had not realized that *bella* was not the right gender for *panorama.*

We walked a bit farther and stopped. The leader put on his rain gear. Everyone followed his lead. A few minutes later we came to a clearing with a nice view of the distant mountains. We stopped, and suddenly people had their knives out and were carving up thistles, offering us morsels of the plant. They were surprisingly good. "White yes, *verde* no," said a woman who had cut several large slices for Mardi and me. I asked the name of the plant and learned that it is called *cara mariano.* It seemed like a good time and a good place to say goodbye to our friends.

"*Arrivederci,*" I shouted to the leader when he resumed hiking. "*Grazie.*"

He turned and waved. Some of the club members followed him, although most seemed content to hang about for a bit of snacking.

"Where is your wife? Come on please, a photo with you," Maria asked.

Mardi somewhat reluctantly joined me as a friend of Maria's snapped a photo of the three of us with Maria's camera. I didn't offer my camera to the woman.

"Nice to meet you," I said to Maria. "Thank you for helping me with my Italian."

"Enjoy your holiday. *Ciao.*" She was suddenly less talkative than she had been. She smiled, turned, and walked slowly away with her friend.

The trekkers did not move off *in massa.* Each of them, one or two at a time, stopped first to say goodbye. The last hiker to leave handed us pieces of marinated jerky, and just like that we were alone in the clearing, surrounded by mutilated white thistles—the green ones still standing.

When the voices had faded to the point where we could hear only the wind, Mardi began singing "Maria," the tune from *West Side Story.* "*I just met a girl named Maria...and suddenly the world will never be the same again.*"

"You're funny. I don't think that's how it goes."

"You won't live this down anytime soon," she said.

"*Ma-ri-a, Ma-ri-a...*" I began singing the song too.

"She has sparkly eyes."

"She has sparkly eyes?" I asked.

"Yes, she does, and she was always shining them at you."

"No, she wasn't," I protested weakly.

"Good thing you were wearing your dorky glasses. If you'd had contacts on, she would have really flipped out." Mardi was walking around the clearing still humming the tune, still eating the stalk of the thistle. I pulled off my rain jacket. The skies were clearing.

"Quite a few of the men were hot on you."

"Yeah, but I didn't dance with them."

"What do you mean you didn't dance with them?"

"I turned down lots of dances."

I thought about that and realized that I *had* danced with Maria quite a few times.

"Mardi, you gotta admit that was fun," I said as we began hiking back the way we had come.

"Yes, it was."

"You can't be mad at me."

"I'm not mad at you, I am just sad because women like you."

I laughed. "No they don't. When she found out how old I was, she was no longer interested."

"Who you kidding? She was *more* interested. She couldn't believe you were that old."

I didn't have a very good hand to play. I changed the subject.

"This would make a good walking stick. My thumb fits right here in this crotch. I'm going to stop and work on it with my Leatherman, smooth it off a bit." I had picked up a branch along the road, one that was not quite as funny-looking as the stick I'd been using since our first hike to Ravello.

We were passing an abandoned stone house, but Mardi felt we'd soon have a better view, so we kept walking. We could hear the voices of the trekkers echoing across the valley. Now that the sun was again shining, the birds were once again singing. The sky overhead had turned completely blue. The intense sunlight turned the raindrops on the leaves and blades of grass into thousands of sparkling jewels. I was thankful that the trekkers had invited us to join them—I had no idea what we would have done otherwise, but it couldn't have been more fun or more beautiful than this hike.

"This is so pretty," Mardi said, spinning in a circle as she said it. It's something she often does in the mountains.

"This is perfect—*bella, bella,*" I said ignoring the distinction. *Bello* to my ear was just not appropriate for the beauty that lay before us. We were also hearing bells on sheep, or maybe cows grazing in a nearby pasture, and that was adding to the perfection of the day, and this moment. I have always been a sucker for cowbells in the mountains.

We soon came to the hilltop with the view that Mardi liked. We could see forever in every direction. I found a large boulder covered in moss to stretch out on. The contours of the rock fit my body extremely well. It was if I'd found a lounge chair on the top of a mountain. I was tucked in out of the wind, basking in warm sun, watching the now-distant shower.

Mardi was looking for a comfortable place to sit down in the field of wildflowers that surrounded us. "I think I've seen this same wildflower on our hikes above Aspen," she said.

"What would you like to eat? We have crackers—and we have crackers," I said.

"This reminds me of our Colorado life. It feels like we're coming full circle," she said as she contributed cheese and apples to our lunch. The wind, whose sound was contributing to the beauty of the day, changed Mardi's mind about where to sit. She chose a rock beside me, protected from the wind. We dined on our simple fare and talked about our similar tastes—how we had both fallen in love with the mountains when we were young and in love—so much so that we had moved from Omaha to Colorado to raise our family.

"More crackers?" I asked.

"We even like the same kind of crackers. What's going on?"

"We're falling deeper in love."

"I tried to be mad at you, but I can't."

"Mardi, I feel bad. I've got such a comfortable spot here. It feels like a bed," I said, trying to steer the subject away from Maria.

"Do you want to marry someone like that if I die?"

"She'd be too young for me. She's just a baby."

I had given an answer that Mardi liked. She smiled and gave me a hug.

"It's fun getting old. I think we're doing it fairly gracefully."

"Falling in love with my wife again. That's a pretty good way to grow old."

"If ever you wanted a moment to last forever," she said, "this would be it."

"Would you put your healing touch on my knee? I'll make room in my bed for you."

"Maybe someday we can live in the mountains again," she said as she snuggled next to me. "At the very least, let's go home and join a trekking club."

Her idea sounded good to me considering the day this trekking club had given us.

"Let's just lie here forever," I said.

"When people ask *Why you go to Accettura,* we should say because it is beautiful, it's old-fashioned, and it celebrates families," Mardi said.

"That's a good response."

"I love it here," she said. We were running out of words to describe our feelings, but the emotion in our voices said it all. We cuddled and reminisced, letting our minds jump where they wanted with memories of our journey together—from love-struck twenty-some-year-olds to soon-to-be-seventy-somethings even deeper in love.

I don't know how long I slept, but when I woke up, Mardi was no longer beside me. I sat up and saw her a short distance away, walking through more fields of wildflowers. The scene was just as beautiful as it had been before I fell asleep. She was probably ready to move on, but she had let me keep napping.

"Shall we go?" I asked after watching her for a while—a woman reliving happy times.

We gathered our things and reluctantly said goodbye to our glorious spot on the mountaintop. We wondered where the trekkers were and if they too had found such a marvelous place to stop and enjoy their lunch.

"This day has reminded me of my childhood, out exploring all the time," Mardi said as we began walking back to Accettura slowly and somewhat subdued. "I wanted to be either a missionary, an explorer, or a park ranger—those were my dreams." But then she suddenly switched to talking about her sister's health—or lack of it—and the problems her sister's husband was having.

"How much older are they than we are?" I asked.

"Mary is nine years older than I am."

"This is a peaceful little stretch of trail, wouldn't you say?" I said, not wanting to stay on the subject of old age.

"I'm feeling very fortunate being able to do this—not having to go to a job or take care of someone," she said.

"You mean walking along a mountain lane in Italy, on a perfectly gorgeous day? *Tu felice?*" I asked.

"*Molto felice.* I am very happy."

"That is Santa Croccia—that mountain right there. They pointed it out to me on the way over. Let's get off the trail and take a peek into this valley—we aren't in a hurry, are we?"

The view from the ridge was spectacular—we were in a clearing surrounded by a dense forest—everywhere we looked we were treated to a different landscape. Only moments before we had been on a sandy slope of an eroded hillside, the kind of land Carlo Levi fell in love with.

"Wow—this definitely reminds me of *Chocolat*—the wind is howling through here," I said as we walked back over the ridge to the lane we had been following and continued in the direction we had been going. But suddenly things didn't look familiar.

"You think we're on the right road?" I asked.

"I was too busy looking at you and Maria to notice the trail, but I probably have enough pictures of the two of you that we could find our way back by looking at them for landmarks."

"You do?" I asked, surprised that she had been photographing us. "I didn't realize you were *such* a jealous person."

"She was infringing on my territory. I loved studying things like that in college—anthropology."

"Oh, about younger women going for old men?"

"It's called territorial imperative," she said as she handed me her phone. "Here are some pictures of you and *Ma Ree Ah*—you can start here."

"That was nice of you to take pictures of me and Maria."

"I wasn't being nice," she said as I began looking at what was quite a collection that began with photographs and even video of me dancing with Maria.

"Cesare was surprised we were going hiking with them," I said. *"Ah, you're making friends,* he said."

"He doesn't know the half of it. My husband is very friendly. He makes friends wherever he goes." She was still trying to be mad at me. "You know I love you. You're kind and loving and..." she seemed to get lost trying to think what to say next.

"You danced with the guy who was walking for a long time next to Maria and me," I said, trying to take the focus off of myself.

"The man I enjoyed dancing with the most was the one who looked like Matt."

"In blue?" I asked.

"Yeah, he had white hair," Mardi said.

I stopped to take a photograph of Accettura shining on the distant hillside—the village was spotlighted in sunlight. Fluffy clouds had formed, changing the character of the day. Mardi continued walking.

I just love you, I thought I heard her say. She was by then far ahead of me.

Not wanting to presume, I yelled, "What?"

She turned around to face me and sent the words through the wind: "I miss Matthew." The words were clear this time. The syllables were the same, the rhythm was similar, but she was not telling me she loved me but that she was lonely for our oldest son. We don't get to see him very often. He flies a lot, and I think he feels we don't appreciate him like we do our other kids, who have intact marriages. He has married twice and divorced twice. He rarely comes to see us. Over the years he has seemed to pull away. We used to be very close. He was the first to fly with me, starting when he was just a toddler. I could tell right away that he'd been born with the gift of flight. He was not heavy on the controls, giving just enough input to keep the wings level and headed toward whatever spot I had given him on the horizon to fly toward. He was and is a natural in the air. I've always been proud of the compliment that he gave me regarding my flying abilities. After he'd been in the Air Force quite a few years and was a highly skilled F-16 pilot, he told me that I was better at landing small planes than he was. I didn't believe it, but I appreciated that he would say such a thing about his old man.

We try to say things that will let Matt know that we love him and appreciate him, but like his compliment about my piloting skills, I don't think he really believes us when we say we love him. He wants kids, I think, and he has dated a few young women—young enough to have children. There was one in particular I think he could envision starting a family with, but the relationship didn't work out. He was devastated and we weren't sure that he had recovered.

We do what we can to try to make him feel appreciated, but it doesn't seem to stick. The same is true in marriage. Love can be offered, but it also has to be accepted. I always wanted our marriage to be great, but until that September day at the YMCA, the love I thought I was offering to Mardi wasn't sticking. She didn't feel lovable. She has told me since that she didn't think we were compatible. I had never thought that in the ultimate sense. I knew in my heart that we were *molto compatibile*. We started out that way, but we drifted apart. I felt unloved and unappreciated. During those difficult years when we were raising children, and I was launching my business, Mardi seemed to want more success than I was giving her. She resented the time I spent on my dreams that didn't always pay off. That's how I felt.

But her feelings changed in one day—and she began accepting the love I was offering—and as Robert Frost wrote, that has made all the difference. Two roads were diverging in the woods, and we took the one that allowed us to believe that we were loved, and because we believed we were loved, we began to love and let one another know of our love as we had never done before. And that has brought us to this, the happiest moment in our lives. We were now secure in the love that we showered on each other. Mardi may still get jealous when a woman like Maria pays attention to me, but she knows that my heart and my love are for her. We have a story to tell, and that story involves all the kids and grandkids who look to us as a team. We are a unit of love. We are a unit of commitment. People depend upon us. We are living not just our story but their *storia* as well. We have a responsibility to make sure that the story our kids and grandkids tell is a good story—a very good story.

We crested a hill and could once again see Accettura in the distance—a town that in only one week had begun to feel very much like the hometown we had always dreamed of finding.

I didn't know how it would happen, but I had been certain since we'd left Florida a month and a half earlier that we'd know when it was time for our journey of a lifetime to end. We both felt it on that windy hilltop as we made our way back to Accettura. Our love for each other had been confirmed and validated. Our lives together had been celebrated. We felt complete. It was time to return to our family. We also knew that we would come back to Italy—that made it easier to think about leaving.

We felt completely loved at that moment, not just by the people of Italy but by the countryside too. As we walked slowly along the ridgetop, the sand on the road and the wind in the trees were making me feel at one with the land. I grew up walking in fine sand, facing into the wind, seeing my hometown far in the distance through the clear air of the high plains. We were doing the same here in Italy. The hometown I knew as a child is gone, at least much of it, but here in Italy I had found a vibrant main street that I cherished. I loved Accettura's sense of community. The people know and love each other. It is probably that way in most towns throughout Italy. It certainly was true of the many towns in Italy I've had the good fortune to visit these past half dozen years. I was certain that this particular little town in Basilicata would figure prominently in the remaining chapters of my life.

We had been welcomed as honorary citizens of *il Bel Paese*—a feeling that just about everyone takes home from Italy. You know when something is right, and on that hilltop, at that moment, life could not have looked or felt any better. We had found what we had always been looking for—a partner to share the journey of a lifetime that we'd set out on together so very long ago. We hoped, of course, that we still had many pages to write, but if God had chosen to end our time on Earth at that moment we would have felt that we had learned the most important thing God and Italy had to teach us—how to love, and how to give that love unconditionally. I felt loved—and I could see in Mardi's radiant face that she felt loved too. When it comes time for the story of our lives to be told, I want the narrator to say that we had a good journey—on that hilltop on that day I was certain that we had.

But our sojourn in Italy could not end on that hilltop. It would have been a perfect ending, but nothing ended on that hilltop with the amazingly clear view of Accettura—certainly not our love for each other. I don't know that we had ever felt closer or more in tune with each other than at that moment. The dry, cool winds of Basilicata may have had something to do with how we felt—our affinity for mountains runs deep in our souls. But despite that feeling of peace, our lives were in Wisconsin, and it was to Wisconsin that it was time to return. Our *luna di miele* had to end sometime—and as we walked back to Accettura, neither of us could imagine a better ending.

"Did we make our reservations, or did Matt?" I asked.

"Matt did. He's just waiting for us to tell him when we're ready to come home. Then he'll check the loads and tell us the best day to fly."

I love it that Mardi remembers the details that define our lives. I look at the big picture. She takes care of the nitty gritty, keeping our dreams alive.

"I dreamed about being a gypsy when I was little," she said.

"My dreams changed depending on how old I was—a clarinet player, a baseball hero, an architect—but I remember that one of my favorite books was *Around the World in Two Thousand Pictures*. I didn't realize it then, but now I see that it combined two loves—travel and taking pictures. It took a while for me to realize that the book also represented a third passion of mine—writing."

"Isn't it funny how early in life our journey is cast?" Mardi asked.

"I think the key thing is to recognize the passions of youth and follow them. I don't think everyone gets to do that," I said.

"If they do, they're fortunate," Mardi said as she offered me her hand.

Fortunate was what we were feeling as we walked to town, basking in the clear light of the mountain air. We had learned a lot about ourselves and each other in our short hike into the hills of Basilicata with those passionate Italians. These hills and the people who lived in them taught Carlo Levi about himself; in fact, they came to define his life. It was to these hills that he returned to be buried. I had felt a deep connection to this land when I read his book, and now that I had hiked through the landscape he loved, I understood why.

"It's still a *Chocolat* kind of day," I said when we got to the edge of town. The wind was blowing hard through the streets of Accettura, just as it had in the mountains. We walked the streets that were becoming increasingly familiar to us, convinced that unless something big happened—an invitation we couldn't pass up—it was time to let the winds blow us out of town and back to the life we'd been living before we set off on this wonderfully improbable Italian journey.

CHAPTER TWENTY-FIVE

Hotel Sangiuliano ~ Monday April 25 ~ 45 & Calm

Is It Time to Say Goodbye?

*"When a man and woman turn to one another in a bond of
faithfulness, God robes them in garments of light, and we
come as close as we will ever get to God himself, bringing
new life into being, turning the prose of biology into the
poetry of the human spirit, redeeming the darkness
of the world by the radiance of love."*
JONATHAN SACKS

▪

*Italy is a country that every man should love once.
I loved it once and lived through it—
you ought to love it once or at least live in it.
It is something like the need for classics.*
ERNEST HEMINGWAY

We woke up not yet convinced our time in Accettura was over. Cesare had
mentioned that he might be able to put together a visit with Giuliano's son,
who had taken over his father's tile-making operation. And of course the
possibility always existed that we'd be invited to another feast like Vittorio's—
although the chance of such a thing happening on a Monday would not be
likely. Nevertheless, we walked hand in hand down the grand marble staircase
of the Hotel Sangiuliano open to whatever fate and the bounce of the pinball
might fling our way.

As the lobby opened up before us we saw only Teresa and Cesare, and the
morning took on a more relaxed feeling, no longer filled with anticipation.

Teresa was carrying a small vacuum cleaner. Cesare was seated in front of the computer. Neither seem rushed.

I greeted them with my best *Buongiorno* complete with a slight roll of the *r*.

"Good morning," Teresa cheerily responded. Cesare looked up and saluted, which I took as a sign of approval for my continued attempts to improve my Italian.

"*Due cappuccino?*" he asked.

"*Si.*"

"Did you sleep well?" he asked in his jaunty Nottingham-laced accent. To my ear it seemed that he turned it on and off at will—when speaking to Mardi and me he seemed to rev it up a notch, especially noticeable when he dropped his *h*'s.

"Yes, very," I said, and then added, "What is a nice Italian phrase for asking if a person has slept well?"

"*Dormito bene?*"

"*Dormito bene?*" I repeated.

"*Dormito benissimo* is how you would respond."

He excused himself to start heating the water for our *cappuccinos*. While we waited I worked through some Italian phrases I'd been studying, such as "Where can I find a cheap hotel?"

When Cesare rejoined us I said with a hint of sternness, "*Mi lasci in pace.*"

His eyes opened wide and he said, "Excuse me."

I smiled and quickly told him I was testing my pronunciation of Italian rather than trying to be rude. He returned my smile and said, "*Bravo.*" I had told him to "leave me alone"—literally translated as *leave me in peace*. But he knew that I was nowhere near fluency, so he switched back to English.

"Was it busy last night?"

"A lot of families came in. The restaurant has been full *every* night. If you could get a hiking club every weekend you'd be all set."

"That reminds me, did you enjoy your hike?"

"It was a blast. We walked a couple of hours with them. They treated us to a thistle."

"I can tell you had fun."

"My husband had a little too much fun."

"I saw you guys dancing. It looked like you were having a good time too, Mardi," Cesare said as he went to finish making our *cappuccinos*.

"I can't believe you didn't tell him about Maria," I said when he was out of earshot.

"I don't want him to know what a rascal you are."

"Paying a little too much attention to the girls, was 'ee?" Cesare asked as he set our *cappuccinos* in front of us.

"Actually, the girls were paying a little too much attention to *him*."

Cesare's eyebrows shot up.

"I'm surprised you didn't push 'im down the stairs this morning."

"They were just practicing their English. That's all it was," I explained.

"Yeah, right," Mardi said.

Cesare was enjoying our little spat. I was too. Mardi showed Cesare some of the photos. I think she quite enjoyed it that a perky, attractive Italian woman almost twenty years younger was flirting with her husband. I could tell by the way her face lit up that she especially loved telling Cesare that Maria thought we were celebrating our twenty-sixth year of marriage, not our forty-sixth.

"Italy is good for you. Italy is good for both of you. You must *coam* back. We will always have a room for you," he said as he left to attend to the needs of the only other guests in the hotel.

"I want to adopt Cesare," Mardi said.

He was about the same age as our oldest son and shared Matt's sharp mind. Her comment about adopting him confirmed that she was getting a bit homesick, and unless something big happened, and soon, we were going to be checking out of the Sangiuliano and working our way toward Rome and a flight to America.

"Mardi wants to adopt you," I said when he returned. "She's missing her boys."

He asked about our family. We gave him a quick synopsis and asked about his wife.

"You haven't met my wife? That's the way it is with Italian men. We keep 'em hidden."

The more we talked about family the more convinced I became that Mardi was ready to return to hers. Cesare made it easy for us. He made no tempting offers. He had discovered that the tile maker's son was out of town. He recommended we go see where *The Passion of the Christ* had been filmed.

"Go to Sassi straight away. You will feel like you've gone back to the Stone Age. But be ready for lots of people—the tourists are about—lots of Chinese and Japanese."

There seemed little doubt where our pinball was bouncing us. The day before a dozen people had told us we must see Matera, and now Cesare had made an impassioned appeal for us to visit Sassi, the oldest part of Matera. To thank him for his hospitality we gave him a bottle of wine from Tramonti and promised we'd be back.

I can't say for sure, but he may still have been hoping that we would be back in a few weeks for the festival. I didn't think we would, but we all were quite certain that our paths would cross again, so our *goodbye* was more like a *see you soon*. We had already surprised him by coming back to Accettura once—he had by then discovered that we were travelers, not tourists.

Cesare had warned us that Matera would be crowded, so when a parking place suddenly opened up in front of us we dove into it. As we got out of the car, it seemed like a normal Italian town—lots of *gelato* shops and sidewalk cafés. Figuring out how to get to Sassi was easy—the flow of people carried us there. The hard part was figuring out how in the span of a block we'd journeyed back two thousand years. As we walked across the *piazza* vendors selling every imaginable souvenir left no doubt we were smack in the middle of twenty-first century consumerism. But when we reached the edge of the *piazza* and looked out over the old city we were thrust instantly into a different age—the color palette changed from gaudy to an absolute monochrome, the color of the sand. The only hint of color was the occasional flash of bright clothing of a tourist in the distance. Otherwise the whole city looked like a movie set. No wonder Mel Gibson chose this place to shoot *The Passion of the Christ*, and no wonder it felt as if we were walking the streets Jesus walked on the way to His crucifixion. Oppression hung heavy in the air.

As we strolled the ancient streets I wondered whether the feelings that had come over me upon catching sight of Sassi were born of my associations with the pain, the passion of the movie, or was there something intrinsic in these gray and tan structures that suddenly transformed my day. Or was my discomfort a reaction to feeling like a tourist as we walked the dusty streets where people, when I was a boy, were living in caves? It felt more like touring a museum than visiting a town. I would have felt much more comfortable in Sassi seventy-five years ago when people lived there—when the feelings of community and tradition and family were strong and vibrant despite the poverty. Now Sassi had been *discovered* and the caves were being taken over by tourist shops and restaurants.

Another possibility for the funk that I felt was my regret that we had left Cesare and Accettura long before I had wanted to. I knew our journey had to end someday and somewhere, and at breakfast I'd felt that it was right that we should go, but as we were climbing the steps to get back up to the level of the new town of Matera a deep sense of sadness swept over me. Suddenly I wanted out of Matera as quickly as possible.

Mardi must have been feeling the same thing. She offered no alternative when I said I had seen enough. She was also on board when I said I didn't feel like eating in Matera. I knew that we had not gotten past first impressions, but it felt as if we were being led to someone or something else on down the road. Or maybe it was the dampness—the light, cold mist that was falling—but when we got back to the car and discovered we had only two minutes left on our parking validation we took it as a sign that it was time to move on.

"I don't even want to get a *gelato*. I don't feel like standing in a line," I said.

"I've got Benevento in the GPS," Mardi said.

"You don't want to go to the coast?"

"No, I want to see more mountains."

"You're sure it's okay with you that we're leaving Matera so quickly?" I asked as I backed out and turned on the windshield wipers. It had begun pouring—yet another sign that it was time to move on.

"Yeah, I'm sure. Look at all the tour buses."

I looked up the street and was surprised to see so many I couldn't even guess at the number. I was sure that Sassi and Matera had a lot to offer a tourist, but sometimes a person is just not in the mood for hordes of people.

"At the roundabout take the second exit..." Dorothy began directing us out of town. Every time I'm in a situation like that I thank God for the techy geniuses, the space program, and everybody else who had anything to do with perfecting the GPS technology that makes it possible to efficiently navigate the dizzying array of streets in an ancient Italian town—to get from *il centro* to the *Autostrada* in minutes.

I know also that if I had not had a GPS I would have had to talk with a local to figure out the best way out of town—and who knows what that might have led to in the serendipitous world of pinball traveling—but on this afternoon I just wanted to get down the road as far as possible toward Rome and our next adventure in the four or five hours of daylight remaining.

"Do you think this is the best route to take us through the mountains?" Mardi asked.

"Let's stop and take a look."

I pulled off in one of the many spots that Italian highways have for that sort of thing, and after sorting through our choices we stayed with Benevento. It looked both direct and promising.

"It will be nice to drive through Puglia, since we love Trader Joe's Puglia bread so much," Mardi said. I was now certain we had made the right choice.

A wind had blown us out of Accettura, and now Mardi had chosen Benevento as a waypoint on the way to Rome, not even knowing that the name means *Good Wind*. Good fortune has many names. Our spirits had lifted now that we were on the road, and had made what seemed like a very fortuitous decision to head toward Benevento. We had no idea how far we would get, but it definitely felt like our steps were being directed.

We liked the rolling countryside. It truly was wheat country, much of it very much like the land I had grown up on—helping my father raise wheat on the open plains of southwest Nebraska. We were passing by tractors, combines, and even grain elevators. This was not the land of terraced plots like the Amalfi Coast or the contoured vineyards and olive groves of Tuscany; this landscape looked like the breadbasket of the center of America.

"Look at this, no wonder there are big John Deere tractors here, look how flat this land is." I felt right at home. Sadly, we were seeing old buildings that had fallen into disrepair. That also reminded me of the plains of America. Two things were very different, though. You won't find ancient mansions in the middle of America's farm belt, and you can't see the Rocky Mountains from the wheat country of Nebraska. But on this drive we were always in sight of rugged peaks as we made our way north and west toward Rome. The only time we couldn't see mountains was when it was raining so hard we could hardly see twenty-five yards down the road.

"It's really not a very good day for anything but driving," Mardi said, rationalizing our decision to leave Matera. We were also second-guessing our decision to head home, wondering how much more deeply in love we'd be with Italy and each other if we kept right on going south, all the way to Sicily. Rick Steves had said that Italy gets more intense the farther south you go, and it seemed to be true. Why should we stop?

But momentum or something seemed to be carrying us north and west. Mardi was right. This was a wonderful day for travel. Changing weather increases the beauty of landscapes. We were driving in and out of rain showers every dozen miles or so. We were even treated to patches of sunlight and rainbows that dramatically drew our attention to fields, mountains, and rivers.

"Does it make sense that it is two hundred thirty miles from Benevento to Rome?" Mardi asked.

"No, but it makes sense that it is two hundred thirty *kilometers*. That would be about two and a half hours. That sounds right."

"Like they say, all roads lead to Rome," she said making me feel that her sights were once again firmly set on places north.

"We're going through a wind farm," I said as the sky began clearing and we could see great distances again—all the way to the big whirling turbines on the ridge lines.

"This is so peaceful," Mardi said as the full sense of being far from a city swept over us.

"Field after field of wheat. I had no idea Italy could look so much like Nebraska. We'll probably see Chimney Rock around the next bend."

"This is an awesome route to Rome. I see now why Puglia has all the good bread—they have all the wheat."

We were enjoying our road trip. The land was incredibly diverse and interesting, bringing back memories of trips we had taken with and without children. That made me think of the many cars we had driven, which once again reminded me of the movie *Two for the Road*, which used cars to signify the passage of time, from an old MG to a station wagon to a little Mercedes roadster. Our marriage could also be timestamped in cars and landscapes—and that was just what this short drive was doing. In the span of a hundred or so miles, it felt as if we had driven through a thousand miles of an American landscape—the landscape between Wisconsin and the Rocky Mountains that we had driven countless times.

"I think we just drove by a FIAT factory," I said, surprised to see such a large factory in Italy's farm country. It also reminded me of my promise to myself to someday drive my own Cinquecento.

"We're leaving Puglia," Mardi announced. She was studying the map, wondering where we were going to spend the night.

"You're right. I just saw a sign that had a line through Puglia and a circle around Campania. Let's see, it's four forty-five." I was trying to judge how close we might be able to get to Rome before dark. We were making such good progress that we were beginning to think Benevento was not in the cards—that we should bypass the good winds, keep driving, and save Benevento for a time when we could walk its streets and let the wind blow us where it would.

We weren't ready to quit for the day, but I was ready for a break. The traffic had become very heavy and very fast. I pulled into a gas plaza. It was crowded with long lines for everything. We bypassed them all and headed for the restrooms. Even those had long waits. Mardi's line was quite long. While I waited for her I wandered around eavesdropping. I was surprised I heard no one complaining about the lines. They must have been normal.

The lines convinced us we could do without a coffee. We left the building and looked around. I had been so busy concentrating on the traffic that I hadn't taken a good look at the terrain. I was surprised to see that the peaks surrounding us were covered with snow.

"You sure you don't want me to drive into one of those villages up there, get a room, and wake up to brush snow off our car?" I asked.

"No—it's beautiful, but I just want to get close to Rome and check the Internet. Matt might have had to schedule us for a flight tomorrow."

I didn't think that would be the case, but I could tell she was quite happy to be looking up at the mountains rather than driving in them, especially if there was a chance we would be driving on snow-packed roads.

"Do you know what the name of that mountain is?" she asked after we'd been back on the road for a few miles. She was oohing and ahhing. I couldn't take my eyes off the road long enough to look at it. The turns and the tunnels and the traffic were keeping me fully occupied.

"What do I do here?" I asked, hoping she'd been following along on the map.

"The highway goes in a circle around Benevento."

"So you don't want to get off in *Centro*?"

"No. It would be easier to get off in a small town."

We passed the downtown exit for Benevento and I suddenly felt like a like a horse that had been given free rein.

"Are we going home?" I asked.

"I think we are," Mardi said.

We both fell silent. I didn't like the idea. But I was feeling what she was feeling—that we had shared an incredible journey, truly the journey of a lifetime, but now it was time to leave Italy. We would not be passing *Go*—our adventures on the rest of this journey would be those that would lead us toward our kids and grandkids and home. The traffic had slowed. I was able to look around a bit. We were driving through spectacular country.

"That was where I was going to take you," Mardi said. "That's why I had Benevento in the GPS. I thought it would get us to these mountains quickly."

"Where are we? What's the name of this town?"

"On the right is Ponte, on the south side is Torrecuso."

"I don't have the clothes for snow," I said as we contemplated the beauty before us and wondered again if we should spend the night in the mountains. Being in the mountains is one thing, but being in mountains covered with snow is quite another. It would be a great addition to our journey of a lifetime and remind us strongly of our ten years in Aspen as young-marrieds.

"I don't either," she replied. I heard in her voice a conviction that our journey was complete—that if you let it, Italy is capable of tempting the traveler forever.

"I'm sure there are a lot of stories in the towns that we're driving by, but it is hard to imagine that they're better than the stories we uncovered in Accettura,"

I said, trying to make myself feel better about what seemed like an almost irreversible decision to close what had been a very good chapter of our lives.

We began talking again of Cesare and his six friends—those seven guys coming together to create a gathering place for visitors and jobs for themselves in their small hometown, but the magnificent countryside soon changed our focus.

"This is going to be beautiful with the sun setting behind us," I said. "Look at the colors on those peaks."

Mardi began searching through *Back Roads Italy*, the book we had planned to leave with Cesare to start his library, but somehow it was in the car with us. There was no doubt now. We would have to return to Accettura to return our library book.

"Have you heard of Palestrina?" Mardi asked. She was reading through possibilities near Rome. The traffic began to speed up, but then inexplicably, it slowed down again.

"Can you believe it? That was a tourist with the audacity to drive the speed limit," I said after we had passed the slow moving car and were once again flying down the road.

"Do you know where Nemi is?"

"I've never heard of it," I said as I drove onto the shoulder as I had done when Sergio was riding shotgun, to make room for two cars coming at us, driving side by side. "In America horns would have been blaring, but Italians think nothing of it." The two cars flew by and I carefully guided our car back onto the road. We were still passing through wheat fields, but they were much smaller than the fields in Puglia.

"Nemi is a tiny medieval town twelve miles southeast of Rome," Mardi continued. "I found a bed and breakfast there, but it's probably booked up. It's called Mama Maria's."

"I like the name. Do you think we can get there before dark?"

If Mardi caught on to my allusion to the two women named Maria who she thought were flirting with me she kept it hidden. She was intently studying her maps. Traffic was slowing. We were on a huge downward slope. I could see at least three miles of bumper-to-bumper traffic in front of me.

"Maybe we should stay in Palestrina. It's probably cheaper," she said.

I didn't say anything. I was trying to figure out whether we'd be able to get to either town before nightfall. I didn't want to be driving on unfamiliar roads in the dark.

"In half a mile merge onto A1 toward Roma," Dorothy directed us.

That was all it took. I imagined bumper-to-bumper traffic all the way to Rome.

"Let's pull into this service station and see if we can get anything lined up," I said.

Mardi read the phone number but I had trouble entering it—a sure sign I had been driving too long. After a couple of misdials I heard *"Pronto."*

"Parli inglese?" I asked and was elated to hear the woman say *Si.* I didn't have the energy to think in Italian.

"I was wondering if you have a room for the night." I had the speaker on so Mardi could hear.

"Yes we do. It is forty-five a night." I could not believe our good fortune— we had found a room so close to Rome and it was the same price we'd raved about on the Amalfi Coast. However, I said nothing to indicate how pleased or surprised I was.

"How did you find us?" she asked.

"Found you in *Back Roads Italy.*"

"Yeah, yeah, yeah. That has been very good for us," she said, her voice gaining more confidence and enthusiasm. She now knew a little more about the kind of people who would be sharing her home.

"I have a room for two nights."

"We would like to stay with you. One night for sure, and maybe two," I said.

"I will give you the address. After eight you can drive into the historical center of town."

"Oh, yes, it will be well after eight by the time we arrive," I said. It was already seven-twenty.

"Perfect—I think you like it. You will be able to park nearby. My name is Maria."

I told her our names, and she told us more about the town and her B&B. I became convinced that we would not only like it but might love it. I hung up feeling that we had just discovered the reason we were so eager to get out of Matera and on down the road as far as we could—as close as possible to Rome.

"Way to go, Mardi. I think you have hit it out of the park on this one." I would never have had the patience to search through our guidebooks long enough to discover this jewel so close to Rome. The timing was also perfect. We'd be able to drive to Fiumicino early on Tuesday or Wednesday morning in time for our flight. Once again our fortune seemed too good to be true.

"We are pronouncing Nemi wrong—it's not Nee-mee, it's more like Nay-mee."

Mardi began reading the description from the book—it seemed perfect for honeymooners. "Ideal for those seeking lakeside calm," she began. "Famous for its strawberries and flowers. It's on the main street. She restored a store."

That didn't sound quite like what Maria had said, but I wasn't worried. We had a place for the night, it was close to Rome, and we were paying less than fifty dollars. Even if the place was nothing like the description Mardi was reading I would be happy to quit driving. I'd be especially satisfied if I made it all the way to Maria's place with neither a speeding ticket nor a dinged-up car.

"The GPS keeps giving me this darned place," I said, frustrated that it wouldn't take the address Maria had given me.

"I'm surprised she has room," Mardi said. "I figured that with a blurb in a book like that she would be always booked up."

I punched the accelerator and took off faster than I should have. My frustration was showing. I had given up getting the GPS to take the address Maria had given me and had accepted a random street in Nemi as my destination.

"Not sure why the GPS says it will take us until eight-thirty to get there," I said. I was beginning to fear that it was not as close to the *Autostrada* as we thought, and that might mean a longer drive to Fiumicino.

"Do you want me to read you a little more about it?" Mardi asked.

"Yes. Do you also have something for me to drink?"

She handed me a fruit drink and began telling me about Castelli Romani... a summer refuge for Popes...a bicycle ride around Nemi that must not be missed...each apartment has two bedrooms and two bathrooms.

"The place sounds excellent," I said, still not believing it could be as nice as it sounded for only forty-five euros a night.

"Sounds like a real peaceful place," Mardi said.

"Do you have any crackers, and maybe some cheese?" I was beginning to feel a little sleepy. We were driving through beauty I never expected this close to Rome. The mountaintops were still lit with alpenglow, and a patch of late evening sunlight bathed the highway—thankfully, the sun was behind us.

"Can I have one more cracker?" I asked.

"You're going to have to have prunes for breakfast," Mardi warned, but she had nothing else to give me. Sunflower seeds are my go-to remedy to keep from falling asleep, but we had not thought that I would ever feel so comfortable driving in Italy that I might get drowsy.

"Here comes the slow-down," I said as I saw ahead an *Autostrada* with every lane filled with bumper-to-bumper traffic. Only moments before we'd been hurtling along at over one hundred forty kilometers an hour and we were still being passed.

"We're fifty-six minutes from an eight-forty arrival, and it says I'm not getting off for twenty-two miles. Does that seem right?"

"You could get off at Valmontone."

"In twelve miles take exit Valmontone," Dorothy said as if she had heard Mardi and suddenly changed her mind. A few moments later the traffic began moving along at a better pace, nothing like the speeds we had been enjoying of over eighty miles an hour, but still fast enough that the Valmontone exit came up surprisingly fast. Despite the fact that the traffic was now flowing smoothly again we wanted to take our chances with the backroads of Italy. It was, after all, a book by that name that had led us to this inexpensive yet fabulous-sounding B&B.

"Do you have any cash for the toll?" Mardi asked.

"How much do I need?" I was thankful I wasn't driving alone. I was getting nervous about whether I would be able to figure out what to do in an automated toll lane. I looked for a lane with a human being at the front and found none. I watched the cars in front of me to see if I could learn anything. "Help me Sergio!" I cried as we got to the head of the line. Mardi laughed.

"Where do you put the money?" I asked, fearing that I was going to hold things up. The Italian instructions weren't computing for me.

"Do you see a button for English?" I didn't know how much money to put in, so I began looking for a credit card reader and saw none. Then I recalled that I had seen the driver in front of me put his receipt in the upper left corner of the machine. I did the same and it took it, but I still couldn't figure out where to put my credit card. I was expecting horns to begin honking. Finally I realized I had to put my credit card into the same slot I had placed the receipt. I did and *Bob's your uncle*—we were free to go.

"Sorry about that, all you folks behind me," I said as we pulled back into traffic. I could not believe that not one driver had honked at me.

"Use the roundabout to make a U-turn," Dorothy directed us.

"Ay yi yi," I said.

After a few more *Recalculatings* Dorothy gave up on getting us back on the *Autostrada* and gave us a new ETA for the route we had chosen. I was amazed at how rural the countryside had become. Only a few miles away hundreds, even thousands, of cars were headed toward Rome, but now it felt as if we were as isolated as we'd been ten hours earlier in the landscape surrounding Accettura. We were amidst tractors, horses, sheep, and hundreds of bales of hay.

"If you had told me before this trip that you could see snow-covered peaks from the outskirts of Rome in late April I would have thought you were crazy," I said. Mardi still had her head buried in *Back Roads Italy*—still noting points of interest in the area.

"I have a feeling you will fall so head over heels in love with Nemi you will want to stay two nights," she said.

"When you told me it was twelve miles from Rome I thought we would be working our way through heavily congested city streets to get there, not dodging cows, horses, and sheep."

I was exaggerating a bit—the animals were all safely on the other side of well-built fences—but I was amazed to see signs along the road warning of cow crossings. As the last pink in the western sky faded to blue we corkscrewed into Nemi on one of the most amazing roads I had ever seen, winding lower and lower. The only thing I could compare it to was a parking garage, but we were not encased in concrete—we were descending into what looked like a huge circular chasm in the earth. And then, all of a sudden, we were in a town, a very ancient town.

"This looks like the main street," Mardi said. "Let's call and tell her we're here."

But I didn't want to give up. It had occurred to me that I might have spelled the name of the street wrong. I stopped the car and did a search.

"I bet I could get out and walk to Maria's from here."

"Ah there it is, G I U," I said. I had been spelling it G U I L I A.

"Directions to Via Giulia," Dorothy said. She seemed to be directing us to go where signs proclaimed we shouldn't go, but I remembered that Maria had said it would be okay to drive into the historical center of Nemi since it would be after eight. We squeezed around the road closure barricades and off we went, only to stop short a few moments later.

"Whoa—go up that?" I exclaimed when I saw where Dorothy was directing us. The street was hardly wide enough for two people to walk side by side.

"Yikes," Mardi said. "You can't get through there."

"*Scusi,*" I said to a man walking toward us. I feared that he'd ask me what the heck I thought I was doing, but he expressed no alarm whatsoever. It was apparently normal for a car to be driving up a street where you have to pull in your mirrors to get through.

I asked him if I was heading toward Via Giulia. He answered, "*Tra piazza.*"

His gesture told me that once I had squeezed through the narrow crack between buildings that we could see ahead, which apparently was actually a street, we'd be in a *piazza,* and once we crossed that *piazza* I would find Via Giulia angling up the hill to the right.

How in the world he conveyed all that to me in one eloquent hand gesture I do not understand—but that is just what Italians do. He gave me the confidence in a five-second exchange to do what Mardi was convinced was sheer madness to even try.

"I'm going to get out and walk," she said half in jest. But she couldn't have followed through with her threat. We didn't have a sunroof. In that chasm between those buildings we didn't even have room to open a door, not even a smidgen.

"This is wild," I said as I inched forward, concerned that somebody would step out of a door. But no one stepped out. No one appeared in front of us either walking or driving. And suddenly we were in that *piazza* the man had mentioned and on the other side of it, just as he had gestured, was another narrow street, but this one was made narrow not by buildings but by cars parked on both sides.

"You can't get through there," Mardi said with tremendous conviction. I didn't argue with her. She had a very good chance of being right. Getting up that street was going to take every bit of situational awareness I could muster. This was going to be even more difficult than navigating the narrow path I'd just driven through, which had been a straight line. Via Giulia was going to require course corrections all the way to the street's end, where Maria had told me we would find her B&B.

I put the car in its lowest gear and began inching forward. The first part of the task was relatively easy. The cars on either side of the street hugged the walls with no room to spare—but just beyond one car projected into the street at an odd angle—a poor job of parking. And just beyond on the other side another car was sticking out into the street. This was going to be like slalom skiing. I wasn't going to be able to just turn around the car when I got to it. I was going to have to set up my turn long before. Getting up that street was a combination of skiing and playing chess, figuring out moves far in advance—that's why I was so darned proud of myself when I finally broke out into a wide opening at the end of the street. I wasn't sure exactly where Maria's door was, but Dorothy confirmed that I'd made it: "Arrived at Via Giulia 911."

I stopped, got out, and immediately heard a woman's voice call out "Allo."

"Hello," I said shocked to hear someone speaking in English.

"How are you?" the woman's voice called and I realized it must be Maria.

"*Va bene.* We are quite proud of ourselves that we got here."

"And you should be. It is not easy," she said as she reached my side and extended her hand. "I am Maria."

"I am James." I shook her hand and turned toward Mardi. "This is Mardi."

We were standing in front of what felt like a huge vine-covered castle. It was completely dark, but I could see that the reason we were in a wide spot was that the street did a one-eighty right in front of her place and climbed very steeply on up the hill. We were definitely in an ancient city. I wouldn't have been surprised to see archers peering down at us from the parapets above. I also saw that I wouldn't be able to remain parked where I was. No one would be able to make the sharp turn.

"I saw an empty parking spot just down the street," I said.

"By all means, if there's a space just there, grab it straight away," Maria said, and I realized why I had thought she was English at first—*straight away* conjures England for me.

I hopped into the car, leaving Mardi and Maria to get acquainted. I should have been able to head the other way with the same finesse I had driven up the street. But for whatever reason I did not. I had three cars to maneuver past, but when I got to that third car I had not taken the right line—I had not planned my moves far enough in advance like a good chess player, but at that point I was too tired to care. I knew my right side mirror was going to hit the third car's mirror, but I didn't reach across my car to pull it in—I just kept going, relying on the fact that modern mirrors are designed to give way. It didn't occur to me until both mirrors had popped back into place that one or both of them might have been scratched by the contact. I chalked that oversight up to being tired. But maybe I no longer cared. I had gotten us to Maria's B&B without incident. Mardi had been impressed with my skill at maneuvering up that crowded street. But now she was no longer in the car—she'd know about this only if I chose to tell her.

All that was left was to execute a perfect parallel parking maneuver into a very tight space that would require the side of our car to be flush up against a brick wall when I was finished. As I worked my way into my initial position I was glad to see that Mardi had come to help. She was directing me, using hand signals as she does when I'm hitching up a trailer.

It would have been a piece of cake to park a FIAT 500 in that space—no wonder that car is so beloved in Italy—but we squeezed our FIAT Punta into it, and with that, our journey to Nemi was over. A tremendous feeling of accomplishment swept over me. I grabbed our overnight bag and my computer and rejoined Maria.

"Very impressive parking. I think you've been to Italy before," she said.

Her compliment made me feel I had passed a test and could now truly claim to be an Italian driver. I smiled.

"Please come in," Maria said as she opened the door.

We stepped in and saw that the wallpaper in the sitting room was the very same pattern as one of the bags Mardi was carrying.

"I think we're going to feel right at home," I said.

"This is delightful," Mardi said.

Maria told us that she would not be able to serve us breakfast but that we'd be able to make tea and coffee. She then showed us the apartment and we were instantly certain we would stay as long as we could. We had a bedroom, a sitting room, a kitchen, a breakfast room, another bedroom, two bathrooms, and a living room. What was not to love?

"Where have you come from?" Maria asked.

"Accettura," I said.

She had not heard of it, so we told her a quick story about the town and the seven young men we had fallen in love with who had opened a hotel. She told us that she had fallen in love with Nemi thirty-five years ago, moved here from Sweden, and eventually opened the first B&B in the area.

"You will love Nemi. I love Nemi—not exploited, so hidden. The temple of Diana is down by the lake. There is so much to see and do." As she left she handed us the room key, which was huge and ancient looking, in perfect keeping with her castle. Her car was perfect too—a nondescript beauty from a former era, and her truck was a classic round-fendered FIAT from the thirties or forties. She seemed proud that she was preserving so much.

"Ain't this something?" I said to Mardi after Maria had gone into her house, leaving us to walk to town to find a restaurant.

"Incredible," was all she could say. I could see that she was reeling from the wonder of it all. "I can't believe we're here."

It really was mind blowing. For one thing, I couldn't imagine that such a place existed so close to Rome, especially one so inexpensive. When we left Accettura, we thought we might get no farther than Matera. So much had happened and we had seen so many different things and different landscapes that it seemed as if it had been days since we had said goodbye to Cesare—but it had been only twelve hours. And now we were walking arm in arm down an ancient street perched high on the rim of an extinct volcano looking for a restaurant still serving food.

"Can you eat pizza for another night if that's all we can find?" I asked.

"I can as long as they also have salad."

"Here's a bookstore," I said.

But we didn't need any more books. We needed something to eat, and right next door we found what looked like a *trattoria,* but it didn't look very popular. I wasn't even certain it was open, but nothing else looked open as far as we could see on either side of the street. Not one person was around. No cars were moving, not even a Vespa. The place was romantic but also eerily empty.

"Do you want to try it?" I asked.

She shrugged her shoulders. I walked through the doors and saw no one. We went deeper into the dark and encountered a young woman who was moving quickly like a waitress.

"Can we get something to eat?" I asked.

I got no reaction. I remembered where I was and resorted to tourist Italian, *"Cena? Mangia, mangia?"*

"Ah, si" she said and indicated that we should follow her. She led us up one flight of stairs and the place now looked like a restaurant. A few tables were occupied, but it was not busy. She seated us near a couple that I took to be tourists, possibly French. They were intensely interested in each other—they took absolutely no notice of our arrival.

Our waitress handed us menus, but I was quite certain we wouldn't choose anything but our usual fare. It was late, we had been snacking to stay awake on the drive to Rome, and I had seen what looked like a very interesting pizza on the way in—it was oblong in shape and so large it took two full-size dinner plates to hold it. When I noticed that it cost less than ten euros I had no doubt that's what I wanted. And Mardi had no doubt that she wanted an *insalata mista.* We ordered no wine, only water. So far not once had we been disappointed with that order in Italy. We had first ordered salad and pizza in Bolzano, Italy, a few days after Thanksgiving the previous year, when the South Tyrolean town was preparing its streets for Christmas. We had chosen a table on a *piazza* that was still bathed in late afternoon sunlight. We were shocked at how little it had cost and how delicious both had been. It was one of the first times we dined out together in Italy. Mardi and I had eaten most of our meals in the kitchens of our hosts. We were exchanging our labor and our expertise for room and board, but on that day, a Sunday, we were on our own wandering around that colorful city, delighted with the feeling of being in a mountain town that felt more like Austria than Italy. The architecture was pure Alps, but the food was pure Italian. We had chosen the spot because it was in the sun and gave us a perfect vantage point to watch the people gathering in the town square to watch Christmas decorations being put up. We had not expected to be treated to what we thought at the time was the best pizza we'd ever eaten.

We no longer remember that pizza as the best we have had in Italy, but we remember it as the pizza that opened our eyes to just how good Italians are at preparing pizza. I have since found three other pizzas that I rank above that first one, the most recent being Donato's Buffalo Doc in Accettura. When this two-platter pizza arrived I had high hopes for it—the presentation was unique and fun—but alas the pizza itself was rather pedestrian. It wasn't bad, and in fact it was better than most pizza you get in the US, but as an Italian pizza, it was just okay. But an okay pizza that night was just fine. Mardi's salad was "okay" too, which was also just fine. We had found a pleasant place to eat; the music was romantic, alternating between American classics and lovely Italian songs; and we were tremendously thankful to have found such a wonderful place to stay. It was hard to imagine that we would not want to return to Maria's every time we passed through Rome. I was even imagining that Maria's would be a good place to come to write. At about fifty bucks a night we could afford to spend a lot of time in Nemi.

"Look Mardi, I just realized those are the lights of Rome twinkling out there—can you believe this?" We were so high that it reminded me of driving out of the mountains and looking down at the lights of Denver.

I asked Mardi again how she had chosen Nemi.

"It just sounded like a place we'd like. Right off the main square. But I thought it would cost a lot. I rationalized that it would be worth it because we would be close to Rome. Think how many hidden backroads places there must be in Italy."

She was right. Every town in Italy probably has a great place to stay and delicious food to eat. All it takes is some courage and curiosity, a willing attitude, a bouncing pinball, and God's grace to find them. I didn't know how the book we had given to Cesare had ended up in our car, but without it we never would have gotten so close to Rome or spent the night in such a pleasant, homey apartment—an unexpectedly delightful exclamation point on a way-better-than-we-had-hoped-for story to share with our kids and grandkids.

CHAPTER TWENTY-SIX

Nemi ~ Tuesday April 26 ~ 52 & Partly Cloudy

A Foretaste?

What we have once enjoyed we can never lose.
All that we love deeply becomes a part of us.
HELEN KELLER

■

Come, let's be a comfortable couple and take care of each other!
How glad we shall be, that we have somebody we are fond of always,
to talk to and sit with.
CHARLES DICKENS

 $\mathcal{E}$nchanting. I don't know a better word to describe the apartment and the town we found ourselves in the last hours of our journey. *Enchanting* implies a storybook quality, and that was exactly what we were feeling—we were living in a castle, surrounded by more luxury and charm than we had dared imagine. If we've been leading a storybook life the past six weeks, an apartment in a castle was a perfect match—a perfect way to end our journey.

We woke up to another cold, misty day, forcing us inside, where we began enjoying again the peculiar pleasures of home—preparing and eating our own food in our own comfortable areas. It was easy to imagine that we *were* home, doing everyday things—the routines that bring so much comfort, especially that cup of perfectly brewed tea enjoyed in a favorite chair looking out at the falling rain. We've loved every place we have stayed on this sojourn, but I'm sure this one will draw us back time and again.

Part of it is logistics: Nemi lies only an hour from Fiumicino and two hours from Civitavecchia for those times that we again cross the Atlantic by boat. We will visit all the other places we have come to love on this trip and our previous journeys, but we won't get to each of them every time we travel to Italy. But this apartment could serve as a comfortable base from which to begin or end all of our trips to Italy. On this adventure we concentrated on the near South—Campania and Basilicata with a drive through a bit of Puglia. Next time we plan to spend time in the far South as well as Sicily and Sardinia. By the time we are eighty, God willing, we will have been to Italy at least ten times and will have visited most of its twenty regions. That will be a lot of trips through Rome, and by then this apartment really will feel like our home away from home.

Logistics is one thing, but the main reason we're sure we'll return to Nemi is that the apartment is perfect for our needs—it instantly felt comfortable. Plenty of room to spread out and write. An efficient kitchen where we can prepare snacks and meals. A living room. A fantastic bed with individual comforters. Midmorning I heard Maria or possibly her husband just outside our window attending to the weekly chores of maintaining a home—bottles clinking into the recycling bin. But that was all I heard—no sound of the city except for an occasional car door shutting as presumably a few folks in the neighborhood were heading off to work in the city.

As I recalled our journey I realized how often I had thought we couldn't find a situation we liked better—but each time we did. It was tempting to keep traveling around Italy to see if Nemi and Maria's enchanting apartment could be topped, but we had to quit somewhere—and this village, which looked so out of place and out of time when we first saw it, seemed like a good choice. We caught a hint last night of its incredible beauty as we walked to the end of Via Giulia, turned at the city walls and proceeded to the Garibaldi Piazza, where we enjoyed pizza and *insalata mista* at the Straccio of Diana. Far below us highlights glistened on the surface of Lago di Nemi, and we could see in the distance the shimmering lights of Rome from our lofty vantage point.

When I had finished making notes of my first impressions of Nemi, and Mardi had begun feeling guilty for sleeping so late and so well, we walked to the heart of the village to find brunch—not in a restaurant, but the ingredients for preparing a meal in our kitchen. We soon discovered that this historic town was known for more than beauty—*fragole*—strawberries are the key to Nemi's livelihood. The fruit and its presentation were perfect, as though an illustrator of children's books had created the displays—the strawberries, blueberries, and raspberries were bigger, fatter, and brighter than any I had ever seen—the colors so intense I thought the berries would explode if I touched them. Only people who have not been to Nemi would be tempted to feel I once again had resorted to hyperbole. Those who have seen the berries of this volcanic region will say *Right on.*

We also found radishes at one of the *frutta e verdura* shops. We didn't know what else we were looking for but we kept walking and looking, figuring we would know it when we saw it. Each time Mardi ducked into a shop to buy more food or just to browse, I took more photographs of the medieval village. Nemi is a photographer's paradise, with or without people. It was mostly without that morning. However, we did notice an affectionate young family in the park. The wife seemed to be heading off to work. As she turned her face toward us after kissing her daughter and husband goodbye, we realized that she was our waitress from the night before. We said *Buongiorno* as we walked by. She returned our greeting, but if she recognized us she gave no indication. There seemed little chance that she would become Nemi's Jessica to us.

On the way back to the apartment Mardi took the low road to look for a *forno* to get some *pane* for our radishes and *prosciutto* and cheese, I took the high road, the exact path we had followed to reach Maria's—a path that I could now see had been unnecessarily difficult. The GPS could have chosen a simpler route, but the high road had added excitement and a bit of a challenge to our introduction to Nemi.

It was fun thinking back to my thoughts of the night before as I worked my way through the streets of what appeared to be a fantasy town, wondering what this forty-five-euro apartment was going to be like—if we ever got to it. I suppose that half-dozen-block drive was a good metaphor, a good capsulation of our whole journey—every time we've been surprised by how well things turned out as we made our way to each new adventure.

Even though Mardi and I had come to the realization it was time to go home, I was in no way tired of Italy, or of wanting to speak the language better, or of learning more about the interesting lives I saw Italians living. I was not looking forward to returning to our American suburb even though, by every standard, we have a very good life there. All but four of our grandkids live very close to us and three of our children live within ten miles. Our neighborhood is quiet and beautiful. I have great cycling friends and terrific roads to bike on. Our church is vibrant. Life is good, but Italy is something else—and if you've been to Italy you know how you define *something else.*

Italy possesses a quality that is duplicated nowhere else in the world that I am aware of. It is the only country other than the US I would want to live in. I may yet discover a country I enjoy or appreciate as much as I enjoy America or Italy, but I haven't found it yet. If we are fortunate we will have the chance to get to know such a country, but that will happen only if we are able to take

at least two trips abroad each year, because I know that each year for the rest of our lives we will live for a while in Italy. We feel too at home to stay away very long. Our trips to Ireland or Iceland or Israel will have to be in addition to our yearly trip to Italy.

As I walked onto Via Giulia, I turned and saw Mardi—she smiled and blurted out what I'd been thinking—*we now have a home in Rome.* The realization that from Nemi we had access to all of Italy was rendering us giddy. Compared to the USA, Italy is quite compact. We could spend time in the Alps with Gianrico and Annika, or in Tuscany with Giovanni and Giovanna, or in Lazio with Eleonora and Luigi before heading to Maiori to see Jessica and the gang at Le Suite, or Minori to see Sergio and Vittorio, or Accettura to find out how the seven young men were doing bringing jobs to their secluded mountain village.

Tutto italia—that was what we now saw awaiting us on our next Italian journey—all of Italy, if we chose. As my mind wandered over the past six weeks I recalled more people than places—the people who had blessed each of our days. Each day seemed to have at least one defining event, from the Sunday dinner with nineteen of Vittorio's friends to the road trip with Sergio, to the hike with the Italian Trekking Club.

We stepped into our apartment, and in a way stepped back into our lives at home. The strawberries didn't remind us of Wisconsin. They were unlike any we had ever eaten, but in every other way the brunch we enjoyed—the yogurt, the croissant, the ham, the radishes, and of course our Earl Grey tea—reminded us of the way we eat at home. While we enjoyed our leisurely brunch I began writing and Mardi began communicating with our family and friends via Facebook and Instagram. It was quite easy to imagine that we *were* home.

The flowers and the vines just outside my window were shining with the moisture of the falling droplets. The paving stones, smoothed by thousands of years of wear, glittered with highlights, even on this, the grayest of days since we arrived in Italy. Mardi opened a window as she left the room. I could hear the rain falling gently in the courtyard. The peacefulness of the day lulled me to sleep.

When I awoke three hours later, the day looked and sounded much as it had before I had fallen to sleep, except that now I could no longer hear Mardi. I presumed she had found a comfortable place to watch the rain and she too had fallen asleep. Everything about that moment seemed perfect, especially the quiet. What a wonderful place for a writer. The rain was all I could hear. My mind whirled with possibilities. I hoped Mardi was loving the apartment as much as I was—she seemed just as content—it was easy to imagine spending not just days here but weeks at a time. Everything we needed—most importantly the produce of the local farmers—was only a few blocks away down Via Giulia.

I began writing again. As I worked I slowly became aware that I could hear Mardi somewhere in the apartment. Just as I was getting up to boil water for tea, Mardi walked in with a pitcher of Earl Grey and cookies. This really was like home.

We spent the rest of the afternoon in the apartment. Mardi marveled at the comfortable surroundings that Maria had created. It was the type of introspective day when you suddenly become aware of how good it feels to be alive and indoors—protected and comfortable—enjoying the most basic of needs. Mardi and I were luxuriating in the quiet company of each other, deeply aware of our abiding love, and our incredible journey.

Ironically, our last full day in Italy turned out to be the kind of day I wished we would enjoy in America. Our little car remained parked. We walked everywhere, yet we had everything we needed. We ventured out for the *passeggiata*, and because we had slept in the afternoon, we dined late into the night. It was a very Italian kind of day.

CHAPTER TWENTY-SEVEN

Maria's B&B ~ Wednesday April 27 ~ 51 & Partly Cloudy

Travel, Like Love, Transforms You

I never knew how much like heaven this world could be,
when two people love and live for one another!
LOUISA MAY ALCOTT

■

Travel is like love,
mostly because it's a heightened state of awareness,
in which we are mindful, receptive,
undimmed by familiarity and ready to be transformed.
That is why the best trips, like the best love affairs, never really end.
PICO IYER

Our departure from Nemi was noted by few. We left at first light to ensure that we would have time to encounter a difficulty or two and still make it to the airport on time. We wrote Maria a note thanking her for the wonderful apartment she had created for travelers and promised that we'd be back. We want to get to know Nemi as well as we know the other Italian towns in which we had sojourned.

I thought we would depart Nemi in the general direction of Fiumicino, but Dorothy seemed certain that we needed to leave town the same way we had come in—and since she was also certain we'd arrive in Fiumicino less than an hour later—we accepted her guidance. We had entered Nemi though the corkscrew tunnel and we left it the same way. I had never before been on a road that did a complete three-sixty. We were delighted to do it again. It was fun. It was memorable.

I wasn't able to figure out at what point we turned off the road that had brought us into Nemi, but within a few miles we were heading toward Rome and Leonardo da Vinci International Airport and no longer back toward the good winds of Benevento. I relaxed. The ETA remained steady and the time to the airport was going down.

The traffic was moving slowly, and calmly. These drivers were nothing like the drivers we had encountered on the Amalfi Coast. They also weren't as good. Ten miles into the journey I slowed up and encouraged a cautious driver to pull onto the highway in front of me. An Amalfi Coast driver would have dived into the traffic knowing that the other drivers would make room for him. But this driver was not only slow in entering traffic, he was slow *in* traffic as well. Our ETA began to climb, but passing him would have been impossible on the busy road so I relaxed and followed him. Unfortunately, I got so used to seeing him in front of me that I followed his tail lights onto a roundabout instead of Dorothy's instructions. I quickly realized my mistake, but not before I was out of the roundabout. I was being shuttled into bumper-to-bumper traffic headed to Rome, which was exactly what I didn't need if we were going to get to the airport on time—who knew when I'd be able to exit the *Autostrada* and get headed in the other direction.

Calling on the bravado I picked up from driving on the Amalfi Coast and the memory of the maneuver of the bus driver on Capri, I executed a one-eighty in the face of two lanes of oncoming traffic. It was a precise maneuver that I had to make in a split second—if I had delayed even momentarily there would have been no opening. It was also made possible by the quick steering and short turning radius of the FIAT. And just like that we were headed back toward the airport. The beautiful thing about the maneuver was that not one driver honked at me as I dove from the off ramp to the on ramp. Italian drivers have a lot more faith and understanding than American drivers—recognizing that were they in the same situation they might have done the same thing. Would a policeman have been as forgiving as the other drivers? I don't know. I just knew that at that moment our arrival at the airport with plenty of time to turn in our rental car and get through security seemed assured.

The next decision, which I had plenty of time to think about, was whether to risk losing time pulling into a gas station. We were getting dangerously close to empty. The FIAT's computer readout said we had ten kilometers to spare, but that seemed like it was cutting it way too close—what if we ran into a traffic jam at the airport? Taking five minutes to get gas seemed like a good idea, but I had yet to accomplish the feat that quickly. As the distance to the airport and the distance to empty became closer and closer to the same number, I got more and more nervous. Each time I had convinced myself that I could pump my own gas, I chickened out and drove past, hoping that at the next station I'd see a lonely attendant with no one to wait on but me. Finally there he was—I swung in and drove right up beside him and asked for *cinque euro di benzina.*

"Chiave?" he said quickly back, sensing my panic.

I shut the car off and chided myself for not handing him the keys and the coins in one motion as I asked for gas. But that slowed us up only a few seconds and in less than two minutes we were back on the road, working our way slowly to Fiumicino Aeroporto.

Our next bit of saving grace was Siri's slowness in figuring out the correct terminal for American Airlines. She complimented us for asking an interesting question. But by the time she had found that we needed Terminal 5, we were already heading toward Terminal 3. While looking for a way to get back to T5 we saw a sign for Hertz returns. We decided to change our plans: instead of dropping Mardi and our bags at the American terminal, we *and* our bags would ride the shuttle.

The lane to the Hertz return wound into a parking garage, and within moments we found a place to park and I was standing in line with my keys and contract in hand. I got to the head of the line a couple of minutes later and turned both over to the attendant. He checked my mileage, returned to his computer, punched a few keystrokes, and said, "See you next year."

"We're done?" I asked, amazed. Just like that our journey had ended and this man who knew us not at all, somehow knew that we would be back to Italy next year.

"Yes. You'll be charged for one extra day," he said.

"That's it?" I asked. "No drop-off charge?"

"Just another day of insurance, the fuel has already been paid for."

"Wonderful," I said. "Hertz has been great. Matteo in Salerno took very good care of us. Thanks. What's your name?"

"Stefano," he said with what I considered an absolutely beautiful accent.

"Mi chiamo James, and I definitely hope to see you again next year. *Ciao."*

And with that we were done. We grabbed our suitcases from the car and wheeled them toward the elevator and the shuttle that would take us to the terminal. A feeling surged through me that I couldn't quite understand. I hadn't wanted this day to come, and now that it had, the finality of it had come much too quickly. I wasn't prepared for the mental letdown. I wasn't prepared to be no longer following pinballs of transformation. This pinball would, barring disaster, bounce us back to our lives in Wisconsin.

"The guy in front of me in the Hertz line had only an hour until his flight," I said to Mardi trying to take my mind off my feelings. "I can't imagine he is going to be able to make it."

"How long do we have?"

"Over two hours."

When we got to an information screen we learned that we had even more than that. Our flight had been delayed. That delay took off the pressure we were feeling about not being able to figure out where Terminal 5 was. The signs seemed to be directing us in a circle.

"Do you know where Terminal 5 is?" I said to a man who seemed to be in no particular hurry.

"Ignore that sign. You have to go out those doors and catch another shuttle bus to get to Terminal 5."

Using my best Italian body language I acknowledged his help with a tip of my head and said, "You have a good command of English."

"I am from the Philippines," he answered.

Since neither of us was in a hurry we chatted a bit. I told him that as a young man I had spent a little time in the Philippines on overnight stops flying to Vietnam, Korea, and Japan. He told me that he doubted that I would recognize much of anything. I thanked him and sat down with our luggage surrounding me and my perplexing thoughts to wait for Mardi, who had gone off in search of a restroom.

I began thinking again what the man had said about Manila and imagined that today many of the places I visited forty-some years ago would look nothing like they did then. Whenever I see old travelogues of Italy or the movies of Roberto Rossellini I wish that I had been able to see Italy in the mid-twentieth century. I love that this country reconnects me with my memories of childhood, of a more community-oriented time in America, but how much more intensely would I have felt the connection if Mardi and I had walked the Amalfi Coast or the streets of Accettura when we truly were newlyweds back in 1970. Sergio had said that going to southern Italy takes you back two hundred years. I'm certain he was exaggerating, but even if he wasn't, I'm convinced that his comment is going to be the pinball flip that is going to propel Mardi and me to Calabria, Sicily, and Puglia, the heel of Italy, on our next journey to *il Bel Paese*.

Mardi returned. We took the bus to our terminal, checked in, and began breathing normally again. She went for a walk. I waited with our luggage and occasionally checked on our flight, which kept getting delayed. As I waited I relived our journey to the airport—thinking of how well the day had gone and how easy it had been to turn the car in at Hertz—when all of a sudden I realized that I'd left the key connector from my man purse on the FIAT keys. I had ruined what had otherwise been a perfect honeymoon. Mardi, doing her part to keep the honeymoon perfect, returned with food as well as presents for our grandkids. She even returned with a great gift for us—*scopa* cards—on our next trip to Italy we'll be ready to play with Cesare.

Mardi wanted to show me some other gifts she was considering. She thought we had until 1300, but I was certain I'd been told that standby passengers would be announced at 1240. Keeping in mind my main job, we went to the gift shop. We arrived back at the gate at 1245. It turned out that for once I was right—our names had been called. An agent who had been on the receiving end of at least four questions from me at four different times in our two-hour, numerous-delays wait said that because we hadn't been there when the standbys were called, we'd been downgraded to seats on the wing. I took that to mean that we already had the worst seats in the plane—not that we had been bumped.

"How about an upgrade instead?" I asked.

"We'll see," the young man working with the agent replied, but I wasn't holding out much hope; he had told me an hour earlier that an upgrade to business or first class was not likely to happen.

"Only by his good graces," I said, and he smiled.

"He knows English well," I said to Mardi, and he smiled again. He did try to make things a bit easier for us. As a consolation prize, he gave us four seats in the middle of the plane to spread out on. But when a flight attendant saw what we had, she took them away—she wanted them for herself. What she gave us in trade turned out quite well—some privacy in the last row of the plane—Mardi loved her window seat on the port side. We caught glimpses of Paris and London and the Scottish coast, and got great service from the flight attendants.

As we flew across Europe, we began reliving our journey. Why, we wondered, do we both feel such a connection to Italy, and not to Ireland or Scotland, where we both have relatives? It is a mystery we hope someday to solve, but it remains a curiosity and not a burning desire. We have for years been talking about going to Ireland, but I strongly suspect that our next journey will again be to Italy.

Mardi told me that she felt we had enjoyed God's grace throughout—that ours had been a perfect honeymoon. It certainly far exceeded my expectations. It had done what Pico Iyer had said travel is capable of—it had transformed us, our relationship, and our marriage.

Our adventure was one day short of forty days. I could easily have stretched it out to fifty. But I had been telling Mardi that my primary job in life was to make her happy, so when everything seemed to be falling into place for us to head home—when Maria's apartment turned out to be available for only two days and it worked out that we could drop the car off at the airport—stopping by Rome for a few days seemed anticlimactic. Why risk spoiling the beautiful memories we already had of the Eternal City?

A plane on our runway at O'Hare didn't respond immediately to being cleared for takeoff, so our pilot aborted our landing and circled the airport. That delay caused us to miss the 1740 bus to Goerke's Corners, a few miles from our home. As I looked back on our journey I realized that go-around and forgetting the key connector for my man purse were the worst things that happened to us on our Italian adventure—unless of course you count that I came back weighing two hundred twenty pounds. But was it realistic to think we could travel about in a country that is known for growing and preparing some of the best food in the world and come home weighing what we did when we left? So what if I had twenty pounds to ride off in the upcoming cycling season—I had the memories of the journey of a lifetime to make the miles fly by and the pounds melt off—miles that would get me in shape for our next Italian sojourn—our next *Two for the Road* adventure.

Wisconsin

Un Nuovo Sogno

*You are never too old to set another goal
or to dream a new dream.*
C.S. LEWIS

■

Be ready to be surprised by grace.
WILLIAM ZINSSER

"Why did we waste all those years not loving each other?" Mardi asked one night in a flash of recognition as we sat sipping wine and gazing at the spectacular Amalfi Coast.

"Before I'd been to Italy I loved Pizza Hut pizza," was my cryptic, cast-no-blame answer, trying to make the point that we didn't know any better—we were getting by with what we had, wishing we could do better, but not quite able to get to the good life we hoped someday awaited us. The moment she asked that question I knew my prayers had been answered, that our journey of a lifetime had given me the very thing I had wanted—a wife who understood that we could love each other better and deeper. My first journey to Italy had taught me the benefits of sacrificial love, and now Mardi was also seeing that there was a better way to live, and to love.

I have been living with the memories of our journey of a lifetime for almost two years now, and the words of Hemingway ring truer and clearer with every thought I have of that mystical land. Hemingway had been overpowered by an epiphany while recovering from injuries suffered driving an ambulance as a volunteer in the Italian army during World War I. *Italy is a country that every man should love once. I loved it once and lived through it—you ought to love it once or at least live in it. It is something like the need for classics.*

Just as suffering was at the heart of Hemingway's epiphany, so too did heartbreak lead to Mardi's revelation. We had many years of just getting by, as well as moments of hostility, to compare to the love we were feeling for each other that night in Maiori. For Hemingway Italy was akin to a well-rounded education—for me what happened to us in Italy was an affirmation of the need to embrace mystery in our lives—being open to forces too wonderful to know—that lie in the realm entered only through faith. Italy and Italians helped me to see what was missing in my life, and then, by God's grace, seven years later Mardi saw it too, which led her in a moment of deep introspection to ask, *Why did we waste all those years not loving each other?*

I can think of nothing she could have said that would have thrilled me more deeply or would have convinced me more of the love she wanted to give me. It was an incredible act of humility and courage. Those few words looked back on years of regret, but they also, with strong resolve, looked forward with great hope.

As I reflect on our sojourn, I am close to proclaiming, with only a slight touch of hyperbole, that there are two stages in life—your years spent on this earth before seeing the Amalfi Coast, and those after. I can say without exaggeration that during that second stage of life you will spend almost every day wishing you could go again to that craggy storybook coast. It casts a magical spell. The people we fell in love there have much to do with our desire to return, but I also know that every time I see one of the photographs I took on the Amalfi Coast I long deeply to return to experience the overwhelming beauty that God and Man have created along that rugged shoreline. You can easily be forgiven for uttering the words *Heaven on Earth* upon witnessing such beauty.

It seems inexplicable that people who are not Italian can feel such a deep connection to a country. I feel it for no other country in the world, but Italy I long to return to with every fiber of my being. I feel at home there. It is the only country I would consider moving to on a semi-permanent basis—the others I only want to visit.

Italy is also the only country I want to explore from the saddle of a bicycle before I die. I would go with no itinerary—only the desire to get to know Italy and Italians better. If I bicycled through all twenty regions of the country that would be grand, but if my journey was measured not by miles or regions checked off, but by the people of Italy who crossed my path I would be pleased. For that is what I truly treasure about Italy—the people. The spirit of Italian people resonates with my spirit. Their passion fuels my passions. I feel at home with their enthusiasms. I could write about Italy for the rest of my life and not come close to exhausting the good stories to tell about this land, these people, and their in-love-with-life *attitudine*.

A journey to Italy once a year for the rest of my life, God willing, is just about the only thing not checked off my bucket list that does not involve family. Even a few of the family dreams also involve Italy, because I would like to someday take all of my children and grandchildren—and great-grandchildren if that many years elapse before we pull it off—to Italy by boat.

Italy is in my blood. I am certain that I will someday explore whether within my family tree it can be shown that I have more than a metaphoric connection to Italy, but for the moment I am willing to accept that it is enough that I am passionate about the country, about learning what Italy and Italians have to teach me. For forty-some years Mardi and I missed an essential truth in our relationship. On my first journey to Italy, as I searched for the essence of what makes an Italian an Italian, I came to understand that sacrificial love is at the heart of the Italian people. Their selfless devotion to the strangers among them during World War II gave me the key to unlock the secrets of their better way to live. I came to understand what sacrificial love did for Allied soldiers being sheltered from the Nazis and I also came to understand what sacrificial love does for relationships. It is at the heart of the greatest story ever told.

Italians give of themselves. They don't necessarily think of it as sacrificial giving. It is just what they do—and I like that—it helps in a marriage to just give and not count the cost or even expect a return. At times throughout the first forty-some years of our marriage we came close to giving sacrificially; at other times we were stubbornly resistant to loving at all—we just went through the motions of survival—but now that we love and serve one another with no reservations, we are supremely happy with each other and with our lives. I only wish it had not taken us almost a whole lifetime to get to that point. But we're there now and we are, to be rather sappy and over the top, head over heels in joy-filled love. Or, as my favorite spinning song, "Wake Me Up," puts it—*Life's a game made for everyone, and love is the prize.*

We lived in Italy long enough that on some mornings I am reminded of the rhythms of our Italian days. Patterns developed, especially in our mornings, in the taking of our coffee and tea, and on some days those memories come flooding back. I may be drinking Italian coffee that Mardi has prepared to Italian standards, and I will be reminded of all the people we came to know, that we shared a *cappuccino* with, but I know that just outside my room I will not hear the sounds of Italy, and that is what I deeply miss. I will not be suddenly thrust into the pulse of an Italian town; I will walk outdoors and hear only birds, not the concentrated conversations of dozens of townspeople starting their day with energy and passion. I miss the intensity of those conversations—the power of Italian expression—the courage of convictions. On such mornings I miss Italy deeply. I want to be engulfed again in that passion—that love of life that Vittorio showed us as he led us on a tour of his beautiful farm—or the intensity of feeling that Sergio and Addolorata expressed as they argued about Italian dialects—or the sadness in Jessica's eyes when she asked why we were leaving Maiori.

Everywhere we traveled we were welcomed as though we were family or old friends. The traditions of Italians are deeply ingrained. They are a hospitable people. They are a loving people. We have discovered that if you want to truly experience Italy, you must go to where the people are—not the tourists. You yourself must not be a tourist to the extent that is possible. If you are truly going to experience Italy, you must be a pilgrim in a land that will at times be foreign to you. You must be open to the all that the people, and the land of Italy have for you. You will be amply rewarded for your pilgrimage, I can assure you.

People who have not been to Italy don't fully understand why Hemingway felt that it was so important to take an Italian journey at least once in your life. This may sound a little self-serving coming from a writer, but people who have not been to *italia* don't understand why writing a book about Italy can be as important as writing a book about history, philosophy, or theology. Writing about Italy allows a writer to express wisdom literature while at the same time conveying the importance of *dolce far niente*—the sweetness of doing nothing. The list of writers who have fallen in love with Italy is very long. Italy possesses a soul that inspires writers.

The most important things I've learned in seventy years on this earth fit seamlessly into a book about Italy, the beautiful country, *il Bel Paese*, as Dante so fittingly called it. I am a driven person who has within him a bit of the German determination to be always productive, but who has in his later years come to see the importance of no longer measuring my days in terms of items marked off a to-do list. Have I loved someone today and have I made that person aware of my love? Italy taught me that.

Writing about Italy also involves giving voice to contradictions, paradoxes, and mysteries. Italians understand the give-and-take of life. They seem to be aware of mankind's sinfulness, of his fallenness, and his need for forgiveness like no other people I have encountered. I love how Italians argue, how passionately they express themselves, yet they accept the foibles of other people, and themselves as well. They know they're not perfect and they don't expect other people to be perfect either, or even close to it. In short, Italians love life, not some Pollyanna version of it. They don't seem to have a script they follow—they go through life improvising as need be, day by day—living life as it is meant to be lived—passionately, lovingly, and enthusiastically.

Vittorio's feast represents for me the essence of Italian living. Whenever I happen to think about that glorious day, or read a book that brings to mind an Italian dinner, or look at one of the dozens and dozens of photographs I took on his farm high above the Amalfi Coast, I am amazed at how like family a group of strangers made Mardi and me feel. More than the monuments of Rome, or the churches of Italy, or the country's natural beauty, that day and so many other moments like it are what keeps drawing us back year after year.

Have our lives changed because of Italy and Italians? I think that even the casual observer would say *yes*. We gave up our American minivan and are now driving a FIAT 500X, a sharp little car that corners like a skateboard yet still has room for my new Italian bicycle when the rear seats are folded down. It's a beautiful bike—a Pinarello—a perfect blend of engineering and art that gives me a thrill every time I take it out for a ride. We attend Italian film festivals and were delighted this past year to see a very funny film that tells the story of Angel Flight—the zip line between Pietrapertosa and Castelmezzano—a story very similar to that of Cesare and his six compatriots taking a bold step to create jobs in their beloved hometown. Remembering the delightful couple of days we spent in Maria's converted castle, we bought a house that we decorated to look like the apartment we rented in Nemi. The house also affords us the conveniences of living in a small Italian village. We can walk to the library, the farmers market, the bank, the post office, the supermarket, the pharmacy, the bike store, the high school, the Wednesday evening concerts in the park, and America's attempt to recreate the peculiar attractions of an Italian bar/ cafe—even its name is derived from the Italian word for bread, *pane*.

But with all the conveniences, including a Roman Catholic church a couple of blocks away that tolls the time, we still deeply miss Italy. We are, however, near our grandkids, and their daily visits mean a lot to us. You might say that we are now looking at the world through an Italian prism colored by an Italian mindset fed by an Italian zest for living.

Having experienced the journey of a lifetime, we now face a quandary— what do we do to top it? How do you replace a dream you've been carrying all your life? As a teenager I fantasized about traveling the world with a beautiful woman I loved, who shared my passion for challenge and adventure.

That dream has been more than fulfilled. I could say that my dream is to do it again, and that would be true, but now that I have found a people who I believe have discovered and continue to pass down the secrets and essence of a life well-lived, my new dream is to master the language of this people I so deeply admire. I don't know that I will ever be able to claim mastery of the Italian language—I'm not sure I have the ear for it—but I do have the desire. The desire to be healthy carries me out each day to bicycle distances that have made it possible for me to carry into my seventies the fitness of a thirty- or forty-year-old. It may be that my deep desire to learn Italian will carry me to a fluency beyond my most fanciful dreams. Certainly the thought of biking twelve thousand miles in one year was once beyond my wildest thinking, but as I write this epilogue in the seventieth year of my life, that is how many miles, plus a few more, that I will have ridden, God willing, when midnight strikes on the thirty-first of December this year.

Having witnessed what once seemed like the miraculous so many times in my years, I am going forth with my dream of one day being able to speak and think in Italian. For the moment I will not dare hope that I might someday *write* in Italian, but who knows. Once one dream is attained a new one must be claimed. I would begin my first book in the Italian language with these words—*Grazie a Italia e al popolo italiano per avermi restituire l'amore della mia vita*—thanking Italy and the Italian people for giving me back the love of my life. Who knows where the story, and the journey, might go from there?

For Roger and Bev,

who have been with us

on much of life's journey,

if, at times, only in spirit.

It is with sadness that I write

that Roger has gone ahead to scout out Heaven.

But as he did so often on Earth

he will be ready with a story to welcome us.

Acknowledgments

𝒜 heartfelt thanks to all the kind and spirited people we've met on our Italian journeys. Italy is vast and beautiful, but the fine character of the people is what makes this great land unique in the world.

I also want to express my gratitude for the encouragement, patience, and superb eye of George Foster, who designed the cover; for the knowledgeable and ever vigilant sharp-eyed copyediting, editing, interior design, and typesetting, as well as the good advice of Sue Knopf; and for the beautiful and evocative drawings of Jonathan Shaw, who has captured the spirit of the Italian people.

It was a joy working with each of you.

About the Author

James Ernest Shaw lives in Wisconsin, in the heart of what John Steinbeck called "the prettiest state I ever saw." He and his wife divide their time among their five children and twelve grandchildren. James is a former filmmaker and for six years wrote a newspaper column, "Another View of Life." His first book, *An Italian Journey: A Harvest of Revelations in the Olive Groves of Tuscany*, tells the story of the people he met during an extended sojourn in Tuscany picking olives and eating with Italians at their kitchen tables. He was searching for the essence of Italy—what makes Italians so uniquely hospitable.

His second book, *An American Journey: Travels with Friday in Search of America and Americans*, is a comparison of America 1962 and America 2012 told through the stories of the people he met on two bike rides across the heartland taken fifty years apart. The first was inspired by John Steinbeck's *Travels with Charley*, and the second was, like Steinbeck's journey, taken during the height of a presidential campaign. In each book, the unique story of America is told through the people that Steinbeck and Shaw met on the roads of America.

James is a product of small-town America. He graduated from the University of Nebraska. After a short stint as a ski bum in Breckenridge, Colorado, he served in the US Army as a cinematographer. He spent his professional career as a filmmaker, shooting and producing award-winning films throughout the world. He is also a pilot with over two thousand hours, and in his never-ending quest for adventure even served a short stint as a bush pilot in Alaska.

James has been greatly influenced by his sojourns in Italy. He now drives an Italian car, a FIAT, and rides an Italian bike, a Pinarello. He and his wife, Mardi, eat like Italians and every year try to live for extended periods of time in Italy.

www.facebook.com/ItalianJourney

www.facebook.com/ItalianLoveStory

www.jamesernestshaw.com

Made in the USA
Columbia, SC
19 August 2022

65697104R00336